Sicily

a photo essay

1 The Cathedral, Palermo

2 Cupola of the cathedral of
  San Lorenzo, Tràpani
3 Archaeological Zone, Syracuse
4 Hills rising directly behind Taormina
5 The ceramic staircase of the Scala di Santa
  Maria del Monte, Caltagirone

7

6

8

9

6 Collegio dei Gesuiti, Mazara del Vallo
7 Palazzo Villadorata, Noto
8 Roman mosaic, Villa del Casale,
Piazza Armerina
9 Temple of Concord, Agrigento

10

11

10 San Giovanni degli Eremiti, Palermo with
   two of its five red cupolas
11 Mosaic inside La Martorana, Palermo
12 Baroque splendour in Ragusa
13 Carved capital, Monreale cathedral cloister

14 The Acropolis, Selinunte
15 Active volcano on Vulcano, Aeolian Islands
16 Orto Botanico, Palermo
17 Lipari, Aeolian Islands
18 Cathedral, old town and the Rocca, Cefalù

17

18

19 Looking across salt pans near
   Tràpani to the Egadi Islands
20 Coastal scene near Scopello
21 The western shores under a
   rainbow, as seen from Erice
22 The Aeolian island of Salina
23 The emptiness of central Sicily, near
   Enna

MARZAPANE

24

25

26

27

3
1,00

Piano

€ 0,60

24 The ubiquitous bougainvillea
25 Fishmarket, Catania
26 Marzipan fruits – frutta alla Martorana
27 Typically plump offerings on a market stall
28 Souvenirs for the devout, Syracuse

29 Architectural detail, Ortygia, Syracuse

Dana Facaros and
Michael Pauls

SICILY

'The mythic garden of Persephone,
an Islamic paradise on earth,
the fairy-tale Norman kingdom...'

CADOGANguides

Contents

About the authors

Dana Facaros and Michael Pauls are old Sicily hands. They first went there in 1980 and have been back many times since. They have written over 30 Cadogan Guides. Dana and Michael now live in a farmhouse in southwest France.

Acknowledgements

This book would not have been possible without the help of good friends: Michael and Brian, who entertained Jackson and Lily for us; Carol and Bob, who loaned us their French postal van, which went places in Sicily that no French postal van had gone before; and Victor, who fixed it in exchange for a few pizzas. Also, we'd like to thank the numerous Sicilians who took the time to talk to us.

About the updaters

Kicca Tommasi and **Kamin Mohammadi** have been friends and travelling companions since they met (at Cadogan) a decade ago. In Sicily they were scared by volcanoes and seduced by islands, and their senses were wooed by the scent of jasmine and taste of orange blossom honey. Kicca takes photos while Kamin scribbles.

Cadogan Guides
Highlands House, 165, The Broadway,
London SW19 1NE
info@cadoganguides.co.uk
www.cadoganguides.com

The Globe Pequot Press
246 Goose Lane, PO Box 480, Guilford,
Connecticut 06437–0480

Copyright © Dana Facaros and Michael Pauls
1994, 1998, 2001, 2004
Updated by Kikka Tommasi and Kamin
  Mohammadi.

Cover and photo essay design by Kicca Tommasi
Book design by Andrew Barker
Cover photographs by John Ferro Sims
Maps © Cadogan Guides,
  drawn by Map Creation Ltd
Managing Editor: Antonia Cunningham
Editor: Tim Locke
Proofreader: Ali Qassim
Page layout: Sarah Rianhard-Gardner
Indexing: Isobel McLean
Typeset by Dorchester Typesetting
Production: Navigator Guides
Printed in Italy by Legoprint
A catalogue record for this book is available
  from the British Library

ISBN 1-86011-153X

Introduction

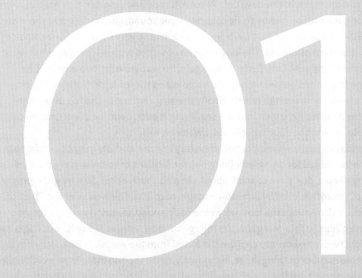

Sicily is the schoolroom model of Italy for beginners, with every Italian quality and defect magnified, exasperated, and brightly coloured... Everywhere in Italy life is more or less slowed down by the exuberant intelligence of the inhabitants: in Sicily it is practically paralysed by it.
Luigi Barzini, *The Italians*

Sicily, eternal triangle of intensity, excess and carnal beauty, sits square at the crossroads of Europe and Africa. Only 4km separate it from the toe of the big boot, ever poised for a smart kick, but these 4km have given the island enough history, customs and personality for an entire continent. Although they are the most Italian of the Italians, as Barzini writes, Sicilians are also the least, the heirs of the ancient Greeks, Carthaginians, Arabs and Normans. Spain, Naples and Rome have ruled it from afar, but never engaged its heart; Sicilians are Latins only by adoption.

Sicily is a deep place, often sombre, ambiguous, feverish, terrible and fascinating; 'surly, stingy with itself, in love with its own silence, closed in its own shell of solitude as if in palace-prison', as Sicily's own Gesualdo Bufalino put it (*see p.341*). Yet when Sicily's destiny has been in the hands of people who cared for it, the island has been the mythic garden of Persephone, an Islamic paradise on earth, the fairy-tale Norman kingdom, more splendid and sophisticated than any in the early Middle Ages. More often the island has been raped by faraway rulers who squeezed out every ounce of wealth and beauty: paradise turns into violent poverty, a fairy tale gone underground and twisted, its hope warped into despair. The Sicilian language is the only one in Europe without a future tense.

One of the best-known Sicilian stories tells of a boy from Messina named Nicola who liked to swim so much that he became part fish, and was known as Cola Pesce. When the king heard about this half-man, half-fish he asked him to swim around Sicily and tell him what he saw. Cola Pesce returned and reported that Messina was built on a rock supported by three columns – one sound, one cracked and the other altogether broken – and that by its lighthouse, on the very tip of Sicily, he could not find the bottom of the sea. The king became obsessed with discovering what lay at the bottom, and sent Cola Pesce down again. He was gone for two days, but he became frightened before finding the bottom and turned back. Nothing the king could say would make him return. Finally the king climbed to the top of the lighthouse and hurled his crown into the sea. 'Bring it back, Cola!' he cried. Cola Pesce dived down into the depths. Sicily still awaits his return.

Nowadays a Sicilian-sized portion of history and melancholy might be more than anyone bargained for on their holiday, but the Sicilians of today, a lively, forward-looking people, don't like to think about the past much either. So why go? A proper plate of swordfish *involtini* is reason enough, of course. The view over the Strait of Messina, with Mount Etna looming in the background, is reason enough, too. You may even see the Fata Morgana, the mirage spun by Morgan le Fay (Count Roger saw it, before he crossed over to capture the island from the Arabs). In fact, Sicily has an incredible number of things that, individually, make the trip more than worthwhile, things you won't see the like of anywhere else: the glittering Cappella Palatina in

Palermo, or Strómboli erupting every eight minutes, the face of Christ at Cefalù cathedral, the spring flowers around Enna or Erice, the acre of Roman mosaics at Piazza Armerina, the poetic solitude of the temple of Segesta, the dreamlike panorama of the Aeolian Islands rising from the sea. If Sicily's past has made it a world apart, it has also left it among the lands most able to provide that old Mediterranean speciality – a wake-up call to the spirit, a straight shot of sensuality to the brain. For the sleepy times we live in, that makes Sicily priceless.

A Little Geography

Sicily is the largest island in the Mediterranean, 9,923sq miles, with a population of just over 5 million. Thanks to Mount Etna, the highest volcano in Europe, the triangle has a somewhat alarming 10,902ft/3,323m-high third dimension as well. A diehard smoker, Etna has been responsible for a good deal of life as well as death, nourishing Sicily on its lava-rich soil. The Arabs thought it was paradise on earth.

Along with Etna, most of Sicily's other mountains are in the east: the Nebrodi, Peloritani and Iblean ranges surround Etna like bridesmaids. The highest of these B-division mountains, the Madonìe, are in the central north and attain enough altitude (6,462ft/1,970m) to be covered with snow most of the winter. In ancient times Sicily had several navigable rivers, although these have all since filled with silt from careless farming and irrigation practices. The oak forests that once covered the island fell prey in ancient times to shipbuilders, and now cover less than 7.5 per cent of the total land area. Despite the ravages over the centuries, Sicily is still very much a garden. Citrus and olive groves, vineyards and palm trees grow along the coasts, and almonds in the south; higher in the hills are the rolling fields of wheat that made the island the bread-basket of ancient Rome.

If all that isn't enough, Sicily has an enviable collection of smaller volcanic islands: north of Milazzo, the seven outlandishly beautiful Aeolian Islands, which include another active volcano (Strómboli) among their many curiosities; Ùstica, a little black island north of Palermo; the three Egadi Islands, west of Tràpani, famous for tuna; Pantelleria to the south, more North African than Italian; and even farther south, the rocky Pelagie Islands, halfway between Malta and Tunisia in a crystal-clear sea.

A Guide to the Guide

Palermo Dusty, noisy Palermo is a fascinating place to spend a few days or more, with its historic centre packed with palaces, museums and churches, as well as markets and restaurants and general air of cheery chaos. Within an easy journey of the city centre are numerous interesting towns and villages, including Monreale, with its unmissable cathedral. Easily accessible by ferry is the island of Ùstica, a floating garden that has become a hotspot for scuba divers.

Western Sicily With a distinctly North African atmosphere, this corner of Sicily offers several remarkable sites, including enchanting Segesta and Motya. The main towns of

Chapter Divisions

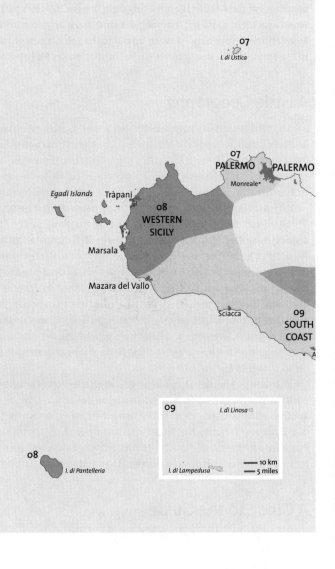

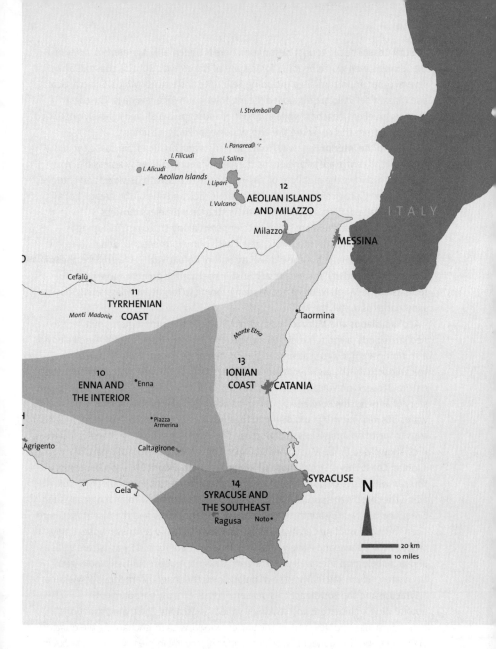

I. Strómboli

I. Panarea

I. Filicudi · I. Salina

I. Alicudi
Aeolian Islands
I. Lipari

I. Vulcano

12
AEOLIAN ISLANDS
AND MILAZZO

Milazzo

MESSINA

ITALY

Cefalù

11
TYRRHENIAN
Monti Madonie **COAST**

Taormina

Monte Etna

13
IONIAN
COAST CATANIA

10
ENNA AND ·Enna
THE INTERIOR

· Piazza
Armerina

Agrigento

Caltagirone

SYRACUSE

14
SYRACUSE AND
THE SOUTHEAST

Gela

Ragusa Noto·

N

20 km
10 miles

Tràpani and Marsala (the best place for a tipple of Marsala wine) are both worth a
visit, but silent, misty Erice is one of the highlights of the island. As you journey west,
the coastline changes from untouched beaches to a moonscape of salt pans. Islands
off the coast are the beautiful Egadis, and Pantelleria, home to the *sesi* culture.

South Coast The big tourist destination here is undeniably Agrigento's Valley of the Temples, well worth heading for in spite of the crowds. But this coast also has several other important sites, including Selinunte and Eraclea Minoa. Sciacca, Licata and Mazara del Vallo are unspoiled fishing towns, fun for a few days. The coast shelters excellent beaches, while inland the landscape is lush and sparsely populated. Accessible from this coast are the arid, windswept Pelagie Islands.

Enna and the Interior Far away from the resorts and bustle of the coast, the hill towns of the centre are as ancient as they're isolated. Enna, easily accessible by public transport, is the highlight of any visit to the island, with its *piazze* and churches. There is also Caltagirone, covered with ceramic tiles, and one of the greatest of all Roman villas near Piazza Armerina, with its strangely timeless mosaics.

Tyrrhenian Coast There are several ancient sites along this coast, including Tindari, Himera and Solunto, interspersed with numerous beaches and resorts, the most beautiful of which is the old fishing port of Cefalù, with its Norman cathedral, soaring Rocca and idyllic sandy beach. Just inland are the greener, more peaceful retreats of the Monti Nebrodi and Madonìe, home to forgotten villages, religious sanctuaries and, still, the Mafia.

Aeolian Islands and Milazzo The port of Milazzo is the jumping-off point for the Aeolian Islands (although they can also be reached from Naples, Cefalù and Palermo), a stunning archipelago scattered in the Tyrrhenian Sea. A particular draw is the volcanic activity: the nightly fireworks displays from Strómboli's active volcano, the natural Jacuzzis on Vulcano and Salina's Pollara beach, where *Il Postino* (the poignant story of a friendship between a poet and a postman) was filmed. Activities are mainly water-based: swimming and diving in the crystal sea, or taking one of numerous boat trips to weird offshore islets and grottoes. The islands also boast archaeological treasures, showcased in the Museo Archeológico Eoliano in the resort of Lipari.

Ionian Coast This is Sicily's most striking coast, with Mount Etna as a backdrop. You can walk, drive or take the train around this unforgettable, smouldering boil. Also along the coast is the popular upmarket resort of Taormina, with its magically sited Greek theatre. Nearby are the excavations of ancient Naxos and the Alcántara Gorge. Then there's crumbling Catania, which has a rewarding old centre, an appealingly broody atmosphere and a lively nightlife. Between Catania and Syracuse are villages and archaeological sites well worth a visit. Messina, much rebuilt, still looks good from a ferry if you sail in from the mainland over the magnificent Strait of Messina.

Syracuse and the Southeast This peaceful corner of Sicily harbours both outstanding architecture and strikingly varied landscapes. The main attraction here is Syracuse, the New York of the ancient world, with its enchanting old quarter of Ortygia, and the Archaeological Zone, offering several impressive ruins. The town of Noto is not to be missed, a masterpiece of Sicilian Baroque. Mòdica and Ragusa are striking hill towns, set in rugged landscapes, and now, along with some other towns in this corner, more energized from their UNESCO world heritage designation. The coast includes miles of relatively untouched beaches and the splendid nature reserve beaches of the Vendicari, although the densely industrialized stretch north of Syracuse is largely to be avoided.

History and Art

History

History is a nightmare from which I am trying to awake.

James Joyce

A Busy Prehistory

The island of Sicily was once connected to North Africa, but it became separated in the Tertiary period, long before the coming of the first peoples, who crossed the Strait of Messina in the Upper Palaeolithic period (*c.* 20,000 BC). Inhabiting mostly the coastal areas, these Stone Age peoples have left us not only simple tools but also beautiful incised drawings in the grottoes of Monte Pellegrino in Palermo and the then contiguous island of Levanzo.

Sometime around 4000–3000 BC, influences from the eastern Mediterranean introduced the first Neolithic culture on Sicily, called Stentinello after the village where Sicily's great archaeologist Paolo Orsi first identified the culture. The **Stentinello people** lived in settlements instead of caves, made weapons of obsidian, and decorated their pottery with incisions or seashell impressions. The most culturally advanced Sicilians of this age made their home on the island of Lipari, whose deposits of obsidian made them wealthy; they traded it across the Mediterranean.

After 3000 BC, the relative cultural unity Neolithic Sicily had enjoyed was shattered by waves of invasion and migration, from the Italian peninsula and from the eastern Mediterranean. The southeast remained the most sophisticated corner of the island, with the **Castelluccio culture** (1900–1500 BC) and the maritime **Thapsos culture** (1500–900 BC), named after the walled town on the Magnisi Peninsula north of Syracuse. Copper and rock-cut oven tombs were in favour during this period, brought over to Sicily from the Aegean. Sicilians were also highly skilled in painted and incised pottery (as they are today). Metal didn't become important until after 1500 BC, when the Bronze Age blew in from the east. In Sicily, as elsewhere in the Mediterranean, this was a time of turmoil; people started moving inland from the coasts for protection, founding new settlements on defensible hills, notably at Pantalica.

Greek historians, especially Thucydides and Diodorus Siculus, hand down a good deal of information about pre-Greek Sicily. Thucydides describes the island (the ancient and proper name for which is Trinacria) as inhabited by three peoples when the Greeks arrived: Sikans, Elymians and Sikels. The **Sikans**, the oldest of the three, had most of western Sicily; the Greeks thought of them as the 'aboriginal' inhabitants, though they were probably Iberians who came from Spain or Africa in the early Bronze Age. The **Elymians**, who settled around Segesta and Erice, claimed descent from the Trojans. The third group, the **Sikels**, chased the Sikans out of the east and made it their own some time after 1200 BC. As the Zakkala, the Sikels are mentioned in records of ancient Egypt, as one of the 'Sea Peoples' who wandered the Mediterranean causing trouble after the fall of Troy (*c.* 1180 BC), along with the Etruscans, Achaean Greeks and Sards.

The Arrival of the Greeks and Carthaginians

In the 8th century BC, Greeks from Chalcis, Eretria, Rhodes and Corinth began to colonize the Bay of Naples, then Calabria and the eastern coast of Sicily. Here the first settlements were at **Naxos** (735 BC), **Catania** and, most importantly, **Syracuse** (734 BC). The reasons behind the push towards Magna Graecia – 'greater Greece' – were twofold: the pressures of a growing population at home, and the need to protect their trade routes in the west. The Greek effort was huge and well financed. The new cities prospered from the start, farming, and trading and buccaneering on the seas.

Relations between the Greeks and the native Sikels were complex. It was no simple matter of settlers and Indians: the Sikels were a strong, civilized people themselves. They were not, however, sailors, and had none of the Greeks' flair for trade. So, while in many cases the Greeks had to fight their way in, taking over Sikel towns, in others the Greeks were at first tolerated, or even welcome. Their cities offered the Sikels a market for their exports, and a window on to a new world of wealth and culture. We know that leading Greek and Sikel families inter-married – probably to cement political and economic alliances.

The colonies thrived, and began to split and create new colonies – spreading Greek culture throughout eastern Sicily – such as **Selinunte**, founded *c.* 650 BC from Megara Hyblea, or **Akragas** (Agrigento), *c.* 581 BC from Gela. Their success meant a growing threat to the Phoenicians, who felt their own sea-trading livelihood threatened. The Phoenicians had established outposts around western Sicily in the 10th century BC. Greek expansion coincided with the rise of Carthage (founded in 814 BC), the Phoenicians' main western trading base, which rapidly became more like an empire in its own right. In western Sicily, the most important Carthaginian colonies were **Motya**, **Solunto** and **Palermo**. Greek aggression on the seas, and attempts to found new colonies in the west, led the Carthaginians to reduce most of the west to a 'protectorate' by 529 BC. Greeks and Carthaginians would spend the next two centuries alternately trading with each other and making war.

The Greek 'New World'

This rivalry between Greeks and Carthaginians first came to a head in 480 BC, when the combined Greek armies of Syracuse, Gela and Akragas defeated the Carthaginians in the great **Battle of Himera**. According to the Greeks, it took place on the very day that the Athenians defeated the Persians in the Battle of Salamis. True or not, these two victories over the 'barbarians' initiated a long period of relative peace, which saw amazing achievements by the ancient Greeks at home and in Magna Graecia.

The beautiful, opulent cities of 5th–3rd-century BC Sicily shared fully in Greece's golden age, contributing Empedocles, Archimedes, Stesichorus and Theocritus; other great figures, such as Plato and Aeschylus, came to visit. After Himera, the cities underwent colossal building programmes, creating the largest of all Greek temples in Akragas, and the largest theatre in **Syracuse**. This city became a major power in the central Mediterranean, with naval bases as far away as the Adriatic. Life would have been sweet but for the Greeks' habit, when not threatened from outside, of battering each other. Within the cities, political factionalism pitted tyrants against oligarchic democrats. Losing factions would often invite in outside enemies to get revenge on their own people; such an incident in 485 BC made the future victor at Himera, Gelon of Gela, also the ruler of Syracuse. When one Greek city conquered another, it was entirely normal to raze it and sell its inhabitants into slavery – Syracuse did this to its own colony, Camarina.

A turning-point for Sicily came with the beginning of the **Peloponnesian Wars** in Greece. When Athens gained the upper hand over Sparta, Greek hubris led the city to target Sparta's ally, Syracuse. In 415 BC, Athens sent the greatest fleet in Greek history against her, the Great Expedition. The fleet's total destruction resulted in the end of the Athenian Empire and foretold the end of Greece's golden age. It also confirmed Syracuse as the dominant power of Sicily – but first, however, it gave Carthage a chance for revenge. Under Hannibal (ancestor of the more famous general), the Carthaginians took advantage of the commotion to sweep along the southern coast in 409 BC, destroying Selinunte, Akragas and Gela. This high-water mark of Carthaginian might was not to last. Under the tyrant Dionysius I, Syracuse recovered, united the other Greeks, and counter-attacked. In 397 BC the Greeks captured and destroyed Motya, after which the Carthaginians were only a minor nuisance.

Still, the Greeks continued their sad practice of factionalism and occasional civil war. A break came in 343 BC, when the exhausted factions of Syracuse, unable to agree on a ruler, sent to their mother-city of Corinth for one. Corinth gave them the remarkable **Timoleon**, an obscure fellow with a philosophical turn of mind and a love of justice. He pacified the island, restored democracy to many cities, and refounded others that had been wrecked in the wars. After his death in 336 BC, things took a while to degenerate to the usual bloody-mindedness. **Agathocles**, an adventurer who seized power in Syracuse in 317 BC, was the sort that gave tyrants a bad name. Oppressive at home, his ambitions brought constant warfare to Sicily. Although successful in conquering most of the island, his empire broke up upon his death in 289 BC.

Under the Roman Boot

After Agathocles, the Carthaginians tried their luck once more. This time Greek Sicily was saved by a surprise man on horseback: **Pyrrhus of Epirus**, who brought his large army to Greece at Syracuse's request, and beat the Carthaginians. But an even bigger bogey was looming on the horizon: Rome. That pathologically violent little republic was just gobbling up the Greek cities of the mainland – it was against the Romans that Pyrrhus won his 'Pyrrhic victories', battles that were rendered meaningless when Rome drove him out of Italy in 275 BC.

A showdown between Rome and Carthage was inevitable. It came with the **First Punic War** (264–241 BC), which started in Sicily. Some of Agathocles' old mercenaries, who called themselves the Mamertines ('sons of Mars'), had set up shop in Messina and Taormina. Threatened by Carthage, they called in the Romans to help. Syracuse wisely favoured the Romans; much of the rest of the island got flattened. The Romans allowed most cities to maintain a façade of independence, but most intelligent Sicilians were busy studying their Latin declensions.

In the **Second Punic War**, Syracuse made the fatal mistake of siding with Carthage. After a long siege, drawn out by the wizardry of Archimedes, the Romans fought their way into the city in 212 BC – while Hannibal and his elephants were still wandering helplessly around Italy. Rome now had its first real colonial possession, and Rome knew how to treat it like one. Roman tribute and taxes strangled the cities' commerce, while the victors divided the countryside among themselves, creating huge estates called *latifundia*. In doing so, they also created Sicily's prime evil – an aristocracy of absentee landowners.

Nor did the pillage stop after victory. It never stopped. Sicily became Rome's bread-basket, supplying the grain handed out to Rome's parasites by the dole. Poverty and Roman law pushed vast numbers of free men into slavery, and they were oppressed so meticulously, so scientifically, on the estates, that they rose up in two desperate **Slave Wars**, in 135 BC and 104 BC, both put down with a calculated maximum of blood and gore. Cities that had survived the Greek anarchy now withered and died under the Roman peace. To the Romans, bestowing the position of provincial governor was an open invitation to take. In the year 73 BC, Sicily got a governor so bad he shocked even the Roman Senate. **Verres**, who literally stole everything in Sicily that wasn't nailed down, including the holy statues in the temples, became famous, because Cicero prosecuted him before the Senate. Cicero won his case, the first time such a thing had ever happened.

Rome was growing up a bit, but Sicily never really recovered. The rich, sophisticated world of the Greek cities was ruined and gone for ever, and the near-total lack of Roman buildings testifies to long centuries of destitution and neglect. Under the Caesars, conditions improved somewhat; in the 3rd century AD many Sicilians finally acquired the rights of Roman citizens. The island remained, however, an impoverished agricultural backwater, a vast slave camp, right to the end.

The end came in the 5th century AD. In 410 the **Goths** arrived, but, there being nothing to steal, they did little harm. Neither did the **Vandals**, who passed through in 440. The chronicles of the time, written by the sons of wealthy families in monasteries, gave the Vandals a very bad press, but for the common people their arrival was often a heaven-sent deliverance, an opportunity to sack the great villas and burn the manor records and the tax rolls. After that, Sicily became part of **Theodoric**'s short-lived Gothic Kingdom. The next barbarians, oddly enough, spoke Greek and marched under the eagles of Rome. Byzantine **Emperor Justinian**'s mad and nearly successful attempt to reconquer the West began with an invasion of Sicily in 535, under his dashing general Belisarius. While the Greek population was initially delighted to see him, it soon became clear that Byzantium was only interested in what she could squeeze out of Sicily.

With the decline in sea-borne trade at this time, Sicily's importance had decreased considerably. Largely unmolested, it remained the boondocks it had been in Roman times. In the three centuries of Byzantine rule, the only memorable event was the visit of **Emperor Constans II** in 663, the first emperor to travel to the West since the fall of Rome. Hard-pressed by the Arabs and Slavs at home, Constans was seriously entertaining the idea of moving his capital to Syracuse – until a courtier killed him in the baths with a soap dish.

Muslim Sicily

By the late 8th century, the Arabs were installed in North Africa and making periodic raids on Sicily. Their chance to take it all came in 827, when a Byzantine governor named **Euphemius** revolted (over a sleazy affair with a nun) and asked the Arabs to help. Around 10,000 Berbers, Spanish Muslims and Arabs landed near Mazara, and within three years they had taken Palermo. The Arabs gradually consolidated their hold, crowning it with the surrender of Syracuse in 878 after a long, grisly siege; even then, the Byzantines held on to a few outposts on the east coast for another century.

Under the Arabs, Sicily bloomed once again. Other conquerors had brought colonists, but the Arabs' great contribution was to ship in farmers. They brought with them the best-known techniques in intensive **farming and irrigation**, along with cotton, silk, oranges, lemons, date-palms and sugar. No longer a backwater, Sicily found itself occupying an important place in the new Muslim world. Trade was reborn, and the cities sprang up again, fresh sprouts after the long Roman-Byzantine drought. The new capital, **Palermo**, became the central Mediterranean's marketplace for goods and ideas.

The Arab policy of religious tolerance suited the island perfectly, with its cosmopolitan population of Greeks, Latins, Jews and Muslims. Non-believers had higher taxes to pay, but in turn were excused military service and generally left alone. Even the Greek monasteries were untouched, and Sicilian scholars did their part in helping transmit the lost learning of classical times, along with the new Arab advances in **science and philosophy**, back to the semi-barbarous West.

One thing the Arabs never were able to achieve was political unity. Although there was an emir for each of Sicily's 'Three Valleys', and an Emir of Emirs at Palermo, a real central authority remained elusive; without one, the lordlings were soon raising hell with each other. In the 10th century, the Aghlabids of Tunisia were overthrown, and the Fatimids moved the capital of the Empire to Egypt; with its central position in the Empire removed, Sicily was laid open to attack.

The Norman Kingdom

By about 900, the Northmen, or Normans, were comfortably settled in the Duchy of Normandy that they had wrested from the French. Unfortunately for everyone else, they were producing plenty of little Normans, all of whom grew up to want a fief of their own. The first to reach southern Italy came as pilgrims to Monte Sant'Angelo in Apulia in 1016. They saw a rich land, with no one very frightening to defend it. Soon

Norman second sons were pouring down to Apulia, hiring themselves out as mercenaries to local barons. In those times, a disciplined, armour-clad Norman knight was the equivalent of a tank, and business was so good that soon many of them did manage to acquire fiefs.

Greatest among the Normans were the 12 sons of a modest landowner in Normandy, Tancred de Hauteville. After serving as mercenaries for and against the pope, they were authorized by Pope Nicholas II to rule whatever pieces of southern Italy they could capture, probably in the hope that these powerful nuisances would self-destruct. But by the time the brothers were through, one of them, Robert Guiscard (1015–85), controlled nearly all of southern Italy as the Duke of Apulia, leaving the conquest of Sicily to the youngest brother, **Roger I** (1031–1101), whose remarkable success, through a combination of fighting skill and diplomacy, won him all of Sicily by 1091, and the title Count of Sicily.

Because Roger wasn't followed by a wave of Norman immigrants, necessity dictated reconciliation with the native populations. Their religions were tolerated, and their languages, Arabic and Greek, and to a much lesser extent Latin, were the official languages of Sicily, while Count Roger spoke Norman French. Both Arabs and Greeks served in the government and armies of Roger, and built – especially under Roger's capable son, **King Roger II** (ruled 1112–54) – the churches and palaces that are one of the wonders of Sicily today. Roger II's rule was a second golden age for Sicily. The king's centralized state included all of southern Italy, and briefly Tunisia, as well as Sicily. Palermo, his capital, was one of the most splendid cities of Europe, the cultural centre of the middle Mediterranean.

Unfortunately, the coming of the Normans also meant a re-feudalization of Sicily. Norman power depended on a body of knights, each of whom had to be rewarded with lands and titles. The two Rogers were particularly skilful in keeping their appetites in check, but in the latter days of the kingdom this baronage caused constant trouble, while its grip over the countryside – encouraging manorial self-sufficiency and discouraging trade and innovation – proved an ever increasing burden on the economy.

Although Roger II's son and grandson, William I, 'the Bad' (ruled 1154–66), and William II, 'the Good' (1166–89 – married to Joan of England, sister of Richard the Lionheart), could not match the great king in intelligence and strength, the island continued to thrive, perfecting its unique mixture of cultures. The first William wasn't particularly Bad: he earned the title for the vigour with which he put down noble insurgencies. Neither was his son Good for much: he was good-looking at least, and well intentioned, but his political incapacities and inability to produce an heir presaged the rapid end of the Norman kingdom. After William the Good's death, many Sicilian barons preferred **Tancred**, Count of Lecce, William's bastard nephew; but William had willed the crown to his aunt Constance, a posthumous daughter of Roger II, and to her husband, **Henry of Hohenstaufen**, son of Emperor Frederick I Barbarossa (Sicilians call Henry, and all the Germans that followed, Svevi, Swabians, after the Hohenstaufen homeland). In the end, Henry became King of Sicily only after Tancred's death, by which time he was the Holy Roman Emperor Henry VI. The Empire

had long been Sicily's arch-enemy, but, amidst chaos on the island, Henry brought
down a German army to enforce his claims to the throne. When he was finally
crowned in Palermo, Henry had only three years to live; he died of dysentery in
Messina in 1197.

The Hohenstaufens and Angevins

At the age of 44, Henry's wife Constance became regent for their three-year-old son
Frederick II (1194–1250). Crowned in 1198, he was left orphaned six months later.
Although the mightiest of the medieval popes, Innocent III, was his appointed
guardian, the German barons took control of Frederick, and it was their grasping
influences which Frederick had to shake off to establish himself as king, and later as
emperor. Called Stupor Mundi ('the Wonder of the World'), in his lifetime he made his
court one of the most brilliant in Europe. The seeds of modern Italian literature were
nurtured in Palermo. Greek and Arabic classics were translated, new scientific theories propounded under Frederick's patronage.

Politically, Sicily felt the power of his awe-inspiring personality and benefited from
his rule while he lived; his domains enjoyed the world's first real constitution, the 1
231 **Constitutio Melfitani**. Prosperity was maintained, though taxes were high – to
assist Frederick in his never-ending quarrels with his former guardian, the pope, and
the cities of northern Italy. At home, there were problems. Religious intolerance
fostered by the Church caused frequent revolts, and led many Muslims into a life of
banditry in the mountains (Frederick resettled 20,000 of them in Apulia and put
them under his personal protection). Feudal rebellions became increasingly common;
the string of castles Frederick built across the island testifies to the difficulties of
maintaining control.

The Sicilian Vespers

Not long after Frederick's death, in 1250, his powerful central administration began
to crumble. His son, Emperor Conrad IV, suddenly followed his father to the grave in
1254, during his campaign to claim the crown of Sicily; his son Conradin was too
young to act for himself, and the throne was claimed by Frederick's illegitimate son
Manfred. Crowned in Palermo in 1258, in the face of papal hostility, Manfred quickly
consolidated his power, and by 1261 controlled much of Italy. The newly elected Pope
Urban IV, hastily hunting about for an alternative candidate to support, hit upon
Charles of Anjou, ruthless younger brother of the King of France. Charles' army
invaded Italy, and in Benevento in 1266 slew Manfred in battle. The last hurrah of the
Hohenstaufen came in the person of the young Conradin, who was enthusiastically
received by the Ghibellines in Rome but was soon captured by Charles and beheaded
in Naples (1268), an unpopular act that tainted the Angevins from the start.

Charles heightened the religious persecutions; his heavy taxes, and his grasping
French entourage, made him extremely unpopular. In 1282 the country's hatred

exploded in the **War of the Vespers**, named after the incident at a Palermitan church that triggered the rebellion. Nearly all the French in Sicily were massacred (they were summarily identified by their inability to pronounce *ci*, evidence of how quickly the Sicilian language had become universal). The Sicilian barons convened a parliament and invited **Peter III of Aragon**, husband of Manfred's daughter Constance, to wear the crown of Sicily; he duly accepted, but he and his Spaniards had to defend their new holding against the French for 21 years.

The Spaniards

Under Peter and his sons Alfonso and James, Sicily was treated as nothing more than a mere appendage, a granary for Aragon. James (ruled 1291–8) eventually tried to return the island to the pope and the Angevins for political reasons. The Sicilian barons and James' younger brother, the Viceroy Frederick, reacted to this by holding a parliament in Enna and crowning Frederick 'King of Trinacria', though he has gone down in history as **Frederick II of Aragon** (just to confuse things, he is often known in Sicily as Frederick III).

Frederick's manoeuvrings kept Sicily politically independent, but the situation was deteriorating quickly: the barons grew more powerful, while trade came under the grasping control of the Barcelona merchants. Frederick died in 1337, and the last vestiges of a strong central power went with him. The Black Death arrived 10 years later – another factor contributing to the disintegration of Sicilian society. Power existed primarily in the hands of two families, the **Ventimiglia**, who sided with the Spaniards, and the **Chiaramonte**, who tried to bring the Angevins back. Civil war and anarchy were the order of the day.

In 1412, Trinacria was reunited with the Aragonese crown; later Aragonese kings used the island as a springboard for their ambitions in southern Italy. **Alfonso V** (1416–58), who conquered Naples, paid close attention to Sicily and gave it its first university, at Catania (1434). After him, however, Sicily was ruled indifferently by viceroys. A disaster for Sicily, as for Spain, was the union of the crowns of Aragon and Castile under **Ferdinand and Isabella**. These two nasty bigots gave the island their Inquisition (1487) and decreed the expulsion of the Jews (1492).

Thanks to Spanish misrule and intolerance, Sicily played almost no part in the cultural life of the Renaissance. In the 1500s, instead of art, Sicily had North African and Turkish pirates, causing the depopulation of most of the smaller islands. Spanish rule was a return to Roman times. The aristocracy now had the island in its pocket, substantially aided by the Church with its clammy hordes of monks and nuns; both institutions found that they had a vested interest in enforcing the continuation of poverty and ignorance.

For all its Baroque frippery, the 17th century marks the rock bottom of modern Sicilian history. The only noteworthy events, typically, are natural disasters: the **1669 eruption of Etna** that buried much of Catania, and the terrible **earthquake of 1693**, which killed at least 50,000 and devastated the cities of the southeast.

With the decadence of Spain, Sicily became a pawn for the powers of Europe. After the War of the Spanish Succession (1713), the diplomats fobbed the island off on the House of Savoy, rulers of Piedmont. In 1720 the Savoyans traded it for the nearer and less troublesome island of Sardinia, and Sicily passed to **Austrian rule**. The Sicilians were relieved when in 1734 the Spanish infante, **Charles of Bourbon**, came and took this southern headache away from Austria, meeting little resistance. Charles stayed a week before moving to Naples.

Hard as they tried, the Bourbons never really made a profit out of Sicily in this Mediterranean Dark Age. Constantly in debt, they were forced, among other expedients, constantly to sell titles of nobility to anyone with a little cash. In 1600, Sicily had one prince, a marquis, two dukes and 21 counts; by Napoleon's time there were 142 princes, 788 marquises and 1,566 dukes and counts. Ironically, while much of the population habitually hovered at starvation level, the island was still exporting lots of grain – all the profits going to the noble landowners. Nor were they content with that: by legal chicanery and outright force, the barons in the 17th and 18th centuries managed to grab almost all the common lands of the peasants – some historians estimate this may have been as much as a third of Sicily.

In the 18th century, under the influence of the Enlightenment, there were some glimmers of hope. **Charles III of Naples** (ruled 1734–59), and later of Spain, was the only intelligent man among the last Bourbons, and something of a reformer. Under his successor, Ferdinand IV, two of Charles' old ministers were viceroys in Sicily and made some significant improvements: **Domenico Caracciolo**, Marquis of Villarmina, abolished the Inquisition, confiscated some monasteries and opened schools in the 1780s; his successor, the **Prince of Caramanico**, eliminated the last vestiges of slavery – which had still existed for bankrupt debtors.

A British Interlude

The advent of the French Revolution, however, turned the Bourbons away from reform. Ferdinand came to be increasingly dominated by his Austrian wife, **Maria Carolina**, whose favourite, a reactionary Englishman named **John Acton**, became chief minister in 1789. The news from France was causing great excitement in the south, especially in Sicily; a radical conspiracy against the Bourbons took shape which has been called the 'first act of the **Italian Risorgimento**'. It included not only enlightened nobles and Freemasons but also many members of the small middle classes and even priests; its discovery in 1794 was followed by a fierce police terror across the island. Acton and Maria Carolina had manoeuvered the kingdom into an alliance with Britain, and the British provoked Ferdinand into war against France in 1793 and again in 1798. On the second occasion, Neapolitan troops entered Rome, but the French counter-attacked and soon conquered southern Italy. The royal family escaped on **Admiral Nelson**'s flagship to Palermo. Although the Bourbons were restored to Naples a year later – followed by the usual bloody reprisals – Napoleon came down to boot them out again in 1806; once more Nelson's fleet evacuated the Bourbons and protected Sicily.

As Sicily's strategic importance in the Mediterranean became increasingly evident, the British took a greater hand in the island's affairs; there was talk in the highest circles of annexing Sicily outright. In 1811, the government sent in a 36-year-old colonial officer named **William Bentinck**. Bentinck assumed *de facto* control over Sicily; this *bestia feroce*, as Maria Carolina called him, forced Ferdinand to abdicate in favour of his young son Francesco, and packed the queen off into exile; in 1812 he called the Sicilian parliament and manipulated it into declaring Sicily independent, and adopting a constitution exactly the same as England's (the first time in history, it has been noted, that the English constitution was ever written down on paper). Bentinck had been quite sincere, but to the government back home it was just part of the game. With Napoleon's defeat, Britain decided to forget all about the abdication and constitution and to reinstall the Bourbons. When Ferdinand IV returned, he started calling himself 'Ferdinand I', to emphasize that he now ruled over a united Kingdom of the Two Sicilies in which the traditional separateness of the one real Sicily was to be forgotten forever.

The Age of Revolts

Sicilians, who had lost a constitution, and for whom the end of British rule had meant a general economic depression, had more reason than ever to be disaffected. In 1820, after revolts in Spain and Naples, Sicily acted; interestingly, this time the rebellion was led by the *maestranze*, the ancient trade guilds of Palermo. These could never agree with the radicals of Naples, or even the rest of Sicily, making it much easier for the Bourbons to come back (with the help of an Austrian army) in 1821. This time the bloodbath of liberals and intellectuals was so severe it shocked even the Austrians.

Ferdinand I died in 1825; his successors, Francesco I and the vicious, illiterate **Ferdinand II** (ruled 1830–59), unluckily proved even worse. Southern Italy degenerated into total anarchy, with near starvation of the populace the background for a little theatre of constant revolt and resulting massacre. A **cholera epidemic** in 1836 carried off one-tenth of Sicily's population. For all that, Sicily wasn't down yet. In fact, the great year of European revolutions, 1848, started in Palermo, on 12 January – inspiring the uprisings in Paris, Naples and everywhere else on the continent. Once again the Sicilians moved quickly to create a liberal, constitutional government. An election among all literate males chose a new parliament, with one of the leaders of the revolt, a retired naval officer named **Ruggero Settimo**, as its president. But, yet again, the island's hopes were doomed. Again with Austrian help, and the even greater aid of divisions among the Neapolitan revolutionaries, Ferdinand II regained control on the continent in the spring of 1849. He then sent his troops to Sicily, ordering the artillery to flatten Messina to set an example (thus earning Ferdinand the eternal nickname of Re Bomba, the Bomb King). The Sicilians held out until May, becoming, along with the Venetians and the Hungarians, the last sad survivors of the continental revolution that failed.

The next chance came in 1860, during the climax of Italy's wars of unification, after the Piedmontese with French aid had defeated Austria and occupied most of northern Italy. **Giuseppe Garibaldi** and his 'Thousand' landed at Marsala in May. Garibaldi, a hero of 1848, had raised a small force of idealists, mostly northerners, near Genoa. Eager for the unification of Italy, and disappointed with the conservative Piedmontese, he meant to force the issue by creating a general uprising in the south. This was the plot that succeeded where others had failed. On arrival, Garibaldi declared himself dictator of Sicily, acting in the name of Piedmontese King Vittorio Emanuele II, and then his motley crew defeated a far larger Neapolitan force at Calatafimi. The effect on Sicily, and Europe, was electrifying. Garibaldi entered Palermo soon after. His Thousand swelled to 10 times that with Sicilian volunteers, fighting their way across the island. They took Messina at the end of July, and Garibaldi crossed the Strait to win a final victory, putting the Kingdom of the Two Sicilies out of its misery once and for all.

Mafiosi and Other Scoundrels

The first hints that unification was not to be all that Sicily desired and deserved were not long in coming. The Piedmontese refused to accept Garibaldi's veterans into the new Italian army, while gladly taking all of the old Neapolitan officers – less educated and therefore more reliable. Sicilians voted overwhelmingly to join the new Italian kingdom, but the new conservative, bureaucratic state had no intention of solving its biggest problems: land reform and lack of investment.

Ironically, while Sicilians came to take more than their share of jobs and power in the government, folks back home became ever more resentful of it, rightfully feeling that unification had been a revolution betrayed. Popular revolts against 'the Italians' occurred as early as 1866. In the countryside, these more often took the form of banditry, although in the 1870s a more politically sophisticated form of protest appeared – the *fasci*, a socialist movement made up mostly of peasants, with large contingents of miners and urban workers. Their efforts were met by unrelenting violence, from the government, and especially from the gangs employed by the landowners to maintain their stranglehold on society. The latter phenomenon had a lot to do with the beginnings of the modern **Mafia** (the word became current in the 1860s). The Mafia style of organization dates back perhaps to the Middle Ages; but now, besides its subsidiary rackets, the phrase took on its more familiar form – the Sicilian ruling class's private police.

Though blood flowed liberally across the island, by the 1890s the *fasci* had become the strongest and best-disciplined movement in Italy. Where the Mafia couldn't do the job, the government decided to send in the army. The prime minister in 1892 was **Francesco Crispi**, who had once been Garibaldi's right-hand man in Sicily. But this former radical was also a Sicilian, and a landowner, a fact that had gradually made him forget about Garibaldi and become a fervent admirer of the Prussian leader Bismarck. Crispi declared martial law in Sicily and sent in 15,000 troops; he outlawed the *fasci* and sent most of their leaders (including some of his former comrades-in-arms) to long prison terms. To his credit, Crispi also started the first system of public education, and even attempted some minor land-reform schemes. To the other Sicilian landowners, this was treason: they met in a congress the next year, and demanded that public education be abolished. They also wanted 'reform' on the high grain tariffs, the greatest factor in keeping most Sicilians on the brink of starvation. They wanted the tariffs put even higher.

Crispi's government fell in 1894, and most of the *fasci* leaders were released. They set themselves to work on all sorts of quieter tasks, such as founding cooperatives, but their efforts were dealt a final death blow by **emigration**. Hundreds of thousands of Sicilians decided the only thing to do was leave; from 1890 to 1920 perhaps a quarter of the entire population, including many of the most intelligent and enterprising, departed for the Americas. In the States, they were soon stereotyped as organ-grinders, gangsters and fruit vendors. Today, grandsons of fruit vendors own supermarket chains, and the one profession in which Sicilians are represented far out of proportion to their numbers is teaching.

Sicily after the start of the 20th century had become a quiet, subdued place; the major event was another disaster, the **earthquake of 1908**, which levelled Messina and killed some 80,000 on both sides of the straits. The Mafia was now free to extend its control over the western half of the island, while its links with the political class in Rome increased greatly. The prime minister of Italy at the end of the First World War, the man who went to Versailles with Clemenceau, Wilson and Lloyd George, was a Sicilian and a Mafioso, **Vittorio Emanuele Orlando**.

Fascism and Postwar Disappointments

Though **Mussolini**, a former socialist, stole the name of his new movement from the *fasci*, Fascism was at first a northern phenomenon without significant support in Sicily. The Fascists, though they had no problems with the status quo on the island, became sworn enemies of the Mafia. Mussolini sent down a determined prefect named Cesare Mori, who waged war on the Mafia all through the 1920s and 30s, by legal and extra-legal means. Mussolini also promoted a huge public works programme, modernizing the railways, creating new industries, and building urban developments such as the civic centres in Ragusa and Enna.

During the Second World War, Sicily was the first territory in Europe to be retaken successfully by the Allies, in **Operation Husky**, in July 1943. After annihilating the bases on Pantelleria by air and sea, the Americans, under Patton, stormed the beach at Gela, and the British, under Montgomery, did the same around Pozzallo, a huge combined operation that covered 160km of coastline. Many Sicilian cities were bombarded; Palermo, Catania and especially Messina (again) suffered the most. The Nazis were finally forced to abandon Sicily on 18 August 1943. Ironically, the vacuum they left was quickly filled by Mafiosi, who helped the Allies against the Fascists who had tried to destroy them. Mafia chiefs who had been in prison were freed, and they were soon back to their old tricks.

Sicilian **separatists**, disillusioned with 80 years of Italian rule, were clamouring for independence. The peasants, intellectuals and even some landowners who supported the separatist cause (which was also promoted by famous bandit **Salvatore Giuliano**) hoped to achieve independence at the end of the war, with a little help from the Allies. However, in 1943 the Italian army, the Communists and the Mafia, each for their own reasons fearing an independent Sicily, joined forces against the separatists. When the United Nations was founded in 1945, the Sicilians could not obtain recognition, and the United States wasn't interested when Giuliano proposed Sicily as the 49th State. The last real separatist guerrilla forces were wiped out by the Italian army in 1945, but such was the power of the separatist movement that Italy had to grant Sicily regional autonomy. The first **regional Sicilian parliament** met in 1947, although the Sicilians will be the first to tell you that it is superficial and ineffective against their many problems. Giuliano and his band went on, employed by the landowners to shoot down leftists, as in the notorious **May Day Massacre** at Portella della Ginestra, near Palermo, in 1947. Giuliano was assassinated in 1950 at the age of 27, probably by his friends.

In the 1950s, Sicily was quiet once more. The **Christian Democrats**, in close alliance with the Mafia and the landowners, gained a tight hold on the region's politics. But times had changed. In a game attempt to make up for the neglect of the past, major economic reforms were initiated in the postwar years, notably the **Cassa per il Mezzogiorno** (Fund for the South), supported by the World Bank and Common Market; though something of a sham, the Cassa helped with enormous industrial schemes such as those around Gela and Augusta, ruining miles of coastline but finally giving the island the beginnings of an industrial base. But very little of the profits stayed in Sicily. Some agricultural reforms were also achieved (50 per cent of the arable land had been owned by 1 per cent of the population). The sums and effort spent by governmental attempts at reform seem pathetic when placed next to the work of a single individual – **Danilo Dolci**. Born in the north of Italy in 1924, after the war Dolci left a promising architectural career to help the poor. In 1950 he arrived in western Sicily. One of the first things he saw was a child die of starvation. Like Gandhi, Dolci began a series of fasts (to change policies towards the poor, and improve their housing conditions) that brought him international recognition. Later, he built a modern residential and educational village at Trappeto, offering training and cultural events. In the face of governmental delay and Mafia opposition, he worked hard for the construction of Sicily's largest dam, on the Iato, which has greatly enhanced the fertility of the surrounding valley.

In the 1950s and 60s, few young Sicilians could find a decent job on the island, and tens of thousands were forced to seek work in northern Italy, or in Germany or Switzerland. Today they still do: **unemployment** hovers around 20 per cent, and very few of the German numberplates you'll see on the roads belong to tourists. Ironically, the tracts of wasteland with crumbling shuttered-up houses, and concrete skeletons of unfinished projects that form the most depressing part of the Sicilian landscape, are a result of a deep love of the land. The emigrants can't bear to sell their last link with Sicily, the symbol of the hope that they may some day be able to return to make a living on the island where they were born.

Sicily Today

How is Sicily doing? Economically, it isn't easy to tell; any statistics you may see will be mere guesses (one that you can believe is the **illiteracy** rate, said to be about 15 per cent, and **unemployment**, running at around 15–20 per cent). The distortion caused by **undercover criminal activity**, especially the billions in drugs money that flow in each year, has created an economy that cannot be controlled by the State, or even under-stood. On the one hand, the primeval, grinding poverty still in evidence in the 1950s has gone; on the other, no one believes that Sicily is keeping up with the rest of Italy, let alone catching up. If statistics are meaningless, then we are left with impressions.

The island seems less dark, less introspective than a decade or two ago. There are new cars on the road. Sicilians definitely know what the **new Europe** is about, and they definitely want to take part. Everyone is moving to the cities, to the coasts. The villages are emptier, though oddly they seem less decayed; there are fewer sharecrop-pers – driven out by **mechanization**, not good intentions – and more modern farmers.

Sicilian history continues to scream out of our daily newspapers, though at this point it is too early to tell if the present flurry of activity is a real revolution or merely another false start. The first serious efforts to **investigate the Mafia**, in the 1970s, led to retalia-tion against prosecutors and judges. Most publicized and most spectacular of the murders was that of **General Dalla Chiesa**, the police prefect, a short time after he assumed office in 1982. From that followed the *maxiprocessi* of 1986, with the familiar sight of hundreds of Mafiosi in their glass cage in the Palermo courtroom. Most were convicted, though many were later released on appeal by corrupt judges. The Mafia stepped up the pressure in 1992 with the car-bomb murders of its two chief tormen-tors, the courageous prosecutors **Giovanni Falcone** and **Paolo Borsellino**; the politicians who dared attend their funerals were jeered by huge crowds and nearly assaulted.

Other capable prosecutors have come forward to take their places. They have since had two important breaks. First, the capture of **Salvatore Riina**, *capo di tutti capi*, in January 1993; the 'most wanted man in Europe', Riina had been living openly in his home village of Corleone for two decades. The other was the explosion of the *tangen-topoli* scandal up north, which had come to involve many national politicians, and shed much light on their Mafia connections. Former seven-times Prime Minister **Giulio Andreotti** lost his parliamentary immunity in 1992, and in 1995, while still a senator, went on trial for the killing of Mino Pecorelli, a journalist who was about to publish his discoveries on the obvious connections Andreotti had with the Mafia. His trial was a classic piece of Italian comic-drama, with the court first clearing him on 1999 for 'lack of evidence', then when the case reopened in 2001 sentencing him to 24 years in prison but only to be over-ruled by a higher court in 2003 which definitively cleared him of any charges.

However, a steady flow of *pentiti*, informants who break with the Mafia's traditional code of silence and testify against bosses in exchange for more favourable treatment from prosecutors, guarantees that the trials will continue. In early 1999, the bands responsible for the assassinations of Judges Falcone and Borsellino, as well as those guilty of setting the bombs that destroyed part of the Uffizi Gallery in Florence and the Church of San Giovanni in Rome in 1993, were sentenced to long prison terms. Throughout 2002 the anti-Mafia squad arrested several key figures of the Sicilian Mafia, including government officials, in raids across the country after a two-year investigation, and in 2003 Salvatore Sciarabba, the top aidee of the 30-years-in-hiding 'Boss of Bosses' Bernardo Provenzano, was arrested in central Palermo, just a few hundred meters from the courthouse.

Investigations into the business dealings of prime minister Silvio Berlusconi involved a raid on his Milan headquarters by anti-Mafia police in 1998 and a hasty trip to Sicily where Berlusconi denied charges of laundering money for the Mafia, though a much-argued law passed by parliament in June 2003 gave Mr Berlusconi immunity as long as he remains in office. Incidentally, Berlusconi's re-election in 2001 had the majority of Sicily's votes and his right wing Forza Italia Party makes much of the immigration that is flooding Sicily's southern islands in particular from North Africa.

Sicily is becoming more relaxed and less politically introverted day by day. What still doesn't seem to be changing, according to some, is the petty corruption of ordinary life: there are claims that you only get a job if you know the 'right' people. While no one can conclude that the Mafia is a thing of the past, there are signs that the tide has finally turned and there is a more open attitude in which people at least admit to the existence of the Mafia. The last two mayoral elections in Palermo were notably different from their predecessors in which the main issue of the campaign related to the city itself rather than the alleged corruption of one or all of the candidates. It is likely that the continuing efforts at making Italy a central player in the European Union should keep up the pressure.

Art and Architecture

The many different peoples who have occupied Sicily make any account of its rich artistic heritage something of a bumpy, stop-and-start ride. Although a tragic amount has been lost through natural disasters, vandalism, wars and neglect, what still stands today is remarkable by any standards. One Sicilian constant throughout all the ages and changes is a love of colour and decoration; the second, perhaps owing to Sicily's unique geography, is an almost magical sense of theatre and harmony in setting a building in its environment, an inborn geomancy that the modern world doesn't understand and has sometimes actively destroyed.

Greeks and Romans

Sicily has more ancient Greek temples than Greece itself, and nearly all are Doric – the style of the Parthenon in Athens. **Doric temples** evolved from wooden models, and are characterized by columns tapering up like the trunks of trees, with broad flutings that narrow at the top. The simple Doric capitals, in Sicily invariably deco-rated only with three incised concentric circles, are topped by a plain architrave, above which runs a carved frieze of square metopes separated by grooved triglyphs that symbolize the end of the wooden beams. Above the frieze is a triangular pediment framing the tympanum, which was often decorated, in early temples, with a prophy-lactic mask of Medusa, protecting the religious secrets within. Decorative plaques stood up from the corners and over the pediments; and (apparently a Sicilian speciality) there were elaborate, ornamental, brightly painted antefixes, which hid the ends of the roof tiles along the eaves and cornices. As with all Greek temples, nearly all but the columns was colourfully painted. Since Sicily has no fine marble,, the columns were made of sandstone and covered with a stucco made of marble dust.

The greatest innovation of Greek temple builders in Sicily was size: among the temples in the valley of ancient Akragas (Agrigento), is the largest in the world. Another at Akragas is one of the best preserved, along with beautiful lonely Segesta. Although the Carthaginians flattened the temples at Selinunte, several of their magnificent metopes (6th century BC) survive in the Archaeological Museum in Palermo, examples of the Greek move from Egyptian models to a more natural sense of movement in **sculpture**. By the next century, anatomy would be completely mastered, in Sicily represented by two remarkably sexy statues: the *Landolina Venus* in Syracuse, and the recently discovered *Charioteer* in Motya.

Greek **theatres** in Sicily are nearly as impressive as the temples for the sheer beauty of their settings. Taormina is only the most spectacular; others are at Tindari, Segesta and Syracuse, the latter carved in the living rock. Both the archaeological museums in Syracuse and Palermo testify to a wide-ranging talent in **painted pottery**, although it was a school of potters on Lipari who first painted in a variety of colours. The Greeks in Sicily were also famous for their elegant **terracottas** (especially Gela and Syracuse).

The Romans took far more than they contributed to Sicily. In the late Empire, however, they did build sumptuous Imperial **villas** the size of small towns on their great proto-feudal estates, especially at Piazza Armerina, where the floors are ablaze with magnificent mosaics. Others are at Patti and San Biagio. **Catacombs** in Syracuse and elsewhere were decorated in a primitive manner by early Christians.

Normans

Little that was built by the Byzantines or the Arabs has survived, but a record of their talent remains in the late 11th–mid-13th-century **churches and palaces** erected by the Normans, who hired local craftsmen. The first small churches (at Palermo) are topped with high mosque-like cupolas; later Norman buildings, more reminiscent of the austere verticals of northern **French Romanesque**, are decorated with intricate polychrome interlacing of **Arab-Byzantine** inspiration. Sculptors from Burgundy and Provence carved capitals and cloisters; Arab craftsmen carved and painted wooden ceilings. Greek mosaicists, and later Venetians, decorated the walls with glimmering **mosaics** that are among the finest medieval works of art anywhere: Cefalù and Monreale cathedrals, and Palermo's Cappella Palatina and Martorana church. Other important Norman works survive near Castelvetrano and in the Greek churches south of Messina; the best is SS. Pietro e Paolo, near Forza d'Agrò.

Gothic and Renaissance

The changing political climate saw to it that the Swabians contributed mostly **castles** to Sicily, bastions of imperial control – Frederick II's Castello di Lombardia in Enna, Castello Maniace in Syracuse, Castello Ursino in Catania, and the Castle of Augusta. These stark, functional, strangely modern castles show a strong influence from contemporary works in the Middle East; it is likely that Frederick brought some Arab architects home with him from the Crusades. The early days of Aragonese rule (late 13th–14th century) saw urbane *palazzi* go up (along with a score more castles); the **Palazzo Chiaramonte** in Palermo gave its name to a widespread local Gothic style that derived ornamental features from the Normans (interlacing arches, polychrome geometric stone work) with arched mullioned windows. Palazzo Sclàfani, San Francesco d'Assisi and Sant'Agostino in Palermo are other examples. In the 15th century, a native of Noto named Matteo Carnelivari introduced the florid grace of **Catalan Gothic** to Palermo, mixed with a few new Renaissance ideas – in Palazzo Abatellis, Santa Maria della Catena, and Palazzo Aiutamicristo, all in Palermo.

Sicilian painters are completely overshadowed by the figure of **Antonello da Messina** (1430–79; *see* p.273), whose exquisite subtlety of colour and understatement make him one of the great masters of Renaissance art. Four paintings remain on his native island, two damaged by earthquakes at Messina and Syracuse, a third at Cefalù, and the fourth, his masterpiece *Annunciation*, at Palermo.

Renaissance sculpture was first introduced in Sicily by the great Dalmatian **Francesco Laurana** (1439–1503), whose subtle geometry of form was too sophisticated to find any disciples on the island (see his bust of Eleanora of Aragon and Mastrantonio Chapel in San Francesco d'Assisi, both in Palermo, his portal of Santa Margherita, Sciacca, and the Madonna in SS. Crocifisso, Noto). It fell to the lesser, more sentimental, talent of Lombard **Domenico Gagini** (*c.* 1430–92) to found a school (mostly through procreation), and spread the gospel of the Renaissance into every other church in Sicily. The greatest of the Gaginis was Domenico's son Antonello, whose many Madonnas and Annunciations are often tender and moving (especially when the gaudy paint has flaked off): fine examples are in the cathedrals in Syracuse, Nicosia and Palermo, and in Tràpani's Santa Maria del Gesù. Antonello's sons, Antonino, Giacomo, Vincenzo and Fazio, often assisted him, and went on to produce their own altars, choirs, façades and pulpits.

Sicilian Baroque

In the 17th and 18th centuries, Sicily was regarded by its rulers as more of a dead-end backwater than a cultural crossroads. Yet this backwater took the new Baroque medium invented in Rome and, finding its theatrical and extravagant luxuriousness very much to its taste, made the style its own. Sicilian Baroque is characterized by its fantasy, dynamism and emphasis on façades and ornamentation, rather than on the complex geometry, structure and play of shadow and light that characterize Baroque in northern Italy. Surviving works from the early 1600s are fairly orthodox (the Quattro Canti in Palermo and Giovanni Vermexio's Municipio in Syracuse), but **Natale Masuccio**'s curvaceous Jesuit church in Tràpani (1636) offers a preview of coming attractions. Masuccio was from Messina and, although everything in his home town was lost in the earthquake, he influenced Sicily's greatest Baroque architect, **Filippo Juvara** (b. 1678, Messina), who left in 1700 for fame in Rome, Turin and Madrid.

Fortunately for Sicily, most of her other native architects stayed at home, although many spent time training in Rome. Nearly all were priests as well, among them the Jesuits who decorated Palermo's lavish Gesù in the 1630s; as was **Paolo Amato** from the little village of Ciminna (1633–1714), author of Palermo's San Salvatore, the first church in Sicily built on a curvilinear plan (1682); and Palermitan **Giacomo Amato** (1643–1732), who introduced Roman High Baroque to his home town (Santa Teresa di Kalsa, Sant'Ignazio all'Olivella). Another early figure was **Giovanni Biagio Amico**, from Tràpani (1684–1754), whose church façades are among the most dynamic and lively in the west (Sant'Anna in Palermo, San Lorenzo in Tràpani). The most innovative of all are the dreamy extravagances in Bagheria; the Villas Palagonia and Valguarnera are by **Tommaso Napoli** (1655–1725), a Dominican monk.

Whatever was built on the east coast prior to 1693 was lost in the cataclysmic earthquake. Fortunately, by the time the towns and cities were ready to rebuild, two architects of exceptional talent were on the scene. **Rosario Gagliardi** (c. 1700–70), a priest born in the southeastern corner of Sicily, created some luscious, sculpted façades (Ragusa's San Giorgio and San Giuseppe, Módica's San Giorgio), and was one of the prime movers behind the re-creation of Noto on its entirely new site, along with his niece's husband, Neoclassicist Vincenzo Sinatra. The second architect was **Giovanni Battista Vaccarini**, from Palermo (1702–70), who studied in Rome and returned in 1730 to remake Catania into a stunning pageant of lively Rococo, in a highly original meld of Borromini and Sicilian panache (see especially Catania's Badia di Sant'Agata, Palazzo Municipale and cathedral). Another original architect working on the east coast was **Andrea Palma**, from Tràpani (1664–1730), who designed Syracuse's cathedral; in Palermo he created a lavish interior in Santa Caterina.

As theatrical as the façades of Sicily's Baroque churches are, they are often matched, if not blown away into immediate amnesia in the visitor's mind, by interiors swimming in coloured marbles and stucco decoration. The latter was the speciality of **Giacomo Serpotta** of Palermo (1656–1732), who left his incredibly lively plaster statues of saints, allegories of the virtues, and hilarious tumbling *putti* in a number of churches and oratories in western Sicily, especially Palermo (his masterpieces are the oratories of Santa Cita, San Domenico and San Lorenzo). Of all Italian sculptors of the period, Serpotta is considered the truest Rococo spirit, with a cheerfulness and grace none of his more drama-prone contemporaries on the peninsula could equal. He had several followers: his brother Giuseppe and Giuseppe's more talented son Procopio, and Vincenzo Messina, whose masterpiece is the oratory in Carini.

Sicilian paintings in the period seem dim next to the accomplishments of the island's architects and *stuccatori*. Early decorations were provided by the prolific, if not inspiring, Giuseppe Salerno, called **Lo Zoppo di Ganci** (1570–1632). Caravaggio spent time in Sicily after murdering a man in Rome, and left some haunting paintings at Messina and Syracuse that inspired the early career of **Pietro Novelli** of Monreale (1603–47), one of the fathers of Baroque painting; one of his best works is in the monastery near the cathedral of Monreale. The 17th-century **Fra Umile da Petralia**, from Petralia Soprana high in the Monti Madonie, had never heard of Baroque, but carved extremely naturalistic wooden Crucifixions that are the treasures of the region's churches. In the 18th century, the saccharine Flemish painter **Wilhem (Guglielmo) Borremans** travelled about Sicily, ladling his sticky sugar-candy art on the ceilings and domes.

Neoclassical and Liberty

As the 18th century reached its close, Sicily's best architect, **Venanzio Marvuglia** (1729–1814), interpreted the fashionable Neoclassicism of the day with touches of Sicilian Baroque (in Palermo's oratory of Sant'Ignazio all'Olivella and in the Botanical Gardens). Other Neoclassical works are mostly impressive for their size, especially the Teatro Massimo in Palermo (1875), designed by Giovanni Battista Basile. A far more important figure is the latter's son, Ernesto (1857–1932). Art Nouveau in Italy is known as Liberty, after the fabrics exported by the famous department store in London; in Sicily its chief interpreter was **Ernesto Basile**, a student of Sicily's medieval decorative tradition. Basile designed not only buildings, but also furniture and details, down to the door knockers, to create a perfect environment. Most of his few surviving works are in Palermo and, although his masterpiece, Villino Florio, was burned out inside, don't miss the salon of the Villa Igiea (also see Ispica and Caltagirone).

In the early 20th century, the major project was the rebuilding of **Messina** after the 1908 earthquake. The 'Borzi plan' for new streets provided a surprisingly elegant network of boulevards and a skilful use of the city's waterfront. **Mussolini**'s programme of public buildings on Sicily was the most ambitious of any region in Italy. The Duce meant well, to make amends for the neglect Sicily had suffered since unification, but the results of his totalitarian Art Deco approach are uneven. Usually made of Roman travertine, with ambiguous slogans about mystic power (now mostly effaced) engraved on their façades, the best examples are the skyscraper, central post office and central fire station of Palermo, big civic centre projects in Ragusa and Enna, and the harbour-front ensemble of Messina. Of Sicilian postwar architecture, typically sprawling suburbs, the less said the better – as is true of the rest of Italy.

Culture

03

Goethe Takes a Holiday

*To have seen Italy without having seen Sicily is not to
have seen Italy at all, for Sicily is the clue to everything.*
                        Goethe, *Italian Journey*

In 1786, at the age of 38, Goethe suffered a severe mid-life crisis at the court in Weimar and bolted for Italy when no one was looking. Famous all over Europe as the author of *Werther*, he travelled under a false name, and did much to blaze the Grand Tour with his *Italian Journey*, published from his letters and notes in 1816. Many have used it as their guide, at least to Naples; but only a minority of Grand Tourists even now take up his challenge to sail on to Sicily.

'To me, Sicily implies Asia and Africa,' he wrote, a sentiment that would make any northern Italian smile in agreement. But Goethe's interests were historical and classical; he longed 'to stand at that miraculous centre upon which so many radii of world history converge'.

Goethe was one of the greatest poets who ever lived, but his *Italian Journey* could have been written by an awestruck insurance salesman; his insights are ponderous and trite, his opinions on art marvels of philistine conformity. Everything is beautiful, or important or simply fills him with emotion. Much of his descriptions apparently hides what he was really thinking about – sex being near the top of the list; its easy availability in Italy did much to make the country irresistible to Romantic poets and artists of all nationalities.

Goethe's adventures would be the envy of any traveller today, who may come home with only the account of a missed airport bus to jazz up their holiday tale. Two hundred years ago it took three or four days to sail from Naples to Palermo; Goethe was so seasick he couldn't stand up, but he still managed to compose an act or two of a play. On the return sail from Messina, his ship came within inches of crashing into the sheer cliffs of Capri; its neutral flag served to keep pirates at bay.

We take cameras to record our travels; Goethe took his own artist. In Naples he hobnobbed with Sir William and Lady Hamilton. In Palermo he impersonated an Englishman to meet the mother and relatives of Cagliostro. He was entertained by the viceroy, counts and princes, and had an amusing encounter with the gruff governor of Messina.

Inns, however, were few and far between, and, in an especially desperate one, Goethe described how the beggars fought the dogs for his sausage skins and apple parings. In other towns, Goethe and his artist had to buy a chicken from a peasant, and hire his pots, stove, dishes and table; they were grateful for a pestilent mattress to sleep on in the barn. Think of that when you can't decide between the lobster or swordfish kebabs on the restaurant menu.

Goethe spent a month and a half in Sicily alone. Few modern travellers have the luxury to dawdle so. But a journey was a far more serious business then, a once-in-a-lifetime experience; not only did Goethe see the sights, but he theorized on the 'primal plant', measured temples and ancient sculpture, read the *Odyssey* in Greek and began a new play. But most of all, Goethe travelled to learn about Sicily, and about himself; and his journey took on the weight of an archetype as old as the *Odyssey* itself: 'If I cannot come back reborn, it would be much better not to come back at all.'

The Magician from Palermo

If, like Goethe, you are determined, you can find his house in the most squalid slum of Palermo's Albergheria quarter, just off Piazza Ballarò and Via Benfratelli, in a dark, wretched alley named after him in 1869: Vicolo Conte Cagliostro. The first house on the corner, not only does it look abandoned, it doesn't even have a door.

By all accounts except his own, Giuseppe Balsamo, alias Count Alessandro Cagliostro, came into the world here on 2 June 1743. He was bright but unruly, gifted in art and chemistry – in those days a subject halfway between science and magic. Booted out of monastic school for blasphemy, he made a living forging theatre tickets. His greatest coup was convincing a goldsmith that he had discovered a cave on Monte Pellegrino full of treasure, but guarded by devils who could only be lured away by 60 ounces of gold. The goldsmith brought the gold, Giuseppe began to dig, and the 'devil' came out of the darkness and hit the goldsmith with a stick, frightening him so badly that he ran home. By the time he took the matter to the police, Giuseppe and the gold were in Messina.

There the young rascal met a famous Armenian alchemist named Altolas. With Altolas, Giuseppe travelled to Greece, Egypt and Malta, where the Grand Master of the Knights let the two seek the Philosopher's Stone in his laboratory. After Altolas accidentally poisoned himself, Giuseppe ended up in Rome, where, thanks to a forged letter, he was taken in by the Maltese ambassador, who set him up in business distilling love potions and beauty creams. In 1768, Giuseppe married a pretty 14-year-old Roman named Lorenza Feliciani who would cheat on him right and left, usually with Giuseppe's pimping connivance.

An intrigue gone sour forced the newlyweds to leave Rome. It was then that Giuseppe Balsamo decided to re-create himself as the greatest magician in Europe. He took the name Cagliostro, and let it be known that he had been born in ancient Egypt and had been raised by the alchemist Salaahim, that he had given Jesus Christ a few pointers, and that he had personally assassinated Pompey.

'To really know a thing, you must become that thing,' wrote Giuseppe Balsamo. Becoming Cagliostro took him years of work, often one step ahead of the law. Real fame and fortune came only when he moved to London for a second time in 1776 (the first time he had been imprisoned for blackmail). He gave a Mr and Mrs Scott some numbers and they won £2,000 at the lottery. Overnight, Cagliostro was famous; people flocked to him for numbers, pills and his 'elixir of long life'. He declared he had found the Philosopher's Stone. He joined the Scottish Rite Masons.

Although the Scotts denounced Cagliostro as a charlatan for not supplying more winning numbers, the count returned to the Continent with his reputation intact. He founded his own Masonic Lodge and was offered the dukedom of Mittau, which he refused. In St Petersburg he counselled Catherine the Great, and in Strasbourg he made the blind see and the crippled walk, until rumours of his works reached the Cardinal of Rohan, a close relative of the King of France. Rohan invited Cagliostro to live in his palace in Paris and told everyone that he had watched him create a diamond out of thin air.

Cagliostro intended to make Paris the headquarters for his Masonic Lodge, but was thwarted by a less happy experience with diamonds. Ironically, in the case of the 'Diamond Necklace Affair', Cagliostro, perhaps for the first time ever, was completely innocent. Rohan, a dupe of the first order, had been completely taken in by a 'countess' claiming to be Marie-Antoinette's trusted confidante. Rohan arranged the financing of a fabulous diamond necklace that the 'countess' led him to believe the queen secretly wanted to buy. When Marie-Antoinette was approached by the jewellers for payment, she blew a fuse and had Louis XVI send Rohan and Cagliostro to the Bastille.

Both were soon acquitted, but it was the beginning of the end for the count. He went back to London only to find mockery: Lorenza had told the truth about his humble past to a journalist. She apologized and insisted they go back to Rome. Cagliostro could never say no to her, and went back to brewing love potions.

He made a splash at Rome's Masonic Lodge in September 1789, when he hypnotized a girl who predicted accurately to within three weeks the beginning of the French Revolution. The Inquisition became very interested in his activities, and Lorenza, obviously immune to her husband's love potions, confessed that the count was guilty of Freemasonry. In December 1789 he was arrested and sentenced to death, a sentence commuted to life imprisonment at the terrible Rocca di San Leo; for four and a half years he slowly went mad in a tiny, dark, rat-infested room, unrepentant to the end, until he finally died in 1795.

The Church forbade his burial in consecrated ground. A few years later, when Napoleon showed up at San Leo, wanting to pay his respects at Cagliostro's tomb, no one could find it. But back in Palermo, around Piazza Ballarò, they knew the truth: that he's tucked somewhere in the Catacombs of the Cappuccini, and that at night the mummies come down off the walls to pay him homage.

Puppets and Mafiosi

The Crusades of the 11th century gave the Normans a taste not only for conquest but also for chivalry. The first appetite they gratified in southern Italy and England, the second in a strict code of honour and the deeds of King Arthur, Charlemagne and Roland, 'Orlando' in Italian. Their new Sicilian subjects devoured the tales, and came to look upon the Norman kingdom as a Golden Age; the Normans stayed and built palaces, while none of Sicily's subsequent rulers even bothered to visit, leaving the day-to-day corruption to viceroys and petty officials.

Dogged by centuries of injustice and misrule, the Sicilians preserved the Norman code of honour amongst themselves. Even the poorest illiterate could follow the adventures of Carlomagno's paladins in the *opera dei pupi*, or puppet theatre, where the moral of the story is always the same: a man's most important possession is his honour. And as the law of the land failed to defend honour or property, landowners hired companies of armed men (*compagnie d'armi*) to do it for them.

Secrecy was essential and, to maintain it, the penalty for any affront, large or trivial, was death. The fact that the landowners were nearly always absent from their estates left the *compagnie d'armi* free to cross over into the brigandry they were supposed to fight. The Mafia was only a step away.

The origins of the name 'Mafia' are said to be the Arabic for protection, *mu'afah*. Sicilians traditionally prefer euphemisms such as the *amici* (friends) or the *onorata società* (the 'honoured society'). Until relatively recently, the Mafia's activities were limited to the western half of Sicily, where feudal agricultural estates survived the longest. And, for a long time, the Mafia preserved some rudiments of chivalry; even the most powerful dons led austere lives, donated large sums to charity, assisted the needy, and came down heavily on freelance crime.

But what useful purpose the Mafia may have served was always balanced by its sinister stranglehold: it has always been ruthlessly efficient, murderously vindictive, diverse and hard to pin down. The Italians compare it to the many-headed Hydra or octopus, *piovra*, who grew a new head or limb whenever one was lopped off. The only person who came close to destroying the monster was Mussolini, who didn't like the competition. The Mafia's hatred of the Fascists made it a strange bedfellow for the Allies, and the collaboration of the US Army and the Mafia under the auspices of Lucky Luciano has already become Italian folklore. Liberation for benighted Sicily meant the return of 'the friends'.

After the Second World War both the *teatro dei pupi* and the old Mafia suffered a decline: both had become anachronisms. New roads, money and jobs were transforming Sicily, and no one cared for the old code of honour; money, a scarcity before, became the new criterion of respect. But while the knightly puppets are now benign folklore, the new Americanized urban Mafia nefariously adapted to the times, infiltrating the government and raking off building funds, expanding protection rackets and, like the American Cosa Nostra, delving into gambling, prostitution and, most notoriously, heroin – activities the old dons would have shunned.

What has also changed are the attitudes of the Sicilians – now that the Mafia has devoted itself wholeheartedly to crime, its latent support has been replaced by a sense of revulsion; the 'friends' have irrevocably become the enemies of the just and honourable. Their poison threatens all of Italy despite the brave efforts of anti-Mafia squads, commissions and judges, the paladins of our day who thwack off one head of the monster after another, and are themselves often the targets of assassination and intimidation. Like the puppet shows, each performance leaves spectators hanging in the air, waiting for the next episode. But for the first time in years, the good guys are often on the winning side (*see* **History and Art**, p.21).

A Sicilian Day

All Italians wear watches as fashion accessories, but down south in Sicily you'll never need one unless you have a train to catch. It will always be more pleasant to follow the natural rhythms of the place, which follow as strict a schedule as any mechanical timepiece, and which probably have not changed much since King Cocalus' day.

In place of alarm clocks, the average Sicilian town has cement-mixers, which begin churning half an hour after dawn. It's a fine thing to be out then, in the cool of the morning, with the rose-tinted early light. The tradesmen are going about their jobs and don't look sleepy at all, while the *galantuomini*, in starched shirts and *fedoras*, stroll past on the way to their sinecures – after a coffee or two. A crisp aroma of fresh bread fills the side streets; the baker, his arms dusted with flour, lounges in the doorway enjoying an early-morning smoke and watching the passing parade.

An hour or so later, and you'll have to keep your wits about you: the ladies upstairs have finished washing the floors, and they'll be dumping their buckets over the balconies. Shopping is their next job, and the place soon becomes as busy as a Sicilian town can ever get, save only on the Sunday of the local festival. Old fellows gesticulate in serious discussion around the newspaper kiosks, and the younger ones, who repair toasters or restore Bourbon furniture, take their work out on to the pavement so as not to miss any of the comings and goings.

You'll know it's past 11.30am when, instead of *buongiorno*, shopkeepers send you off with *buon appetito*. The approach to the day's climax, the midday meal, begins with a majestic traffic jam that balloons to total gridlock by 11.55. The town's constabulary dons white gloves and rushes on to the streets.

Gradually the mess is sorted out, and by 1pm your Sicilian town has assumed the uncanny quiet of the grave. It will stay that way for about three hours. The burning sun commands the deserted town like a lion; passing a human being, you feel an urge to stop and talk, like travellers meeting in the desert. At least one bar remains open, to offer an iced coffee or *granita* to poor souls marooned in the void.

Once the worst of the day's heat has passed, rebirth begins with a small swarm of Fiats, suddenly buzzing around the fountain like flies around a light bulb, startling the Sicilians from their afternoon reverie. The streets are full again by 5pm, though without much of the delight and purposefulness of the morning. People go out to do what must be done. The old fellows now are subdued into wooden chairs in front of the local headquarters of their political party or community centre. The bars are busy, and ice cream disappears in impressive quantities.

At dusk comes the day's last landmark, the *passeggiata*, or promenade. It's a constant revelation for the visitor to see how the often dour, inscrutable Sicilians quietly celebrate the sense of living together and enjoy each other's company.

That's all there is. The *passeggiata* fades into a peaceful night. There may be a dull, decorous political rally, or an outdoor concert for the teenagers, but, if it isn't a big town, most likely the streets will be empty again by 11pm. Nights are for rest: they'll all want to be up with the cement-mixer again tomorrow.

Sicily's Goddess

*...they neither plow
nor sow by hand, nor till the ground, though grain –
wild wheat and barley – grows untended, and
wine-grapes, in clusters, ripen in heaven's rain.*
                                       Odyssey, Book 9

In the 8th century BC, about the time when the Homeric epics were taking the form in which we know them, the Greeks were scouting the coasts of Sicily for settlement. Old legends of Cyclopes and cannibal Laestrygones could not frighten them away, for, as everyone knew, Sicily was the earthly paradise, where the crops grew of their own accord and the scent of the flowers was so thick and strong that hunting dogs could not follow a trace.

According to the Sicilian-born writer Diodorus Siculus (*c.*90–21 BC), in the 1st century BC wild wheat could still be found on the rich plains around Lentini (that would be rare: wheat is something of a mystery, and has never been found in a wild state anywhere). Grain had been the special gift of Demeter, goddess of the earth, to the island she loved above any place on earth. The aboriginal Sikans claimed that she had once lived among them, and besides their food she had also given them their laws. By whatever name she had among them, the Greek settlers recognized the similarity of the ancient Sicilian goddess to their Demeter, the golden-haired sister of Zeus.

The Sikans must have had some other tales that rang a bell with the Greeks. In fact, the Sikans knew the very place where Kore (Persephone), Demeter's daughter, had been carried off by Hades, Lord of the Underworld. Everyone knows this story. Young Kore had been picking flowers on the shore of Lago di Pergusa, near Enna. Her Uncle Hades, who had heard of her beauty, broke through the earth with his chariot and carried her off, returning down below at the fountain of Cyane, near Syracuse. Her distraught mother, not knowing what had happened, roamed the Earth in search of the girl. When she was told by the one witness to the rape, Triptolemus the shepherd, she was so angry that she forbade the fruits of the earth to grow. The land became barren; men were dying and the gods of Olympus no longer received the honour of their sacrifices. Zeus commanded Kore's return, and Hades agreed, provided the maiden had not tasted any of the food of the underworld during her stay. But those seven seeds of the pomegranate Kore tasted did her in; in the divine compromise that was worked out, Kore and Demeter would be reunited, but Kore would have to return to Hades for three months of the year. Thus the barren season – though in the Mediterranean this is not the mild green winter but the wretchedly dry late summer after the grain harvest. Go to Sicily in August or September and you'll understand.

As in so many Greek myths, there is a good deal of late literary embroidery here, superimposed on ancient faith. Demeter and Kore were originally not so much mother and daughter as – along with all the other female deities of the Mediterranean – aspects of the same transcendent Great Goddess. Demeter at harvest, and Kore at the *anodos*, the 'rising of the maiden' in the late autumn (or spring, in cooler climes), when life returns to the Earth. Keep her in mind, for she is the necessary protagonist of this book or any other book about Sicily.

In any of the island's Greek cities there were numerous temples – most, in that increasingly secular age, little more than civic monuments, treasuries or public art galleries. The one that counted, the only one that inspired any real religious emotion, was outside the walls, the sanctuary of Demeter and Kore, where archaeologists find thousand upon thousand of ceramic ex-voto offerings. On this most religiously conservative of islands she survived the coming of Christianity to reappear as the Virgin Mary: the festival processions, with her image on a cart, or perhaps a maiden of the village on a white horse, differ little from those of two millennia or more ago.

And so she presides over the eternal Sicilian melancholy; you may feel her mourning for her lost daughter, or son, for everything that has been lost or spoilt over the centuries. The wild flowers and the rich crops still come each year without fail; Sicily's abundance makes its poverty that much harder to understand. There's no reason to think that the contradictions will cease until some greater *anodos* brings a saner life and culture to this unhappy island. Abundance and poverty, brilliant sunlight and sinister shadows, almond blossoms and death.

Volcanoes

One of the world's most important schools of vulcanology is in Catania, but anyone who travels among Sicily's islands can get a free extension course in the steamy science. Imagine, *à la* Disney's *Fantasia*, a time-lapse film of the islands over the past four millennia: with volcanoes, earthquakes and assorted cataclysms, it would have all the frenzy of a rock video. Three of Europe's most active volcanoes would provide the thumping rhythms to Stravinsky's *Rite of Spring*: mighty Etna, the bass, bursting forth with irregular but awesome thunder, accompanied by the boisterous choir of 300 minor craters on its flanks; the three craters of Vulcano like the Andrews Sisters, erupting into song every hundred years or so; and Strómboli, a *piccolo continuo*, sputtering with the reliable festival of fireworks that has earned it the nickname 'lighthouse of the Mediterranean'.

Many of Sicily's other islands are dead or dormant volcanoes. There are certain advantages to living with the big blisters and the vomit of lava they spew forth: light, airy pumice goes into soap and glass, while hard obsidian and basalt were the 'steel' of prehistoric man. Easy-to-slice tufa is perfect for building houses, and even run-of-the-mill lava comes in handy as nearly indestructible paving stones. Let the ash mellow, and you have some of the most fertile soil in the world, perfect for vines, pistachios, citrus, almonds and vegetables. Volcanic hot springs and mud pools soothe arthritis and a host of other ailments. The snows of Etna cooled the sherbets of the emirs and chilled the ice cream before the advent of refrigeration.

Of course, volcanoes can make unruly neighbours. Vulcano is due to erupt any day now, keeping the population at a minimum; Etna has nearly destroyed Catania on more than one occasion, while the densely populated villages on its slopes have fared less well. Each village has an emergency supply of holy relics, to ward off molten lava flows in their direction, and even today, despite all the study that's gone into vulcanology, saintly intervention remains the best and often the only civil defence available.

Etna scoffs at mere human attempts to make sense of its activities and predict its violence. In 1971 an eruption destroyed the vulcanology school's observatory by the main crater, in 1983 another engulfed the cable car to the main crater, and in 1992 it nearly gobbled up the village of Zafferana Etnea, before Nostra Signora di Divina Provvidenza took the matter in hand. The eruption of December 2002 again destroyed the cable car service from Sapienza to the crater.

Odes on Wheels

'A cart is like a poem,' wrote the French novelist René Bazin at the start of the 20th century – an odd statement unless, like Bazin, you've been to Sicily, where traditional carved and brightly painted carts are works of art. From Istanbul to the Philippines to New York City, the urge to tart up everyday transport is universal; in Sicily it began under the Bourbon government in 1830, when the first ruts dignified by the word 'road' were laid out across the island to exploit its resources better. The main means of transport also improved, from mule train to cart.

These vehicles had to be sturdy, and were crafted with as much care as a Venetian takes constructing a gondola: different woods for the different parts, iron axles, all perfectly balanced to take extreme pre-*autostrada* conditions. Each area of the island developed its distinctive shape and structure.

The result was fairly costly, and it wasn't long before customers began to have painters embellish their investments with pictures from history and legend that were familiar to even the most rustic, uneducated Sicilian: scenes from *Orlando Furioso* and the Sicilian puppet theatre, famous operas, the battles of Napoleon and Garibaldi, Norman Crusaders and Saracens, and so on, bordered by floral and geometric designs that dazzle the eye with their bright primary colours, and can indeed be 'read' like a poem by the illiterate. The most lavish have spokes carved like intricate totem poles. Traditionally, these carts are pulled by horses decked out in plumes, tassels, bells and bright embroidered trappings.

In the 1930s, there were 5,000 carts in Palermo alone. Although all the painted ones have been banished to folklore museums and tourist haunts, you'll still see a few weatherbeaten examples rumbling behind ponies through old medieval streets, laden with garlic or tomatoes or pots and pans, driven by weary old men who call out their wares in strange mournful street cries that will soon be lost, like so many things in Sicily.

Food and Drink

*Your people err in the meagreness of their diets; for they live on so much celery and
fennel that it constitutes almost all their sustenance; and this generates a humour
which putrefies the body and brings it to the extremes of sickness and even death.*
                              Peter of Blois, 1173, writing to Richard Palmer in Sicily

It's hard today to imagine Sicilians dining on celery, if they ever really did. With its
seas brimming with tuna and swordfish, lobster and red mullet, its abundant fresh
produce, its citrus, olive and almond groves, the island has always been a larder of
inspiration to chefs, from the ancient Greeks to the modern Sicilian exponents of *la
nuova cucina* (2,600 years ago, cities such as Akragas and Syracuse offered state
prizes for the best new sauces). Even the bread is better than that of nearly
anywhere else in Italy, baked in a dozen varieties that shame the stolid medieval
loaves of Tuscany.

Generally Sicilian food comes hotter, spicier or sweeter than in the rest of Italy. The
longest-lasting gastronomical influence has been Arabic, with a decided leaning
towards aubergines/eggplants (introduced by the Saracens), olives, pine nuts,
anchovies, and especially capers whenever feasible. Sicilian capers (*capperi*) are highly
esteemed, especially those that grow on exceptionally barren and rocky grounds
close to the sea (Pantelleria and the Aeolian Islands are top-class providers). Sicilian
capers are larger and more voluptuous than the French *non pareilles* variety, and they
are normally preserved in sea salt rather then vinegar brine. *Pasta con le sarde*, the
most typical dish on the island, was said to have been invented by the first Saracen
chefs to feed the conquering army; when properly prepared, it combines sardines,
wild fennel, olive oil, currants or raisins, pine nuts and saffron – an unusual but tasty
concoction, but beware some of the cheaper versions. Western Sicilians wholeheartedly adopted the semolina couscous of the Saracens, here called *cùscusu* or *cuscus*
and served with fish; this is the great speciality of Tràpani and Mazara.

The origins of pasta are ancient and obscure, but it's possible that the whole thing
started with the Greeks of southern Italy, who had a dish at funeral feasts called
makaria – the ancestor of *macaroni*. The Greeks also seem to have invented the
rolling-pin, and were turning out something like *tagliatelle* and *lasagne* around
600 BC. Some Sicilian patriots, however, claim that pasta is a Sicilian invention from
centuries earlier, and that the Sikans and Sikels taught it to the Greeks as a convenient way of preserving freshly milled wheat. In the Middle Ages, pasta had probably
already reached something like its current level of sophistication; *vermicelli* is
recorded as a favourite at Trabía, on the north coast, by an 11th-century writer.

The most popular way of doing pasta today is simple *spaghetti alle vongole*, with
the delicious baby clams that seem to be peculiar to Italy; any good restaurant on the
coast will have it at the top of the menu. Sicilian cooks are especially ingenious with
pasta, which varies in shape and texture from town to town, and often serves as
part of more elaborate preparations, such as *timbali* (savoury pies). Some other
memorable first courses are *pasta con le fave*, with fava beans, tomatoes and fennel
seed, and pungent *pasta ca'anciova e muddica*, with anchovies and toasted breadcrumbs. *Pesto trapanese* is a popular western pasta sauce, made from fresh tomatoes,

almonds, garlic and basil, ground together in a mortar. In eastern Sicily the favourite pasta dish is supposedly named after Bellini's opera: *pasta alla Norma*, featuring fried aubergine, fresh tomato sauce, basil and salted *ricotta* cheese – ingredients that are to the region 'normal', or *norma* in dialect, the true origin of the name. What you won't see on many menus is *maccu* (mush of dried fava beans), the staple of poor Sicilians for centuries; the Sunday-dinner version includes a couple of sprigs of wild fennel, *macaroni* and grated cheese.

Not surprisingly, seafood also dominates the list of Sicilian *secondi*. The humble sardine is dressed up to star in *sarde a beccafico*, filled with breadcrumbs, pine nuts and currants, and baked in the oven with orange juice and bay leaves. In late spring, there are fresh tuna (*tonno*), their deep-red flesh deliciously grilled or marinated in olive oil, lemon and herbs. All year round you can enjoy salt-cured tuna roe (*bottarga*), grated over pasta. The real king of Sicilian seafood, however, is the swordfish (*pesce spada*), usually grilled with lemon, olive oil and oregano, a sauce called *salmoriglio*, or as *involtini* (flat slices rolled with a filling of breadcrumbs, onions, spices, etc.). *Involtini* are also the most popular way to serve beef, pounded thin and filled with breadcrumbs, cheese, ham and maybe pine nuts and raisins, cooked on a spit. The larger gourmet version, *farsumagru*, includes hard-boiled eggs.

Sicilians save most of their artistry for sweets and desserts. Most famous of these are *cannoli*, pastry tubes filled with fresh *ricotta*, bits of chocolate, and candied fruit, and the rich *cassata* (another Arab innovation) made with sweetened *ricotta*, almond paste, sponge cake and candied fruit. In the summer, delicious lemon or coffee *granita* (slushy ice), homemade *gelato* (ice cream) with fresh fruit, and fruit sorbet help keep the temperature down. Sicilians like to think they have the best ice cream on the planet, and they may be right.

The most prominent displays in any pastry-shop window (especially around Palermo) are of candied fruit and *frutta alla Martorana*, which is marzipan shaped and painted expertly to look like figs, fennel, tomatoes, bananas, clams, or even spaghetti or fried eggs. Invented by the nuns at La Martorana in Palermo, they're genuine works of art, and so accurate that the story goes the nuns once hung them in trees and fooled a visiting archbishop who was amazed to see fruit in the winter. For festivals, little mannequins of pure sugar are made with exquisite skill; for St Joseph's Day (19 March) elaborate bread rolls in fantastical shapes are used as ornaments; at Christmas there is *buccellato* (ring pastry with almonds, walnuts and dried figs). A year-round treat are the sesame-coated *biscotti regina*.

Snack foods in Sicily are impressive even by Italian standards. In the bars and *tavole calde* there are all manner of delights that can easily take the place of a full meal. An essential part of the Sicilian experience is the orange that's not an orange, the *arancino*, a deep-fried breaded ball of rice with a tomato, meat and vegetable filling, or just butter (*bianco*). Beyond these, there are all sorts of good sandwiches, *tramezzini* (finger sandwiches on white bread that are usually much better than they look), and many varieties of pizza *a taglio* (by the slice). Every bar that makes food has its own specialities; you may encounter such traditional foods as *sfincione*, thick pizza with warm onions and anchovies. *Panelle* (fried square patties of chickpea) and *pani cu' la mensa* – *focaccia* filled with thinly sliced sautéed beef spleen, *ricotta* and sharp *cacio-cavallo* cheese – are popular street food in Palermo.

Although archaeologists tell us that Sicilians have been making wine since about 1400 BC, the origins of the wine made today in Sicily go back to the Normans, who replanted vineyards long neglected by the Arabs. Sicilian wines on the whole are sundrenched and strong; a few are downright volcanic.

In recent years Sicilian wine has experienced something of a revolution and a fine bottle such as Santa Cecilia made of Nero d'Avola grapes is a revelation. Sicilian grapes such as the Nero d'Avola, Catarratto, Grecanico and Pignatello are being used to create modern wines that can hold their own against international labels. Sicily is now one of the rising stars of the wine world and has been called the new California, its transformation having taken place in such a short time. It is possible to visit wine estates and some of the best can be found in Sicily's south-eastern corner: ask for details at the tourist office in Catania, they have comprehensive guides.

Specialist wine tour operator Arblaster & Clarke offers a one week autumn holiday that takes in eight wine estates as well as traditional sites on a Sicilian itinerary (for details see p.49).

Appreciative imbibers should try Corvo, a dry, fruity white or very respectable red; Etna, a dry white, and excellent, lusty red produced by villages under the volcano; red Faro and Mamertino from Messina, a favourite of the ancient Romans; Alcamo, a dry white to complement any seafood; Regaleali, a dry white or red, among Sicily's best; and red or white Cervasuolo, from Vittoria in Ragusa province. Or there are various Marsalas, from the sickening sweet to a dry wine that you can drink as an aperitif; sweet, amber Moscato and Passito from Pantelleria, Noto or Syracuse, each with its own character; the dessert wine Malvasia delle Lipari, especially from the islands of Salina and Strómboli; or the more unusual almond wine from Taormina called *vino alla mandorla*. The house wine served up in most restaurants is very drinkable, and much better than in most parts of southern Italy across the straits.

Sicily also has its own brewery which produces Messina beer, which like all Italian beer is thin fare. For something more potent, round off a meal with a snort of Averna from Caltanissetta, one of the nation's favourite *digestivi* (Italian post-prandial medicine), or put a volcano in your tank with a glass of Fuoco dell'Etna.

Restaurant Generalities

Sicilian restaurants are open from noon to 3 or 4pm and from 7 or 8 until 11pm. Although traditionally a **trattoria** is a cheaper, simpler place than a **ristorante**, in reality they are often exactly the same, both in quality and price, the only difference being, presumably, that a *ristorante* has more pretensions. Be careful with *trattorie* though: the name is beginning to define something more rustic and authentic than your average restaurant (a form of inverted snobbery that classes some *trattorie* as 'chic'). Most restaurants display a menu outside so that you know what to expect, at least as regards the price.

The *rosticceria*, *tavola calda*, or *gastronomia* are quite similar, the latter now the more popular name for the counters of prepared hot and cold food, where you choose what looks good, eat, pay and go. Some of these are quite elaborate, while the modest ones don't even have chairs or stools. If you're used to eating a light lunch instead of a major Italian midday feast, they're the answer. Most *pizzerie* are open only at night; look for one with a wood-burning oven.

Service in *ristoranti* and *trattorie* is always obligatory, either already included in the prices or added as a percentage (generally 10 per cent) of your bill at the end. Tipping comes on top of that, but is a matter of a few euros left on the table and not a fixed percentage of the bill, as in other countries. Most restaurants charge a modest *pane e coperto* (cover and bread charge) per person. **Tax law** in Italy orders restaurants and bars to give patrons a receipt (*ricevuta fiscale*) for everything they eat or drink, which you are supposed to take out of the restaurant with you and carry for 300m in case the receipt police intercept you. Only in Italy...

Menu Vocabulary

Antipasti
These before-meal treats can include almost anything; among the most common are:

antipasto misto	mixed antipasto
bruschetta	garlic toast (sometimes with tomatoes)
carciofi (sott'olio)	artichokes (in oil)
frutti di mare	seafood
funghi (trifolati)	mushrooms (with anchovies, garlic, lemon)
gamberi ai fagioli	prawns (shrimps) with white beans
mozzarella (in carrozza)	cow/buffalo cheese (fried with bread in batter)
prosciutto (con melone)	raw ham (with melon)
salsicce	sausages

Minestre (Soups) and Pasta

agnolotti	ravioli with meat
cappelletti	small ravioli, often in broth
crespelle	crêpes
frittata	omelette
orecchiette	ear-shaped pasta, served with turnip greens
panzerotti	ravioli with mozzarella, anchovies, and egg
pasta e fagioli	soup with beans, bacon, and tomatoes
pastina in brodo	tiny pasta in broth
penne all'arrabbiata	quill-shaped pasta with spicy tomato sauce
polenta	cake or pudding of corn semolina
spaghetti all'Amatriciana	with spicy pork, tomato, onion and chili sauce
spaghetti alle vongole	with clam sauce
stracciatella	broth with eggs and cheese

Carne (Meat)

agnello	lamb
anatra	duck
arrosto misto	mixed roast meats
bollito misto	stew of boiled meats
braciola	chop
brasato di manzo	braised beef with veg
bresaola	dried raw meat
carpaccio	thinly sliced raw beef
cassoeula	pork stew with cabbage
cervello	brains
cervo	venison
coniglio	rabbit
lumache	snails
manzo	beef

Many places offer *prezzo fisso* (set price) or *menu turistico* meals – often a real bargain, but more in terms of quantity than quality. Keep a sharp eye on where Sicilians seem to go; in most cases, the fewer languages on the menu, the more likely you are to eat a worthy meal. Posh joints with gourmet pretensions sometimes offer a *menu degustazione*, a fixed menu of the chef's specialities, which can be a real treat and is usually good value. Of course you can always order *alla carta* (from the menu), which is divided into the following categories:

Antipasti (*hors d'œuvres*) are often sumptuously displayed to tempt you the minute you walk in. Common starters are seafoods, vegetables, salami, ham, olives, etc. Sicilian specialities are *panelle* (chickpea fritters), *cazzilli* (potato croquettes), *peperonata* (peppers sautéed in olive oil and served cold) and olive *fritte* (eastern Sicilian fried olives).

Primi are soups or pasta dishes. Most Italians choose to have either an *antipasto* or a first course, but you are welcome to try both. There is almost always a particular shape

osso buco	braised veal knuckle	*polipi/polpi*	octopus
pancetta	rolled pork	*sarde*	sardines
piccione	pigeon	*sogliola*	sole
pizzaiola	beef steak in tomato and oregano sauce	*squadro*	monkfish
		stoccafisso	wind-dried cod
pollo	chicken	*tonno*	tuna
polpette	meatballs	*vongole*	small clams
rognoni	kidneys	*zuppa di pesce*	fish in sauce or stew
saltimbocca	veal, prosciutto and sage, cooked in wine	**Contorni (Side Dishes, Vegetables)**	
scaloppine	thin slices of veal sautéed in butter	*asparagi*	asparagus
		carciofi	artichokes
stufato	beef and vegetables braised in wine	*cavolo*	cabbage
		ceci	chickpeas
tacchino	turkey	*cetriolo*	cucumber
vitello	veal	*cipolla*	onion
		fagiolini	French (green) beans
Pesce (Fish)		*fave*	broad beans
acciughe or *alici*	anchovies	*funghi* (*porcini*)	mushrooms (boletus)
anguilla	eel		
aragosta	lobster	*insalata*	salad
baccalà	dried salt cod	*lenticchie*	lentils
bonito	small tuna	*melanzane*	aubergine
calamari	squid	*patate* (*fritte*)	potatoes (fried)
cappe sante	scallops	*peperoni*	sweet peppers
cozze	mussels	*peperonata*	stewed peppers
fritto misto	mixed firied fish	*piselli* (*al prosciutto*)	peas (with ham)
gamberetto	shrimp	*pomodoro(i)*	tomato(es)
gamberi	prawns	*porri*	leeks
granchio	crab	*rucola*	rocket
insalata di mare	seafood salad	*verdure*	greens
merluzzo	cod	*zucca*	pumpkin
ostriche	oysters	*zucchini*	courgettes
pesce spada	swordfish		

of fresh pasta in any region of Sicily – ask what is made in-house. *Risotto* is a dish borrowed from Northern Italy, and is better sampled there.

Secondi (second courses) consist of meat or fish. The fish (*pesce*) is often according to availability, since it is always fresh. Frozen stuff usually only insinuates its way on to a Sicilian menu in such dishes as a mixed seafood grill (*grigliata mista*). Two special treats in Sicily, besides tuna and swordfish, are red mullet (*triglia*) and the clawless Mediterranean lobster (*aragosta*). Fish is often priced according to weight before cooking. Meat (*carne*) includes chicken, rabbit, beef, lamb, veal and pork. With meat or fish, you get a *contorno* (side dish) of your choice – typically this will tend to be salad, vegetables or potatoes. Famous Sicilian *contorni* are *caponata*, an aubergine/eggplant stew with tomatoes, olives and capers, and *frittedda*, fried onions, artichokes, baby peas and fava beans.

And finally... **dolce o frutta** (dessert or fruit).

Formaggio (Cheese)

bel paese	soft white cow's cheese
cacio/caciocavallo	pale yellow, often sharp cheese
caprino	goat's cheese
gorgonzola	soft blue cheese
parmigiano	parmesan cheese
pecorino	sharp sheep's cheese
provolone	sharp, tangy cheese; *dolce* is less strong
stracchino	soft white cheese

Frutta (Fruit, Nuts)

albicocche	apricots
ananas	pineapple
arance	oranges
banane	bananas
ciliege	cherries
cocomero	watermelon
fragole	strawberries
frutta di stagione	fruit in season
lamponi	raspberries
limone	lemon
macedonia di frutta	fruit salad
mandorle	almonds
mele	apples
more	blackberries
nocciole	hazelnuts
noci	walnuts
pesca	peach
pesca noce	nectarine
pinoli	pine nuts
pompelmo	grapefruit
prugna/susina	prune/plum
uva	grapes

Dolci (Desserts)

amaretti	macaroons
crostata	fruit flan
gelato (*produzione propria*)	ice cream (home-made)
granita	flavoured ice, usually lemon or coffee
panettone	sponge cake with candied fruit and raisins
semifreddo	refrigerated cake
spumone	a soft ice cream
torta	cake, tart
zabaglione	whipped eggs and Marsala wine, served hot
zuppa inglese	trifle

Bevande (Beverages)

acqua minerale con/senza gas	mineral water with/without fizz
aranciata	orange soda
birra (alla spina)	beer (draught)
caffè (freddo)	coffee (iced)
cioccolata (con panna)	chocolate (with cream)
frizzante	fizzy mineral water
latte (interno/scremato)	milk (whole/skimmed)
succo di frutta	fruit juice
tè	tea
vino (rosso, bianco, rosato)	wine (red, white, rosé)

Wine is the most popular accompaniment to dinner. *Vino locale* (house wine) is the cheapest and usually quite good, and this is what you'll be given unless you order a specific label. **Mineral water** (*acqua minerale*) comes under as many labels as the wine, with or without added or natural carbonization (or *gas*, as the Italians call those little bubbles; *frizzante* denotes fizzy). Italian **beer**, always served cold, is just about passable, and of course you can always order the ubiquitous Coca Cola or Fanta. A small, black *espresso* coffee and/or *digestivo* puts the final touch to an Italian meal.

Note: Prices quoted for restaurants throughout this book are the average for one person, including two courses plus dessert or *antipasto*, cover charge and service (but not wine or drinks).

Bars and Cafés

These have little in common with American bars or English pubs, and can be anything from luxurious open-air cafés to dingy back-alley meeting places. All serve primarily **coffee** in the form of *espresso* (small, stormy and black), *cappuccino* (with hot foaming milk, and never, never drunk by the natives after a meal) or simply *caffè latte* (coffee with more milk) served in a glass. Many people have **breakfast** at a bar, snatching *cornetti* (croissants) or whatever other pastries are available.

Bars are a godsend in hot Sicilian summers, when your sightseeing turns into an eternal but not unpleasant bar crawl in search of relief; they'll always have *granita* (ices flavoured with lemon, mint, orange or coffee), iced coffee (*caffè freddo*) or tea (*tè freddo*, flavoured with mint or peach), cold drinks and ice cream. A great Sicilian treat is *latte di mandorla*, almond paste dissolved in water, served cold. Don't be embarrassed to ask for a plain glass of water; people do it all the time.

Alcohol is cheap, as long as it's not imported; drinking wine by the glass in a bar, surprisingly, is eccentric behaviour in Sicily, although *enoteche*, or wine bars, have begun to appear in the most fashionable resorts and cities. Standing at the bar is about a third cheaper than sitting at a table to be served. The *scontrino* is the **receipt**, and you may be asked to collect one from the *cassa* (cashier) before being served, especially in the big cities.

Travel

Getting There

By Air

From the UK

Flying is obviously the quickest and easiest way of getting to Sicily. It can also, if you are not careful, be by far the most expensive, though the **low cost airline** revolution has touched Sicily too; Ryanair now flies to Palermo. There can be an alarming difference in price between **scheduled** and charter flights. The major carriers, Alitalia and Meridiana, operate between three and four flights a week from Gatwick, Heathrow and Manchester to Palermo, and charge anything up to £700 return in high season, dropping to around £250 in low season. British Airways and Air Malta each have three direct flights weekly from London Gatwick to Catania, with prices from around £130.

Charter flights can be a cheap option. High-season prices range from £190 to £240, although Italflights sometimes has special deals for as low as £130.

Ryanair's **low cost flights** to Palermo are usually the most cost-effective, particularly if you book when they have one of their 'sales' on. Otherwise, expect to pay from £80 and keep an eye on their website (the cheapest deals tend to be a month or so in advance, midweek and off-season).

Another option is to take a **flight to Naples**, and take the train or ferry from there. At the time of writing, Easyjet was offering flights from London Stansted from as little as £80 return (cheapest some weeks ahead).

For car hire, ask your airline or travel agency about fly-drive deals. Other options are available through the holiday operators: try **thinkSicily**, The Thinking Traveller Ltd, 91-95 Brick Lane, London E1 6QL, **t** (020) 7377 8518, *www.thinkSicily.co.uk*.

From Ireland

There are no flights from Ireland to Sicily, and precious few to the Italian mainland either. The cheapest and easiest way is to fly to London from Dublin or Belfast and take a charter from there. Aer Lingus can take you as far as Milan or Rome from around £280 return in the high season, or try Alitalia.

Airline Carriers

The UK and Ireland

Scheduled Flights

Aer Lingus (Ireland): **t** (01) 705 3333, *www.aerlingus.ie*.
Air Malta: **t** 0845 607 3710, *www.airmalta.com*.
Alitalia: **t** 0870 544 8259, *www.alitalia.co.uk*.
Alitalia (Ireland): **t** (01) 677 51 71, *www.alitalia.ie*.
British Airways: **t** 0345 222 111, *www.british airways.com*.
British Airways (Ireland): **t** (0141) 222 2345.
Easyjet (for flights from London Stansted to Naples): **t** 0871 750010, *www.easyjet.com*.
Meridiana (UK): **t** (020) 7839 2222, *www.meridiana.it*.
Ryanair: **t** 0871 246 0000, *www.ryanair.com*.

Charters, Discounts and Special Deals

Italia nel Mondo (UK): **t** (020) 7834 7651.
Italflights (UK): **t** (020) 7405 6771.
Italy Sky Shuttle (for the UK): **t** (020) 8241 5145.
United Travel (for Ireland): **t** 01 288 4346.

The USA and Canada

Scheduled Flights

Air Canada: USA, **t** 800 776 3000; Canada, **t** 800 555 1212, *www.aircanada.ca*.
Alitalia: USA, **t** 800 223 5730; Canada, **t** 800 361 8336, *www.alitalia.com*.
British Airways: USA, **t** 800 247 9297; Canada, **t** 800 668 1055, *www.britishairways.com*
Delta: USA, **t** 800 241 4141, *www.delta.com*.
KLM: USA, **t** 800 374 7747; Canada, **t** 800 361 5330, *www.klm.com*.
Lufthansa: USA, **t** 800 645 3880; Canada, **t** 800 563 5954, *www.lufthansa.com*.
TWA: USA, **t** 800 892 4141, *www.twa.com*.

Charters, Discounts and Special Deals

The cheapest tickets are available only a few days before departure. You may also have to pay a club membership fee to have access to the best bargains, but the amount you save usually makes it worthwhile. Some of the largest discount specialists are:

From the USA and Canada

There are no direct scheduled flights from North America to Sicily. You can fly to either Rome or Milan from New York, Boston, Miami, Chicago, Los Angeles, Toronto or Montreal and catch a connecting flight or train from there. Alitalia has the most options available and runs all the connecting flights; a July round-trip ticket from New York to Rome costs just under US$1,500, from Montreal or Toronto CA$1,360. Fares dip considerably between November and March (and March is a very good month to visit Sicily) and cost less if you fly mid-week instead of on a weekend. Another option is to take one of the many competitive flights to London and pick up a charter flight from there (*see* above).

By Sea

You can save a long, fatiguing drive through Italy by catching a ferry to Sicily from Genoa, Livorno or Naples, but book months in advance if you're transporting your car. Travelling by sea has become fashionable in recent years and ferry companies are now busy transforming their image.

Caronte (**t** 0904 14 15 in Messina) offers ferries from Villa San Giovanni to Messina round the clock; foot passengers are free. Tickets are on sale at kiosks at the port.

FS (**t** 0906 75 234 in Messina) runs frequent inexpensive ferries from Villa San Giovanni (25mins) and Reggio di Calabria (20mins) to Messina. Tickets are on sale at kiosks at the port.

Grandi Navi Veloci (**t** 01 05 89 331 in Genoa, **t** 0916 11 22 42 in Palermo, *www1.gnv.it*) runs ferries from Genoa to Palermo (about 19hrs) three times per week. In the UK contact them through Viamare Travel, Graphic House, 2 Sumatra Rd, London NW6 1PU, **t** 8704 106040.

Grandi Traghetti/Grandi Navi Veloci (**t** 05 86 40 98 04 in Livorno, **t** 09 15 87 404 in Palermo) sail Livorno–Palermo in 17–19hrs, three times a week. In the UK contact them through Viamare Travel (*see* above).

Siremar (**t** 09 15 82 403, *www.gruppotirrenia. it/ siremar*) has ferries at least once a week, and as many as five or six a week from July to September, from Naples to various Aeolian Islands and Milazzo (in Naples, contact Tirrenia di Navigazione SPA, Stazione

---

Air Brokers International: USA, **t** 800 883 3273.

Interworld: USA, **t** (305) 443 4929.

New Frontiers: USA, **t** 800 366 6387; Canada, **t** (513) 526 8444.

Stand Buys: USA, **t** 800 331 0257.

Travel Avenue: USA, **t** 800 333 3335.

Unitravel: USA, **t** 800 325 2222.

Student and Youth Travel

If you're under 26 or a full-time student under 32 with an International Student Identity Card to prove it, you're eligible for student/youth charters and can save big money by booking through one of the following specialist agencies.

Campus Travel: 52 Grosvenor Gardens, London SW1, **t** 0870 240 1010; with branches at most UK universities: Birmingham, **t** (0121) 414 1848; Bristol, **t** (0117) 929 2494; Cambridge, **t** (01223) 360 201; Edinburgh, **t** (0131) 668 3303; Manchester, **t** (0161) 833 2046; Oxford, **t** (01865) 242 067.

Council Travel, 205 E. 42nd St, New York, NY 10017, **t** 1800 2COUNCIL, **t** (212) 822 2700; with branches in most major US cities.

STA Travel

In the **UK**, 86 Old Brompton Rd, London SW7 3LH, **t** 0870 1600599; Bristol, **t** (0117) 929 4399; Manchester, **t** (0161) 834 0668; and many other branches in the UK. In the **USA**, 5900 Wilshire Bd, Suite 2110, Los Angeles, CA 90036, **t** 1800 777 0112; other branches in New York, Boston, San Francisco and Honolulu. In **Australia**, **t** (02) 9212 1255.

Travel Cuts, 187 College St, Toronto, ON M5T 1P7, **t** 1800 667 2887, **t** (416) 979 2406; with other branches.

USIT, 19–21 Aston Quay, O'Connell Bridge, Dublin 2, **t** (01) 679 8833; Fountain Centre, College St, Belfast, **t** (028) 9032 4073; Cork, **t** (0214) 270 900; Galway, **t** (091) 565 177; Limerick **t** (061) 415 064; Waterford, **t** (051) 872 601.

Marittima, Molo Angioino, t 08 15 80 03 40). In the UK contact them through Serena Holidays, 40–42 Kenway Rd, London SW5, t (020) 7244 8422.

SNAV (t 0817 61 23 48 in Naples, t 0903 64 044 in Messina, *www.snav.it*,) offers an impressively short 5hr trip (including embarking and disembarking) from Naples to Palermo. Tickets in high season cost around €60 for a single and €135 for a car and driver. SNAV also runs hydrofoils from Reggio di Calabria to Messina (15mins).

Tirrenia (t 09 16 02 11 11 in Palermo, t 08 17 20 11 11 in Naples, *www.gruppotirrenia.it*) sails nightly at 8pm from Naples to Palermo, and once a week between Palermo and Cagliari. In the UK contact them through Serena Holidays (*see* above).

By Train

This is a long haul from the UK (at least 38hrs from London to Catania with a change of stations in Paris and trains in Rome), costs as much as a charter flight (around £200

Train Tickets and Passes

In the UK and Ireland
Rail Europe, Travel Centre, 179 Piccadilly, London W1, t 0990 300 003, *www.rail europe.co.uk*.
International Rail Centre, Victoria Station, London SW1, t 0990 848 848.
Italian State Railways Agents (for FS tickets and passes), Marco Polo House, 3–5 Lansdowne Rd, Croydon, Surrey, t (020) 8686 0677, *www.fs-on-line.com*.

In the USA and Canada
Rail Europe, 226–30 Westchester Av, White Plains, NY 10604, t (914) 682 2999, t 800 438 7245, *www.raileurope.com*.
Italian State Railways Agents USA (for FS tickets and passes), 666 5th Av, 6th Floor, New York, NY 10113, t (212) 697 2100, *www.fs-on-line.com*.
Italian State Railways Agents Canada (for FS tickets and passes), 1450 City Councillors St, Suite 750, Montreal H3A 2E6, t (514) 954 8608, *www.fs-on-line.com*.

return), and is only recommended for people terrified of aeroplanes, masochists, or if you mean to break your journey. You can save a bit of money and a lot of train fatigue by transferring to a ferry to Palermo at Genoa, Livorno or Naples (*see* 'By Sea', above).

Buying an international rail card before leaving home (**Inter-Rail** from the UK, **Eurail** from North America or Australia) is rarely worthwhile if you're simply travelling to Sicily or even just around Italy, but if you're a student or under 26 it can work out to your advantage if you plan to do a lot of train travelling elsewhere. An Inter-Rail pass covering one zone costs £223 (£159 for under-26s) for 16 days, two zones £303 (£215) for 22 days and all zones £415 (£295) for a month. Zones cover more than one country (for example Italy, Turkey, Greece and Slovenia is one zone).

Fares on the Italian State railway, the FS (Ferrovie dello Stato), are among the lowest in Europe. Children between 4 and 12 pay half-price, and under-4s travel free. If you intend to travel mainly by train, **Trenitalia Pass** is a special ticket valid for up to 10 days of travel within a two-month span. They are sold in all main stations and can be bought up to two months in advance to the first day of validity; the pass can be used by up to five people (thus five people going 100km would count as one trip and 500km on the pass). These passes are also available before you leave for Italy from the FS agents in your country (*see* 'Train Tickets and Passes').

By Bus

National Express/Eurolines, t 0990 808 080, *www.nationalexpress.com*, offer an excruciating service from London to Rome (33hrs), from where you'll have to catch another coach or train down to Sicily. A second-class adult return to Rome is around £140 (if booked 2 weeks in advance), a single around £95. If you adore riding the coach, you can continue down to Palermo (12hrs), Syracuse or Messina with the Segesta bus company from Rome's Stazione Tiburtina, nightly at 9.30pm (€70 return; tickets and information at Bar La Favorita, t 06 44 24 59 05 in Rome, or call the Palermo office on t 0916 16 79 19, t 09 13 20 757, t 09 16 16 90 39).

Self-catering and Special Interest Holidays

The UK and Ireland
Aeolian Friends/Sicilian Experience, 6 Palace St, London SW1 E5HY, **t** (020) 7834 7651. Apartments etc. on the Aeolian Islands.

Art History Abroad (AHA), 66 Camberwell Road, London SE5 0EG, **t** (020) 7277 4514, *www.arthistoryabroad.com*. Art history tours.

Arblaster & Clarke, **t** 01730 893 344, *www.arblasterandclarke.com*. Offers a one-week autumn wine tour of Sicily.

Alternative Travel Group, 69–71 Banbury Rd, Oxford OX2 6PJ, **t** (01865) 513 333. Walking holidays.

Citalia, Marco Polo House, 3–5 Lansdowne Rd, Croydon, Surrey CR9 1LL, **t** (020) 8686 5533, **f** (020) 8681 0712. Self-catering holidays.

Magic of Italy, 12–42 Wood St, Kings Place, Kingston-upon-Thames KT1 1JS, **t** (020) 8939 5453. Apartments in Taormina.

The Owners' Syndicate (020) 7801 9807, *www.ownerssyndicate.com*, for rooms/apartments rented directly from the owners.

Ramblers Holidays, Box 43, Welwyn Garden City, Herts AL8 8PQ, **t** (01707) 331 133. Walking holidays based in Francavilla, near Mt Etna.

Swan Hellenic Art Treasure Tours, 77 New Oxford St, London WC1A 1PP, **t** (020) 7800 2200. Visits to all the historic sites.

thinkSicily, The Thinking Traveller Ltd, 91–95 Brick Lane, London E1 6QL, **t** (020) 7377 8518, *www.thinkSicily.co.uk*. Villa specialists and tailor-made holidays.

The USA and Canada
Amelia Tours, 17 Woodberry Rd, Hicksville, NY 11801, **t** (516) 433 0696, **f** (516) 822 6220. Cultural, archaeological, wine and culinary tours for groups or independent travellers.

Bike Riders, PO Box 130254, Boston, MA 02113, **t** (617) 723 2354, **f** (617) 723 2355. Cycling tours.

Great Travels, 5506 Connecticut Av N.W., Suite 23, Washington DC 20015, **t** (202) 237 5220, **f** (202) 966 6972. Sailing holidays around the Aeolian Islands on a tall ship.

By Car

To bring a GB-registered car into Italy, you'll need your car registration, valid driving licence, and insurance. Make sure everything is in excellent working order, or your slightly bald tyre may enrich the coffers of the Swiss or Italian police – it's not uncommon to be stopped for no reason and have your car searched until the police find something to stick a fine on.

Note that by law you are required to carry a portable triangular danger sign (available from ACI offices; *see* 'Getting Around', below). Also beware that spare parts for non-Italian cars are difficult to come by. US citizens wishing to drive in Italy should have an International Driving Licence.

Be careful when parking: illegally parked cars are frequently towed away, and recovering your vehicle is a long and expensive procedure. Parking in Palermo can be almost impossible, and it's less hassle to visit the city without a car.

You have the choice of various long and short ferry crossings between the Italian mainland and Sicily (*see* 'By Sea', above).

Entry Formalities

Passports and Visas
EU nationals with a valid passport can enter and stay in Italy as long as they like. Citizens of the USA, Canada, Australia and New Zealand need only a valid passport to stay up to three months in Italy; if you wish to stay longer or to work, get a special visa in advance from an Italian embassy or consulate (*see* **Practical A–Z**, pp 55–6).

Customs
Those arriving from another EU country can now import a limitless amount of duty-paid goods as long as they're for personal use. Those arriving from outside the EU have to pass through the Italian customs, which are usually benign – they'll let you be if you don't look suspicious and haven't brought along more than 200 cigarettes or 100 cigars, and not more than a litre of hard drink or three bottles of wine, a couple of cameras, a movie camera, 10 rolls of film for each, a tape-recorder, radio, record-player, one canoe less than 5.5m, sports equipment for personal use,

and one TV (though you'll have to pay for a licence for it)! Pets must be accompanied by a bilingual Certificate of Health from your local veterinary inspector.

You can take the same items listed above home with you without hassle – except of course your British pet. US citizens may return with $400 worth of merchandise – so do keep your receipts.

Getting Around

By Air

The only flights really worth taking in Sicily are from Palermo to the Pelagie Islands or from Palermo or Tràpani to Pantelleria. Domestic flights are on **Alitalia** (for contact details, *see* 'Airline Carriers', above), the national airline, or several smaller companies, including **La Med Airlines, t** 0923 54 98 24, **Meridiana, t** 0953 46 966, **Alpi Eagles, t** 0953 49 297, and **Air Sicilia, t** 0923 84 14 23. Major airports in Sicily are Palermo, Birgi (Tràpani/Marsala) and Catania. For information on how to get into the cities appears in the respective chapters on each city (*see* p.71 for Palermo, p.124 for Tràpani/Marsala and p.296 for Catania).

On Alitalia domestic flights, children under 2 fly at a 90% discount; for ages 2 to 11 they receive a 33% cent discount, and for ages 12 to 25 discounted rates depend on dates and destinations. Weekend travel is often discounted for all passengers.

By Sea

Most of the islands off Sicily's coast are served by hydrofoils (*aliscafi*) as well as ferries (*traghetti*). Hydrofoils tend to be twice as fast and twice as expensive as the ships, and are even more choosy about the state of the sea. Siremar, subsidized by the regional government of Sicily, has *aliscafi* and ferries to every island; usually there's a private competitor to keep them on their toes. *See* 'Getting There' under individual islands for details of crossings. *See* 'By Sea', above, for ferries from the mainland to Sicily.

Sailing

Most of the islands have some facilities for yachts, though they may not be equipped for a long stay. The harbour master (*capitaneria di porto*) at your first Italian port of call will give you a document called a *costituto*, which you will have to produce to purchase tax-free fuel. For further information contact the Italian State Tourist Office (*see* p.62) or write to either of these organizations:

Federazione Italiana Vela (Italian Sailing Federation), Porticciolo Duca degli Abruzzi, Genoa, *www.federvela.it*.

Federazione Italiana Motonautica (Italian Motorboat Federation), Via Cappuccio 19, Milan, *www.fimconi.it*.

Several UK yacht-charter companies have bases in the Italian islands. Look in specialist magazines for listings, or contact:

Nixe Yachting, Via Catania 146, Palermo, **t** 0916 25 79 90.

Siciliamare Yachting Service, Via Lodi 6, Messina, **t** 0906 92 344.

Helpful guides to the Italian coasts include *The Tyrrhenian Sea* by H. A. Denham and *Round the Italian Coast* by P. Bristow.

By Train

Sicily's trains pass through all important centres but tend to take their sweet time, whether you take the intercity (the fastest, with a mandatory supplement on top of the regular fare), or the *diretto*, *regionale* and *espresso* (which make a few stops). The regular services between Messina and Palermo, and Messina and Syracuse, are perfectly adequate. Chances that a *sciopero* (strike) will interrupt train service are much slimmer than ever before, but there is the odd exception. Regular train tickets are good for two months from the date of purchase and must be validated just before use – be absolutely sure to stamp them before you get on the train, in the little yellow machine at the side of each track or in the station. For discount passes, etc, *see* p.48.

If you are embarking on a potentially long journey, remember that there are often no buffet cars on trains. Anything can happen on a Sicilian train. A few years back, we were the only passengers on an Enna–Agrigento run.

The train pulled into a tunnel and stopped; without a word, the driver and the conductor turned off all the lights, locked the doors and disappeared. We fell asleep, and two hours later when the train started again, there was an umbrella hanging on the back of our seat.

By Bus

In Sicily a score of bus (Pullman) companies offer an extensive network across the island to towns and villages where trains don't go. When they directly compete with train routes, buses are almost always the better deal, with comparable prices and the ability to let you off smack in the centre of town, while the train is liable to dump you a few miles away, at a station served by one very expensive old taxi cab. Bus companies can be difficult to contact by phone, and operators rarely (never) speak English. The local tourist office should have information about local bus connections.

Riding the Pullman has its memorable moments too. Once, half an hour after arriving in Gela, one of the authors noticed he had lost his pocket watch. He ran back to the station at top speed and found the bus had been waiting – never mind the schedule – and the passengers who had seemed so grim and taciturn an hour ago broke out into cheers and applause. With a flourish, the conductor pulled a carved wooden box from under the dashboard; inside was a red velvet bag, from which he produced the watch, every *centesimo* of the change that had fallen into the seat with it, and two cinnamon sweets that someone had contributed for our baby.

On town-to-town buses you can nearly always purchase a ticket on board; or get one at the bus company office at the stop, if there is one. For city buses you must purchase tickets from tobacconist shops or news-stands and 'obliterate' them in the machines on the bus. Vendors of the tickets will know how many you need to reach your destination.

By Car

The easiest way to see the Sicilian countryside is by car, although putting up with Sicilian motorists, an absurd amount of traffic in the towns, and some of the most expensive petrol in Europe comes with the deal. In the cities, a red traffic light usually means go into second gear; stop at one the locals have ignored for years, and you'll have your ears hooted off. But for anyone with a game heart, getting used to Sicilian **driving habits** will take about five minutes. What at first seems murderous anarchy turns out to have an impeccable logic to it. The first rule is: keep moving, no matter what. Assume that everyone else is sharp and on their toes, and that when you barge into their space they will make way. If they see you in time, they will; as aggressively as they drive, Sicilians are much more courteous about letting you in than northern Europeans. The second rule is: cars are only projections of their drivers, so traffic proceeds like a crowd of pedestrians, only faster. On main roads, it is considered bad manners to be in the far left lane if someone else wants to drive faster than you; expect that car to pull right up behind you and sit a yard or two off your rear bumper until you move over.

Everyone has their own peculiar way of reaching their destination, so constantly look out for other vehicles approaching from every direction, at every moment. The only problem with this way of doing things is that it requires everyone's total attention at all times. One mistake and there's carnage.

Sicilian **towns** were not built for motor vehicles. There are usually only a few streets fit for cars, and the traffic will be terrific – in any town of more than 20,000, that means traffic jams at least eight hours of the day; 10am–1pm and 4–9pm will be the worst times to try to enter or leave. Do not try to navigate the old centres of towns: it's always best to leave your beast in a central *piazza*, or one of the badly signposted parking lots. The authorities do try to mark paths through the medieval street plans but one wrong turn and you'll be descending a rough-cobbled vertical grade into a quarry, from which, even if you survive, no escape is possible.

Road signs, in town or in the country, carry little if any meaning. They'll slow you down to 10km/h for a tiny bump on a motorway, and neglect to mention when paving ends, or when traffic is merging from six directions. Little blue arrows pointed leftwards are installed at random, as if to say 'do not drive off the highway and into the trees'. Patience and humour are essential travel companions if you are driving in Sicily.

Flash your headlights in the daytime to proclaim that you are passing, that you desire someone to make way, or to warn oncoming traffic that the police are up the road, which is truly rare. The **police** of course may have you for any infraction (posted speed limits are often ridiculously low, and consequently ignored); the infrequent interventions of the law are entirely arbitrary, and should be taken as bad luck. Do be prepared, however, to cough up your driving licence, car insurance and passport, instantly.

Like their Roman forefathers, the Italians love to build **roads**. The biggest of these are the *autostrade* – supermotorways. In Sicily these are built on lofty piers for miles on end. Tolls are charged on the *autostrade* but the Catania–Palermo–Mazara del Vallo *autostrade* (A19 and A29) are free. Other main roads are called *strade statali* (SS).

The ACI (Automobile Club of Italy; **t** 06 49 98 234) is a good friend to the foreign motorist. For any motoring difficulty you may have, dial their assistance number, **t** 116; English-speaking operators are on duty 24hrs to answer your questions. If you need a tow, your car will be taken to the nearest ACI garage within 45mins. It is also possible to get an ACI membership (which includes reduced road service rates), but it's probably only worth doing if you are planning on a lot of driving in a very dodgy car.

Car thefts and thefts from cars is a chronic problem. If you're going to visit an island for several days, leave your car in a guarded garage. and do not leave any valuables visible

Hiring a Car or Camper

Hiring a car is simple but not particularly cheap. In Italian it's called *autonoleggio*. There are both large international firms through which you can reserve a car in advance, and local agencies, which often have lower prices. Air or train travellers should check out

possible discount packages. Rates vary considerably with the season, size of the car and the day of the week (best deals are at the weekend). It is often less expensive to make your reservations from abroad than in Italy. Check insurance policies and small print, as cheaper deals tend not to cover theft or damage done to the vehicle in the absence of a third party. Most companies will require a deposit amounting to the estimated cost of the hire and will have a minimum age limit of 21 (23 in some cases). A credit card makes life easier. You must show your licence and a passport when you hire. Perhaps try one of the following international firms:

Avis: UK, **t** 0870 6060 100; USA and Canada, **t** (741) 690 360; Ireland, **t** 01 605 7500, *www.avis.com*.

Hertz: UK, **t** 0990 996 699; USA, **t** 800 654 3001; Canada, **t** 800 263 0600; Ireland, **t** 01 660 2255, *www.hertz.com*.

Eurodollar: UK, **t** (01895) 233 300.

Travel Line: UK, **t** (020) 7499 4433.

Thrifty: UK, **t** 01494 751 600, *www.thrifty.co.uk*.

Taxis

Unfortunately, Sicilian taxi drivers often see visitors as fair game and will invariably overcharge. Even when they have meters, as in Palermo, it's a fight to get them to turn them on. If you're out in the countryside where there are no meters, negotiate the price first.

Motorcycles and Bikes

It's hard to rent either a motorcycle or bike, except on the smaller islands. What you're more likely to find, and then only at resort areas, are Vespa scooters and mopeds, which are fine for getting around and cost €35–40 a day (no special licence needed).

Hitch-hiking

Not recommended (especially for women), though it's legal to thumb a ride anywhere in Italy except on the *autostrade* (you can hitch on the roads leading up to the toll-booths however). Sicilians themselves rarely do it, and off the main roads you may have a long wait.

Practical A–Z

Average Temperatures in °C/F						
	Jan	March	May	July	Sept	Nov
Caltanissetta	7/44	10/50	14/57	23/74	20/68	11/51
Strómboli	13/55	13/55	17/63	24/76	22/72	14/57
Syracuse	12/53	13/55	18/64	25/77	23/74	14/57

Climate and When to Go

Sicily enjoys a Mediterranean climate, although it can get diabolically hot in the summer: Africa is only 80 miles away and in foul moods blasts Sicily with the hot, suffocating *scirocco*. February (when the almonds bloom), March and April are the best times to visit. The winter rains diminish, the hills are a glorious green and covered with wild flowers in every imaginable hue, and there are a score of interesting Easter festivals to attend. May and June are quite good as well, hot enough for swimming but not at all crowded. Late summer is the true 'winter' in Sicily: the floral riot gives way to parched, brown landscapes, and Sicilians hide indoors from the sun as much as they can. Yet July, August and September are the most crowded with tourists; in many places hotel prices double. In the autumn it stays warm enough to swim, in some places until early October. Winters on the coast are mild enough, if often wet; in the interior hill towns, fog often comes and stays for weeks. Beginning in December, snow falls in the Monti Madonìe and upper Monti Nebrodi, as well as on Etna; a skiing holiday in Sicily sounds odd but is certainly possible.

Crime and the Police

Anyone who fears going to Sicily because of what they see on the news is being silly. It doesn't have a monopoly on car bombs and assassinations, and the quaint way in which the Mafia conducts its internal politics has nothing to do with you.

On the other hand, there is a good deal of **petty crime**, especially in the cities. Unemployment, drugs and the alienation of youth are fairly serious problems here. Pickpocketing has always been a thriving business, in markets, in crowds, and on city buses. So don't carry any loose gear, and keep your eyes open; a bit of common sense and alertness goes a long way. Most common of all, however, is **car theft and thefts from cars**, not only in the big cities but also in smaller towns and especially tourist resorts.

The one thing that can get you in a jam in Sicily is **drugs** – and quite understandably, in a very conservative country awash with hard stuff thanks to the Mafia. Don't expect any tolerance from anyone on anything to do with drugs. Another, unexpected way of meeting the police is rough **camping in coastal areas**: Sicilians consider it an environmental menace, and you may be fined.

The police in Italy come in 31 flavours: dial t 113 in an **emergency** for the cop nearest you. The **Carabinieri** and **Polizia Statale** are the national forces who take care of business in rural areas. Every sizable town has its own police, too. The general rule is, if you need directions, need to find a hotel or a restaurant with good *spaghetti alle vongole*, or anything else, ask the cop on the corner.

The **Guardia di Finanza** is the tax police (only in Italy...). You'll see quite a lot of them, patrolling the coastal waters for smugglers and haunting the towns for businesses cheating on their income statements. It's true that they stop people outside bars and ask to see their receipts – they once fined an eight-year-old boy on a beach for buying an ice cream cone and not taking away the *scontrino*. The case was dismissed because the boy hadn't actually got any pockets in his swimming trunks.

You might also see **soldiers** protecting courthouses and other public buildings, and also occasionally in the countryside – often their only purpose is cosmetic, an effort by the government to make people in the Mafia areas feel a little more confident and secure. The tall fellows with the little feathers in their alpine hats are the *bersaglieri* (sharpshooters), Italy's elite troops.

Disabled Travellers

Italy is way behind northern Europe in providing access for the disabled, and Sicily is behind the rest of Italy, although things have begun improving slightly of late. The annual hotel listings from the provincial tourist boards list which have facilities; and enquire at the national tourist office if any operator has begun tours of Sicily with the disabled in mind. At the time of writing, no one has.

Organizations in Italy
Centro Studi Consulenza Invalidi, Via Gozzadini 7, 20148 Milan. Publishes an annual guide, *Vacanze per Disabili*, with details of suitable accommodation in Italy.
CO.IN (Consorzio Cooperative Integrate), Via Enrico Giglioli 54a, 00169 Rome, **t** 06 23 26 75 04, **f** 06 23 26 75 05, *andi.casaccia.enea.it*. Their tourist information centre offers advice and information on accessibility. They also publish a quarterly magazine in Italian and English for disabled visitors. *Open Mon–Fri 9–5.*

Organizations in the UK
Holiday Care Service, 2nd Floor, Imperial Buildings, Victoria Rd, Horley, Surrey RH6 7PZ, **t** (01293) 773716. For travel information and details of accessible accommodation and care holidays.
RADAR (Royal Association for Disability and Rehabilitation), 12 City Forum, 250 City Rd, London EC1V 8AF, **t** (020) 7250 3222. Publishes *Holidays and Travel Abroad: A Guide for Disabled People* (£3.50) listing hotels with facilities, specialist tour operators, self-catering apartments and more.
Royal National Institute for the Blind, 224 Great Portland St, London W15 5TB, **t** (020) 7388 1266. Its mobility unit offers a *Plane Easy* audio cassette with advice for blind people travelling by plane. It will also advise on finding accommodation.
Tripscope, The Courtyard, Evelyn Rd, London W4 5JE, **t** 0345 585 641. Offers practical advice and information on every aspect of travel and transport for elderly and disabled travellers. On request, information can be provided by letter or tape.

Organizations in the USA and Canada
American Foundation for the Blind, 15 West 16th St, New York, NY 10011, **t** (212) 620 2000, **t** 800 2323 5463. The best source of information in the USA for visually impaired travellers.
Jewish Rehabilitation Hospital, 3205 Place Alton Goldbloom, Montreal, Quebec, H7V 1R2, **t** (514) 688 9550, ext 226. Can post guidebooks and information.
Mobility International USA, PO Box 10767, Eugene, OR 97440, **t** (541) 343 1284, **f** (541) 343 6812, *info@niusa.org*. Organizes educational and study-abroad programmes for disabled travellers ($35 membership).
SATD (Society for the Advancement of Travel for the Disabled), 347 5th Av, Suite 610, NY 10016, **t** (212) 447 7284. Offers advice on all aspects of travel for the disabled, on an ad hoc basis for a $3 charge, or unlimited to members ($45, concessions $25).
Travel Information Service, Moss Rehab Hospital, 1200 West Tabor Rd, Philadelphia, PA 19141, **t** (215) 456 9600. Telephone information service supplying travel advice to people with disabilities.

Organizations in Australia
Australian Council for the Rehabilitation of the Disabled (ACROD), 24 Cabarita Rd, Cabarita, New South Wales, **t** (02) 9743 2699, *www.acrod.org.au*.

Embassies and Consulates

In Italy
Australia: Via Alessandria 215, Rome, **t** 06 85 27 21.
Canada: Via Zara 30, Rome, **t** 06 45 981.
Ireland: Via del Pozzetto 108, Rome, **t** 06 67 82 541.
New Zealand: Via Zara 28, Rome, **t** 06 44 03 028.
UK: Via Cavour 121, Palermo, **t** 09 15 82 533. Via Francesco Crispi 122, Naples, **t** 08 16 63 511. Via XX Settembre 80a, Rome, **t** 06 48 25 441.
USA: Via Re Federico 18b, Palermo, **t** 09 16 11 00 20. Via Veneto 121, Rome, **t** 06 46 74 13.

Calendar of Events

January
1 Lively celebration with fireworks, Capri; also in Taormina, with concerts and traditional performances.
6 Byzantine-Orthodox Epiphany celebrations, Piana degli Albanesi and Mezzojuso.
15 San Mauro, Aci Castello.
17 San Antonio, Nicolosi.
20 San Sebastiano, Syracuse.

February
Early Sagra del Mandorlo in Fiore (Festival of Flowering Almonds) with folklore, bands and processions in costume, Agrigento.
3 San Biagio, where pasta figures are given to the kids, and adults scramble up slippery poles for prizes, Salemi.
3–5 Sant'Agata, Catania, climaxing with the Cannelore, a procession of large wooden floats, some 5m high, carried on the men's shoulders, with elaborately decorated tableaux of scenes from the life of Sant'Agata. The procession stops at various places in the city associated with the saint.
Week before Ash Wednesday 'The most beautiful carnival in Sicily' takes place in Acireale, but also in Tràpani, Taormina, Giardini-Naxos, Paternó, Sciacca and Caltanissetta; a very traditional carnival with parades and masks takes place in Castellana Sicula. These festive events are a last chance to indulge in eating meat and behaving raucously before the strictness of Lent takes over.

March
19 San Giuseppe, when elaborate altars are decorated with holy figures made out of bread, Salemi.

25 Madonna of the Annunziata, Trapani.
Last Friday A 'miraculous' crucifix dating from 1610 is transported through town by 33 hooded monks, San Marco d'Alunzio.

April
Holy Week Celebrations on the island often have a Spanish flavour, with processions of floats carried by robed and hooded members of local confraternities. Among the most fascinating are in Enna.
Maundy Thursday Procession with participants dressed as characters from the Passion and girls (Veronicas) magnificently dressed and dripping with gold, Marsala; medieval procession of the Misteri, with musical bands from all over the province, Caltanissetta.
Good Friday Processions in traditional costumes, in Acireale, Messina, Ragusa and Vittória; procession of Misteri in Erice, Agrigento, Tràpani and Procida; procession of the Lords of the City, Caltanissetta; Festa dei Giudei, a very old and archaic carnival in which men dress up as 'Jews' in red costumes and masks and blast on trumpets, San Fratello.
Easter Sunday Abballu di li Diavuli (Dance of the Devils) in which masked figures of Death and Devils dance to pagan rhythms with a procession of the Madonna, until dispatched by avenging angels, Prizzi; Passion Play, Adrano; Festa di li Schetti, in which young men lift and swing huge tree trunks, along with traditional music and dancing, Terrasini.
Orthodox Easter Traditional celebrations in costumes, Piana degli Albanesi.
23 San Giorgio parade, in Piano degli Albanesi and Ragusa.
Last week Windsurfing festival, Mondello.

Abroad
Australia: Level 45, Macquarie Place, Sydney 2000, NSW, t (02) 9392 7900.
509 St Kilda Rd, Melbourne, t (03) 9867 5744.
Canada: 136 Beverley St, Toronto, t (416) 977 1566.
Ireland: 63–5 Northumberland Rd, Dublin, t (01) 660 1744.
7 Richmond Park, Belfast, t 028 668 854.

New Zealand: 34 Grant Rd, Wellington, t (04) 473 5339.
UK: 3 King's Yard, London W1Y 2EH, t (020) 7312 2200.
32 Melville St, Edinburgh EH3 7HA, t (0131) 226 3631.
USA: 690 Park Av, New York, NY 10021, t (212) 737 9100.
12400 Wilshire Bd, Suite 300, Los Angeles, CA, t (310) 820 0622.

May

Early Sagra del Lago with local folklore and fireworks, Pergusa.

3 'Third of May' festival, at the Santuario di Santa Maria delle Vittorie, Piazza Armerina; Santa Lucia, Syracuse.

4 Naked children in procession of San Sebastian, Melilli.

9 Foot race up to Trecastagni from Catania for the Three Holy Brothers.

Last week Sfilata del Carretto, with painted carts and puppet shows, Taormina.

Last three days Il Raduno del Costume e del Carretto, Taormina.

June

All month La Mattanza, the tuna fish massacre, Favignana.

3 Madonna della Lettera, Messina.

Mid-month Sagra delle Ciliege, cherry festival, Castelbuono.

19–21 The patron saint of Alcamo, Maria SS. dei Miracoli, with a pilgrimage up Monte Bonifato.

24 Festa dei Muzzini, decorated amphorae and harvest ceremonies from pagan times, Alcara Li Fusi.

27–29 Festa del Mare, Sciacca.

29 SS. Pietro and Paolo, Pantelleria.

June–July International ballet festival, in the Greek theatre (every second year), Syracuse; festival of underwater activities, and mural-painting contest (even-numbered years only), Ùstica.

June–Aug Music, dance and theatre performances in the Greek theatre, Taormina; handicraft exhibition in Pantelleria.

July

All month Estate Musicale Trapanese, outdoor opera at Villa Margherita, Tràpani.

First Sunday Beginning of week-long celebration of Santa Venera, Acireale; San Calogero festival, with local folklore and exhibitions, Agrigento.

Second week Medieval and Renaissance music festival, Erice.

10–13 The Feast of the Three Maries, Pantelleria.

12–15 U Fistinu, or feast of Santa Rosalia, one of the most spectacular in the Mediterranean: parades, fireworks and other delights culminate in a torch-lit pilgrimage to the saint's sanctuary on Monte Pellegrino, Palermo.

23 San Giacomo, Caltagirone.

End of month International film festival, Taormina; Sant'Anna, Ischia Ponte.

Last Sunday Palio del Mare, Syracuse; Santa Venera, Avola; fishermen's festival, Aci Trezza.

July–Aug Estate Ennese, operettas in the Castello di Lombardia, Enna; Pirandello performances, Agrigento; theatre and music festival, Taormina.

August

All month 'The Iblean August', folklore and sport festivities throughout the month, culminating in a celebration in honour of St John the Baptist on 29 August, Ragusa.

First Sunday Marine *palio* around Ortygia Island, Syracuse.

8 Pilgrimages to the Madonnas of Tindari and Gibilmanna.

Second week Festa della Spiga, corn festival with floats in honour of Ceres, music, folkdancing, theatre, fireworks, Gangi; La Castellana, costumed procession of historical characters, Cáccamo.

13–14 Il Palio dei Normanni (Norman joust), Piazza Armerina: major medieval fête in

Festivals and Events

A century ago, Giuseppe Pitrè, Sicily's great student of folklore, wrote, 'In Sicily the past is not dead, but rather accompanies one from cradle to grave, in festivals and games, in spectacles and in church, in rites and in traditions...' Nearly all Sicily's festivals are religious in origin; many have distinctly pagan pedigrees, with only a thin veneer of Christ-

ianity applied to rites once devoted to Pan or Persephone. The simplest *feste* are marked by an extra Mass, and streets decorated with coloured lights; stalls offer toys and local delicacies. After Mass, the saint's statue or relics are carried in a procession; dances and fireworks follow in the evening. **Holy Week** is the climax of the Sicilians' religious calendar, when many towns have solemn processions of wooden scenes (*misteri*) from Christ's

Sicily; hundreds participate in medieval costume, re-enact Count Roger's taking of Piazza Armerina and the tournament presented before him between four teams representing the four quarters of the town. The winning team in the various competitions receives a standard from 'Roger' which they keep in their parish church for the year. The locals take their pageant very seriously, and the competition is fierce.

13–15 Assumption and Giganti processions with 6m giants representing the 'legendary procreators' Mata and Grifone, in Messina; also the Fiera di Messina with folklore, sports and exhibitions; Feast of the Assumption, with puppet shows, Tràpani; Madonna dell'Alto, Petralia Sottana; processions, Randazzo.

15 Horse race around the lake, Pantelleria; boat procession in which a statue of the Virgin Mary is taken on a cruise of blessing to the lighthouse, followed by boats overflowing with devotees and lights, Capo d'Orlando.

16 Sagra del Tortone, a feast that takes place in the large space in front of the ancient castle; the celebrations culminate in medieval music and folk dancing, Sperlinga.

24 San Bartolomeo, one of the most popular saints on the islands, with important festivities at Ùstica, Lipari and Alicudi.

29 San Giovanni Battista, Ragusa.

29–3 Sept Madonnina delle Lacrime pilgrimage, Syracuse.

Last Sunday San Corrado, Noto; San Vito, processions of boats, Mazara.

September

6–7 Sagra di Buon Riposo, horse racing, sausage feasting and animal fair, Calascibetta.

8 Large pilgrimage to the Mother Church, followed by a sausage picnic, Altavilla Milicia.

Mid-month Festival of Hazelnuts, Polizzi Generosa; Ntaccalora e lu Triunfu di la Manna, country revelry at Cáccamo; Cuscus Festival, San Vito Lo Capo.

22 La Madonna di Porto Salvo, with a pilgrimage to the sanctuary, a procession and other events, Lampedusa.

29 St Michael's Fair, Caltanissetta.

October

Every weekend Ottobrata Zafferanese, weekends devoted to autumnal feasting, with dishes based on honey, mushrooms, wine and chestnuts, Zafferana Etnea.

2 Sant'Angelo, Vulcano.

22 Since 1600, in Capo d'Orlando, on this day there has been a feast with a market and a fair dedicated to the Virgin Mary. The original sacred image of the Madonna was stolen in 1925: it has been replaced by a small silver statue and worship goes on unperturbed.

November

1 All Souls toy fair, with sugar figurines for the children, Palermo.

First week A week of sacred music, Monreale.

11 San Martino, Catania.

December

All month Display of *presepi*, or Christmas cribs, Acireale.

13 Santa Lucia, in which a silver relic is paraded through the streets beneath colourful fireworks, Syracuse.

24 Procession of characters from the Nativity, Salemi.

Passion, borne by men in hooded robes, a reminder of the centuries of Spanish occupation. (Or did the Spanish learn it from the Sicilians?) Sicilian **music**, with its eerie quarter tones more reminiscent of Greek music than 'O Sole Mio', is played on instruments such as the *guartara* (a terracotta wind instrument), *ciaramedda* (the shepherd's goatskin bagpipe), *friscalettu* (reed flute) and *tambureddu* (skin drum). Palermo and Catania have regular

opera seasons, and performances of all sorts are often staged in Sicily's ancient **Greek theatres** in the summer.

Food and Drink

Sicilian restaurants are open from noon to 3 or 4pm and from 7 or 8 until 11pm. Most restaurants display a menu outside so that

Restaurant Price Categories	
expensive	over €40
moderate	€25–40
inexpensive	under €25

you know what to expect, at least as regards the price. **Service** in *ristoranti* and *trattorie* is always obligatory, either already included in the prices or added as a percentage (generally 10 per cent) of your bill at the end. Tipping comes on top of that, but is a matter of a few thousand lire left on the table and not a fixed percentage of the bill, as in other countries. Most restaurants charge a modest *pane e coperto* (cover and bread charge) per person. **Tax law** in Italy orders restaurants and bars to give patrons a receipt (*ricevuta fiscale*) for everything they eat or drink, which you are supposed to take out of the restaurant with you and carry for 300m in case the receipt police intercept you.

In this guide we have divided restaurants into several price categories. Prices are the average for one person, including two courses plus dessert or *antipasto*, cover charge and service (but not wine or drinks). Cafés and other places for snacks are not categorized by price.

For further information about eating in Sicily, including local specialities, wines and a menu decoder, *see* the **Food and Drink** chapter.

Health and Emergencies

Police: t 112
Ambulance (*ambulanza*) or any emergency service: **t** 113
Fire brigade: t 115

Citizens of EU countries are entitled to free healthcare in Italy's national health service, and a 90 per cent discount on prescriptions (bring a Form E111 with you). The E111 does not cover all medical expenses (no repatriation costs, for example, and no private treatment), and it is advisable to take out separate **travel insurance** for full cover. Citizens of non-EU countries should check carefully that they have adequate insurance for any medical expenses, and the cost of returning home. Australia has a reciprocal healthcare scheme

with Italy, but New Zealand, Canada and the USA do not. If you already have health insurance, a student card, or a credit card, you may be entitled to some medical cover abroad.

Less serious problems can be treated at a *pronto soccorso* (casualty/first aid department) at any hospital, or at a local health unit (*unità sanitariale locale – USL*). Airports and main railway stations also have first-aid posts. If you have to pay for any health treatment, make sure you get a receipt.

Pharmacies are generally open 8.30–1 and 4–8. Pharmacists are trained to give advice for minor ills and administer simple first aid. Any large town has a pharmacy that stays open 24 hours; others take turns to stay open (the address rota is posted in the windows of pharmacies).

No specific vaccinations are required or advised for citizens of most countries before visiting Italy: the main health risks are the usual travellers' woes of upset stomachs or the effects of too much sun. Take a supply of useful medicaments with you (e.g. insect repellent, anti-diarrhoeal medicine, sun lotion and antiseptic cream), and any drugs you need regularly. Stick to bottled water (dehydration is a serious risk in the summer).

Maps

If you intend to explore on foot or by bike, invest in a good, up-to-date regional map before you arrive, available from any of the following bookshops:
Stanford's, 12–14 Long Acre, London WC2 9LP, **t** (020) 7836 1321, *www.stanfords.co.uk*.
The Travel Bookshop, 13 Blenheim Crescent, London W11 2EE, **t** (020) 7229 5260.
The Complete Traveller, 199 Madison Av, New York, NY 10016, **t** (212) 685 9007.

Excellent maps are produced by Touring Club Italiano, Michelin and Istituto Geografico de Agostini. They are available at all major bookshops in Italy (e.g., Feltrinelli) or sometimes on news-stands. Italian tourist offices are helpful and can often supply good area maps and town plans.

Money and Banks

The euro is the official currency in Italy and 10 other nations of the European Union. Banknotes come in denominations of €5, €10, €20, €50, coins in €2, €1, 50 cents, 20 cents, 10 cents, 5 cents, 2 cents and 1 cent. At the time of writing, the euro was worth UK£0.70, US$0.85 and C$1.58.

It's a good idea to have a wad of euros in hand when you arrive in Italy, the land of strikes, unforeseen delays and quirky **banking hours** – usually Mon–Fri 8.35am–1.20pm and 3–4pm, closed weekends and on local and national holidays (*see* below). But it has never been easier to get money while travelling in Sicily. Even though you pay a small transaction fee, the **ATM** is the easiest way to get cash, and the exchange rate is always better than what you would get at a change bureau. The machines are everywhere now, even in many small towns. Go to a bank to change **travellers' cheques** and/or to draw euros against your credit card. Hotels, private exchanges in resorts and FS-run exchanges at railway stations should be your last resort, but are open outside of banking hours.

Major **credit cards** are accepted at most moderate and luxury hotels in Sicily, resort area restaurants, shops and car hire firms, but there is frequently the odd exception. Don't expect to use plastic at petrol stations, nor in most restaurants. To cancel any **lost or stolen card** in Italy, call t 16 78 22 056.

In an emergency, you can have **money transferred** in a day to the main post office in the area (*vaglia telegrafica*), or transferred through an Italian bank, although it will take 10 days to arrive if you're lucky, even if it's sent urgent *espressissimo*. Make sure it arrives with your passport number and you bring said document to pick it up, or you may have to punch the clerk in the nose to get it.

Museums and Churches

National museums are generally open from 9am to 1pm; the larger ones also open in the afternoon a few days a week. Outdoor sites (archaeological excavations, castles, etc.) generally open from 9am until an hour before sunset. Be warned that **opening hours** can

National Holidays

Most museums, banks and shops are closed on the following national holidays:

1 January (New Year's Day)
6 January (Epiphany)
Easter Sunday and Monday
25 April (Liberation Day)
1 May (Labour Day)
15 August (Assumption, also known as Ferragosto, the peak of the Italian holiday season)
1 November (All Saints' Day)
8 December (Immaculate Conception)
25 December (Christmas Day)
26 December (Santo Stefano)

change according to an array of variables, ranging from the time of year to local holidays and the ever common 'restoration'. If you are really set on seeing a place, or are going out of your way, it is advisable to call the local tourist office to get the latest information. **Admission prices** in Sicily are very low compared to those in the rest of Europe (average €4.50 for museums; most archaeological sites are free). If you're under 18 or over 65 you get in free if you are from one of the countries that has a reciprocal agreement with Italy (including all EU countries, but not the USA).

Churches are usually open 8–noon or 12.30, and 4 or 5–evening mass (6.30 or 7); exceptions are noted in the book. A frustrating number are only open early in the morning or in the early evening for Mass, when it's not very polite to go prowling around; other churches have been closed for restoration for the past 20 years.

Post, Fax and Email

Dealing with *la posta italiana* has always been a risky, frustrating, time-consuming affair. One of the scandals that has mesmerized Italy in the past few years was the one involving the minister of the post office, who disposed of literally tons of backlog mail by tossing the letters in the Tiber. When the news broke, he was replaced – the new minister, having learned his lesson, burned all the mail the post office was incapable of delivering. Not surprisingly, fed-up Italians viewed the invention of the fax machine like a gift straight from the Madonna.

Post offices are usually open from 9am until 1pm, or until 6 or 7pm in a large city. To have your mail sent *posta restante* (general delivery), have it addressed to you at: Fermo Posta, Ufficio Postale di (city). To pick up your mail you must present your passport and pay a nominal charge. Stamps may be purchased in post offices or at tobacconists (*tabacchi*, identified by their blue signs with a white T).

Most Sicilian towns now have a **fax** office. For international faxes the cost is around €0.50 a page, plus the call cost. Have a look at *www.cyberiacafe.net/cyberia/guide/ccafe.htm* for **internet cafés** in Sicily – all of the cities and resorts now have them.

Shopping and Crafts

Italian **shops** are generally open Mon–Sat 9am–1pm and 4–7.30pm, although most supermarkets are closed on Wednesday afternoon, and clothing shops are typically closed Monday morning. Measurements and sizes are in many cases different in Italy, and it always pays to try on what you are buying, especially since shops in Italy don't have returns policies. Italians tend to have narrower feet for the length of the shoe, and their waists tend to be smaller than those of British and American women. **Clothing, leather and shoes** are always attractive buys in fashion-enslaved Italy. Apart from the glittering designer boutiques of Palermo, Catania and Taormina you may find some good bargains in the open-air markets, especially in Palermo.

Some age-old Sicilian crafts have yet to disappear, and some are even being revived. The Arabs introduced **wrought iron** to Sicily, but it was in the age of Baroque that it really blossomed, especially on balconies. Today three craftsmen still work in Giardini-Naxos, producing everything from ornate headboards for beds, to bell wheels and traditional Jew's harps (*marranzanu*). It was also the Arabs who refired the kilns of the ancient Greeks, refounding the **ceramics** and terracotta industries on the island. Three main centres survive: Sciacca, Caltagirone and Santo Stefano di Camastra, producing colourful pottery of all

kinds though the best by far seem to be from Sciacca. Although Sicily's great banks of **coral** were seriously depleted in the 19th century, coral is imported from the Bay of Naples and made into necklaces and other pretty things in Tràpani, Palermo, Catania and Messina.

The art of making **wooden puppets** has declined somewhat in recent years, along with the puppet theatre, but if you look carefully you can still find handsome hand-made Paladins and Saracens – some as tall as 2m, alongside the cheap industrial-made souvenir models.

Colourful rustic **carpets** called *frazzata* are made by the women of Erice, and **lace** is the speciality of San Cataldo, near Caltanissetta. In Castiglione (near Catania), Vittória (near Ragusa) and Sortino (near Syracuse), women still do intricate **embroideries**, heirs of the Arab silkworkers who worked in the royal workshops (*tiraz*) of Palermo, and produced in 1133 the magnificent mantle of tigers attacking camels for Roger II (now on display in Vienna's Kunsthistorisches Museum).

Telephones

Orange **payphones** may be found along major streets and in bars. Most phones take *schede telefoniche* (prepaid phone cards), available from tobacconists, bars and post offices in various denominations. You must break off the perforated corner before using a new card, and don't forget to take it with you when you have finished your call. In smaller villages and islands, you can usually find a telephone *a scatti* (with a meter) in at least one bar. Try to avoid telephoning from hotels, which often add 25 per cent to the bill. **Directory enquiries** is available in Italian by dialling t 12 (there is no charge from payphones which are not in booths or bars).

Direct **international** calls may be made by dialling the international prefix (for the UK 00 44, Ireland 00 353, USA and Canada 00 1, Australia 00 61, New Zealand 00 64). Lowest rates are generally after 10pm and on Sundays. The international code for Italy is 39 and you do have to dial the initial 'o' in the number. The exception is with mobile phones: the zero that you dial in Italy will have to be skipped if you phone from abroad – a tricky business if you don't know whether or not a number starting with zero is an area code or a mobile one. There is good coverage for mobile phones in Sicily so if you are able to use your phone in Italy, you should get good reception on the island.

Time

Italy is one hour ahead of Greenwich Mean Time, and seven hours ahead of Eastern Standard Time.

From the last weekend of March to the end of September, Italian Summer Time (daylight saving time) is in effect.

Tourist Offices

Tourist information offices, known as EPT, APT or AAST, are generally open Mon–Fri 8–12.30 or 1 and 3–7, possibly longer in summer. Few open on Saturday afternoons or Sundays. They provide hotel lists, town plans and terse information on local sights and transport. Queues can be maddeningly long. English is spoken in the main centres. If you're stuck, you may get more sense out of a travel agency than an official tourist office.

The Italian national tourist office can be found at *www.enit.it*, or contact one of the following addresses:

Australia: Level 26, 44 Market St, Sydney 2000, NSW, **t** (02) 9262 1666.

Canada: 17 Bloor St East, Suite 907, South Tower, Toronto M4W 3R8, **t** (416) 925 4882.

Ireland: 47 Merrion Square, Dublin 2, **t** (01) 766 397.

New Zealand: c/o Italian Embassy, 36 Grant Road, Thornton, Wellington, **t** (04) 473 5339.

UK: 1 Princess St, London W1R 9AY, **t** (020) 7408 1254.

USA: 630 Fifth Av, Suite 1565, New York, NY 10111, **t** (212) 245 5095.
500 North Michigan Av, Suite 2240, Chicago, Illinois 60611, **t** (312) 644 0996.
12400 Wilshire Bd, Suite 550, Los Angeles, California 90025, **t** (310) 820 1898.

Where to Stay

All accommodation in Italy is classified, with prices regulated by the provincial tourist boards. On arrival, you will be asked for your passport for registration purposes. Quality has improved across the board in the past few decades, and there are quite a few spanking-new hotels on the coast with every comfort. Nostalgic visitors can still find a few old-fashioned Sicilian hotels kicking around on the third floors of Baroque *palazzi*, with rusting balconies, mile-high ceilings, wardrobes the size of elephants, cement pillows, and a simpering Madonna looming overhead.

Hotels

These are by no means evenly distributed in Sicily: the coast is fairly well endowed but many towns in the interior have only one hotel, if any. Price lists are posted on the back of the door of every room (or inside the wardrobe), along with the prices of continental breakfast or full- or half-board, the cost of adding an extra bed, and air-conditioning if it is considered an 'extra'. Heating, if called for, is free of charge, although in the most modest establishments you may pay for a shower.

In Italy the hotel rates are now adjusted every year, so we can't guarantee exact prices for rooms. Many hotels boost prices during the tourist season (Easter, and July to mid-September). Beach-side resort hotels tend to close down altogether between September and June. **Reservations** are always a good idea in summer, and essential for a major resort. Fax numbers are listed here where possible, but be warned that faxed enquiries are rarely answered promptly (if ever).

Pensioni are generally rated one or two stars, and are often (but not necessarily) family-run and located on one or several floors of a

Hotel Prices
Throughout this book, prices listed for hotels are for a standard double room in high season. As a general guide, expect to pay around:

luxury	over €200
expensive	€120–200
moderate	€90–120
inexpensive	€60–90
budget	under €60

building. **Rooms in private houses** can be had in most resort areas and islands (ask at the tourist offices first). **Single travellers** should be aware that a hotel that gives a double room as *uso singolo* (single use) cannot legally charge more than the maximum rate for a single room. An extra bed cannot add more than 35 per cent to the rate of the room.

Note that many pensions and hotels in resort areas have **half-board requirements** (when they have restaurants, that is – some do not) and have **minimum stays** in August; these requirements are noted in this book accordingly.

In Sicily, a stay in a lowly pension may be an unforgettable adventure – do make the owners show you the room and WC before you commit yourself. Mysterious wall and wardrobe growths lend many a dingy but palatially high-ceilinged room a nasty but natural texture. But even in the worst dive, the sheets will be spotless. In the hotter months, it might be wise to buy an **anti-mosquito device** (in *casalinghi*, houseware shops) to keep away the major summertime nuisance.

In this book, the official star ratings are also given for hotels. Beware, however, of assuming anything at all about a hotel by its classification. Owners of the hotels are given enough discretion in rating their hotels to make guidelines useless. Some hotels are deliberately classed lower to attract the bargain-minded traveller, although they may charge as much as a hotel with double the number of stars.

Tourist Villages

There are tourist villages (*villaggi turistici*) sprouting up along the coasts; almost all consist of separate units (white Mediterranean bungalows or Polynesian grass huts) near a beach, and offer a number of recreational facilities in Club Méditerranée style, chiefly attracting a youthful sun-and-fun crowd. Lists can be obtained from tourist offices.

Mountain Refuges

In Sicily, Club Alpino Italiano operates refuges on the main mountain trails around Mount Etna, and in the Monti Nebrodi and Madonìe. These offer simple accommodation, often with restaurants. Each province has a listing, or check the Club Alpino Italiano website on *www.cai.it*, **t** 02 26 14 13 78. Charges average €10 a night, with a 20 per cent increase between December and April.

Camping

Sicily and its islands have some 90 official campsites and some are very beautiful, but bear in mind that the majority of Italians take their holidays in August, when the sites are bursting at the seams. If you can go any other month, do, and you may have the place to yourself. Note also that campsites congregate around popular tourist sites – there are very few in the island's interior.

Most campsites have beaches near by, and facilities include anything from toilets and showers to tennis courts and swimming pools. Prices, if inexpensive by resort hotel standards, are not a bargain compared to cheap hotels: two people with a car and tent can easily pay €20 a night. Touring Club Italiano, Corso Italia 10, Milan, **t** 02 85 26 245, publishes a guide to campsites.

Agriturismo

Urban, urbane Italians occasionally have an irresistible longing to seek out their country roots by spending a week or two in a country apartment in accommodation known by the generic term of *agriturismo*. This is a growing trend in Sicily, but you need some Italian under your belt before committing yourself to a few days in a rural olive grove. The advantage is getting to meet people in their own environment (horse riding, fishing and other rural activities are often included) and rooms are often large and come with their own kitchen. For a book of listings of farm accommodation (though be warned that these are by no means comprehensive as the *agriturismos* have to pay to be included, so do check out sites on the Internet too like *www.farm-holidays.it*, *www.sicilia-agriturismo.com* or *www.agriturismoonline.com*), contact Agriturist, Via A. di Giovanni 14, Palermo, **t** 0913 46 046, *www.agriturist.it*.

Women Travellers

Italian men, with the heritage of Casanova, Don Giovanni and Rudolph Valentino as their birthright, are very confident in their role as

Great Latin Lovers, but the old horror stories of gangs following the innocent tourist maiden are way behind the times. Sicilian men these days are often exquisitely polite and flirt on a much more sophisticated level.

Still, women travelling alone may frequently receive hisses, wolf-whistles and unsolicited comments or 'assistance' from local swains – usually of the balding, middle-age-crisis variety. A confident, indifferent poise is usually the best policy. Failing that, a polite 'I am waiting for my *marito*' (avoiding damaged male egos), followed by a firm '*Vai via!*' (Scram!) will generally solve the problem.

Flashers and wandering hands on crowded buses may be an unpleasant surprise, but rarely present a serious threat (unless they're after your purse). Risks can be reduced if you use common sense and avoid lonely streets or parks and stations after dark. Choose restaurants within easy walking distance of public transport. Travelling with a companion of either sex will buffer you considerably from such nuisances (a guardian male, of course, instantly converts you into an inviolable chattel in Italian eyes). Avoid hitch-hiking alone in Sicily or anywhere else in Italy.

Palermo

07

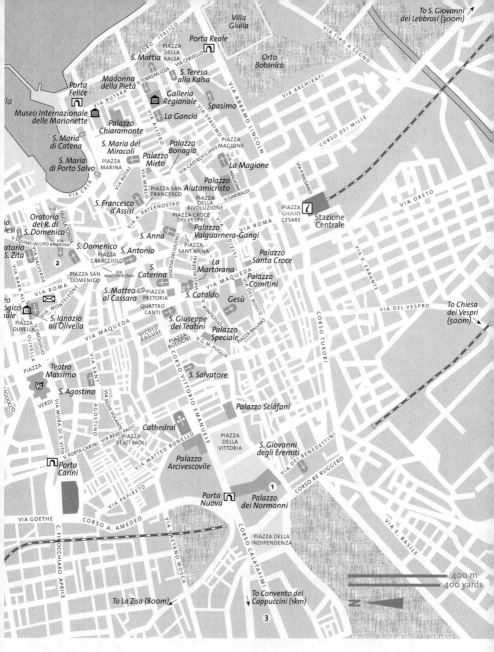

Highlights

1 Palermo's masterpiece of 12th-century craftsmanship, the Cappella Palatina inside the Palazzo dei Normanni

2 Serpotta's saucy stucco flight of fancy, the Oratorio del Rosario

3 The grinning corpses in the unforgettably gruesome Convento dei Cappuccini

4 A boat trip through the magical grottoes of the island of Ùstica 67km north of Palermo

Of all of Italy's great art cities, Palermo is the most underrated. It is also the most likely to fill you with wistful melancholy or alarmed dismay or both. For the periods when Palermo has fulfilled the promise of its superb location and exuberant natural talent, it has blossomed like a rare orchid in a unique hothouse of Mediterranean and northern cultures. Today the most outstanding of these flowerings to have survived – the superb syncretic monuments of the Normans, the medieval palaces, the Baroque churches and oratories, the Art Nouveau-Liberty villas and hotels – often stand like islands in a stagnant sea of desolation. The historic centre though, is slowly being renovated and Palermo is coming out of the slumber of corruption and stagnation, once again to wear its fineries like the jewels they are.

Palermo, like all capitals, tends to reflect the best and the worst of the land. It may have too many cars, too much noise, too much crime (of the petty variety – all you're likely to see of the Mafia is what is splashed across the headlines of the papers), and some of western Europe's most squalid slums, but it also has a near overkill of art, architecture and atmosphere, lush gardens, a long sandy beach and teeming markets. A troubled history has given Palermo a touching belief in saintly miracles (expressed most deliriously in the July festival of Santa Rosalia) and in less saintly magic as well: the services offered in the omnipresent handbills and hoardings by the *magi*, or sorcerers, are a constant reminder that this was the home town of Cagliostro, where anything is possible. After all, fatalism is really a form of optimism, perhaps best expressed in the celluloid fairy tales of Frank Capra, the Palermitan who moved to Hollywood.

History

The first known inhabitants of what is now Palermo were the Upper Palaeolithic artists who left lovely engravings of a dance in Grotta dell'Addaura on the north slope of Monte Pellegrino, the magnificent promontory that closes Palermo's harbour on the north. Despite this superb location Palermo was colonized relatively late by Sicilian standards (in the 8th century BC), by the Phoenicians as a trading port and counterbalance to the advance of the Greeks in western Sicily. Its Punic name is unknown; the Greeks called it Panormos ('the all-haven') for the safe anchorages formed by the two rivers that once flowed on either side of modern Corso Vittorio Emanuele, main axis of the city since the beginning. The Phoenician town stood at the top of the peninsula, in the area of the modern Palazzo dei Normanni, which even then was probably the chief citadel. This was Paleopolis, the old city; later Neapolis, the new city, grew up towards the port.

Rome fought hard for Palermo in the First Punic War, finally capturing it in 254 BC. With the fall of Rome the city was occupied by the Goths until AD 535, when the great Byzantine general Belisarius seized it by pulling his ships up to the walled port with archers bound high to the masts. The Goths gave up; the Byzantines called their conquest Balarma.

Arab and Norman Palermo

Palermo's history as a city proper begins in 831 with the Arab conquest. The Arabs immediately recognized the potential of the site and made Palermo the splendid capital of an emirate and an important commercial centre. Under their reign the city quickly grew to a population that has been estimated at as high as 200,000 – mostly Arabs, but also sizeable minorities of Greeks, Jews, Persians, Slavs, Lombards and black Africans. From the Al-Qasr quarter (known as *il Cassaro* today and meaning 'the citadel') – old Paleopolis with its repaired Roman fortress, the great mosque (on the site of the present cathedral), souks and markets – Palermo spread in all directions. After 940 the emir and his nobles (*el-Halisah*, 'the elect') moved to another walled area near the sea, an administrative quarter of public buildings still known as the Kalsa. Old Neapolis, the area near the port and Piazza Marina, became an elite residential quarter for merchants, called the Cassaro. Travellers' accounts tell of Palermo's beauty and wealth, its 300 mosques and seething markets. All around the city were pleasure palaces immersed in gardens, orchards and orange groves fed by clear fountains. It had the first known paper mill in Europe, an art the Arabs had learned from the Chinese with their conquest of Samarkand in 707.

The first Norman attempt to seize Palermo, in 1064, ended in tragicomedy when they bivouacked on a hill swarming with a species of tarantula whose bites caused painful farts. But by 1072 Robert Guiscard and his younger brother, the future Count Roger, were back, and after a siege took the city. Much to the surprise of the Palermitans, they were neither killed nor enslaved by their Norman conquerors, but left in peace to follow their own religion and laws. Although Count Roger spent most of his time in Messina, owing to the frequent need to squash rebellious barons in Apulia and Calabria, his widow Adelaide and son, King Roger II, made Palermo their multilingual, multiracial capital. Roger and his successors increased the splendour of what was already one of the most extraordinary cities in Europe, assimilating the best of each culture they met, in architecture, politics and scholarship.

Palermo continued its role as a cultural centre under the Swabians, especially under Emperor Frederick II, whose centralizing schemes gave the capital more power than it ever held under the Normans, although the delicate racial balance in the city created by the Hautevilles would never be regained. All Sicilians did unite, however, against the hated Angevins in the Sicilian Vespers, a rebellion that broke out in 1282 at a church in Palermo. After massacring all the French, the barons of Sicily held a parliament in the Orthodox church of La Martorana, where they voted to offer the crown of Sicily to Peter of Aragon.

Spanish and Bourbon Palermo

When the destructive War of the Sicilian Vespers ground to a halt in 1302, the Aragonese proved to be little better than the Angevins. Instead of pleasure domes, the nobles of the 14th and 15th centuries built fortified palaces. Palermo remained a stagnant backwater until it became the seat of the Spanish viceroys in the 1500s. The nobility flocked to their court, and competed with each other to decorate the new wider streets and squares with the most splendid palaces, while the Inquisition wiped up any last vestiges of tolerance. Religious orders thrived, with immense sums to lavish on their churches; if the Baroque churches of Noto and Ragusa are more original, Palermo's have interiors awash with colourful marbles, semi-precious stones, frescoes and some of the most extraordinary stucco decorations on this planet.

By the 18th century Palermo had 200,000 people, making it the second or third largest city in Italy. Foreign travellers, of whom Goethe is only the most famous, flocked here, and sent tantalizing descriptions back home. The King of Naples, Ferdinand IV, moved his court to the city when the French occupied Naples (1799–1805 and 1806–15). The increasingly brutal tyranny of Ferdinand and his successor prompted three revolts in Palermo. First, in 1820, the uprising of the 72 guilds (*maestranze*) which turned into a futile class war when the rest of Sicily failed to join in. The second, in January 1848, of Palermo's poor, begun by Giuseppe La Masa, which turned out to be the first revolt of that revolutionary year in Europe. Ruggero Settimo, a retired naval officer, became its leader, and the rest of Sicily joined him in chasing the Bourbon army off the island, except for the fortress in Messina. The revolt lasted for almost a year and a half, long enough to strike fear into the wealthy nobles. The third revolt, in 1860, brought Garibaldi down to Sicily to save the day and begin the unification of Italy.

If unification proved to be more of a problem than a solution for the average Sicilian, the aristocracy and millionaires in the capital enjoyed a luscious Belle Epoque twilight. It also signalled the start of the abandonment of the old centre for the wider streets of 'new addition' around Piazza Ruggero Settimo. The best of the new *villini* built here were by Liberty architect Ernesto Basile. The decay was accelerated a hundredfold after a rain of Allied bombs in August 1943. Even today you'll find a few bomb-shattered buildings untouched since the war along Via Messina.

Palermo Today

Some million people live in Palermo and its periphery, a number that continues to swell every year, mostly at the expense of the once-idyllic Conca d'Oro, where gardens and farms are being crushed under creeping suburbia. Only a few thousand Palermitans, from poverty or stubbornness, have refused the allure of a new concrete flat to remain in the exquisite cadaver of old Palermo. Responsibility for its neglect falls firmly on the shoulders of the Mafia and the corrupt governments it has controlled, which do not give a fig for historic restoration, and have long found building and new property speculations the easiest way to launder ill-gotten gains.

But there is hope. A combination of factors – lack of room for new urban growth, the purge of corrupt politicians, and sustained pressure on the Mafia thanks to the courage of ex-Mayor Leoluca Orlando – may well have brought about a new spring-time for Palermo. New Mayor Diego Cammarata puts urban renewal at the top of his priorities but with unemployment in the city running at 29 per cent (three times the national level), he has other worries. Cammarata insists that his programme of public works and focus on tourism will bring in 37,000 jobs in the next five years, but there are also those who say that the Mafia have gone back to their old ways – extortion and controlling public works, so the boom in construction projects could also be an

Getting There

By Air

Palermo's Falcone-Borsellino airport is at Punta Raisi, 30km west of the city. For flight information, call toll free **t** 848 865 643.

There's a regular Prestia & Comandè **bus** (**t** 091 580 457) to the airport and back from Stazione Centrale in front of the Hotel Elena, and from Piazza Ruggero Settimo, in front of the Teatro Politeama Garibaldi. There are no buses after midnight. There is also a shuttle train that goes to the main train station in Palermo every 6 minutes from 5.40am to 11.40pm. It takes 55 mins; tickets (around €5) are bought on board. Find the train opposite the baggage hall.

A **taxi** from the airport to the centre of town should cost about €50, **t** 091 591 662.

By Sea

There are regular **ferry** services to Naples and Cagliari on Tirrenia (Via Molo, **t** 091 602 1111, *www.tirrenia.it*). There are also ferry and **hydrofoil** connections to Ùstica with Siremar (Via F. Crispi 118, **t** 091 582 403, *www.gruppo tirrenia.it/siremar*), as well as occasional SNAV summer hydrofoils to the Aeolian Islands and Cefalù (Via Principe di Belmonte 53, **t** 091 631 7900, *www.snav.it*).

For connections with other Italian destinations contact Grandi Navi Veloci, Via Marinai d'Italia, **t** 091 587 404.

By Train

Stazione Centrale, on Piazza Giulio Cesare, is Palermo's main station (**t** 091 603 1111, travel information on **t** 892 021, *www.trenitalia.com*). From Palermo you can pick up a train to all corners of Sicily. The left-luggage service (**t** 091 603 3040) is open daily 6am–10pm.

By Bus

Small towns near Palermo are generally served by AST, from Corso Re Ruggero or Piazza Lolli (**t** 091 680 0030/680 0031, *www.azienda sicilianatrasporti.it*).

Other major lines depart from Via Paolo Balsamo 16, near the Stazione Centrale, for example SAIS (**t** 091 616 6028, *www.saisauto linee.it*) for Catania, Enna and Messina.

Next door at SAIS Trasporti (Via Paolo Balsamo 20, **t** 091 617 1141, *www.saistrasporti.it*) buses go to Caltanisetta, Cefalù and Sciacca. For Agrigento, try Cuffaro buses (**t** 091 616 15 10, *www.cuffaro.it*).

Segesta (**t** 09 16 16 79 19, *www.segesta.it*) goes to Tràpani, Syracuse, Alcamo and Catania.

Getting Around

By Bus (AMAT)

As elsewhere in Italy, buy municipal bus tickets (*€1 for two hours, transfer as often as you like, but frank them in the machine only once, on the first journey, on boarding*) at a tobacconist or news-stand. Ask at the tourist office for the latest AMAT map, or call **t** 091 729 1111 for information.

By Metro

The underground line (**t** 848 888 088) runs from 6.10am to 8.35pm every 25 minutes. It's not amazingly useful for tourists, but it stops at Stazione Centrale, Piazza Vespri, Via Notarbartolo, Via Imperatore Federico, Via Autonomia Siciliana and Piazza Giacchery, near the port, and may come in handy.

By Taxi

Finding a cab at a stand is easier than trying to hail one on the street; or phone Autoradiotaxi **t** 091 512 727, Radio Taxi Trinacria **t** 091 225455. Expect to be charged at least an extra €2, depending on the distance. therwise, the start-up charge on the meter is €3.10, and a supplement of €1.29 will be added on Sundays and holidays, €1.55 after 10pm. Cab drivers are licensed by the city and must use their fare meters; don't be shy about reminding them. Unlicensed cabs should be avoided. Complaints should go to the *Vigili Urbani*: **t** 091 695 4111.

By *Carrozza*

A *carrozza* is a horse-drawn carriage, a few of which are still in business. They can be found by the Stazione Centrale, Palazzo dei Normanni and Teatro Politeama Garibaldi, and can be a fun way to explore the historic centre. Fares are set (*€50 per city tour, there is room for five passengers*), but also negotiable.

Parking

Driving in Palermo is nightmare enough, but finding a safe parking place will drive you round the bend. Some *piazze* in the historic centre are used as guarded car parks (San Domenico and Piazzale Ungheria); there are garages near the Stazione Centrale on Piazza Giulio Cesare, in Via Paolo Paternosto (near the Teatro Politeama Garibaldi), on Via Principe di Belmonte (near the port) and at Piazza XIII Vittime. Usually €1 per hour up to 8pm.

Tourist Information

Piazza Castelnuovo 35, near Piazza Ruggero Settimo, t 091 605 8111, *www.palermo tourism.com (open Mon–Fri 8–2 and Thurs only 2.30–6, Sat 8–2)*.
Stazione Centrale, Piazza Giulio Cesare, t 091 616 5914 *(open Mon–Fri 8.30–2 and 2.30–6)*.
Falcone Borsellino Airport, t 091 591 698 *(open Mon–Fri 8am–midnight, Sat–Sun 8–8)*.
Additionally you will find tourist information booths at various locations.

There's a bi-monthly publication available free at the tourist offices, *Agenda*, which has a comprehensive listing of events and updated museum opening times, with a portion translated into English.

Useful Addresses

All-night chemist: Di Naro, Via Roma 207, t 091 585 869.
American Express: Via Emerico Amari 40, t 800 864046.
Hospital: Ospedale Civico, Via Carmelo Lazzaro, t 091 666 1111.
Internet access: There are lots: Accademia Internet, Via Cala 64, t 091 611 8483. Near the main tourist office is @Internet Point, Via Dante 5, t 091 662 2085.
Lost property: Stazione Centrale (t 091 603 3040).
Library: Archivio di Stato, Corso Vittorio Emanuele 31, t 091 740 6010.
Police: Questura Centrale, Piazza della Vittoria 8, t 091 210 111 (to pick up the form you need for your insurance if something is stolen).

Post office: Via Roma 322, with a fax machine *(open Mon–Fri 8am–6.30pm, Sat 8.10am–1.20pm)*.
Towed-away cars: AMAT, t 091 350 262, Vigili Urbani t 091 695 4295.
UK Consulate: Via Cavour 117, t 091 326 412.
US Consulate: Via Vaccarini 1, t 091 305 857.

Orientation

Palermo stretches northwest–southeast along the sea. The promontory of Monte Pellegrino is the chief landmark to the north; inland is the fertile, mountain-rimmed basin of the Conca d'Oro ('golden shell'), overlooked by the hill town and cathedral of Monreale.

The north–south division between historic and new Palermo is abrupt. North from Via Cavour and on either side of the main axis Viale della Libertà are modern apartment blocks and offices; bright commercial streets and boutiques; Palermo's largest lung, Parco della Favorita; and, behind Monte Pellegrino, the long beach of Mondello Lido.

To the south of Via Cavour lies the historic centre, with all the superb churches and palaces – and all the squalor. The main crossroads here is the Quattro Canti, where the main 16th-century north–south street Via Maqueda meets Palermo's most ancient thoroughfare, now called Corso Vittorio Emanuele, which links the old port of La Cala to the Palazzo dei Normanni.

Tucked into each quadrant of the four corners of Quattro Canti are neighbourhoods of narrow medieval lanes and stairs, often with no street signs. We've written this section as little walking tours with the idea of keeping you from getting too lost in the labyrinth; you may also want to invest in a city map from a news-stand (the free tourist office map only has a few street names).

If you're planning only a brief stay in Palermo, you can scratch the surface fairly deeply by concentrating on the southwest quadrant of the historic centre (the first section described below, the Albergheria), as well as the excellent Museo Archeológico Regionale and Galleria Regionale della Sicilia, and at least one Serpotta oratory (Santa Cita or the Rosario) and Monreale.

Parks and Open Spaces

Città dei Ragazzi, Viale Duca degli Abruzzi, (*open Tues–Sun 10–8, spring and summer only*).
Giardino Inglese, Viale della Libertà (*open Mon–Fri 9–6, Sat & Sun 9–1*).
Parco della Favorita, Piazza Leoni (entrance).
Villa Giulia and Orto Botanico, Via Lincoln, t 091 623 8111 (for the garden), *www.orto botanico.palermo.it* (*open Mon–Sat 9–6, Sun 8.30–1.30; adm*) t 091 740 40 28 for the Villa Giulia (*open daily 8–8*).
Villa Trabia, Via Salinas (*open daily 9–7*).

Markets

Ballarò, Piazza del Cármine. Fish, groceries and household goods at one of Palermo's most interesting markets.
Calderai, Via dei Calderai. Metalwork and handicraft. *Open daily except Sundays.*
Capo, Via Beati Paoli, Via Porta Carini, Via S. Agostino. Food and clothing market dating back to Arab times. Better in the mornings.
Mercato delle Pulci, Piazza Domenico Peranni. Flea market. *Open Mon–Sat 8–4, Sun 8–1.*
Mercato Ittico, Via F. Crispi, t 091 740 6321. Fish market.
Vucciria, Piazza Caracciolo and surroundings. Palermo's most established market. In the old days you would have been able to find anything from sheep's brain to dog's tail; today this meat market is a tamer affair. Though you can find it all day, there is more activity in the morning.

Where to Stay

The one time when rooms may be hard to find is mid-July, during the festival of Santa Rosalia. If there are two prices listed below, the higher one will be the rule in July and August. Palermo has some renowned old establishments that truly deserve the appellation 'Grand Hotel'.

Most of Palermo's less expensive, older hotels are in walking distance of the Stazione Centrale (not an inviting area at night), and some occupy one or more floors of a *palazzo*. Some buildings contain several hotels.

Luxury
****Centrale Palace**, Corso V. Emanuele 327, ✉ 90139, t 091 336 666, *www.centralepalace hotel.it*. Ideally located in the centre, near the cathedral, and beautifully refurbished, it offers TV, mini-bar, air-conditioning, a car park at the rear, and a fabulous roof-garden restaurant; excellent service, too.
*****Grand Hotel Federico II**, Via Principe Granatelli 60, ✉ 90139, t 091 74 95 052, *www.classicahotels.com*. The newest addition to Palermo's luxury contingent, this newly converted palazzo opened in 2003. The roof terrace gives it an edge so near the historic centre of town.
****Grand Hotel et des Palmes**, Via Roma 398, ✉ 90139, t 091 602 8111, *www.despalmes.thi.it*. Wagner supposedly found the inspiration for completing his *Parsifal* in this centrally located hotel's salons, which are all time-capsules of early 1900s Belle Epoque elegance. Later guests included Lucky Luciano, who made the hotel his HQ. The whole hotel is just starting to undergo renovation so plan your visit from 2005 on.
*****Grand Hotel Villa Igiea**, Salita Belmonte 43, ✉ 90142, t 091 631 2111, *www.villaigiea.thi.it* (*see p.95*). Immersed in gardens running down to a little bay on the northeastern periphery of the city, complete with pool (and tennis courts nearby). It is too far from the town centre for some but its mirrored, frescoed salons have hosted half the crowned heads of Europe. Some of the room are looking tired though and service can be patchy. The hotel restaurant La Terrazza di Villa Igiea (*expensive*) has views over palm trees and the sea and serves gourmet dishes based on the freshest seafood.

Expensive
****Politeama Palace**, Piazza Ruggero Settimo 15, ✉ 90133, t 091 32 27 77, *www.hotelpoliteama.it*. A quiet and modern hotel in the city centre.

Moderate–expensive
***Cristal Palace**, Via Roma 477, near Piazza Ruggero Settimo, ✉ 90139, t 091 61 12 580. A modern hotel with parking, and situated in

the centre (unlike most of Palermo's three-star offerings, which are inconveniently located in the north part of town).

★★★★**Jolly Hotel del Foro Italico**, Foro Italico 22, ✉ 90133, **t** 09 16 16 50 90, *www.jollyhotels.it*. A hotel beside the sea with every comfort, and the added plus of a pool.

★★★★**Hotel Principe di Villafranca**, Via G.Turrisi Colonna 4, ✉ 90141, **t** 091 61 18 523, *www.principedivillafranca.it*. Recently opened hotel in the centre of the new town; nearTeatro Politeama Garibaldi. All the rooms are decked out with Sicilian antiques and the individual touch of great taste. Probably Palermo's best value for such elegant surroundings and friendly service.

Inexpensive–moderate

★★★**Tonic**, Via Mariano Stabile 136, **t** 091 581 754, *www.hoteltonic.com*. A good central choice, quite recently renovated.

Inexpensive

★★**Joly**, Via M. Amari 11, ✉ 90129, **t** 091 611 1766. Clean, modern, dependable and overlooking Piazza Florio.

★**Letizia**, Via Bottai 30, ✉ 90133, **t/f** 091 589 110, *www.hotelletizia.com*. A reliable little hotel near Piazza Marina.

★★**Moderno**, Via Roma 276, ✉ 90133, **t/f** 091 58 86 83. Has exceptionally nice high-ceilinged rooms and an English-speaking owner.

★★**Sausele**, Via Vincenzo Errante 12, ✉ 90127, **t** 091 616 308, *www.hotelsausele.it*. A convenient, clean and safe option next to the station; also has access to a pay-parking garage.

★**Sicilia**, Via Divisi 99 (just off Via Maqueda), ✉ 90133, **t/f** 091 616 8460. Set in a Baroque palace with an enormous stair and spacious rooms.

★★**Villa Archirafi**, Via Abramo Lincoln 30, ✉ 90133, **t** 091 605 5308. Towards the sea, near the Orto Botanico, this is a quiet choice, as long as you don't sleep on the street side.

Budget

★**Alessandra**, Via Divisi 99, ✉ 90133, **t** 091 616 7009, *www.albergoallesandra.it*. Just above the Sicilia, in the same Baroque palace, and with similar facilities.

★**Elena**, Piazza G. Cesare 14, ✉ 90127, **t** 091 616 2021. Noisy – and Palermo is a hell of a city for sirens at all hours – but only a stone's throw from the station, this place is clean and convenient.

★**Orientale**, Via Maqueda 26, ✉ 90134, **t** 091 616 1193. For character and a touch of early 18th-century atmosphere and lack of mod-cons (like heating), there's this hotel spread out across the *piano nobile* of Giacomo Amato's Palazzo Cutò. Some wonderfully cavernous rooms, plus smaller ones over-looking the courtyard.

Mondello and Sferracavallo ✉ 90151

★★★★**Mondello Palace**, Via Principe di Scalea 2, **t** 091 450 001 (*moderate–expensive*). As with all of the more expensive hotels at Mondello, this one has access to a beach; tennis, pool, sailing and windsurfing are on offer as well.

★★★★**Splendid Hotel La Torre**, Via Piano Gallo 11, **t** 091 450 222 (*moderate*). Large, luxurious, air-conditioned, with a pool and tennis, etc.

★★★**Hotel Villa Esperia**, Viale Margherita di Savoia 53, **t** 091 684 0717 (*moderate*). Very good value; air-conditioned.

★★★**Hotel Bellevue del Golfo**, Via Planto 40, Sferracavallo, ✉ 90148, **t** 091 530 083, *www.gattei.it/bellevue* (*budget–inexpensive*). Good value and perfectly comfortable; near the beach.

Degli Ulivi, **t** 091 530 247. One of the two closest campsites to Palermo, 13km west of Mondello at Sferracavallo (from Palermo's Stazione Centrale, take bus 101 to the end of the line, and then bus 628 to the Post Office at Sferracavallo).

Internazionale Trinacria, **t** 091 691 2630. The other campsite in Sferracavallo, 13km west of Mondello. *Closed Nov–April.*

Eating Out

When Palermitans dine out, they drive miles from the centre to obscure, hard-to-find addresses they heartily recommend. This is rather frustrating for visitors, but you won't starve: the addresses below are all in town and accessible by foot or bus.

Expensive

Acanto Blu, Via Torrearsa 10, **t** 091 320 444. One of Palermo's best restaurants lies in a shady courtyard in the undistinguished north part of town near Teatro Politeama Garibaldi.

La Cambusa, Piazza Marina, **t** 091 584 574. Long been thought of as the best spot in the historic centre for a seafood feast, and don't all the tourists know it. *Closed Mon.*

Gourmand's, Via della Libertà 37E, **t** 091 323 431. This stylish, contemporary place matches its décor with delightful forays into Italian *nuova cucina*, unheard of elsewhere in Sicily. *Reservations suggested. Closed Sun.*

Santandrea, Piazza Sant'Andrea, **t** 091 334 999. Close to the Piazza San Domenico, in good weather tables are set out in the atmospheric piazzetta. Menus reflect seasonal availability. Palermitan favourites are presented with a twist. *Reservations suggested. Closed Tues and January.*

Stella (ex Hotel Patria), Via Alloro 104, **t** 091 616 1136. In the historic centre, not far from the Galleria Regionale, with tables spread out in a genteelly dilapidated courtyard under a palm tree and tumbling jasmine. Solid cooking and pizza is served. *Closed Sun eve in July–Sept, Mon in Oct–June.*

Moderate

Al 59, Piazza Verdi 59, **t** 091 583 139. A popular spot to the north, near Teatro Massimo, with a lovely shaded terrace; try the *ravioli verdi con salsa di carciofi. Closed Wed.*

Il Biondo, Via Carducci 15, **t** 091 583 662. Ring the bell to be admitted into this restaurant in the Piazza Ruggero Settimo area which is a very popular with Palermitans. *Closed Wed.*

Kursaal Kalhesa, Foro Umberto I 21, **t** 091 616 2282. As well as serving up fine Sicilian food, this restaurant, stylish bar and bookshop is a live music venue. Great fun, Near the Piazza della Kalsa. *Closed Mon lunch and Sun eve.*

Mandarini, Via R. da Partanna 18, **t** 091 671 2199. This little place offers excellent *cucina Siciliana* like Mamma used to make. *Closed Sun in July–Oct, Mon in Nov–June.*

Peppino, Piazza Castelnuovo 49, **t** 091 324 195. A good bet in the vicinity of Piazza Ruggero Settimo, often crowded at lunch. *Closed Wed.*

Primavera, Piazza Bologni 4, **t** 091 329 408. This is a fine old-fashioned and popular place up towards the cathedral, with tables spilling out into the Baroque square in the summer. There's a good selection of pastas and meat dishes, while the fish and seafood is divine. Try the roasted squid prepared in its own ink. No credit cards. *Closed Mon and Sun eve.*

A'Vucciria, Via dei Chiavettieri 7, **t** 091 611 8347. Round the corner from Piazza Marina, this seafood restaurant in the heart of the Vucciria. Be sure to try the tagliatelle with swordfish and almond pesto, or their specialty, *spaghetti a'vucciria.*

Inexpensive

Bellini, Piazza Bellini 6, **t** 091 616 5691. Situated by La Martorana in the ex-theatre, eating outdors here is one of Palermo's most delightful ways to while away the evening; everyone else thinks so too, so get there before 9 to beat the rush. *Closed Tues in Nov–Feb.*

Casa del Brodo, Corso Vittorio Emanuele 175, **t** 091 321 655. One of the classics in the historic centre, founded in 1890, with big pots of different kinds of *brodo* (broth) simmering on the stove; wonderful food and service. *Closed Thurs in winter.*

Shanghai, Vicolo dei Mezzani 34 (between Piazza Caracciolo and Corso V. Emanuele), **t** 091 589 702. Don't expect Chinese food, this famous/infamous place is Sicilian all the way. On a balcony overlooking the colourful Vucciria market; mafiosi in the not-too-distant past would come here to recruit hit men. No credit cards. *Closed Sun.*

Trápani, Piazza G. Cesare 16, **t** 091 616 1642. An old favourite next to the Stazione Centrale. *Closed Sun.*

Snacks, *Pasticcerie* and *Osterie*

Antica Focacceria San Francesco, Piazza San Francesco 4, **t** 091 320 264. An authentic old tavern (founded 1834) with marble tables, marble mirrors, wrought iron, and old woodwork (or sit out in the old square). Slices of *focaccia* and other snacks.

Bar Mazzara, Via Gen. V. Magliocco 19, **t** 091 321 443. Near Piazza Ungheria, this was where Giuseppe di Lampedusa would come to work on *The Leopard* over his favourite jasmine-perfumed melon sherbet; his old booth is preserved, if not much else. Besides the ice cream, try *sfincione*, a deep-fried *calzone* filled with ricotta and anchovies.

Pasticceria d'Asta, Via Mariano Stabile 83, **t** 091 328 248. Good chocolate and pastries.

Gran Café Nobel, Via della Libertà 35. Visit this atmospheric place for a *latte di mandorla* (almond milk) or a *granita* and a *brioche*.

Osteria Paradiso, Via Serradifalco 23 (west of the city centre). One of the city's fine examples of that vanishing Sicilian amenity, the *osteria*, with enormous, dusty wine barrels of *vino locale* stacked up to the ceiling; food is provided mostly to keep you sober enough to drink more. *Closed dinner and Sun.*

Mondello

The seafood in Mondello is fresh – in the morning the restaurateurs buy it straight from the stalls in front of the lido.

Charleston, Mondello Lido, **t** 091 450 171 (*expensive*). Long established as the best and classiest restaurant in Palermo – perhaps in all of Sicily – Charleston moved out permanently to its old holiday pad, this old palace overlooking Viale Regina Elena, a few years ago. Diners are treated to rarefied versions of Palermitan favourites, and for dessert the most divine almond pastries on the island. *Reservations suggested.*

Bye Bye Blues, Via Garofalo 23, **t** 091 684 1415 (*expensive*). A reliable address for fish about 10km from Palermo on the road to Mondello.

Da Totuccio, Via Torre 26A, **t** 091 450 151 (*moderate*). Eat good seafood *antipasti* here at less blistering prices. *Closed Mon.*

Il Giardino dei Melograni, Via Tolomea 13, **t** 091 454 912 (*moderate*). A popular place for pizzas and fish specialities in the evening. *Open Wed–Sun for dinner, and Sun lunch.*

Antico Chisco, Piazza Mondello. Try this place for dessert or some Sicilian sweets.

Puppet Shows

Palermo is a good place to catch a traditional Sicilian puppet show (*see* **Culture**, p.30–2). There are performances at the Museo delle Marionette but try one of the following for a more genuine experience:

Cuticchio Mimmo, Via Bara all'Olivella 52 (near Teatro Massimo), **t** 091 323 400. Shows Sat and Sun at 5.30pm. *Closed Aug.*

Teaotro Ippogrifo, Vicolo Ragusi 6 (off Corso Vittorio Emanuele), **t** 091 329 194. Traditional puppet shows once a week.

Compagnia Argento, Via P. Novelli 1, **t** 091 611 3680. Call for their schedule of shows.

Other Entertainment and Nightlife

As much of the old centre shuts down tight by 9pm, you have to head north for any kind of bar nightlife – **Mondello**, packed in the summer, is the easiest place to aim for without a car. Alternatively, the sidestreets north of Piazza Ruggero Settimo, off Viale della Libertà, are posey and crowded, but cars have been banished from **Via Mazzini** (off Viale della Libertà) and **Via Principe di Belmonte** (off Via Ruggero Settimo) and both have open-air bars and cafés. The city's youngsters gather on **Piazza Castelnuovo** on weekend evenings, giving the place a festival atmosphere. For listings for **music**, **plays** and **films** (nearly always dubbed) have a look at the city's daily paper, *Il Giornale di Sicilia*.

The following is a selection of the city's venues for dance, drama and music:

I Candelai, Via Candelai 65, **t** 091 327 151. Cultural centre: live music, avant-garde theatre, tango nights and internet café.

Metropolitan, Viale Strasburgo 358, **t** 091 688 7513. Music, ballet and drama.

Santa Maria dello Spasimo, Via Spasimo, Piazza Magione, **t** 091 616 1486. This bombed-out church is also an art gallery and a live music venue.

Teatro Libero, Piazza Marina, **t** 091 617 4040. Ring for details of their programme.

Teatro Luigi Orione, Via Don Orione 5, **t** 091 544 525. Comic theatre and popular satire.

Teatro Massimo, Piazza Verdi 9, **t** 091 605 3515, *www.teatromassimo.it*. Ballet and opera, and open for tours.

Teatro Politeama Garibaldi, Piazza Ruggero Settimo, **t** 091 605 33 15. Concert venue.

Teatro della Verdura, Viale del Fante, **t** 091 688 41 37. Outdoor opera and ballet in the summer only.

open invitation to the Mafia. It remains a long and complex process, rooting out the Mafia from Palermo's very heart so the city can enjoy a spring which will last and last. The two are after all, fatalistically connected.

The Historic Centre

The heart of old Palermo is Piazza Vigliena, better known to everyone as the **Quattro Canti** (*buses 101, 102, 103, 104*), the 'four corners', where Via Maqueda, laid out in the 1580s, crossed one of Palermo's most ancient streets, Via Cassaro (from the Arabic Al-Qasr, 'fortress'), now known as Corso Vittorio Emanuele. Inspired by the Quattro Fontane in Rome, the Viceroy Vigliena commissioned the four buildings at this crossroads in 1611, and had their corners adorned with three-storey façade screens. Each screen is decorated with fountains, allegories of the four seasons, the four kings of Sicily, and the saintly patronesses of the four quarters which the Quattro Canti defines. For centuries these four quarters – the **Kalsa** (southeast), **Amalfitani** (northeast), **Sincaldi** (northwest), and **Albergheria** (southwest) – were so clannish that marriages between the quarters were rare. Before the invention of the automobile, the Quattro Canti were creamy white instead of grimy grey, and were a favourite meeting place of the Palermitani. Today you can't even stand back to look at the allegories without the risk of being squashed like a bug.

Around the Quattro Canti

Piazza Pretoria

The Quattro Canti decorations are so high that you hardly notice the huge church begun a year later just behind the Albergheria screen: **San Giuseppe dei Teatini** (*open Mon–Sat 7.30–11 and 6–8, Sun and hols 8.30–12.30 and 6–8*) built by Giacomo Besio. The interior, done in the 17th and 18th centuries, is Baroque at its noisiest – all blast and no content, with little of the virtuosity that makes nearby Santa Caterina such a gem. Eight massive monolithic columns support the dome with its fresco *The Triumph of Sant'Andrea Avellino* (1724) by Borremans. Note, too, the 18th-century altar of inlaid marbles in the sacristy and, in the chapel to the right of the altar, a Crucifix by Fra Umile da Petralia that looks uncomfortable in its gaudy setting.

San Giuseppe's flank closes off the Via Maqueda end of **Piazza Pretoria**, locally known as the Piazza della Vergogna ('of shame') for the flagrant nudity and rapt pubic interest displayed by the three dozen leprous marble nymphs, satyrs, mermen and mermaids gathered around the 16th-century **Fontana Pretoria** (*under restoration*). This handiwork of two loony Florentine Mannerists, Michelangelo Naccherino and Francesco Camilliani, was commissioned by Viceroy Don Pedro di Toledo for his Tuscan villa. His son, who had better taste, flogged it off to Palermo in 1573, whose leadership, keen on ogling its goofy charms as much as possible, put it right in front of their headquarters, the Palazzo Pretorio (1463, but often remodelled). This is now the town hall, or **Municipio**, itself often enough the source of shame in Palermo history. A statue of St Rosalia shares the façade with a collage of historical plaques, commemorating everything from Garibaldi's speech in 1860 to a visit by Pope John Paul II. The north end of the piazza is occupied by the huge flank of **Santa Caterina** (1566–96), the church of the 13th-century Dominican monastery that occupies the entire block. It's worth coming back on a Sunday to get inside: for two centuries the Dominicans spared no expense in the effort to create a sumptuous preview of paradise. The walls are an intricate fusion of polychrome marbles, sculpture and inlaid scenes from the Old Testament; the ceiling and dome are covered with *trompe l'œil* frescoes. Palermitan Giacomo Amato designed the choir and altar, and his associate Andrea Palma is responsible for the extraordinary chapel of St Catherine, with its statue by Antonello Gagini.

La Martorana and San Cataldo

Santa Caterina's main façade looks on to **Piazza Bellini**, which also boasts one of the oldest and loveliest ensembles in all Palermo, set in an exotic garden of palms on an ancient Roman wall: the church of Santa Maria dell' Ammiraglio, better known as La Martorana, with its handsome Norman belltower, and San Cataldo with its bijou red domes. **La Martorana** (*open Mon–Sat 8–1 and 3.30–5.30, Sun and hols 8.30–1; best-lit in the morning*) is the most beautiful Greek church in Sicily, founded in 1143 by Roger II's 'Emir of Emirs' George of Antioch, whose career on the high seas brought fame and fortune to Norman Sicily and heaped such glory on the title of Emir that it was adopted into various languages for the chief general of a fleet – in English, admiral (*amir al-bahr*, 'commander of the ocean'). His church, however, takes its familiar name from a nearby convent founded in 1146 by Eloisa de Marturanu, whose nuns were given the church in 1233.

These are the same nuns who invented the marzipan delicacies you see in Sicilian *pasticcerie* windows, the *frutti alla martorana*, shaped and coloured perfectly to imitate peaches, prickly pears, oranges or apples (or sometimes practical joke dishes of marzipan spaghetti or fried eggs). What the same nuns did to the Admiral's church, however, was not very sweet at all. They demolished the narthex and atrium. They turned its once beautiful exterior into banal Baroque. They destroyed the main apse and mosaics in 1683 to replace it with a wretched frescoed chapel. In 1935, Mussolini returned it to Sicily's Greek Orthodox population.

The sections that the nuns refrained from redecorating, however, are covered with dazzling **mosaics**, done by the same great but anonymous group of Greek artists imported from Constantinople by Roger II to decorate Palermo's Capella Palatina and Cefalù cathedral. Here they achieved 'the most perfect charm which can be found in any surviving medieval decoration on Italian soil. They gave as it were the quintessence of what was gentle and lovely and intimate in the great art of Comnenian mosaic decoration' (Otto Demus, *The Mosaics of Norman Sicily*). Even the circus contortionist archangels, wedged in about the central figure of Christ Pantocrator, have a rare endearing quality.

The wall near the entrance has rare portraits of the two leading players of the day: George of Antioch, lying at the feet of the Virgin, head and limbs emerging out of a cocoon or shell – the result of an inept restoration – and brown-haired King Roger II (Rogerios Rex, as the Greek letters say), handsome and melancholy, receiving a jewelled crown from Christ, a conceit adopted straight from Byzantium.

The adjacent **San Cataldo** (*open Mon–Fri 9–3.30, Sat 9–12.30, Sun and hols 9–1*), of the rosy cupolas, was founded in 1154 by Maio da Bari, William I's efficient but hated emir, whose high-handed ways provoked Matteo Bonnello's *coup d'état* (*see* 'Cáccamo', p.215). The nuns used it as a chapel, the 19th century as a post office; it now belongs to the Knights of the Holy Sepulchre. Pop in to see the few traces of stalactite ceiling.

The Albergheria

From La Martorana to the Cathedral

From Piazza Bellini, cross Via Maqueda into the Albergheria Quarter and turn briefly south (left) to Via Ponticello, which curves round to Sicily's first Jesuit church, the **Gesù** (1564–1636; *open daily 8.30–12, Mon, Wed and Sat afternoons 4–7*), badly damaged in the war but since restored. The Jesuits sought to mask the totalitarian nature of the Church during the Counter-reformation with high theatre, overpowering any potential doubters with the weight of sheer opulence and pageantry, taking the late Renaissance/Mannerist architecture of the cinquecento to its most fantastic extremes. Baroque, after all, was originally known as the Jesuit style, and the interior of the Gesù is their masterpiece in Sicily. Most of it was actually designed and made by the priests themselves: in the 1630s, 14 Jesuits laboured to coat every square inch with stuccoand marble (their work survives in the presbytery, apse and chapel of Sant'Anna, just to the left of the high altar). The church is sometimes called Casa Professa, although this is actually the building with the elegant portal of 1685 just to the right; through its elegant cloister you'll find the Biblioteca Comunale, installed here after the subtle brethren were expelled from Sicily in 1776.

From here, Via Casa Professa continues west to the **Ballaró market**, where you can pick up food, fabrics and second-hand clothes. If you're not in a shopping mood, take Vicolo Casa Professa to Salita Raffadali; at the intersection with Via G. M. Puglia stands the handsome late Catalan-Gothic **Palazzo Speciale** (1468). Via G. M. Puglia then continues down to **Piazza Bologni**, one of Palermo's most elegant Baroque squares. A statue of Emperor Charles V stands in the centre of a rectangle of *palazzi* loaded with coats-of-arms: note especially the classical façade of **Palazzo Belmonte-Riso** (1784) across the busy *corso*, by Neoclassical master Venanzio Marvuglia. The façade in fact is all that remains after its innards were blasted away in the war.

From here walk west (left) up the Corso V. Emanuele, passing little boutiques selling second-hand books, *carabinieri* uniforms and big-eyed policeman dolls. You may well run into a wedding spilling out of **San Salvatore**, at No.431 (*open daily 9.30–12.30, closed Tues*), a Norman foundation transformed in 1682 by Paolo Amato into an oval-shaped church sheathed in marbles, with a frescoed cupola, galleries and opera-like loges. Such churches were constructed with acoustics in mind, the better to hear the oratorios and concertos of Alessandro Scarlatti (born in Palermo in 1660) and his followers, and today San Salvatore is chiefly used as an auditorium and wedding venue. Farther up the Corso stands the 16th-century **Palazzo Castrone-Santa Ninfa** (No.452), the architectural equivalent of the shameless Fontana Pretoria; pop into the courtyard to see its fountain of Perseus and Andromeda.

The Cathedral

Open Mon–Sat 7–7, Sun and hols 8–1.30 and 4–7. Open for groups at 9.30. Buses 104, 105, 108, 110, 118. www.cattedrale.palermo.it.

Opposite the palace is Palermo's cathedral, begun in 1185 on the same site as the Byzantine church that the Arabs had converted into their great Friday Mosque. The cathedral is the work of an Englishman, Walter of the Mill (charmingly Italianized as Gualtiero Offamiglio), whom Henry II had sent to Sicily to tutor William the Good when he was chosen to wed Joanna Plantagenet. The unscrupulous Walter went on to become Emir and Archbishop of Palermo in 1168, 'less by election than by violent intrusion' as one chronicler put it, and he began this new cathedral when William II challenged his authority and dignity by founding Monreale. Walter lacked not only the king's bulging purse but his posthumous luck: while time has barely tampered with Monreale, Walter's cathedral was mangled in the 18th century by Ferdinando Fuga. From the outside Fuga's worst crime is the dome, which swells atop the cathedral like a sore bunion.

Thanks to Fuga's bungling busywork, only parts of the exterior are as Walter built them; look at the striking east end in particular, with its complex interlacing designs and strange Islamic-inspired forms. The main door to the west in Via Bonello lies in the shadow of an elevated passageway crossing over to the tower of the Palazzo Arcivescovile – a quick escape route that came in handy when Stephen du Perche, Regent Margaret of Navarre's unpopular French chancellor, was besieged by a mob in the palace: he fled over the bridge and successfully fended off his attackers from the cathedral's belltower. It took the cathedral builders 200 years to finish what is now the main entrance, the exquisite **Catalan-Gothic porch** on the south side in Piazza della Cattedrale. Incorporated in the left-hand column is an inscription from the Koran, a survivor from the Great Mosque. Even older is the mosaic of the Virgin over the door, believed to date from the original Byzantine church.

After this, the **interior** is stale fare; Fuga tore out the side walls for chapels, demolished the wooden ceiling and whitewashed everything else. Originally the apse was covered with mosaics, but they fell victim to an earlier vandal in the 1500s. Originally the **royal tombs** held pride of place in the right transept. Now they are tucked in the dim recesses in the back: Roger II (d. 1154) and his daughter Constance (d. 1198) in two poorly made sarcophagi and, in the two finer Roman ones that Roger II had set up in Cefalù and that Frederick II (Stupor Mundi) stole and brought here, the Hohenstaufen husband of Constance, Emperor Henry VI (d. 1197), and their son, Stupor Mundi himself (d. 1250). Frederick shares his fine tomb with the idiot Peter II of Aragon (d. 1342) and an unknown woman. Also, set in the wall are the tombs of Duke William of Aragon (d. 1338), son of Frederick II of Aragon, and Constance of Aragon (d. 1222), a 24-year-old widow when she wed the 14-year-old Emperor Frederick II here in the cathedral. Despite the age difference, they were happy, and after her death few could draw the unfathomable Frederick out of his solitude.

The lavish chapel to the right of the choir contains a **silver reliquary** with the bones, the pious say, of Palermo's patron saint Rosalia, but the pathologists say, of a goat. Scattered everywhere else in the cathedral are **statues by Antonello Gagini**, all part of a superb retable that stood on the high altar before Fuga got his hands on it and broke it to bits. The **treasury** to the right of the choir contains items from the tomb of Constance of Aragon, including her crown – a cap with jewels stuck on it, the royal diadem of the Norman kings of Sicily.

Across Via Bonello, the **Palazzo Arcivescovile** was given a face-lift in the 18th century, although the restorers left the beautiful Catalan-Gothic door and mullioned window intact. The palace contains the splendid Museo Diocesano housing works of art salvaged from Palermo's churches bombed in the war. You may, however, find something of interest in the nearby **fleamarket** (*open Mon–Sat 8–4, Sun 8–1*) – take Via Bonello to Via Papireto and Piazza Papireto.

If instead you cross the *corso* from the Palazzo Arcivescovile, and walk along the edge of the gardens of Villa Bonanno, you'll find **Palazzo Scláfani**, one of Palermo's four great medieval mansions. This was begun and finished in one year, 1330, by Matteo Scláfani, and is decorated with a lively interlacing of arches set in tufa, twin-light windows, and an elegant portal topped with an eagle that leads into a large atrium. In 1435 the palace became a hospital, a period when the atrium was decorated with the magnificent *Triumph of Death*, relocated after the Second World War to the Galleria Regionale. The palace is now a military headquarters.

The Palazzo dei Normanni and Cappella Palatina

The *corso* continues past Villa Bonanno to the **Porta Nuova**, a triumphal arch built in 1535 to celebrate Charles V's victory in Tunisia, with a pair of unhappy bound and armless captives on either side. The narrow arches force Palermo's already insane traffic into a strait-jacket. Beyond the gate the street becomes Corso Calatafimi, leading to the Convento dei Cappuccini (*see* 'West Palermo', p.99).

Looming off to the left is the large ill-defined mass of the Palazzo Reale or **Palazzo dei Normanni** (*entrance all the way round off Piazza della Indipendenza; open Mon, Fri, Sat 9–12; other days by arrangement call t 091 705 7003; buses 104, 105, 139, 225, 824*). Originally a Phoenician fort rebuilt by the Romans and Arabs, it was chosen by Roger II as his chief residence. Alterations continued throughout the centuries, so that today from the outside only the blind arcades of the **Torre di Santa Ninfa** recall the men of northern France. This tower made history in 1801 when, from its copper-domed observatory, Giuseppe Piazzi discovered the first asteroid, which he named after Sicily's first patroness, Ceres.

Today the palace houses Sicily's Regional Parliament, and only small sections are open to visitors, but to miss them would be to miss the crown jewel of Palermo: the intimate, utterly incandescent **Cappella Palatina** (*open Mon–Fri 9–11.45 and 3–4.45, Sat 9–11.45, Sun 9–9.45 and 12–12.45 all year except Easter Monday and 26 Dec*), the royal chapel built by Roger II between 1132 and 1143. Roger, so tolerant that he was accused of being a secret Muslim during his lifetime, made certain in this chapel that each of the chief religions and peoples of his kingdom would be represented daily before his eyes. Greek masters made the lovely gold ground **mosaics** that cover the dome and apse, of Christ Pantocrator and the angels. The magnificent wooden **ceiling** was exquisitely carved by Roger's Arab craftsmen, and painted with rare (especially for Muslim artists) fantasies: human figures and scenes from daily life in the 12th century that are best seen with a pair of binoculars. The Cosmati-work inlaid floors, marble walls, the magnificent pulpit, and amazing 15ft paschal candlestick, decorated with a hundred animals carved in white marble, were made by Roman and Norman craftsmen. Later additions, especially the mosaic saints with Latin inscriptions added by his son William I, are all by Italian artists. The dais at the back supported the thrones of the kings, who themselves sat beneath a mosaic of Christ enthroned.

The *palazzo* also contains the **Royal Apartments** (*same hours as Palazzo dei Normanni*), a series of sumptuously dull rooms culminating in the small **Sala di Re Ruggero**, actually built by Roger II's son William I. Its upper sections glitter with the secular counterpart to the Cappella Palatina mosaics: delightful, exotic leopards and peacocks lined up in formal symmetry, Persian style, under orange and palm trees; twin centaurs armed with bows and stags face each other as if in a mirror.

San Giovanni degli Eremiti

Open Mon–Sat 9–7, Sun 9–1.

Across Piazza della Pinta from the Palazzo dei Normanni on Via dei Benedettini rise the striking five red 'Eunuch's bonnet' cupolas of **San Giovanni degli Eremiti**, a church straight out of the *Arabian Nights* and the symbol of Palermo. Founded by Roger II in 1142, it was once the church of the wealthiest monastery in Sicily, whose abbot was confessor and chaplain of the king himself. In its stripped-clean interior there's little to see beyond traces of a 12th-century fresco. The courtyard and one room were originally part of a mosque; don't miss the delicate paired columns of the cloisters (1190s), nearly overgrown with luxuriant citrus and pomegranate trees, roses and bougainvillaea.

The Kalsa

Under the Arabs, the Kalsa, or southeast quarter of old Palermo, was the walled seaside residence of the emir and his ministers. In the Middle Ages, as merchants, nobles and the Spanish viceroys moved in, the Arab walls were destroyed, although for a long time one tower remained, the Torre di Manau, haunted by a giant and wicked Saracen ghoul, who used his beautiful daughter as bait to bring in men to eat and women to rape, until a Christian knight finally cut off his head, accidentally killing the daughter as well by making the sign of the cross. The curse of Manau seems to linger to this day: the Kalsa is still down at heel, its canyon streets fragrant with a surreal jumble of debris (a recent stroll revealed half an alligator in an alley). Piquant, picturesque and dying before your eyes, it rivals only parts of Catania (*see* pp.293–301) as the least restored neighbourhood in Europe. Poking around off the main streets after dark is not a good idea: the labyrinth is badly lit, badly signposted, and who knows what you'll meet around the corner.

San Francesco d'Assisi, the Oratorio di San Lorenzo and Palazzo Mirto

Beginning once again at the Quattro Canti (*see* above), walk east down the *corso*, across busy Via Roma – a street rammed through the historic centre in 1922 – and turn right down curving Via Paternostro. This will lead you to the little *piazza* in front of the 13th-century **San Francesco d'Assisi** (*open Mon 9–12, Tues–Fri 9–4, Saturday 9–12; buses 103, 105, 139, 225, 824*), with its magnificent rose window and portal. The quattrocento chapels on the left-hand side are particularly lovely, the first with a doorway and statue of the Madonna and child by Domenico Gagini (1480s), and the fourth, the superb **Cappella Mastrantonio**, carved in 1468 by Francesco Laurana and Pietro da Bonitate, Palermo's first and one of its best examples of Renaissance art. Eight statues by Serpotta adorn the nave; eight others by 18th-century sculptor Giambattista Ragusa are in the multicoloured marble chapel to the right of the high altar.

Nearby, at Via Immacolatella 5, the **Oratorio di San Lorenzo** (*ask at San Francesco*) is the masterpiece of Serpotta's mature years (1699–1710), a captivating, endlessly imaginative extravaganza of stucco decoration based on the lives of SS. Lawrence and Francis, with a lavish amount of allegories and *putti*. Until it was stolen in 1969, Caravaggio's *Nativity with SS. Francis and Lawrence* hung over the altar.

From Piazza San Francesco, take Via Merlo to No. 2, **Palazzo Mirto** (*free guided tours; open Mon–Sat 9–7.30, Sat 9–1, Sun 9–1.30*), to see on what scale a typical princely family lived in Palermo. Most of the furnishings and collections date from the 18th and 19th centuries. There's an elaborate Baroque seashell fountain in a little courtyard and a pretty Salottino Cinese, where Palermitan artists interpreted the Chinese style fashionable in the 18th century. Two works by Italy's great Neoclassical sculptor Canova, donated to the state in 1983, have unfortunately been locked away in the palace's stables.

Piazza Marina

Via Merlo gives on to Piazza Marina, occupying a section of the port La Cala that silted up in the 10th century. Here the Aragonese held their jousts and fairs, and the Inquisitors staged their autos-da-fé. A garden called Villa Garibaldi occupies the centre of the *piazza*; on the ashes of the poor heretics grow banyan trees, the mastodons of the rubber plant family, each tree supported by a cluster of smaller trunks. These natural pavilions provide welcome shade to the garden's card sharps, who play each card with a stinging snap of defiance.

Architecturally, Piazza Marina is dominated by the massive and magnificent **Palazzo Chiaramonte**, or Steri (*open for exhibitions only, t 09 13 34 139 for the programme*), on the southeast corner, built in 1307 by Sicily's most flamboyant princely family. This palace gave its name to the graceful, highly decorative Chiaramonte style; note especially the **twin- and tri-lobed windows**, adorned with a zigzag pattern, that lighten the fortress-like ground floor. The Chiaramonte didn't get to stay for very long: in 1396, the family scion Andrea was beheaded just in front of it for rebelling against King Martin I of Aragon. The palace went on to become the seat of Sicily's viceroys, then in 1601 the courts of the Inquisition (in its dungeons, entered through an inner courtyard, you can still see the forlorn graffiti dug into the walls by its victims). The Holy Office was replaced in 1779 by Palermo's civil law courts. It is now owned by the university, and has been restored; note the beautiful wooden ceiling (1380) of the **Sala Maggiore**, inspired by the Islamic workmanship in the Cappella Palatina.

Three Renaissance churches dedicated to the Virgin occupy the other corners of Piazza Marina: the 16th-century **Santa Maria dei Miracoli** near Via Merlo; **Santa Maria di Porto Salvo** just across Corso V. Emanuele, attributed to Antonello Gagini (1526) – although partly mutilated by the widening of the *corso*, it retains the lovely star vaulting in the old presbytery and a fine triptych from the 1500s; and just to the east is the 15th-century Catalan Gothic-Renaissance **Santa Maria della Catena** (*open Mon–Fri 9–1; buses 103, 105, 139, 225, 824*), named after the chain that once closed La Cala port every evening. Attributed to Matteo Carnelivari, it has an elegant Renaissance portico at the top of a flight of steps.

Porta Felice and the Museo delle Marionette

Farther east, the *corso* meets the harbour at the monumental **Porta Felice** (1582), named after a viceroy's wife who was famous throughout Palermo for her infidelity. In the next century the overhead arch was removed to permit the passing of the 80ft-high *carrozza* of Santa Rosalia during her July procession. Beyond the Porta Felice lies what was once the most beautiful promenade in Palermo, the Marina, with views over the harbour to Monte Pellegrino, only now it's bisected by the heaving Foro Italico and a funfair. For a hint of its former elegance, walk along the **Mura delle Cattive** (*open daily 10–7*), a last remnant of the old Kalsa wall, decorated with statues and paved with green and white tiles; its name, the 'Wall of the Nasty Women', refers to the crabby old spinsters who used to watch the goings-on disapprovingly out of their windows. In the 18th century, there was certainly plenty to disapprove of. After the decadent Venetians, the Palermitans were perhaps the most sexually liberated people in Europe. Ladies had only to wear a mask to be absolved from any responsibility when they came to the Marina to meet their lovers, certain that their husbands were doing exactly the same thing in the dark; the rule was that all carriage lights were extinguished beyond that gateway of infidelity, Porta Felice. Palermitans still like to come here in the evening, especially teenagers in groups of at least 10, eating ice cream from **Ilardo**, Foro Italico 12 (*open winter weekends, summer daily 2pm–2am*), the oldest *gelateria* in Palermo, or munching a Palermitan special, tripe sandwiches (*pane cu' la meuza*), while sizing up each other's clothes.

Back inland, the first street is Via Butera. The **Museo Internazionale delle Marionette**, at No.1 (*open Mon–Fri 9–1 and 4–7; buses 103, 105, 139, 225, 824*), has nearly 3,000 puppets on display, especially from Palermo, Catania and Naples, their last strongholds in Italy. Besides regular performances for tourists, the museum sponsors the Festival di Morgana, with puppet shows from around the world (*usually in Oct, shows always in Italian*). Via Butera is the best address in old Palermo. Opposite the museum stands the magnificent 17th-century **Palazzo Branciforti di Butera**, where Goethe stayed, and where some of the most illustrious and wealthiest families in Sicily lived, enjoying the magnificent view over the back terrace and Mura delle Cattive; their descendants still live here today. Next to it is the **ex-Albergo Trinacria**, from 1844 to 1911 one of the finest hotels in Palermo (now a court building), and the one chosen by Giuseppe di Lampedusa for the death scene of 'the Leopard' Don Fabrizio. It was an area the author knew well: after the family mansion was bombed in the war, the prince bought the small 18th-century Palazzo Lampedusa next to the hotel and lived his last 10 years there.

Amato's Churches and the Villa Giulia

To the south, Via Butera meets Via Alloro, which continues up to the Galleria Regionale (*see* below). The crossroads is occupied by one of the masterpieces of Sicilian Baroque, the **Madonna della Pietà** (1689, consecrated 1723) by Giacomo Amato, who worked in Rome for 10 years; this church, with its two tiers of columns, was inspired by the highly articulated façade of Rome's Sant'Andrea della Valle. If it's open, go in to see the trompe l'œil ceiling of *The Glory of the Dominicans*, framed in stuccoes by Procopio Serpotta.

Beyond, Via Butera becomes Via Torremuzza and passes another Amato façade, this belonging to the ready-to-topple-over **Santa Mattia** (1686). Beyond, in Piazza della Kalsa, is **Santa Teresa alla Kalsa** (also 1686), another excellent work by Amato, and one that helped enlighten his fellow Palermitan architects. The **interior** (*open for services*) has been left pretty much as Amato intended it, adorned with stuccoes and statues by Giuseppe Serpotta (brother of the greater Giacomo) and his son Procopio, paintings by Borremans and much more. The peculiar ruined **Palazzo Forcella** on the opposite side of the *piazza* is a 19th-century Arab-Norman folly built over a medieval gate.

In Piazza della Kalsa, Via Torremuzza turns into Via N. Cervello and pierces another of the Kalsa's gates, the elegant **Porta Reale** (1787). Across busy Via Lincoln from here is the **Villa Giulia**, a formal pleasure garden laid out in 1777 and named after the wife of another viceroy. In the centre are four Neoclassical frescoed exedrae and a fountain with a sundial. Goethe thought the Villa Giulia was one of the loveliest places on earth, but not so very long ago it was a wasteland of rubbish, dying shrubs, alcoholics and assorted human detritus, its pavilions crumbling into Cinema Verità film sets. Over the past couple of years, however, it's been spruced up, and you can take the children there without fear of bacterial or social contamination. From April to September, you may even catch a concert, financed by a bequest from the music-loving Prince of Paternò in the 1700s.

Adjacent is the lush green oasis of the **Orto Botanico** (*open Mon–Fri 9–6, Sat–Sun 8.30–1.30; buses 139, 221, 224, 250*), founded in 1785 and laid out by Léon Dufourny and Venanzio Marvuglia, with an enormous variety of plants from the tropics and elsewhere (don't miss the century-old *ficus magnolioides*, similar to a baobab).

Frenchman Dufourny had come to Sicily to study its Doric temples, the better to produce authentic Neoclassical buildings back home, but before he left he erected the large Gymnasium here for the gardens, now used as a library.

Galleria Regionale Siciliana

Open all year Mon–Fri 9–2; Tues, Wed, Thurs 3–8; Sun and hols 9–1.
Buses 139, 225, 824.

Sicily's finest art collection is in Via Alloro, the most important street in the Kalsa (from Villa Giulia, backtrack along Via N. Cervello), lined with *palazzi* in various stages of decrepitude. At No.4 stands the grandest of them all, Palazzo Abatellis (1488), a highly original creation of Matteo Carnelivari, its main portal a fanciful Renaissance reworking of Catalan Gothic; the tower has an elaborate head-dress and elegant triple windows. Restored after the war, it is the home of the Galleria Regionale della Sicilia.

One of the first rooms of the gallery is devoted to a remarkable, beautifully restored fresco entitled **The Triumph of Death** by an unknown 15th-century painter who was certainly in the avant-garde in the art of foreshortening. It originally occupied the wall of the Palazzo Scláfani – at that time a hospital, although it's not a subject guaranteed to lift the spirits. In the centre Death the Archer rides a ghostly horse with ribs protruding like the coils of a steam radiator as he plucks off high and mighty bishops, kings and fair ladies. Yet the colours are fresh and spring-like, and the elegant pretty people, unaware of their fate, go about playing music, chatting by a splashing fountain or hunting. Only the poor, the diseased and crippled on the left are aware of Death, and seem to be entreating him for release; above them two men, perhaps the artist and donor, gaze back out at the viewer, as if they are aware on yet another level – that it's all just a painting.

Beyond are odds and ends surviving from Arab Sicily, and the remarkable 15th-century *Bust of Eleonora di Aragona* by **Francesco Laurana**. Laurana is best remembered today for these portrait busts, combining an effortless naturalism with a subtle geometrical generalization of form that outshines all the Gagini works in the same room.

Next are a few rooms of early Tuscan gold ground paintings, and works by two talented late 15th-century Palermitani – frescoes by Tommaso di Vigilia and painted Crucifixes by Pietro Ruzzolone. Contemporary with all these paintings, but light years ahead in its power of expression, is **Antonello da Messina**'s *Annunciation* (1476), painted after his return from Venice to Messina. Unlike most Renaissance Annunciations with their props – lilies, haloes and Angel Gabriels – this is far more of a portrait: the oval-faced Virgin, quiet and radiant, is shown looking up from her reading, left hand modestly holding her hauntingly blue mantle, her right poised in space, in a unique gesture of acceptance and understanding. None of the later paintings can match the *Annunciation*, but there are some gems, especially the extraordinarily detailed 16th-century Flemish *Malvagna Triptych* of the Virgin with angel musicians by Mabuse. Others include a richly coloured *Coronation of the Virgin* by Riccardo Quartararo of Sciacca (1445–1506), a *Dispute of St Thomas* attributed to Mario di Laurito, and, from the 1600s, the Caravaggesque *Angel Liberating St Peter from Prison* by Pietro Novelli.

Next to the gallery is the austere 16th-century Santa Maria degli Angeli, better known as **La Gancia** (*open Mon–Sat 9.30–12 and 4–6, Sun 10–12, but you may have to track down the custodian*), containing works by Antonello Gagini, Serpotta (in the chapels by the high altar) and Vincenzo da Pavia.

La Magione and Palazzo Aiutamicristo

Opposite La Gancia is the refreshing vision of a palace undergoing restoration; a few streets up, at Via Alloro 54, is the sad sight of the bombed-out **Palazzo Bonagia**, where a fibbing sign states restoration will begin in 1987. Look through the gate, however, past the debris, weeds and ruins, to the enchanting vision of its frothy pink and white stone stair that miraculously survived the bombs, a witty piece of virtuoso Baroque that still outshines all others in this city of grand stairs.

At Via Castrofilippo turn left for the vast desolate bomb-born square of several names. The blasts spared two old churches on its fringes. The first is the **Spasimo** (1508; *open daily 9–10.30*), in the far southeastern corner, off Piazza Spasimo (the 'spasm' is the pang felt by Mary on seeing Jesus crucified). Raphael painted his *Spasimo di Sicilia* for the high altar (it's now in the Prado), and the church is used as an exhibition centre and concert venue. Flanking Piazza Magione are the interlacing blind arcades of the Norman **La Magione** (*open daily 8.30–12 and 3–6.30, closed Aug; no admission during weddings; buses 139, 221, 224, 250*), founded in 1160 by the Grand Protonotary Matteo d'Ajello, counsellor of the regent Margaret of Navarre. In 1193 Henry VI handed it over to the Teutonic Knights, who left a few tombs behind. Although badly damaged in the war, La Magione has been sensitively restored to its original form – a fine example of the later, more austere Romanesque style, with thick piers and arches dividing the naves and a mostly original painted wooden ceiling. The potted palms by each pier echo the rows of palms planted in front of the church.

From the gate in front of La Magione, continue up Via Magione to Via Garibaldi. Here stands the enormous **Palazzo Aiutamicristo** (1490), designed by Matteo Carnelivari. The street and inner courtyard (*ask the porter to let you have a look*) are graced with fine Catalan-Gothic details under a few later additions, all good enough in 1535 to house Emperor Charles V while resting after his campaign in Tunis. From here Via Garibaldi continues, as Garibaldi and his Thousand did on 27 May 1860, to picturesque **Piazza della Rivoluzione**. This was originally the Fiera Vecchia, a desperately poor area with a market square. In the centre is the funky **Fontana di Panormo** (1684), sporting a statue of an old king clutching a snake to his bosom, said to represent the genius of Palermo. He has certainly witnessed the city's genius for uprisings. All three revolts against the Bourbons were begun here, in 1820, 1848 and 1860.

Piazza Croce dei Vespri and its Palazzi

An earlier revolt is celebrated in the nearby **Piazza Croce dei Vespri** (from Piazza della Rivoluzione, carry straight on to Via Alloro, and turn left). The shattered marble cross in the midst of the parked cars is a 19th-century replacement of the original, erected over the mass grave of some 2,000 French residents of the long-gone palace of Jean de Saint-Rémy, Angevin Prefect of Palermo, all of whom were massacred in the uprising of the Sicilian Vespers on 31 March 1282 (see the ancient plaque on the wall). Opposite is one of the most beautiful and well-preserved palaces in Palermo, the 18th-century **Palazzo Valguarnera-Gangi**, its luscious rounded courtyard and sweeping stair guarded by a gate and slavering guard dog. Behind its walls is hidden the fanciest ballroom in all Sicily, although practically the only way to see it is in Visconti's film version of *The Leopard*.

Adjacent to Piazza Croce dei Vespri in Piazza Sant'Anna there's another fine Baroque façade by G. B. Amico to admire, the strikingly undulating concave, convex **Sant'Anna** (1736). Just west of here runs Via Roma; if you cross it and walk a street to the south (left), you'll find **Via dei Calderai**, since medieval times the street of metal-workers, although now lined with more trinket shops than forges. Via dei Calderai curves up to Via Maqueda. Turn left to see two of the city's most impressive 18th-century palaces, standing at the intersection of Via Maqueda and Via Santa Rosalia/ Via del Bosco: the Baroque **Palazzo Celestri di Santa Croce**, falling to bits while awaiting restoration, and the **Palazzo Comitini** (1771; *visits by appointment, Mon and Fri 9–1.30*, **t** *09 16 62 83 68*), well-restored by Mussolini. The interior is a Sicilian Rococo romp, with its light-hearted frescoes and painted panelling, chandeliers, stuccoes and marble floors, including bits salvaged from less fortunate palaces. It's open for visits when its current owner, the Provincial Council, is not in session; if you're not up to negotiating the intimidating security system, ask for times at the tourist office.

The Amalfitani

Beginning once more at the Quattro Canti (north along Via Maqueda from Palazzo Comitini), turn east (right) down Corso Vittorio Emanuele. Three streets down on your left, **San Matteo al Cassaro** wears a fine sculpted 17th-century façade in grey marble, decorated with statues; if it's open, go in to see the scattering of stucco statues by Giacomo Serpotta, lavish frescoes, marbles, and high altar glittering with precious stones, lapis lazuli and agate. At Via Roma turn left; near the corner, small 13th-century **San Antonio** was destroyed in the 1823 earthquake but restored to its original Chiaramonte style.

Steps next to San Antonio descend into the bowels of Palermo's oldest market, the **Vucciria** (from the French *boucherie*, 'butcher'), covering a dozen narrow, labyrinthine streets. It manages to insult or tempt every sense at once, with steaming cauldrons of boiled potatoes, live eels and swordfish carved up on slabs topped with ingenious whirling devices to keep the swarms of flies at bay, cascades of tripe and brains, heaving piles of fruits and vegetables, and a vast assortment of non-edibles of the order of smuggled Marlboros, plastic buckets and counterfeit designer handbags. The market is on mornings only (not on Sundays). The area comes into its own after dark, when it is illuminated by strings of bare light bulbs; the pungent odor of the Vucciria at the end of the day lingers in the memory like no other smell in Palermo.

San Domenico and the Oratorio del Rosario

The Vucciria's Via Maccheronai emerges into the light of day in *piazza*-cum-car-park San Domenico, with its towering landmark, the **Colonna dell' Immacolata**, high over Via Roma. The *piazza* was specially cut out of medieval Palermo to set off Tommaso Maria Napoli's theatrical 1726 façade (restored in 1998) on the vast church of **San Domenico** (1670; *open Mon–Sun 9–11.30 Sat and Sun 5–7; buses 101, 102, 103, 104, 105*). The interior is in expensively boring good taste, full of tombs that have given it the nickname 'Sicily's Pantheon'; great men buried here include prime minister Francesco Crispi, painter Pietro Novelli, and folklorist and scholar Giuseppe Pitrè. Off the left aisle is the much lovelier **cloister** (recently restored) of the original 14th-century San Domenico. The **Museo del Risorgimento**, at No.2 on the *piazza* (*open Mon, Wed and Fri 9–1, closed Aug*), has a collection of weapons and uniforms, pictures and documents from Garibaldi's sweep across Sicily in 1860.

The real lure in the area is behind San Domenico, at Via Bambinai 2: the 17th-century **Oratorio del Rosario di San Domenico** (*currently closed but there is talk that it will reopen soon; ask at the tourist office for details*). The interior is delightful enough to disarm even the most ardent Baroqueaphobe: this is stucco wizard Giacomo Serpotta's last oratory, and his most playful and graceful, the allegorical figures of the virtues saucily modelling the most extravagant, opulent fashions (note Serpotta's signature lizard on the column under the second figure on the right, Fortezza), while the walls are covered with chubby, anarchic putti riding piggyback on each other and yanking one another's willies. The beautiful altarpiece, the *Madonna of the Rosary* (1628), is by Van Dyck and shows the Virgin in the company of St Dominic and the four Palermo patronesses. Other wall paintings are by Pietro Novelli and Luca Giordano.

Oratorio di Santa Cita (or Zita)

The streets behind San Domenico have colourful names. Via Tavola Tonda ('round-table street') is south of the oratory, and Via Bambinai turns into Via Squarcialupo ('rip open the wolf street'). There are good buildings here: **Santa Maria Valverde** (1635; *open Tues–Sat 9–1, closed August*) by Mariano Smiriglio, with a grand marble interior, and 16th-century **Santa Cita** (or Zita; *currently closed*), heavily damaged in the war but somehow preserving fine works by Antonello Gagini, especially the triumphal arch in the apse and a smaller one in a chapel to the right of the altar.

Again, however, the main attraction is not precious marbles but the stuccoes behind the church, in Giacomo Serpotta's magnificent **Oratorio di Santa Cita**, Via Valverde 3 (*currently closed; for latest news, check with the tourist office*), entered by way of a late Renaissance loggia. Serpotta decorated it off and on between 1686 and 1718, its programme combining the Mystery of the Rosary, fashionable allegorical ladies and exuberant putti with the Battle of Lepanto, all in the drapery-swathed relief, embellished with stucco swords, blunderbusses, putti running amok with armoured torsos, helmets and a lion; the ships' riggings are made of fine wire.

Via Squarcialupo continues down to dusty **Piazza XIII Vittime**, named after the 13 leaders of the 1860 revolt, executed not long before Garibaldi's arrival. This was the centre of the Castelmare Quarter before it became a prime target during the war. Only the fine Renaissance church of **San Giorgio dei Genovesi** (*Tues–Sun 9–1, closed Aug*) has survived, designed in 1581 by Giorgio di Faccio for the Genoese colony in Palermo. Inside are paintings donated by merchants, whose tombs pave the floor. In the traffic island of Piazza XIII Vittime is a monument to Palermo's contemporary martyrs – those killed in the fight against the Mafia – surrounded by tattered, windswept banners reminiscent of Tibetan prayer flags.

Piazza Olivella

Backtrack to Via Valverde by the Oratorio di Santa Cita and continue up it towards Palermo's Kafkaesque **central post office**, a Mussolini-era white elephant that takes up the entire block. The brute power of the Corporate State demands its homage: an endless, oppressive flight of steps leads up to the enormous doors, the weight of which is enough to defeat all but the most determined postal customer, who, once inside, may wait half an hour before finally, triumphantly, mailing a postcard that may never arrive.

To the right of this temple of doom, Via Bara all'Olivella leads back to elongated Piazza Olivella, named after the handsome Baroque **Sant'Ignazio all'Olivella** and its exceptional Neoclassical **Oratorio dell'Olivella**, designed by Venanzio Marvuglia. The church is usually open for services, worth attending not only for the oratory but for some of its chapels, glowing with semi-precious stones and paintings. To the right of the church, in Via Monteleone, is the **Oratorio di Santa Caterina** (*ring to enter*), filled with delightful, detailed stuccoes (1719–26) on the saint's life by Procopio Serpotta, Giacomo's nephew.

The Museo Archeológico Regionale

Open all year Mon–Fri 8.30–6.30, Sat, Sun and holidays 8.30–1. Buses 101, 102, 103, 104, 122, 124.

On Sant'Ignazio's left, the ex-Philippine convent now contains the Museo Archeológico Regionale. Sicily has two of Italy's best archaeology museums, one in Syracuse and the other here in Palermo. The most important pieces are on the ground floor: off the first cloister, two marble Phoenician female sarcophagi (5th century BC) found at Cannita, possible site of archaic Soluntum; beyond are finds from Motya (*see pp.144–7*), two statues of Bes, several steles of a two-headed Zeus Meilichios (representing the terrifying and the gentle aspects of death, a survival of a primitive chthonic cult in Selinunte and Athens), and the 'Palermo Stone', inscribed with a shopping list from a pharaoh of the Old Kingdom (*c.* 3000 BC) left behind by a Phoenician trader. Other rooms keep you up to date on recent discoveries from the entrails of Palermo. Off the tropical garden of the back cloister are the greatest finds from western Sicily: the huge, colourful pieced-together Gorgon's head from Selinunte's Temple C (570 BC), followed by 19 of the original 59 ferocious, snarling lion's-head waterspouts from Himera's Doric Tempio della Vittoria.

Salone di Selinunte

Beyond is a large room devoted to works from Selinunte (*see* pp. 162–5), one of the artistic capitals of Greek Sicily. In the centre stands the magnificent bronze kouros, the ephebe of Selinunte (470 BC), brought here after it was stolen from Castelvetrano. On the walls are remarkable sets of metopes, the stone reliefs set above the columns of a Doric temple. The oldest, the highly stylized archaic 'metopes Salinas' from Temple C (580 BC), shows the gods of Delphi, the Sphinx, the Rape of Europa, and Hercules with the Bull of Marathon. Three slightly later metopes (550 BC) from the same temple are carved with Apollo's chariot, Perseus slaying the Gorgon, and a subject very rare in Greek iconography: Hercules dangling the laughing Cercopes twins from a pole over his shoulder in punishment for disturbing his sleep in the form of blue-bottle flies. And why are the Cercopes laughing? Because their mother had always warned them to watch out for 'Old Black Bottom', and, hanging upside down, that was just what presented itself to view – Hercules' lion pelt wasn't long enough to cover his bum, so it was leathery and sunburned, not to mention scorched by fire-breathing monsters. Hercules asked the Cercopes just what was so funny, and when they told him he burst out laughing himself and let them go.

This exuberant vitality evolved under Ionian influences into the ideal beauty and serenity of the classical age by 460 BC, the date of the four metopes from Temple E against the far wall: Hercules and the Amazon, the sacred marriage of Zeus, Artemis and Actaeon (about to be torn apart by his own hounds), and Athena and Enceladus – one of the Titans who warred against Olympos. Athena flattened Enceladus with a missile, and he became the island of Sicily.

Etruscan Art

Beyond lies the beautiful Collezione Casuccini of Etruscan art from Chiusi in Tuscany, acquired by a Sicilian historian who was convinced that the Etruscans and Sikans were the same people (they might have been related after all). There is a room of Etruscan funerary urns, some in tufa, others magnificently carved in alabaster, some retaining patches of paint. The favourite motif shows the deceased lounging at a feast, enjoying the afterlife; in the second room, note the fragments of a circular cippus (6th century BC) decorated with dance and fight scenes.

First and Second Floors

The first floor contains thousands of terracotta votive offerings from the Santuario di Demeter Malophoros in Selinunte, finds from Soluntum and from other sites in western Sicily. But the pieces that really stand out are from elsewhere: a magnificent Hellenistic bronze ram that once decorated the gate of Syracuse's Castello Maniace, a small, beautiful bronze of *An Athlete Subduing a Stag* from Pompeii, and a fragment from the Parthenon frieze.

The second floor has a prehistoric collection, including casts of the sensuous Upper Palaeolithic engravings from the Addaura Grotto on Monte Pellegrino. There's a Roman mosaic of Orpheus enchanting the wild beasts, discovered under Palermo's

Piazza della Vittória, and above all an exceptional collection of Greek ceramics, some imported from Greece and others made locally from the 7th–5th centuries BC: among the finest are a red figure *Hercules Fighting the Hydra*, a black figure *Fighting Hoplites* and *Dionysiac Scene*.

The Sincaldi

Teatro Massimo and the Capo

For something completely different, from the Museo Archeológico follow Via Bara all'Olivella west to Via Maqueda and Piazza Verdi. Palermo celebrated the unification of Italy with typical Sicilian excess, building not one, but two of the largest theatres in Europe: the one in front of you, vast, unwieldy **Teatro Massimo** (1875–97), was designed by Giovanni Battista Basile with the second largest stage in Europe, after the Paris Opéra. After almost 20 years of on-and-off restoration, it has re-opened as an opera and ballet venue (*tours daily 10–3.30 except during rehearsals; adm*). You may recognize it as the set from the opera scene in Coppola's *Godfather III*. Giovanni Battista's more talented son, Ernesto Basile, Palermo's great Liberty architect, supplied the *piazza*'s two **kiosks**, using a vocabulary inspired by Palermo's Arab-Norman past.

While here, consider a dip into the **Capo**, Palermo's densest, most untouched popular quarter, and one with an unsavoury reputation ever since it was inhabited by slave dealers. Get there by walking up Via Mura di San Vito behind the theatre; at the end, you'll see to your right one of Palermo's medieval gates, **Porta Carini**, looking as squalid as the rest of the Capo. At this junction, take Via Porta Carini to the left, a market street (and a good one for a freshly grilled mackerel snack), then carry straight on to Piazza Beati Paoli, where you'll be rewarded with the pretty 17th-century façade of **Santa Maria del Gesù**. From in front of the church, take Via Sedie Volanti ('flying chairs street') to its end, past the Monti di Pietà (municipal pawnshop), and turn left into Via Sant'Agostino. Here stands the 14th-century church of **Sant'Agostino**, built by the Chiaramonte family, whose stoneworkers seemingly embroidered the elegant rose window and laid lava mosaics around the door; inside are Serpotta's very last stuccoes, executed with his pupils. From here Via Sant'Agostino continues east back to Via Maqueda.

19th- and 20th-century Palermo

Just north of Teatro Massimo, Via Maqueda turns into Via Ruggero Settimo, marking the end of the historic centre and the beginning of Palermo's 'new addition', laid out in 1778. At the crossroads·with Via Mariano Stabile is the dour **Fascist skyscraper** in Piazzale Ungheria. Not a few of Palermo's public buildings were put up by Mussolini and Co., each stamped with a striving symbolic relief and a bewildering inscription from the Duke of Delusion's slogan machine.

Piazza Ruggero Settimo

Via Ruggero Settimo continues north into vast Piazza Ruggero Settimo (*buses 101, 102, 103, 104, 106, 107, 122, 124*). Just to the left is another **Liberty kiosk** by Ernesto Basile, while in the centre is the recently restored 19th-century **Palchetto della Musica**. These are the last two reminders that this *piazza* was once surrounded by graceful buildings, all since fallen prey to speculators.

The east side of the square is occupied by Palermo's other monster theatre, the Neoclassical **Teatro Politeama Garibaldi**, designed in 1867–74 by Giuseppe Damiani Almejda and crowned with a bronze quadriga by Mario Rutelli. Some of its bulk houses the **Galleria d'Arte Moderna** (*entrance from Via Turati; open Tues–Sat 9–8, Sunday 9–1, open all year*). The works here are Sicilian efforts from the 19th and 20th centuries; among the more interesting paintings are those by Giuseppe Sciuti (1834–1911), whose vast visions of ancient Sicily presage Cecil B. de Mille.

Villa Malfitano and Villino Florio

Other examples of Liberty architecture survive in the sidestreets, especially Via Dante. It runs west out of Piazza Ruggero Settimo past two Liberty villas, **Villino Favaloro** (1889) by Giovanni Battista and Ernesto Basile (at the intersection with Via Malaspina), now a government office building, and, at No.159, **Villino Caruso** (1908), by Filippo La Porta, now the home of the mayor, with a carriage gate in the back made of wrought-iron tendrils.

Via Dante continues to the luxuriant walled gardens of the neo-Renaissance **Villa Malfitano** (*open Mon–Sat 9–1; buses 106, 110, 122*), built by the Marsala wine baron Pip Whitaker in 1889, just after his marriage to Palermitan Tina Scalia. When their daughter Delia died in 1971, she left this villa, along with the island of Motya, to the Whitaker Foundation. Delia willed that the villa's furnishings be left unchanged, offering visitors a glimpse into the rarefied world of wealthy English Palermo – Louis XV and XVI furniture, a ballroom with a hand-painted clavichord (1700), billiards room, coral sculptures, Gobelin tapestries, and more.

The Whitakers' Marsala rivals, the Florios, were such a force in late 19th-century Palermo that the city was nicknamed Floriopolis. Not far from Villa Malfitano, at Viale Regina Margherita 38, they hired Ernesto Basile in 1891 to build their **Villino Florio**, a charming piece of floral confectionery with medieval towers and a gabled roof. It is considered to be Ernesto Basile's masterpiece.

In 1962 it mysteriously caught fire – set alight, more likely than not, by a property speculator, destroying the interior that Basile had especially created to fit the house – from the furniture to the dinner menus. You can still see it from the outside. The architect's nephew, Luigi Basile, a leading member of the Salvare Palermo committee (devoted to restoring the city's monuments), has been trying for years and years to have it repaired.

La Zisa

Piazza Guglielmo il Buono (across Piazza P. Camporeale from Villino Florio), bus 124; open Mon–Sat 9–6, Sun 9–1; free guided tours (ask for Paul, who grew up in New York).

Here, as oft as thou shalt wish, thou shalt see the loveliest possession of this kingdom, the most splendid of the world and of the seas. The mountains, their peaks flushed with the colour of narcissus...Thou shalt see the great King of his century in his beautiful dwelling place, a house of joy and splendour which suits him well. This is the earthly paradise that opens to the view; this King is the Musta'iz; this palace the Aziz.
                                    The Arabic inscription at the entrance to La Zisa

Some 750 years before Sicily's British mercantile dynasties built their villas in this neighbourhood, their Norman cousins were installed in the pleasure dome of La Zisa. *Aziz* means 'magnificent' in Arabic (still current in modern Sicilian as *zizata*) and it perfectly fits this Norman pleasure palace, begun by luxury-loving William the Bad in 1160 and completed by William II. Damaged in the Sicilian Vespers, La Zisa was converted into a fortress by the Ventimiglia family, who added the crenellations; in 1635 it was converted into a residence at great cost to its original interior. In 1971 the north wall collapsed. Since then, the regional government of Sicily has restored La Zisa and reproduced as much of its original appearance as possible. Although at the time of writing only the structure of the fish pond remains in the dusty front courtyard, restoration work has begun on the gardens, which are expected to be in good shape before too long.

La Zisa is a tall peculiar-looking building, its windows set in shallow arches. The central entrance, the Sala della Fontana, is the only section to retain any original decoration: the Arabic inscription, a frieze of golden mosaics similar to those in the Sala di Re Ruggero, carved capitals, stalactite ceilings in the corner, and a fountain, similar to ones at the Alhambra, that fed the fish pond. A small collection of Islamic art from the period occupies several rooms which were cooled by a natural ventilation system; the windows had intricate wooden screens to filter the sun (Ottoman screens in places suggest what they may have looked like). Unfortunately, it was impossible to restore what must have been the most magical room at the top, an arched pavilion open to the sky, with views of the sea and mountains.

North of Piazza Ruggero Settimo

There are three other Liberty villas worth looking up, just north of Piazza Ruggero Settimo: at the corner of Via XX Settembre and Via XII Gennaio, the whimsical Art Deco **Palazzo Dato**, with a moulded skin (1904) by Basile's student Vincenzo Alagna; Norman-inspired **Villa Utreggio** (1903; *no admission*), at the corner of Via XX Settembre and Via Siracusa; and Basile's own house, **Villino Basile** (1904), with colourful tiles and a dainty corner balcony, at Via Siracusa and Via Principe di Villafranca.

Via Siracusa continues east as Via Archimede to Via C. A. Dalla Chiesa, named after the Sicilian Prefect of Police gunned down by the Mafia; from here you can see

Palermo's most notorious landmark, the high-security **Carcere dell'Ucciardone**, the prison where, until recently, the Mafiosi inside conducted business with nearly the same ease as their confrères outside the walls. This in spite of the fact that Ucciardone has three times the number of guards of any other prison in Italy. An underground passage from the prison leads to the special fortified courtroom built in 1986 to try 500 suspected Mafiosi at the famous *maxi-processi*. Another Mafia victim, **Giovanni Falcone**, is remembered at his residence to the west of here. Take Via Duca della Verdura, which becomes fashionable Via Notarbartolo. Judge Falcone lived at No.23A; the tree in front is covered with testimonials and flowers.

At No.52 Viale della Libertà, the boutique-lined main boulevard in new Palermo, is the site of the **Fondazione Mormino**, in the Banco di Sicilia (*open Mon–Fri 9–1 and 3–5, Sat 9–1 all year; buses 101, 106, 806*), with a well-arranged archaeological collection, coins, stamps, majolica, paintings, old prints and more.

If your shoe leather is holding up, another destination in the area is the **Arsenal**, east of the Ucciardone on Via Cristoforo Colombo, a building designed by Mariano Smiriglio in the 17th century. Continuing along the sea towards Monte Pellegrino, there's a little English (read Protestant) **cemetery** a block inland on Via A. Rizzo. The real draw in the area is Ernesto Basile's seaside **Villa Igiea** on Salita Belmonte 43, now a grand hotel where you can pop in for a well-deserved drink and especially to savour the Salone Basile, the most remarkable survivor of Palermo's halcyon Liberty days. Originally the hotel dining room, the Salone is a fantastical, asymmetrical, almost disconcerting piece of total design. Even the smallest details were carefully worked by Basile and his two collaborators: Ducrot, responsible for exotic, sinuous boiseries; and Ettore De Maria Bergler, who painted the languid maidens in fields of flowers that dominate the walls.

Parco della Favorita and Museo Pitrè

Viale della Libertà makes its way north into the old artistocratic suburb of Piana dei Colli and Palermo's largest park, **La Favorita** (*buses 101, 106, 107*). In 1798, when Napoleon's troops were storming Naples, Bourbon King Ferdinand IV and his Queen Maria Carolina fled to Palermo aboard Lord Nelson's flagship *Vanguard*, with Sir William and Lady Hamilton for company. Upon arrival, the royal couple purchased for their residence what is now La Favorita and the old house in the grounds, known as the 'Villa of Bells'. The bells gave Ferdinand the idea of having the villa redone in chinoiserie, the fashion then sweeping Europe. This, the **Palazzina Cinese**, still stands by Piazza Niscemi, the park's main entrance. It's currently under restoration, but even from the outside this crazy, half-Neoclassical, half-Chinese Palermitan Xanadu is worth a look. The ground level forgets to be Chinese, with a portico of orange-striped Gothic arches; flanking twin stairs in little fairy-tale stone turrets lead up to the pagoda Piano Nobile, where the original furnishings survive in typical Palermitan neglect. Half the rooms continue the Chinese theme, with Oriental frescoes, silken walls and lacquered furniture; half are done in another, later 18th-century fad, the Pompeiian, while the king's bedroom somehow combines both styles. Most extraordi-nary of all was the dining room, where Nelson and the Hamiltons were frequent guests at the great oval table. To keep their conversations private, the table was equipped with a winch that lifted the food directly up from the basement kitchen. If someone wanted seconds, the king would inform the staff below with a complicated code of knocks.

Underground passages connect the palace to the stables, servants' quarters and chapel, also decorated with chinoiserie. These house the **Museo Etnografico Pitrè** (*entrance in Via Duca degli Abruzzi; open Mon–Thurs and Sat 8.30–7.30, closed Fri and Sun*), Sicily's biggest and best ethnographic collection, dedicated to the island's great student of folklore, Giuseppe Pitrè. There's a captivating selection of painted carts from all corners of the island, puppets and a puppet theatre, costumes, lace, torture instruments, carriages, masks, ceramics, ex-votos, a bust of Palermo's infamous 18th-century Old Lady Vinegar, who made a career out of poisoning people with 'louse vinegar', and a wooden model of the famous 18th-century Carrozza di Santa Rosalia, one of the most unroadworthy vehicles cooked up by humankind. Vaguely ship-shaped, it towered 80ft high on metal wheels; piled on top were a complete orchestra and several smaller bands, a garden, a cupola surrounded by angels in wooden clouds, and a huge statue of the saint. It took 56 of Sicily's finest mules to pull the contraption through the streets of Palermo for several hours every 15 July.

North Palermo

Monte Pellegrino and the Santuario di Santa Rosalia

La Favorita park stretches just below Palermo's holy mountain, the 1,818ft **Monte Pellegrino**, the ancient Heirkte and, according to Goethe, the most beautiful promontory in the world. Palermitans with cars (which seems to be all of them) head up here on Sundays to get above the smog. You can do the same by way of bus 812 from Via Filippo Turati (next to Teatro Politeama Garibaldi). En route the bus winds past the 1930s **Hotel Castello Utreggio** (now an international management school) with marvellous views over Palermo.

The bus will deposit you before the gauntlet of tacky religious souvenir shops that announce the **Santuario di Santa Rosalia** (*open daily 7–7*).

Rosalia (1132–66), a niece of King William I, renounced the world in 1159 when her father was killed in Bonnello's revolt. According to legend, she retreated to a hermitage on Monte Pellegrino, where she died. In 1624, when Palermo was caught in the grip of a deadly plague, a holy man had a vision regarding Rosalia's relics; these were duly found in a cave and marched around the city three times on 15 July. The plague at once receded. Rosalia's cave, a former sanctuary of the Phoenician *femme fatale* Tanit, was immediately converted into a chapel, where miraculous water (the only source on the mountain) drips down the wall and an alabaster statue of the saint reclines in golden robes amid a pile of loot donated by devotees. Goethe thought she 'seemed rapt in ecstasy, her eyes half veiled, her head softly fallen back on her right hand, covered with rings. I could not get my fill of looking at her, as if she had an extremely singular charm.' The charm was so strong that, when the

Around Palermo

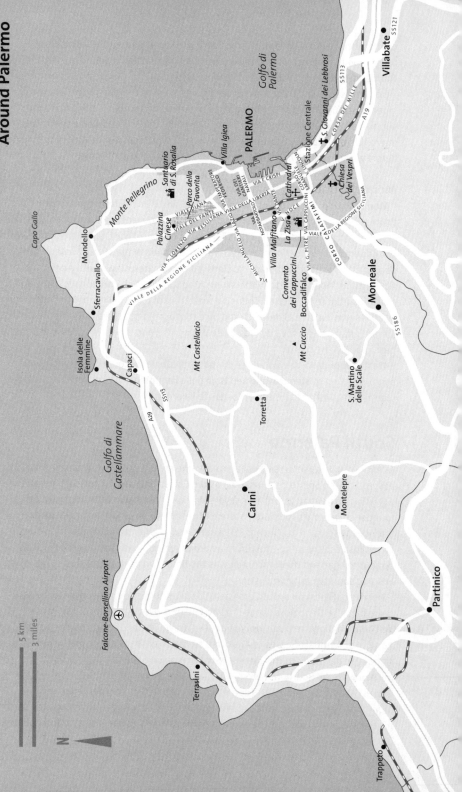

N

5 km
3 miles

Golfo di Castellammare

Capo Gallo

Monte Pellegrino

Mondello

Sferracavallo

Isola delle Femmine

Capaci

Falcone-Borsellino Airport

Terrasini

Trappeto

Partinico

Carini

Torretta

Montelepre

S. Martino delle Scale

Mt Castellacio

Mt Cuccio

Boccadifalco

Convento dei Cappuccini

Villa Malfitano

La Zisa

Palazzina Cinese

Santuario di S. Rosalia

Parco della Favorita

Villa Igiea

PALERMO

Golfo di Palermo

Cathedral

Stazione Centrale

S. Giovanni dei Lebbrosi

Chiesa dei Vespri

Monreale

Villabate

SS121

SS113

A19

CORSO DEI MILLE

CORSO DELLA REGIONE SICILIANA

SS186

A29

SS113

VIALE DELLA REGIONE SICILIANA

VIALE DEL FANTE

VIALE DIANA

VIALE DI S. LORENZO

VIA RESUTTANA

VIALE DELLA LIBERTA

VIA DEL CANTIERI NAVALI

VIA IMPERATORE FEDERICO

VIA BARTOLO

VIA F. CRISPI

VIA DANTE

VIA MICHELANGELO

NOTARBARTOLO

VIA G. PITRÉ

VIA CAPPUCCINI

CORSO CALATAFIMI

CORSO CALATAFIMI

VIA V. EMANUELE

CROCE

VIA ROMA

enlightened Viceroy Domenico Caracciolo (who had abolished the Inquisition) attempted to limit her festival to a mere three days in 1783, he found the Palazzo dei Normanni surrounded with posters reading '*O festa o testa*' ('The festival or your head').

From the sanctuary there is a choice of roads – one to the cliff's edge, where a gigantic statue of Santa Rosalia watches over her city; another leading up to the summit of Monte Pellegrino, with views across the Conca d'Oro; and a third leads down the mountain by way of the Scala Vecchia, which passes the Castello Utreggio before zigzagging down to Le Falde, site of the Fiera del Mediterraneo.

Mondello Lido

Mondello Lido, Palermo's resort annexe, is a half-hour ride from the Teatro Politeama Garibaldi on bus 806. If you're driving, however, take the scenic shore road along the foot of Monte Pellegrino. This passes by way of the Upper Paleolithic **Grotta di Addàura** (*closed indefinitely for restoration; casts are in the Museo Archeológico*), decorated *c.* 17,000 BC with rare incisions, human figures, drawn with a beautiful flowing line. Mondello Lido, with its long, long sandy beach, can be a welcome and relaxing antidote to Palermo. There is a scattering of Liberty villas, but the main thing to do is swim, eat a seaside lunch and ogle the fashion-obsessed Palermitans. On a summer night this is the city's favourite place to be, and there are buses well into the night back to the centre.

West of Mondello, the road dives inland to circumvent Monte Gallo, where you can continue along to **Sferracavallo** and **Isola delle Femmine**, both small fishing-villages-cum-resorts, with the closest campsites to Palermo.

South Palermo

On the opposite, south side of Palermo, in the cemetery of Sant' Orsola in Via del Vespro, is Santo Spirito, better known as the **Chiesa dei Vespri** (*open daily 9–12; buses 243, 318; metro Piazza Vespri*). This severe Norman church was built in 1173 by the founder of Palermo's cathedral, Walter of the Mill. A pair of Sicilian newly-weds attended Vespers on 31 March 1282, Easter Tuesday, when an idle Angevin soldier rudely insulted the bride – this, from a hated oppressor, was too much for Sicilian honour to bear, and the Frenchman was the first of an estimated 8,000 to die in the ensuing spontaneous combustion.

A walk southeast on broad Corso dei Mille from the Stazione Centrale follows the route taken by Garibaldi's Thousand into Palermo, passing by way of the **Ponte dell'Ammiraglio** (*closed, but visible from the street*). The bridge was built in 1113 by Admiral of Admirals George of Antioch over the River Oreto, although the river has since been diverted. On this fine piece of Norman engineering Garibaldi's troops skir-mished with the Bourbons before entering Palermo. Farther down Corso dei Mille (No.384), at Via Cappello, is the domed church of **San Giovanni dei Lebbrosi** (*open Mon–Sat 4–5.15pm; buses 226, 227, 231*), founded by Count Roger I in 1072 on the site of his first victory in Palermo. The church's name refers to its later use as the chapel of a leper hospital. Although the rest of this area of Palermo is now as dreary as can be, Norman chroniclers described it as 'an earthly paradise', where the rough knights from the north walked in disbelief through the luscious gardens and palaces, the greatest of which was Palazzo di Favara, the 10th-century estate of the Emir Giafar, surrounded by an artificial lake and nicknamed Maredolce, the 'Sweet Sea Palace'. Under the Normans Maredolce continued to be the greatest of 'the palaces which circle the valley of the city like a string of pearls on a maiden with a firm breast'. Here the future emperor Frederick II spent his precocious childhood studying Greek, Latin and Arabic in preparation for his career as the first true Renaissance prince.

West Palermo

The Convento dei Cappuccini

Open daily 9–12 and 3–5.30 all year. Bus 327. Leave a donation.

From Piazza Indipendenza, walk 1km up Via Cappuccini to the sign for the catacombs of the Convento dei Cappuccini, a peculiar institution that mummified 8,000 clients between the 16th century and the early years of the 20th. Capuchin friars elsewhere in Italy, especially in Rome, appreciate the aesthetics of Death more than most, and have a knack for arranging curious tableaux of bones and skulls. Here they developed several techniques to preserve as much of the mortal coil as possible. One involved laying fresh corpses out on a system of terracotta tubing for eight months. Afterwards the body would have a wash in vinegar and herbs, and be laid out in the sun to dry completely; then it would be dressed up and hung on the catacomb wall according to station – monk, soldier, lawyer, virgin, spinster and so on. They're still there, and, like a Palermitan of yore, you can make a pleasant excursion (obviously not suitable for children) through the corridors to visit the grinning remains all dressed in their Sunday best. The number of little children is striking and sad; the last to be entombed, in 1920, was a little girl given a special embalming treatment – invented by a Palermitan doctor who took the secret recipe to his own tomb – and well nicknamed 'The Sleeping Beauty'. As you leave, the plump, good-natured friars will want to sell you colour postcards, useful for sending greetings to relatives you don't like. Fans of Giuseppe di Lampedusa can visit his tomb in the cemetery behind the catacombs.

La Cuba

From here it is a short walk down Via Pindemonte to Corso Calatafimi, the main thoroughfare from Porta Nuova up to Monreale. Behind the barracks walls at No.100 stands **La Cuba** (*open Mon–Sat 9–6.30, Sun 9–1*), a pleasure palace built by William II in 1180, in what was then the enormous park of the Maredolce palace (*see* 'South Palermo', above). Only the structure remains, which in form resembles La Zisa, massive and rectangular, embellished with shallow columns and arches; originally it was topped by a dome. Farther up Corso Calatafimi, at No.217, stretches the vast 18th-century **Albergo dei Poveri**, or poorhouse, its size nearly as depressing as all the

Love in La Cuba

Boccaccio used La Cuba as a setting for one of the tales in the *Decameron* (5th day, no.6), in which a young girl from Ischia is carried off by Sicilian brigands and installed in La Cuba for the delectation of King Frederick II of Aragon. Her sweetheart Gianni managed to locate her and to enter La Cuba secretly, where the two were caught making love. Frederick ordered the lovers to be burned at the stake, but at the last minute learned that Gianni was the nephew of Giovanni da Procida, who had acted as middleman between the Angevin-oppressed Sicilians and the Crown of Aragon. Well aware that he owed the uncle his crown, the king released Gianni and his sweetheart for a fairy-tale happy ending. Even more surprising, historians say the story's true.

children in the catacombs. Today it is occasionally used for temporary exhibitions. And next to No.443 is **La Cubula**, a domed summer kiosk that once stood in the gardens of La Cuba. From here Corso Calatafimi continues up to Monreale.

Around Palermo

Monreale

The Norman kings had each endowed important religious foundations in Sicily, and the last of them, the elusive, stay-at-home William II, who liked to be called al Musta'izz bi' Ilah ('He who seeks exaltation in God'), was determined to outdo them all. In 1174, at the age of 20, he claimed that the Virgin revealed to him in a dream the location of a great treasure at the little hill town of Monreale, overlooking the glorious Conca d'Oro. In return he would use the treasure to build a cathedral – a story that neatly tidied away any objection to the huge sums of money William meant to lavish on the project. Pope Alexander III gave Monreale his special blessing, going over the head of Palermo's powerful, arrogant English Archbishop and Emir, Walter of the Mill. Walter was so furious at this royal undermining of his authority and prestige (which was William's other reason for building Monreale) that he declared he would rebuild Palermo cathedral at the same time, although he could not compete with the fabulous resources of al Musta'izz bi' Ilah. The result at Monreale has given rise to a local saying: 'Anyone who comes to Palermo without seeing Monreale arrives as a donkey and leaves as an ass.'

The Cathedral

Open daily 8–12.30 and 3.30–6.

The cathedral is an easy 5min walk from the bus stop. From the outside it is stern, stale fare, with an 18th-century porch tucked between two towers, only one of which was ever completed. Walk round the back, however, to see the three **apses**, covered

Getting There

Monreale is an easy 20min **bus** ride for the cost of a city bus ticket on no.389 from Via Mariano Stabile or Corso Calatafimi; it brings you to the cathedral and Corso Vittorio Emanuele. A **taxi** to Monreale costs around €20, but there are no cabs in Monreale, so you'll have to call one to get you back down.

Virga buses (**t** 09 14 18 021) depart from Palermo's Piazza Verdi for San Martino (five daily), or you can go direct from Monreale on bus 2. Báida can be reached by bus 462 from Piazza Principe di Camporeale or bus 534 from Piazzale Giotta in Palermo. Partinico and Carini are served by AST buses (**t** 091 680 0031) from Piazza Lolli, while AST buses for Montelepre go from Piazza Marina.

Tourist Information

Monreale: by the cathedral, Piazza Vittorio Emanuele 4, **t** 091 656 4570, *www.azienda turismopalermomonreale.it* (*open Mon–Sat 9–1.30 and 2.30–6.30*).

Terrasini: Piazza Duomo, **t** 09 18 68 28 19 (*open Mon–Sat 9–1 and 4–7*).

Where to Stay and Eat

Monreale and San Martino ✉ 90046

★★★Carrubella Park, Via Umberto I 233, **t** 091 640 2188 (*expensive*). Monreale's one central hotel, with parking, air-con and a garden.

★★Messina, Via della Regione 108, **t** 091 418 149 (*budget*). A pleasant hotel in San Martino, with modest prices and a restaurant.

La Botte, SS186 at Contrada Lentizzi, **t** 091 414 051 (*expensive*). The best restaurant in the area, with superb food in a cosy setting.

You'll need a car to get there, though. *Closed Mon, Sun eve and July and Aug.*

Castellaccio, **t** 091 640 37 58 (*inexpensive*). It's best to book for the set lunch served at this refuge five minutes' drive from Monreale.

Di Chiara, **t** 091 418 103 (*inexpensive*). The place to go for a pizza in San Martino delle Scale. *Closed Mon.*

La Panoramica, Via Ruffo di Calabria, **t** 091 223 706 (*inexpensive*). This trattoria in Báida does good pizzas and more. *Closed Tues.*

Villa Tre Fontane, Via Circonvallazione (*inexpensive*). In walking distance of Monreale, with tasty Sicilian food and pizzas.

Terrasini, Carini and Montelepre

★★★Porto Rais, Via Piraineto 125, Carini, ✉ 90044, **t** 091 869 34 81, *portorais@ infinito.it* (*expensive*). In Villa Grazia, Carini's seaside extension, also with a private beach, as well as tennis courts and comfortable air-conditioned rooms.

Casale del Principe, Contrada Damusi, Monreale, **t** 091 857 9910, *www.casaledel principe.it* (*budget–inexpensive; restaurant moderate*) Great value at this *agriturismo* set in 16th-century monastery in its own park and farmland. Has kept its original structure and each room is individually decorated, with a balcony. Pottery courses, horse riding and walks, plus organised children's activities. Home-grown produce including wine are on offer in the restaurant.

★★Villaggio Agli Androni, Via Cala Rossa, at Agli Androni, Terrasini, ✉ 90049, **t** 091 868 33 15 (*inexpensive*). The smallest and most affordable of the three hotels in Terrasini. 62 rooms beside the beach and sports from windsurfing to horse riding. The day's catch is grilled, stewed or fried in a variety of styles and served in a pretty garden.

with an Arab-Norman network of interlaced ogival arches and incrustations of lava and limestone.

Two other things to look at before entering are the **bronze doors**. Those on the front, set in a richly carved portal with tiny human and animal figures and mosaics, have 46 charmingly earthy panels on the Old and New Testaments by Bonanno da Pisa (1186). On the north side, under a long marble colonnade built by the Gaginis, are the smaller doors by Barisano da Trani (1179), whose sophisticated, intricate work owes more to the Byzantine prototypes: the panels show battle scenes, saints, animals and three rather incidental scenes from the life of Jesus. Bronze doors like these, following a Byzantine custom, were a major art form of medieval southern Italy, especially in Apulia; surprisingly, these are the only examples in Sicily.

The interior of the cathedral makes you feel like a tiny ant straying across a glowing illuminated manuscript. The only section that is not original is the roof, which caught fire in 1811; most of the other decorative features are modelled after the Cappella Palatina, but enlarged 10 times. The magnificent **mosaics** alone cover 7,583sq yd – over 2,000 more than St Mark's in Venice. Exactly who made them and when has long been a subject of scholarly dispute. Greek mosaicists, or their Sicilian pupils, were most likely responsible for the Byzantine figures in the apse, including the giant figure of Christ Pantocrator in the centre vault, over 22ft high and looming over the traditional hierarchical ranks of Virgin, angels and saints like a zoom shot from heaven. Amongst the saints lined up below the seated Virgin, stands Thomas à Becket, canonized soon after William II's own father-in-law, Henry II, had him murdered. But rather than a lapse in good taste, the presence of St Thomas here may have been an expiatory gesture on the part of Joanna, William's wife, who as a girl knew Becket well.

On either side of the arch are the thrones of the king and archbishop, each topped with a mosaic: one of William II crowned by Christ (in the manner of his grandfather Roger, in La Martorana) and the other showing William II offering his cathedral to the Virgin. Contemporaries describe William possessing the 'beauty of an angel', but here he looks like a bank manager after a lost weekend.

Note the magnificent **marble screens** by the thrones, decorated with lions and griffons. Later mosaics (believed to date after William's death in 1189) line the nave and walls like huge cartoon strips. They seem to tell every possible story from the Old and New Testaments, with a flowing naturalism and movement rare in Greek mosaics – hence the belief that they were made by Venetian mosaicists who were sent to Sicily by the popes. The lower scenes on the back wall – the *Destruction of Sodom*, the *Miracle of St Castrense* and *SS. Casto and Cassio Refusing to Worship the Idols* – were completed in the last half of the 13th century, and show the same elongated manneristic touches and narrative style as their contemporaries in St Mark's; note the difference between these and the older, simpler, more powerfully poetic scenes of Adam and Eve just above.

William II had intended to make the **choir chapels** the burial place of the Hauteville dynasty (a dynasty that he sadly proved too slow in the sack to continue), beginning with the sarcophagi of his mother Margaret of Navarre, his brothers, and his father William I, all of which were severely damaged in the 1811 fire. William II had a fine porphyry model made for himself, but when he died the incorrigible Walter of the Mill seized both sarcophagus and body for the Palermo cathedral. By the time Monreale got the remains after years of fighting, the sarcophagus was lost and William II now lies near his father in the right chapel, in a white marble tomb of 1575.

If you can avert your eyes from the mosaics there are other things to see: the original Cosmatesque floor in the presbytery; the antique cipollino marble columns and Corinthian capitals dividing the nave; and, to the left of the choir, a marble altar containing the heart and internal organs of St Louis, who lay here in state in 1270, after he died of plague while crusading in Tunis. Nearby, steps lead up to the treasury, although none of its contents can match the explosively frothy marble and *pietra dura* Baroque chapel of the Crucifix (1680s) at its entrance.

Also within the cathedral you can also buy a ticket to climb up the tower to the roof for a quite stupendous view over the cloister, city and the coastal plain.

The Cloister

Open all year Mon–Sat 9–6.30, Sun and hols 9–1

Just to the right of the cathedral is the second wonder of Monreale, the lovely 12th-century garden cloister that once belonged to its Benedictine monastery. Each arcade consists of 26 ogival arches, each supported by a pair of twin slender columns, either carved or smoothed or encrusted with glittering geometric mosaics. Even more remarkable are the vigorously carved capitals, full of Romanesque imagination and originality (done by sculptors from either Burgundy or Provence) – Norman knights, scenes from everyday life, from the Bible, animals, birds, monsters, foliage and, most magnificent of all, the dedicatory capital, showing William offering his church to the Virgin, with the Lamb of God, Faith, Hope, Charity and Justice. One capital even shows Mithras sacrificing a bull.

One corner of the cloister has an enchanting pavilion with a fountain shaped like a palm tree without fronds, where water flows in thin jets from little lions' mouths. (Because of scarcity of water, the fountain is turned off in the afternoon, and occasionally all day long in the summer.)

Castellaccio, San Martino delle Scale and the Convento di Báida

The road above Monreale continues for 5km to the path for the Norman castle, **Castellaccio** (*currently closed to visitors*), built by William II for the Benedictines as a citadel monastery, and now in a bit of a sorry state. The 30min walk isn't too difficult; there are good views at the end.

After another 10km, the road continues to the delightful pine-forested Valle del Paradiso, where **San Martino delle Scale** is a popular summer refuge for overheated Palermitani. Theatrically dominating the valley is the vast white Benedictine **Abbazia di San Martino** (*open Mon–Sat 9–12 and 4.30–6.30, Sun 9–11 and 5–6.30*), according to legend founded by Pope Gregory the Great in the 6th century. Destroyed by the Arabs in 829, it was rebuilt in 1346, and enlarged off and on until Venanzio Marvuglia added the finishing touches in 1770. In its day a major cultural centre, the abbey is still in part occupied by Benedictines, while the rest now houses an orphanage and college. Two works, Marvuglia's elaborate grand staircase and Marabitti's *St Martin and the Beggar* near the same, steal the show, although the 16th-century church has a fine intagliato wooden choir and plenty of paintings by Giuseppe Salerno.

Farther north, on an isolated spur near Boccadifalco, the **Convento di Báida** (*ring bell*) was founded in 1377 for the monks of Castellaccio by Manfred Chiaramonte when he took over their old home. The church has a marble Renaissance portal by Antonio Vanelli (1507) and one of Antonello Gagini's finest pieces, *John the Baptist*. Báida ('white' in Arabic), is itself a pretty hill village, the heir of the 10th-century Saracen original.

Terrasini

Beyond the long tentacle of Palermo sprawl that stretches west to Monte Pecoraro and the airport lies **Terrasini**, overlooking the splendid Golfo di Castellammare. A pleasant fishing village with sandy beaches, it has an ambitious Museo Civico, spread out in three sections. The **Antiquarium** (*open May and Oct Fri and Sat 8–2, Mon–Thurs 8–2 and 4–7; June–Sept daily 8–2 and 4–7*), in the Municipio in Piazza Falcone-Borsellino, houses finds from Davy Jones' locker, especially from Imperial Roman ships that foundered on the rocky coast. The **Museo di Storia Naturale**, Via Cala Rossa 8 (*open Mon–Sat 9–1 and 3–7, Sun 9.30–12.30*), covers local natural history; and the **Museo Etnográfico**, Via Carlo Alberto dalla Chiesa (*open June–Sept Mon–Sat 9–8, Oct–May Mon–Sat 9–12.30 and Sun 4–7*), displays a collection of hand-painted carts from all over Sicily. If that's not enough, a plastic surgeon runs his own private attraction in Terrasini, the **Zoo-Fattoria** (*open daily 9am–sunset*), with 400 animals, including lions, tigers and bears.

Carini, Montelepre and Partinico

In the lonely mountainous confines west of the glittering Conca d'Oro, the hill town of **Carini** is famous in Sicilian lore. Founded in the 10th century by the Arabs near ancient Hyccara, a city destroyed by the Athenians in 415 BC, it forms the setting for the 16th-century epic of passion, jealousy and murder written in Sicilian vernacular called *The Baronessa di Carini*.

The baroness in question was Caterina La Grua Talemanca, who lived in Carini's **Norman castle** (*open Sat and Sun*) and fell in love with her cousin, and was murdered by her husband in 1563; the poem, however, makes her father the killer. The castle was last rebuilt in the 1500s; you can still see the La Grua arms carved over its gate. Carini also has a pair of churches worth seeking out: the **Chiesa Madre**, with Florentine Mannerist Alessandro Allori's *Adoration of the Shepherds* (1578), and the **Oratorio del Sacramento**, with lavish 18th-century stucco decorations by Vincenzo Messina.

South, on the other side of Monte Saraceno, **Montelepre** is a grim introduction to Sicily's most hopelessly poor and downtrodden area. The village was feudal well into this century, symbolized by its fort built in the 15th century by its overlord, the Archbishop of Monreale. It was briefly the kingdom of Sicily's tragic Robin Hood, Salvatore Giuliano, who in the 1940s appointed himself the defender of Montelepre and spent most of his life hiding out with his band in these hills. He gave his henchmen military rank, and enforced a primitive etiquette that caught the fancy of the press.

Giuliano was brave but gullible. The feudal overlords he started off fighting cleverly tricked him into thinking that the real cause was Sicilian separation from Italy, a cause supported by the overlords' Mafia henchmen as well. Then along came the Christian Democrats, who promised the landowners that nothing would change their privileges if they could keep the peasantry from embracing Communism. By 1947 Giuliano was so completely their puppet that he and his band massacred the very people they started out defending, at a May Day fête near Piana degli Albanesi.

Partinico, south of Montelepre, comes from the same desperate mould, although it found a completely different post-war champion for change in a Turin lawyer named Danilo Dolci. His books – *Waste* (1959), *Outlaws* (1961) and *To Feed the Hungry* (1963) – provide a chilling account of the poverty, exploitation, violence and corruption that for decades were the lot of most western Sicilians.

Ùstica

The 3sq miles that make up the black island of Ùstica lie about 40 miles to the north of Palermo, looking for all the world like a giant turtle swimming away from the city. It managed to get far enough away to float in an absolutely transparent sea, amid bright submerged gardens of aquatic flora and fauna. These have made Ùstica's fortune: since 1960 scuba divers from around the world have gathered here every July for the 'International Festival of Underwater Activities'. In 1986, its coast was made Italy's first and most important underwater natural park; in 1992 the Mediterranean's first underwater archaeological trail was set up. But Ùstica has charms for landlubbers, too. Its volcanic origins have endowed it with striking scenery, easily accessible on foot or by donkey. Wild flowers cover the island, except in the hottest months, and capers, figs, lentils and vines grow where the land is level enough for farming. Although the wild coastline has magnificent grottoes and rocky coves, don't expect to find any sandy beaches.

History

Ùstica was inhabited in 2000 BC by a people with close cultural links with both Sicily and the Aeolian Islands. Their settlements were at Falconiera and near the present Saracen castle, and they buried their dead in the nearby Grotta dell'Uomo. The first historical record of the island comes from the Greeks, who called it Osteodes ('island of bones'), from the remains of 6,000 mutinous Carthaginian soldiers who were abandoned here to die of hunger and thirst. The Romans improved somewhat on this dismal name with Ustum ('burned'), referring to the charred volcanic rock of Ùstica. After the Romans, Ùstica became a nest of pirates. The Normans managed to chase them out long enough to build a monastery and a church, although by the 14th century the Saracens had destroyed all, and were once again using Ùstica as their base to plague the coast. In 1760 Ferdinand IV sent a group of settlers to Ùstica; two

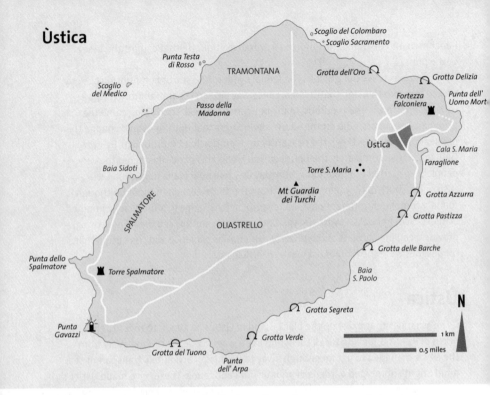

Ùstica

years later the pirates returned and, after a three-day rampage, only two men escaped to tell the tale. The Bourbons wised up and fortified the island before sending a new group of colonists from the Aeolian Islands, the ancestors of the 1,000 people who live on Ùstica today. In September 1943, British and Italian commanders met secretly on the island to discuss Italy's switch-over to the Allies during the war.

Ùstica, Port and Town

Lively Ùstica town contains 90 per cent of the island's population, who live in houses brightly painted with murals. Tree-filled **Piazza Umberto**, the social centre, often doubles as an informal training ground for baseball: Ùstica has one of Italy's finest youth teams. The church, **San Bartolomeo**, has been decorated with colourful ceramic saints. The small **Museo di Archeológia Sottomarina** nearby (*open summer, winter by appointment*) holds items from offshore wrecks. Above the church, on the site of an 11th-century Benedictine monastery, the **Palazzo del Comune** of 1763 is Ùstica's grandest building. Overlooking all are the interesting ruins of a **Saracen castle** on Falconiera, a 20min walk uphill, from which you can see Sicily.

Around Ùstica by Boat

Ùstica's port, **Baia Santa Maria**, has been in use since ancient times, when the Phoenicians constructed a long mole of volcanic rock where the concrete mole stands today. It's easy to hire a boat or find someone to take you on an excursion; the glass-

Getting There

Siremar **ferries** serve Ùstica (one daily June–Sept, six daily between Oct–May, 2hrs 20mins); they also run **hydrofoils** (1hr15mins, two daily Sept–May, three daily June–Aug). Get information and tickets in Palermo at Via F. Crispi 120, **t** 091 749 3111; on Ùstica, Via Capitano Vincenzo di Bartolo 15, **t** 091 844 9002.

Tourist Information

Ùstica has no tourist office, but the Centro Accoglienza per La Riserva Marina, Piazza Vito Longo, **t** 091 844 9456 (*open June–Sept*), has some useful information, and organizes water activities and boat trips. Diving Centre Ùstica, Via Vittorio Emanuele 4, **t** 091 844 95 33 (*open June–Sept*), handles scuba lessons and rentals.

Where to Stay

Ùstica ✉ 90010

Tourism on Ùstica has increased with the general interest in diving, but the season is short and intense, from June to September.
★★★Punta Spalmatore, Spalmatore, **t** 091 844 9482, *www.lirial.it/spalmatore* (*luxury*). A large and well-equipped tourist village with cottage accommodation for 4,000 people and a good selection of sport facilities. *Closed mid Sept–mid June. For reservations call* **t** 02 58 39 63 25; *one week minimum rental.*
★★★★Grotta Azzurra, San Ferlicchio, **t** 091 844 9048, *www.framonhotels.com*

(*expensive–luxury*). A swish hotel with modern air-conditioned rooms perched over its own bay with a nice pool and sun terraces cut into the rocks below and more. *Closed Oct–May.*
★★★Clelia, Via Magazzino 7, **t** 091 844 90 39, *www.hotelclelia.it* (*inexpensive–moderate*). Reasonably priced, this rates as one of Ùstica's nicer options.
★★Ariston, Via della Vittoria 5, **t** 091 844 90 42 (*inexpensive*). Small and reasonably priced hotel. Half or full board only between June and September.
★Diana, Contrada S. Paolo, **t** 091 844 91 09 (*budget*). One of the older hotels, but comfortable, with a good restaurant, pool, tennis and pebble beach.
★★★Stella Marina, Via C. Colombo 33, **t** 091 844 90 14 (*budget*). A favourite central base of diving teams in summer, and one of the few hotels open all year.

Eating Out

Ùstica's specialities are its Albanella wine, the day's catch, and quail (*April–May and Sept–Oct*).
Mamma Lia, Via San Giacomo 1, **t** 091 844 95 94 (*moderate*). A good bet for fish (what else?). *Closed Nov–March.*
Da Mario, Piazza Umberto I 21, **t** 091 844 95 05 (*moderate*). Another place recommended for its fish dishes. *Closed Mon and Oct–May.*
Locanda Clelia Hotel, Via Magazzino 7, **t** 091 844 90 39 (*inexpensive*). Has a good restaurant, where *lenticchie all'usticese* (Ùstican lentils) is a speciality.

bottomed boat tour of the marine reserve is organized by the Centro Accoglienza (*see* 'Tourist Information', above).

Just south of the port are steep ochre cliffs of stratified lava and Ùstica's most famous sea cave, the 300ft-long **Grotta Azzurra** derives its extraordinary iridescent colour from the reflections of light off the sea. The next sea cave, the stalactite **Grotta Pastizza**, is almost as lovely behind its great pyramidal rock. Near it, just under the water, are a large bank of petrified shells and the half-submerged entrance to another grotto, Naiada. Farther south is the majestic **Baia San Paolo**, with a giant lava arch and yet another grotto, known as the **Barche** ('boats'), where fishermen beach their boats during storms. The entrance to the **Grotta Segreta** ('secret cave'), next to Punta Segreta, will keep its secrets, since its mouth has been blocked by a chunk of lava, but the exquisite turquoise colour of the water inside the nearby **Grotta Verde** is impressively visible. Next are the rich fishing grounds of Cala Sciabica and Punta dell' Arpa, and a long stretch of rugged coast towards the Punta Gavazzi and a lighthouse. Beneath the lighthouse is the **Piscina Naturale**, a natural sea pool that attracts scores of swimmers and sunbathers in the summer.

The **Torre Spalmatore**, an 18th-century defensive tower, overlooks numerous inlets and pebbly beaches. The next cove, **Baia Sidoti**, is the most striking of all, with its Scoglio del Medico a little way out to sea; its name, 'the doctor's rock', supposedly recalls a physician tortured and murdered here after failing to save the life of a Saracen princess. Orange cliffs of tufa encompass the bay, and its waters brim with fish and other sea creatures. The steep cliffs north of Sidoti are coloured a deep red at the Testa di Rosso precipice; at the bottom is a small pebbly beach. Following this you pass a series of fantastic volcanic rocks – the Colombaro, or Faraglione, made of black and green crystals, the Sacramento rock, with its unusual stratification, and two grottoes with curious mineral formations in their walls.

Around Ùstica on Foot

If you prefer to explore the island rather than merely admire it from a boat, you can easily circumnavigate it on foot (9km) within three or four hours. By land, you can take in many of the aforementioned sights along the coast from new and sometimes better angles. Signs of a prehistoric (1200 BC) village remain at **Contrada Tramontana** (*visitable by appointment: call the comune, t 091 844 90 45*). The **Passo della Madonna**, with its sheer precipices, is the most dramatic part of the journey – that is if you don't encounter the red bees of Spalmatore. These pesky little blossom-suckers like to buzz around your head and legs when you cross their turf, but they rarely sting.

Western Sicily

08

Western Sicily

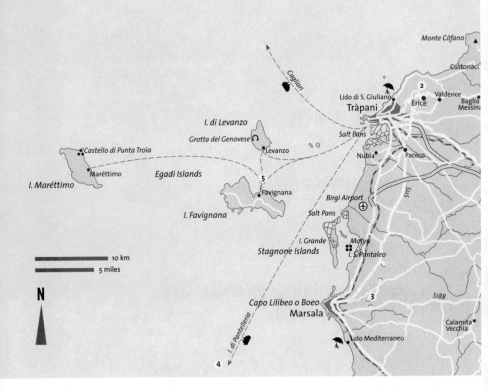

No matter where you go in Italy, you'll hear people joking about the exact borders of Africa. The Milanese will tell you it begins in Florence, the Florentines say it begins in Rome, the Romans Naples, and so on. The truth is that it begins just west of Palermo, in western Sicily, where the sunlight is purer and the air whipped clean by the wind, where spaghetti gives way to couscous , and nearly every town or village can trace its name back to the Arabic. Tunis, after all, is only about five hours by hydrofoil from Tràpani.

If eastern Sicily remained predominantly Greek until the late Middle Ages, western Sicily was predominantly North African and Arab. It is the historic stomping ground of the Phoenicians and Carthaginians, who made Motya and Lilybaeum great sea

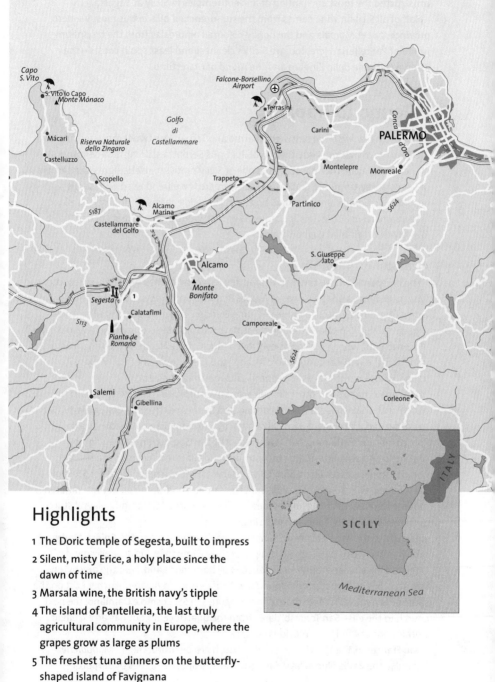

Highlights

1 The Doric temple of Segesta, built to impress
2 Silent, misty Erice, a holy place since the
  dawn of time
3 Marsala wine, the British navy's tipple
4 The island of Pantelleria, the last truly
  agricultural community in Europe, where the
  grapes grow as large as plums
5 The freshest tuna dinners on the butterfly-
  shaped island of Favignana

ports, and the mysterious Elymians, who made Love their greatest god at Erice and constructed the most enchanting of ancient temples in Sicily at Segesta.

Half of all Sicilian wine comes from the sun-drenched hills in this most western province, sweet Marsala and the honey-coloured ambrosias from the fascinating island of Pantelleria. Here, too, are Sicily's cleanest and least spoilt coasts – the Riserva Naturale dello Zingaro and the island of Maréttimo.

Palermo to Tràpani

Just off the *superstrada* between Palermo and Tràpani are two tempting detours: Alcamo, a rarely visited wine town with lustrous Serpotta stucchi, 18th-century churches and little thermal spas; and one of Sicily's most majestic sights, the temple of Segesta. The turquoise Golfo di Castellammare is well-endowed with sandy beaches, including some of Sicily's prettiest. The wild charms of Zingaro, the island's first nature reserve, are an added plus, as are the world's-end delights of San Vito, a low-key resort framed by mountains.

Alcamo

The prosperous white town of Alcamo, the Saracens' Manzil Alqamah, or resort of lotus fruit, broods on the slopes of Monte Bonifato over vineyards that produce white wines from tiny Catarratto grapes – Fiume Freddo, Coda di Volpe (fox tail) or, most exquisite of all, Rapitalà. Although these days Alcamo's best-known son is Mafia capo Vincenzo Rimi, who in the 1960s controlled much of the North Africa–American drug trade, it is the 12th-century Ciullo d'Alcamo, the first known poet to compose in Italian, whose name graces the central sausage-shaped piazza.

Alcamo's notables put most of their economic surplus into an exceptionally fine clutch of churches. Piazza Ciullo is dominated by the massive dull **Collegiale**, but, at the other end, the elegant **Sant'Oliva** (1723; by Giovanni Biagio Amico) has a delightful Rococo interior containing two lovely works by the Gagini clan, a *Sant'Oliva* by Antonello and an *Annunciation* by Antonino and Giacomo. Alcamo's main street, Corso VI Aprile, passes along Sant'Oliva's flank; take it five blocks west for **SS. Paolo e Bartolomeo**, which has an interior from the same period, but in an entirely different mode, covered with colourful frescoes by an artist named Grano, and playful stucco putti by a crew led by Vincenzo Messina.

If you take the *corso* east from Sant'Oliva, you'll soon come to the **Chiesa Madre**, rebuilt in the 1700s but keeping its 14th-century campanile. Inside are a crowd of Gaginis, typically saccharine vault frescoes by Borremans and, near the presbytery, two stuccoes by Serpotta, who found plenty of patrons in Alcamo. Farther east on the same street you'll find two more of his allegories in **SS. Cosmo e Damiano**; the next church to the east, **San Tomaso**, dates from the quattrocento but has an excellent Gothic doorway from the previous century.

San Francesco, the last church on the *corso*, has a beautiful Gagini *Magdalene*. Behind it, the **Badia Nuova** lays claim to Alcamo's finest stuccoes by Serpotta –

Getting Around

Take the bus – Alcamo and Calatafimi have train stations, but the first is 5km from town, the second 3km. If you insist, there are about a dozen **trains** a day that connect the two with Tràpani and Palermo, only one in each direction stopping at Segesta's station, 20 minutes' walk from the site.

Buses run from Tràpani to Calatafimi, with a direct morning bus to Segesta (from Piazza Garibaldi); others stop at Alcamo en route to Palermo. From Alcamo you can reach the coast, by way of Alcamo Marina. There are also Segesta buses (**t** 0916 16 79 19) from Palermo to Calatafimi, Segesta and Alcamo.

AST buses (**t** 0923 23 222) run eight times a day (no service on Sunday from late Sept to early June) from Piazza Malta in Tràpani to Castellammare and San Vito Lo Capo. In summer there are direct Russo buses (**t** 0924 31 364) from Palermo's Piazza Marina to Castellammare, Scopello and San Vito Lo Capo (reduced service on Sundays).

Tourist Information

Alcamo: at the Biblioteca Comunale, Vicolo Grillo 5, **t** 09 24 59 02 87 (open Mon, Wed and Thurs 8–2 and 3.30–6.30; Tues and Fri 8–2).

Castellammare del Golfo: Via A de Gasperi 6, **t** 0924 59 21 11 (open Mon, Wed, Fri 9–2, Tues, Thurs 9–1 and 4–6).

San Vito Lo Capo: Via Savoia 58, **t** 0923 97 24 64 (open Oct–May Mon–Sat 9–1 and 5–7, June–Sept daily 9–1 and 4–midnight), www.sanvitolocapo.it.

Where to Stay and Eat

Alcamo ✉ 91011
Miramare, Corso Generale Medici 72, **t 09 24 21 197 (budget). A basic hotel on the edge of town.

Calatafimi ✉ 91013
*Mille Pini, Piazza Vivona 2, **t** 09 24 95 12 60, www.millepini.it (expensive). Offering the basics, along with a fine view over the mountains. Sicilian specialities are served in the trattoria for €15 or even less.

Castellammare del Golfo ✉ 91014
Castellammare del Golfo mainly caters for Sicilian families on holiday.

***Al Madarig (the Arab name for the town), Piazza Petrolo 7, **t** 0924 33 533, www.almadarig.com (moderate). This new seaside, air-conditioned hotel is the choice of Castellamare; it also has one of the best restaurants in town.

Punta Nord Est, Via Leonardo da Vinci 67, **t 0924 30 511, www.puntanordest.com (inexpensive–moderate). Big family hotel on the seafront with clean if somewhat impersonal rooms

---

allegorical figures as well as the saints around the altar. From here Via Navarro leads to the 14th-century **Castello dei Conti di Módica**, the citadel of Alcamo's feudal bosses, with Catalan Gothic windows and a rose window. The ruins of the Saracen castle of **Alqamah** are 5km up the road on pine-forested Monte Bonifato; here too is the **Madonna dell'Alto** chapel and a superb, panoramic view.

Below Alcamo, a short walk from the station will take you to the little **Stabilimento Gorga** (**t** 09 24 23 842; open daily 8.30am–midnight) with a natural hot-water pool..

Calatafimi

Travellers in days of yore knew Calatafimi as the nearest town to Segesta, although by their descriptions 'sinkhole' would be a more apt title. Whether or not they exaggerated is hard to tell: in January 1968 the earthquake known as the Terremoto del Bélice knocked most of Calatafimi over. It failed, however, to knock out the town's

Scopello ✉ 91010

There's no fussing for accommodation in Scopello – everything is one-star only.

La Tavernetta, Via A. Diaz 3, **t** 0924 54 11 29 (*budget–inexpensive*). This little *locanda* has air-conditioned rooms with bath.

Angelo Bed and Breakfast, Via Marco Polo 4, **t** 0923 531 667 *www.angelobedand breakfast.it* (*budget*). For rooms in the heart of Scopello.

★Torre Bennistra, Via Natale di Roma 19, **t** 0924 54 11 28 (*budget*) This place has also the best restaurant in town (*moderate*) serving *pasta con sarde e finocchiella* (with fried sardines and wild fennel), tagliatelle with shrimp, oven-cooked fish, and white wine from the hills of Alcamo.

★Tranchina, Via Diaz 7, **t/f** 0924 54 10 99 (*budget; restaurant moderate*). A few steps along from La Tavernetta is this restaurant-*pensione* serving *pasta con le fave* (fava beans), lentil dishes, fish soup and meat done over the open fire.

San Vito Lo Capo ✉ 91010

No lack of hotels and campsites here, but be warned that they tend to be packed to the gills from mid-July to September.

★★★★Capo San Vito, Via San Vito 1, **t** 0923 97 21 22, *wwwcaposanvito.it* (*expensive*). The top of the list, offering luxurious air-conditioned rooms on a private beach. *Closed Nov–Easter*.

★Ocean View, Via Gen. Arimondi 21, **t** 0923 97 26 13, *www.hotelsabbiadoro.it* (*budget–inexpensive*). A reasonable option, clean though basic.

★★Miraspiaggia, Via Lungomare 44, **t** 0923 97 22 63, *www.miraspiaggia.it* (*inexpensive*). The best among the numerous two-star pensions. Rooms have private balconies overlooking the beach.

★★★Hotel Mediterraneo, Via Gen. Arimondi 61, **t** 0923 621 062, *www.hotelmediterraneo online.com* (*budget*). North-African style hotel with a private beach.

★★Pocho, Contrada Macari, **t** 0923 972 325, *www.sicilian.net/pocho* (*budget*). At 4 km south of town this small, good-value hotel has friendly staff and a worthwhile restaurant.

El Bahira, **t** 0923 97 25 77, *www.elbahira.it*. One of Italy's four-star campsites, on the beach at Salinella near Mácari.

Camping Soleado, **t** 0923 97 21 66. A campsite usefully placed right on the beach at the edge of San Vito.

Alfredo, Zona Valanga, **t** 09 23 97 23 66 (*moderate*). San Vito has its own speciality, *busiati alla sanvitese*, a kind of homemade *fusilli* (corkscrew pasta) with tuna roe. This and other seafood specialities are served in Alfredo's garden. *Closed Mon and mid-Sept–mid-June*.

Thaam, Via Duca degli Abruzzi 32, **t** 09 23 97 28 36, *www.sanvitoweb.com/thaam* (*moderate*). One of the best places to eat couscous in Sicily, under a tented terrace or in the painstakingly tiled restaurant. They've opened a **hotel** (*inexpensive)* next door with nice and airy rooms.

Festa del Crocifisso, celebrated every three, four or five years in May since 1657. A miraculous Crucifix is the spiritual focal point of the procession, but there are good costumes, especially those of the Ceto delle Maestranze, an organization formed under the auspices of the Church in 1728 when the Bourbons passed a gun-control edict. They are immaculately dressed in black suits, white waistcoats and gloves – and carry rifles at their hips.

If Calatafimi's Ceto delle Maestranze thumbed its nose at the Bourbons, Garibaldi mangled them here on 15 May 1860. His famous Thousand, an untrained crew of students and industrial workers from the north (the youngest was 11, and one was a woman), were armed with a few rusty rifles, outdated muskets and bayonets, and had marched in four days in a roundabout route from Marsala where they had landed.

Waiting for them on the Pianta de Romano, just southwest of Calatafimi, stood a crack, newly armed professional Bourbon army. Garibaldi, perhaps the greatest romantic hero of the 19th century, never blinked, and against all odds his Thousand bayoneted their way to victory. The news of the unexpected Bourbon débâcle galvanized Italy and brought thousands of volunteers to Garibaldi's banner. The Bourbons had scarcely time to recover when, on 27 May, Garibaldi entered Palermo itself. In 1892 Ernesto Basile designed the **Pianta de Romano** obelisk commemorating the Battle of Calatafimi.

Segesta

Open daily 9am until one hour before sunset, adm.

Fortunately the earthquake that shook Calatafimi spared the striking, proud and lonely temple of Segesta. It's easy to reach from either the A29 or SS113, and is best seen either at 9am, when it opens, or very late in the afternoon, when the colours of the surrounding hills are deep and swallows swirl like mad things through the temple's empty spaces.

The city of Egesta, as it was originally known, is believed to have been founded on the slopes of Monte Barbaro in the 12th century BC by the Elymians, a shadowy people who claimed descent from the Trojans. Virgil puts them down as refugees who followed the hero Acestes (Egestus), and certainly the date fits the traditional fall of Troy. Thucydides claims the Trojans intermarried with the neighbouring Sikans to create a new race, the Elymian, which adopted Hellenic fashions (the earliest writings found at Egesta are in an unfathomable language but using Greek letters), although as people they never really got on with the Greeks – understandably enough if they were really Trojan. The Egestans certainly got their revenge for the Trojan horse.

The story begins in the 6th century BC, when Egesta began to quarrel over borders with the more powerful city state of Selinus (Selinunte). When Selinus allied itself with mighty Syracuse, the Egestans sent messengers to Athens (450 BC), boasting of their wealth and power, and offering a mutual self-help treaty. When Athens sent envoys to inspect these claims, the Egestans collected all the gold and silver drinking cups from their territory and secretly sent the whole lot around to each house the Athenians visited, tricking them into believing Egesta was exorbitantly wealthy. In 416 BC, new troubles flared up between Egesta and Selinus, and the Egestans invoked the treaty. Dutifully, the Athenians sent their Great Expedition to clobber Selinus and Syracuse, only to discover that Egesta had reneged on its promise to pay all the expenses for the venture. It was to be only the first of the Greeks' many Sicilian disappointments.

After the Athenians were devoured at Syracuse, the wily Egestans summoned their other great ally, one they had discreetly failed to mention to the Athenians: Carthage. The Carthaginians proved more effective by totally annihilating Selinus (409 BC), and they defended Egesta from the wrath of Dionysius of Syracuse. Revenge for Selinus had to wait over a hundred years, until 307 BC, when the tyrant Agathocles of Syracuse captured Egesta, slew 10,000 of its inhabitants, and sold the rest as slaves.

He repopulated it with Greeks and named it Dikaiopolis, but before long it drifted back to Carthage. When Rome took the upper hand in the First Punic War, the Egestans massacred the Punic garrison and pledged allegiance to Rome. The Romans, inveterate social climbers, were so proud to have these long-lost cousins of their own mythical founder Aeneas that they freed them from ever paying taxes. They also insisted for some unfathomable reason that the city put an S in front of its name. In the 10th century the Saracens wiped it off the map.

The Temple

The Egestans may have gone down in history (written by Greeks, mind you) as devious to the core, but they left behind one of Sicily's most majestic sights and one of the Mediterranean's great Hellenic wannabe monuments, the Doric temple of Segesta. The setting couldn't be more perfect, although the car park and the highway looping over the nearby hills have shattered the poetic solitude that so struck travellers when mules from Calatafimi were the only transport.

As no ancient writings about the temple have survived, it has fuelled a good deal of speculation. No one knows to which god it was dedicated, or why it was never finished (the 36 columns are unfluted, the cella and roof were never built, the knobby bits on the stairs, used to transport the stone, were never sawn off, no holes were left in the architrave for roof beams). The most recent exploration suggests that the Egestans abandoned work around 420 BC, destroying the old theory that the temple served some indigenous open-air Elymian cult. What may well have happened is this: the building was just a charade, another ploy to impress the Athenian envoys and flatter their Hellenic pride with a beautiful copy of a Greek temple. And once the Athenian war machine was imprisoned in the quarries of Syracuse and no further use to Egesta, the Elymians laid down their tools and walked away.

The Theatre

A map by the temple lays out the unexcavated town of Egesta, which was vast. If it's very hot, you may want to opt for the shuttle-bus for the 2.5km up Monte Barbaro to Segesta's second attraction, the theatre. Built in the 3rd century BC after the city fell to Agathocles, it measures 2,082ft in diameter and has 20 rows of seats that face north for an extraordinary view over the Golfo di Castellammare. The Laboratorio di Dramma Antica presents Greek and Roman plays in the summer of every odd year (in even years the plays are performed in Syracuse). Unfortunately, the ancient passage under the orchestra, from which actors could suddenly pop out from the 'underworld', is no longer in use.

There's a third site at Segesta, but it's a serious hike along the rough road east towards the hamlet of Magno. Here waits the sprawling, partly excavated, partly overgrown **Sanctuary of the Elymians**, where the real religious action took place. Although built in the 6th century BC, it was here that a large deposit of 8th-century BC potsherds was found, covered with mysterious Elymian inscriptions. Alternatively, you can perspire just as much sitting still at the sulphurous **Terme**

Segestane (*t 09 25 30 057; open daily 3–11pm*), 4km north at Ponte Bagni, said to have been much appreciated by the Greeks.

Castellammare and Scopello

Although there are beaches from Trappeto to Alcamo Marina, it's worth waiting for the fishing village of **Castellammare del Golfo** near the mouth of the River Freddo. The ancient port of Segesta, Castellammare has one monument: an **Aragonese castle** with a round tower, with sandy beaches on either side. Its present tranquillity belies its sordid Mafia past, when feuding inspired Mario Puzo to write *The Godfather*, and an estimated one in three men in town had committed at least one murder.

West of Castellammare, **Scopello** ('reef' in Greek) has a long, sheltered pebble and sand beach and an irresistible picture-postcard pocket-size port packed with Palermitani on weekends. The little seaside hamlet grew up around a *tonnara* (tuna trap), first documented in the 1200s and only recently abandoned. Two so-called **Saracen towers** defend it still. The upper part of the village, or Scopello di Sopra, grew up around an 18th-century *baglio*, a manor house with a huge courtyard with a fountain, now occupied by a ceramics manufacturer, bars and *trattorie*.

Riserva Naturale dello Zingaro

Open daily 8.30am until one hour before sunset.

In 1981, the 7km of plunging marble shore north of Scopello was designated the Riserva Naturale dello Zingaro, the haunt of kestrels, Bonelli's eagles, and peregrine falcons. Ironically it owes its pristine state to the Mafia. For decades its coves, crannies and delicious beaches were the mob's private drug-smuggling base, and no developer would touch it with a ten-foot pole. In the 1970s the government decided to force a road along the coast – one of the last virgin stretches in Sicily – and in 1976 managed to build a half-mile stretch before environmental groups occupied the area and rallied enough opposition to kill the project. However the battles continues as every year arsonists try to push the project through and in the summer of 2003 were successful in burning some 40 per cent of the reserve.

Leave your car in the car parks at either the Scopello or San Vito entrances (note that the San Vito entrance is 20km from civilization: don't get stuck walking south–north and hoping to find transport late in the day). There are several paths of varying difficulty, taking in an extraordinary variety of landscapes; drinking water exists but is rare. Clumps of dwarf palms are the most common plant, but there are some 600 others, several endemic to the area (pick up the detailed free brochure published by the Worldwide Fund for Nature and Sicilian forestry service). To the dismay of the nature-lovers, most visitors come for the beautiful beaches: from south to north they are Punta di Capreria Grande, Cala Marinella, and the two sandy strands at Uzzo, near a ruined *tonnara* and its watchtower.

San Vito Lo Capo

Since you can't drive through the nature reserve, you have to circle 24km around to the west to reach the towns along the cape of San Vito – approaching from the east, turn off at Baglio Messina. It isn't long before the looming promontory of Monte Cófano comes into view, the twin of Palermo's Monte Pellegrino. Botanists know it for its rare flora, including 19 endemic species. Castelluzzo is the chief town near Monte Cófano, but it's the little medieval hamlet of **Scurati** that sticks in the mind, its recently abandoned houses and paved street sheltered in a cave. Two other grottoes near Castelluzzo, **Miceli** and **Mangipane**, have Upper Paleolithic graffiti. The nearest beach, **Cornino**, has striking views over the promontory; it is 2km below Custonaci, where Cófano's marble is quarried.

After skirting Monte Cófano, the road rejoins the coast by the bizarre rock forma-
tions of **Mácari**, then continues up to San Vito Lo Capo, a sugar-cube village at the tip of the mountainous cape. With a long beach of white sand that takes on rosy tints in the setting sun, and another promontory, Monte Mónaco, as a dramatic backdrop, it has had little trouble evolving from a coral fishery and *tonnara* to a seaside resort. The old Saracen castle in the centre of town was converted long ago into the church of **San Vito**, the patron saint of epilepsy and nervous disorders. Legend goes that the persecuted S. Vito fled Mazara only to be caught by a severe storm but managed to take haven in the bay sheltered by the promontory now called S. Vito Lo Capo.

Although the present town of San Vito was laid out in the 18th century, the Phoenicians and Romans were here, while some time around 12,000 BC inhabitants decorated the **Grotta Racchio** west of town with deer and human figures. Next door to the tourist information office is the **Museo del Mare** (*open Oct–May Mon–Sat 9–1 and 5–7, June–Sept daily 9–1 and 4–midnight*), which contains the cargo of a 12th-
century Norman ship which sunk in the vicinity – mainly amphorae and anchors. The town comes out for processions and great festivities in honour of its patron saint on 15 June. In the third week of September, San Vito Lo Capo hosts the **Festival Internazionale del Cuscus** (five days), with free tastings.

Erice

Suspended 2,495ft above Tràpani and the sea on Monte San Giuliano, Erice is one of the great landmarks in the western Mediterranean. The locals claim that, on the clearest of days, you can make out Cape Bon in Tunisia and the very summit of Etna. It is also one of Italy's most beautiful medieval villages, one that could easily pass for a hill town in Umbria, and certainly, when the fog curls around the mountain, it isn't hard to imagine yourself in that misty, mystical hilly region in the centre of Italy. And no wonder: Erice has been a holy place since the dawn of time. Although now clearly marked on western Sicily's tourist maps, it still has an uncanny atmosphere, perme-
ated with the eerie silence that marks many ancient religious sites. This is in spite of the fact that Erice has gone over to science in a big way, hosting a calendar of

Getting There

Buses from Tràpani make a circular route via Paparella to Erice in about an hour (about 14 daily). If you're **driving**, there's parking just outside Erice's walls.

Tourist Information

Viale Conte Pepoli 11, near the Porta Tràpani, t 0923 86 93 88 (*open Mon–Sat 8–2*).

Where to Stay

Erice ✉ 91016

There are few things more atmospheric than staying up at Erice and strolling its silent, misty lanes when the day-trippers have gone. ★★★**Elimo**, Via Vittorio Emanuele 75, t 0923 86 93 77, *www.charmerelax.com* (*expensive*). Offers 21 lovely rooms near the centre, with beams, marble fittings and old tiles, and superb views from its rooms and terraces (the car park at Porta Tràpani is a short walk away; leave your car there rather than try to negotiate the narrow lanes).
★★★**Moderno**, Via V. Emanuele 63, t 0923 86 93 00, *www.pippocatalano.it* (*moderate*). Larger, recently renovated, boasting a magnificent roof terrace and an excellent restaurant specializing in fish couscous.
★★**Edelweiss**, Cortile P. Vincenzo, t 0923 86 94 20 (*inexpensive–moderate*). Cosy, quiet and central, with 13 rooms; mountain views.
★★★**Baglio Santa Croce**, Contrada Ragosia da Santa Croce, ✉ 91019, t 0923 89 11 11 (*moderate*). Down the mountain 9km east of Erice, in Valderice, this wonderfully atmospheric old farm dates from the 17th century. Rooms, furnished with antiques, have their original terracotta tiles and beams. There's a pool, a delightful citrus grove and a fine restaurant.
Maria Luisa, Via Luigi Barberi, 347 789 36 51 *web.tiscali.it/bberice* (*budget*). A pretty bed and breakfast in the heart of Erice, just next door to the Madre church. English is spoken.
Ostello della Gioventù, Viale delle Pinete, t 0923 86 91 44 (*budget*). Has small dormitory rooms by the Campo Sportivo.

Eating Out

Monte San Giuliano, Vicolo San Rocco 7, t 0923 86 95 95 (*moderate*). Another of Erice's best; try the chef's speciality, *busiati al pesto trapanese*, and the seafood. *Closed Mon.*
Taverna di Re Aceste, Viale Conte Pepoli 45, t 0923 869 084 (*moderate*). Long one of the best in Erice, serving *spaghetti alle vongole*, good *couscous* and other Trapanese specialities. *Closed Wed.*
La Prima Dea, Corso V. Emanuele 17, t 0923 86 92 23 (*inexpensive*). Although it looks more touristy, this restaurant is less expensive and a good bet if *antipasti* are your favourite part of a meal. *Closed Mon in Oct–May.*
Pasticceria Maria Grammatico, Corso V. Emanuele. Here you can recharge on heavenly *sospiri* ('sighs') and other delights made with almonds and dried fruit; the shop will mail treats back home for you.

important international congresses every year at its Centro di Cultura Scientifica Ettore Majorana.

Don't come up to Erice unprepared. Wear sturdy shoes to negotiate its rough cobbled streets, and bring something warm: on average Erice is 10°F cooler than Tràpani down below.

History

When Zeus castrated his father with the sickle that became Tràpani, his genitals fell into the sea and gave birth to the goddess of love – the Phoenician Astarte, Greek Aphrodite, or Roman Venus, the orgiastic queen bee goddess of the western

Mediterranean, surnamed Erycina, 'of the heather'. Her temple at Erice (ancient Eryx) was known far and wide in the classical world. It was the holy of holies for the shadowy Elymians; after all, Venus Erycina married Anchises and became the mother of Aeneas, the hero of the Trojan race, from whom the Elymians claimed descent. Virgil mentions the temple as a landmark in the *Aeneid*. And there is a Sicilian story as well: to make her lover Adonis jealous, Venus spent several nights in Lilybaeum with Butes 'the bee-keeper', an Argonaut whom she had rescued when he jumped overboard to join the Sirens. She thus became the mother of Eryx, king of the Elymians, who founded her cult on this mountain. A later legend tells how Eryx met an abrupt end when Hercules, herding the stolen cattle of Geryon in one of his Labours, found one had strayed on to Eryx's land. In the ensuing wrestling match over the cow, Hercules dashed Eryx to the ground and killed him – a fabricated story to justify several 6th-century BC colonies in the area, founded by Greeks who claimed descent from big Herc.

Not surprisingly, Erice long had a reputation for being impregnable, but in 260 BC Hamilcar Barca seized and destroyed Eryx and moved its population down to Drepanon/Tràpani. The Romans captured it not long after and sent 200 armed slaves to guard the sanctuary; later Tiberius and Claudius rebuilt the temple. When the Arabs captured the town, they too felt the holiness of the place and named it Gebel Hamed (Mohammed's mountain). While besieging it, Count Roger ran into some difficulty, and called upon St Julian for assistance. Julian obliged by sending a white horseman in a halo of light, which frightened the Saracens and did the trick, and in gratitude Roger renamed the town Monte San Giuliano. In 1934 Mussolini re-christened it Erice.

A Stroll through Erice

The fact that Erice is shaped like an equilateral triangle has itself provoked a certain amount of mystical mumbo-jumbo. You scarcely notice it at street level, however: the ancient lanes and stairs twist back and forth and you can easily spend a few hours exploring crannies and *vanelle*, alleys that are so narrow that only one person at a time can pass down them. The houses have secretive stone façades, but when the doors are open they reveal delightful courtyards full of flowers, cats and sometimes a pretty girl. Whether or not the goddess of love has a hand in the matter, the women of Erice have long had a reputation for their looks. As the Arab geographer Ibn Jubair wrote: 'They are said to be the loveliest of the whole island – may Allah deliver them into the hands of the Faithful!' They are also famous for their brightly coloured *frazzate*, carpets with geometric designs: you can find them, and the old wooden looms they are made on, at **Bottega di Penelope**, at Via Cordici 10.

Erice is entered by way of the Porta Tràpani, built, like all of the town's walls and gates, by the Normans over 8th-century BC Elymian fortifications. Just north of the gate is the **cathedral** (*open daily 9–12 and 3–6*), the most important of Erice's 10 churches, founded by Frederick of Aragon in 1312, with a campanile that long did duty as a watchtower. The façade and porch date from 1426 but the dimly lit interior was redone in 1865. Its chief treasure is a beautiful *Madonna and Child* attributed to Francesco Laurana.

Via Vittorio Emanuele, Erice's former Via Regia, leads into Piazza Umberto I, where the Municipio houses the small **Museo Comunale Cordici** (*open Mon–Sat 8.30–1.30 and 3–5*), with a lovely *Annunciation* by Antonello Gagini, a 4th-century BC head of Aphrodite, Punic and Greek bronze sculptures, and coins from ancient Eryx inscribed with doves. White doves were sacred to the goddess and lived in her temple, and would be released every year in the direction of Erice's sister shrine, the temple of Astarte at Sicca Vernia (Tunisia). The doves inevitably returned nine days later with a red dove, a symbol of fertility, in the lead.

The Castello di Vénere
Open daily 8–1.30 and 3.30–6.30.

Dominating the easternmost corner of town, above the communal Giardino del Balio, are two medieval towers, the **Torretta Pepoli** and the **Castello di Vénere**, the last with stupendous views over the Egadi Islands. When Count Roger conquered Erice, he ordered the destruction of all traces of the pagan temple to Venus, and his Normans did their work well, cannibalizing the stone for their walls and this castle. Now only the base remains of the temple of Venus Erycina on the northeast side. Unlike most Greek temples, which are oriented east–west, this temple was aligned northeast–southwest, perhaps with the rising of the midsummer sun, an important event in the bee-goddess cult.

Diodorus Siculus wrote that the base and walls of the sanctuary were strengthened by Daedalus, who subsequently offered the goddess a golden honeycomb he had crafted perfectly to resemble a real honeycomb. It was only one of the many golden treasures stored here – treasures that the Elymians of Segesta borrowed to dupe the Athenians (*see* p.115). As in the sanctuaries of Venus in Corinth and Cyprus, the real allure for Greek and Phoenician sailors and togaed Roman senators on holiday were the *ierodules*, the temple's sacred prostitutes, who plied their trade along what is now Via San Francesco.

Tràpani

It is said that Tràpani arose on the sickle that Ceres dropped while she wandered desperately around the world seeking her daughter Persephone, ravished by Pluto, or alternately that it was created by Saturn, who deliberately came down from Mount Olympos to found it. What is certain is that numerous more or less real or imaginary peoples settled here.

Excerpt from a Tràpani tourist brochure

For whatever reason, be it Saturnian or leftover weirdness bequeathed by the slightly more tangible Elymian founders from lofty Erice, Tràpani does have a dream-like air to it. Several of its anonymous streets come straight out of a De Chirico

Tràpani

N

250 metres
250 yards

Torre di Ligny

Tyrrhenian Sea

VIA TORRE DI LIGNY

VIA CAROLINA

PIAZZA SCALO D'ALLAGIO

PIAZZA SCIO

VIA COLOMBO

VIALE DUCA D'AOSTA

VIA CORALIA

VIA N. NASI

CORSO VITTORIO EMANUELE

Pescheria

VIA LIBERTA

VIA TENENTE GENOVESE

S. Lorenzo

VIA TINTORI

VIA GEN. GIGLIO

Collegio dei Gesuiti

S. Francesco

VIA D

VIA S. FRANCESCO D'ASSISI

Palazzo Cavaretta

VIA TORREARSA

Font di Sa

Purgatorio

VIALE REGINA ELENA

PIAZZA GARIBALDI

S. Agostino

Lazzaretto

Molo di Sanità

Port

painting. Vast salt pans stretch to the south, shallow and empty, dotted with wind-mill giants worthy of a seaborne Quixote.

Piled on its narrow hook of land beckoning towards Tunis, Tràpani's name is derived from the Greek *drepanon* ('sickle'). The satirist Samuel Butler produced some clever if wacky arguments that the *Odyssey*, more novel than epic, was written in Drepanon by a woman, perhaps named Nausicaa, whose purpose was to displace the original myths in order to 'whitewash Penelope'. Another English writer, Robert Graves teased the idea even further in his own novel, *Homer's Daughter*.

Because of its proximity to Africa, Tràpani's fortunes began in the Crusades. The city made the big time in the 1500s, when the port of Marsala, its chief rival in western Sicily, was blocked up by Charles V. Crowned heads of Europe popped in and out with some regularity: King Theobald of Navarre died in Tràpani in 1270 from a Tunisian fever; Edward I landed here on his return from the Crusades and learned that he had

inherited the throne of England; Peter of Aragon disembarked here in 1282 to accept the crown after the Sicilian Vespers; Emperor Charles V arrived in Tràpani after conquering Tunis, and granted it special privileges.

For centuries, Tràpani's chief industries produced tuna (canned tuna was invented here), salt and carved coral knick-knacks; but only the salt industry remains. Tràpani was once the semi-glamorous seaside town preferred by the Mafia, but that presence has faded as well. Tourism is minimal, but to pass straight through for the Egadi Islands or Erice would be to miss the discreet charms of one of Italy's quirkiest provincial capitals.

Corso Vittorio Emanuele

Although Tràpani's postwar sprawl is as bland as any in Italy, with streets that seem wide and empty after the craziness of Palermo, the historic centre on the narrow

Getting There and Around

By Air
Tràpani is served by flights to Palermo, Rome and Pantelleria. The airport is at Birgi, 23km south, t 0923 84 25 02. A bus goes there from the bus station on Piazza Montalto.

By Sea
Tràpani is the principal port for the Egadi Islands (see pp.127–37), with **ferries** and **hydrofoils** every day. Tirrenia (t 0923 21 896) has a ferry to Tunisia every Monday at 9am which takes about 7hrs. For a shorter passage, but only in high season, Ustica lines (t 0923 27 397) has hydrofoils several times a week.

By Train
Trains run to Alcamo, Castelvetrano, Mazara del Vallo, Palermo, Segesta, Marsala and Agrigento (connection in Palermo) from Stazione Centrale in Piazza Umberto I, t 0923 28 071.

By Bus
The bus station is near the train station, in what was once Piazza Malta, now Piazza Giacomo Giaccio-Montalto, or, more simply and to the point, autostazione. Segesta goes to Palermo and Alcamo (t 0923 21 956, t 09 16 16 79 19); AST to Erice and San Vito Lo Capo (t 0923 21 021); Lumia to Agrigento and Sciacca (a slower bus also stops in Marsala, Mazara del Vallo and Castelvetrano, t 09 22 20 414);

Tarantola goes to Segesta, Calatafimi and Castellammare del Golfo (t 09 24 31 020).

Tourist Information

Piazza Saturno, t 0923 29 000 (open Mon–Sat 8–8, Sun 9–12 and 3–6). www.apt.trapani.it
Boat tours: You can tour the seas off the Riserva Naturale dello Zingaro on the Leonardo Da Vinci, t 09 24 34 222.

Where to Stay

Tràpani ✉ 91100

Expensive–Luxury
★★★★**Crystal**, Piazza Umberto I, t 0923 20 000, www.framonhotels.com (expensive–luxury). This dazzling place in front of the station has every creature comfort, and would be more suited to Texas.

Inexpensive
Agriturismo Duca di Castelmonte, Via Salvatore Motisi 3, Xitta, t 0923 52 61 39, www.ducadicastelmonte.it. You'll need a car stay at this nicely converted baglio just outside town. It comes with pool, children's play area and an assemblage of farm animals.
★★**Cavallino Bianco**, Lungomare D. Alighieri, t 0923 21 549, www.initalia.it. If you have a car this is a good choice by the sea.

sickle is well kept and secretive. Its long straight spine, Corso Vittorio Emanuele, was laid out in the 1200s and is closed off at its east end by the grandly Baroque **Palazzo Cavaretta** (or Senatorio, 1701), with its columns, statues and plaques recalling Garibaldi's cry of 'Rome or death!' from the balcony in 1860. Here Tràpani is only a few streets wide: north along Via Torrearsa are the arcades of the restored fishmarket, the **Pescheria**, and south is the port for the islands.

Tucked just behind Palazzo Cavaretta is a little piazza named after its **Fontana di Saturno** (1342), honouring the presumed father of Tràpani. Here, too, is stark **Sant'Agostino**, a Templars' church of the same period. The syncretic Templars must have felt at home in Sicily, with its traditions of tolerance and learning, although this is one of the few buildings associated with them to survive on the island. Tràpani has far more ornate churches, but the rose window of Sant'Agostino burns in the memory – an Islamic geometric pattern of arabesques, converging in a mystical vortex.

***Nuovo Albergo Russo**, Via Tintori 4, t 0923 22 166. On the main pedestrian street; some rooms overlook the cathedral.

***Vittoria**, Via F. Crispi 4, t 0923 87 30 44, *www.hotelvittoriatrapani.it*. Offers comfortable, air-conditioned rooms closer to the sea; the higher up, the better the view.

Budget

****Ai Lumi**, Corso V. Emanuele 71, t 0923 87 24 18, *www.ailumi.it*. Just three rooms in a 18th-century *palazzo* overlooking a quiet courtyard and centrally located. The friendly owners of this B&B give guests a discount to eat at their restaurant next door.

****Maccotta**, Via degli Argentieri 4, t 0923 28 418. Just behind the Palazzo Senatorio, with nine rooms.

Ostello G. Amodeo, 2km along the road to Erice, t 0923 55 29 64 (*dorms and private rooms*). Open to all, its rooms offering a fine view over the sea. You'll need transport to get here, though.

Eating Out

Couscous served with broth and a variety of fish is the speciality of Tràpani, usually eaten at noon as a first course; other fish, especially swordfish, is often served with a sauce of cucumbers, olives, celery and capers.

P & G, Via Spalti 1, t 0923 54 77 01 (*expensive*). Tràpani's swordfish speciality is delicious here; other dishes include a wide variety of *antipasti* and the local pasta favourite *busiate al pesto trapanese*, finishing up with a fine example of Sicilian *cassata*. *Closed Wed*.

Ai Lumi, Corso V. Emanuele 75, t 0923 87 24 18 (*moderate*). An elegant old tavern frequented mostly by locals and serving some of Tràpani's best food. *Closed Sun*.

Da Felice (or Trattoria del Porto), Via A. Staiti 45, t 0923 54 78 22 (*moderate*). You can sit outside and watch the day trippers pour off the island ferries as you tuck into some excellent, reasonably priced food at this very popular *trattoria*. *Closed Mon and Sept–June*.

Taverna Paradiso, Lungomare Alighieri 22, t 0923 22 303 (*moderate*). This place close to the fish market offers the freshest seafood and fish. Try the *spaghetti ai ricci* (sea urchin).

Calvino, Via N. Nasi 77, t 0923 21 464. (*inexpensive*). Here they make delicious pizzas to eat in or take away. *Closed Mon*.

Safina, Piazza Umberto I, t 0923 22 708 (*inexpensive*). Often serving couscous, this is one of the least expensive places in town, across from the station. *Closed Mon*.

Gelateria Gino, Piazza C. A. Della Chiesa 4, t 0923 22 502. Infinite variety of ice-cream flavours, but the local speciality to try is jasmine.

Pasticceria 900, Via Fardella 84, t 0923 22 502. With the very best cakes and pastries in Tràpani, cookie monsters should come here to gratify a sweet tooth. *Closed Mon*.

The *corso* itself is punctuated by two Baroque statements, or rather exclamation marks: first, the **Collegio dei Gesuiti** (1636) by Natale Masuccio, a Jesuit from Messina, whose grotesque masks and caryatids add movement and zest to the prim order of columns, pilasters and broken pediments; and second, a few steps down, the cathedral **San Lorenzo** (1635), an undulating building hemmed in, in 1740, by an angular portico with a cupola by Giovanni Biagio Amico. Amico was also responsible for the church **Purgatorio** (1683; *open Tues 10–12, Fri 10–12 and 5–7*), just south on Via Gen. Giglio, although it seems as if the saints on the façade themselves are the ones in purgatory, wasting away and amputated by time. Come to see the 21 life-size wooden figures of the Misteri, mostly carved in the 18th century and each representing a scene from the Passion. Owned by Tràpani's guilds, on Good Friday they make their annual outing with brass bands in one of Sicily's best-loved Easter festivals (*open daily 4–6.30*).

West of the Purgatorio, on Via San Francesco d'Assisi, past the forlorn 17th-century prison with its four leprous telamones, the church of **San Francesco** has a fine wooden Crucifix by Trapanese sculptor Millanti, who also made the stucco virtues lining the nave. Farther west, on the very northern tip of the sickle, the Torre di Ligny was erected to honour the arrival of Sicily's Spanish viceroy in 1671, and now houses the **Museo del Mare and the Museo di Preistoria** (*closed at the time of writing*), a fine collection of fossils, and palaeontological and archaeological finds from across Tràpani province, including photographs from Levanzo's Grotta del Genovese if you don't have the time or energy to see the real McCoy.

Around Santa Maria del Gesù

The old quarter north of Via A. Staiti took the most licks from Allied bombs. One landed square on the convent of **Santa Maria del Gesù** in Corso Italia, but the church founded by Emperor Charles V was spared, along with its Renaissance door and its chief treasure, the lovely terracotta *Madonna of the Angels* by Andrea della Robbia, protected by a marble baldacchino by Antonello Gagini (1521).

Tràpani's ghetto lay to the north of Corso Italia, and there you'll find the **Palazzo della Giudecca**, built by a noble Jewish family, the Ciambra. One of the most important Jewish buildings to survive the Spanish-decreed expulsion of 1492, it was often rebuilt, in the 16th century with Spanish Plateresque windows, grimacing faces and nubby diamond-pointed stones. Farther north, near Via Garibaldi, **San Domenico** (*open daily 3.30–7*) was rebuilt in the 17th century but conserves many traces of its medieval origins: its rose window and apse, containing the sarcophagus of Manfredi, son of Frederick III of Aragon (1318); 14th-century frescoes in two chapels; and, in a polychromatic marble extravaganza by Giovanni Biagio Amico, a 13th-century Spanish *Crucifixion*. It has recently been restored and converted into an exhibition space and conference centre, but the decorations are still there to be admired.

At the end of Via Garibaldi is the **post office**, an elaborate Liberty-style confection from 1924, and, just beyond, the public garden, **Villa Margherita**, with a small zoo for the tykes (*open dawn to dusk*), and opera *alfresco* in the summer for the grown-ups.

The Santuario dell'Annunziata

It's a long boring walk or a short bus ride (no.25 from Piazza Umberto I) out along Via G. Fardella and Via Conte Pepoli to Tràpani's holy of holies, the **Santuario dell'Annunziata** (*open daily 7–12 and 4–7*), a church founded in 1315 to house a lovely sweetly smiling marble Madonna, a product of the great medieval Pisan school of sculpture, and perhaps even from the chisel of Nino Pisano himself. This Madonna was the most precious treasure of a Pisan Knight of Jerusalem, who commissioned her and took her to the Holy Land. It wasn't long before the Saracens made it hot for the Christians there and, to keep his statue safe, the knight decided to return with it to Pisa. Off Tràpani a storm brewed; the knight prayed to his Madonna and she landed the ship safely in port. Then, according to the Pisans, the Trapanese absconded with their miraculous Madonna; according to the Trapanese, the knight had vowed to leave her at the first place they came to shore. By building her a church so far inland, the good burghers at least made certain the Pisans would have a hard time stealing her back.

As an important pilgrimage shrine, the Annunziata has often been altered. The delicate rose window and Norman Gothic door survive from the early 1400s, and the ponderous campanile was added in 1650. Although the interior was unfortunately redone in 1750, three chapels escaped. Two especially ornate ones were built out of tufa in the 16th century, one dedicated by fishermen and the other by sailors; the Madonna's own chapel is coated with coloured marbles and framed in a marble arch carved with prophets and sibyls by Antonino and Giacomo Gagini (1537).

Museo Regionale Pepoli

Open Mon – Sat 9–1.30 and 4–8; Sun 9–12.30; adm.

Adjacent to the Annunziata, the imposing 16th-century Carmelite convent now houses the Museo Regionale Pepoli, named after its benefactor, Count Pepoli, whose obsession it was to collect the decorative arts and crafts of western Sicily, especially works in coral from the 16th to 19th centuries, when coral-fishers could rake it in by the pound from the great reefs off Tràpani and San Vito Lo Capo. Now practically extinct in the region, Tràpani's coral survives in extraordinary dust magnets that were once the rage in Europe, mostly carved by local artists: reliquaries, Christmas cribs (including a charming one from the 18th century, combined with marble, shell and gold), holy plaques and two virtuoso pieces from the 1630s by a Franciscan named Matteo Bavera – a tall hanging lamp in coral, copper and enamel, and a perfectly tasteless Crucifix, with the figure of Christ carved from one large piece of coral, on a cross of ebony and mother-of-pearl.

Besides the count's vast collections of silverwork, *presepi* (Christmas crib figures) and other bric-a-brac, the museum offers an archaeological section; a flock of Gagini sculptures, starring Antonello's *St James the Greater* (1522); and a painting gallery featuring Counter-reformation religious blood and guts, a *St Francis Receiving the Stigmata* (1530) by Titian, a serene 15th-century panel from the Maestro of the Tràpani Triptych, and a *Pietà* (1380), one of the most important surviving works by the southern Italian Roberto di Oderisio.

The Egadi Islands

The three members of the Egadi archipelago – Favignana, Levanzo and Maréttimo – are just a hop and a skip off the west coast of Tràpani. Each has a unique beauty and personality of its own. Favignana, the largest and by far the most populated, is the island of tufa, tuna and tourism; dinky Levanzo is dry and rocky, but has the prize Palaeolithic engravings; mountainous Maréttimo has fascinating rock formations and sea grottoes, and a fishing village scarcely touched by the passing of time.

As islands go, all are relative newcomers. Maréttimo, the farthest out, was split apart from Sicily 600,000 years ago during the Quaternary period, while Favignana and Levanzo, both inhabited by 10,000 BC, were parted from Sicily *c.* 5000 BC, a

Getting There

Tràpani is the principal port for the Egadi Islands (*see* pp.127–137). SIREMAR (Via A. Staiti, **t** 0923 27 780, *www.siremar.it*) runs **hydrofoils** (*aliscafi*) and **ferries** (*traghetti*) to the Egadi Islands. Hydrofoils leave from Molo Dogana, taking 20–60mins; ferries leave from Molo Sanitá, taking 1–3hrs. A third ferry serving the Egadi Islands when you least expect it, is a cadmium yellow tub called the *Vulcano* (two

trips daily in winter, three in summer), which sells tickets on board or through the offices of EGATOUR (Via A. Staiti 13, **t** 0923 21 754). From Marsala there's a daily *motonave* service to Favignana and Levanzo (**t** 0923 95 34 34).

The only island even to consider bringing your **car** to is Favignana. However you go, you're better off buying a one-way ticket: both companies have the same prices, and you never know which one will have the departure you want.

divorce caused not only by earthquakes but by the melting of glaciers and subsequent rise in sea level. Only the highest hills in between have kept their heads above water. These uninhabited islets are called the Formiche ('ants'), although one is crowned by an abandoned tuna cannery.

History

The earliest human traces on the islands are concentrated in the caves of Favignana and Levanzo, many of which remained inhabited up to the 18th century AD. Nothing left by the later residents, however, can match the first graceful incisions in Levanzo's Grotta del Genovese, where 12,000 years ago Upper Palaeolithic artists drew bulls, fluid dancing figures, an ass and a deer. Later Neolithic artists added their simple black and red paintings that look crude in comparison.

The Egadi Islands, sitting on an important Africa–Europe trade route, were colonized by the Phoenicians, although they were never as important as Motya just to the south (*see* pp.144–7). During the 20 years of the First Punic War, the islands witnessed many sea battles between Rome and Carthage, including the greatest one in 241 BC, when both Rome and Carthage decided to stake their fleets on a great showdown at Lilybaeum (Marsala). The two armadas met just northeast of Favignana, the Romans with 200 new warships, the Carthaginians with 400 ships crammed full of soldiers coming to succour and reinforce Lilybaeum. Before the Carthaginians could reach land, however, the Romans demolished them, sinking 120 ships and capturing 10,000 prisoners. So many dead Phoenicians washed ashore at Favignana that their blood dyed the sea red, giving Cala Rossa ('red cove') its name.

Although the islanders adopted Roman ways, at least on the surface, several inscriptions from the 1st century BC found in Favignana's grottoes are in Punic characters. These same grottoes bear the graffiti symbols of the first Christians (4th and 5th centuries). One inscription found in the Grotta della Stele was linguistically important for determining the evolution of languages in the Mediterranean, as well as offering an insight into the pathetic life of the island's troglodytes: translated it means 'House, tomb, stable'.

After the decline of Rome, the Egadi Islands vanish from history. The Saracens used them as a base for their conquest of Sicily; the Normans fortified Favignana and

Maréttimo. Under the Aragonese, the islands were hired out as a port of call for Genoese merchants, and in the 15th century they were granted to Giovanni de Karissima, who took the proud title 'Baron of Tuna'.

The Spanish were the first to exploit the great banks of coral around the islands, although all the profits went to Tràpani. Spain's never-ending wars caused ever-increasing debts, and to help pay them off the Spanish sold the Egadi Islands to the Marquis Pallavicino of Genoa in 1637. The Pallavicini did much to develop the islands economically and, for the first time, the Favignanese were able to leave their caves to found a town around the Castello San Giacomo (the modern penitentiary).

In the latter half of the 19th century, Favignana had its golden age, thanks to its new tuna canneries and tufa quarries, the stone being exported to Tunisia and Libya. Between the wars, however, the economy nosedived, and many islanders emigrated to northern Italy and the New World. Only the advent of tourism in the late 1960s and 1970s has turned the tide of decline and kept at least some of the young people at home.

Favignana

A charmer of many names – the Phoenician Katria, the Greek Aegusa and the medieval Faugnana (from 'Favonio', the name of a wind) – Favignana is the biggest (at 7sq miles) and most populated (3,500 souls) of the Egadis. Tourist brochures emphasize the island's butterfly shape, although the 'wings' hardly match – the eastern wing is a level plain pitted with abandoned tufa excavations, and the western wing is mountainous. Visit in May or June and you can watch the ancient ritual of the tuna kill, the *mattanza* (contact the tourist office in Tràpani).

Favignana Town

Sun-bleached Favignana is a bright, busy tufa town that effortlessly combines the needs of its residents with the café and *gelateria* requirements of its visitors. As you sail into port, however, the first buildings you'll notice are empty and melancholy: the large tuna canneries by a rocky beach and the proud mansion of their founder, the **Palazzo Florio**. Built in 1876, and surrounded by a scraggly garden with only two palms and a pine tree, it is a symbol of fallen grandeur.

Ignazio Florio, scion of the Marsala dynasty, bought the Egadi Islands from the last of the Pallavicini in 1874 and applied his father's industrial know-how to invent canned tuna. He built canneries on Favignana and the islet of Formica, handsome Alhambras of industry complete with soaring arches, vaults and ogival doors. His son Vincenzo, through high living and personal tragedy, lost the business to a Genoese company in 1937. Now the galleries of Florio's canneries are empty and haunted; the haul from Favignana's *mattanza* is either served fresh or exported. It is a gourmet item (honestly, it is more delicious than any tinned tuna you've ever tasted before) and available at special stands in Favignana town.

Getting Around

Three **bus** lines departing regularly from the port cover most of the asphalted roads on Favignana. At least a dozen shops in town hire out **bikes**, the favourite mode of transport among locals and visitors alike.

Tourist Information

Pro Loco, Piazza Matrice 8, t 0923 92 16 47 (*open April–Oct Mon–Sat 9–12 and 5–8, Sun 9.30–12*), *www.egadi.com*.

Where to Stay

Favignana ✉ 91023

Favignana is the only Egadi Island equipped to handle a large number of visitors. The tourist office has a list of private rooms and mini-flats.

***L'Approdo di Ulisse, Cala Grande, t 0923 922 525, *www.apprododiulisse.it* (*moderate–expensive*). One of two isolated resort hotels with pretensions along the coast; a favourite with scuba divers. *Closed Oct–May.*

**Aegusa, Via Giuseppe Garibaldi 11, t 0923 92 24 20, *www.aegusahotel.it* (*inexpensive*). A *palazzo* transformed into hotel, and with its own restaurant.

**Egadi, Via Cristoforo Colombo 17, t/f 0923 92 12 32 (*inexpensive*). Recently spruced up, this is one of the better choices in town. The restaurant is rather plain but the food is some of the finest in Sicily (*expensive*).

Villaggio Quattro Rose, t 0923 92 12 23 (*moderate; half board mandatory*). Halfway to Lido Burrione, on the C. Molino a Vento, this tourist village has a strip of motel rooms, Favignana's cheapest campsite, with shade, a restaurant, discotheque and a 'singing room' for playing music, including Sicilian songs.

Miramare, Strada Provinciale Punta Sottile, *www.villaggiomiramare.it*, t 0923 92 22 00. A four-star campsite 1km from town towards the beach, with bungalows on the beach and windsurf rentals.

Eating Out

Expect to see plenty of tuna fish prepared in a hundred different styles, along with swordfish and Trapanese couscous. There are also snack bars at Cala Azzurra and Burrone.

El Pescador, Piazza Europa 38, t 0923 92 10 35 (*moderate*). A good restaurant: do order their special spaghetti *al pescador*, with capers, thyme, olives, marjoran and pine nuts.

La Tavernetta, Piazza Matrice 54, t 0923 92 16 39 (*moderate*). The best place to find local specialities, a little dearer than the rest, but worth it. *Book ahead.*

La Bettola, Via Nicotera 47, t 0923 92 19 88 (*inexpensive*). A no-nonsense *trattoria* with various tuna and swordfish specialities.

Camarillo Brillo, Via Vittorio Emanuele 18. A wine bar with live music and delicious appetizers, very popular for the *aperitivo*.

Giabar Cavallo, Zona Cavallo. A bar created inside a disused tufa quarry. where you can listen to live music while sitting under palm trees in their candle-lit garden.

In central **Piazza Europa**, Favignana is still watched over by a statue of its portly benefactor Ignazio Florio. A busy street of shops leads from here to enlongated Piazza Madrice, with the **Chiesa Madrice** tucked away at the far end. When it was built in 1704, the Marquis Pallavicino insisted that it should be out of range of **Forte San Giacomo** directly opposite. Today a maximum-security prison, the fortress was founded in 1120 by King Roger II, rebuilt in 1498 by the King of Aragon, Ferdinand the Catholic, and converted into a prison in 1837 by the Bourbons, who, thanks to their rotten ways, always had a surplus of prisoners. Favignana took its status as a penal colony in its stride. Naturally kind and tactful, the islanders earned a reputation as ideal prison guards.

To the right of the church, the **Rione Sant'Anna** is the oldest part of town, with houses made of native tufa. Just behind this are several abandoned tufa quarries, unremoved golden blocks carved in the walls and a luxuriant wild garden invariably at the bottom, protected from the wind. Easy to work, tufa has provided everything from dovecotes to well covers to sculptures (Favignana always seems to have a resident tufa sculptor – these days he's Antonino Campo). Some of the newer tufa buildings have been whitewashed, as modern architecture in the Mediterranean seems to dictate.

Eastern Favignana: Punta San Nicola and Cala Rossa

A short walk along the shore west of town is tufa-rich **Punta San Nicola**. Caves here have been inhabited from Palaeolithic times to the 18th century, and its cemetery has received the island's dead since ancient times. Despite such rare continuity, Punta San Nicola is unkempt, awaiting funds for exploration and conservation that may never come. Look out for the **Grotta del Pazzo** ('madman's cave'), with its late Punic and early Christian inscriptions, and the **Grotta degli Archi**, housing Christian tombs from the 4th and 5th centuries. To the right of the Cala San Nicola is the **Bagno delle Donne**

Favignana

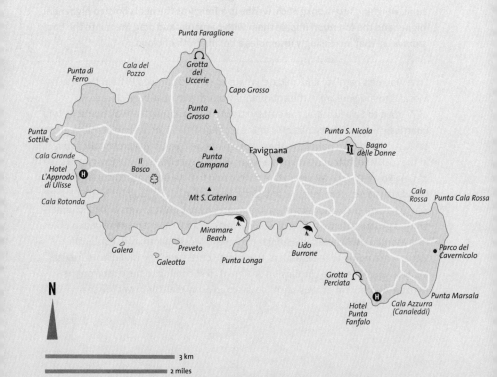

The *Mattanza*

Every spring, tuna migrate through the Straits of Gibraltar to breed in the warmer waters of the Mediterranean. As they circle Sicily, the currents funnel thousands of them into the strait between Favignana and the Formiche islets, so many in fact that catching them is not called fishing, but a *mattanza*, the Spanish word for slaughter. It is a wild, bloody ritual, perhaps dating back to the Phoenician times. Traces of Roman *tonnare* (tuna traps) have been found in several places along the coast; the contemporary *mattanza* has a vocabulary dating from the Arabian occupation.

Less than a century ago, Sicily had 50 *tonnare*, but now only one remains active, at Favignana. Competition with Japanese fishing boats, the lack of skilled *tonnaroti*, or tuna butchers, to work a couple of months a year, and the decline in the numbers of tuna have decimated the industry. In Florio's heyday 150,000 tonnes of tuna would be canned each year by 350 employees. These days the catch varies between 1,000 and 1,500 tonnes.

Favignana holds the last ritual *mattanza* in Sicily. It has also become something of a tourist attraction and may well be the most legally violent sight you'll ever see (contact the tourist office in Tràpani for details). The hapless tuna swim into the trap of the *tonnara*, a long corridor of nets anchored at sea and on shore, through which they are siphoned from chamber to chamber until driven into the last corral, surrounded by the flat boats of the *tonnaroti*. Led by the priest-like *rais*, the men rhythmically chant sacred songs, the *cialoma*, then at the order '*Rivirsata di la tunnina dda dintra!*' raise the floor of the great net. Jammed tightly together, the tuna, weighing 140–400kg each, writhe in a frenzy as the net is hoisted higher and higher and the *tonnaroti* impale them with harpoons and drag them into the boats from a sea that increasingly resembles a boiling froth of blood.

('the women's bath') of Roman date, where water was pumped in from the sea. Mosaics found here are in the antiquarium, but this too has been closed.

The road to Cala Rossa, at the eastern tip of Favignana, passes two enormous **tufa quarries**, carved with the patterns of the great quarried blocks, their depths a green oasis. An overgrown path from the electric plant here leads to a **prehistoric tomb** cut in the rock, and farther up there is a ledge with an excellent view of Favignana's coast. At **Cala Rossa** the crystal-clear waters were said to have become red during the bloody battle between Romans and Carthaginians in 241 BC (during the first Punic war). The tufa excavations form an imaginary city of Cubist towers and long underground galleries. Come before dawn on a hot day and you may see Favignana's own **Fata Morgana**, when mirages similar to those in Messina form over Punta San Vituzzo. According to the islanders, the mirage once saved the island from Turkish pirates, when it formed the illusion of a great fleet coming to the rescue on the horizon. At other times they say it looks like an army marching over the sea, or a pack of Godzillas.

The road continues east to Orsa Maggiore and Favignana's newest attraction, the **Parco del Cavernicolo,** where an entrepreneur has found a use for abandoned tufa quarries – as a swimming-pool complex complete with a garden and menagerie of exotic birds.

Lido Burrone

From Favignana town it's a 15min walk south to Lido Burrone, a long stretch of sand facing a shallow, transparent sea. This is one of the most popular spots on the island and in summer it can get quite crowded. To the west it is sheltered by the 'head' of the butterfly, the promontory of Punta Longa; to the east the road continues up an increasingly rugged shore to the seaside **Grotta Perciata** ('pierced cave'), where a tiny port is capable of holding three small fishing boats. The road continues east for Cala Canaleddi, better known as **Cala Azzurra** for the intense blue of the sea next to the almost snowy whiteness of the rocks around it.

The Butterfly's West Wing

From Favignana town a mule path zigzags up the mountain to Forte Santa Caterina, but don't take it unless you have special permission to visit the military zone. Founded by the Saracens, renovated by King Roger II, and expanded in 1498 and 1655, it was used by the Bourbons to imprison Risorgimento celebrities.

The mountain it sits on, Monte Santa Caterina (942ft), forms an effective barrier to the western half of the island; the one paved road skirts the extreme southern edge of the mountain, past the little beach at **Miramare**. It leads to **Il Bosco** ('the wood'), really nothing more than several acres of abandoned farmland. Near the Case Casino the paved road forks, one branch leading to the south side of Cala Grande and the **Villagio Approdo di Ulisse**, where you can see an ancient well with a pendulum mechanism, still used by the few farmers who live in the area.

The right fork leads to Punta Sottile to the north of Cala Grande. An unpaved track to the right passes the barren landscapes of Calazza for the steep cliffs of **Faraglione** with close-up views of Levanzo. Just below Faraglione is the entrance to the **Grotta delle Uccerie** (take a torch) with coloured stalactites. There are two chambers, the second less desecrated by souvenir-hunting shepherds.

Levanzo

At 2.2sq miles, Levanzo is the midget of the Egadi Islands. The Saracens called it 'dry' (Gazirat al ya bisah), and in the Renaissance it became Levanto, named by Genoese sailors after their home town near Genoa. Unlike Favignana and Maréttimo, Levanzo has no source of fresh water, which keeps its population down to a minimum (about 200), all concentrated around the port at Cala Dogana, where houses gaze over the sea towards Favignana, and the dogs have nothing better to do all day but sleep in

Levanzo

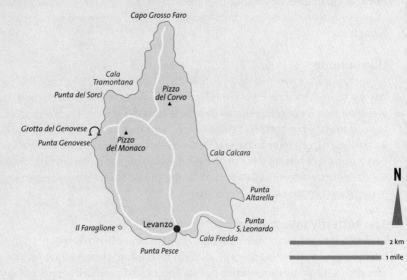

Capo Grosso Faro

Cala Tramontana
Punta dei Sorci
Pizzo del Corvo

Grotta del Genovese
Punta Genovese
Pizzo del Monaco

Cala Calcara

N

Punta Altarella

Il Faraglione
Levanzo
Punta S. Leonardo
Cala Fredda

Punta Pesce

2 km
1 mile

the streets. And yet Levanzo gets its share of tourists thanks to its famous Grotta del Genovese.

Grotta del Genovese

To see the *grotta*, make an appointment with its custodian, Natale Castiglione, who lives directly above the dock (*t 339 7418 88 00*) and will take you in his boat if it's not too windy. The larger the party, the cheaper it is per person. You can also walk to the cave along the pretty inland path and meet Signor Castiglione there.

The Grotta del Genovese, 100ft above the sea, was named after the Genoese sailing ships that anchored offshore here. The cave has always been known, but no one saw the prehistoric art inside until 1949, when an artist on holiday, Francesca Minellono, picked it out; until the early 1900s, the belief that 'cavemen' were far too primitive to draw pictures had made people blind to them. They are among the most important discovered in Italy. Made while Levanzo was still part of Sicily, 10,000 years ago, the carvings of 29 animals and four human figures, who seem to be dancing, are as fragile as they are magnificent; the beautiful deer beside the entrance is under a protective glass because the slightest touch causes the stone to crumble. Less skilful are the confused rows of stylized black paintings of men and women, unfinished animals and tuna fish (their first known representation in art) added 5,000 years later, in the Neolithic era; apparently their magic was of a different variety.

Where to Stay and Eat

Levanzo ✉ 91010
*Paradiso, Via Lungomare 8, t 0923 92 40 80 (*moderate*). Has 15 rooms (all with shower) and a terrace overlooking the sea. There is also a restaurant serving traditional fare.

**Pensione dei Fenici, Via Calvario 18, t 0923 92 40 83 (*budget*). Newer of the two hotels in Levanzo, offering 10 rooms (all with shower) and a restaurant.
Il Nautilus, t 0923 92 40 08 (*inexpensive*). This restaurant serves average food on a pleasant terrace.

The Rest of Levanzo

The entire coastline is rocky and inaccessible, except for a few inlets with rocks to swim off at **Cala Fredda, Cala Dogana, Punta Pesce, Cala Minnola, Cala Tramontana** and **Cala Calcara** (easier to reach by boat). One of the nicest tracks to walk is through Levanzo's **valley**, used as pastureland for a score of dairy cows. It's surrounded by hills, the highest called Pizzo del Monaco (909ft). Another walk along the track west of the port takes you in 20mins to the **Faraglione**, an odd-shaped rock off the rugged coast; from here you can continue to the Grotta del Genovese.

Maréttimo

Maréttimo, the first of the Egadi Islands to break away from Sicily, is also the furthest – and not only in distance. The 80 islanders, nearly all fishermen, have little to do with Sicily or even Favignana; proud, soft-spoken and independent, they stick to their magnificent rocky island, their simple houses, their families and their brightly painted boats. Most of its waters are a marine reserve. The tourist industry holds no attraction for them and, even though central planners long ago made plans for the construction of x number of hotels, the islanders haven't made any moves towards that goal. Visitors are kindly received into their own homes; several Italians from the mainland have built summer villas on Maréttimo. And that's it. Few places are more beguiling.

The Greeks named it Iera (sacred), and under the Arabs it became Malitimah (whence Maréttimo). In his *The Authoress of the Odyssey* cranky Samuel Butler

Where to Stay and Eat

There are a few rooms at the fishermen's houses on Maréttimo, as well as several furnished houses to rent for longer stays.
La Rosa dei Venti, Contrada Crocilla, t 0923 92 32 49, *www.isoladimarettimo.it* (*budget*). Has rooms for rent and also organizes island tours, both inland and by sea. Lobster, when available, is the prize dish on the island.
Il Veliero, Via Umberto 22, t 0923 92 32 74. (*moderate*) A good restaurant serving a great fish soup.

Il Pirata, Via Scalo Vecchio, t 0923 92 30 27 (*moderate*). Lobster soup and fish couscous shine among the dishes served in this not-so cheap restaurant
Onda Blu, Piazza Umberto I, t 0923 92 31 02 (*inexpensive*). Open in summer only, with tables on the square and serving the freshest pasta with tuna, aubergines and zucchini. In particular don't miss the *granita ai gelsi*.
La Scaletta, Via Telegrafo 4, for those late-night ice cream urges.

Maréttimo

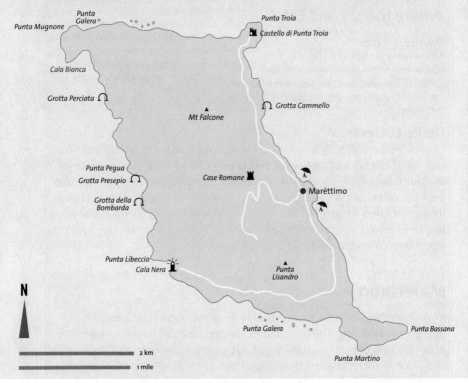

claimed that Maréttimo was the Ithaca of Odysseus (*see* p.122), a proposition that makes the Maréttimese smile. Their island is really more of the order of Capri; take one of the offered **boat excursions** around the island (in about three hours) for the close-up views of its dramatic coves, cliffs and deep blue grottoes. It looks even better with the aid of a snorkle.

Everyone lives in the village of Maréttimo, founded in the 1800s, although its growth is limited by the mountains. Two piers protrude on either side of town: the Scala Nuova for the delicate hydrofoils, and the Scala Vecchia, the fishermen's port, with the fine red, white and blue fishing smacks – some purchased with money raised in Anchorage, Alaska.

There are **beaches** both sides of town.

Treks around Maréttimo

Once you've visited the coast by sea, you may want to plod into the steep mountainous hinterland, taking care to start early and otherwise avoid sunstroke. One bumpy track winds up to the abandoned **Semaforo** and the **Case Romane**, about 45mins up from the port. The Case aren't houses, but a well-preserved late Roman fort. Next to the fort stands an anonymous, crumbling little lost church probably built by Byzantine monks under the two Rogers. Its form was inspired by the Arabs, with barrel vaulting and central rounded drum, a design rare in Italy.

The road south of the village ends up at the lighthouse. Pine trees provide some shade, although the road is often tortuous. The scenery is splendid, especially on the western coast, where lofty vertical cliffs plunge into the sea. Just beyond the lighthouse, a path winds down to **Cala Nera**, where you can swim off the rocks.

A rather hair-raising track north of the port skirts the shore and **Monte Falcone** (2,250ft), by far the highest peak in the Egadi Islands, covered in Aleppo pines, holm oaks and a macchia of thyme, rosemary, heather, lentisk bushes and an endemic species called *Daphne oleifolia* that doesn't grow on Sicily. The path ends at the **Castello di Punta Troia**, built on a precipice over the sea. There is a welcome spring of fresh water near the winding climb up to the castle. The original tower on this site was built by the Saracens in the 9th century; Roger II enlarged it, and the Spanish completed the building in the 17th century. They also constructed cisterns, a church, and a prison so inhuman and cruel that when Ferdinand II visited it in 1844 he ordered it closed – a rare act for a Bourbon. Marvellous views over Maréttimo and the sea wait from the castle terrace. Steps from the path lead down to a secluded **beach**; take a boat if you're subject to vertigo. On the other northern side at **Cala Bianca** you'll find the most spectacular bay of the island with its white chalky cliffs plunging perpendicularly into the turquoise waters.

Pantelleria

Been wondering where Italian fashion victims in the know sneak off to? Get out your map and look 112km southwest of Sicily and 80km east of Cape Bon, Tunisia, and look no further. Round volcanic Pantelleria's 32sq miles merit a dot on most maps. Until the 1990s, its distant location attracted few outsiders apart from the scholars: archaeologists who study its Megalithic *sesi*; anthropologists who come to examine the last truly agricultural community in Europe; students of architecture who come to examine the *dammusi*, square houses built of volcanic stone, with shallow domes and thick white walls that stay cool in the summer; ecologists who come to observe the islanders' admirable management of natural resources. And last off the boat, the fashion designers and the fashionably designed.

In short, Pantelleria is a most unusual island. Despite determined efforts by some to develop it as a typical holiday paradise, with the same bright white hotels you see everywhere else around the Med, there is an even more determined group of people who want Pantelleria to retain its ethnological identity, encouraging visitors to stay in the traditional *dammuso* houses, to understand a way of life that once existed throughout the Mediterranean. It isn't easy, however, to compete with the easy money that tourists will pay to lie in the sun. At the moment, 60 per cent of Pantelleria's income still comes from agriculture (zibibbo grapes, wine, capers and lentils), while 40 per cent derives from tourism. Perhaps both sides can claim victory from these figures.

Getting There and Around

The SIREMAR **ferry** from Tràpani (Agenzia Rizzo, Borgo Italia 12, Pantelleria, **t** 09 23 91 11 04) makes the 6hr trip daily in the summer, and every day but Saturday from September to June. **Hydrofoils** make the trip in half the time but cost as much as one of the cheaper **flights**: Air Sicilia (**t** 09 23 84 14 23) and La Med (**t** 09 23 54 98 24) from Palermo and Tràpani all year round.

Travel agencies charter day **excursions by air** to Tunis, and others offer **boats to hire**. **Buses** depart from the church for Scauri and Tracino every half-hour; several firms by the quay hire out **mopeds**.

Tourist Information

Via San Nicola, **t** 09 23 91 18 38, *www.pantelleria.it*.

For information on the cultural aspects of Pantelleria, contact the Gruppo Etnologico Pantesco, Corso Umberto 66, **t** 09 23 91 10 29. In July, you can talk to the professors at the Centre for Advanced Studies in Environmental Design, Cala Tramontana.

Where to Stay

Pantelleria ✉ 91017

Quelli di Pantelleria, Contrada Bonsulton, **t** 0923 91 83 06 (from October to May call their Rome office, **t** 06 8621 2315; (*€250–450 per week for two people*). Try this for something more ambitious. It offers weekend or weekly stays in a *dammuso*, along with horses to explore the island paths from June to September.

Miryam, Corso Umberto 1, **t 0923 91 13 74, *www.myriamhotel.it* (*inexpensive*). One of the most comfortable of the more traditional hotels in Pantelleria.

***Port' Hotel, Borgo Italia 43, **t** 0923 91 12 99, *porthotel@pantelleria.it* (*budget–inexpensive*). A comfortable modern building with air-conditioned rooms.

Blue Marino Residenziale, **t 0923 91 28 22 (*budget–inexpensive*). A small secluded place on a cliff 1 km from town, with a garden and pool.

***Hotel Mursia, **t** 0923 91 12 17, *www.mursia.it* (*inexpensive–moderate*). Situated on a private beach in Mursia, with swimming pools, tennis courts and easy access for the disabled; some rooms have air-conditioning. Owned by the same people the nearby *****Cossyra** is at Cuddie Rosse, with similar facilities and prices.

Eating Out

Pantelleria is famous for its high-octane (16%) wines, especially a nectar called Zibibbo di Pantelleria that lifts creamy Italian desserts, and in particular *cannoli di ricotta*, into a culinary stratosphere. Even more refined is Moscato, a sweet, fragrant amber wine made from zibibbo or moscatellone grapes. When made from raisins, the wine is known as Passito, with a scent ranging from dried figs and almonds to apricots and honey. Two of the best of many cellars to seek out are Salvatore Murana, Contrada Khamma 276, **t** 0923 96 96 73, and Cantina Casano, **t** 0923 91 29 48. Other less ambrosial but still very drinkable table wines come from the vineyards near Scauri, both reds and whites.

Local specialities to go with all this wine are cow's milk *tumma* cheese, similar to ricotta in flavour but harder; North African *cuscus*; *pesto pantesco*, a sauce made from tomatoes, garlic, pepper and basil, served with *ravioli amari*, made with delicious cow's ricotta and mint.

Favarotta, Contrada Favorotta, **t** 0923 91 53 47 (*moderate*). One of the best places to taste the traditional local dishes, such as roasted hare and *caponata*. *Closed Wed.*

I Mulini, Località Tracino, **t** 0923 91 53 98 (*moderate*). In a former mill; serves a menu changing daily according to the catch.

Il Cappero, Via Roma 31, **t** 0923 91 26 01 (*inexpensive*). A local favourite serving fish and pizza. *Closed Mon in winter.*

La Risacca, Via Padova, **t** 0923 91 29 75 (*inexpensive*). Like Il Cappero, it serves simply prepared fish dishes and pizza.

Isola nell'isola, Contrada Mueggen. A wine bar in an old *dammuso* with the best local wines selection and yummy appetizers.

Oxidiana, Armani's favourite disco on the island is entirely buit from lava and has an Arab feel to its décor.

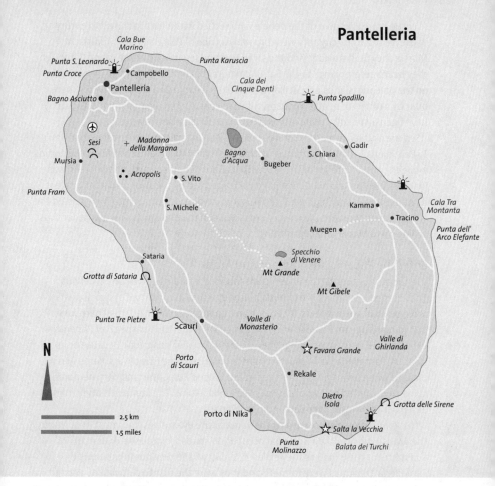

Pantelleria

Come in May, June, September or October, when the coastal flora – *helichrysum* and *trifolium* in particular – is in bloom, and it's not too hot to walk in the afternoon. The sea stays warm enough for swimming (the island has no real beaches) well into October. These months are also the best for spotting migratory birds – uncommon species such as the Iberian fantailed warbler and Algerian great tit pass through Pantelleria and nowhere else in Italy.

History: the *Sesi* Culture

The elusiveness that characterizes Pantelleria begins with its history. The product of innumerable volcanic eruptions, the island may once have been land-locked between Sicily and North Africa before the continents drifted apart. Volcanic eruptions continued after the first humans showed up; a hand-worked stone found under the basalt of an eruption *c.* 30,000 BC suggests an aboriginal people.

A little more is known of the people who settled Pantelleria in the 18th century BC. These Neolithic immigrants were probably a tribe of Pelagians from Tunisia. At Mursia they built a village and the strange stone *sesi* unique to the island. Although they bear a resemblance to the Sardinian nuraghi and the Megalithic monuments on the Balearic Islands, the Sicilian archaeologist Paolo Orsi believes the *sesi* were built by a different people; more primitive in construction and technique, they may have been inspired by more refined structures found elsewhere.

Sesi are circular domed structures made of natural volcanic rock, somewhat similar to Pantelleria's modern *dammusi*. Within the thick walls themselves are niche-tombs, while the actual interior of the *sesi*, with its floor of beaten earth and pebbles, was inaccessible. The *sesi*-builders' village was protected by the strong wall that gave it its name, Alta Mura ('high wall'). An upsurge in volcanic activity may have caused the village's abandonment. Never very prosperous, in the end it was only a base for those sailing on to bigger and better things.

Enter the Phoenicians, Romans and Arabs

In the 7th century BC, the Phoenicians founded a trading colony on Pantelleria. They named it Hiranin ('isle of birds'), although the Greek name Cossyra appears more often in ancient texts. It became an important outpost, its small harbours providing refuge for Phoenician vessels in bad weather. One of the chief Phoenician exports were massive grinding wheels carved out of volcanic rock. Because of its location, Pantelleria was a much sought-after prize in the Punic Wars; Rome was so pleased when it was finally captured in the Second Punic War that commemorative coins were minted and a holiday was declared in Rome. The Romans found it handy as a place of exile for over-demanding legionaries.

The Romans were succeeded by the Vandals, the Byzantines and, most importantly, the Arabs, who over their 400-year occupation shaped Pantelleria, or Bent el rion ('daughter of the wind') as they called it. Unlike all the previous inhabitants of Pantelleria, the Arabs were farmers, and they were the first to cultivate its rich red volcanic soil. They introduced vineyards, cotton, vegetables, citrus and palm trees, and barley, from which they baked a long-lasting hard bread, common until recently. They also built irrigation systems and *dammusi* to be near their fields, and secret pleasure gardens protected by high walls. Their language lingers in place names such as Zighidi, Khagiar and Bugeber, and in the local dialect.

Union with Sicily

When the Normans conquered Sicily they took Pantelleria as well, and ever since then it has been administered from Tràpani. The island was given to various nobles who had done the King of Sicily a good turn; one family, the Requesens, proudly attached the title of 'Prince of Pantelleria' to their leading male. Their presence was noticeable only at tax time. Under their regime, only 12 per cent of the land was half-heartedly cultivated.

In 1845, feudal rights were abolished in Sicily and the land was redistributed among the people, so that by the start of the 20th century 50 per cent of the island was under cultivation. Because both male and female children were now equally entitled to inherit, the farms of Pantelleria were gradually divided into small holdings – a problem partly solved today by having fewer children.

During the Second World War the Fascists made Pantelleria their main base in the central Mediterranean, fortifying it and building an airport. When North Africa fell to the Allies, the base became crucial to both sides; the Allies had to take it before beginning the invasion of Sicily. On 8 May 1943, the bombs began to fall, day and night. Pantelleria held out until 11 June; then, flattened and blockaded, the 11,000 soldiers stationed on the island surrendered and were taken prisoner.

Pantelleria Town

Pantelleria has one souvenir of the war that won't go away: the concrete reconstruction of its main town, after the pleasant original was bombed beyond repair (see the photos in the lobby of Hotel Agadir). If you sail into Pantelleria, it's a wretched introduction to an otherwise exceptionally charming island. The one old building still standing, the black, reconstructed **Spanish castle**, isn't even very interesting. Nevertheless, as the sun goes down, the whole place heaves into action: the bars and seaside promenade fill up as the darkness discreetly hides the battle scars and other assorted junk.

Along the road towards the airport, a branch to the right leads up to Cossyra's Roman **acropolis**, where excavations from 2000 onwards uncovered three marble heads dating from the first century AD and identified as Giulio Cesare, Agrippina and a young Tito. Another road before the airport leads to the church **Madonna della Margana**, dedicated to the patroness of the island, represented in a 15th-century painting salvaged from a shipwreck. When the oxen pulling the cart with the picture reached Margana, they refused to budge, so a church was built on the spot. These days the Madonna winters, without too much of a fuss, in the town's **Chiesa Matrice**.

Around Pantelleria

The ideal way of seeing the rest of Pantelleria is to take one of the two buses to some point in the countryside, and then walk. It takes time to absorb what is special about the island, the subtle beauty of the domed *dammusi*, the patterns on the landscape formed by drystone walls, and the neat vineyards, trained to hug the ground owing to the violence of the wind. In the centre of the island towers Montagna Grande (2,508ft), the volcano that last erupted in 1891, while all around is the crystal blue of the clean sea, rich in lobsters, sponges and coral. In places you can see the old Arab irrigation system and the cisterns, some of which were originally catacombs – on Pantelleria nothing is wasted.

Into the Interior: Siba and Montagna Grande

Past the airport, the road leading into the interior of Pantelleria passes the ancient town of **Siba**, site of the oldest *dammusi* on the island, with barrel roofs; the weight of the dome rests on the two longer walls of the houses. A rough track from here, suitable for jeeps or horses, leads through forests of Aleppo pine to the summit of

Montagna Grande, with a panorama of the entire island and near neighbour Monte Gibele, an extinct volcano. Added to the views, however, are some volcanic curiosities: 24 *cuddie*, or baby spouts; *stufe*, volcanic steam vents; and, in the crater itself, a miniature lake called the Specchio di Venere ('Venus's mirror'), where the water, supplied by a hot spring, is a sizzling 50°C, and health and beauty freaks come to butter their bodies with volcanic mud. On the other hand, the Monte Gibele crater (2,310ft) is a cool oasis, even in August.

Below Montagna Grande lie two of the finest agricultural valleys on Pantelleria, a paradise for hikers or riders: the **Valle di Monastero**, named after a derelict Benedictine abbey with catacombs, and the **Valle della Ghirlanda** to the east, where Neolithic tombs and grottoes lie partly hidden in the greenery. Ghirlanda has the most fertile soil on the island, where the grapes grow as large as plums.

East Along the Coast from Pantelleria Town

Buses make this trip, and one of the first stops is **Campobello**, where the shore is level enough to permit bathing – but don't expect any wide stretches of sand. The shallow round lake near Campobello, **Bagno d'Acqua**, is in another old crater, 1,766ft in diameter. The emission of volcanic vapours, fed by the sea, makes the shores of the lake white, warm, sulphurous and highly alkaline; smearing its mud over your body before a dip is a recommended beauty treatment. In August, the fastest horses on Pantelleria take part in the festive races around the lake. The road along the shore ends up at the ancient town of **Bugeber**, with the best view over the constantly changing colours of the lake.

The main road (and the bus) continues east towards the strikingly savage **Cala dei Cinque Denti** ('inlet of five teeth'), where the craggy blocks of lava under the cliffs do indeed resemble a set of dragon-size canines. Just past the lighthouse is **Gadir**, with its little bay, the prettiest fishing village on Pantelleria, which has attracted the likes of Giorgio Armani, whose villa sits on the cliffs. The mildly radioactive black sand and hot springs just offshore make for a remarkable rustic spa. Still farther east is **Khamma**, a sprawling village just above the **Arco dell' Elefante Coricato**, a rock formation that resembles an elephant lying low to take a drink from the sea. The innovative *dammusi* in Khamma have been studied by the students of the Environmental Design Centre in nearby Tracino (the bus terminus), but even people who know nothing about 'environmental design' can appreciate the skill of the native builders. Above Khamma a path leads up to **Muegen**, a fascinating ghost village of very old *dammusi* on the slope of Montagna Grande. Off the coast here is another oddball rock formation spewed out long ago by the volcano, the **Scogli del Formaggio** ('cheese reef').

The extreme southeast coast of Pantelleria is known as **Dietro Isola**, the 'back of the island', a harsh, unpopulated dry area. One of the coves here, Balata dei Turchi, was supposedly the place where Turkish pirates landed and were thwarted by the islanders. Another landmark to the west is a 594ft precipice towering over the sea known as the **Salta la Vecchia** ('old lady leap').

The Southwest Coast

The holiday side of Pantelleria is concentrated a few kilometres from the capital by the beaches at Mursia, unfortunately near the ruins of the Pelagian village and the *sesi* themselves. Originally Pantelleria had some 500 of these mysterious giant igloos of volcanic rock; after centuries of being cannibalized by *dammuso*-builders, only 27 have survived in a sorry state of neglect. The grandest is called the Seso del Re. At Khazen, the closet-like natural sauna called **Bagno Asciutto** was carved out long ago, perhaps even by the *sesi*-builders, but still does the trick in a few hot minutes. At **Punta Fram** to the south you can see the Pelagians' obsidian mines.

The **Grotta di Sataria** farther down the coast contains a notable hot spring, where the water flows into a Roman basin. Here the lava formed canals of volcanic glass known as 'liparite' after the same material on Lipari (Pantelleria, too, has lent its name to a volcanic rock, cossyrite).

Another sea cave, the **Grotta dello Storto**, may be entered by boat, but quietly: it is the nesting place for numerous birds. **Scauri**, the bus terminus, has been the second port on the island since Phoenician times, although the town itself stands on a shelf some 300ft above the sea. The attractive white church forms the focus of the typical cluster of *dammusi*. Paths lead down to the Valle di Monastero (*see* above) and to the fumaroles and 100°C hot springs at **Favara Grande** on the other side of the Torrente Nika, which only runs from Montagna Grande in winter and when Pantelleria gets a bit of rain. The lack of fresh water has long been a bugbear for Pantelleria; farmers would condense the vapours of the favara to water their livestock. By the beached fishing boats at Scauri another hot spring is collected in two basins, where it is possible to bathe.

Yet another hot spring rises in the **Grotta di Nika** near the tiny village of the same name. Best reached by boat, Nika is a good base for a tour of the splendid **sea grottoes** on this part of the coast and the awesome cliffs of **Dietro Isola**. Above Porta di Nika lies the scarcely visited village of **Rekale**, another of those places on Pantelleria that does not seem to be a part of the modern world.

Tràpani to Marsala: a Salty Interlude

Spread along the coast from Tràpani south to Marsala are the shallow mirrors and sparkling heaps of Sicily's salt pans, first exploited by the Phoenicians and now a half-derelict, barren landscape dotted with giant windmills. At twilight, the dying sun turns the salt pans into molten patchwork patterns of red and orange that take on a special magic when seen from the stupendous natural balcony of Erice.

It takes 80 to 100 days to produce about 6cm of salt in the pans – barring a storm. Sicilian sea salt still goes into much of Italy's cuisine, and the growth of fish farms is attracting new economic interest in the area. You can learn all about the history of salt and the tools used to extract it at – where else? – the **Salt Museum** (*t 0923 86 74 42, t 0923 86 71 42; generally open 9–1*), housed in the 16th-century mill of the Salina Calcasi, at Nubia near Paceco (5km south of Tràpani).

The Stagnone Islands

The *stagnone* (big lagoon) extends along the coast from Birgi Airport almost to Marsala. One island, Isola Lunga, encloses it; two smaller ones, Isola San Pantaleo and Isola Santa Maria, shelter inside. San Pantaleo is the one that matters: in ancient times it was the city of Motya (Mozia in Italian, Mtwa to the Phoenicians), once the major Carthaginian base in Sicily and now, thanks to the excavations of a determined English amateur, the major Carthaginian archaeological site.

In the 4th century BC Isola Lunga was connected to Sicily at Capo San Teodoro; by the 3rd century BC the Carthaginians had dug two canals (*fretum*) through Isola Lunga, dividing it in two and separating it from the mainland, although not at Punta di Tramontana but across the present salt pans. Today Punta di Tramontana and San Teodoro are separated by a strait less than 1,200ft wide. Even more remarkable is the road 3ft under the sea, built by the Phoenicians, connecting San Pantaleo (ancient Motya) to the mainland necropolis at Birgi, near where the airport is today. Of all the islands in this book, San Pantaleo is the only one you can walk to if you don't mind getting your trousers wet. All three islands belong to the *comune* of Marsala and are uninhabited except for the caretaker and his family on San Pantaleo.

Isola Lunga

Isola Lunga, strangely, horizontally beautiful, with its salt flats, lagoons and numerous windmills, has been declared a nature reserve. The few men who still work the salt pans live on the mainland. What the park authorities are really interested in, however, is fish farming on or near the island. Archaeologists, for their part, have a treasure trove off the coast of Isola Lunga: here archaeologist Honor Frost discovered the Punic ship dating from the wars with Rome that is now in Marsala's Museo Archeológico.

Motya

The island, along with the excavations and museum, t 0923 71 25 98, is open to visitors April–Oct daily 9–12.30 and 3-6.30, Nov–Mar daily 9–3.30, and from the car park there is a regular boat service for the 10min crossing (€5.50 total for parking, ferry and entrance to the island and museum). Access by train or bus from Tràpani/Marsala.

At the beginning of the 20th century, one of the great English wine merchants of Marsala, Joseph (Pip) Whitaker, took an interest in the island of Motya, then known as San Pantaleo. Unusual stones had been found under the roots of vineyards planted there, and Whitaker, fascinated by the excavations of Troy and Crete, bought the island in order to do some archaeological research of his own. Sneaking away to San Pantaleo whenever business permitted, he gradually discovered that the nearly circular island had once been a city. His finds, patiently assembled over the decades, have been as important as anything from Carthage or the Middle East in helping to

Catapults and Other Marvels

At the turn of the 4th century BC the tyrant Dionysius was holding the reins in Syracuse. Dionysius was one of antiquity's craftiest politicians: he faked a peace treaty with Carthage, then summoned engineers from all corners to invent new weapons (founding history's first ordnance department), while skilfully using propaganda and diplomacy to unite the independent Greek cities against the barbarian threat. After nine years all was ready, and in 397 BC the Greeks set sail with a powerful fleet to destroy Motya, the heart of Phoenician power in Sicily.

The ensuing battle was one of the most curious in ancient history. The Motyans boxed themselves in on their tiny island, walled up their gates and cut their marvellous road to Birgi, then sent to Carthage for help. At this time Isola Lunga was a huge peninsula surrounding Motya, and the only outlet to the sea was to the south, near Marsala. It was so narrow that only one ship could pass through at a time.

Dionysius landed 80,000 soldiers, who camped at Birgi. They destroyed the Carthaginian-Elymian strongholds of Segesta, Eryx and Soluntum, and repaired the underwater road to Motya to transport their secret weapons. Carthage meanwhile sent a fleet to attack Syracuse, to lure Dionysius from Motya. But Syracuse was well defended, and Dionysius couldn't be distracted from his prey. Himilco, the Carthaginian general, then decided to make a sneak attack on the Greek ships, beached at Punta Palermo.

At dawn the Carthaginians struck. Dionysius quickly brought his army from Birgi to Punta Palermo, along with his secret weapons – the catapult, huge spiked flaming projectiles and other war machines never seen or used before. These caused such destruction and panic among the Punic fleet that Himilco had to withdraw, but he still controlled the straits. The Greek fleet was left trapped in Motya's unusual harbour, sitting ducks for the Carthaginians.

Quickly assessing the situation, Dionysius had a brilliant idea. He left part of his army to hold off the Punic fleet with their catapults, and ordered the others to chop down hundreds of trees and lay the trunks across Isola Lunga to the open sea. As Himilco and the Carthaginians watched in disbelief, the Greeks then rolled their entire fleet across land and in turn began to surround them. At that Himilco had had enough. He ordered a quick retreat and sailed for Africa to escape the Greeks' monstrous weapons and ships that 'sailed across the land'. Without even giving battle, he left Motya to its fate.

Dionysius destroyed the city and its inhabitants with a vengeance. The Greek residents of the city who took refuge in Motya's Greek temple were either spared to become slaves, or, according to another account, crucified. The island city was never rebuilt: when the Carthaginians returned they chose Lilybaeum (Marsala) for their new base.

recapture the lost world of Phoenician civilization. Whitaker spent so much time digging on the island that he built a villa, and planted the trees that beautify the island today.

The island and the excellent little museum Whitaker built are administered by the Whitaker Foundation. To visit, look for the shed with the sign *'Parcheggio per Mozia'* on the coastal road north of Marsala.

History

The Phoenicians founded Motya in the 8th century BC – not long after Carthage itself – and it soon became their most important trading post in Sicily, connecting Carthage with its Elymian allies, and with the Etruscans of central Italy. Motya soon became a force to be reckoned with in western Sicily, and the rapid colonization of the eastern part of the large island by the Greeks gave them much concern. When a company of Greeks from Cnidos attempted to settle Lilybaeum (Marsala), Motya and Segesta, its Elymian ally, joined forces to kick them out. The few Greek survivors ended up on Lipari (*see* p.244).

To keep the Greeks on their own side of Sicily, Carthage and Motya mounted a successful campaign between 560 and 550 BC. The island was heavily fortified, while the city on it had become so large that the necropolis had to be transferred to the mainland at Birgi – hence the famous submerged road, which ox-carts carrying goods could use as well as funeral processions.

In 510 BC, Motya and Segesta again united to drive out a hopeful Greek colony on the west coast. This was the beginning of the long-drawn-out war between Greeks and Carthaginians for total control of Sicily. When the united Greek forces defeated the Carthaginian army in the Battle of Himera (480 BC), the Greeks took the usual prisoners and demanded ransoms and fines, and also ordered the barbarians to stop sacrificing babies.

Motya survived the war and continued trading with the Greek cities – one of the reasons, perhaps, why the Greeks didn't eliminate the Phoenicians once and for all from Sicily when they had the chance. They probably wished they had when in 409 BC Motya assisted Segesta and Carthage in destroying Selinunte, and, three years later, Akragas. Only the outbreak of plague in the Punic army prevented the destruction of Syracuse and the rest of Hellenized Sicily. No one at the time could have foreseen that Motya had in fact little more than a decade left to live (*see* 'Catapults and Other Marvels').

The Excavations

The ruins of ancient Motya are scanty, half excavated but fascinating nonetheless. They occupy most of the island and can easily be explored in an hour or so. Near the southern tip are remnants of the **city walls**, and the **cothon**, a small artificial harbour safe inside the walls (Carthage itself had one like it). At the northern end is a **cemetery** dating from the 8th–6th centuries BC, before the necropolis was established at Birgi. There is also a **tophet**, dedicated to the goddess Tanit, where the Phoenicians sacrificed the lives of their first-born. Near this is the **north gate**, with the beginning of the submerged highway to Birgi, as well as an enclosed court full of building foundations that may have been the most important religious sanctuary of the city, at a spot called 'Cappiddazzu'.

In the residential areas of Motya are the ruins of numerous houses, some with mosaics, especially the **Casa dei Mosaici** near the museum, with a particularly fine black and white pebble floor of lions fighting a bull.

The Whitaker Museum

More than 1,000 small **burial urns** (some still containing the tiny bones of the victims) and grave-marking **steles** carved with the various fashionable symbols of cruel Tanit have been uncovered in Motya. Many of these decorate the garden courtyards of Pip Whitaker's little villa and the adjacent museum.

It's a small museum, full of wonders, with finds from Motya and all over the Mediterranean. Whitaker, who had a good eye for such things, bought relics from dealers; unfortunately he never wrote down what they were or where he got them, driving later curators crazy. As in the Greek cities, much of the art is in terracotta: masks, divine images and ex-votos that show influences from Greece and Egypt. One memorable image is of the smiling god **Bes**, the only likeable figure in the Phoenician pantheon. There is a lot of **pre-Punic pottery**, some showing the neat, concentric-circle motifs of the native Sicilians, and many fine painted Greek works. From one of Motya's gates come the two stone lions killing a bull, a motif common in the Middle East. Where the Phoenicians really excelled, though, was in the dainty things of **domestic life**: pretty coloured glass bottles and jewellery, a painted ostrich egg, carved Egyptian scarabs for good luck, or the tiny decorated braziers where Motyan ladies would burn their myrrh and spikenard for perfume.

In whatever medium – ceramics, marble or bronze – from whatever culture or century, what stands out are the faces, the expressions of delight or pain, of necessity and wisdom. Most seem tantalizingly eager to tell you everything they know about life in the streets and parlours of their lost city, 2,500 years ago.

Undoubtedly, *The Man with a Tunic* is the main attraction. Italians call him Auriga, a charioteer. Both titles reflect a lack of precise knowledge as to the subject portrayed, but this is the finest Greek statue in Sicily, and one of the most remarkable ancient works of art anywhere. It is one of those sculptures with the pure perfection of line that is intimidating to us mere mortals of the Iron Age. The skill of the artist communicates a kind of masterful arrogance as much as the pose of the male figure itself. The Phoenicians, like everyone else in the Mediterranean, appreciated the genius of Greek art and imported it in quantity. This statue dates from the early 5th century BC. If not a charioteer, informed guesses would have it either as a political figure of Carthage, or else Hercules-Melkarth, a god with many names, common to both the Greeks and the Phoenicians. From the little holes in his head, it is supposed that the figure once wore a bronze hat, or a crown, and the pose of his broken right arm suggests he was displaying something in his hand.

Marsala

On the ground, Marsala (pop. 85,000) is nothing but confusion; with a map, it resolves as a perfect square of walls, with a tidy grid of narrow, lively streets within. Ancient Lilybaeum rose from the ruins of Motya here, on Capo Boeo, the westernmost point of Sicily. It thrived under the Romans and Arabs, and in the 18th century it found the destiny the fates had planned for it all along – selling wine to the English.

History

Ironically, the Greeks were the first to settle at the natural harbour of Lilybaeum, although they were soon wiped out by the Carthaginians. Survivors from Motya, along with native Sicilians, refounded the city after 397 BC, and it remained the main

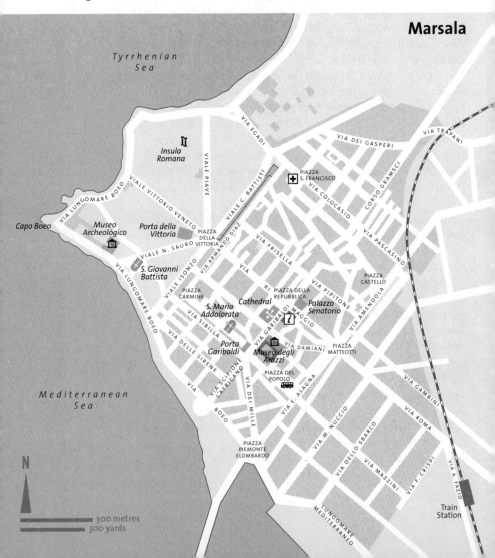

Marsala

Tyrrhenian
Sea

Insula
Romana

Capo Boeo

Museo
Archeológico

Porta della
Vittoria

PIAZZA
DELLA
VITTORIA

S. Giovanni
Battista

PIAZZA
CARMINE

S. Maria
Addolorata

Cathedral

Porta
Garibaldi

Museo degli
Arazzi

PIAZZA DEL
POPOLO

Mediterranean
Sea

PIAZZA
PIEMONTE
ELOMBARDO

VIALE PIAVE

VIALE VITTORIO VENETO

VIA LUNGOMARE BOEO

VIALE N. SAURO

VIALE ISONZO

VIA LUNGOMARE BOEO

VIA SIBILLA

VIA DELLE SIRENE

VIA SCIPIONE L'AFRICANO

VIA DEI MILLE

VIA BOEO

VIA EGADI

VIALE C. BATTISTI

VIA ARMANDO DIAZ

PIAZZA
S. FRANCISCO

VIA DEI GASPERI

VIA TRAPANI

CORSO GRAMSCI

VIA COLOCASIO

VIA PASCASINO

VIA FRISELLA

VIA

PIAZZA DELLA
REPUBBLICA

XI

VIA PIPITONE

PIAZZA
CASTELLO

Palazzo
Senatorio

VIA GARIBALDI

VIA MAGGIO

VIA DAMIANI

PIAZZA
MATTEOTTI

VIA AMENDOLA

VIA E. ALAGNA

VIA GAMBINI

VIA ROMA

VIA M. NUCCIO

VIA DELLO SBARCO

VIA MAZZINI

VIA F. CRISPI

VIA A. FAZIO

LUNGOMARE
MEDITERRANEO

Train
Station

N

300 metres
300 yards

Getting There and Around

By Air

Fifteen kilometres away, between Marsala and Tràpani, the airport of Birgi has flights to Rome (75mins, two daily) and Pantelleria (30mins, one daily).

By Train

Marsala is regularly connected by train with Tràpani; the line continues south to Mazara del Vallo and Castelvetrano, then loops back up to the north. From Castelvetrano there is an erratic service along the coast to Selinunte, Menfi, Sciacca, Ribera and Montallegro and on to Agrigento.

By Bus

Marsala's no.4 city bus goes to the Motya landing and on to Birgi airport five times a day, from Piazza del Popolo. This square also has the stop for inter-city routes: four or five a day for Tràpani and Mazara, and less frequent services to Agrigento and to the villages of the interior.

Tourist Information

Piazza Repubblica, Palazzo VII Aprile, **t** 0923 71 40 97 (*open Mon–Sat 8–2*).

Where to Stay

Marsala ✉ 91025

****New Palace Hotel, Lungomare Mediterraneo 57, **t** 0923 71 94 92 (*expensive*). A villa built in the 19th century by an Englishman and converted in 1998 into a hotel with all modern comfort and luxuries.

***President, Via Nino Bixio 1, **t** 0923 99 93 33 (*moderate–expensive*). Like most of the hotels in Marsala, prices here can seem a little dear, although it does have its own pool.

***Villa Favorita, Via Favorita 27, **t** 09 23 98 91 00, *www.villafavorita.com* (*inexpensive–moderate*). A 19th-century villa set in beautiful park with great views over the Egadi and Stagnone islands.

Baglio Vajarassa, Contrada Spagnola 176, **t** 0923 96 86 28, *www.bagliovajarassa.com* (*budget*). A traditional manor house hotel 6km north of town with just four rooms and furnished in style.

Garden, Via Gambini 36, **t 09 23 98 23 20 (*budget*). A small hotel, the least expensive in Marsala and near the train station.

Eating Out

Bacco, Via Trieste 5, **t** 0923 73 72 62 (*expensive*). Just 3 km out of town, this started as a simple *trattoria* and is now a renowned restaurant serving specialities like *casarecce with patelle e gamberi* or tuna with mint and fresh tomato.

Villa Favorita, Via Favorita 27, **t** 0923 98 91 00 (*expensive*). The restaurant of this hotel (*see* above) may be the top choice in town; a genuine old Liberty-style villa, good seafood and everything a chef could possibly do with Marsala wine.

Divino...Rosso, Via XI Maggio, **t** 0923 71 17 70 (*moderate*). Just opposite the *palazzo* Fici you can sit outdoors and taste local cuisine, mostly fish based. Over 150 labels in their extensive wine list.

Marinella 'Gnaziu 'U Pazzu, Contrada Stagnone 800, **t** 0923 98 97 92 (*moderate*). Offers tasty seafood concoctions and other dishes.

Mothia, loc. E. Infersa 13, **t** 0923 74 52 55 (*moderate*). A fish restaurant located off the road that connects Marsala and Tràpani, overlooking the windmills and salt beds. *Closed Wed.*

Carthaginian base in Sicily until the Romans conquered it in 241 BC, during the First Punic War. The Romans had besieged it unsuccessfully for nine years, and only took it by treachery during the peace that followed their victory at Erice. Cicero described it as a splendid city, and in 204 BC Scipio Africanus and his fleet sailed from Lilybaeum to conquer Carthage.

The Saracens renamed the town Marsah-al-Allah ('the port of God') and made it their main port in Sicily. Marsala continued to do well through the Middle Ages; Renaissance engineers under Aragonese rule gave the city its unusual square of walls, with a gate in the centre of each side. Emperor Charles V, despoiler of so much in the Mediterranean, blocked up Marsala's port, and the city languished until John Woodhouse started the English wine trade in 1773. Largely by chance, Garibaldi and his men landed at Marsala in May 1860, making it the first city of united Italy; ever since then Marsala has been known as the Città dei Mille, the 'City of the Thousand'. Its strategic position did it dirty in the Second World War, however, when much of the city was destroyed in bombing raids.

Lilybaeum

The seaside half of ancient Lilybaeum today is a broad, flat wasteland between the city walls and the sea. In Mussolini's time there were great plans for the area, and three boulevards, Viale Vittorio Veneto, Viale Piave and Via Nazario Sauro, were laid across it. Caught between the government, the developers and the archaeologists, however, nothing ever happened, and it remains a bizarre void, conducive to halluci-nations in the afternoon when populated only by a few woebegone tourists trying gamely to find the archaeological area. Some of them eventually do find their way to the **Insula Romana**, an area of excavations off the northern tip of the area on Viale

Marsala Wine

Being a sailor in the British Royal Navy wasn't a bed of roses, but one of the perks was a glass of wine at sunset. To keep on long sea voyages, the wine had to be forti-fied, and until the 18th century the wine of choice was port. As the Mediterranean fleet expanded alongside British interests in the region, the navy began to cast about for an easily obtainable local wine.

Enter a soap merchant from Liverpool, John Woodhouse, who noticed that Sicilian wine, when fortified with a bit of strong alcohol before the long trip to England, was much better than the plain wine. He moved to Marsala, and shipped the first batch to England in 1773, where it became a roaring success – his biggest customer was Nelson. In 1806 Benjamin Ingham opened another winery; in 1833 Vicenzo Florio opened a third. For the next hundred years the three firms ruled the industry, their seafront warehouses, or *baglios*, the city's landmarks. In the 1920s, the Cinzano firm of Turin bought them, though it continues to bottle the wine under the old labels.

You can learn all about Marsala wine at the Florio Winery (*open daily 10.30–1 and 3.30–6*) south of the town, on the Lungomare Mediterraneo, with abundant tastings provided.

The sweetest of the sweet wine brewed in those great wooden casks is that famous sexual boost-'er-up Marsala all'Uovo – with egg yolks. Others have various flavours added; Marsala Secco – dry only by Marsala standards – may be your favourite as an aperitif. Besides Florio, there are a number of other wineries along the roads to Selinunte and the airport.

Vittorio Veneto. The Roman-era ruins uncovered include not only an *insula*, a block of flats, but a **public baths** with some good mosaics on display.

The Museo Archeológico

Open Mon, Tues and Thurs, Fri 9–2, Wed, Sat and Sun 9–2 and 3–6. Adm.

Set in the old Anselmi wine *baglio* on the seafront, the museum is visible from anywhere in the empty zone. And it's worth the trouble to find, a well-planned and lovingly arranged trip into the past.

Baglio, as you'll learn here, comes from the Latin word *ballium*, used in medieval Italy for any sort of enclosed, fortified manufacture, such as works that produced sugar or olive oil. Both word and building form evolved through the centuries, and the Anselmi *baglio*, with its open quadrangle, is typical of the great houses of Marsala's golden age. You'll also learn a lot about ancient Lilybaeum, which did well all through Roman times, at least until the bad earthquake of 365 (the Vandals passed through and trashed what was left in 440). The city's mix of Phoenicians, Greeks and Romans made it a very cosmopolitan place, and its mixing of customs and religions is reflected in many of the items on display, such as the *edicole*, the little painted shrines that were erected on many tombs. Other works range from **Roman mosaics** (one good one with lions and tigers and their prey) to the peculiar **oil lamps** made in the shape of feet, and cast with anatomical precision. There is also a model of the Roman insula mentioned above, and a collection of objects found in Motya's tophet. It seems that the women of Lilybaeum often aborted their firstborn to serve up to Tanit. Tophet collections from less sophisticated outposts (as on Sardinia) are full of children's toys.

A separate hall of the museum houses the famous **Phoenician galley** reclaimed from the shallows off Motya. Kept in a plastic tent, it's really only about five per cent of a ship – the bottom of the hull – but an impressive reconstruction nevertheless. It may have been sunk in the Battle of the Egadi Islands, which, in 241 BC, ended the First Punic War. Measuring 105ft and manned by 68 rowers, it is a unique example of classical warships. Articles from the wreck and drawings showing how the ship may have originally looked are also present.

The Cave of the Lilybaean Sibyl

Of the Sibyls, legendary prophetesses of antiquity, three lived in Italy: at Tiburtina (Tivoli), near Rome; at Cumae, near Naples; and a rather minor Sibyl here in Lilybaeum – just across the street from the Museo Archeológico in fact, underneath the church of **San Giovanni Battista** (*ask for the key at the Pro Loco on Via Garibaldi*). These shadowy priestesses, representatives of a pan-Mediterranean religious tradition that no one now really understands, were a favourite subject in Renaissance art for the legend that they all in some way foretold the coming of Christ. In the crypt, where the Sibyls would chew laurel leaves and inhale the smoke of an unknown herb to go into their prophetic trances, there are only bits of mosaic and, as at Cumae, an underground spring.

Inside the Square

The proper way to enter Marsala is through the **Porta della Vittoria**, facing the archaeological area and the sea. This grand entrance was done up in Mussolini's time, probably meant to serve as a grand city centre, uniting the old town with the new Marsala that never got built; its only Mussolini monument is the weirdly grandiose **Cinema Impero**, recently restored and again in use as a movie theatre. Inside the gate is Via XI Maggio, main street of the city since ancient times. This leads you to **Piazza della Repubblica** in the city centre, where Garibaldi kicked off the unification of Italy in 1860 with a rousing speech to the Marsalans.

Today the city's gentlemen of leisure shoot the breeze all day under the arcades of the 18th-century **Palazzo Senatorio**, facing the Baroque **cathedral**, dedicated to St Thomas of Canterbury. It's only fair – the supporting columns were on their way from Corinth to Canterbury when the ship carrying them took refuge in Marsala in a heavy storm. The columns were considered to be too heavy and were consequently left behind. The bright, airy interior, which was completely rebuilt in 1628, contains Gagini statues of St Vincent Ferrer, St Thomas and others, and the tomb of native son Antonio Lombardo (died 1595), who was Archbishop of Messina and ambassador to Spain. Another Lombardo, a poor man named Pasquale, emigrated from Marsala to New York at the start of the 20th century and made it big; as the inscriptions outside attest, he came back home to pay for the completion of the cathedral façade, left half-finished for over 300 years. Essentially Baroque as it looks, the work was only finished in 1954.

Around the back of the cathedral on Via Damiani there's a real surprise, the **Museo degli Arazzi** (*open Tues–Sun 9–1 and 4–6*). Spanish King Philip II gave Archbishop Lombardo the set of eight fine Flemish tapestries (*arazzi*, or arrases) exhibited here. They tell the story of Rome's conquest of Israel, as narrated by the Jewish historian Josephus: detailed scenes show the capture of Jerusalem, the victorious general Vespasian's accession to the Imperial throne, the destruction of the temple, and Vespasian's son Titus making a sacrifice to Jehovah in atonement. At the end the guide does a trick with the lighting to show how the Flemish master weavers sewed an illusion of depth into their works.

On Via XI Maggio are the **Palazzo Fici**, with a Baroque courtyard, and the **Pinacoteca**, at No.15 (*open daily 9–1 and 4–8*), dedicated to contemporary Sicilian artists.

In the southern part of the city, **Porta Garibaldi** is adorned with a nasty-looking imperial eagle from the reign of the mad Spanish King Charles II. Just inside it are the colourful **marketplace** and the lace-like 18th-century façade of **Santa Maria Addolorata**. Marsala, like Syracuse, has **early Christian catacombs**, but you're not likely to see them. One is under the railway line to Tràpani; another can be entered from the ancient church of Santa Maria della Grotta, near the stadium. These are damp and dangerous, but if you can find the sacristan he might let you have a peek.

South Coast

09

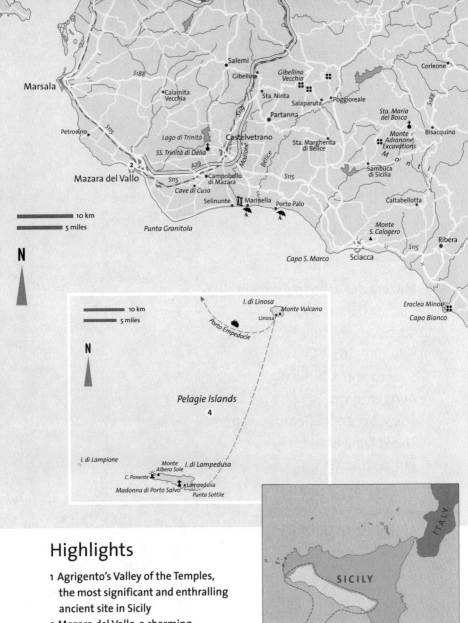

Highlights

1 Agrigento's Valley of the Temples, the most significant and enthralling ancient site in Sicily
2 Mazara del Vallo, a charming fishing port with unexpected Baroque delights
3 Shopping for pottery in the pretty seaside town of Licata
4 The Pelagie Islands, wind-whipped and floating in the cleanest seas in Italy

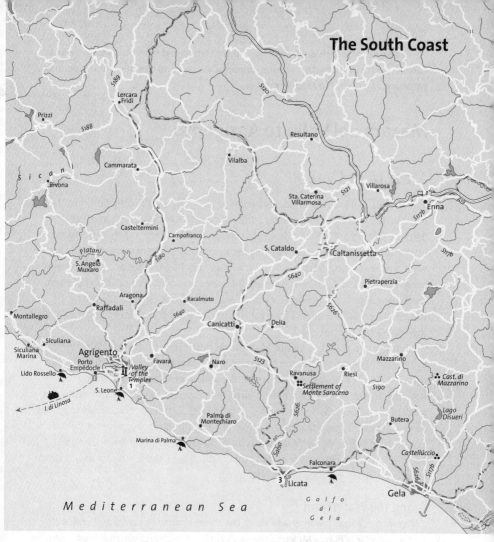

Not as green or as scenic as the other coasts, and much more sparsely populated, the part of Sicily that faces Africa definitely has a more exotic air to it. Palms and cacti punctuate long lonely miles on the coastal Via Siculana, the SS115. Along the way, the main attractions are ruins and beaches – usually right next to each other, so you can get your swimming and sightseeing in on the same day. Both are first-rate: endless miles of warm sand, usually uncrowded and clean, and the ancient Greek cities of Selinunte, Eraclea Minoa and Agrigento. There are three seldom-visited modern cities along this stretch – Mazara del Vallo, Sciacca and Licata; all are unpretentious, unspoiled fishing towns, and all are good fun.

The Greeks were attracted to this coast by some of Sicily's richest farmland. If you dip inland you'll see endless vistas of treeless hills planted in grain; alive with wildflowers in the spring, they turn a memorable golden colour by July.

This chapter also includes two little-known islands, lost out in the sea halfway to Tunisia: pretty Linosa with its pastel-coloured houses, and woebegone Lampedusa, aqualung capital of the Mediterranean.

Mazara del Vallo to Agrigento

Mazara del Vallo

Of all the unknown, unheralded wonders of Sicily this salty fishing port must be near the top of the list. Its ancient centre is a delight to walk in, with a collection of Baroque monuments at least as good as those of Noto. Mazara (pop. 55,000) gets little attention in most books, possibly because its historic centre was decayed and neglected for so long. Mazara's on its way back now. Its churches and palaces have been restored, and its citizens have gradually been redoing the houses in between, one by one. Signs of a growing civic pride are everywhere – specifically, the neatly hand-lettered signs residents have taped up on many corners beseeching their fellow townsmen not to litter.

Originally a colony of Selinunte, Mazara was destroyed at the same time as that city by the Carthaginians. In 827 the Arabs conquered Mazara, their first territory in Sicily. Under their rule it developed into 'a singular and magnificent town, lacking for nothing', according to the traveller al-Idrisi, who marvelled at its opulent baths and gardens, its great walls and its overflowing markets. Count Roger took it in 1075, and 20 years later the town saw the first Norman parliament. Throughout the period of Spanish and Bourbon rule, Mazara was an important Church centre, housing a number of wealthy monasteries and other institutions – the reason for its unexpectedly rich ensemble of Baroque architecture.

Along the Waterfront

Mazara has a lovely **promenade** along the shore, lined with palms and seafood restaurants. Near **Piazza Mokarta**, the city's centre, is a carefully maintained fragment of wall with a pointed arch, the only survival of the Norman castle built by Count Roger. Mazara is full of the unexpected; facing the seafront park called the Giardino Jolanda is the **Museo Ornitologico**, a little pavilion full of stuffed birds that seems to be open all day and all night.

Opposite this, on the great Baroque façade of the **cathedral**, you'll notice a 1534 relief of Count Roger spearing a Muslim, just over the main portal. Founded by the Normans in 1093, the church was substantially rebuilt in the 1690s. Inside, besides the fanciest carved-wood church pews in Christendom, are two Gagini works: a tomb by Domenico (1485) and a *Transfiguration* by Antonello (1532). On the floor, part of the original Norman pavement has been uncovered and is displayed under glass, and at the side entrances are some interesting ancient sarcophagi: one with that favourite Sicilian subject, the Rape of Persephone, another with an Amazonomachia (battle of

Getting There

Mazara train station is at the east end of the old town, at the top of Via Crispi, from where there are frequent **train** connections to Campo-bello di Mazara, Castelvetrano, Marsala and Tràpani. **Buses** (about 12 daily) depart from the station or Piazza Matteotti pretty much to the same locations, plus Palermo and Agrigento.

Tourist Information

Piazza Santa Veneranda 2, t 0923 94 17 27 (*open Tues and Thurs–Sat 8–2, Mon and Wed 8–2 and 3–6*); *www.comune.mazara-del-vallo.tp.it*

Where to Stay and Eat

Mazara del Vallo ✉ 91026

For dinner, head for the Lungomare around the cathedral. Mazara gets the pick of the catch, and the townspeople come out to enjoy it at a very competitive row of restaurants, all with adjoining outdoor tables.

****Villa Fontanasalsa**, Via Salem km 6,800, t 0923 94 22 98 (*expensive*). A small 19th-century villa with seven rooms, set in a garden with pool and tennis courts.

****Baglio Basile**, SS115, Petrosino, t 0923 74 17 05, *www.delfinobeach.com/baglio_basile* (*moderate*). A 19th-century *baglio* offering nine rooms and one suite with period furniture and all modern conveniences.

***Hopps Hotel**, Via G. Hopps 29, t 0923 94 61 33 (*inexpensive*) *hoppshotel@tiscali.it*. One of two good hotels near the seafront in Mazara, with a pool and a quite unusual garden.

Alla Kasbah, Via Itria 10, t 0923 90 61 26 (*expensive*). Tunisian-influenced restaurant offering specialities such as fish couscous.

Baby Luna, Via Punica, t 0923 94 86 22 (*moderate*). This busy place is one of several good fish restaurants on the Lungomare beside the cathedral.

Il Gambero, t 0923 93 29 32 (*moderate*). Another of the competitive restaurants on the Lungomare, with outdoor tables and the pick of the catch.

Il Pescatore, Via Castelvetrano 191, t 0923 94 75 80 (*moderate*). Liberty-style decor and traditional Sicilian food, with an emphasis on fish and seafood.

Lo Scoiattolo, t 0923 94 63 13 (*moderate*). Come here for buffet *antipasto* (a bit extra), pasta or risotto, and a main course with couscous (you'll get a strange look if you order anything other than a grilled fresh fish); also situated on the Lungomare.

the Argonauts and Amazons). And don't miss the little treasure in the last chapel on the right near the altar – a well-preserved 13th-century fresco of Christ Pantocrator.

Piazza della Repubblica

Round the back of the cathedral, you can see the original apses of the Norman building, near the entrance to perhaps one of the most beautiful piazzas in Sicily (unfortunately marred by parking), a composition in the contrast of warm sandstone and white stucco that is the basis of Mazara Baroque. All the buildings, save only the modern atrocity at the short end of the piazza, are from the early 1700s: the elegant campanile of the cathedral, the arcaded Seminario dei Chierici, and the Palazzo Vescovile, connected to the cathedral by a graceful stone passageway over the street.

From the far end of the piazza, Via XX Settembre leads to another attractive, if less spectacular square: **Piazza Plebiscito**. On one side, the simple domed Norman church of **Sant'Egidio** has been deconsecrated and houses the **Museo del Satiro**, the town's newest museum (*Mon, Tues and Thurs 9–2; Wed, Fri–Sun and holidays 9-2 and 4–7; adm*), its highlight the bronze statue of *the Dancing Satyr*, found in the waters between here and Pantelleria in 1998 and beautifully restored. Over 8ft high, it is the largest of its kind and thought to be a 3rd–2nd century BC copy of a Greek original. On the other side of the piazza the baroque church of **Sant'Ignazio** adjoins the imposing quadrangle of the **Collegio dei Gesuiti**, now containing the municipal offices and the **Museo Civico** (*t 0923 94 02 66; open daily 9–1*), with a small collection of architectural fragments – winsome marble elephants and lions from Mazara's old churches before the Baroque rebuildings – and a collection of local painting.

Santa Veneranda and San Michele

The great advantage Mazara's architects had over those of Noto was the lack of an earthquake. With a clear space to build upon, Noto's architects laid out a primitive grid, the sort of plan least able to provide an artistic setting for buildings. In Mazara, they were constrained to fit their works into an existing jumble of streets and squares that went back at least to Muslim times. The result was an agreeably bastard mix of flagrant Baroque architecture and subtle medieval town planning. It's never more than 500 yards in any direction across the historic centre of Mazara, but the intimate, enclosed web of streets makes it seem an enormous world unto itself – with a sweet surprise round every corner.

There's no sense trying to give precise directions through it, but in a casual hour's walk you'll see everything (it's even better to walk it at night, when the streets are empty and the churches are illuminated).

Closest to Piazza del Plebiscito, to the north, is the most ornate of all Mazara's churches: **Santa Veneranda** (begun in 1650; completed 138 years later), its unique façade highlighted by a splash of green- and gold-chequered tiles on its twin belfries; on the little alley to the left of the façade, the unrestored **Casa dei Scuderi** has an odd cylindrical tower from the 1400s.

Via San Michele leads to the next piazza and **San Michele**. The adjacent convent, with its exquisite loggia and tower, is still in use; inside the church is an intriguing series of allegorical statues by followers of Serpotta – what the allegories represent you can guess for yourselves. And behind San Michele and to the left, **Sant'Agostino** occupies the site of Mazara's ancient synagogue; a plaque from the 1930s recalls the 'glorious memory' of the city's substantial Jewish community, chased out of their homes by the Spaniards in 1492.

The Porto Canale

In any Arab or Norman city, every nation had a quarter to itself. The Jews lived around Sant'Agostino, the 'Latins' around the cathedral. The Arabs inhabited the northern quarter, in the warren of arched alleys the people of Mazara call the **Casbah**; today, fittingly, many of the inhabitants here are recent immigrants from North Africa. **Via Porta Palermo**, in this area, is one of the most animated streets of old Mazara; one incredible new apartment block here, with its terraces, spiral staircase and hanging gardens, makes an argument that modern Mazara is quite capable of making its recent revival live up to the grace of its past.

The fourth nation, the Greeks, kept their homes near the **Porto Canale**, the wide mouth of the Mázaro River that has always served this city as a harbour. Mazara today is arguably Italy's leading fishing port. In the morning, when the boats come in, the dock along **Molo Comandante Caito** is a noisy, chaotic epiphany of tired fishermen, carting off the treasures of the sea in rainbow colours. The cats of the town will be waiting at the **fishmarket**, just to the north on Piazza dello Scalo. Overlooking the scene from its pedestal above the Molo is one Sicily's most beautiful Norman monuments, the church of **San Nicolò Regale**, its square plan little changed since its building in 1124. In medieval times this was the Greek Orthodox church of Mazara.

Castelvetrano and Around

Most visitors to this corner of Sicily make a beeline for the ruins of Selinunte (*see* p.162–5), but if you have the time or the fancy to explore there are a few things to see along the way. There were considerably more before the night of 14 January 1968, when an earthquake (Terremoto del Bélice) cut a terrible swathe of destruction through the area, leaving some 400 dead and 50,000 homeless. The gaping scars remain to this day – a large percentage of the allocated rebuilding funds went straight into the pockets of the Mafia and politicians.

Castelvetrano

East of Mazara, Castelvetrano is a wine- and furniture-making centre with some small pretty things to offer if you're passing through. Outside the **Chiesa Madre** (completed 1579) is a lovely Baroque fountain called the **Fontana della Ninfa**, built in 1615. The church itself contains an altarpiece by Orazio Ferraro and works by Serpotta. Another church, **San Domenico**, contains some of the earliest examples (1570) of fancy Sicilian stucco decoration.

Castelvetrano seems to have been a Greek town, though it was refounded by the Romans, who settled a colony of retired legionaries on it and gave it its present name – the castrum of the veterans. Salvatore Giuliano was gunned down in Castelvetrano on 5 July 1950, a murder claimed by his cousin and lieutenant Gaspare Pisciotta, who himself was murdered before he could spill the beans and implicate more than one high-ranking member of the government. The macabre scene of Giuliano's mother on her knees licking his blood off the pavement burns in the memory of many Sicilians; the fact that analysis proved the blood belonged to a chicken makes it even stranger.

To see one of the finest of all Sicily's surviving Norman churches, ask a few score Castelvetranesi for directions to the Lago di Trinità, a man-made lake just west of town. It isn't well signposted, and you'll have a hell of a time finding the road, but it's worth a little aggravation to see **SS. Trinità di Délia** (*ask for the key from the Favoritia family, adjacent to the church*), set in a garden just to the south of the lake. Built in the 12th century and restored to its original state, the church is neatly squarish, though with three aisles and three apses: a clever trick of combining a Byzantine central plan with the basilican form favoured by Latins. This is one of the last Norman churches

Getting Around

Castelvetrano is on the main **train** line between Mazara and Agrigento, and to Alcamo in the north. Salemi and Gibellina Nuova share a station on the Alcamo line, but it's far from Salemi: you're better off taking the bus from Castelvetrano. Five **buses** a day in winter (more in summer) leave Castelvetrano for the beach at Marinella Lido and the magnificent and romantic ruins of Selinus (in Italian, Selinunte). There are also frequent buses to Sciacca and Agrigento.

Tourist Information

Selinunte: at the entrance to the archaeological area, t 09 24 46 251 (*open Mon–Sat 8–8, Sun 9–12 and 3–6*).

Gibellina Nuova: Museo Civico, Viale Segesta, t 09 24 67 877 (*open Mon, Tues and Thurs–Sat 8–2, Wed 8–2 and 3–6*).

Where to Stay and Eat

Castelvetrano ✉ 91022

**Zeus, Via Vittorio Veneto 6, Castelvetrano, t 0924 90 55 65 (*budget*). The only hotel in Castelvetrano, this has a restaurant.

Marinella ✉ 91022

***Alceste, Via Alceste 21, Marinella, t 09 24 46 184, *www.sicilyhotelsnet.it* (*inexpensive*). Set in a residential area not too far from the beach, the staff is friendly and breakfast is served on a lovely terrace. Good no-nonsense fish restaurant.

***Garzia, Via Pigafetta 8, Marinella, t 0924 46 024, *www.hotelgarzia.com* (*inexpensive*). You can stay right on the seafront at this sharp, modern hotel just a few minutes' walk from the ruins.

**Lido Azzurro, Via Marco Polo 98, Marinella, t 0924 46 256, *lazzurro@freemail.it* (*budget*). This white and green villa is the bargain choice in the centre. It's a clean, small family-run place near the beach with pretty, sea-facing rooms and a seafood restaurant on the terrace. A bit noisy in the summer.

Miramare, Via Pigafetta 2, Marinella, t 0924 46 31 00 (*moderate*). Next to the Hotel Garzia, this restaurant has a wide choice of dishes, starring of course local grilled fish and *cuscus al pesce*. Closed 10 Jan–10 Feb.

Pierrot, Via Marco Polo 108, Marinella, t 0924 46 205 (*inexpensive*). Has fish dishes and a tasty *gatto' di ricotta* (Sicilian cheese-cake) at good prices.

Salemi ✉ 91018

***Florence, Via 4 Stagioni, località Monte delle Rose, t 0924 68 511 (*budget*). The only hotel in Salemi, but a nice one, a local favourite for weddings and ceremonies.

Al Cavallino, t 0924 68 511 (*inexpensive*). Part of the Florence hotel, this restaurant serves Sicilian favourites and pizza with Salemi's delicious white wine.

with a strong Arab influence in its decoration: a small pink dome, and lovely stone latticework in the apse windows.

Castelvetrano's most recent claim to fame among food-lovers is the success of the excellent olive oil produced at Tenuta Rocchetta, which won the first prize in the 1997 Italian olive oil competition.

Campobello di Mazara

South of Castelvetrano lies wine-making Campobello di Mazara, where the parish **church** contains a 17th-century Crucifix by Fra Umile da Petralia. From here take Strada di Tre Fontane to the **Greek quarries** at the caves of Rocche di Cusa (from N115, turn off at Principe–Torre Cusa). It was from here that Selinunte took the stone to build its temples, and some of the column drums, still waiting to be taken in ox carts to Selinus, lie forlorn amidst the trees. The Carthaginian invasion in 409 BC interrupted the work on Temple G, and the quarries have not been used since that day.

Salemi

One of the biggest bones of contention between ancient Selinunte and Segesta was Salemi, the modern incarnation of the Sikan-Elymian hill town Halicyae. Its Arabic name, Salem, 'place of delights', offers a clue to its pre-earthquake charms, now a distant memory in Salemi's narrow alleyways and shattered buildings, some still untouched since the day of the earthquake. A heartier survivor is the 13th-century **Swabian-Norman castle**, rebuilt by Frederick II. It earned its allotted 15 minutes of fame in 1860 before the Battle of Calatafimi (see p.114) when Garibaldi slept here and declared himself dictator of Sicily – in the name of Vittorio Emanuele – in effect making little Salemi the first capital of united Italy for the whole of three days. One of the greatest artistic losses in the earthquake was Salemi's early Baroque cathedral, built next to the castle on the site of Halicyae's temple of Venus, and now itself in ruins.

Works of art from the cathedral, as well as those from Salemi's other damaged churches, have been moved to the **Museo Civico d'Arte Sacra** (open Mon–Sat 9–1.30 and 3.30–7) in the monumental ex-Collegio dei Gesuiti (1600). Two sculptures tenuously attributed to Laurana, and various Gagini pieces, hold pride of place among the religious works; the archaeology section has pieces dating back to the 12th century BC; another section has mementos from the Risorgimento.

Gibellina

East of Salemi is a cluster of villages that had to be completely rebuilt after the earthquake – Santa Ninfa, Salaparuta and Poggioreale, where excavations on Monte Castellazzo have revealed the ruins of ancient Elymian Entella. The only one that really tempts a visit is Gibellina, an agricultural town of 5,000 that was flattened into rubble. Its tragedy made it the symbol of the earthquake and, when Gibellina was rebuilt 18km west of the ruins near the superstrada, artists throughout Italy and Sicily combined to create not only a new town, but one completely different from any town anywhere, a kind of open-air art museum supposedly defying the destructive force of Ma Nature – a lofty aim somewhat circumvented by painfully dated 1970s design and penny-pinching on the quality of building materials.

Contemporary paintings and models of the sculptures and monuments of new Gibellina are housed in the **Museo Civico d'Arte Contemporanea**, Viale Segesta (t 09 24 67 855; open Tues–Sat 9–1 and 3–7, Sun 10–1 and 4–7).

Old Gibellina has hardly been forgotten, either. Older memories (a reconstructed farmhouse, tools, etc.) are stored in the **Museo Etnoantropologico della Valle del Bélice**, in Via Vespri Siciliani (open Tues–Sun 10–1). The still terrible ruins of **Gibellina Vecchia**, in the meantime, have become a canvas for artist Alberto Burri, who has covered the labyrinthine remains with a thin layer of concrete tracing out the old streets. A stage here, the **Teatro dei Rúderi** ('theatre of ruins'), set up on scaffolding, is the striking setting for a summer festival of theatre and music called the Orestiadi.

Closer to Castelvetrano, **Partanna**'s long 14th-century **castle** was spared by the earthquake, and is now open to visitors (t 09 24 87 058; open daily 9–2). The 17th-century

cathedral with its twin campaniles was partly damaged; inside are stucchi by the Messina and Serpotta clans, and a holy-water font carved by Francesco Laurana.

To the east, **Santa Margherita di Bélice** was the childhood summer home of the writer Giuseppe di Lampedusa, whose family would come down from Palermo to stay in his grandmother's 17th-century palace in the elegant tree-filled *piazza*. Lampedusa renamed it Donnafugata in *The Leopard* and wrote of it long and lovingly. The earthquake, however, has made a literary pilgrimage a poignant experience: only one palace wall remains, and a bit of the church, all overgrown and almost forgotten.

Monte Adranone

East of Santa Margherita di Bélice and 8km north of Sambuca di Sicilia, Monte Adranone was the site of ancient Adranon, where recent excavations have revealed a settlement dating back to the Iron Age, Hellenized by Selinunte and destroyed in the Carthaginian terror tour of 409 BC. It was rebuilt under the Carthaginians, only to be wrecked again by the Romans in the First Punic War. The **archaeological area** (*open daily 9–7.30*), with temples, walls, a barracks and sanctuary, dates from the time of the Carthaginians.

Selinunte

Ancient Selinus, lying between the Rivers Modione and Cottone, was the most westerly of all Greek colonies, founded by Megara Hyblaea around 650 BC. Selinus' name derives from the Greek word for the wild celery (*selinon*), the symbol of the city, which still grows on the fertile plain.

This plain that attracted settlers so far westward was the cause of the city's prosperity in the 6th and 5th centuries BC, as well as its woes, for the Elymians of Segesta coveted the land and ceaselessly fought for it by fair means and foul; for over two centuries Selinus' existence depended on the astuteness of its diplomats in dealing with the neighbouring Carthaginians and Segestans. In 409 BC, the Segestans formed an alliance with Carthage, which sent 100,000 men in a surprise attack against Selinus, capturing the city in nine days using tall siege towers. The conquerors showed a barbarity exceptional even for the standards of the time. Tens of thousands of Selinus' citizens were butchered, the rest sold into slavery.

Hermocrates of Syracuse later attempted to found a new settlement, but this plan failed and the site returned to Carthaginian hands. Carthage occupied the site as a garrison town until the Punic Wars, but Selinus never was rebuilt; its buildings were shaken down by earthquakes over the centuries, and the once-great city disappeared under the soil.

The site itself was totally lost, re-identified only in the 1600s; the diggers, beginning with two Englishmen named Walter Harris and Samuel Angeli in the 1820s, have brought it painstakingly back into the light a little at a time.

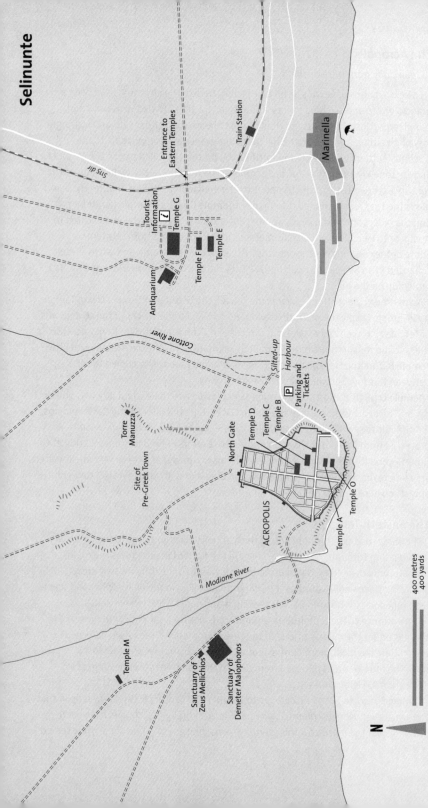

Selinunte

Entrance to
Eastern Temples

Train Station

Marinella

Sts dir

Tourist
Information

Temple G

Temple E

Temple F

Antiquarium

Cottone River

Silted-up
Harbour

Parking and
Tickets

Temple D

Temple C

Temple B

North Gate

Torre
Manuzza

Site of
Pre-Greek Town

Temple O

Temple A

ACROPOLIS

Modione River

Temple M

Sanctuary of
Zeus Mellichios

Sanctuary of
Demeter Malophoros

400 metres
400 yards

N

The Acropolis

Open daily 9am until dusk.

The excavations of Selinus lie on hills facing the sea. The city must have been a grand sight to approaching sailors: a steep, narrow hill crowded with walls and temples, two little harbours (now silted up) beneath it on either side, and a straight row of gleaming temples on the hill to the right, Selinus' religious sanctuary.

Selinus' settlers levelled off and fortified the prominent hill between the Modione and Cottone Rivers for the seafront acropolis. The remains of the walls (begun 6th century BC) are mostly reconstructions by the archaeologists. Dominating the acropolis is the 1927 reconstructed colonnade of **Temple C**, a large temple (208ft by 79ft) and the oldest one in the city (mid-6th century BC); it may have been dedicated to Apollo or to Hercules. The Archaic metopes in Palermo came from this temple. Some of the columns were monoliths instead of divided drums, and when these collapsed in an 8th-century earthquake they flattened a Byzantine village that had grown up on the hill.

Across the ancient street towards the sea are the vestiges of **Temple O** and **Temple A**. Of Temple O only the platform (stylobate) remains, while pieces of the 36 columns of Temple A, as well as its stylobate, can be seen. Both temples date from 490–480 BC, the last and most refined temples built in Selinunte. Only the base remains of little **Temple B** from the Hellenistic period. Selinus' agora probably occupied the space between this row of temples and the eastern wall.

Temple D (185ft by 69ft), on the main street leading to the ancient city, was built in 535 BC. The nearby ramparts of the **North Gate** were built later by the Carthaginians. It's difficult to see in the confused ruins on the site, but this double gate, well protected from every angle, was an impressive example of military engineering at the time. Beyond it to the north, where the hill slopes upward again, is a vast unexcavated area where most of Selinus' people lived, on a rigid grid of streets. A Sikel town probably stood here before the Greeks ever arrived.

The Eastern Temples

The same road that brought you to the acropolis takes you back to the sanctuary area, passing through the Cottone Valley. To the right of the road was the main harbour, now completely silted up. To the left was an unhealthy, marshy area; according to ancient historians the Selinuntians called in the philosopher and scientist Empedocles, who found a way to drain it and paid for the job himself.

The entrance to the temple area is unmarked; look for a car park with narrow tunnels under the railway tracks. Of the three temples on the eastern bank near the station, the most prominent is **Temple E** (480–460 BC), reconstructed in 1958. The four metopes removed from here to the Palermo museum suggest a dedication to Hera.

Temple F, next to Temple E, belongs to the mid-6th century BC, and is unique in that the spaces between its columns were filled in with 9ft walls. Scholars have been puzzling over the reason for this for many years; one guess is that the temple served as a treasury, which was a common function for Greek temples, and being outside the walls it was closed up for extra security. Another guess is that the temple was dedicated to Dionysos, and therefore needed to be walled up in order to conceal the sacred but often somewhat unseemly rites within. If this was the case, then the adjoining Temple E probably belonged not to Hera, but to Aphrodite. There was a similar extramural pair of temples dedicated to the goddess of love and the orgiastic god of the vine in Megara, Selinus' mother city in Greece.

In any case, these unusual stone screens may have inspired the architect of the huge Temple of Olympian Zeus at Agrigento when faced with the knotty problem of holding up such a large structure. As to size, the Agrigento architect was competing with the grandeur of **Temple G** on the other side of the road. Begun in the 5th or 6th century BC, this vast edifice measures 373ft by 178ft and was lined with columns 10ft in diameter, now broken and lying about like a giant's broken toys; like the Temple of Zeus, to which it is second in size, it was still unfinished when the Carthaginian bully-boys came to town. Over the years of its construction, fashions changed, and the temple is partly archaic, partly classical. Only one column still stands, built of 100-ton drums.

Sanctuary of Demeter

To the west of the acropolis, on the other side of the ancient River Selinus (modern Modione), a path leads to the **Sanctuary of Demeter Malophoros** ('the bearer of fruits'). The walled sanctuary was built around 575 BC, replacing an older one. Outside the sanctuary worshippers set up carved stelae, and more than 12,000 votive figures of Demeter have been recovered, attesting to the importance of the cult; a vast necropolis is spread around the sanctuary, and, for several miles to the west along the coast, tombs are visible.

Marinella and the Bélice Estuary

Only a stone's throw from the acropolis, bathers lounge on the fine beach of **Marinella Lido**, an extremely pleasant, laid-back resort, with all the facilities if you want to stay overnight.

Farther east, coastal dunes and marshy lagoons mark the evocative **Bélice Estuary**, a protected natural area easy to explore from Marinella or the next beach resort, Porto Palo. Although swept by the sirocco and crossed by the train line, it is an attractive and largely unspoiled area, rich in herons, ducks and other waterfowl; marine turtles use the beach to lay their eggs.

Sciacca and Around

Sciacca (pop. 43,000) started out as Thermai Selinuntinai, a dependency of Selinus that was popular as a spa with both the Greeks and the Romans. Under the Arabs it become a very prosperous town, acquiring its modern name (*xacca* meant 'from the waters'). It has been a fairly quiet place since then, though any Sicilian town is good

Getting There and Around

The train only gets as close as Castelvetrano and Selinunte; from there, several **buses** a day go to Sciacca and other coastal towns. Autolinea Gallo (**t** 09 25 21 086) run eight buses a day to Palermo from Viale della Vittoria 27, near the spa establishment. Autolinea Alumia (**t** 09 25 20 414) runs to Agrigento from Viale delle Terme. Eraclea Minoa is accessible only by car, but there are fairly frequent buses to Caltabellotta and the *grotte* from Sciacca.

Tourist Information

Corso Vittorio Emanuele 84, **t** 0925 86 247 (*open Mon–Sat 8–2 and 4–7*).

Where to Stay

Sciacca ✉ 92019

Because of its status as a thermal spa, Sciacca has a number of places to stay.

****Grand Hotel delle Terme di Sciacca**, Viale Nuove Terme 1, **t** 0925 23 133 (*moderate*). Smack next to the spa, also with sea views, this is conveniently located for those patrons suffering from indigestion pains that Alka-Seltzer just can't handle.

****Villa Palocla**, contrada Raganella, **t** 0925 90 28 12 (*moderate*). A country house constructed in 1750, with some of its late Baroque features. Lovely garden with orange grove and pool.

***Torre Makauda**, on the SS115, 9km from town, **t** 0925 96 88 25 (*inexpensive–moderate; half board only*). One of the big modern resort hotels, with a central building and bungalows overlooking the sea; tennis courts, beach, pool, and children's activities.

***Garden**, Via Valverde 2, just off the SS115, **t** 0925 26 299 (*budget*). A less expensive choice not far from the Villa Comunale.

Paloma Bianca, Via Figuli 5, on the SS115, **t** 0925 25 130 (*budget*). Cheap and convenient.

Baia Makauda, Contrada Tranchina, 7km from Sciacca, **t** 0925 99 70 01 (*€10 for a two-person tent*). One of several campsites in the vicinity. *Closed Oct–mid-June.*

Siculiana ✉ 92010

Paguro Residence, Via Principe di Piemonte 37, **t** 0925 81 55 10 (*budget*). Siculiana's sole hotel.

Eraclea Minoa ✉ 92010

Eraclea Minoa Village, **t** 0925 84 73 10 (*camping €10 in a two-person tent*). An attractive tourist village near the ruins at Eraclea Minoa, with camping under the pines, two-bed bungalows and a bar and restaurant, set on the beach under the chalk cliffs. *Closed Nov–Apr.*

Eating Out

Hostaria del Vicolo, Vicolo Sammaritano 10, **t** 09 25 23 071 (*expensive*). The popular choice in Sciacca, proposes traditional cooking with an experimental touch (fish with green tea and lemon). *Closed Sun eve and Mon.*

Il Gambero Rosso, Corso Vittorio Emanuele (*moderate–expensive*). Near the Villa Comunale.

Bella Napoli Seconda, Viale della Vittoria 14, **t** 0925 25 448 (*inexpensive*). A simple pizzeria, also close to the Villa Comunale. *Closed lunch.*

Al Faro, Via Porto 25, **t** 09 25 25 349 (*inexpensive*). Next to the fishmarket, this restaurant gets the pick of the catch down by the port, where there's lots more seafood. *Closed Sun.*

for at least one impressive explosion. Sciacca's came during the 15th and 16th centuries, with one of the island's greatest feuds: the Caso Sciacca, which grew to the extent that it divided the town's population into factions loyal to the Aragonese family Luna and Norman Perolla. The feud left the town devastated and decreased its population by half.

Today it's quiet again, a pretty town on a hillside sloping up from the sea, living on fish, the thermal waters, and traditional pottery – Sciacca's ceramic artists are some of the most talented in Sicily; they have shops in the port area and along the main road, Via Licata.

Santa Margherita and Palazzo Steripinto

The traditional way of entering this terraced town overlooking the sea is through the grandiose **Porta San Salvatore**, built in the 16th century within the older fortifications. The lower town contains many fine churches – first among them the unexpected Renaissance jewel **Santa Margherita** (1342, rebuilt in 1595), just inside the gate. This subtle and elegant rectangle – hardly a Sicilian's idea of what a church should be – retains two relics from its earlier incarnation: a simple front portal with two little monsters, and a glorious Gothic side portal (currently under restoration), with bas-reliefs of 1486 by Francesco Laurana. The unusual cornice with its gargoyles is a Renaissance addition.

Across the street, the peculiar church of the **Carmine** looks for all the world like a picture in a book with a torn page, so abruptly does its 18th-century restoration stop midway up. One street to the left of this façade is an equally peculiar one, the 1501 **Palazzo Steripinto** with its rasp-like surface of diamond-pointed stone. Buildings like this were a short-lived fad in the 1500s; no one knows where it started, but examples turn up from Naples to Spain.

The Terra Vecchia

Everyone in Sciacca comes for the *passeggiata* in **Piazza Scandaliato**, facing the town hall and overlooking the sea. A block east, the **cathedral**, from the early 12th century, has since been modified with a curly Baroque façade, decorated on the outside with five statues by Antonino and Gian Domenico Gagini, while the east side of the church is original. The interior, from the 1600s, has a *Madonna* by Laurana in one of the chapels on the right. A street leads down from the front of the cathedral, through the walls and down the stairs to Sciacca's mouldering but picturesque **port** quarter, a nest of narrow alleys with no churches at all save the fishermen's church on the waterfront, naturally dedicated to St Peter.

There are more quarters like this in the old centre, the **Terra Vecchia**, above Via Licata (the main SS115). Via Santa Caterina takes you up to the oldest parts of town and the derelict church of **San Nicolò**, built by Count Roger though much altered since. **Santa Maria Giummare**, nearby on Via Valverde, also retains some traces of its Norman origins, along with 18th-century stucco work inside.

Farther up, along Sciacca's eastern walls, is the **Castello Luna**, built in 1380 and named after one of the feuding families (they were a branch of the famous family that produced the anti-pope Benedict XIII). At the top of the town is another interesting old quarter around Piazza Noceto and the 16th-century church of **San Michele**.

There are beaches at Stazzone, Lido Salus and La Foggia, but the places to go are **San Marco** and **Contrada Sobareto**.

The Baths and Monte San Calógero

The **Grotte Vaporose di San Calógero**, Via Agatocle 2 (*t 0925 96 11 11, t 0925 96 12 11; open daily*), run by the Azienda Autonoma delle Terme di Sciacca, are thermal baths which have been used to cure skin diseases and arthritis since pre-Roman times – the remains of the world's oldest heating system (17th century BC) were found there, including a (still visible) 'sweating cave', in which canals conducted the steam. The seats and water channels were hollowed out in ancient times. Legend has it that Daedalus made the baths, while other sources claim that St Paul sent San Calógero to Sicily to put an end to a plague raging there, and during his stay he found the caverns in the mountain that bears his name, as well as the natural saunas which are reputed to cure rheumatism. A second version of the story has it that San Calógero made the water gurgle out from the mountain to scare away the devils who lived there. The *grotte*, 7km north of Sciacca on Monte San Calógero, have been restored and are now part of the complex. Beneath the steam baths, where the sulphurous vapours are more concentrated, lie two underground caverns, open since very ancient times, where archaeologists and speleologists have discovered huge Copper Age jars and the tiny arm bones of children sacrificed as an offering to the terrible gods inside.

Perhaps the strangest of all the stories concerning San Calógero involves a small uncharted island offshore. In 1831, British seamen discovered it and claimed it for Britain. The French spotted it too, as did of course the Kingdom of Naples. All three were sending warships toward the island, and it looked like trouble. But before any of them could reach it and cause an international incident, the island sank out of sight, vanishing as mysteriously as it had appeared.

At 2km east of Sciacca, in the **Castello Incantato** (*open Tues–Sat 9–12 and 3–7*) thousands of stone heads crowd an olive grove, a totally bizarre open-air gallery created by sculptor Filippo Bentivegna who devoted his life to carving the heads of his imaginary enemies up till his death in 1967.

Caltabellotta

The castle atop the lofty, gloomy village of Caltabellotta saw the 1302 signing of the peace ending the War of the Vespers. Twenty kilometres from Sciacca, controlling the approaches to the Monti Sicani, Caltabellotta is one of the highest towns in Sicily, over half a mile in the air. The Greeks defended it, as did the Arabs, who gave it its name ('castle of the oaks'). Among the buildings in the medieval town is the Norman **Chiesa Madre**, containing some ornate stucco decoration and two works by the Gaginis: the *Madonna della Catena* and a *St Benedict*. The castle where Frederick of Aragon and Charles of Anjou made their deal is little more than ruins today, but at the top of the village is the little **Cappella di San Pellegrino**, built near an ancient holy cave in the cliff. Pellegrino is an obscure saint, but a good man to have around. When he came to Caltabellotta there was a dragon in the cave gobbling up all the village's maidens; he went right off and gave the dragon a good bashing, and that was that.

King Minos in Sicily

The old place name Minoa recalls ancient Crete and the legend of Daedalus and the labyrinth. According to the Greeks, King Minos came to Sicily with his mighty fleet in search of Daedalus, the master smith and builder of the labyrinth, who had escaped Crete with the aid of his man-made wings. Daedalus took refuge secretly in Sicily with the legendary King Cocalus, and made the famous golden honeycomb as a votive offering to Aphrodite at Erice. He also made some mechanical dolls for the king's daughters, which delighted them greatly.

Not knowing where to find Daedalus, Minos had been roaming the Mediterranean with a triton shell offering a reward to anyone who could draw a linen thread through its spiralling chambers. Arriving at the coast at Heraclea, he proceeded inland to Cocalus' capital, Camicos (*see* 'In the Interior', p.185). The Sicilian king accepted the challenge, and naturally gave the shell to Daedalus, who bored a hole at the small end, tied the string round an ant, and let the ant do the rest. Minos knew only one man was capable of such a trick, and he demanded the return of his wizard. With such a big navy off his shores, Cocalus could hardly refuse – but his daughters, unhappy about losing the fellow who made them such pretty toys, poured boiling water in Minos' bath and cooked him.

In the battle that followed, the Sicilians burned Minos' fleet. Minos got an impressive tomb at Camicos, while the surviving Cretans founded Heraclea Minoa, though some wandered inland and founded another city (possibly Nicosia or Troina). Just how much history can be sieved out of all this is hard to say – probably quite a bit, although no Minoan finds have yet been made in Sicily. The Cretans, with their sea empire, probably had a lot to do with Sicily after *c.* 2000 BC; Diodorus Siculus wrote that Theron of Akragas discovered the tomb of Minos in the 5th century BC, and restored his remains to the Cretans.

Eraclea Minoa

The Greeks certainly had a good eye for picking sites for cities – aesthetically, at least. There may not be much to see of Eraclea Minoa, a Selinuntan colony founded in the 6th century BC that was abandoned by Augustus' time, but the location is superb. Low hills by the sea, an extravagant beach and shining white cliffs – do come, even if by this point the last thing you want to see is more ruins. The town as it exists was founded in the 6th century BC by Selinunte; the name commemorating Hercules was added later, perhaps in the 4th century BC when the city belonged to Akragas. During the Carthaginian Wars, Eraclea Minoa was depopulated, as the River Plátani (the ancient Halykos) formed the dangerous boundary between Greek and Punic territory. Timoleon repopulated the city with a mixed Greek-Carthaginian population; it changed hands a few times and suffered so much in the 1st-century Slave Wars and from the depredations of Verres that it was abandoned for good.

The Greek Theatre

Open 9am until one hour before dusk, adm.

The excavations date mainly from Timoleon's rebuilding in the 4th century BC and include remains of the city walls and a few streets. The interesting theatre, built of easily erodable soft marl and now protected with a plastic covering that reproduces the shape of the original seating, was designed after the main theatre in Athens. Restored in the 4th century, when there was still a taste for theatre, it was abandoned in Roman times. Nevertheless, austere and dignified, this is the best example of a classical theatre in Sicily; with its view over the sea it would be the perfect place to see a play by Euripides or Aeschylus now, if only the seats were real. An **antiquarium** on the site contains a few items from the digs and a plan of the ancient city, which is still being excavated.

Farther east towards Agrigento, **Siculiana** has a large castle (privately owned) dating from 1356. The **beaches** at Siculiana Marina are among the most peaceful and uncontaminated of all southern Italy, a long stretch of fine sand backed by white chalky cliffs and umbrella pine woods..

Agrigento

Ancient Akragas, one of the most opulent cities of the ancient Greeks, sprawled gracefully from its high acropolis down to the sea. Since the Dark Ages, however, the

Getting There and Around

Agrigento is connected by **train** directly with Caltanissetta, from which the lines branch off for Palermo or Catania (via Enna); connections to other towns are patchy – one or two trains a day, with a change to make. The station is on Piazza Marconi, in the exact centre of the city.

All inter-city **buses** leave from nearby Piazza Roselli, where there is also a parking space. The bus is almost quicker than the train for any destination. Regular city buses (no.10 among others) make the circuit of the Valley of the Temples, starting from Piazza Marconi. No.10 also goes to the beach at San Leone; no.12 descends to Caos and Pirandello's house. Others descend every 30mins for Porto Empédocle.

Driving in the old town can be a major adventure. The only main street, Via Atenea, is for pedestrians 9–2 and 4–8, and the only route through for cars (one way) begins with Via Gioieni, next to the Standa on central Piazzale Aldo Moro, and circles through the town. One wrong turn and you'll be headed down a stairway, but be bold: you can do it.

Tourist Information

Via Cesare Battisti 15, t 0922 20 454.

Where to Stay

All the cheaper possibilities here are in the old town, actually much more convenient for spending your evenings after the sightseeing.

Agrigento ✉ 92100

★★★★**Baglio della Luna**, Contrada Maddalusa, t 0922 51 10 61 (*luxury*), bagliodl@oasi.it. Beautifully restored with timbered ceilings and antique furniture. The restaurant has an extensive wine list.

★★★★**Grand Hotel Corte dei Vescovi**,Contrada Maddalusa, 92 t 0922 40 61 11 (*luxury*). A manor house dating back to the 19th century. and set in a park with lemon groves town has cowered shyly on its small citadel. Today, with a population of 60,000 and growing, it's still up there – and bursting at the seams. Agrigento's reluctance to expand much down on to its ample plains has created one of Italy's most remarkable urban landscapes. Arriving from the sparse hills of the interior, you'll suddenly cross over a long dizzying viaduct into what seems a cloud-island of densely packed tall buildings, finally and abruptly to be dumped in the middle of one of the slickest and most up-to-date cities on the island. This hilltop Agrigento is a delight, but from anywhere in it with a view down to the sea you'll enjoy a broad panorama of the real attraction: the Valley of the Temples, the most significant and most visited archaeological site in Sicily.

History

Colonists from Gela and Rhodes founded Akragas in 581 BC, on the plain between the Rivers Akragas (San Biagio) and Hypsas (Sant'Anna). The early colonists must have been very confident about Akragas' future, for, unlike most ancient cities, it is thought the new colony was laid out with a large plan to grow into, and its extensive walls were built all at once in the 6th century BC.

Though the youngest of the Greek colonies, Akragas soon became one of the major cities in Sicily, owing to an early tyrant, Phalaris, who reigned until *c.* 550 BC. Credit is given to him for the city walls and grand building programme, and for annexing large territories, including the city of Licata, from the Sikans. Pindar, who lived as a guest in Akragas under the later tyrant Theron, wrote that Phalaris roasted his enemies alive

and umbrella pines. Stunning 360-degree views of the sea, the Valley and Agrigento.
★★★★Villa Athena, Via dei Templi 33, **t** 0922 59 62 88 (*luxury*). The only hotel actually located in the Valley of the Temples is this elegant and serene place built around an 18th-century villa and garden overlooking the Temple of Concord. Its restaurant is the finest in Agrigento.
★★★★Dioscuri Bay Palace, Lungomare Falcone e Borsellino 1, **t** 0922 40 61 11, *www.framon hotels.it* (*expensive*). A winter garden pool and restaurant with panoramic views.
★★★★Hotel Kaos, Contrada L. Pirandello, **t** 0922 59 86 22 (*expensive*). A new hotel built on the site of an old villa, with lovely old gardens, tennis courts and an generously sized pool.
★★★Colleverde Park, Via Passeggiata Archeologica, **t** 09 22 29 555, *www.colleverde hotel.it* (*moderate–inexpensive*). Farther up the slope and with a beautiful garden looking down on part of the valley.

★★Akragas, Viale Emporium 16, **t/f** 09 22 41 40 82 (*inexpensive*). A simpler option, also close to the beach at San Leone.
★★★Hotel del Viale, Via del Piave (Piazza Cavour), **t** 09 22 20 053 (*inexpensive*). This clean and comfortable hotel is a wise choice if you want to stay in the historic centre and still be close to your parked car.
★★★Pirandello Mare, Via Giorgio de Chirico 17, **t** 09 22 41 23 33 (*inexpensive*). Close to the beach at San Leone, with a restaurant. A bit noisy in the summer months.
★★Bella Napoli, Piazza Lena 6, **t** 0922 20 435 (*budget*). Farther west in the old town (behind the Tribunale on Via Atenea), this is a good choice for this price bracket.
★★Belvedere, Via San Vito 20, **t** 0922 20 051 (*budget*). Just off central Piazzale Aldo Moro, this is an austere-looking but tolerable place, with the bonus of private parking for an extra €5 a day; some of the rooms have views over the valley and the sea.
★★Concordia, Piazza San Francesco 11, **t** 0922 59 62 66 (*budget*). This basic hotel is

in a large bull made of bronze, a recurring theme in Rhodian legends but not very likely to have happened in reality.

Under Theron, who ascended to power in 488 BC, Akragas expanded its territories up to Himera (Imera) on the north coast of Sicily, provoking the mass Carthaginian attack on that city. Theron and his ally, Gelon of Gela, won a sweeping victory here in 480 BC, and the captives and disbanded soldiers of this campaign were set to work erecting the temples and other public works. The city became fabulously wealthy – ironically, through peaceful trade with the empire of the Carthaginians. To commemorate the Battle of Himera, the Temple of Olympian Zeus was begun, largest of all Greek temples. 'The people built temples as if they would live forever, but lived as if they would die the next day,' marvelled an ancient writer. Akragas was famous for its horses, which often won at the Greek games and were depicted on the city's coins. Akragas also had a reputation for decadence second only to that of Sybaris; during one war the sentries on the walls are recorded as going on strike for softer pillows.

At this time Akragas gave the world Empedocles. Scientist, engineer and poet, as well as a man of affairs who played an important role during the city's brief period of democratic rule, he is best known for his philosophical writings. His concept of matter as divided into the Four Elements – Earth, Water, Fire and Air – was a foundation of scientific thought for the next 2,000 years (he was also the first to consider air as a material substance). Empedocles explained the problem of motion – the obsession of the early philosophers – with the poetic idea that all the events and movements of the world could be seen in terms of Love and Strife, attraction and repulsion, Eros and

cheapest in town and is on the other side of Piazzale Moro, towards the heart of the old town.
Internazional San Leone, Contrada le Dune, t 0922 41 61 21. Campsite. *Closed off-season.*

Eating Out

Agrigento isn't particularly known for any special dishes; one local speciality is *cuscusu* – not couscous as in Tràpani, but a sweet of almonds and pistachios made only by the nuns at the convent of Santo Spirito.
As with the hotels, the fancier places are down by the temples.
Le Caprice, Via Panoramica dei Templi 51, t 0922 26 469 (*expensive*). Besides the aforementioned Villa Athena, this is one of the best – a seafood palace with perfect swordfish *involtini. Closed Fri.*
Taverna Mosè, at San Biagio, just east of Agrigento on the SS115, Contrada Mosè, t 0922 26 778 (*expensive*). Good for atmosphere, a view of the temples, and their own

scaloppine Pirandello, fave specialities and local sole. *Closed Mon.*
Concordia, Via Porcello 8, t 0922 59 62 66 (*moderate*). Specializes in fish; one of a number of similar touristy but less expensive *trattorie* on the side streets around Via Atenea.
Trattoria dei Templi, Via Panoramica dei Templi 15, t 0922 40 31 10 (*moderate*). A smart trattoria situated near the Temple of Concordia: it has vaulted ceilings and terracotta floors and offers an imaginative menu where fish features in particular.
Atenea, Via Ficani 32, t 0922 413 23 66 (*inexpensive*). With tables out on a little *piazza*, they offer a passable full meal here – even fresh fish, but don't expect a culinary masterpiece. *Closed Sun lunch in summer, all day Sun in winter.*
Pizzeria Vetro, Via delle Ninfe 61, t 0922 41 22 42 (*inexpensive*). The popular favourite in San Leone, a nice family place with excellent pizzas, and a full menu.

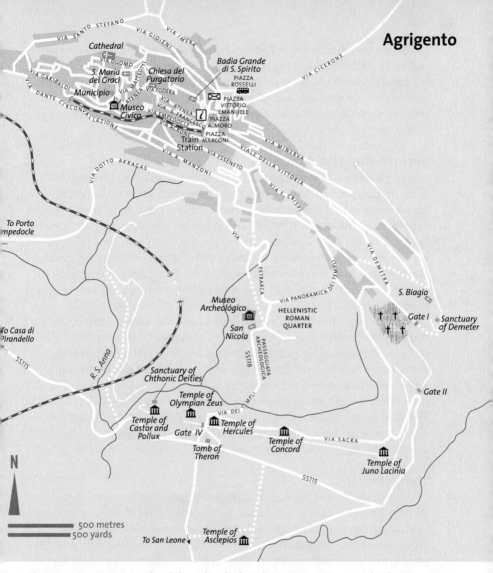

Agrigento

Cathedral
VIA SANTO STEFANO
VIA GIOIENI
VIA IMERA
VIA DUOMO
S. Maria dei Graci
Chiesa del Purgatorio
Badia Grande di S. Spirito
PIAZZA ROSSELLI
VIA CICERONE
Municipio
VIA GARIBALDI
VIA MATTEOTTI
VIA FODERA
VIA ATENEA
PIAZZA VITTORIO EMANUELE
Museo Civico
VIA ATENEA
VIA S. FRANCESCO
PIAZZA A. MORO
VIA DANTE
CIRCONVALLAZIONE
VIA EMPEDOCLE
VIA ACRONE
PIAZZA MARCONI
Train Station
VIA MINERVA
VIALE DELLA VITTORIA
VIA A. MANZONI
VIA ESSENETO
VIA DOTTO AKRAGAS
VIA F. CRISPI

To Porto Empedocle

VIA

VIA DEMETRA

Museo Archeológico
PETRARCA
VIA PANORAMICA DEI TEMPLI
HELLENISTIC ROMAN QUARTER
S. Biagio
Gate I
Sanctuary of Demeter

To Casa di Pirandello
SS115
San Nicola
SS118
PASSEGGIATA ARCHEOLOGICA
Gate II

R. S. Anna

Sanctuary of Chthonic Deities
Temple of Olympian Zeus
VIA DEI TEMPLI
Temple of Castor and Pollux
Gate IV
Temple of Hercules
Temple of Concord
VIA SACRA
Tomb of Theron
Temple of Juno Lacinia
SS115

N

500 metres
500 yards

To San Leone
Temple of Asclepios

Thanatos. One story says the philosopher died studying Mount Etna; another has it that he was hanged after a political coup.

For all its wealth and accomplishments, time was running out for Akragas. When the city's great enemy, Syracuse, defeated the Athenians, the Carthaginians saw their chance to exact revenge for Imera. They besieged Akragas for eight months before capturing it. Many of the citizens took refuge in the Temple of Athena and set fire to it and themselves as the Carthaginians looted the city. Later the Carthaginians allowed some inhabitants to return. The city became independent, was rebuilt by Timoleon in 340 BC, and eventually enjoyed a bit of its old prosperity under the Romans, when it was the only survivor among the once-great Greek cities of the southern coast.

In the 3rd century AD, however, Agrigentum, as the Romans called it, began its long decline. By the 8th century there was nothing more than a little village atop the ancient acropolis. Its revival began under the Arabs, and has proceeded slowly and gradually up to the present day. Until 1927, the town was known by its mangled medieval name Girgenti. Mussolini, in his name campaign, changed it to Agrigento in 1927.

Via Atenea and Old Agrigento

Sloping **Piazzale Aldo Moro** just north of the station (Piazza Marconi) is the centre of the city and one of the few green spots in old Agrigento. At the bottom of the square, Via F. Crispi leads down to the Museo Archeológico and the temples; on the opposite side is **Via Atenea**, a lively, attractive pedestrian thoroughfare with most of Agrigento's shops and restaurants, the main artery of the old town. On this street, the 17th-century church known as the **Chiesa del Purgatorio**, with fine stucco-work allegorical figures by Serpotta, stands over the entrance to a complex underground system of cisterns of the 5th century BC; stone removed from here was used to build the temples.

The **Municipio**, farther down Via Atenea, is in a pretty 17th-century convent, sharing Piazza Pirandello with the Teatro Pirandello and the **Museo Civico** (*open daily 9–1.30 and 4.30–6.30*), containing a variety of paintings from many centuries. Up the stairs and alleyways from here you reach the old whitewashed **Greek quarter** of town, which indeed looks more Greek than Italian; signs will direct you to the former Orthodox cathedral, **Santa Maria dei Greci** (*usually open daily 8–12.30 and 4.30–7.30*). This little church with a lovely portal was constructed in the 12th century and incorporated a temple, perhaps of Athena. Six bases of Doric columns remain inside, as well as part of the original pavement, and some fragments of Byzantine frescoes.

The Cathedral

Farther up you will find the Via del Duomo and the large 14th-century cathedral at the very top of Agrigento. This and the diocesan museum next to it were damaged in a landslide in 1966 and the museum's collection has since been moved to the Museo Archeológico. Founded by San Gerlando, Roger I's bishop, the church was dedicated to him in 1365 and contains his relics in a silver casket. Partly painted, partly coffered, the ceiling offers the main interest in the interior, along with the grand arch in the nave. The phenomenon known as *porta voce* allows someone in the apse, beneath the cornice, to hear whispering in the main doorway, and so the priest could discreetly listen to comments on his sermon as the parishioners departed. Stranger still is a letter from the Devil himself, in a fantastic, incomprehensible script of magic signs and symbols, but said to be addressed to a virgin of Agrigento, to whom he offered all the treasures of the world in exchange for her virtue. She stood firm, and, as the story goes, foiled his designs completely when she turned the letter over to the priest. Just behind the cathedral is the **Biblioteca Lucchesiana**, founded in 1765 by the Bishop of Agrigento as a public library, now containing 40,000 volumes including many rare documents and manuscripts.

The finest church in Agrigento, however, lies towards the east side of the old town, at the top of dead-end Via Fodera, not far from the round *Fascista* **post office**. Known as the **Badia Grande**, the Cistercian convent and church of Santo Spirito was founded by Marchisia Chiaramonte in 1290. The church preserves a beautiful doorway (on the west), a white interior with stuccoes by Serpotta, and a *Madonna* by the school of Domenico Gagini. The cloister, recently restored, houses a museum of local crafts.

Viale della Vittoria

Agrigento's modern quarter, running along the ridge of the Rupe Atenea, lies on the opposite side of Piazzale Aldo Moro from the old town, along a broad and elegant boulevard called Viale della Vittoria. There are many places with excellent views over the Valley of the Temples, and at the far end of the *viale* is the medieval church of San Biagio and the Sanctuary of Demeter (*see* below).

The Valley of the Temples

Even more than Selinunte, ancient Akragas must have been a splendid sight from the sea. The Greeks definitely planned it that way; important temples (like the Parthenon) were always sited with regard to the seafarer's view. The term 'Valley of the Temples', probably invented by the tourist board, is misleading enough: it isn't a valley at all. The great temples of Akragas were sited on a long cliff, just inside the southern walls; it's an unusual plan for a Greek city, as if the flashy Akragans wanted to put their jewels right up front where everyone could see them. From here, the city sloped upwards on a broad grid of streets to the other temples on the Rupe Atenea – as the historian Polybius noted, almost every house in Akragas had a sea view.

The Archaeological Zone below Agrigento (Via F. Crispi) is always open, with the exception of the Temple of Zeus and the Temple of the Dioscuri (*open 9am–dusk*) and the Hellenistic quarter, by the church of San Nicola (*open daily 9–12 and 3–7, until 6 in winter*). Every night the temples are illuminated.

The Museo Archeológico

Open Wed-Sat 9-1.30 and 3-6. Mon, Tues and Sun 9-1.30, adm.

Spread across 3km in the valley, the temples take a good part of a day to explore, and you may consider stopping first at the Museo Archeológico near the 15th-century cloisters of **San Nicola** – the bus's first stop en route to the temples.

This fabulous collection of vases, statues, coins, etc. found on the site makes a fine introduction to the splendour of ancient Akragas and its unique temples. Particularly good are the **Greek vases**, and the heads and one body of the giant **telamones** of the Temple of Zeus. Beside these a display of models offers various conceptions of what this monstrous temple used to look like. Among the sculptures there is a Praxitelian torso and the Phaedra sarcophagus of the 2nd century AD, moved here from the damaged cathedral.

A small Greek theatre was discovered next to the museum during its construction, and near the so-called Oratory of Phalaris, actually a shrine dedicated to an unknown woman of the 2nd century BC, converted to a chapel in the Middle Ages.

Across the Passeggiata Archeológica, the main road to the temples, lies the **Hellenistic-Roman Quarter**, where along the grid of streets some of the houses have been unearthed, with good mosaics (under protective coverings) and reconstructed columns of their peristyle courts. From here you can continue south on the Passeggiata to the main temples on either side of the Posto di Ristoro café, or back-track a bit to the north, turning east (right) for the Via Panoramica and the Via Demetra; this, along with some ancient wheel ruts, leads up to San Biagio at the edge of the Rupe Atenea shelf.

The Sanctuary of Demeter

Like Santa Maria dei Greci, **San Biagio** incorporates parts of a Greek temple. The Normans built the church over an important Temple of Demeter and Persephone, begun shortly after the Greek victory at Himera in 480 BC. Of the temple, part of the foundation can be seen by the chapel, and two round altars remain to the north; in one of them, a hole called the bothros received the wine, piglets, male members made of dough, etc. offered to the chthonic (underworld) gods, to whom the cult of Demeter and Persephone was closely attached.

Even more interesting in this respect is the rock **Sanctuary of Demeter** (*if the gate is locked, the key is held by the obliging Colagero Alaimo, at Via Bottighella 2, in Agrigento; leave a tip*) below San Biagio (steps in the rock). Pre-dating the temple of Demeter and the Greek colony of Akragas itself by 200 years, the sanctuary is of Sikan origin, although the walls they built demonstrate how Greek influences infiltrated Sicily very early on. The sacred area consists of three natural caves, once filled with votive statues of Demeter and Persephone of various periods, the oldest dating back to the early 8th century BC, when water deities apparently were worshipped (channels and drains for the water can still be seen in the caves). Timoleon added a nymphaeum to the existing source and cisterns.

A short walk south of here, by the wall of the cemetery, is the first of eight city gates, **Gate I**, and a V-shaped bastion located at a particularly vulnerable point in the defences.

Gate II and the Temple of Juno Lacinia

The Via Panoramica heads south from here, taking you past **Gate II** (known as the Gela Gate), from which the ancient road to the mother city can still be seen. At this important gate, more votive offerings to Demeter and Persephone have been uncovered. The **Temple of Juno Lacinia**, the easternmost of the great temples, comes clearly into sight as you descend to the south. Its name derives from an 18th-century confusion with another temple, and its original dedication is unknown. Built around 460 BC, the temple still shows signs of the sack of 409 BC, when the Carthaginians set fire to it; the Romans later restored it, only to have their good work undone by an earthquake. Only 25 of the original 34 columns remain, windblasted on the southeast by the sirocco; the temple is currently undergoing restoration and cannot be entered.

Gate III and the Temple of Concord

Between the Temple of Juno Lacinia and the Temple of Concord, **Gate III** has suffered the borings of Byzantine tombs. These continue throughout the natural rock wall up to the **Temple of Concord**, which along with the Theseion in Athens is one of the best-preserved Greek temples in the world, owing to its conversion into a church by the 6th-century Bishop of Agrigento, San Gregorio delle Rape ('of the turnips'). Dismantled in the 18th century, the church left this Doric structure of the mid-5th century BC almost intact, with its 34 columns, stylobate, cella, etc. Like all Agrigento's temples, this one was originally coated with powdered marble stucco and painted in bright colours that have long since worn away; the rough, dull-golden limestone beneath surprises people who expect all temples to look like the Parthenon or their local bank branch.

The Temple of Hercules

Still heading west you cross an unusual, deeply cut street known as the **Street of Tombs**, which passes through an early Christian cemetery. The **Roman catacombs** north of here were adapted by the Christians in the 3rd century, and continue all the way to the garden of the Villa Aurea, the old **Antiquarium** (whose collections have been transferred to the main Museo Archeológico). The columns near here, rising above the Passeggiata Archeológica, belong to the oldest temple in the valley, the **Temple of Hercules**. Built around 500 BC, on an artificial platform, it measures 221ft by 82ft – longer than most. The Carthaginians burned it and the Romans repaired it, although the predatory Praetor Verres did his best to make off with a famous statue of Hercules that once graced the temple. For once the outrage of the citizens deterred him. In 1923 eight of the temple's columns were re-erected by Sir Alexander Hardcastle.

Gate IV and the Temple of Asclepius

The Passeggiata leads south to the **Tomb of Theron**, which you can see from the Temple of Hercules. Like almost everything else it is erroneously named, for this two-storey monumental tomb belongs to the 1st century BC. It is located just outside the city walls, where the city's main gate, Porta Aurea (**Gate IV**), once stood. A large Roman cemetery, partially destroyed by landslides, spreads out over the hill from the gate. South of the Tomb of Theron, on the other side of the SS115, lies the **Temple of Asclepius**, built in the 5th century and different from the other temples in that it has solid walls instead of columns. Asclepius was the god of healing, and this temple, along with all others dedicated to him, is built beside a spring with curative properties. The treatment offered by the priests consisted of dream interpretations, restful surroundings, and taking of the waters. The success of this simple cure is attested to by the great popularity of the cult throughout the Greek world.

The Temple of Olympian Zeus

The next temple within the walls, across the Passeggiata and next to the Posto di Ristoro, is the Temple of Olympian Zeus, the largest Greek temple in the world and one of the most remarkable. Although totally ruined by an earthquake, its stone quarried to build Porto Empédocle, the remains are still very impressive, measuring 373ft by 278ft (larger than a football field). The columns, thought to have been 53ft tall, were made of small stones plastered over to look like whole marble pillars – the flutings in these, as Goethe noted, are wide enough to hold a man with his shoulders scarcely touching the sides; it would take 20 men standing in a circle to embrace the pillar's great girth. Walls and buttresses filled the spaces between the mock columns and on top of these stood the enormous telamones, or stone giants, supporting the architrave. A copy of one of these Atlas-like figures lies within the temple, to give you an idea of the vast scale the Carthaginian slaves were forced to work on: columns, telamones and architrave combined, the whole thing stood over 100ft high. Begun in 480 BC, the temple was still unfinished in 409 BC when the Carthaginians invaded the city.

Gate V and the Sanctuary of the Chthonic Deities

To the west, the newly excavated **Gate V** once had a tall projecting tower, designed as many of these gates were to hamper the shield arms of opponents trying to enter. Here also are four temples dating from the foundation of Akragas, known collectively as the **Sanctuary of the Chthonic Deities**. The first two temples, begun in the 6th century BC, were never completed; the third, commonly known as the **Temple of Castor and Pollux** or of the Dioscuri, was finished at the end of the 5th century BC. In 1836 four columns and a piece of architrave were pieced together for picturesque effect but without any attempt at historical accuracy: it's a mishmash of items from the numerous ruins of altars and sanctuaries that litter the area, some of which date back to the Sikans (like the Sanctuary of Demeter), and one altar is prehistoric. The fourth temple, with its platform and fallen columns, is from the Hellenistic period. Below this sacred area the River Hypsas runs through some extraordinary countryside.

If you're a well-shod enthusiast, you can continue along the difficult path from the sanctuary (look for the signpost) to one last sanctuary, the **Temple of Vulcano**, beyond the railway. Just two columns of this temple remain standing; it is thought that it was never completed, and was certainly not dedicated to the smith god. Gates VI–IX are also in this area if you are intent on making the complete circuit of the ancient walls.

Pirandello and Porto Empédocle

Just below Agrigento on the road to Porto Empédocle, Italy's most important modern playwright, Luigi Pirandello (1867–1936), was born in a hamlet called **Caos**, a fitting name for the birthplace of a student of the absurd, and one borrowed for the film based on Pirandello's short stories – the Taviani brothers' *Kaos*. Although the Nobel-prize winning author of *Henry IV* and *Six Characters in Search of an Author* left Sicily as a student and returned only in the summer, he is well remembered in the

Casa Natale di Pirandello (*open daily 9-1 hr before sunset, adm*) by memorabilia and photographs; as he wished, his ashes are buried under a pine near the house. In August his plays are performed here in a Settimana Pirandellana.

From Caos you can look down into **Porto Empédocle**, Agrigento's port, named after the famous philosopher. On the harbour stands an 18th-century tower partly made from the stone of the Temple of Zeus, as was the mole. Porto Empédocle is one of Italy's main mineral ports and the port for the islands of Lampedusa and Linosa. Unless you have to go there, avoid this town: there isn't a good word to be said for it.

The nearest beach to Agrigento is the developed lido at **San Leone** (*city bus every half-hour from the station*). There's another fine, less developed beach just outside Porto Empédocle to the west – **Lido Rossello**, fortunately isolated from the industrial sprawl by a hill. There are ruins of a Roman villa near the beach.

The Pelagie Islands

The remote and arid Pelagie archipelago (from the Greek Pelagia or 'sea islands') consists of two sparsely populated islands, Lampedusa and Linosa, and the uninhabited Lampione. Flat, pistol-shaped and wind-whipped, Lampedusa is the largest of the

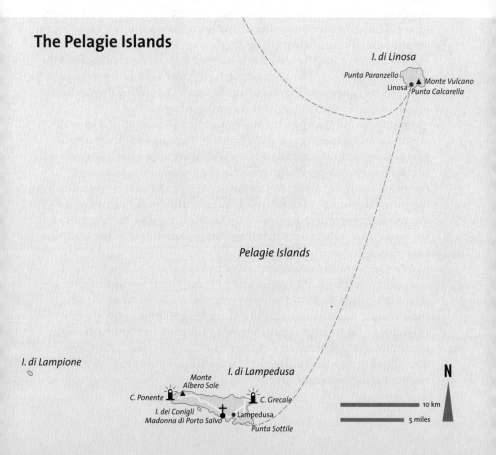

The Pelagie Islands

I. di Linosa

Punta Paranzello
Linosa Monte Vulcano
Punta Calcarella

Pelagie Islands

I. di Lampione

Monte Albero Sole
C. Ponente
I. dei Conigli
Madonna di Porto Salvo

I. di Lampedusa

C. Grecale
Lampedusa
Punta Sottile

10 km
5 miles

N

Getting There

There are 1hr **flights** from Palermo's Falcone-Borsellino airport (*see* **Travel**, p.46 and p.50) to Lampedusa (2–3 daily in the winter, 15–16 daily in the summer), or charter flights from Milan, Bergamo or Rome.

There's also the Siremar **ferry** from Porto Empédocle near Agrigento (**t** 0922 63 61 10). The service runs daily in the summer (less frequently in the winter), an overnight trip that calls at both Linosa (6hrs) and Lampedusa (8hrs). In Lampedusa, **t** 0922 97 00 03; in Linosa, **t** 0922 97 20 62.

group and the southernmost point of the Italian Republic, just a mile closer to Monastir in Tunisia than to Porto Empédocle in Agrigento Province; in all Europe, only Crete is farther south. Geologically, Lampedusa belongs to North Africa, while Linosa, a volcanic island, is the last tiny cone to the south of the great volcanic chain stretching from Etna to Vesuvius and the Pontine Islands. Only recently have the Pelagie Islands attracted many visitors, who come almost exclusively for 'the cleanest sea in Italy', and for the miles and miles which lie between these islands and the industrial regions of the rest of Europe.

History

Although finds prove that Lampedusa and Linosa were inhabited in ancient times, nothing is really known about the islands until 813, when the Saracens established small colonies on them. In 1430, King Alfonso V of Aragon ceded the islands to the barons of Caro di Montechiaro, under whom Lampedusa made its first appearance in literature, as the scene of a tremendous duel in Ariosto's *Orlando Furioso* (1516). One of the few people during the Renaissance who probably never read *Orlando* was the Turkish pirate-governor of Tunis, Dragut, who in 1553 paid a visit to Lampedusa and carried off the entire population of 1,000 as slaves. A few years later the Montechiari built a fortress to defend Lampedusa from similar outrages.

In 1630, Carlos II of Spain gave the title 'Prince of Lampedusa' to Giulio Tomasi di Lampedusa, who passed it down to the author of *The Leopard*. In 1800, the then prince allowed some Maltese colonists, the Gatt family, to farm Lampedusa. Ten years later the Gatts subdivided the island with an Englishman named Alexander Fernandez, who brought another 300 colonists. Today it's hard to believe that in those days Lampedusa had trees, fertile soil, deer and wild boar – a fragile environment which has been devastated by deforestation and improper farming, causing all the topsoil simply to blow away. But Lampedusa appears to have prospered in these early years.

In 1839 the princes of Lampedusa changed their minds and told the Gatts and Fernandez to clear off. As the Bourbons were helping neither to maintain nor to defend Lampedusa, the Tomasi family offered to sell the depopulated Pelagie to England as a companion piece to nearby Malta. When King Ferdinando II got wind of the proposition in Naples, he quickly intervened and purchased the islands himself for 12,000 ducats, sending a group of colonists in 1848. Thirty years later, the new Italian Republic did what it usually did to islands – made them into penal colonies, much to the colonists' resentment.

During the Second World War the people of Lampedusa were evacuated and the island was turned into a fortress. On 12 June 1943, the Allied fleet surrounded and bombarded it non-stop until the troops surrendered the next day. The peace treaty of 1947 stipulated that all fortifications on the island be destroyed; a minor point, as it was already shot to hell.

Lampedusa

Lampedusa is a 7.7sq mile ecological disaster area, an extreme example of neglect and misuse of natural resources. Only a few of the oldest inhabitants can recall the days when the neat drystone walls enclosed rich farmland instead of piles of rock. One of the biggest jokes on the island is the 'national park' – two scrubby trees forever dwarfed by the wind and lack of rainfall. However, the lush greenery and flowers around the Santuario della Madonna di Porto Salvo and a few vineyards recently planted demonstrate that the children of Lampedusa needn't grow up on such a lunar landscape.

Some 5,000 people live on this world's end; 70 per cent earn a living from the very rich fishing grounds surrounding the island, catching more fish than the small ice-packing plant can freeze. The ever-growing tourist industry employs another 15 per cent of the work force – the lack of greenery apparently does not deter visitors in search of immaculately clean seas.

Lampedusa Town

Most of the inhabitants of Lampedusa live in the town, only one minute's walk from the airport or the Siremar ferry quay. The width of the main street (Via Roma) and quantity of telephone booths would better suit a grand boulevard in Rome; out of season, it wants only tumbleweeds to complete the air of total desolation.

The houses on the sidestreets are plain and unadorned, each with a padlocked little cistern resembling an oven, rarely used; most of the island's nasty-tasting water comes from a desalination plant.

It is a 15min walk from here to the fine sandy **beach** at **Guitgia** on the other side of the fishermen's port. Most of the hotels are here, as well as the former prison, converted into a garage. Just west of Guitgia is **Cala Croce**, another good beach which gets slightly less crowded.

Around Lampedusa by Land

The rest of Lampedusa is shared by a few Italians, some wild rabbits and two species of poisonous snake. You can stroll along the windswept coasts and beaches, or make the one excursion to the centre of the island and the **Santuario della Madonna di Porto Salvo**, a garden spot with real flowers and bushes. The legend behind the venerated statue of the Madonna claims that it was sculpted in Cyprus in the 8th century. The ship carrying it from Jerusalem during the Crusades foundered off Lampedusa, and the statue was rescued and taken to a grotto that had long been

Tourist Information

Tourist office: Via Roma, t 0922 97 13 90 (*open Apr–Oct*), *www.lampedusa.to.*
Forza Dieci Diving Center 0922 97 54 62 one of the most reliable of the island.

Where to Stay

Lampedusa ✉ 92010
★★★Guitgia Tommasino, Via Lido Azzurro, contrada Guitgia, t 0922 97 08 79, *www.paginegialle.it/guitgia* (*luxury*). A smaller hotel with a patch of garden. The room on the first floor have balconies facing the sea.
★★★Lido Azzurro, Via Lido Azzurro, Contrada Guitgia, *www.mediatel.it/lidoazzurro*, t 0922 97 02 25 (*expensive–luxury*). A pleasant, family-run place with a good restaurant.
★★★Baia Turchese, Via Lido Azzurro, t 0922 97 04 55 (*expensive*). Just outside Lampedusa town on a beach, with 42 tidy, air-conditioned rooms, all with shower and balcony.
★★Il Gattopardo, Via Beta 6, Contrada Cala creta, t 0922 97 00 51 (*expensive*). An ultra exclusive *dammuso* (see 'Pantelleria', p.137) village retreat, purposely minus telephones or televisions, but with every other refinement, boat excursions and delicious meals. The complex was begun by the notorious Giuseppe Sindona, the Sicilian who caused the Franklin National Bank of New York to go under when millions of dollars were unaccountably lost. After being on the run for a long time, Sindona was captured in Italy in 1981; somebody slipped him a poisoned espresso in prison before he could implicate any accomplices. For over a decade the *dammuso* village stood abandoned, before current owner Roberto Merlo took over the project.
★★Belvedere, Piazza Guglielmo Marconi 4, t 0922 97 01 88 (*inexpensive*). One of a number of basic *pensioni*; opposite the harbour.
★★★Le Pelagie, Via G. Bonfiglio 11, t 0922 97 02 11 (*inexpensive*). A reasonable deal.
★Sardina, Via Pollini, t 09 22 97 01 73 (*budget*). Only stay here if you don't mind being squeezed into a sardine tin.
La Roccia, Contrada Madonna 84, *www.wel.it/laroccia*, t 0922 97 00 55. The best campsite.

Eating Out

Seafood is everywhere: in *pagghiata di pesce* (a sort of paella with rice and several different kinds of fish), spaghetti with sardines, and grilled tuna fish. Try them at the following:
Gemelli, Via Cala Pisana 2, t 0922 97 06 99 (*expensive*). Fish soup and seafood paella on the menu of this Arab-inspired restaurant.
La Lampara, Via Madonna 28, Porto Nuovo, t 0922 97 16 17 (*expensive*). Tunisian-influenced dishes like fish couscous and more traditional Sicilian ones like spaghetti with sardines, wild fennel and fresh tomatoes.
Il Saraceno, Piazza Castello 3, t 0922 97 16 41. (*expensive*). Eat on the big terrace overlooking the harbour. *Spaghetti al nero di seppia* (squid ink) and daily catch.

a hiding place from pirates and slave traders. In 1619, a sailor from Imperia was enslaved by Barbary pirates and forced to cut wood on Lampedusa. He escaped to the grotto, and there he carved a canoe of sorts in which he managed to flee Lampedusa, using a painted banner of the Madonna, Child and Santa Caterina as a sail. In gratitude for his miraculous escape, he turned the grotto into a sanctuary. A more mundane account claims that, when the Bourbon colonists arrived, the statue was found broken on the floor of the church, and that the September festival actually celebrates the anniversary of the first colonists' arrival.

The road continues to the far western end of Lampedusa, where the old US Coast Guard station and a lighthouse may be found. Halfway there, a track branches off to the left, leading down to a lovely white **sand beach** with turquoise waters opposite

A Stirring Chapter in American Naval History

The most recent foreign attack on Lampedusa came in 1986, when Colonel Gaddafi lobbed over a few Russian-made missiles. All of them fell harmlessly into the sea short of their target, which was the only European base of the United States Coast Guard. What vile imperialist plot, you may ask, brought these boys so far from America's coasts? As they explained it to us, they were there to send out a radio signal for ships to navigate by in the Mediterranean. It was a job that one man could do – simply minding the transmitter – but from long experience the service knew that one man alone on a foreign island would surely go bats in a few months (on Lampedusa, frankly, it could happen in a few days).

So the Coast Guard sent out 16 Guardsmen, just to keep each other company; their commander was the first woman officer in the service's history (this'll teach her a lesson, the brass must have thought). As it happened, out at their 'Lampedusa Hilton' on the farthest point of the island, they were never lonely. On a good day, half the island's population would be queued up outside the base to use the gym and the pool table, amazing novelties for an island where the only entertainment was a bizarre disco, set above a car garage in the middle of a junkyard.

Most days, the Yanks would abandon the place to the Lampedusans and drive into the village, there to sit a few hours and wait for the daily plane from Palermo, hoping against hope that some good-looking girl might finally turn up. The cost of the trip was the ride back, after dark, a subject which gave the Coast Guardsmen the shudders. 'Them rocks, they walk by night – they just come rolling out in front of the truck,' one of them told us. 'They're out to get us,' another added. The rest nodded their heads in silent agreement, not wishing to discuss the matter any further. After Gaddafi's missiles, the Americans moved the station to a safer island, and Lampedusa has been a quieter and sadder place.

the nature reserve **Isola dei Conigli** ('rabbit island'), which in summer is off-limits to protect rare loggerhead turtles (*Caretta caretta*) who come to lay their eggs.

Circumnavigating Lampedusa by boat is rather more picturesque than the trip by land. Among the excursion's highlights are the steep cliffs of **Albero Sole**, at 452ft the highest point on the island, with its *faraglione* just a few feet out in the crystal-clear sea. Just to the west are the stratified cliffs of **Punta Parise**, full of grottoes and boasting a curious rock formation resembling a Madonna and Child. The north coast of Lampedusa has jagged bare precipices dotted with fish-filled grottoes.

Linosa

Nearly 50km north of Lampedusa lies its round baby sister Linosa (almost 2sq miles). The two islands have little in common: if Lampedusa is part of North Africa, Linosa consists of three extinct craters – Monte Vulcano, the tallest (610ft), Monte Rosso and Monte Nero, also known as Monte di Ponente – the last and southernmost

Where to Stay and Eat

Linosa ✉ 92010
***Algusa, Via Alfieri, **t** 09 22 97 20 52 (*inexpensive*). This is the one real hotel on Linosa; it's fairly boring but decent enough.
Linosa Club, Contrada Calcarella, Punta Levante, **t 0922 97 20 66, **t** 06 94 64 138 out of season (*inexpensive*). Another option is this tourist village with bungalows, swimming pool and tennis courts. It also has a restaurant which is open all year. *Accommodation closed Oct–May.*

Anna, Via Vittorio Veneto 1, **t** 0922 97 20 48 (*budget*). The owners of this local trattoria provide visitors to the island with another choice of accommodation – an array of studio apartments available all year.
Errera, Via Scalo Vecchio 1, **t** 0922 97 20 41 (*budget*). Another trattoria with apartments and rooms to let. *Closed Nov–April.*

points of the great volcanic chain beginning at Mount Vesuvius. These volcanoes have not only enriched the soil but have also prevented the wind from blowing it away. The slight disadvantage to all this becomes obvious in summer, when the lack of wind and the black soil and rock sometimes roast the Linosians alive – it is one of the hottest places in Italy. Unlike Lampedusa, where the seabed slopes gradually, the waters around Linosa drop down quickly to great depths.

Ancient cisterns and other scanty traces reveal that Linosa was inhabited in the Roman era, then by the Arabs, and again in the 16th century, when it was a refuge for pirate and slave ships. In 1845 the first real settlers arrived, Bourbon colonists, mostly from Agrigento. They cultivated the good earth, fished and built their brightly painted little village (pop. 400) between two craters and the sea. In the 1940s the government built a now abandoned prison on the island, and until quite recently used it to dump off terrorists, Mafiosi and other *personae non gratae*.

Linosa today is as far out of the way as you can get in Italy, an idyllic isle of peace and quiet. Here is civilization in miniature: a couple of miles of road, a tiny church, a few cars, 40 telephones and one tobacconist.

There are several **lava 'beaches'**, the spectacular cliffs of **Pozzolana di Ponente** plunging into the green water and the three **craters** to explore, adorned in spring with several species of wildflowers.

Lampione

The uninhabited islet of Lampione lies to the west of Lampedusa and Linosa. Like Lampedusa it is geologically part of North Africa, and has almost no vegetation at all. The tiny islet (about 320 acres) is popular with scuba divers, for the fish are exceptionally large in these unfrequented waters, which are also dangerously alive with all sorts of sharks.

Lampione can be reached in two hours in a small boat from Lampedusa.

Agrigento to Gela

In the Interior

In the centre of Agrigento province, near the small village of **Sant'Angelo Muxaro** in the Plátani Valley, domed tholos tombs have been excavated which seem to link the site to Camicos, ancient capital of the legendary King Cocalus, who lived, if he lived at all, around 2000 BC (*see* 'King Minos in Sicily', p.169). Long famous in Greece before Sicily was even colonized, King Cocalus supposedly had Camicos built by Daedalus. None of the wonderful things made by the inventor of the labyrinth remain, although some of the ceramics and gold found in the tomb bear a remarkable resemblance to items in the eastern Mediterranean, suggesting a link between Greece and Sicily a few centuries before the first colonies. The rock-carved tombs in the walls around the modern town also show Eastern influences, the lower ones dating back to the 10th century BC. The largest of these is known as the **Tomba del Principe** (*enquire in Sant'Angelo for directions*). It is well worth the effort to see this: it is the finest such tomb in Sicily.

In **Aragona**, south of here, you can find a guide to visit the **Macalube** – funny little volcanoes only a few feet high, bubbling with mud. Nearby **Raffadali** has a Roman sarcophagus in the church, in an ancient necropolis on Busone Hill. **Cammarata**, to the east, is an increasingly popular mountain resort, although it has only one hotel. **Racalmuto** (from the Arabic Rahal-maut) was the birthplace of the late novelist and conscience of Sicily, Leonardo Sciascia.

Nondescript **Canicatti**, to the east, is an important wine centre, though nowadays the whole area is coated with plastic (for strawberries and such) during the winter, as if all the farmers had been inspired by Christo. South of Canicatti, the seldom-visited village of **Naro** was long an important monastic centre, and consequently has a nice ensemble of Baroque buildings to go with its medieval walls and Chiaramonte castle.

Getting Around

There are **trains** from Agrigento to Racalmuto and Canicatti (and onwards to Enna). Trains from Canicatti run to Licata and Gela (and onwards to Ragusa and Syracuse).

Buses from Agrigento go to Canicatti, Sant'Angelo Muxaro, Naro, Palma di Montechiaro, Licata and Gela.

Trains take 2hrs 40mins from Agrigento to Enna; to get from Agrigento to Gela by train, travel to Canicatti (45 mins), and change for Gela (1hr 40mins). Buses take 1hr from Agrigento to Licata, and 1hr 30mins from Agrigento to Gela.

Where to Stay and Eat

Licata ✉ **92027**

★★★Al Faro, Via Dogana 6, t 0922 77 55 03 (*budget*). Near the port of Licata, with air-conditioning and a restaurant.

★Roma, Corso Ferrovia 54, t 09 22 77 40 751 (*budget*). Central, well-kept but rather noisy.

Lido Giummarella, on the beach of the same name (*inexpensive*). If you don't eat at one of the seafood restaurants around the port area, head for this place just outside town. It has a €10 lunch menu, and serves pizza in the evenings.

Between Naro and Canicatti, **Delia** is believed to occupy the site of ancient Petiliana. About a kilometre from the centre of town, its narrow **castle** seemingly growing out of the rock was first built by the Romans and enlarged by the Normans in the 12th century. It has been restored and equipped with steps and platforms.

Along the Coast

Eastwards from Agrigento, the next town along the coast, **Palma di Montechiaro** with its fine Chiesa Madre, was founded in 1637 by an ancestor of Giuseppe di Lampedusa, who inherited it. There is a beach at the **Marina di Palma** below.

Forty-four kilometres from Agrigento, and located at the mouth of the River Salso (known as the Himera in ancient times), **Licata** developed on the site of ancient Phintias, a colony of Agrigento named after its founder, who transferred the inhabitants of Gela here when that city was destroyed. The city prospered discreetly under the Romans and Arabs. But you won't get much of a sense of the past here. This town is all present – crowded, chaotic and rather joyfully alive, especially in the morning, when the market's on and the fish and tomatoes seem to be flying in every direction.

The ambience is terrific, though monuments are few. Prehistoric and Greek finds are kept at the **Museo Civico**, in Piazza Linares (*open Tues-Sat 9-12.30 and 4-7*). In Piazza Progresso, at the centre of Licata, the **Municipio** is a late eclectic work of Ernesto Basile (1935), not one of his best. The **Palazzo Canarelli** on the *corso* is embellished with monstrous heads, while the **Chiesa del Carmine** at the end of the street is a Baroque church with a pretty medieval cloister.

A wide sandy beach at **Mollarella Bay** attracts its share of sun- and fun-seekers in the summer. Along the coast from here to Agrigento totters a ruined string of medieval defences. North of Licata on the bank of the River Salso, near the village of Ravanusa, are the ruins of a proto-historical settlement on **Monte Saraceno** (*to visit the site, go to Ravanusa and ask for precise directions*), later Hellenized by Gela and Agrigento. Little of the town has been excavated; you can see the acropolis on top, vestiges of a temple and the town plan on the hillside.

Getting There and Around

All bus and train connections start from Gela's train station on the northern edge of town. There are frequent **trains** west for Licata, Canicatti, Caltanisetta and onwards to Enna; and east for Ragusa, Syracuse and the east coast. Gela is a major hub for **bus** connections along the coast and inland. There are frequent buses for Butera.

Tourist Information

Via Palazzi 211, t 0933 823 107 (*open Mon–Sat 8–1 and 4-7*).

Where to Stay and Eat

**Hotel Sole, Via Mare 32, Gela, t 0933 92 52 92 (*budget*). You wouldn't go out of your way to spend a night in Gela, but if you end up there this is the only central place to crash.

**Lido degli Angeli, off the SS115, Falconara Sicula, t 0934 34 90 54 (*budget*). An alternative is the Lido at Falconara Sicula, where this is a modern, reasonably priced hotel.

Due Rocche, Falconara Sicula, t 0934 34 90 06. This campsite has a market and pizzeria.

Britannia Pub, on the main square, Butera. Butera has neither a hotel nor a restaurant, but this place is good for pizza and snacks.

Gela

When we first saw Gela, many years ago, the prospects for this ancient yet brand-new city seemed dim: dust, trash and concrete everywhere, and squalid streets of half-built, ugly buildings. In the evening the surreal *passeggiata* on the main street brought out thousands of industrial workers, weary Sicilian and North African immigrants in grey caps, without a single woman or child present.

But time can heal all wounds, even the construction of a gigantic oil refinery on a once-pristine coast. Gela today is almost beginning to look like a real city. The unfinished blocks now have laundry hanging out on the balconies, the dust is more or less settled, and children are everywhere. It isn't going to be a gracious city for a long time, but Gela is a prosperous and hard-working place. It's part of Sicily's future, a chance for thousands of village boys with no hope for a job to avoid that sad trip to Stuttgart or Hamburg. Gela today, with its 79,000 inhabitants, has probably equalled its total in the days of the Greeks. For a short time, before bad luck and the Carthaginians wiped Gela off the map for two millennia to come, this city had threatened to become the greatest power in Sicily.

History

Gela was founded by colonists from Crete and Rhodes in 680 BC. From the beginning the city prospered, producing wine, oil, grain and ceramics: not only pots, but terracotta figurines and plaques for religious offerings. By the 6th century BC the southern coast of Sicily belonged to Gela, and to handle the overflow the Geloans founded Akragas in 581 BC.

In 498 BC the grasping tyrant Hippocrates seized control of Gela, and he and his mercenaries proceeded to conquer half of Sicily. Jealous of their harbour, Hippocrates defeated the Syracusans, but later returned their city to them in exchange for the colony of Camarina. At this point Gela was the strongest city on the island. Hippocrates attempted to force the native Sikels into Greek ways and caused the one and only national uprising among the Sikels, who were led by Ducetius. Hippocrates died in a Sikel battle and was succeeded by his cavalry commander, Gelon.

With his father-in-law, the tyrant of Akragas, Gelon defeated the Carthaginians at Himera in 480 BC. Subsequent political turmoil in Syracuse provided Gelon with a chance to muscle in, and he took control of that city, taking the unusual step of moving half of Gela's population to Syracuse. He realized that Syracuse, with its fine harbour, was Sicily's natural capital.

A few years later, though, the Gelans were allowed to go home, and the city prospered once more, on terracotta and literature – Aeschylus wrote his Oresteia trilogy here, and died in Gela in 456 BC when an eagle dropped a turtle on his head; the eagle wanted to break the turtle's shell, and apparently thought the poet's bald pate was a stone. Another poet, the comic Apollodoros, was born and brought up in Gela.

In 405 BC the Carthaginians destroyed Gela. Timoleon, the good tyrant of Syracuse, had Gela laid out anew in 338 BC and sent colonists to repopulate it. However, by the ascendancy of Agathocles, Gela had allied itself with Carthage, and Agathocles conquered the city, putting 7,000 Gelans to death. The town was again destroyed by the Mamertines in 282 BC, after which Phintias of Akragas removed the remaining Gelans to what is now Licata. A wasteland until Frederick II built a castle on the site in 1233, it was known as 'Terranova' until 1928, when Mussolini restored its old name.

During the Second World War, Gela was the focal point of the Anglo-American landings on 11 July 1943, and was the first town in Europe to be liberated. After the war, the big oil refinery appeared in the midst of the lonely beaches.

The Museo Archeológico

Open daily 9–1 and 3–6, adm.

The best treasures of ancient Gela are housed here, at the eastern end of the long main street, Corso Vittorio Emanuele. The museum contains some excellent examples of Gela's terracottas, coins and vases, and two magnificent horse heads. Next door is the **Mulino Vento Acropolis**, with remains of Hellenistic houses from Timoleon's recolonization. A Doric column in a garden is all that remains of a temple of Athena.

Capo Soprano

At the other end of town are the **Capo Soprano fortifications** (*open daily 9am–dusk, adm*). These 5th-century BC Greek walls are the best preserved in the world, having been covered by 65ft sand dunes until they were excavated in 1954–8 (in some places the walls are still 25ft high). The fortifications have been covered in part by a plastic shield to protect them from the sea winds, especially the upper parts of the walls which are made of brick rather than stone. Very near Capo Soprano, next to the hospital on Via Europa, are the sheltered **Greek public baths** (*always open*). Dating from Timoleon's time, they are the only ones found in Sicily and the only hot baths to have seats. The huge sandy beaches of the **'Gela Riviera'** stretch all along the bay, and you have the choice of bathing with the crowd or on your own (the farther from the city and its oil refinery, the better).

Inland from Gela

On a low hill by the junction of the N190 north to Caltanissetta stand the lonesome, romantic ruins of **Castellúccio**, a castle built by Frederick II. North of here, near Lago Disueri, is a Pantalica-like oven-tomb **necropolis** of the late Bronze Age. A by-road north of Gela will take you the 19km to **Butera**, the prettiest town in the undistinguished province of Caltanissetta, built on a steep hill dominated by an 11th-century **Norman castle**. Its artistic treasures, a Renaissance triptych and a painting of the Madonna by Filippo Paladino, are in the **Chiesa Madre**. In the Middle Ages the princes of Butera, the Barresi, controlled most of the region. They founded **Mazzarino**, 17km north along the N190, where their palace still exists, and there's another Barresi palace at **Pietraperzía**. Southeast of here is a site known as Sofiana or **Castellazzo**, where some 1st-century thermal baths have been discovered; they remained in use until the 4th century. A small basilica and necropolis have also been excavated, their contents now at the Gela museum.

Enna and the Interior

10

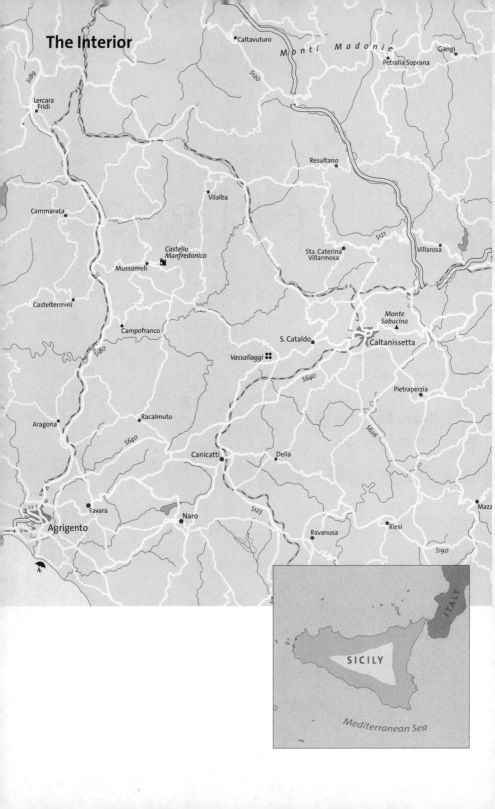

The Interior

Caltavuturo

Monti Madonie

Gangi

Petralia Soprana

S189

Lercara
Fridi

S120

Resultano

Vilalba

S121

Villarosa

Cammarata

Castello
Manfredonico

Sta. Caterina
Villarmosa

Mussomeli

Casteltermini

Monte
Sabucina

Campofranco

S. Cataldo

Caltanissetta

S180

Vassallaggi

S640

Pietraperzia

Aragona

Racalmuto

S640

S636

Canicattì

Delia

Favara

Naro

S123

Mazz

Agrigento

Ravanusa

Riesi

S190

ITALY

SICILY

Mediterranean Sea

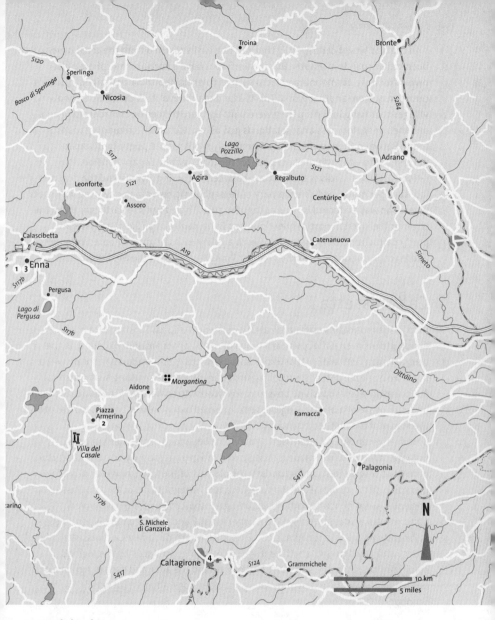

Highlights

1 The lovely *piazze* of Enna, an unforgettable hill town lost in the clouds

2 Salami-sellers, fishing cupids and bikini girls, all appearing in the Roman mosaics
   at the Villa del Casale near Piazza Armerina

3 The spectacular view from the Torre di Federico II in Enna

4 Caltagirone, decorated throughout with a rainbow of majolica tiles

All the odd bits of central Sicily that can't be easily reached from the coast have been collected in this chapter. But the area does have a special atmosphere of its own. After busy, cosmopolitan places such as Palermo, Taormina or Agrigento, Sicily's centre may seem another world. This is a land of primeval, forbidding cities, and villages that hang in the air. They were built up there to keep out invaders long ago, and their very aloofness and isolation is just as successful at discouraging tourists today. Between them come empty, formidably silent spaces, poetic landscapes beyond doubt – though the best poet for the job might be Edgar Allan Poe.

Nowhere else in Sicily is the contrast between the spring Floralia and the desert of late summer more vivid. The memory of Persephone is never far away – the very spot where she was abducted is here, at Lago Pergusa. Three towns in particular make the trip into the interior worthwhile: cloud-top Enna, centre of all Sicilian mysteries; pretty Caltagirone, defying the odds with a splash of its brightly coloured ceramics; and Piazza Armerina, one of the greatest Roman-era sites in the Mediterranean.

Caltanissetta

Up in the mountains north of Licata, the provincial capital Caltanissetta is a nice enough town, even if it does have a touch of comic-opera absurdity about it. In the central Piazza Garibaldi, preposterous Baroque architecture frames a fountain where a marble Neptune defends himself against bug-eyed, water-spitting sea monsters. A block away, aged shoeshine boys wait for tycoons to come out of the Banco di Sicilia under the gaze of a bronze King Umberto I, decked out in helmet and epaulettes like the leader of the firemen's band.

From Norman times Caltanissetta's economy depended on the sulphur and potassium mines which made it modern and prosperous (pop. 65,000), but unfortunately not very interesting for tourists. The old part of the town, however, has a few memories of its medieval and Baroque heritage. Thought to be located on the site of ancient Nissa, whence its name 'Kalat an-nisa' – the 'Ladies Castle' – is derived, Caltanissetta was captured by Count Roger in 1086 and presented to his son. In the 15th century it fell into the hands of the Spanish Moncada family. Caltanissetta only grew into a city during the 19th century, on the money produced by the region's sulphur mines; there are still some of these around the area, and even in Agrigento, but before they were undercut by foreign competition Caltanissetta was briefly the 'sulphur capital of the world'.

Around Piazza Garibaldi

On central Piazza Garibaldi, the 17th-century **Cattedrale di Santa Maria la Nuova** is proudest of its saccharine ceiling paintings by the Flemish artist Wilhelm Borremans (1720); the paintings, damaged by bombing in the war, were restored in 2002 to their original state. Across the square, **San Sebastiano** has a quirky late Baroque façade with the eye of God staring down from the top. From here, just up Corso Umberto, is a third Baroque work, the pretty façade of **Sant'Agata**, the former Jesuit church, now

Getting There

The **train** station is on Piazza Roma, downhill at the western edge of town; service is very slow but frequent from Agrigento, and there are also trains from Palermo, or Enna and Catania. The main Sicilian train line passes just north of the city at a junction called Caltanissetta-Xirbi, and you may have to change there.

Buses for all points leave from Piazza della Repubblica, including about 14 daily for Palermo and 10 daily for Catania, which beat the trains, and one early-morning bus in season for Cefalù. There are also buses for other towns in the interior, including Enna, Caltagirone and Piazza Armerina.

Tourist Information

Viale Testasecca 20, just north of the train station, t 0934 421 089 (open Mon–Fri 9–1, Wed 9–1 and 4–7), www.apit.cl.it.

Where to Stay and Eat

Caltanissetta ✉ 93100

Hotels in the nearby towns being rare, you may end up passing a night here, but the few choices mostly cater to salami salesmen.

★★★★**San Michele**, Via Fasci Siciliani, t 0934 55 37 50, www.hotelsanmichelesicilia.it (*moderate*). Somewhat fancy, and with a swimming pool.

★★★**Plaza**, Via B. Gaetani 5, t 0934 58 38 77 (*inexpensive*). A nondescript modern place near San Sebastiano.

Delfino Bianco, Via Gaetano Scovazzi, t 0934 25 435 (*moderate*). Of the restaurants, which are also not that numerous, this place is the favourite for lunch. It's in the centre, just off Piazza Garibaldi. *Closed Sun.*

Moby Dick, Corso Vittorio Emanuele 140, t 0934 58 39 72 (*moderate*). Specializes in fish – there's even a water tank from which to choose crustaceans from. *Closed Mon.*

Cortese, Corso Sicilia 166, t 0934 59 16 86 (*inexpensive*). Traditional Sicilian food. *Closed Mon.*

protected by the aforementioned statue of Re Umberto. The **Museo Archeologico**, on Via Napoleone Colajanni 3 (*open daily 9–1 and 3.30–7, adm*), contains finds from the province, mainly from Sabucina; the early Bronze Age figures are the oldest found in Sicily. Adjacent to the church of San Pio X is the local **Folklore Museum** (*open by appointment, ask at tourist office*).

One of the most interesting parts of Caltanissetta is **Viale Regina Margherita**, an elegant early 20th-century boulevard south of Piazza Garibaldi which rather oddly runs into a dead end at the edge of a cliff. Most of the public buildings are here, along with the town park, the **Villa Amedeo**. Caltanissetta's most striking monument is the **Castello di Pietrarossa**, whose ruins from the 1567 earthquake are perched high on a crag. During the war between the Chiaramonte and Ventimiglia families, Frederick II found shelter here, and the castle became a favourite residence of the Aragonese king Frederick III. Just east of the town, the **Abbazia di Santo Spirito** has a church founded by King Roger and Queen Adelaide, and consecrated in 1153; three apses survive from the original building, which contains some good 15th-century frescoes (*if church is locked, ring the bell at the gate on the right*).

Around Caltanissetta

Caltanissetta province is the least visited in Sicily. However, some of the hill towns are quite charming and certainly untainted by tourism, and there are a few minor archaeological sites scattered throughout the area. One of these is **Monte Sabucina** (*to visit the digs, ask at the Museo Civico, Caltanissetta*), 9km northeast of Caltanissetta,

The Mayor of Villalba

For an illustration of just how tenacious Sicily's feudal heritage can be, you need only look at a map. Northwest of Caltanissetta, the little village of Villalba is an island of Caltanissetta province entirely surrounded by Palermo and Agrigento territory. By ancient right and custom Villalba belonged to Caltanissetta, and so it remains to this day.

There's not much reason to go to Villalba; Luigi Barzini called it a 'little stage, ready for Cavalleria Rusticana to begin'. But it does have its stories. Near the village rises a peak called Pizzo di Lauro: up on top, they say, is hidden the greatest treasure in the world, guarded by fairies who live in a golden palace, passing their days and nights in amours and revelry. Many have tried to climb the peak to seize the treasure; none came back, and their enchanted souls could often be heard, groaning in the night:

Pizzu di Lauru, pri la to ricchizza
Nni pirdemu la vita e la salvizza
'Pizzo di Lauro, for your riches
We have lost our lives and our salvation'

But Villalba's greatest fame came in the postwar years, when it was the *de facto* capital of western Sicily. Don Calò Vizzini, one of the last of the old-style Mafia czars, was a Villalba native. Often in prison under Mussolini's rule, in 1943 he was installed as mayor of his home village under the Allied occupation, allowing him to exercise his functions with dignity and respect in his declining years. A little man, 'dressed in the velveteen suit of a well-to-do farmer, with a cloth cap on his head', as Barzini saw him, Don Calò would hold court each morning at the café on the village *piazza*, granting favours with a nod or a few words to the humble countrymen who came to kiss his hand. The more important petitioners – the ones from Palermo – made their visits more discreetly.

Most of Don Calò's relatives were priests or even bishops; he himself was a staunch Christian Democrat, undoubtedly the founder of the close Mafia-Democristiano alliance that was forged under his reign. A redoubtable killer in earlier days, Don Calò knew just how to deal with the Communists and trades unionists, unleashing a wave of terror that made the Rome politicians and the Americans grateful. He died in 1954, at the age of 77; thousands of top Mafiosi, politicians, barons and businessmen came to Villalba for one of the fanciest funerals Sicily had ever seen.

by the Salso River. Inhabited originally by Sikels in the first millennium BC, the site was later Hellenized and fortified. Excavations have uncovered the 6th-century BC town, huts and tombs from the Bronze Age, and a small Sikel temple outside the town wall.

Nearby **Vassallaggi** is another archaeological site, spread over five hills. This was a Greek settlement in the 5th century BC, under the wing of Agrigento; you can still see the sanctuary, the fortifications, part of the town, and a rich necropolis that has yielded fine painted vases and urns, now in the museums of Gela and Agrigento.

High on a crag at **Mussomeli**, northwest of San Cataldo, looms the striking Castello Manfredonico, built by Manfred III of the Chiaramonte family around 1370.

Enna

You can catch glimpses of Enna from points all over central Sicily, but from a mile away you might not see it at all. Even when it's not lost in the clouds (as it is most of the winter), this mountain-top city is so high and isolated you can literally stand in the fields of poppies underneath it and not realize the city is there. At 2,844ft above sea level, Enna is the highest provincial capital in Italy (pop. 29,000). The ancient 'navel of Sicily' and the vortex of all Sicilian secrets, it is a town so old no one even tries to guess when it was first settled. Favoured by both Frederick II of

Getting There

Enna's station lies along the Palermo–Catania **train** line; a bus timed to meet the train will soon arrive to take you up (this bus also connects Enna with Calascibetta). Train connections along the main line are easy; travelling to or from Agrigento and the south will probably mean a stop at the junction called Caltanissetta–Xirbi.

Enna's new **bus** station, with connections for Piazza Armerina, villages in the province (including Leonforte and Calascibetta) and the rest of Sicily, is in the newer part of the city, in Viale Diaz. There are 12 buses daily to Palermo, four to Caltanissetta and four to Catania. City buses run to Pergusa.

If you're **driving**, the motorway will lead you to Enna from either Catania of Palermo in less than 2hrs. The latter stretches that run along the Monti Madonie are nothing short of spectacular.

Tourist Information

Via Roma 411, **t** 0935 52 88 28 (open Mon–Sun 8.30–1 and 3–7), www.apt-enna.com.

Where to Stay

★★★**Grande Albergo Sicilia**, Piazza Colajanni 7 (just off Via Roma), ✉ 94100, **t** 0935 50 08 50, www.hotelsiciliaenna.it (moderate). Until someone has the inspiration to reopen the wonderful Art Deco Hotel Belvedere, this is unfortunately the only hotel in Enna. It's modern and comfortable nevertheless.
★★★**Azienda Agrituristica Gerace**, Contrada Gerace, **t** 339 604 76 39,

www.agrigerace.com (budget). A peaceful agriturismo offering pool, tennis courts, horse riding and a peaceful view of the valley. Closed Nov–Mar.
★★**Miralago**, Via Nazionale, Contrada Staglio, ✉ 94010, **t** 0935 54 12 72 (budget). The alternative is staying out by Lago Pergusa, where this simple but nice place is the least expensive. It has a restaurant-pizzeria.

Eating Out

Ariston, Via Roma 353, **t** 0935 26 038 (moderate). In the same range as the Centrale, and also worth a try. Closed Sun.
Centrale, Piazza VI Dicembre 9 (off Via Roma), **t** 0935 50 09 63 (expensive). An old favourite (they'll show you Mussolini's signature in the guestbook) where they have unusual vegetable pasta dishes. Closed Sat in winter.
La Brace, on the SS290 1km out of town (inexpensive). A family-run trattoria with pizza from a wood-burning oven in the evenings. Closed Mon.
Centrale, Via Ree Pentite 6, **t** 0935 50 09 73. (inexpensive) Decent value, and a good choice for local specialities.
Family Trattoria (inexpensive). Situated round the corner from the Torre di Federico II, off Via Libertà, here the portions of pasta are plentiful and inexpensive; the Enna football team eats here regularly, win or lose.
San Gennaro, Via Belvedere Marconi 6, **t** 0935 24 067 (inexpensive). Offers outdoor tables with a view, located near Piazza Crispi. Closed Wed.
Il Dolce, Piazza S. Agostino 37. Make your way here for delicious pastries such as sfogliatine alla ricotta and cannoli.

Hohenstaufen and Frederick II of Aragon for its unique position, Enna has not only marvellous panoramas in all directions, but fine medieval towers and churches.

History

Ancient Sikan Henna, in one of the most strategic positions in Sicily – high in the Monti Erei, almost in the dead centre of the island – was also the centre of the cult of Demeter and her abducted daughter Persephone. Near the border of Sikel lands, Henna knew constant strife as long as anyone could remember. It also saw one of Europe's first attempts to settle things diplomatically: Diodorus Siculus mentions an 8th-century BC peace treaty between the Sikans and Sikels, one of the oldest recorded treaties in history.

Enna was gradually Hellenized by Greek colonists who lived in peace with the natives (Via dei Greci still runs through the ancient Greek quarter), and Gelon built a temple of Demeter here in 480 BC. The Romans called Enna 'Castrum Hennae', and their government of the town could hardly be termed happy. In 214 BC the Consul Pinarius had the leading citizens massacred, fearing they would side with Carthage, and in 135 BC a slave from Enna named Euno led the First Slave War, giving the Romans no end of trouble until they recaptured the city two years later. In 859 the Saracens took Enna from the Byzantines only by scaling the cliffs and creeping one by one through the main sewer by night – so impregnable was Enna's position. Under the Saracens, the town's name was corrupted to 'Kasr Janna'. Count Roger took Enna, one of the last Muslim strongholds in Sicily, in 1087, only after capturing its defending army out on the plain. The Normans called it 'Castrogiovanni', but in 1927 Mussolini reinstated its classical name and made it a provincial capital.

Via Roma

The main street, Via Roma is strung with lovely *piazze* like pearls on a necklace. In the first (at the western end of Via Roma), **Piazza Vittorio Emanuele**, is the church of **San Francesco** with a fine 15th-century tower. The adjacent **Piazza Crispi** has an extraordinary belvedere, with views towards the neighbouring, equally lofty hill town of Calascibetta; in the *piazza* is a copy of Bernini's *Rape of Persephone* (the original is in Rome's Galleria Borghese). Continuing east along Via Roma, the intrusive Fascist public buildings of **Piazza Garibaldi** stand out like a sore thumb.

The next square, **Piazza Coppola**, takes its name from the Arabic cupola on the elegant tower of San Giovanni. Just round the corner there is the **Museo Varisano** (*open daily 9–6.30, adm*) in an old palace. None of the finds is of special interest, but it will provide a good background to the region's ancient history.

The Cathedral

Open daily 9–12 and 4–7.

Still heading east along Via Roma you will come without warning upon the cathedral. Founded in 1307 by Eleonora, wife of Frederick III of Aragon, it caught fire in 1446 and wasn't restored until the following century, which may account for its idiosyncratic façade and the few remaining Gothic elements on the south side, including the walled-in Holy Portal. Inside, the iron gate of the baptistry is said to have once guarded the Saracen harem. The two columns near the entrance, carved with puzzling allegorical monsters, were produced by one of the Gagini – a peculiar work to have come out of that normally tradition-bound clan of Sicilian masters. Another Gagini work, the font, rests on a pedestal of ancient origin, perhaps from the temple of Demeter. Filippo Paladino painted the scenes in the choir and the nave ceiling in the 16th century, and Giovanni Gallina – a local artist – sculpted the marble pulpit. Amongst the paintings are three by Borremans.

Across the street from the cathedral, spread about the rooms of a house, is the **Museo Alessi** (*open daily 8–8, adm*). It contains a good collection of coins and a few antiquities from Enna province, along with some neglected paintings and the remarkable cathedral treasury, with Renaissance trinkets in gold, silver and crystal such as the enamelled gold 'crown of the Madonna'.

Castello di Lombardia

Open daily from 8 until 1 hr before sunset.

Via Roma ends at the Castello di Lombardia, constructed by Frederick II, and used as a residence by Frederick III of Aragon, who proclaimed himself 'King of Trinacria' here and summoned the Sicilian parliament in 1324. 'Lombardia', an unusual name in Sicily, is thought to derive from the Lombard troops that Frederick or some later ruler quartered here to keep them out of trouble. Six towers remain of the original 20, the tallest of which – the Torre Pisano – can be climbed for its commanding view of the surrounding countryside. Below, in the courtyard, where excavations are in progress, is an underground chamber with mysterious prehistoric incisions of upside-down tridents, not unlike the mysterious symbols found in Upper Paleolithic caves such as Lascaux. Legend has it that the shadowy King Sikanus and the goddess Demeter are buried together under the castle.

Rocca di Cerere

Beyond the castle, at the very tip of Enna's tall plateau, there is a rugged crag called the Rocca di Cerere (or di Demeter; Ceres is her Latin name). Long before the Greeks ever arrived, this massive boulder poised 1,200ft over the plain below was one of the holiest sites on the island, the centre of the worship of the Great Goddess. The Greeks associated her with their Demeter, and Gelon built a temple to her on the rock after the Battle of Himera; later rebuilt at least once, it remained a famous religious centre throughout classical times. Cicero wrote that it featured giant statues of Demeter and Triptolemus, the King of Eleusis. Triptolemus alone witnessed the rape of Persephone, and, in gratitude for revealing what he knew, Demeter taught him the art of agriculture and sent him around in a serpent-drawn chariot to spread the knowledge. Not a trace of the temple remains today, though the site is wonderfully evocative and the views spectacular even for Enna.

The Torre di Federico II

To visit the lower town, take Via Roma south of the Piazza Matteotti, passing the churches of **San Tommaso**, with a distinguished altar, and the **Carmine**, a block west on Via Trieste. Both have 15th-century campaniles (the good people of Enna like their church bells and ring them often). Farther down, on a knoll in the public garden, is the **Torre di Federico II** (*under restoration*). Scholars believe that 'Stupor Mundi' built this 'tower of the winds' to mark the crossroads of ancient Sicily's three main thoroughfares, symbolized in the three legs of the Trinacria symbol. Considered to be in the absolute centre of the island, the tower (as well as the rest of Enna) acquired the name Umbilicus Sicilae ('Sicily's navel') and served to divide the island into three districts: the Val Demone, the Val di Noto, and the Val di Mazara – the same Three Valleys used by the Arabs to partition the island. The tower itself is octagonal with three floors. It is rumoured that at the bottom there is an underground passage to the Castello di Lombardia. A spiral stairway leads you up inside the 10ft-thick walls to the top unfinished floor, and the most spectacular view of any place in Sicily. From here, on the clearest of days, the three corners of Trinacria are visible.

The Celestial Temple of Sicily

Frederick's tower was not the first on this site, and it is an open question whether the subtle emperor was aware of the true significance of this spot. But Frederick also built a famous castle in Apulia, the Castel del Monte, a work that, for its mathematical proportions, its lack of any discernible purpose and its surpassing strangeness, has given rise to all manner of crazy theories, a veritable Great Pyramid of mystery. Some have speculated that the emperor built it for the meetings of a secret philosophical society over which he presided. Like Castel del Monte, the tower of Enna is octagonal, has no known purpose, and is rugged and plain outside but delicately vaulted within.

But the puzzle certainly doesn't stop here. Forty years ago a Sicilian historian, Umberto Massocco, propounded a theory that this spot was the centre of a giant geomantic construction, covering the whole of Sicily, created before the arrival of the Greeks. Like the leys of Britain (which Massocco appears not to have known about), there is a network of alignments of holy places and landmarks, meeting at right angles and running the length of the island; the long axes are oriented towards the midsummer sunrise. Massocco, with the aid of aerial surveying and the writings of Diodorus Siculus, discovered that many of the oldest sites on the island – Monte Erice, Segesta, Selinunte, Ortygia Island and Eraclea Minoa among them – fall along these alignments.

He called the work the *Templum Caelesti*, an attempt to make the whole of the island into one great geometrical temple. In Enna, he notes that the two central alignments that cross at Frederick's tower pass through the churches of San Marco (Piazza VI Dicembre) and San Bartolomeo (Piazza San Bartolomeo) and that these three sites form a neat Pythagorean triangle of sides proportionately 3, 4 and 5.

Trinacria and Ancient Sicily

N

50 km
25 miles

Catana ● Site
Thapsos ● Excavated site

Charybdis
Scylla
Zancle (Messina)
Fretum Siculum
VIA VALERIA
Mylae (Milazzo)
Neptunium Montes
Naxos
Callipolis
Acis
Tauromenion
Catana
I. Strongyle
I. Lipara
Lipara
I. Didyme
I. Hiera
Tyndaris
SNOW
ETNA
Symaethos
Agathyrnum
Apollonia
Manolito
Centuripae
Erice
Palica
Boreas
Nebrodes Montes
Halaesa
Henna
Umbilicus Siciliae
CARDO MAXIMUS
Morgantina
L.Pergusa
Casimenae
Megara Hyblaea
Thapsos
Syracusae
Euro
Helorus
I. Pachynus
Leontinoi
Pantalica
Akrai (Palazzo Acreide)
Netum (Noto)
Cava d'Ispica
Motyca
Hybla (Ragusa)
Gela
Camarina
Cephaloedion (Cefalù)
Himera
DECUMANUS MAXIMUS
M. Saraceno
Phintas (Licata)
Mendris
Solus
Panormos (Palermo)
Ietae
Camicos (?)
Akragas (Agrigento)
SIKANS
Heraclea Minoa
M. Adranone
Thermae Selinuntae (Sciacca)
Entella
Selinos
Zefiro
ELYMIANS
Segesta
Eryx
Drepanon (Trapani)
I. Aegusa
Motya
I. Phorbantis
Lilybaeum
Mazara

Calascibetta and Persephone's Lake

The exotic-looking hill town you saw across the valley from Enna's Piazza Crispi is **Calascibetta**, its Arabic origins apparent both in its old reddish buildings and in its name. It's a quiet, brooding place. To the north, the **Necropolis of Realmesi** has oven tombs hollowed out of the rock, dating back to the 9th century BC.

On the edge of **Leonforte**, northeast of Calascibetta, the lavish great fountain, **La Gran Fonte** (1651), has 24 spouts along its unusual length and two sides: one for people, the other for animals. Leonforte was founded by Prince Niccolò Branciforte in the 17th century. His family's funeral chapel is in the **Capuchin church** on Piazza Margherita; also in the chapel is *The Election of St Matthew* by Pietro Novelli. **Assoro**, 19km east of Enna off the N121, is worth a visit for its 14th-century church of **San Leone**. On the exterior, note the late Gothic portal; inside are a fine wooden ceiling and floral reliefs decorating the pillars.

South of Enna, the village of **Pergusa** borders on the lake of the same name, famous in ancient times for its beauty and the abundance of wildflowers on its banks. But don't expect any classical epiphanies on this spot, where dark Hades of the underworld abducted the spring goddess Persephone from her flowery fields. In perhaps the greatest atrocity visited on any classical site in Italy, the lake is now encircled by a motor speedway, and motor-boats and waterskiers noisily skim over the old demons patrolling the sullen depths.

Around Enna

Enna Province, the only province in Sicily without a coast, in compensation has six large natural and man-made lakes, and beautiful mountain scenery. Its inland position has also made it less vulnerable to outside influences and change, and almost all the towns retain a medieval aspect.

Nicosia

Beyond Leonforte, another 19km north on N117 will take you deeper into the mountains, through some of the quietest, loneliest corners of Sicily, to beautiful Nicosia, as fine a medieval backwater as one could hope to find. As a free city, Nicosia prospered under the Arabs and then the Normans, who settled the town with Lombard and Piedmontese colonists, whose northern origins still flavour the local *argot*. Before the coastal road was completed, only in the 19th century, Nicosia was a key stronghold along the main road from Palermo to Messina.

Upon a crag above the town stand the ruins of the **Norman castle**. The town itself is full of ambitious churches, monasteries and palaces (particularly along Via Salomone), though almost all of them were damaged in an earthquake in 1967, and restoration work has been haphazard at best. In **Santa Maria Maggiore** (Via Francesco Salomone) is an early 15th-century marble polyptych of the Virgin's life, by Antonello Gagini, as well as the throne used by Emperor Charles V when he visited Nicosia in 1535. Another unusual Gagini work can be seen in the church of **San Biagio**. The

Getting Around

All these villages have **bus** services from Enna, but don't expect them to run frequently. Nicosia also has buses to Catania, Palermo, Mistretta, Petralia, etc. There are buses between Troina and Agira.

Where to Stay and Eat

Restaurants and hotels are almost impossible to find in this seldom-visited region.

**La Pineta, Via S. Paolo, Nicosia, ✉ 94014, t 0935 64 70 02 (*budget*). A modest hotel.
*Aurora, Via Annunziata, Agira, ✉ 94011, t 0935 69 14 16 (*budget*). Another euro-saving place.
Orchidea, at Contrada Castile outside Troina (*expensive*). Most of the better places to eat are on the edge of town or in the country, where folks go to celebrate or have a pizza: this trattoria-pizzeria is a good example.
La Cirata, on the SS117 outside Nicosia (*moderate*). A good place to come for solid home-cooking. *Closed Mon.*

Cattedrale di San Nicola has a lovely 14th-century façade and campanile, the only parts remaining from the original medieval building; inside are some impressive wood-carved choir stalls from the 1700s.

Just west of Nicosia rises picturesque **Sperlinga**, with its medieval **castle** perched atop its mountain. The only safe refuge the French found after the Revolt of the Vespers (hence the local saying, 'Whatever pleases Sicily, only Sperlinga denies'), Sperlinga's occupation goes back to prehistoric times (1300–900 BC), as evidenced by the mad warren of **tunnels** and chambers hollowed out of the sandstone mountain (some of these, communicating with the outside, were inhabited not too many years ago). The castle and tunnels can be visited, along with a crafts museum the village has installed inside.

Troina and Agira

The 32km by road from Nicosia east to **Troina** takes in some impressive scenery as it climbs to its goal. Troina qualifies as one of the highest towns in Sicily, 3,090ft above sea level. Roger I captured it from the Arabs in 1062, though he, his family and his knights had to endure a bitter siege the first winter. The castle was the Norman base before the conquest of Palermo. The village retains many Norman souvenirs, including **San Basilio**, founded by Roger himself in 1082, making it the first Norman diocese in Sicily. The **Chiesa Madre**'s tower is also Norman, and its treasury contains a famous 13th-century silver pastoral staff. Inhabited since the Sikels, Troina still has a few parts of its Greek walls.

Agira, the ancient Sikel Agyrion, is another picture-postcard hill town, 30km south of Troina. From the west, Agira's needle-like hill offers the strangest skyline in Sicily, packed to the very top with houses. In 339 BC Timoleon of Syracuse captured and Hellenized Agyrion, the birthplace of the great Diodorus Siculus, the 1st-century historian who was the first to attempt a history of the world. In later days San Filippo Siriaco (or 'of Agira') performed many legendary miracles here – actually thought to be the deeds of ancient Agyrion's patron god Hercules in Christian clothing. The church of **San Salvatore** contains a good treasury.

Regalbuto and Centúripe

Regalbuto, 14km east of Agira, is only a few kilometres from the large artificial **Lago Pozzillo**, a favourite of anglers. In 1261 the inhabitants of Centúripe decimated Regalbuto, which had been populated largely by the hated Swabians. The present town was rebuilt by Manfred. To the east the old enemy **Centúripe** is magnificently situated in front of Mount Etna and the sea; Garibaldi nicknamed it the 'balcone della Sicilia'. As ancient Kentoripa it was the site of an important Sikel town, and in the 1st century it was the birthplace of the physician Celsus. Despite this antiquity, the present town dates back only to 1545, as both Frederick II and Charles of Anjou razed Centúripe for its defiance. During the Second World War the Nazis made the town a key base, and its fall to the 38th Irish Brigade forced the Germans to abandon Sicily. (There are a few Allied military cemeteries in the area, including one on the shores of Lago Pozzillo.) Centúripe has a small but extremely interesting **Museo Civico** (*open daily 9–1 and 3–7*) housing the distinctive locally produced polychromatic pottery and ceramics renowned in Hellenistic times. On the outskirts of town a road leads to the so-called **Mausoleo Romano**, a 2nd-century ruin, perhaps of a tomb or tower.

Piazza Armerina

Before the surprise discovery of the great Roman villa in 1950 put this town on everyone's Sicilian itinerary, no one ever came to Piazza Armerina (pop. 23,000). Nevertheless, it's a graceful old town, set in the richly forested countryside south of Enna that could pass for northern Italy. Piazza's excellent hill site was inhabited in antiquity, but only became important in the Middle Ages, when Roger I built a fortified camp. In 1161 King William the Bad destroyed the old town in retaliation for a massacre of Saracens by its citizens, but three years later the Normans rebuilt what they had demolished and the new town prospered. In 1240 Frederick II elevated Piazza to one of his 11 imperial towns at the Parliament of Foggia. In mid-August the town hosts one of the major festivals in Sicily, the Norman Joust.

On Piazza's Piazzas

The **Piazza Garibaldi** is the heart of the old town, with the Municipio, the church of San Rocco (1613) and various palazzi. Turn west up Via Vittorio Emanuele for the Baroque **Sant'Anna** and the 14th-century **Aragonese castle** where Martin I of Aragon once resided. At the summit of the city, in the **Piazza del Duomo**, is the **cathedral**, built in 1627 with funds donated by Baron Marco Trigona, whose portly statue and *palazzo* also adorn the square. The Catalan campanile is a hundred years older than the cathedral, and the façade is some hundred years later. Inside is a Byzantine icon of the Madonna given to Count Roger by Pope Nicholas II, and a medieval Crucifix painting on wood by an unknown artist. The treasury contains a rare statue of Roger among the more typical vestments and reliquaries.

Of the many other churches in this elegant town, the best are the 13th-century **San Giovanni di Rodi** (*ring for entrance*), a chapel of the Knights of St John, who lived

Getting There

There's no train to Piazza Armerina, but the **bus** stop for Caltagirone and Aidone (six buses daily to each) is in Piazza Marescalchi on the SS117. There are also buses to Enna, Gela and Palermo, a daily bus from Syracuse (day trip unfeasible), and tour buses to the Villa del Casale from Taormina.

Tourist Information

Via Cavour 15, t 0935 68 02 01 (*open Mon–Sat 8–2*), *www.aziendaautonomapiazza.com*.

Where to Stay

Piazza Armerina ✉ 94015

Piazza's hotels are not all that special. There's a campsite near the Villa del Casale on the Barrafranca road.

★★★Park Hotel Paradiso, Loc. Ramaldo, t 0935 68 08 41, *www.paginegialle.it/photelparadiso* (*moderate*). One option north of town with pool and all mod cons.

★★★Villa Romana, Via Alcide de Gasperi 18, t 0935 68 29 11, *hotelvillaromana@piazza-armerina.it* (*moderate*). A slightly cheaper alternative right in the town centre.

★★Mosaici, Contrada Paratore 11, t 0935 68 54 53 (*budget*). A friendly place located 4km out of town, so you will need transport.

★★Ostello del Borgo, Largo S. Giovanni 6, t 0935 68 70 19, *www.ostellodelborgo.it* (*budget*). This restored cloister in the old centre is a wonderful alternative to the other places listed. The nuns' cells have been transformed into good-value private guest rooms with bathrooms, and there are even cheaper beds in dormitories. The staff are very helpful.

Eating Out

Al Fogher, C. da Bella (SS117), t 0935 68 41 23, (*expensive*). This cordial establishment is a little far from the centre, so you'll need some means of transport. Come here if you can for your evening meal. *Closed Mon.*

Al Ritrovo, on the SS117b, t 0935 68 19 80 (*moderate*). This attractive, if remote, restaurant makes a pleasant spot to have lunch after you have visited the Villa del Casale. Particularly good are the *tagliatelle* with a special thick sauce (*ragù*) and the kid cooked over the open fire. *Closed Fri.*

La Ruota, Contrada Paratore-Casale, t 0935 68 05 42 (*moderate*). Not far from the Villa del Casale, with tables outside in the summer; all the pasta is made in-house. *Lunch only.*

Da Totò, Via Mazzini 29, t 0935 68 01 53 (*moderate*). Excellent pasta from the oven and some very good local wines. *Closed Mon.*

La Tavernetta, Via Cavour 14, t 0935 68 58 83 (*inexpensive*). A place of genuine character on a steep lane towards the top of town.

Al Teatro, Via del Teatro 6, t 0935 85 662 (*inexpensive*). Fantastically crispy pizzas at large tables outside. *Closed Wed.*

Pasticceria Restivo, Via Mazzini 21. Makes some of the area's best pastries and sweets, including *torroni* and the ubiquitous *cassata*.

Club La Belle Aurore, Piazza Castello 5, t 0935 68 63 33, *labelleaureclub@yahoo.it*. This stylish bar spills out on to a private courtyard. The cocktails' main ingredient is the formidable *fuoco dell'Etna* (fire of Etna).

on the island of Rhodes before being chased to Malta; the **Collegium** of St Ignatius; and, north of the town, the church of **Sant'Andrea**, begun in 1096 by the Normans and containing some intriguing early Sicilian frescoes.

Villa del Casale

Open daily from 8am until one hour before sunset; adm.

The excavations of the Roman villa of Casale are 4km southwest of Piazza. Buses run on the half-hour (9–11 and 4–6) between April and September. Unless there are many in your party, a taxi isn't much of a bargain, and the walk is very pleasant if it's not too hot. But whatever the means, go: at the end of the journey lie the most magnificent Roman mosaics in the world. Unfortunately they are not being kept in the best state: the perpex coverings placed on top of the mosaics is creating a green-house effect with temperatures reaching 40 degrees C and humidity as high as 80 per cent thus leading to their fast fading. Matters are not helped by the presence of an underground stream that with heavy rains swells up and causes the tesserae to jump out. The mosaics are now one of the sites deemed at risk of disappearing by UNESCO.

Scholars generally hold that the villa was built as a summer retreat near the end of the 3rd century AD for a member of the Imperial family, perhaps even for Maximilian, Diocletian's co-emperor, who ruled from 286 to 305 – it would have gone up at the same time as Diocletian's great palace, still largely intact, in the centre of Split, Croatia. Maximilian, the junior Caesar, probably had a smaller bank account, but this 1,000ft-long hideaway was the most impressive residence built in Italy since the time of Nero's Golden House and Hadrian's Villa at Tivoli. It speaks volumes about the decadence of the late 3rd-century West – such a bauble, at a time when the Empire was bankrupt and everything was going to pieces. Diocletian at least sited his palace in a strategic place, close to the borders; Maximilian built his as far away from trouble as possible. The few rich landowners of the time, who had appropriated almost all of the West's land and wealth to themselves, lived in smaller versions of this ultimate suburban dream house, far from the degraded and collapsing cities; they decorated them from the profits they had made pressing the rest of the population into serfdom.

Imperial successors, especially Constantine, probably spent time here. Later the Arabs made some use of it, as did the Normans, and William the Bad probably destroyed it along with the town in 1161. A landslide covered it, and only since 1950 have serious excavations revealed the treasures that were buried.

The Mosaics

There are some 40 mosaics in all, covering 38,000sq ft of floor, the whole shielded by a clear protective roof following the design of the building. They are the most vivid and masterful representatives of what is known as the African tradition. Before the arrival of the Romans, North African artists were immersed in the romantic, vivid emotions of Hellenistic art, and many of the more ambitious mosaics here are believed to be derived from Hellenistic paintings or cartoons, with colour used to suggest modelling and foreshortening; the fact that many of the tesserae are from Africa suggest parts of the mosaics may have been prefabricated there. On the other hand, the white backgrounds to the scenes are derived from the Italian black-and-white tradition. It may have been here that the two styles met and merged for the first time.

Beyond the ruins of the aqueduct that once supplied the villa is the monumental entrance and the **baths**, where the mosaics represent various stages of the elaborate Roman bath ritual and some mythical sea creatures. The remains of the plumbing are visible in the *tepidarium* (warming room), where the floor was built on brick pillars, allowing heat to rise into the room through vents (the hypocaust). The central latrines are also nearby. The vestibule contains damaged mosaics of guests being welcomed into the house, and leads into the large rectangular court, or **peristyle**, with mosaic animal heads along the side floors and a fountain in the centre. Following the walkway to the left, the **Hall of the Circus** (*palaestra*) is named after its mosaics depicting a chariot race at the Circus Maximus in Rome, the four contestants bearing the colours of the four circus factions of Rome – red, green, blue and white. Note the salami-seller in the stands.

A series of **bedchambers** with intricate geometric designs follows, and then the **Room of the Small Hunt**, with realistic scenes of a local hunting expedition and the hunters' subsequent picnic. Whimsical mosaics of fishing cupids, a very popular theme of the age, follow this, before the 200ft-long **Hall of the Great Hunt**, whose mosaic masterpiece depicts the hunt and capture of wild animals to be slaughtered in Rome's amphitheatres – scenes remarkable not only for their lively and realistic details, but for their powerful sense of action and movement. At either end are allegorical figures of Africa and the Middle East, the two principal sources of the beasts. Not long after these mosaics were made, the Romans would hunt several of the species you see here (like the North African lion) to extinction. An adjacent room contains the bland but very famous *Bikini Girls*, disporting themselves on some Roman lido, while the next room has a mosaic floor that shows Orpheus enchanting the savage beasts.

The walkway leads out to the **Elliptical Courtyard** where the mosaics portray industrious putti harvesting grapes, pressing wine and fishing. Entering the villa once more, the walkway ascends into the **Banquet Hall** (*triclinium*), with powerful mosaics of the labours of Hercules. The five giants, struck by Hercules' arrows and writhing in pain, are reminiscent of Michelangelo. Another remarkable room follows, with its 'painting in stone' of Cyclops and Odysseus; the wily Greeks are offering Polyphemus wine, hoping to intoxicate him and thus make their escape. Next is the so-called **Chamber of the Erotic Scene** (i.e. a kiss and a bare bottom), followed by the private apartments that compose the rest of the villa, including two charming **nursery** mosaics, one showing *The Children's Hunt*, with youngsters chasing rabbits and ducks, the other showing *The Small Circus*, with children racing carts pulled by birds in imitation of their elders. There is also a room with mosaics of Greek instruments and musical notation, and another representing the myth of Arion the musician.

Morgantina

Other important excavations are northeast of Piazza Armerina at Morgantina, a few miles from the old Lombard village of Aidone; the latter's name is yet another reminder of the Demeter and Persephone myth, from Aidoneus, another title for Hades, the King of the Underworld. This Sikel-Greek town of the 6th century BC rebelled against the Romans in 211 BC and was given to their Spanish mercenaries. Located at the Serra d'Orlando, the **excavations** (*signposted; open daily from 8am until one hour before sunset, adm*) include the large agora, with stoas, a market building and a trapezoidal stairway, an adjacent bouleuterion (council house) and theatre. Also near the centre are a sanctuary of Demeter and Kore, a gymnasium and Hellenistic houses, many with mosaics. Finds from Morgantina are housed in the **Museo Archeológico** (*open daily 9–6.30, adm*) in an old Capuchin convent in Aidone.

Caltagirone

Caltagirone, 32km southeast of Piazza Armerina, has the sobriquet 'Queen of the Hills'. It spreads out over three hills in the shape of an eagle, some 1,890ft above sea level, and the eagle is reproduced on the city's coat of arms. Inhabited since remotest antiquity, it was Hellenized by the Syracusans. The name 'Caltagirone' dates from the Arabic occupation (*kalat*, or castle, and *gerum*, or caves). The Normans conquered it in 1090, and the 1693 earthquake destroyed it, occasioning a grand Baroque rebuilding. Bombs in 1943 caused more damage and 700 deaths.

Caltagirone's other nickname is the 'Faenza of Sicily' from its ceramics, a tradition in the town since ancient times. Its golden age came, as in many ceramic towns, from the 16th to 18th centuries, when demand was high for its typical blue, green and yellow painted ware. By the early 20th century, the art was on the verge of dying out, when local priest and folklore student Luigi Sturzo gathered the surviving craftsmen and founded Caltagirone's school of ceramics. Don Luigi, after whom you will see streets and *piazze* named all over Sicily and even on the mainland, went on to become a longtime mayor of Caltagirone, and a progressive Christian politician active in the land-reform movement. Sturzo is credited as one of the founding fathers of the Christian Democrat Party – representing the idealistic ambitions the party forgot before its well-deserved implosion in 1993.

Majolica Museums

With the warm sandstone of its domes and towers sloping up its hills, Caltagirone is a grand sight. Seen close up, the people's habit of using their colourful tiles to decorate the buildings, the church towers and even the bridges makes it one of the most striking towns in Sicily. In the valley at the foot of the hills, the boundary between new town and old, the **Giardino Pubblico** (*open daily 8–7, longer hours in summer*), full of exotic plants and ceramic knick-knacks, is also the site of **Museo della Ceramica** (*open daily 9–6.30, adm*), containing crafts from prehistoric potsherds to the 19th century.

Via Roma leads from here into the old town, passing one of the major works of the Baroque rebuilding, the church and convent of **San Francesco**. From here, the lovely 17th-century **Ponte San Francesco** leads to the **Museo Civico** (*open Mon, Wed and Thurs 9–1; Tues and Fri–Sun 9–1 and 4–7*), in an old Bourbon-era prison, with more ceramics, many by modern artists, paintings and archaeological finds. Around the corner is the central Piazza Municipio, with the town hall and a decorous Baroque building called the **Corte Capitanale**, decorated by members of the Gagini family (Antonello is thought to have lived part of his life in Caltagirone); this was once the

Getting There

Caltagrione's **train** station, with connections to Gela, Catania and Grammichele, is in the new town off Viale Principe Umberto I. Most **buses** (a few each day), for Enna, Piazza Armerina and Palermo, depart from there. Those for Ragusa go from Piazza Municipio.

Tourist Information

Via Libertini 3, t 09 33 53 809 (*open Mon–Fri 8–2 and 3.30–6.30, Sat 3.30–6.30; plus Sat–Sun 10–1 in summer*).

Where to Stay and Eat

Caltagirone ☑ 95041

★★★**Grand Hotel Villa San Mauro**, Via Portosalvo 14, t 0933 26500, *www.framon hotels.com* (*expensive*). Part of the Framon hotels group, this functional modern-looking hotel is on the hills outside town. Pool, panoramic terrace and a non-smoking floor.

★★★★**Agriturismo Gigliotto**, SS117 km60 (Svincolo per Mirabe), t 335-8380324/337-889052, *www.gigliotto.com* (*moderate*). Set on a hill with breathtaking views, this *masseria* dates back to the 14th century. The

15 rooms are furnished in Sicilian style with lovely terracotta floors, and they even have one room specifically for disabled, a rarity on Sicily. *Open all year.*

★★★**Pomara**, Via Vittorio Veneto 84, 95040, t 0933 977 090, *www.hotelpomara.com* (*moderate*). Twelve kilometres north of Caltagirone, on the SS124 towards Piazza Armerina, the little village of San Michele di Ganzaria has become something of a resort in the woods, with this one rather swanky modern hotel with pool and all amenities.

★★**Monteverde**, Via delle Industrie 11, t 0933 53 682 (*inexpensive*). A cheaper option just south of town and with a good restaurant.

La Scala 2, Piazza Umberto I 1, t 0933 51 552 (*budget*). Rooms to rent right in the centre of town, on the main square. A bit noisy.

La Scala, Scalinata Santa Maria del Monte, t 0933 57781, (*expensive*). The fabulous setting of this restaurant, at the bottom of the stairs and with a stream running through it, makes it more expensive than it should be. Still, the food is good and service pleasant. *Closed Wed.*

L'Arcata, Via Nazionale (*inexpensive*). A fine pizzeria in Caltagirone town.

Scivoli, Via Milazzo 121, t 0933 23 108. The local pastry shop – worth a stop for a quick bite. *Closed Tues.*

seat of the Bourbon governors. Next to it stands the **cathedral** (*under restoration*); this is another Baroque work – though its façade was so badly done it had to be completely rebuilt, finished only in 1954.

The Scala di Santa Maria del Monte

From the far end of Piazza Umberto, the two 'wings' of Caltagirone spread on either side, along Via Vittorio Emanuele and Via Luigi Sturzo. The former leads to the church of **San Giacomo**, another Baroque rebuilding, with some Gagini statues inside salvaged from the original church. Via Sturzo leads to the northernmost quarter of town; from it, the first street to the right takes you to one of the best of the city's churches, curvaceous **Santa Chiara** (*under restoration*), designed by Rosario Gagliardi, the architect of Ragusa and Módica; across from it is a 1908 **Liberty-style building** by Ernesto Basile. Farther up Via Sturzo, **San Domenico** contains some florid decoration and Don Sturzo's tomb.

Back at Piazza Municipio, besides the two 'wings', there is a third possible direction: straight ahead, up Caltagirone's pride and symbol, the **Scala di Santa Maria del Monte**. The stair was rebuilt in its present form in 1953, the runners of its 142 steps adorned with colourful ceramic designs, reproducing the colours and motifs of local designs from the 10th century on. On July 24th and 25th, it is brilliantly illuminated with oil lamps for the *festa* of San Giacomo. Many of the city's majolica artists have their shops around the stair, and at the top is the church of **Santa Maria del Monte**, another Baroque work, replacing the Norman original; its main altar is decorated with the 13th-century Tuscan *Madonna di Conadomini.*

Grammichele

Just east of Caltagirone on the SS124, Grammichele often receives special mention in books on urban design. The modern town is built on the site of Occialà, which was destroyed in the earthquake of 1693. The new town was designed in a strict hexagonal form by Nicola Branciforte, after a book by Tommaso Campanella (*Civitas Solis*), reviving an idea of radiocentric city planning that Baroque writers falsely believed was common in ancient Babylonia. Campanella, who began as a Dominican monk, ended up a mystic philosopher, astrologer and leader of a fierce revolt in Calabria against the Spaniards in 1599. For decades afterwards, though imprisoned, he remained one of the most influential thinkers in Italy; he wrote in defence of Galileo during his famous trial for heresy. Campanella's 'City of the Sun' was a sibylline prophecy of a Utopian future, and Grammichele was an attempt to realize this in stone.

From the air it is a perfect geometric symbol, the streets a series of concentric hexagons. Grammichele is divided into six wards, or *sestiere*, like the sections of an orange, each with its own *piazza*. At the centre, where the six main avenues meet, is the completely paved central square, also hexagonal; it lacks only a few De Chirico mannequins in heroic poses for total metaphysical weirdness. Originally there was an iron gnomon in the middle, making the *piazza* a giant sundial; this was removed in the Catholic reaction after the Napoleonic Wars. There isn't much of a Utopian air about the town today: Grammichele has become just another forgotten Sicilian backwater, best known for its dried figs.

Tyrrhenian Coast

11

The Tyrrhenian Coast

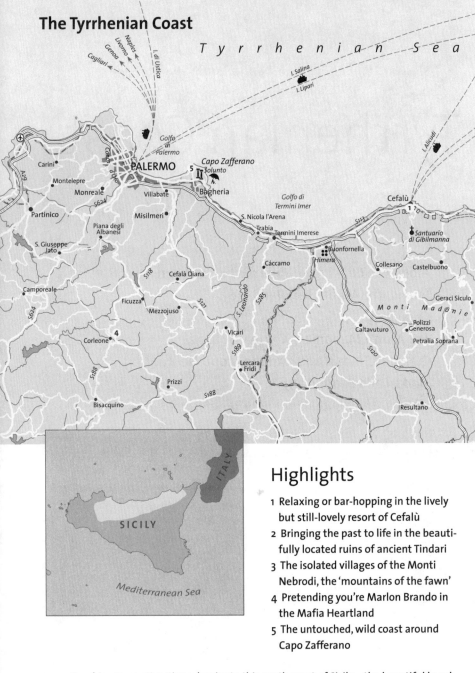

Highlights

1 Relaxing or bar-hopping in the lively but still-lovely resort of Cefalù
2 Bringing the past to life in the beautifully located ruins of ancient Tindari
3 The isolated villages of the Monti Nebrodi, the 'mountains of the fawn'
4 Pretending you're Marlon Brando in the Mafia Heartland
5 The untouched, wild coast around Capo Zafferano

Two big-name attractions dominate this north coast of Sicily – the beautiful beach resort of Cefalù, with its soaring Rocca and Norman cathedral, and Tindari, of the holy shrine and ancient ruins. Unfortunately, many other stretches of this often lovely

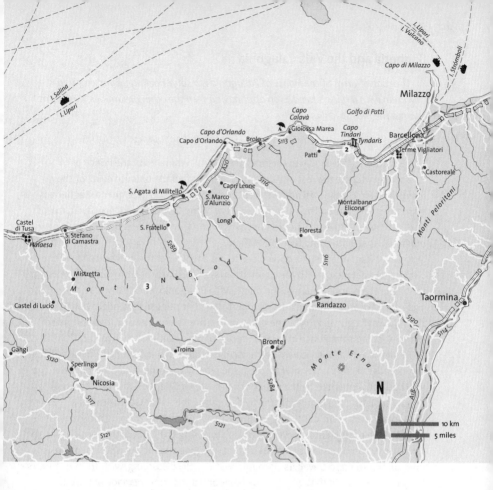

coast have been marred by intensive, uninviting *abusivo* building and holiday sprawl. Yet veer just inland to the hidden towns of the Monti Nebrodi and Madonìe, and you'll enter another, cooler, greener, older world that hardly seems to have anything to do with pizza or ice cream or even the Mediterranean, full stop.

Along the Coast from Palermo to Cefalù

This stretch of the Tyrrhenian immediately east of the capital offers a typical Sicilian pot-pourri of cultures. First chronologically are two important and rewarding classical sites, Greek Himera and Carthaginian Solunto. Then there are architectural flourishes: a tremendous medieval castle at Cáccamo, and a half-mad Baroque villa in Bagheria. The area is visually scruffy in parts, but the startlingly abrupt mountains rising from the coast are a compensation, and there are worthwhile beaches at Trabía as well as some beautiful swimming off Capo Zafferano.

Bagheria and the Villa Palagonia

... the coat-of-arms of the House of Pallagonia is a satyr holding up a mirror to a woman with a horse's head. Even after having seen the other absurdities, this seems to me the most peculiar of all.

Goethe, *Italian Journey*

Goethe didn't take kindly to the mad and playful whimsies of the Prince of Palagonia, who, like the rest of Palermitan nobility, fled the unloved court of the Spanish viceroy in the 17th and 18th centuries to build villas in Bagheria. Bagheria is 15km from Palermo, on the easternmost edge of the Conca d'Oro. Once idyllic, full of citrus and palm groves, it's now a dusty, sprawling town intruded upon by ugly new buildings, speculators and feuding Mafiosi.

However, Bagheria is still a good place to get a feeling of the pampered life of the old Sicilian aristocracy, with the dark extremes of the Baroque imagination thrown in for free in the one villa open to the public, **Villa Palagonia** (*open daily 9–12.30 and 3.30–5.30*). Located off main Corso Umberto, and hemmed in by modern buildings, the villa was begun in 1705 by the great, innovative Palermitan architect Tommaso Maria Napoli for the Prince of Palagonia, one of the wealthiest men in Italy.

The villa is a deliciously curving virtuoso piece, although much of the initial effect is lost because visitors now enter through the rear. By the time of Goethe, however, the villa had been inherited by the prince's grandson, Ferdinando Gravina, who was rapidly depleting the family fortune by decorating it in what Goethe called a 'Palagonian paroxysm' of crudely leering, writhing, snarling, grinning monstrosities – 62 of the weirdest creatures ever carved in stone ring the garden. The cornices are topsy-turvy, tormented with figures of dragons, gods and monkeys. The neglected interior, according to travellers' accounts, was equally disturbing, with strange mirrors (only one survives, in the ceiling of the ballroom) and furniture made of broken teapots. There are frescoes on the labours of Hercules in the elliptical vestibule; the marble busts are said to represent various members of the Gravina family. Gone, however, are the chairs with spikes hidden under the cushions. Some say Gravina was jealous of his young wife, and had the works made to torment her and drive her crazy; others say he was a proto-Surrealist genius.

Just opposite Villa Palagonia is the entrance to another villa by Tommaso Maria Napoli, the lovely **Villa Valguarnera** (1721), still owned by a descendant, a lofty, rectangular palace with a sweeping double stair, its curves echoed in the semicircular colonnade embracing the front courtyard. Still set in its own garden, you can only really see it from the hills behind Bagheria. Other villas in Bagheria include the one that set the trend, Giuseppe Branciforte's 1658 **Villa Butera**, on top of Via Butera, a fine, more severe house despite later Baroque touches; its little crenellated tower adds a warlike feel. Adjacent was an 18th-century pavilion called **La Certosa**, where visitors would come to stare at waxwork figures of famous people, all dressed in Carthusian habits. On the Palermo road, **Villa dei Principi di Cattolica** (*open Tues – Sun 9.30 – 7*), also from the 17th century, has a gently concave façade and an elliptical stair.

Getting Around

Trains between Palermo and Messina stop at Bagheria, Altavilla Milicia and Términi Imerese; the first two are also served by AST **buses** from Palermo's Piazza Lolli, t 09 16 88 29 06. Cáccamo and Santa Flávia (Solunto) are reached by Randazzo buses from Via Paolo Balsamo, Palermo, t 09 18 14 82 35. Himera and Cáccamo can be reached by bus from Términi Imerese.

Where to Stay and Eat

Bagheria

Trattoria Don Ciccio, Via del Cavaliere 87, t 09 19 32 442 (*moderate*). About as typical an eating place as you can get, with time-tested offerings which never stray from tradition. *Closed Wed, Sun and Aug.*

Santa Flávia ✉ 90017

★★★Kafara, Litoranea Mongerbino, north of town at S. Elia, t 0919 57 377, *www.kafara hotel.it* (*moderate–expensive*). The name of this modern hotel is the Phoenician name for nearby Solunto. It has a private beach, tennis, air-conditioning and more.

Trattoria dell'Arco Franco 'u Piscaturi', Porticello, t 09 19 57 758 (*expensive*). Down at Santa Flávia's little fishing port, this restaurant serves the freshest fish, deliciously prepared. *Closed Mon.*

Al Faro Verde, Porticello, t 0919 57 868 (*moderate*). Another delightful fish restaurant at Santa Flávia's little port. *Closed Tues.*

Trabía ✉ 90019

★★★Hotel Torre Artale, Contrada S. Onofrio, t 0918 11 35 57 (*moderate–expensive*). An old farm village surrounded by lovely gardens. Meals on the terrace with panoramic views.

★Lido Vetrana, Via Nazionale 87, t 0918 12 53 01 (*budget*). Offers a long row of simple motel rooms, with porches directly on to the beach; the restaurant-pizzeria (*inexpensive*) is packed in the summer.

Términi Imerese ✉ 90018

★★★★Grand Hotel delle Terme, Piazza Terme 2, t 0918 11 35 57, *ghterme@hotmail.com* (*moderate–expensive*). A posh spa establishment where you can take the waters with the Italians – who get reimbursed by their national health insurance.

La Petite Marseilles, Via Porta Erculea (*moderate*). This restaurant above Piazza Terme has good seafood and a terrace.

Cáccamo ✉ 90012

★★La Spiga d'Oro, Via Margherita 78, t 09 18 14 89 68 (*budget*). This pleasant little place is Cáccamo's only hotel.

This is now the **Galleria Comunale d'Arte Moderna** (*open same as above*), founded in 1973 by Expressionist painter Renato Guttuso (1912–87), a native of Bagheria and a vigorous crusader against the Fascists during the war, and the Mafia after the war. Besides social themes, Guttuso took a keen interest in the history of art, and often 'quoted' from other painters. His works dominate this collection.

Solunto

Open Mon–Sat 9–6, Sun and holidays 9–2.

Bagheria is shielded from the wind by lumpy Monte Catalfano, where the ancient city of Solunto (Soluntum) is situated in a spectacular position on the mountain's heel, high over the sea, 3km from Bagheria. Soluntum was the child of Solus (one of the three main Phoenician settlements, along with Palermo and Motya), which stood some 5km to the southwest at Cozzo Cannita. Very little remained of this earlier town, after Dionysius of Syracuse obliterated it in 398 BC in his campaign to ethnically cleanse Sicily of non-Greeks. The Carthaginians later returned and laid out a new town, Soluntum, in a classic grid plan, and invited Greek mercenaries, abandoned by Agathocles, to come and live with them (307 BC), completing the Hellenization of the town.

During the First Punic War the Romans annexed it as a *civitas decumana*, but it never prospered, and in the 2nd century AD it was abandoned. At the entrance of the excavations, the **antiquarium** contains a plan of Soluntum, coins, stele and a few capitals (everything else is in Palermo). The residential district was quite a jammy place to live. The re-erected column and peristyle called the **Gymnasium** are actually part of a residence. Other houses have fine **mosaic floors**, one with Leda and the swan, another with a unique 2nd-century BC picture of Archimedes' orrery. The public area of Soluntum includes a temple, perhaps dedicated to Baal, ruins of the agora, the theatre, and a semi-circular building that could have been the odeon or senate chamber (a bouleuterion).

From Solunto, the view of the castle of Solanto, the Casteldáccia vineyards and Cefalù along the coast, is spectacular. Nearby **Santa Flávia** is a fishing village and small resort, but the coast to the north around **Capo Zafferano** is still wild and beautiful – the first piece of undeveloped coast as you leave Palermo.

Eastwards, the coast is largely built up with the summer houses and *pizzerie* of the Palermitani. Two small castles are at **San Nicola l'Arena** (now a nightclub) and **Trabía**, this one dating back to the Arabs. Off the *autostrada* in **Altavilla Milicia**, the ruined church of San Michele, called the Chiesazza, was built by Robert Guiscard in 1077, on the site where he defeated the Saracens; just below is a little Arab bridge.

On the western outskirts of Términi Imerese, you can see several tiers of the **aqueduct of Cornelius** (east, on the Cáccamo road) the best-preserved on Sicily.

Términi Imerese

Overlooking a gulf of the same name, Términi Imerese (Thermae Himerenses) began as a colony of neighbouring Himera before being expropriated by Carthage. Its hot (42°C) **mineral springs** were much appreciated in antiquity: Diodorus wrote that three nymphs created them and that Hercules, on his way back from his fight in Erice (*see* p.120), was the first to bathe in them. Located in the lower town near the station, the waters are still used to treat urological problems; according to the Italians, they're also the secret ingredient of Términi's good pasta. You can see remains of the Roman baths and marbled pools in the **Stablimento Vecchio** and **Grande Albergo delle Terme**.

After the defeat of the Carthaginians and Pompey, Augustus made Términi a Roman colony; the lines of its forum remain in the long **Piazza del Duomo** in the attractive upper city (*buses every half-hour from the station*). At the end of the square near the belvedere is the 17th-century **cathedral**, its façade designed to fit four early 16th-century statues. On the altar there's a Crucifix by Ruzzolone painted on both sides (1484), and there's a Jesus with real hair in one of the chapels. The curves in Vias San Marco and Anfiteatro trace the lines of Términi's Roman amphitheatre. Nearby, **Santa Caterina d'Alessandria** contains naïve frescoes from the 15th–16th centuries with inscriptions in dialect. The **Museo Civico** (*open Tues–Sat 9–1 and 3–6, Sun 9–1*), founded in 1873 in an old hospital in Via di Museo, contains both an art collection – a

Byzantine triptych and other medieval works, and paintings by Caravaggio's pupil, Mattia Preti – and archaeological finds from the area, including lions' heads from Himera's Tempio della Vittoria, Imperial portraits, lead pipes from the Roman baths – testimony to Imperial plumbing – reliefs, sarcophagi, columns and mosaics.

Cáccamo

In the 5th century BC the Carthaginian citadel, high on a spur of Monte San Calógero at Cáccamo, often niggled ancient Himera. In the 12th century, a magnificent, spiral-shaped **castle** (*open daily 9–12 and 3–6.30*) replaced it and was used as the seat of the local dukes into the 20th century. One of the largest castles in Italy, piled on the edge of the sheer escarpment, it is crowned with the swallow-tail crenellations of the Ghibellines, the emperor's party. Some of its well-preserved rooms house a collection of arms and art. The best-known room is the Sala della Congiura, where the castle's lord, Matteo Bonnello, plotted with his fellow Norman nobles to overthrow William I the Bad, in 1160, a coup that frightened William badly and left Bonnello blinded, hamstrung and, shortly after, dead in the king's dungeon.

Cáccamo has a number of interesting churches. The Norman **cathedral** of 1090 was rebuilt in 1614 and contains a few Renaissance works – *quattrocento* marble panels attributed to Francesco Laurana, a painted Crucifix, and a baptismal font by Domenico Gagini. The **Annunziata** dates from the Middle Ages, and was given a half-hearted 17th-century facelift; inside, its treasure is the *Pala dell'Annunciazione* by the Flemish painter Borremans. Best of all, however, is the pavement in **San Benedetto** (1615), depicting marine and country scenes, done in fantasy majolica tiles by Niccolò Sarzana of Palermo.

Himera

If you're taking the coastal *autostrada*, the exit for ancient Himera is the Agglomerato Industriale, at a desolate seaside factory near Buonfornello; from here find your way to the SS113, keeping a sharp lookout for a tiny sign pointing up to the Museo d'Imera (*closed for restoration*). Just beyond is a burned wasteland of barbed wire, scrubby weeds and a few reconstructed six-inch walls; the rest is off limits.

Himera means 'day' in Greek, and it has known better ones. It was founded as a colony of Zancle (Messina) in 678 BC, the only important Greek city on this Carthaginian coast – their eastern outpost, Solunto, is only 30km away. Himera's territory extended from modern Cefalù to Términi Imerese. It gave birth to the great lyric poet Stesichorus, whose destiny was foretold as a child, when a nightingale alighted on his lips and sang. And Himera even had the gumption to boot out its tyrant, Terillo. Furious, Terillo turned to Carthaginian Palermo for assistance.

The Carthaginians didn't need to be asked twice: their general, Hamilcar, raised an army of 30,000, threatening to destroy not only Himera but all the Greeks in Sicily. In response, Theron of Agrigento (who had supported the citizens of Himera against Terillo) summoned the aid of his brother-in-law, Gelon of Syracuse, and in 480 BC their combined armies crushed Hamilcar in a decisive battle at Himera. In despair, Hamilcar dramatically flung himself on the funeral pyre of his dead warriors; the Greeks won great spoils and gained sufficient security to indulge in their favourite pastime –, fighting one another.

In 409 BC, Hamilcar's grandson, Hannibal (not the one who worried Rome, but an ancestor), took his revenge on the Greeks. He captured Himera, demolished the city, slew 3,000 prisoners on the spot where his grandfather had died so dramatically, and sent the survivors as slaves to the Carthaginian town of Thermae Himerenses (Términi Imerese). Himera was never rebuilt.

Only a tiny part of the **excavations** are open to visitors (*open 9am–one hour before sunset, adm*), near the museum; elsewhere excavations in 1963 uncovered remnants of temples of the 7th, 6th and 5th centuries BC, tombs, and 16 paved streets, which produced some remarkable ceramics and votive offerings, decorated with cockerels, then symbol of the city. Below, on the other side of the SS113, is the large base of the so-called **Tempio della Vittoria** (Temple of Victory; 205ft by 82ft), all that remains of lower Himera, which once had a port near the mouth of the River Grande. Erected between 470 and 460 BC, this large Doric temple was long believed to have commemorated the Victory of Himera. The ruined cella and drums of the columns remain; its rows of snarling lions' heads have been moved to the Museo Civico in Términi Imerese.

True warriors, it is said, have a sixth sense when it comes to old battlefields. While the Allies fought for Himera in August 1943, the ghosts of the Carthaginians and Greeks rose up out of the ground and refought the Battle of Himera for the sole benefit of General Patton – no one else present could see them.

Inland: the Mafia Heartland

Just west of Bagheria at Villabate the SS121 wends its way south towards Agrigento, passing up into bandit country and through some of the finest inland scenery that Sicily has to offer. The roads dip and rise with the contours of the grassy slopes through utterly serene pastures, as motionless as oil paintings. Take a picnic and a bottle of heady Corvo wine, find a shady tree and listen closely for the tinkling of bells, as niggled goats are goaded to new grazing grounds.

Misilmeri and Piana degli Albanesi

The first town of consequence is **Misilmeri** (from the Arabic Menzil el Emir – 'the village of the Emir'), which saw Count Roger's great victory over the huge Saracen army of Emir Ayub in 1068. The Normans captured the carrier pigeons of the Saracens, and Roger had the idea of releasing them to take the news of the defeat back to Palermo, each pigeon bearing a blood-soaked piece of cloth on its leg. As a piece of psychological warfare it was amazingly effective: Ayub fled to North Africa and left his leaderless people in despair. After Misilmeri, the Norman conquest of Palermo was only a matter of time. As a mute memorial to the battle, the ruined walls of the **Arab-Norman castle** dominate the town. The polygonal towers were added in the 14th century by the Chiaramonte princes – the fierce rivals of the

Getting Around

Palermo is the terminus of **buses** serving this region. Sicilbus, **t** 09 16 16 79 19, go to Misilmeri. from Via Paolo Balsamo in Palermo.

For Cefalà Diana, Bisacquino, Lercara Friddi, Corleone, Prizzi and San Giuseppe Jato/San Cipirello there's AST from Piazza Lolli, Palermo, **t** 09 16 88 29 06.

For Piana degli Albanesi, there are Prestia buses also from Via Paolo Balsamo, **t** 09 15 80 457.

If departing from Via Paolo Balsamo in Palermo, this bus departure area is just east of the main train station; allow time to find the right bus, as the layout of bus stops is confusing in the extreme.

Where to Stay and Eat

★★Miravalle, Contrada Segretaria, Misilmeri, ✉ 90036, **t** 0918 72 27 88 (*inexpensive*). A simple hotel with clean rooms with bath.

★★★Belvedere, Contrada Belvedere, Corleone, ✉ 90034, **t** 0918 46 40 00, *www.corleoneworld.it* (*budget–inexpensive*). Comfortable, and air-conditioned.

Casa Mia Pollara, on the Roccamena road, near Corleone, **t** 0918 96 31 97 (*inexpensive*). A farm at Malvello; fairly traditional.

Mulinazzo, at km237.5 on the SS121 Palermo–Agrigento road, **t** 0918 724870 (*expensive*). Traditional Sicilian food with a creative twist and a good wine list. *Closed Sun eve, Mon, last two weeks in Feb.*

Ventimiglia just to the east. Misilmeri produces white Passito wine, good strong stuff, but otherwise there's no need to linger here.

To the west, the road runs over a desolate landscape of lonely shepherds to the most important Albanian settlement in Sicily: **Piana degli Albanesi** (pop. 6,200), settled in the late 15th century by Albanian refugees from the Ottomans who were given permission by Juan II of Spain to settle the then empty spaces of western Sicily. The street signs are in two languages, and many people still speak Albanian at home, attend Greek Catholic (Uniate) services, and bring out their beautiful old costumes for weddings, baptisms and feasts. The biggest events, Epiphany and Easter, when the ancient liturgical rites are followed, draw hundreds of tourists. At other times you can check out the collection of tools in the **Museo Antropologico**, in Corso Castriota (*open Tues–Sun 9–1 and 4–7*). The water of nearby **Lago Piana degli Albanesi**, a beautiful artificial lake, is sent to Palermo as drinking water and to irrigate the last remaining crops and orchards of the Conca d'Oro. Just above the lake is the infamous **Portella della Ginestra**, where Salvatore Giuliano gunned down the revellers from Piana degli Albanesi and San Giuseppe Jato (14km west).

San Giuseppe Jato was called Ietas, an Elymian-Greek settlement dating back to the 6th century BC. Excavations since 1971, on the west flank of Monte Jato, have revealed the small theatre, arcaded agora, bouleuterion, houses, and temple dedicated to Aphrodite (*to visit, contact Signora Quiescenti, t 09 18 57 39 88*). In **San Cipirello**, adjacent to San Giuseppe, the **Museo**, Via Roma 320 (*open daily 9–1 and 3–7*), contains caryatids, telamons and ceramics from the site.

To the east, little **Cefalà Diana** (just west of the SS121) is named after a head-shaped buttress rock, crowned by a ruined Arab castle. Just north, the rectangular bath building called the **Bagni di Cefalà** has long mystified historians, with its traces of kufic inscriptions. Some say it is Arab; others say the thick outer walls were built by the Romans, and rebuilt by the Normans with Arab labour. Farther south, on a wooded slope is **Mezzojuso** (from the Arab Manzil Jusuf – 'Joe's village'). In the 1400s, it became a haven for Albanian Greek refugees and hence has two 'mother' churches, one Greek, **San Nicola**, which has some late Byzantine icons, and one Latin, **Annunziata** (*both open Sundays for mass*). In 1650, Greeks took over the monastery of **Santa Maria delle Grazie**, now used as a workshop to restore ancient books; the church has 15th-century icons, and frescoes of the Orthodox Doctors of the Church.

The Bosco della Ficuzza and Corleone

Around here stretches the last surviving forest in western Sicily, the 10,000-acre **Bosco della Ficuzza**, its chestnuts and oaks set aside as a boar-hunting reserve for Ferdinando III. The royal hunting lodge, the **Casino di Caccia**, designed by Venanzio Marvuglia in 1803, is an elegant little palace in warm sandstone, strikingly set against a tall limestone bluff; today it is the headquarters of the local forest rangers. There are several woodland paths to take from the hamlet of Ficuzza, one leading to the infamous **Rocca Busambra**, a formidable cliff from which Corleone's Mafia bravos have tossed countless victims.

The main town south of here, **Corleone**, will ring a bell for anyone familiar with Mario Puzo's *The Godfather*, and in reality the town has been blood-stained by more Mafia feuding and vendettas than any other in Sicily since the war. Overlooking the main Palermo–Sciacca route and a fertile valley, set among craggy rocks and a natural rock pinnacle, Corleone was an important military outpost of the Saracens. The Normans granted it to the abbey of Monreale. In the early 13th century, Frederick II introduced a large population of Lombards who, in the Sicilian Vespers massacre, acquired a reputation for their gusto for violence. Corleone has been the cradle of recent top Mafia bosses: the late Luciano Liggio and his henchman and successor since 1974, Salvatore Riina. The most wanted man in Italy for years, he was picked up on a street in Palermo in 1993. Riina may continue to claim that he has never even heard of the Mafia, but investigators hold him responsible for the deaths of Palermo's special judges, Giovanni Falcone and Paolo Borsellino, plus a good hundred other murders. Yet Riina had been living openly in Corleone ever since becoming the 'boss of bosses'. The police were only able to circumvent the corrupt politicians shielding him because Riina's own driver turned him in.

So don't be too surprised if the Corleonese eye you suspiciously in the cobbled streets, and fall silent when you walk into a bar. There is a pair of churches to seek out, **San Martino** (1382, enlarged and redecorated in the 18th century) and the 17th-century **Santa Rosalia**, both used as repositories of painting and sculpture gathered from abandoned churches. Look for the statue of St Francis in one of the *piazze*; his frustrated expression and outstretched arms suggest he is bemoaning the loss of a big, prize fish, the one that got away.

Prizzi and Lercara Friddi

Prizzi sits proudly in the breezy hills, even higher (3,267ft) and colder than Lercara Friddi (from *freddo*, or cold). Now a household name thanks to the Mafia *film noir* starring Jack Nicholson, Prizzi overlooks a lake and some unusual 'drunken' rocks to the west. Farther west, **Bisacquino** is another panoramic mountain town founded by the Arabs; the **Museo Civico** (*open daily 9–2*) in Via Orsini has a few Punic and Greek finds from the surrounding hills, and ethnographic exhibits on pastoral and agricultural life in the area. Seven kilometres west, you can visit the melancholy but panoramic remains of the once grand Olivetan **Abbazia di Santa Maria del Bosco**, built between 1401 and 1646, and ruined in the 1968 earthquake that devasted so much of western Sicily. The views stretch for miles to the west.

Farther east, you'll find **Lercara Friddi** (2,165ft), an important sulphur town in the 19th century, although postwar competition has forced the closing of the mines. It gave the world the mobster Lucky Luciano, who was later deported to Palermo by the United States. Luciano thought that as an American big-shot he would immediately have a high ranking back home in Sicily, and he swanned about with the most powerful bosses on the island. He was a fish out of water. The real Mafia conned him into investing in a sweets factory, and rigged it so that, the more caramels it sold, the more money Luciano lost.

Cefalù

Of all the resorts along the Tyrrhenian Coast, Cefalù is the loveliest, squeezed between a long sweeping curve of sand and the massive peak, the Rocca, that the Greeks thought resembled a head (*kephalos*, hence Cefalù). It is a singular sight, most striking when viewed across the bay from the west, where Roger II's lofty cathedral stands out like a stepping stone between rock and sea.

The skirts and the crown of the Rocca have been continuously inhabited since the 9th century BC, when the Sikels founded their town of Cephaloedium. In the 5th century BC it became the fortified western outpost of Imera. In Byzantine times Cefalù was the seat of a Greek bishop, but, by the 8th century, pirate raids drove the inhabitants to move to the top of the Rocca for defence. They stayed up there under the Arabs (858–1063), and only came back down again in 1131, when Roger II rebuilt the town by the sea at the same time as his great cathedral.

Nowadays it's a lively place. Shops close around midnight in summer, and bars are often still open at dawn. Avoid Cefalù in August if you can; without a hotel booking you will find yourself on the beach or in the car for the night. The best beach extends west to Santa Lucia, with sands and easy bathing. East of La Rocca there's less swimming and the coast is marred by the presence of a sewage farm.

The Cathedral

Open daily 8–12 and 3.30–7.30; women must cover their arms.

Cefalù's Norman cathedral is located in a spacious *piazza* along the main Corso Ruggero. According to legend, Roger II ran into a violent storm while sailing to Palermo in 1131, and vowed that if his ship reached shore safely he would build a cathedral where he landed. In the thick of the storm St George appeared and helped him safely to port in Cefalù. Accordingly, Roger made Cefalù a bishopric and pulled out all the stops to build a beautiful cathedral, which he declared would hold his

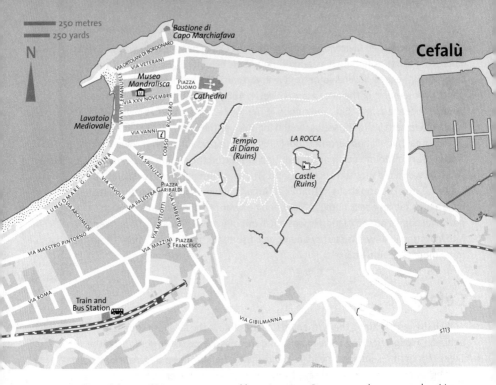

tomb and those of his successors, and he set up two Roman porphyry sarcophagi to that effect. He took a deep personal interest in the project, to the extent of building a palace nearby to supervise the work (*see* 'Around Old Cefalù', below).

It just so happened that the miraculous rescue also conveniently suited Roger politically. The fact that he had been crowned king by an antipope, Anacletus, who was supported by no other ruler but Roger himself, made his legitimacy somewhat tenuous. As a future bargaining chip in dealing with the next pope, he not only infringed on the right claimed by Rome to appoint bishops in Sicily, but also defiantly made Cefalù his royal church in place of Rome-recognized Palermo.

When Anacletus died in 1139, and even Roger had to acknowledge Innocent II as his rightful pope, he managed to have his crown confirmed in an unexpectedly direct manner – by capturing Innocent II on the battlefield and holding him ransom in exchange for recognition of his kingship. In revenge the popes refused to acknowledge the bishopric of Cefalù, which was the reason why, after Roger's death, Palermo refused to give up his body. Cefalù continued to insist on its rights, to no avail. Seventy years later, Roger's grandson, Frederick Stupor Mundi, launched a surprise night raid on Cefalù and made off with the sarcophagi before anyone knew what had happened. To this day they remain in Palermo cathedral.

The cathedral in Cefalù took 100 years to complete. The magnificent façade, with its golden patina in the late afternoon light, the pair of mighty towers, the interlaced brickwork and blind arcades, were designed in 1240 by Giovanni Panettera; in the same year the church was consecrated by a Monsignor Chat, whose arms of a cat rampant can still be seen. It's hard to imagine a more perfect setting, atop the gentle rise of a *piazza* filled with palm trees, and the Rocca looming just behind. A colourful 6th-century Byzantine mosaic, recently discovered under the cathedral's west entrance, has shown that the same site had been used by the Greeks.

The Mosaics

At first the long nave, with its 16 Roman columns, pointed arches and timber ceiling (built by Arab carpenters, who left some hard-to-discern paintings on the beams), looks a bit bare. The interior decoration was never completed in the Middle Ages (although don't miss the two large **capitals** swarming with monsters, near the crossing), and the Baroque encrustations added later have been stripped away.

The result is that nothing distracts from the shimmering magnificence of the golden mosaics in the presbytery and over the altar. These are the oldest Byzantine-Norman mosaics in Sicily, completed in 1148, six years before Roger's death (currently partly being removed for restoration). The traditional Byzantine figure of the Pantocrator in the apse is one of the most memorable portrayals of Christ anywhere, holding a book with the legend 'I am the Light of the World' in Greek and Latin, while blessing the congregation. Despite his dominance and size in the overall scheme, this is a gentle, compassionate Christ, divine yet human, noble yet merciful. Even in his features, Sicilians see Roger's tolerance and syncretism: his hair is blond like a Norman, his beard and brows black like an Arab, his nose and mouth Greek. Below him stands his mother, arms outstretched in prayer, and four archangels in Byzantine court dress; below them are the 12 apostles.

From Roger's day are the **marble thrones**, one for the bishop and one for Roger, the priest-king. There's a lovely cloister, the model for Monreale, but it's been under restoration for the better part of 20 years; wicked tongues say it's been dismantled and put in boxes that have disappeared off the face of the earth.

Museo Mandralisca

Open daily 9–7, Sun 9–1; adm.

Just below the cathedral, in Via Mandralisca, the eclectic collections of Enrico Piraino di Mandralisca are on display in the Museo Mandralisca. Its greatest prize is the *Portrait of an Unknown Man* (c. 1460), the earliest known portrait by Antonello da Messina; the man's enigmatic, ironic, mocking smile has no counterpart in 15th-century portraiture, and perhaps even incited the angry scratches that someone clawed on his arrogant face. Here too are Greek vases from Lipari (including a charming crater showing a fishmonger slicing off a slab of tuna for a customer), seashells, Arab ceramics, an ancient coin collection and Chinese boxes.

Around Old Cefalù

The Museo Mandralisca is in the heart of medieval Cefalù, its narrow lanes softly lit in the evening for romantic strolling. Towards the sea, in Via Vittorio Emanuele, which runs along the beach, a secret underground stream makes an appearance at the foot

Getting There

Cefalù lies on the main bus and **train** routes between Palermo and Messina. **Buses** leave from the train station (south of the town centre) for Gibilmanna (three daily), for Castelbuono (six daily) and Geraci Siculo and Gangi (one daily). In summer SNAV runs a daily **hydrofoil** service to the Aeolian Islands of Lipari and Vulcano; check with the tourist office for timetables or go to *www.snav.it*.

Tourist Information

Corso Ruggero 77, **t** 0921 21 050, *www.cefalu-tour.pa.it*, (*open Mon–Fri 8–2 and 4–7, Sat 8–2*). Ask for *30 Footpaths in the Madonìe*, a detailed and comprehensive description of the roads, paths, *refuges* and facilities in the Monti Madonìe, for bikers, trekkers and common mortals.
Useful website: *www.cefaluonline.com*.
Internet access: Corso Ruggero 38, **t** 0921 42 17 53, *baco@online*.

Where to Stay

Cefalù ✉ 90015

Several hotels in town spread along the best beach, to Santa Lucia in the west (Caldura in the east is less ideal). The higher prices are in force July–mid Sept. There are three campsites near the sea, but too near the train tracks for a good night's sleep.

★★★Paradiso Club, Via dei Mulini 18, **t** 0921 42 39 00, *www.paginegialle.it/paradisoclub* (*expensive–luxury*). If you have a car, consider the Polynesian huts and huge pool at this place up in the hills above Cefalù. The hotel also hires out windsurfers, sailing boats and yachts, and can get you scuba classes.
★★★Le Calette, Via Vincenzo Cavallaro 12, **t** 0921 42 41 44, *www.lecalette.it* (*moderate–luxury*). At 2 km from the centre with a pool surrounded by palm trees and overlooking a white pebbly beach. The only drawback is the railway line running at the back of it.
★★★Baia del Capitano, Contrada Mazzaforno, **t** 0921 42 00 03/5, *www.baiadelcapitano.it* (*moderate–expensive*). Modern, air-con hotel immersed in a century-old olive grove 4km west of Cefalù, this is one of the many in the area with a beach.
★★★Kalura, Via V. Cavallaro 13, **t** 09 21 42 13 54, *www.kalura.it* (*moderate–expensive*). Built directly over the dramatic coast at Caldura, it has a private beach, pool and a good dozen other activities for adults and kids alike. Modern and a bit impersonal but with friendly staff.
Azienda Agrituristica Arione, C. da Pozzetti, Collesano ✉ 90015, **t** 0921 42 77 03, *arione@agriturismoarione.it* (*rooms and apartments vary in price; most are moderate*). Set in the cacti-covered hills towards Làscari and close to the Madonie Regional Park, there is a swimming pool and an officially recognised riding school at this

of a curving stair at the **Lavatoio Mediovale**, where, in the Middle Ages until fairly recent times, the women did their laundry in a series of stone basins under an arcade; it still looks in working order. **San Gregorio**, in the same street (*open for services*), has a Norman façade. One of the classic views of Cefalù is from the little fisherman's beach just below here, where the houses stand in a solid front against the sea; another, of the coast and what remains of the city's megalithic fortifications, may be had from the **Bastione di Capo Marchiafava**, at the very northern tip of the city, near the top of handsome 17th-century Via Ortolano di Crispi.

Heading south along Corso Ruggero from the cathedral, note the **Purgatorio** (*open for services*), with its 15th-century portal decorated with skulls and souls languishing in pots of flames. What remains of Roger II's residence – especially the windows – has been incorporated into the splendidly restored **Osterio Magno**, on the corner of Via Amendola (*open daily 9–7*), now open for exhibitions.

agriturismo farm. Rooms and apartments vary in price; most are moderate.

***Astro, Via Roma 105, t 0921 42 16 39, www.astrohotel.it (*inexpensive–moderate*). Modern, air-conditioned, and in a pleasant spot 100m from the sea and just west of the train station. Has its own private lido.

**La Giara, Via Veterani 40, t 0921 42 15 62, www.paginegialle.it/hotellagiara (*inexpensive–moderate*). A restored *palazzo* in one of the narrow cobbled streets in the heart of Cefalù, just northwest of the cathedral. There is a large terraced roof with spectacular views over the sea and the cathedral, though rooms tend to be a little noisy. Enjoy wonderfully prepared Sicilian specialities for either lunch or dinner.

**Pensione delle Rose, Via Gibilmanna, t 0921 42 18 85 (*inexpensive*). A quiet modern retreat among the olives, with splendid views, a 20min walk from town.

*Locanda Cangelosi, Via Umberto I 26, t 09 21 42 15 91 (*budget*). A good choice if you're watching pennies; it has four basic rooms and staff with erratic mood. Just south of Piazza Garibaldi.

Eating Out

The seafood-lover will be gratified to learn that Cefalù is still a fishing village. As you may have noticed, the arms of the town show three fish holding a loaf on their noses.

Da Nino, Lungomare G. Giardina, t 0921 42 25 82 (*expensive*). Run by two brothers in a former salt warehouse by the beach, 300m south of the cathedral, it offers a heaving table of cold and warm *antipasti*, plenty of seafood, and excellent pizzas as well. *Closed Tues in Nov–Dec.*

La Botte, Via Veterani 6, t 0921 42 43 15 (*moderate*). Small, cosy and particularly good restaurant, at the north end of town, with delicious fresh seafood and local wines. In the summer months they set tables out on the pavement.

La Brace, Via XXV Novembre 10, t 0921 42 35 70 (*moderate*) Another great place, just west of the cathedral, with a menu that changes with the seasons. *Closed Mon.*

Al Gabbiano, Lungomare G. Giardina, 0921 42 14 95 (*moderate*). Serves the freshest of pasta and seafood, and is frequented by a less touristy clientele, near Da Nino. *Closed on Weds.*

Al Giardino, Lungomare G. Giardina, t 0921 92 12 90 (*moderate*). An unpretentious trattoria-pizzeria set in a lush, semi-tropical garden on the beach at the southwest edge of town. *Closed Thurs.*

Vecchia Marina, Via Vittorio Emanuele 73, t 0921 42 03 88 (*moderate*). Sit on the little terrace overlooking the fishermen's beach and enjoy a recent catch. *Closed Tues and Nov.*

L'Antica Corte, Corso Ruggero 193, t 0921 42 32 28 (*inexpensive*). An excellent trattoria, tucked away in a beautiful *cortile*, very convenient for the museum and the cathedral. *Closed Thurs.*

Up on the Rocca

Farther south along Corso Ruggero, Piazza Garibaldi divides new from old Cefalù. From here signs point the way up to the Rocca – a hard slog in the heat of August, though for part of the early stages you have the welcome shade of trees. The reward is a bird's-eye view of the city and its bays directly below, and a wander through its recently restored Arab and feudal fortifications, past remains of cisterns and ovens to the ruined castle on top. In classical times, the Rocca was the acropolis of Cephaloedium, with a temple of Hercules on top. One feature that has survived the centuries of stone quarrying is a megalithic structure of huge trapezoidal blocks, known, probably erroneously, as the **Tempio di Diana**. It has a distinctive Mycenaean air to it; studies have shown that it underwent three phases of construction, from the 9th to the 4th century BC. And that's all anyone knows.

The Magician of Cefalù

One of the funniest of Sciascia's short stories, *Apocryphal Correspondence re Crowley*, not to mention Somerset Maugham's *The Magician*, is based on real-life happenings that mesmerized Sicily in the early 1920s. Just under the Rocca, in a stone cottage called Villa Agnello, a certain Aleister (Edward Alexander) Crowley from Leamington, England, founded the 'Abbey of Thelema', to hold the rites that he declared would be the successor to Christianity. The cult was devoted to as much drugs and sex as possible, with a dash of ancient rites, mumbo-jumbo and black magic thrown in. Over the door was an inscription: 'Do as you please; the law is yours.' One of Crowley's chief disciples was Leah Faesi, the Grand Priestess, known as the Scarlet Woman. Crowley shaved his head and wore gold earrings and called himself The Beast. He looked more like Mr Clean. He painted pornographic murals on the walls of Villa Agnello and wrote a book, *Diary of a Drug Addict*, in which he calls Cefalù Telephilus. Some saw him as a superhuman genius revealing a new world age, or perhaps an English D'Annunzio.

The townspeople and local peasantry were fascinated by Crowley's doings, and in 1923 were sad to see The Beast and his followers expelled on Mussolini's orders. When Crowley died in England in 1947, he asked in his will to be buried on the Rocca by the Tempio di Diana, with an epitaph reading: 'Come across the sea, from Sicily and Arcady, wandering like Bacchus, with fawns, pards, nymphs and satyrs as guards. On the milk-white donkey come to me! Come with Apollo, in your nuptial garment. Do as you please, as only a god can!' For some reason, Cefalù said no thanks.

The Monti Madonìe: a Circular Tour

High above Cefalù are the Monti Madonìe, pitching up in places to over 5,700ft. Under these rocky crests begin the fertile, rolling hills of the central Sicilian bread-basket that helped feed the insatiable maw of Imperial Rome. In the Middle Ages this was the treasured fief of the Ventimiglia, one of the three families of 'semi-kings' who ruled post-Angevin Sicily. Their castles dot the Madonìe's lofty villages, where, as in the Monti Nebrodi to the east, a number of pagan festival rites have survived almost intact.

In 1989 the Parco Regionale delle Madonìe was created, incorporating the area between Castelbuono, Gangi, Caltavuturo and Collesano. An extensive network of walking, riding and mountain-bike paths cross some of the highest mountains in Sicily: ask the tourist office in Cefalù for their list of stables, and a map, *Madonie: Carta dei Sentieri* (do check out paths before you attempt them; some plunge over limestone cliffs and are no light undertaking). For guided tours ring Museo Ambientalista Madonita t 091 55 10 09.

Gibilmanna and Castelbuono

The religious centre of the Madonìe is the **Santuario di Gibilmanna** (*monastery open daily 9–1 and 3–5*), a panoramic spot 14km above Cefalù, on a hill called 'Gibel el Iman'

('The Mount of Faith') by the Arabs after they witnessed a miracle performed by the Madonna there. The monastery is said to be much older, one of six founded in Sicily by Gregory the Great in the 6th century. In 1535, Capuchin friars rebuilt it, and have been there ever since; the new church was rebuilt in 1624. The monastery has a **museum** of religious art and vestments.

From here the SS286 continues up to **Isnello**, a summer and winter resort with the closest skiing to Palermo, at Piano degli Zucchi, 'Pumpkin Plain' (3,300ft). The road then veers east for **Castelbuono**, the metropolis of the Madonie, a handsome mountain town chosen by the Ventimiglia of Geraci as their new seat in 1316. They built themselves an austere **castle** in 1438 (*open Mon 9–1 and Tues–Sun 9-1 and 4–7, adm*), lightened up with stucco decorations in the chapel, believed to be by Giacomo Serpotta. Pretty Piazza Margherita has a fountain and a Renaissance church, the **Matrice Vecchia**, with a marble ciborium, or canopy, over the altar, enthroning a polyptych by Antonello da Messina's nephew, Antonello de Saliba. The 13th-century **San Francesco**, with its Gothic portal, was built as the Ventimiglia funerary chapel.

Gangi

Beyond Geraci lies the old Palermo–Catania highway, now the SS120. Take it a few kilometres east to medieval Gangi, famous in Sicilian lore for its **Sagra delle Spighe** (second Sunday in August), when ears of wheat tied in red ribbons decorate the city in a rite straight from the days of Demeter. Gangi, too, is dominated by a Ventimiglia castle; their 14th-century tower now doubles as a campanile of **San Nicola**. Gangi was the birthplace of the prolific Giuseppe Salerno (1570–1632), better known in these mountains as Lo Zoppo di Gangi ('the lame man of Gangi'), who graced San Nicola with his own version of Michelangelo's *Last Judgement* (1629). On the steps of Via Matrice, 17th-century **SS. Salvatore** has a superb Crucifix by Fra Umile da Petralia. Don't miss **Via Vitale**, with its medieval arcades.

Petralia Sottana and Petralia Soprana

The same SS120 leads 13km west to the two charming Petralias: lower Petralia Sottana and older, upper Petralia Soprana, set in the most densely forested region in Sicily, with a long-range view across to Etna. Hardly low, at 3,000ft, **Sottana** was founded in the Middle Ages as a defensive outpost for Soprana. Its two old churches stand face to face, one with a **sundial**, the other with a **model metre**, embedded in the wall in 1860 to teach the townspeople the new unit of measurement. Farther up, the handsome **Chiesa Madre** dominates the town, with its campanile built over an archway; inside are more paintings by Lo Zoppo. The Sunday after Ferragosto (15 August), a re-enactment of an ancient wedding dance, **La Cordella**, is staged here, while SS. Trinità is the scene of the festival of the **Madonna dell'Alto**, with a nocturnal procession through the streets (16 August).

Some 350ft above Sottana, **Petralia Soprana** has been inhabited since the 3rd century BC. A monument in the centre honours its most famous son, 17th-century sculptor Fra Umile Pintorno. Too poor to work in marble, he carved in wood, making his name for a unique series of passionate life-sized Crucifixes; one hangs in the

Getting There and Around

The Monti Madonìe are served better by **bus** than many inland areas. SAIS TRASPORTI, Via Balsamo 16, Palermo, **t** 09 16 17 11 41, run from Palermo to Cefalù, Castelbuono, Geraci, Gangi, Petralia, Siculo and beyond to Nicosia. AST, **t** 0916 88 27 83, run from Cefalù and Palermo (Corso Re Ruggero) to Collesano and Isnello (no service Sun). La Spisa, **t** 0921 42 43 00, make the run up from Cefalù to Gibilmanna (no service Sun). Buses from Cefalù also run (one daily Mon–Sat) to Polizzi Generosa and Caltavuturo.
Useful website: *www.parcodellemadonie.com*.

Where to Stay and Eat

Gibilmanna ✉ 90015
**Bel Soggiorno, t 0921 42 18 36 (*inexpensive*). The only hotel in Gibilmanna. *Closed Nov–May.*
***Fattoria Pianetti, Contrada Gratteri, **t** 0921 42 18 90, *fattoriapianetti@yahoo.it* (*inexpensive*). This *agriturismo* on the hills has seven rooms and offers a variety of courses and horse-riding excursions. Excellent food (*inexpensive*) using home-grown organic produce.

Isnello ✉ 90010
***Baita del Faggio, Acque del Faggio (4,100ft), **t** 09 21 66 21 94, *www.baitdel faggio.com* (*inexpensive*). This cosy place is the highest of several comfortable, all-season resort hotels around Isnello.
***Piano Torre Park Hotel, Piano Torre, **t** 09 21 66 26 71, *www.pianotoreparkhotel.com* (*inexpensive*). Offers swimming in the summer, skiing in the winter, tennis and other sports. The hotel restaurant is a good place to sample local mushrooms in season.
Rifugio Ostello di Piano Merlino, Piano Battaglia (5,510ft), **t** 09 21 64 99 95 (*budget*). This hostel high up in the woods is run by the Club Alpino Italiano and provides meals.

Castelbuono ✉ 90013
*****Relais Santa Anastasia, Contrada Santa Anastasia, **t** 0921 67 22 33, *www.santa -anastasia-relais.it* (*luxury*). If luxury is what

you are after, stay in this restored manor. Plush furnishing, reading rooms and pool.
***Milocca, Contrada Piano Castagna, **t** 0921 67 19 44, *www.albergomilocca.com* (*inexpensive; half-board only in Aug*). A resort hotel on the outskirts of Castelbuono, with a pool and tennis – one of the most comfortable hotels in the mountains.
Villa Levante, Via Isnello, **t** 335 639 45 74 (*inexpensive*). Wooden beams and stone walled rooms in this 19th-century castle. Splendid views of the mountains and the coast.
*Ariston, Via Vittimaro 2, **t** 0921 67 13 21 (*budget*). A more modest choice in town with eight rooms.
Il Romitaggio, 4km from Castelbuono on the San Guglielmo road, **t** 0921 67 13 23 (*moderate*). Some of the best food in the area is served at this old cloister, which has typical Sicilian dishes, and pizza in the evening. *Closed Wed.*
Al Vecchio Palmento, Via Failla 2, **t** 0921 67 20 99 (*moderate*). Mushroom-based recipies are served in this restored 13th-century *frantoio* (oil mill). *Closed Mon.*
Bar Fiasconaro, Piazza Margherita. A good place to try the local dessert called *testa di turco* (Turk's head), a delightful fried pastry, also made in most restaurants in the area.

Gangi ✉ 90024
Tenuta Gangivecchio, Gangivecchio, **t** 0921 68 91 91, *www.gangivecchio.it* (*moderate*). Just outside town, this former Benedictine monastery is the best place to eat or stay, and could be the ideal spot from which to explore the mountains if you have transport. The staff are friendly, there is a swimming pool and the food is superb – the owner's mother and sister have written books on Sicilian cuisine.
Miramonti, Via Nazionale 13, **t/f 09 21 64 44 24 (*budget*). A nondescript hotel just below town.

Petralia Sottana ✉ 90027
Madonìe, Corso Paolo Agliata 81, **t 0921 64 11 06 (*inexpensive*). A simple option in the centre of town.
Pomieri, Piano Pomieri, **t 0921 64 99 98, (*budget–inexpensive*). A resort hotel outside town with a pool in its garden.

ornate stuccoed **Chiesa Madre**, built in the 1300s by the Ventimiglia. The 18th-century **Santa Maria di Loreto** occupies the site of the Norman castle, its two 14th-century tower-campaniles adorned with colourful majolica tiles.

Polizzi Generosa and Caltavuturo

From the Petralias, the SS643 veers north to another picturesque town, stretched along the spine of a mountain, **Polizzi Generosa**, which was given its title 'generous' by Frederick Stupor Mundi. It is more than generously endowed with churches, at one time 76 in number. The best of the survivors, the **Chiesa Madre**, houses a lovely 16th-century Flemish triptych by the mysterious Maître au Feuillage Brodé, a Venetian organ, and sculptures salvaged from other churches.

Caltavuturo is 12km west on the other side of the A19. The most ancient section perches beneath a Saracen castle, **Kalat-Abi-Thur**, captured by Roger I. This area, called **Terra Vecchia**, is picturesque, jumbly, and nearly all the streets consist of stairs. In the 'new' village, dating from the 16th and 17th centuries, is **Santa Maria di Gesù**, with another of Fra Umile's wooden Crucifixes.

Back towards the coast lies **Collesano**, another medieval town that has kept its fabric intact, especially around the ruins of its castle. Among several old churches, the most notable is 15th-century **Santa Maria la Nuova** on Corso Vittorio Emanuele, with a Gothic-Catalan portal on the right, and frescoes from the 1600s.

Cefalù to Tindari and into the Monti Nebrodi

A string of resorts dot the Tyrrhenian coast beside sandy beaches, interrupted by such natural features as the picturesque big orange rock of Capo Calavà.

Just inland, the isolated villages in the Nebrodi, the gentle 'mountains of the fawn' (*nebros* in Greek), have resolutely avoided keeping up with the times. They present an unexpected side to the island of the sun: covered with deciduous forests, including the southernmost beech woods in Europe, and fauna that ranges from foxes to wild cats and eagles. Charcoal-burning, carpet-weaving and sheep-herding are age-old occupations; ancient customs and dialects have lingered here longer than anywhere else in Sicily. Two mountain towns near the coast, Mistretti and San Marco d'Alunzio, are especially worth a visit for their Baroque churches and *palazzi*.

Ancient Halaesa, Santo Stefano di Camastra and Mistretta

On the coast some way east of Cefalù, near pretty **Castel di Tusa**, stood Halaesa, founded in 403 BC by Archonides of Herbita, a Sikel. In 263 BC Halaesa was the first city in Sicily to ally itself with Rome, and in return Rome granted it special tax privileges; Cicero described it as one of the cities most faithful to Rome, and one of the wealthiest, at least until the predatory praetor Verres stripped it clean. Under the Arabs it disappeared altogether.

The **excavations** (*open daily 9–1 hr before sunset, adm; 3km from Castel di Tusa – there's no bus*) have unearthed its regular grid street plan, part of the agora, walls, the remains of the temple to Apollo (chief god of the city), and, in the necropolis, a colombarium dated early Empire. Up in **Tusa** proper, note the **Chiesa Matrice**, with its medieval campanile and Gothic door, and the 14th-century **San Nicola**. You will note, however, that not everything is ancient in this neck of the woods: Castel di Tusa is surrounded by an open-air museum of giant works of art called the **Fiumara d'Arte**. The big blue rectangle with an erection is only the most unmissable.

Santo Stefano di Camastra's chief industry is displayed the whole length of the road through town, lined as it is with bright, colourful **ceramics**. The clay here is among the best in Sicily – second only to that of Caltagirone; prices are reasonable, and the styles range from the traditional to the outlandishly contemporary. If you're short of time, you may want to head straight for the excellent Ceramiche Fratantoni on the Via Nazionale. The town, behind the bright plates and jugs, dates from the 18th century, with a street plan said to be copied from the gardens of Versailles. For an overview of the history of ceramics in this area, visit the **Museo delle Ceramiche**, in Palazzo Trabia (*open Mon–Fri 9–1 and 4–8*).

Just south of Santo Stefano, **Mistretta** is heir of ancient Greek Mitistrata, a handsome town of showy provincial 17th-century churches and palaces, and a favourite base for excursions into the Nebrodi, especially through the watershed Portella del Contrasto, or to Castel di Lucio. Built around one of the most decrepit castles in Sicily, Mistretta's chief architectural monument is its **Chiesa Madre** in central Piazza V. Veneto, a 17th-century fort of a church with an ornate Renaissance portal and an Antonello Gagini inside. On holidays, two warrior giants named Kronos and Mitia (said to have been introduced by the Hapsburgs, of all people) make an appearance; the rest of the year they're guarding an icon of the Virgin.

Sant'Agata di Militello, San Fratello and Alcara li Fusi

Sant'Agata di Militello is a down-to-business and no-frills market town, with a long seafront and a sandy beach, where stands an 18th-century castle meant some day to house the collections of the little **Museo dei Nebrodi** (*closed at the time of writing*). In **Acquedolci**, a seaside hamlet just to the west, the **Grotta di San Teodoro** was inhabited in the Upper Paleolithic era, when this area was rich in hippopotami; a museum is planned to contain the discoveries (*for information call the tourist office t 0941 72 61 10*).

Just west of Sant'Agata, you can take the SS289 13km up to a Nebrodi town, **San Fratello**. This was founded by Adelasia (Adelaide) di Monferrato, third wife of Roger I, for her Northern Italian countrymen. Although the medieval town was destroyed by a mud slide in 1754, the handsome church founded by Adelasia, the **Santuario dei SS. Fratelli** (dedicated to the three martyred brothers, Alfio, Filadelfio and Cirino), has survived in a superb spot on Monte Vecchio.

For centuries, San Fratello was so isolated that its inhabitants have retained traces of their French-Lombard speech; other Nebrodi villagers will tell you they even look different – taller, blonder, more blue-eyed. They've also retained a curious old 'Feast of the Jews' (Maundy Thursday–Good Friday), when young men don red costumes with masks, and blast trumpets in the streets – the exact opposite of the usual Sicilian

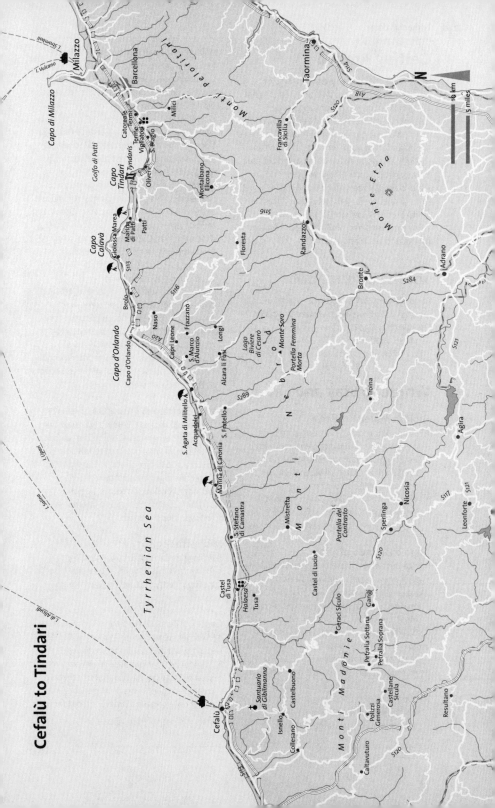

Cefalù to Tindari

N

10 km
5 miles

Tyrrhenian Sea

I. di Alicudi
I. Filicudi
I. Salina
I. Stromboli
I. Vulcano

Milazzo
Capo di Milazzo
Barcellona
Catoreale Termi
Terme Vigliatore
S. Biagio
Tyndaris
Oliveri
Capo Tindaris
Golfo di Patti
Capo Calavà
Marina di Patti
Gioiosa Marea
Patti
Montalbano Elicona
Milici
Francavilla di Sicilia
Taormina
Brolo
Naso
Capo d'Orlando
Capo d'Orlando
Capri Leone
Frazzanò
S. Marco d'Alunzio
Longi
Alcara li Fusi
S. Agata di Militello
Acquedolci
S. Fratello
Marina di Caronia
S. Stefano di Camastra
Castel di Tusa
Halaesa
Tusa
Mistretta
Castel di Lucio
Geraci Siculo
Gangi
Petralia Sottana
Petralia Soprana
Castellane Sicula
Polizzi Generosa
Castelbuono
Isnello
Collesano
Caltavuturo
Resuttano
Cefalù
Santuario di Gibilmanna

Floresta
Randazzo
Bronte
Adrano
Monte Etna
Monte Soro
Lago Biviere di Cesarò
Portella Femmina Morta
Nebrodi
Monti
Troina
Nicosia
Sperlinga
Leonforte
Agira
Portella del Contrasto
Monti Madonie

Monti Peloritani

Golfo di Patti

S113
S116
A20
S289
S117
S120
S121
S284
S115
S116
A18
A19
S120
S121

Getting Around

The **train** line runs along this stretch of coast, stopping at Capo d'Orlando, Sant'Agata di Militello, Acquedolci, Santo Stéfano di Camastra, Castel di Tusa and Cefalù. You really need a **car** to explore the mountains, but there are **buses** (often quite infrequent) from train stations along the coast: from Capo d'Orlando to Naso; from Sant'Agata di Militello to San Fratello, San Marco d'Alunzio and Alcara li Fusi; from Acquedolci to San Fratello; and from Santo Stéfano to Mistretta and Nicosia.

Covemar runs **hydrofoils** from Sant'Agata di Militello to Lipari and Vulcano.

Tourist Information

Capo d'Orlando: A. Volta corner Via Amnedola, t 0941 91 27 84, *www.aastcapodorlando.it* (*open daily 8.30–1.30 and 5–8*).
San Marco d'Alunzio: Via SS. Annunziata, t 03 39 64 65 077, t 03 30 67 74 55.

Where to Stay and Eat

Gioiosa Marea ✉ 98063
★★★Capo Skino Park, Skino, t 0941 30 11 67, *www.hotelcaposkino.it* (*expensive–luxury*). Resort-type hotel immersed in the pines off the SS113 near Capo Calavà, with views, tennis and a pool. *Closed mid-Sept–mid-June.*
★★Villa Smeralda, Calavà, t 0941 30 27 81 (*inexpensive*). A pleasant place, some of the rooms have views over the Aeolian Islands.

Capo d'Orlando ✉ 98071
★★★La Tartaruga, Lido San Gregório, t 0941 95 50 12, *www.hoteltartaruga.it* (*moderate*). On the beach and with its own pool, this hotel also has the best restaurant (*expensive*) on this stretch of the Tyrrhenian, where under a seaside arcade you can dine on *pasta alla marinara*, superb fish and traditional ice cream or *granita* desserts.
★★★Il Mulino, Via A. Doria 46, t 0941 90 24 31, *www.agatirno.it/mulino* (*moderate*). A modern hotel overlooking the sea in the middle of town with the rarity of non-smoker rooms. Its restaurant is popular.

★★Villaggio Testa di Monaco, Via Nazionale, t 0941 95 50 16 (*inexpensive–moderate*). For something cheaper, with pleasant rooms among the trees and right by the sea, head out to Testa di Monaco on the SS113. *Closed Oct–April.*
★★Villa Nazareth, Contrada Certari e Crocevia t 0941 91 19 27, *0941911927@iol.it* (*budget*). *Agriturism* on the hill just above town with fantastic views over the Capo.
La Tettoia, Contrada Certari, t 0941 90 21 46 (*moderate*). This pleasant, family-run place is the trattoria of choice in the area. *Closed Mon in Sept–June.*
Matteo, Lido San Gregório, t 0941 95 50 29. (*moderate*) Try this place for fresh fish and seafood, just across from the nicest stretch of beach in Capo d'Orlando.
Giulio, Via Amendola 25, t 0941 91 25 46. Just opposite the Tourist Office, come here to have the best pistacchio ice-cream in town.
Pescaturismo, Lido San Gregório, t 0941 95 51 57, *www.agatirno.it/sea2love*. If you are a fishing enthusiast, you can get accommodation, boats and all the equipment you need at this specialist place.

Santo Stefano di Camastra ✉ 98077
★★La Plaja Blanca, Via Fiumara Marina, t 0921 33 12 48 (*inexpensive*). Close to the sea, and with a swimming pool and tennis courts, this is a good place to stay if you want to linger amongst the ceramics.
★Locanda U Cucinu, Via Nuova 75, t 0921 33 11 06 (*budget*). An utterly basic alternative – you won't find cheaper.

Mistretta ✉ 98073
★Sicilia, Via Libertà 128, t 0921 38 14 63 (*budget*). This is the only choice in Mistretta. It offers plenty of character and simple comforts.

Castel di Tusa ✉ 98079
★★★Atelier sul Mare, Via C. Battisti 4, t 0921 33 42 95, *www.ateliersulmare.it* (*moderate*). Original beach-front hotel in which 15 rooms have been designed by different artists to create a unique 'living-art'experience. You can choose to have a different room for each night of your stay.

Holy Week processions. In the green hills around the village look for the prized *cavalli sanfratellani*, direct descendants of Norman mounts, bred with the local Arabians.

The cool oak, beech, ash and yew forests stretch from San Fratello to the scenic pass, **Portella Femmina Morta**, and up to the Nebrodis' highest peak, Monte Soro (5,541ft), to form the **Parco dei Nebrodi**. This encompasses the curious little mountain-top lake north of Monte Soro, **Lago Biviere di Cesarò**.

From Sant'Agata buses run up to **Alcara li Fusi**, at the foot of a huge bulging rock, overlooking the Valle del Rosmarino. Alcara is famous for its fountains and its harvest festival on 24 June, the Muzzini, believed to have come down intact from the ancient Greeks. Broken amphorae are placed on little altars and decorated with bright cloth and golden necklaces; in front of them friends link pinkie fingers and make solemn pledges to share everything except death.

San Marco d'Alunzio and Frazzanò

A turn-off from the coastal road squirms up into the foothills and natural belvederes to **San Marco d'Alunzio** (Hellenistic Aluntium), a commanding site inhabited since prehistoric times – the locals call it 'a second Taormina' and wonder why so few visitors come up to visit its 24 churches. At the top of the town are the ruins of the very first **Norman castle** in Sicily, built by Robert Guiscard in 1061. In another commanding spot, an impressive Hellenistic temple of Hercules has better withstood the ravages of time, converted in the 7th century into the church of **San Marco**. Another temple, Roman this time, provided the base for 17th-century **San Salvatore**; a few ancient columns and capitals have recently been uncovered. Another church, the Byzantine **Badia Piccola**, is built in the shape of a Greek cross crowned with a little cupola. When not ancient, the fabric of San Marco d'Alunzio is pure grassroots Sicilian Baroque: don't miss the 17th-century **Aracoeli**, its nave and aisles separated by monolithic columns made from the locally quarried red marble, *rosso aluntino*. Like the Aracoeli, **Chiesa Madre** has impressive portals and interiors.

Set in a lovely spot overlooking the Aeolian Islands a short way east, **Frazzanò** is graced with its tottering Basilian abbey of **San Filippo di Fragalà** (1090). Roger I made it his syncretic policy to fund new Orthodox religious houses in Sicily, and architecturally San Filippo was a model for many later foundations, with its decorative brickwork and three apses; there are even traces of Byzantine frescoes. Plans have been bruited about to restore it as a religious centre of some kind. **Longi**, another 7km up, has a wild river canyon that is *de rigueur* for serious trekkers in the Nebrodi.

Capo d'Orlando, Brolo and Naso

Capo d'Orlando, has a name going back to Charlemagne's paladin Roland (Orlando), who, according to legend, founded the castle on its sea-swept promontory, last rebuilt in the 14th century. Here the great Catalan admiral Roger de Lauria, with the fleets of Anjou to back him up, defeated Frederick II. The church next to the castle dates back to 1598. Just east of Capo d'Orlando is a unique beach, **San Gregório**, where the fine sand is strewn with odd-shaped boulders. Not far from San Gregório is a place called **Bagnoli**, the remains of a thermal structure belonging to a Roman villa,

Getting Around

This stretch of coast between Capo d'Orlando and Tindari is well covered by both trains and buses, with Messina the chief base (*see* pp.267–74). **Trains** run along the coast, from Milazzo to Barcellona, Oliveri-Tindari (from which it is a long walk to Tindari, so take the bus from Patti train station instead), Patti, Capo d'Orlando, and onwards to Cefalù and Palermo. There are **buses** from Barcellona to Castroreale.

In the summer, Alioth, Via C. Colombo 159, t 0941 36 13 91, runs **motor-boat** excursions to the Aeolian Islands from Marina di Patti.

Tourist Information

Patti: Piazza Marconi 11, t 0941 24 11 36 (*open Mon–Fri 9–1 and 4–7, Sat 9–1*).
For Tindari: Via Teatro Greco 15, t 0941 36 91 84 (*open Easter–Sept daily 9–7, Oct–Easter daily 9–1 and 4–7*).

Where to Stay and Eat

Marina di Patti ✉ 98066

***Hotel La Playa**, Via Playa 3, t 0941 36 13 98 (*moderate–expensive*). Recently renovated, with a pool and up-to-date comforts right on the beach. *Closed mid-Oct–mid-Mar.*
***Park Philip**, Via Zuccarrello 55, t 0941 36 13 32 (*moderate–expensive*). A big yellow place with a pool and comfortable rooms.
*Villa Romana, Via Playa, t 0941 36 12 68 (*budget*). Another pleasant place near the sea, with a garden, restaurant and pizzeria.

Cani Cani, t 0941 36 10 22 (*inexpensive*). For good, Messina-style seafood continue west 4km on the SS113 for Saliceto to track down this oddly named place. *Closed Tues in Oct–May.*
Bar Jolie, Piazza Mario Sciacca, Patti. For a delicious snack, track down this bar and try the *cardinali alla ricotta*.

Oliveri ✉ 98060

*La Mimosa, Via Fiume, t 0941 31 31 54 (*inexpensive*). Just to the east of Tindari, and not far from the sea, this is a pleasant hotel with a good restaurant.
*La Corda, Via Spiaggia Mare, t 0941 31 31 40 (*budget*). The budget option in Oliveri.

Castroreale

****Grand Hotel delle Terme**, Via Stabilimento 85, ✉ 98050, t 090 978 10 78 (*moderate–expensive*). Serving the baths in luxury, this hotel has a nice garden and tennis court. *Closed Dec–April.*
****Green Manors Country Hotel**, Porticato, t 090 974 65 15, www.greenmanors.it (*moderate–expensive*). This *agriturismo* is up on the hills surrounded by a lush park with swimming pool.
*Lido Marchesano, Via Marchesana, ✉ 98050, t 090 978 12 11 (*budget*). For much less, you can come here to stay down by the sea and beach.
Ostello della Gioventù delle Aquile, t 090 974 60 65, www.ostellionline.org (*budget*). Frederick's tower in Castroreale is now home to this youth hostel. *Closed Nov–Mar.*

which came to light in 1987. No walls are left but the layout is clear. The polychromatic mosaic flooring is fascinating. Also worth seeing in Capo d'Orlando is the **Piccolo di Calanovella** museum foundation, situated in an elegant late 19th-century villa. Author Giuseppe Tomasi di Lampedusa spent a lot of his time here writing his masterpiece *The Leopard* (*Il Gattopardo*). The museum holds paintings, photographs, ceramics and nostalgic momentos.

Brolo, farther east along the coast, has the distinction of a hexagonal medieval tower with swallow-tail crenellations, a giveaway that it was built by the Ghibellines, the emperor's party, as opposed to the Guelphs, or pope's party, who built their crenellations square. Near the excellent beaches at Capo Calavà, the resort of **Gioiosa Marea** has one of the area's main concentration of hotels.

One of the main roads into the mountains, the SS116, begins at Capo d'Orlando and leads up (11km) to **Naso** ('nose'). The etymology of the village's name is a little more interesting than its translation may suggest: some say the name is a derivation of the Greek word *nasu* ('forgotten'), recalling the coastal inhabitants who took refuge here from the invasions of the Saracen hordes in 901 BC. Nowadays it is a small village immersed in sprawl, but with a beautiful 15th-century church, **Santa Maria di Gesù**, just outside the town, housing the Renaissance tomb of Artale Cardona (died 1477) and its attendant allegorical statues of the virtues. Don't miss the enchanting view of the Sinagra Valley from the central *piazza*. The SS116 continues 36km to **Floresta**, at 3,825ft the highest town in Sicily, remote and grey, with Etna for a backdrop.

Patti

Farther east along the striking coast-hugging road is the lofty hilltown of Patti, and its beach extension, Marina di Patti. Patti has gone down in the annals for having been burned twice, once by Frederick II of Aragon for its loyalty to the Angevins, and once by Barbarossa in 1544, as part of a pirate's day's work. At the highest point of Patti, Roger II founded a church to house the remains of his beloved mother, Adelaide, who died in Patti in 1118. A few bits of the Norman church are incorporated into the façade of the 18th-century **Cattedrale di San Bartolomeo**. In the last chapel on the right is the sarcophagus of Adelaide, re-made in the Renaissance, with a winsome melancholy effigy of the queen. She had good reason for her blues: having done a notable job of raising her son and ruling Sicily after the death of Count Roger, she married King Baldwin of Jerusalem (1113), offering a priceless dowry. The impecunious Baldwin spent it, then had to confess he was already married; he sent her back to Sicily with little ceremony, and very little of her goods. She died the following year. It was an insult that her son Roger never forgave in his relationship with the Crusader states.

In 1973, while digging a base for an *autostrada* pier above Marina di Patti, the engineers came across the extensive ruins of a late Imperial **Roman villa** (*open daily 9am–one hour before sunset*). Covering nearly three acres, this luxurious hideaway is rich in colourful mosaic floors from the 4th century, the best of it carpeting the vast hall with three apses reminiscent of the villa in Piazza Armerina, built in the same period. Part of the baths has been excavated to the northeast. Badly damaged in a 5th-century earthquake, the villa never recovered its former splendour, although the site was inhabited until the 9th century. The little antiquarium on the site should open any day to hold the rich trove of works in gold and precious stones found in the necropolis.

Tindari and Around

A local tourist brochure in English describes the famous promontory of Tindari better than we ever could: 'Tindari...lonely mythical and sacred, facing on to the eyes of the dead waters among long brilliantly white streaks of sand, tells of the hard vast stones of its sleeping unknit body, moving Christian legends and severe Greek and Latin idleness...its external layer is made of an airy terrace that speaks words of millennia, its horizons are sweet islands and bays like the lying bodies of maidens, its roads bordered with walls that only slaves and cyclopses could construct.'

History

In 396 BC, Dionysius of Syracuse found this promontory an ideal place for a garrison town. Most of the first settlers were veterans from the Peloponnesian War, and they named the new colony Tyndaridae, after the husband of Ledo and the putative father of the Dioscuri – the divine warrior twins Castor and Pollux, patrons of soldiers, who were fittingly chosen as the new town's protectors.

Although captured by Carthage in 264 BC, during the First Punic War, Tindari was regained by Rome 10 years later and remained a loyal ally ever after. Under Augustus the town became one of Rome's five colonies in Sicily. A century later, Tindari suffered a terrible blow when, with an ear-shattering roar, half the city suddenly fell into the sea. The remaining half never really recovered from the shock, but survived well into the Christian era, when it became the seat of a diocese. All was demolished by the Arabs in 836 and, when it was safe enough to re-establish a settlement on the coast, Roger I chose the present site of Patti.

The Santuario della Madonna Nera

Open Mon – Sat 6.45–12.30 and 2.30–7, Sun 12.30–8

The beautiful ruins of ancient Tyndaris are not, however, the magnet for the thousands of daily visitors, nor are they responsible for the extraordinary gauntlet of stands selling flicker pictures of Jesus, lava ashtrays, Pope John Paul II thermometers, *double-entendre* bathroom tiles, and tambourines the size of dustbin lids bearing the portrait of Santa Rita, who, after a wretched marriage, became a nun, only to develop such a foul-smelling sore on her forehead that none of the other sisters would come near her.

No. All these come as an accompaniment to the Santuario della Madonna Nera. The sanctuary was founded in the 16th century to house a miraculous Byzantine black-faced icon of the Virgin that, according to legend, was being transported to another country when the ship came ashore here and absolutely refused to budge until the icon was unloaded. Her most famous miracle was the rescue of a child who fell over the cliff on to 'an unexpected mattress of sand caught by the entreating blowing of the mother's desperate prayer'. This pink Grand Central Station of Sicilian Mariolatry, last rebuilt in the darkest age of religious art – the 1960s – is decorated with superbly ugly mosaics, frescoes and stained glass, which elevate the Madonna to the position once held by God the Father. The sanctuary occupies a holy place, the ancient acropolis of Tyndaris.

Whatever the qualities (or otherwise) of the Santuario itself, the view from the sanctuary is stunning, taking in as it does a long stretch of sand and the Marinello lagoons far below.

The Archaeological Zone

Open daily 9am until one hour before sunset.

The modern village occupies what was Tindari's agora, and beyond are the excavations, covering one of the most ravishing sites in Sicily. Near the entrance is an **antiquarium**, housing a massive head of Augustus, a model of the theatre, terracotta figurines, glass, a winged Victory and an assortment of headless statues in togas. Although the Christians must share some of the blame for their decapitation, chances are they were first sculpted this way: just as the Communist Party chairmen used to obliterate their predecessors, provincial Romans would knock off the block of a dead governor or emperor and replace it with a politically correct head sent from Rome's bust factories.

The decumanus leads to the huge arches of a partially restored 4th-century AD structure called the **basilica**, although most archaeologists now believe it was originally the monumental entrance from the town to the agora. Originally a gallery with nine vaults, its massive stones were cannibalized in later years for the all-important fortifications; the impressive remains of walls, towers and gates are scattered all over the promontory. The upper terrace of the town was occupied by a thermal establishment, with floors decorated with mosaics of the Dioscuri, dolphins, a marine centaur, Dionysus and a panther. Below are two terraces occupied by two luxurious **houses**. The lower one, a mansion of the 1st century BC, has retained sections of the peristyle of the atrium, the triclinium and the impluvium, where the residents saved precious rainwater. The lowest excavated terrace proved to be a row of *tabernae*, where it's easy to imagine the inhabitants, in their 'severe Greek and Latin idleness', sipping honey and wine coolers while watching the sun set into the sea below.

They also must have done plenty of idling in the **theatre**, which was built in the late 4th century BC by Dionysius' first colonists, then adapted and enlarged by the decadent Romans for gladiatorial contests and wild animal 'hunts', which required a corridor between the spectators and the dangerous activities in the ring. Only the theatre in Taormina has the more striking permanent stage set; from Tindari spectators could see the Aeolian Islands and, on a clear day, Mount Etna. It is a magical place, or, as the tourist brochure breathlessly concludes: 'The most intensive fascination of Tindari, however, is caused by its silences among a fragile hubbub of very distant voices that pant the subtle breaths between the wind and the rocks.'

East of Tindari: Castroreale and a Roman Villa

Rickety medieval Castroreale, 10km from Milazzo (*see* pp.240–2), up in a panoramic position in the Monti Peloritani, was named after a royal castle rebuilt in 1324 by Frederick II of Aragon, who spent a good deal of his time hunting here. However, little has survived beyond a stumpy **cylindrical tower**, slapped around by too many earthquakes, and the oft-restored **Porta Ranieri**. Castroreale's heyday came later, in the 16th century, when Emperor Charles V granted it the privileged status of city, igniting in the townspeople a fierce desire to build more churches than they could ever fill.

Chiesa Matrice, with its crenellated campanile, was restored in the 1600s but retains its Renaissance interior, a *Madonna and St Catherine of Alexandria* by Antonello Gagini, and a 17th-century inlaid choir. Other Gaginis are in **Sant'Agata** (*ask for the key from the town library*) and the **Immacolata** (*closed*).

Most visitors who spend any time in Castroreale these days have come to indulge in two favourite Italian pastimes – soaking in therapeutic mud, and flushing their livers with mineral water, both done in coastal **Terme Vigliatore**. Three kilometres west of Castroreale, at **San Biagio**, the remains of a 1st-century AD **Roman villa** (*open daily 9–one hour before sunset, adm*) were discovered in 1953; they include a section of the ancient baths, the peristyle, and various rooms paved with black and white mosaics, the best of which shows a fishing scene.

Milici, inland from San Biagio, was a flourishing Sikel town known as Longane that was destroyed by Messina in the 5th century BC. It has never been excavated, but you can see megalithic walls and a temple foundation. Another squiggly mountain road, just west of San Biagio, leads up 35km to **Montalbano Elicona** (*buses from Terme Vigliatore*), where no one ever goes. It has another example of Frederick II's 14th-century castle-building spree, this one particularly well-preserved. Some of the original frescoes survive in the chapel, if barely.

Aeolian Islands
and Milazzo

12

The Aeolian Islands

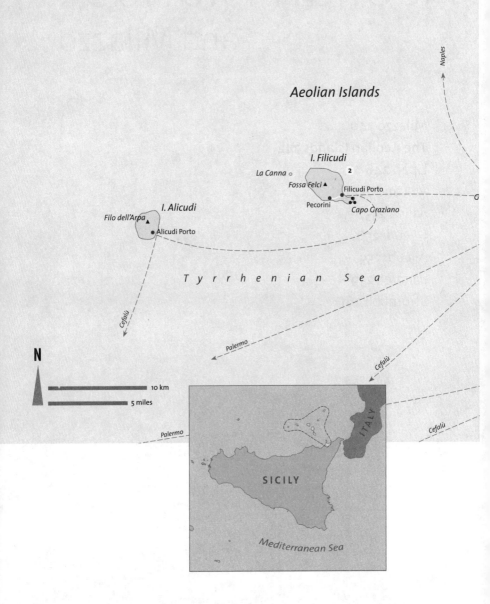

Aeolian Islands

I. Filicudi

La Canna ○

Fossa Felci ▲   **2**

Pecorini ● ● Filicudi Porto

Capo Graziano

I. Alicudi

Filo dell'Arpa ▲

● Alicudi Porto

T y r r h e n i a n   S e a

Naples

G

Cefalù

Palermo

Cefalù

N

10 km

5 miles

Palermo

Cefalù

Cefalù

ITALY

SICILY

Mediterranean Sea

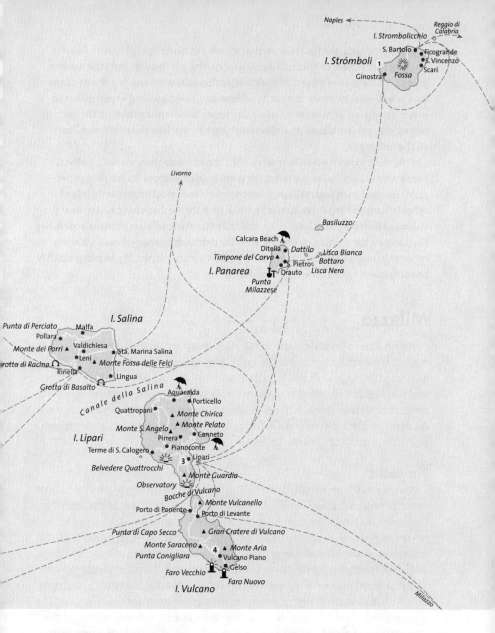

Highlights

1 The nightly fireworks display on Strómboli, the only Aeolian Island with an active volcano
2 Diving in the crystal sea around peaceful Filicudi
3 The fascinating Museo Archeológico Eoliano in the resort of Lipari
4 Bathing in the natural Jacuzzis on bubbling, sulphur-stinking Vulcano

West of Messina, the first feature that stands out along the Tyrrhenian Coast is the long thin trigger of Milazzo's peninsula, curling out towards the little Aeolian Islands. Scattered like a burst of buckshot, sculpted by wind and fire, the Aeolians have a feeling of intimacy rare for an archipelago. Few travelling experiences can match sailing out of Milazzo on a fine day, to see their forms rise up on the horizon one by one, green mountains and eccentric rock formations floating dreamlike on the indigo sea.

In the early 1970s the Aeolians were still a secret destination, even for Italians. Those who did visit were the rare birds who could do without Italian necessities – stainless-steel bars, smart shops, motor-scooters and, most importantly, lots of other Italians to keep them company. Since then the Aeolians have had to bear the stigma of fashion: prices have risen, and the natural friendliness of the islanders has been somewhat blunted by dealing with the demands of anonymous throngs in reflecting sunglasses. August and early September are the months to avoid. Lipari is the only island with a tourist information office.

Milazzo

There is little to detain you on the half-hour drive from Messina west to Milazzo, the main port for the Aeolian Islands. At first glance, there doesn't seem to be anything in Milazzo to detain you either – its eastern suburbs are occupied by the hulking tanks and pipelines of Sicily's largest industry, a huge oil refinery, and there's an inordinate amount of postwar sprawl to traverse to reach the centre by the sea. But once there it's a pleasant enough city and a naturally strategic one, protected by a narrow 6km promontory pointing towards the Aeolians.

The Castle

Milazzo was the ancient Mylai of the Greeks, who came over from Messina to colonize it in 716 BC. Whatever remained of its acropolis on the hill was obliterated when Frederick II Hohenstaufen built his great castle here in 1239 (*open Tues–Sun, Mar–May 10–12 and 3–5, June–Sept 10–12 and 5–7, Oct–Feb 9–12 and 2.30–3.30, guided tours several times a day*). It was enlarged a few decades later by Jaime of Aragon, who added the handsome ogival gate between two towers at the top of pedestrian-only Salita Castello. This, one of the most important strongholds of Sicily, once contained all of Milazzo and offers superb views over the modern town and sea.

Today wildflowers surround its remaining structures, the loveliest of which is the stately **Duomo Vecchio** (*closed*), built in 1608 and a rare example of Mannerism in Sicily. Adjacent are the ruined 14th-century **Palazzo dei Giurati**, once Milazzo's town hall, and, farther up, the old **Sala del Parlamento**. A late Bronze Age **necropolis** just north of the castle produced a number of important finds, now housed in Lipari's archaeology museum.

Besides the castle, there are a handful of churches of minor interest to explore while waiting for your boat: 15th-century **San Giacomo** near the port, with the rich

Getting There

Avoid the **train** if you can – Milazzo's station is miles from anywhere, although city buses make cameo appearances to link it to the port. However, there are trains from Palermo, Cefalù and Messina. Giunta **bus** from Via Terranova 8 in Messina stops in front of the port. City buses from Milazzo make the trip out to Capo di Milazzo. If you're flying into Catania airport between April and September, a Giunta bus, t 090 673 782, connects the airport with the hydrofoil port in Milazzo, daily at 4pm.

It's risky leaving a **car** with foreign number-plates parked overnight in Milazzo port. Ask at the ticket office about garages, although if you mean to spend at least four days on Lipari it costs less to take your car along.

Tourist Information

Piazza Caio Duilio 20, t 090 922 2865 (open Mon–Fri 8–2 and 4–7, Sat 8–2, also Sun 8–2 in July–Aug).

Where to Stay

Milazzo ✉ 98057

*****Eolian Inn Park**, Via Cappuccini 25, t 090 928 61 33 (expensive). A large and luxurious choice beneath the castle, with a pool, garden, tennis court and more.

*****Riviera Lido**, Contrada Corrie, t 090 928 34 56 (moderate–expensive). If you have a car, this smaller place on the promontory's Strada Panoramica is cheaper and has a beach as well.

****La Bussola**, Via XX Luglio 29, t 090 922 12 44 (moderate). Provides comfortable air-conditioned rooms in the centre of town.

*****Petit Hotel**, Via dei Mille, t 090 928 6784, www.petithotel.it (inexpensive). Friendly and good value hotel right by the port, particularly if you have an early boat to catch.

***California**, Via Sole 9, t 090 922 13 89 (budget). Next door and twin sister to the

Central (see below), the only difference being that all double rooms come with a private bath or shower.

***Central**, Via del Sole 8, t 090 928 10 43 (budget). A nice, friendly little hotel near the port, with showers down the hall.

Villaggio Cirucco, Capo di Milazzo, t 090 928 4746. An excellent campsite with bungalows in an olive grove, a private beach and a pizzeria overlooking the sea; the Milazzo bus stops at the entrance.

Eating Out

Salamone a Mare, Strada Panoramica, t 090 928 12 33 (expensive). One of many places to eat along the promontory, and probably the finest for seafood. The chef uses the freshest fish and lobster, served on a seaside terrace. Closed Mon.

Villa Esperanza, Via Baronia 191, t 090 922 29 16 (expensive). Out near the capo, this exclusive restaurant is the place to go for a splurge, especially on a Friday night in the summer, when dinner is accompanied by live jazz or ethnic world music. Closed Mon.

Il Covo del Pirata, Via Marina Garibaldi 2, t 090 928 44 37 (moderate). For delicious swordfish and other specialities of Milazzo, this restaurant is at the top of the list. Closed Wed.

Marinaio, Via Largo Buccari, t 090 928 7485 (inexpensive). This place near the port does delicious, economical seafood: €25 will get you everything from antipasto to wine and coffee.

L'Ugghiularu, Via Acquaviole 137, t 090 928 43 84 (inexpensive). Anyone who has visited Italy for more than a decade will have noticed the decline of an old cheap standby – simple, untarted-up bistros called vini e cucine. This one, however, survives in Milazzo. You can dine plentifully here for around €15. Closed Wed.

Pasticceria Majorana, Via Colossi 39. Serves Milazzo's best granite di limone and other sweet treats.

marble intarsia altar from the Duomo Vecchio, or the **Duomo Nuovo**, with some better than average Renaissance paintings, including an Adoration by Antonello de Saliba, nephew of a more famous Antonello – da Messina.

Capo di Milazzo

The most memorable thing to do is drive or take the bus out along the promontory's Strada Panoramica to Capo di Milazzo for its view of the islands, the Sicilian coast, and the sea where Caius Duilius defeated the Carthaginians in 260 BC, Rome's first naval victory and one that led to the annihilation of the Greek civilization on the Aeolian Islands (*see* below). Olive groves line the cliffs, although here and there small beaches are tucked along the cape. Just before the lighthouse, steps descend to the cave-sanctuary of **Sant'Antonio da Padova**.

The Aeolian Islands

Like the seven stars of Pleiades, one of the loveliest constellations of the night sky, the seven Aeolian sisters of Lipari, Vulcano, Salina, Panarea, Filicudi, Alicudi and Strómboli form one of the earth's most enchanting archipelagos. All betray the strange, unworldly beauty of their volcanic origins in fantastical formations and colours – smouldering Vulcano and exploding Strómboli, actively so. The differing activities of these two in particular is responsible for the Aeolian Islands' presence on UNESCO's World Heritage list. The sea surrounding them is the most violent in the Tyrrhenian, swept by winds that have devoured the rock: within a mile of soft, rolling green hills plunge inhuman regions of unmitigated white – see the blinding pumice slopes of Lipari – or infernal black at the Sciara del Fuoco, where Strómboli's volcano vomits its daily ration of fire and molten crud. On calm days each island has its own little cloud over its highest peak, like a genie, or ghost of some ancient volcanic emission. Clustered in the few hospitable nooks are villages, farms and hamlets made of narrow lanes or stairs, with houses built in what's known as the Aeolian vernacular: simple, cubic, whitewashed or pastel, almost as if, deep in the recesses of their builders' imagination, they remember the Aeolians' Greek past.

History

Homer was the first to mention the Aeolian Islands, when Odysseus landed here after passing through the terrors of Scylla and Charybdis in the Strait of Messina. Aeolus, the king of the islands and god of the wind, welcomed him and gave him a useful gift to speed his voyage home to Ithaca – a bag of wind. Overcome with curiosity, the Greek sailors opened the bag as soon as they left port, and the wind rushed out, pushing them right back to Aeolus. Seeing his great gift so squandered, the king berated them and sent them on their way.

Diodorus Siculus puts Homer in historical perspective, writing that, at the time of the Trojan War, Liparo, son of King Auson of central Italy, left home to found a colony on the islands, which he named after himself. One of his companions was Aeolus, who married a girl on either Lipari or Strómboli and stayed there as king when Liparo returned to Ausonia. According to Diodorus, it was Liparo who entertained Odysseus and whose sons founded other towns in Calabria and Sicily.

Getting There

You can reach the Aeolian Islands by ferry or hydrofoil. Although they take cars (reserve well in advance in high season), the ferries are primarily used for transporting goods to the islands. Only Lipari and Salina are large enough to justify the expense of bringing a car, but they also have efficient bus services, as does Vulcano on its one stretch of road. Panarea, Strómboli, Filicudi and Alicudi all have virtually no roads to speak of. The main advantage of the ferries is their lower prices and leisurely pace, which allows you to drink in your fill of delicious island scenery.

From Milazzo

The main port for the Aeolian Islands is Milazzo (for how to get to Milazzo, *see* p.241), and **ferries/hydrofoils** from there are the cheapest option. Three companies serve the islands from Milazzo; timetables are constantly changing so always double check with the companies themselves and don't just rely on the tourist office's information.

Siremar, Via dei Mille, **t** 090 928 32 42, *www.gruppotirrenia.it/siremar*, runs numerous hydrofoils and ferries; these sail from Milazzo to Naples (15hrs) several times a week Oct–June, daily in July–Aug, calling at most of the Aeolian Islands on the way. There are also services three times a week to Lipari, Panarea and Strómboli (6hrs); five times a week to Lipari, Filicudi and Alicudi (6.5hrs); two a day to Lipari and Vulcano (2hrs); and one a day to Vulcano, Lipari and Salina (3.5hrs). **SNAV**, Via L. Rizzo, **t** 090 928 45 09, *www.snav.it*, runs only hydrofoils. **NGI**, Via dei Mille, **t** 090 928 4091, operates ferries only.

The Milazzo–Naples ferries leave at night, arriving in Lipari for lunch. So you save a night in a hotel and get a free fireworks show from Strómboli to boot.

From Messina

Several SNAV **hydrofoils** a day in summer, and one a day in winter, sail from Messina in 1.5hrs (Cortina del Porto, **t** 090 364 044).

From Cefalù

June–Sept, **hydrofoils** sail from Cefalù to Vulcano and Lipari in about 2hrs, several days a week, **t** 092 42 15 95 (tickets can be bought either at the port or at Corso Ruggero 82).

From Palermo

Hydrofoils chug to Lipari by way of Cefalù (Wed–Fri only) in about 3.5hrs, or directly to Lipari in 3.5hrs, twice daily, from June 15 to the end of September only (tickets are sold at the SNAV office, Via Belmonte 51–5, **t** 091 631 7900, or before departure at the port – Molo Vittorio – with a reservation).

From Reggio di Calabria

You can reach Lipari and Vulcano by **hydrofoil** in about 2.5hrs, **t** 096 529 568, several times daily in the summer, and once a day in the winter (tickets at the port).

From Naples

Once a day, June–Sept, you can take a **hydrofoil** from Naples in 6hrs; information at Via Giordano Bruno 84, **t** 08 17 61 23 48 (tickets at the port). Year round, there are Siremar **ferries** to the islands, **t** 091 690 25 55.

Tourist Information

The only tourist office is on Lipari. Don't count on finding a place to change money on Salina, Filicudi and Alicudi, or on Panarea, Strómboli or Vulcano out of season. Bring your ATM card as increasingly, ATMs can be found on even the small islands.

Prehistory

Since 1948, excavations inside the portside castle of Lipari have revealed an extraordinary stratified record of the island's prehistoric settlements; thanks to dust borne by the wind, the ground level rose rapidly enough to entomb the remains of each successive culture as neatly as a layer cake. As a result, we know a bit more about the early inhabitants of the Aeolian Islands than did Diodorus.

Lipari was first inhabited late in the 5th millennium BC by people from Sicily, who settled in the Castello Vecchio area. They were drawn to Lipari by a natural resource as sought after back then as petroleum is today: obsidian, or black volcanic glass, harder than and superior to flint for making tools. Lipari's Monte Pelato was an extremely good source of obsidian, and the islanders mined and exported it on a large scale, attracting the attention of a people from the Adriatic Coast (the Ripoli culture) who invaded Lipari around 3900 BC. This was followed by a third and final Neolithic period which saw the settlement of the fertile Diana plain below the castle, the first part of the island to be cultivated. At this stage (3000 BC), Lipari's obsidian trade peaked, when it found a market not only in Italy but also in France, Spain and Malta. Settlements were founded on Filicudi and Panarea.

Around 2500 BC, the demand for obsidian collapsed with the discovery of copper and metallurgy. Lipari's flourishing civilization seemed to vanish overnight, to be succeeded by a much poorer one known as the Aeolian Medieval Period.

Business picked up again in the Bronze Age (2000 BC), when new settlers, Greeks from Aeolia, developed the islands as ports on the important east–west trading route between the Aegean and Tyrrhenian. Settlements were founded on Salina, Panarea, Strómboli and, most importantly, Capo Graziano on Filicudi, which lent its name to the period. After 1550 BC the inhabitants were wealthy enough to import Mycenaean ceramics as well as building methods – see Lipari's tholos-sauna at San Calógero. This was the period remembered in the *Odyssey*.

Some time around 1430 BC, people from Sicily introduced a new culture, named after Punta Milazzese on Panarea. Contacts with the Aegean continued, but new trade links developed as well, with the Apennines. In 1270 BC this backfired when one Apennine tribe, the Ausonians, invaded the islands, burned all the settlements and killed or enslaved the inhabitants. These new masters of the islands are remembered in Diodorus' *Liparo and Aeolus*. As the Aegean had entered its post-Trojan War dark age, the Ausonians traded extensively with the *nuraghi*-builders of Sardinia (cultures known as Ausonia I and II). Yet like the civilization the Ausonians destroyed, theirs too met a sudden end. In 850 BC everything burned, leaving a population existing at subsistence level.

Greeks Versus Etruscans

Diodorus then picks up the tale again: in 580 BC Dorian Greeks from Cnidos attempted to colonize the west coast of Sicily, but were pushed out by the Segestans and Carthaginians. Discouraged, the Cnidians made for home, stopping at Lipari on the way. The 500 surviving islanders, plagued by Etruscan pirates, were glad to see them and convinced them to stay by offering to divide their land with them.

The first thing the Cnidians did was to refortify the castle against the Etruscans; the second was to establish their own fleet. For a century, Lipari fought a sea war with the Etruscans. They eventually won, according to Pausanias, thanks to a tip from Apollo. When asked how to defeat the Etruscans, the oracle at Delphi told the Liparesi that they should fight with the bare minimum of ships. When the Etruscan captain saw only five Liparian ships defending the island against his squadron, he confidently sent only five ships against them. They were all captured. Again the captain sent five ships, with the same result, then another five, and another five – all captured by the Liparesi. In disbelief, the Etruscans withdrew to escape the 'sea devils' while they could. In thanksgiving, the islanders built a treasury at Delphi and dedicated a gold statue of Apollo for every ship they had captured.

The First Communists

With the decline of the Etruscans, the islanders perfected a unique, communal system of self-government that stands in stark contrast to the rule of tyrants in Sicily and the ideal republic that Plato tried to set up in Syracuse. All land, ships, houses and other goods were owned in common and redistributed amid great festivities every 20 years. The inhabitants of the Aeolians divided themselves into 'people of the earth', who farmed not only the islands but parts of the mainland as well; and 'people of the sea', fishermen, pirates and defenders. Whatever loot was captured was shared by all, and annual tributes were sent to Delphi.

Even the Aeolian pirates never forgot Lipari's debt to Apollo. In 396 BC, they ambushed a Roman ship in the Strait of Messina. When the Liparesi captain found out that its cargo consisted of golden ex-votos for Delphi celebrating the Roman victory over Etruscan Vei, he not only returned the ship to the Romans, but escorted it to Delphi. In gratitude the Roman senate made the pirate captain an *ospitum publicum* – an honorary citizen of Rome.

But All Good Things Must Come to an End

The Liparesi, faithful allies of Syracuse for many years in their battles against Carthage, were caught unawares when the cruel tyrant of Syracuse, Agathocles, landed in 304 BC in the guise of a friend, then proceeded to pillage the island's rich temples of Aeolus and Hephaestos, filling 11 ships with their gold. The wind god Aeolus got his own back by blowing up a storm that sank all 11 ships. Only Agathocles' ship escaped destruction, leaving the tyrant to die a more lingering, unpleasant death from plague.

Outraged by Agathocles' duplicity, Lipari changed sides and joined Carthage, which soon proved to be an unfortunate choice. In 260 BC, during the First Punic War, the Carthaginian fleet was defeated by Caius Duilius at Milazzo. The Romans let the islanders squirm for nine years, then, with 'that monstrous inferiority to which they always gave way when confronted with Greek culture' (John Julius Norwich), sent 60 ships to destroy the islands methodically, leaving a handful of survivors to tell the tale.

Modern Times

After the Romans, the history of the Aeolians more or less follows that of Sicily, until 1544, when the Turkish pirate Barbarossa killed or enslaved everyone. Because of their strategic position, Emperor Charles V had the islands recolonized a few years later, and ordered a new castle to be built on Lipari for their protection. In the early 20th century, the state converted the castle into a prison. The islanders opposed it from the start, and in 1926 they stormed the prison and destroyed it. A few years later, when the Fascists began to send their political undesirables to Lipari, the islanders made them welcome, and the prisoners not only shared the islanders' toil but founded a lending library in the little town.

After the war, accounts of the Aeolian Islands told of extreme destitution: the score of families who hadn't emigrated struggled to survive on their windswept rocks, scratching out a living in the pumice mines, or fishing. The first hydrofoil arrived like the Lone Ranger to the rescue in the early 1960s, and every year since tourism has formed a larger chunk of the local economy, although not all the profits go into the pockets of the islanders, who occasionally feel like plunderers plundered.

Lipari

The largest of the Aeolian Islands (13sq miles), Lipari is the offspring of seven volcanic eruptions. The last occurred around the 18th century BC, when Monte Pelato spewed out the lava that solidified into the Rocche Rosse and obsidian streams, as well as the snowy pumice slopes on the northeast of the island, which occupy about a quarter of its entire surface area. Today the volcano is dormant.

That may be the only sleepy thing about the island. Endowed with all the essentials – gorgeous scenery and beaches, a charming port, a few posey cafés, bars, good restaurants, stylish hotels and a fair amount of nightlife – Lipari is one of the most popular resorts in Sicily. A fascinating archaeology museum is an added attraction.

Lipari Town

The only real town on the island, Lipari is the seat of the *comune* of the Aeolian Islands – which includes all the islands except Salina, which is autonomous. Arriving by hydrofoil, you are left in the charming, lively, intimate **Marina Corta**, wedged between the castle walls, a natural rocky mole and a church of 'the Souls in Purgatory'. This prim reminder of the wages of sin does not at all deter any of the Proud, Lustful and Greedy from swilling Campari and flirting in the many bars and cafés lining the waterfront.

A few streets back, long **Corso Vittorio Emanuele** is a busy shopping street that neatly divides Lipari town into new and old. At its northern end is the small bay of **Marina Lunga**, the ferry port and bus terminal, closed off at the far end by Monte Rosa. The narrow, older lanes of Lipari town are dominated by the high walls of the castle, reached by way of a grand pebble stairway off Via Garibaldi (which runs beneath the walls).

The Castle

The castle was built in the 16th century by the Spanish after Barbarossa's rampage, amply re-using the massive blocks of a Greek tower of the 4th century BC. It sits on a

Getting Around

URSO **buses**, t 090 981 12 62, leave Marina Lunga fairly frequently for Canneto, the pumice quarries, Acquacalda, Quattropani, Pianoconte and Quattrocchi, and at least three times a day for Pirrera, Serra, Lami, Monte and Pianogreco. Three times a day they offer a tour around the entire island. **Taxis** can be ordered on t 090 981 2216.

A number of companies on Lipari hire or charter sailing **boats**, motor boats and yachts by the hour, day or week; contact the tourist office for listings. You can hire **Vespas**, mopeds, jetskis, zodiacs or boats from Roberto Foti, Via F. Crispi 31 at Marina Lunga, t 090 981 23 52.

Tourist Information

Corso Vittorio Emanuele 202, t 090 988 00 95 (*open Sept–June Mon–Fri 8–2 and 4.30–6.30, Sat 8–2; July–Aug Mon–Sat 8–2 and 4–10, Sun 8–2*). Note: this is the only tourist office on the Aeolians.

Where to Stay

Lipari ✉ 98055

The higher prices listed below are for July, August and early September, when bookings are essential. Note that half-board is usually obligatory in the summer, which can easily add €40 per head to the bill. Accommodation may be found in private houses, but remember that in summer the island reaches saturation point, so phone in advance.

★★★**Carasco**, Porto delle Genti, t 090 981 16 05, *www.carasco.it* (*expensive–luxury*). One of the most spectacularly sited hotels on the island, south of town, with its own private stretch of rocks overlooking the sea, and superb views across to the town from its seawater pool decked with bougainvillea. A bus shuttles guests to the Marina Corta. *Closed Nov–March.*

★★★**Giardino sul Mare**, Via Maddalena 65, t 090 981 10 04, *www.netnet.it/conti* (*expensive–luxury*). The third choice in town is this pleasant family-run hotel right on the sea, with a pool, garden and terrace. *Closed Dec–Feb.*

★★★★**Villa Meligunis**, Via Marte 7, t 090 981 24 26, *www.villameligunis.it* (*expensive–luxury*). Built in the 1700s in a vaguely Spanish style, with an enormous roof terrace overlooking the bijou Marina Corta. Completely restored a few years ago, it is furnished with every comfort, most rooms with wrought-iron beds, though the snob factor also runs high.

★★★**Gattopardo Park Hotel**, Viale Diana, t 090 981 10 35, *gattopardo@netnet.it* (*moderate–expensive*). A pleasant resort hotel from which to send home impressive postcards. *Closed Nov–Feb.*

★★★**Villa Augustus**, Via Ausonia 16, t 090 981 12 32, *www.villaaugustus.it* (*moderate–expensive*). Also central and surrounded by luxuriant gardens, endowed with balconies and a roof terrace overlooking the town and the sea.

★★**Neri**, Via Marconi 43, t/f 09 09 81 14 13, *www.pensioneneri.it* (*moderate, in Aug half-board only and minimum one-week stay*). A charming old pink villa with a garden, overlooking the ancient sarcophagi of the necropolis, 100m west of the *corso*.

★★★**Oriente**, Via Marconi 35, t 090 981 14 93, *www.hotelorientelipari.com* (*moderate*). Five minutes from the port, this is a modern hotel with a shady garden terrace, close to the Neri.

★★**Villa Diana**, Via Tufo 1, t/f 09 09 81 14 03, *www.villadiana.com* (*moderate*). A rustic option outside town with pretty views over sea and town run by the friendly South African Diana. *Closed Nov–Easter.*

promontory overlooking the sea, a spot inhabited ever since Neolithic times, when Lipari was the queen of Tyrrhenian obsidian. Along the cobbled streets of the castle are excavations with explanatory placards about the strata of millennia they have revealed; the lowest layer, dated the late 5th millennium BC, lay 30ft below the

***Poseidon**, Via Ausonia 7, t 090 981 28 76, www.hotelposeidonlipari.com (*inexpensive–moderate*). A charming choice just off the *corso*, with white rooms off a delightful courtyard.

*****Europeo**, Corso Vittorio Emanuele 98, t/f 090 981 1589 (*budget–inexpensive*). A simple yet quiet choice. *Closed Oct–March.*

Youth Hostel, t 090 981 15 40 (*budget*). An excellent place inside the castle with fine views over the sea, run by Antonio, a wannabe opera star. *Closed Nov–Feb.*

Baia Unci, at Caneto, t 090 981 19 09. As the only campsite on the island, it tends to be packed; buses pass near by. *Closed Oct–Easter.*

Eating Out

There are some very good restaurants on Lipari, which gets enough tourists both to stimulate competition and keep prices reasonable. Nearly all close by the end of October, however. Seafood holds pride of place, especially *stoccafisso* in *ghiotta* sauce, a lively blend of olive oil, locally produced capers, tomatoes, garlic and basil. Black rice, given its colour by the *seppia*, or inkfish, and dishes with octopus and swordfish are other favourites. Another speciality is *spaghetti all'eoliana*, with a delicious sauce made of nothing but fine olive oil and fresh basil. The local wine, red and white and a dessert Malvasia that has earned DOC status, is worth a try; **Eolivino**, on Corso V. Emanuele near Marina Lunga, serves it correctly with little anis-flavoured biscuits. There's even an island *digestivo* called Amaro Eolie, made from 'marine herbs'.

Lipari Town

Filippino, Piazza Municipio, t 090 981 10 02 (*expensive*). For one of Sicily's gourmet treats, make your way up to the Filippino's garden terrace, near Marina Lunga. It has been the gastronomic jewel of the archipelago since 1910, with a choice of *risotti*, a delicious *pasta alla Filippino* with a wealth of goodies in it, and some very refined *haute cuisine* main courses. *Closed Mon in Oct–March and all Nov.* Book in summer.

E' Pulera, Via Diana, t 090 981 11 58 (*moderate*). Also good for Aeolian specialities – and run by the same family as the Filippino – this restaurant is set in a pretty garden, a way west from the town centre. *Coniglio all'Aeoliana* (rabbit in a caper and olive oil sauce) is usually on the menu. *Closed lunch and Nov–May.*

La Nassa, Via Franza 36, t 090 981 13 19 (*expensive*). A local favourite for delicious pasta and seafood, just out of town near the hospital. *Closed Mon in Nov–March.*

D'Oro, Via Umberto I (between Corso V. Emanuele and the castle), t 090 981 13 04 (*inexpensive*). Popular with the Liparesi. *Closed Sun in Nov–March.*

A Sfiziusa, Piazza Sant'Onofrio, t 090 981 12 16 (*inexpensive*). A trattoria south of Marina Corta whose tables totter on the sidewalk. It draws a young crowd and the food is good and inexpensive, if not particularly original.

Around Lipari

La Ginestra, Via Stradale 10, t 090 982 22 85 (*expensive*). An exceptional choice in Pianoconte. Giacomo and Marisa Biviano offer both traditional Aeolian/Messinan cuisine and innovative dishes, accompanied by the best wine list on Lipari. *Closed Mon in Oct–April.*

Da Lauro, t 090 982 10 26 (*moderate*). A good bet in Acquacalda, specializing in fresh grilled fish. *Closed Fri in Oct–April.*

A Cannata, t 090 982 20 58 (*inexpensive*). Also in Pianoconte, this trattoria serves local cuisine and pizza.

surface. Such excellent time capsules are so rare that the potsherds found here are used to date discoveries elsewhere in the Mediterranean. In classical times, this was Lipari's acropolis, crowned by the temples of Aeolus and Hephaestos that were so futilely pillaged by Agathocles; all that remains is the bothros of Aeolus, a deep cavity cut out of the rock like a cistern, topped with a lava cover carved with a lion (now in the museum) and two holes for offerings.

The Museo Archeológico Eoliano

Open Mon–Sun 9–1.30 and 3–7, adm.

Spread out in several buildings in the castle, the Museo Archeológico Eoliano houses one of the finest Neolithic collections in the world. It is chronologically arranged, beginning in the former bishop's palace (rooms I–XII) with Lipari's oldest finds, from Castello Vecchio (*c.* 4200 BC): pottery decorated in the **Stentinello style**, with simple incisions, similar to that made in eastern Sicily. The next rooms contain the three-toned, **spiral-decorated ceramics** from the castle itself (4th millennium BC) and, from the last Neolithic period, the lustrous red ceramics called the **Diana style** (3000–2500 BC, named after the Contrada Diana, just below the castle). Subsequent **Copper Age pottery** from Pianoconte (2500–2000 BC, when the obsidian economy nosedived) looks primitive in comparison.

Beyond, the rooms devoted to the **Bronze Age and Ausonian cultures** (2000–850 BC) contain cups with the bulls' horns symbol that dominated so much Mediterranean art at the time, lamps and reconstructed necropolises from the Middle Bronze Age Ausonia I cultures. From the first Greek residents are finds from the bottom of the bothros of Aeolus, including a **depiction of Greek warships**.

Section II

Finds from the smaller Aeolian Islands are housed in an adjacent pavilion (rooms XIII–XV). The most important discoveries are from **Piano Quartara on Panarea** (*c.* 2300–1800 BC), **Capo Graziano on Filicudi** (2000–1500 BC), characterized by ceramic imports from the Aegean, and **Punta Milazzese on Panarea** (1400–1270 BC), which shows striking similarities to the Thapsos culture of Sicily.

Section III

This section, in a pavilion north of the cathedral, houses the disarmingly beautiful **artefacts from the necropolises** of Lipari (rooms XVI–XXV). It begins with the re-construction of an Ausonian II necropolis, followed by Greek- and Roman-era sarcophagi and their burial treasures. The oldest tombs contained ceramics imported from Greek Attica or Syracuse, but by the late 4th century the proto-Communists of Lipari had their own workshops, dominated by the prolific 'Pittore di Lipari', who specialized in painting feminine subjects, with far more colours than the average Greek vase painter. In his – or her – wide shallow *lekanai*, note the dreamy melancholy of souls in the form of winged young women in the after-life.

Equally fascinating are the 1,200 pieces of 4th–3rd-century BC painted terracotta and stone **theatrical masks and figurines** representing characters from the dramas and satires of the day, the largest collection of its kind. All were discovered in the tombs. The masks suggest that the New Comedy of Menander was especially appre-ciated on Lipari – 250 are from his plays alone – although the dramas of Sophocles, Aristophanes and Euripides are represented as well. The small figurines – some sombre, others goofy, pot-bellied caricatures – are displayed in model theatrical sets.

There are few archaeological museums where you walk out saying to yourself, 'How happy they must have been!', but this is one.

Sections IV and V

But there's more, if you have the energy. The same building houses Section IV, with **finds from Milazzo**, with the reconstruction of its two necropolises, one from Middle Bronze Age (1300 BC) and one that puzzles the experts, the only Late Bronze Age (8th century BC) cemetery ever found on Sicily. Section V is devoted to **underwater archaeology**, especially finds from a ship from the Capo Graziano period that sank between Lipari and Filicudi.

Cattedrale di San Bartolomeo

Between the museum buildings, as you will have already noticed, stands the Cattedrale di San Bartolomeo, patron saint of the Aeolian Islands, after whom half of the male islanders seem to be named. The body of the Apostle San Bartolomeo, or the rather unpleasant remains of it after he suffered martyrdom by being flayed alived in the Near East, is said to have floated ashore in a marble coffin at Porto delle Genti on Lipari in 264.

The cathedral was founded by King Roger in the 11th century and, as depicted on the doors, San Bartolomeo once saved the town from fire. He could do nothing about Barbarossa, however, and the church had to be completely reconstructed after the pirate's passing in 1654. Inside are 18th-century frescoes and a silver statue of San Bartolomeo rather charmingly carrying his skin under his arm, as well as a fine late 15th-century *Madonna of the Rosary* by Girolamo Alibrandi. The nearby Baroque church of the **Addolorata** (*under restoration*) is built on an older, Byzantine plan.

When you leave the castle, take the steps down to the north to **Piazza Municipio**, with its garden and blocks of lava carved with the verses from the *Odyssey* referring to Lipari (XII, 55) in ancient Greek and Italian. Other odds and ends in town include a **1st-century BC statue of a woman**, displayed near the place where it was found in the garden of the Esposito house in Via Garibaldi, and a collection of **Greco-Roman sarcophagi** along Via Marconi.

A Walk to the Geophysical Observatory

The classic walk from Lipari town is the hour's stroll south to the observatory. It passes the great **necropolis** that provided many of the contents of the Museo Archeológico, and **Porto delle Genti** (or Portinente) and its church of San Nicola, with an ancient architrave, and then a **promontory** formed by Monte Giardina and Monte Guardia, volcanic cupolas born in a relatively recent eruption of Monte Sant'Angelo.

Press on through vines and caper plantations to the UNESCO-funded **Geophysical Observatory** (*Via Serra; visits by appointment, t 09 09 81 10 81*). This looks dramatically over the standing sea rocks and down into the crater of Vulcano a kilometre away, pouting publicly for all to see, and across to Salina, Alicudi and Filicudi – a view that becomes pure enchantment at twilight. This is the vulcanological hub of the area.

Scientists here keep track of all the active volcanoes in the Mediterranean, chart seismic activity under the Tyrrhenian Sea, and correlate volcanic and seismic phenomena.

Around Lipari

If at all possible, take one of the available **sea excursions** around Lipari, or at least to the southernmost part of the island, where the dashingly coloured cliffs loom over the intense blue of the sea, and monumental rocks such as Le Formiche and the monolithic 258ft-high Pietralunga lend a fantastical air to the seascape.

Two routes leave Marina Lunga for **Canneto** to the north, the prettier one being farther inland, the shorter one through the tunnel. Canneto, Lipari's second largest settlement, is a fishing town with a long pebble beach and also one of white sand, the Spiaggia Bianca at the end of town. Behind the village a road leads up to the old obsidian fields of **Forgia Vecchia** and the tiny hamlet of **Pirrera** beneath Monte Sant'Angelo.

The coastal road from Canneto runs for 3km to the white slopes of **Monte Pelato** (1,416ft), made of Lipari's famous pumice, formed when obsidian is filled with volcanic gas while being cooled. It is the lightest rock in the world: it even floats. It has diverse uses, in the soap, toothpaste, electronics, chemical and glass industries; remember when you next see Chicago's Sears Tower that part of it came from here. The pumice, mined in long galleries, is shipped from the docks beneath Monte Pelato. Mussolini's political prisoners were sent to these mines, and forced to work in horrendous conditions that killed them in a few months; his derelict installations are at La Cava.

Farther north, at **Porticello** the beach is made of pumice and obsidian, the veins of which are red and black. These obsidian streams can be seen most spectacularly at the **Rocche Rosse** of Monte Pelato, where huge blocks of it remain in the old quarries. To visit the site, take the path up from Porticello or Acquacalda – but take care: obsidian is as sharp as glass. Other pumice quarries are behind Acquacalda on the slopes of Lipari's highest mountain, **Monte Chirica** (1,806ft). **Acquacalda** has a long pebble beach, but few people make it all this way to use it.

Quattropani and Pianoconte

Quattropani, with its simple church, the Chiesa Vecchia, overlooks the island of Salina. Quattropani presents yet another aspect of Lipari – scattered white houses, gardens, vineyards and orchards give this whole area a contented rural appearance.

The road south winds toward Pianoconte, then branches off to the **Terme di San Calògero** (*closed*). According to legend, St Paul sent San Calògero to Lipari, where he discovered the spring – obviously a special knack of his. The truth is the spa considerably pre-dates the good saint by about 1,500 years – a portion is built of huge blocks from the Mycenaean era, in the same shape as a tholos tomb. As far as anyone knows, it is the oldest thermal establishment in the world.

From **Pianoconte** a path winds up to the extinct crater of **Monte Sant'Angelo** (1,782ft). Although the path is steep, the climb rewards your effort with lovely views of the entire island and the unusual stratification inside the crater. Next to Pianoconte you may also visit the **fumaroles**, or little volcanic steam kettles, at Bagno Secco.

South of Pianoconte the **Belvedere Quattrocchi** offers a magnificent, much photographed panorama of Vulcano and the four craggy towers sculpted by nature, the Faraglioni, shooting up from the sea between the two islands. Another path descends from here to the **Valle Muria** and a lonely beach.

Vulcano

Nearest to the mainland and Lipari, Vulcano, in ancient times Iera (the sacred island) or Thermessa (the warm island), has at present plenty of what the experts call secondary volcanic activity – increasingly busy every year – but no active volcanoes. This certainly wasn't true in the past: Aristotle, Diodorus Siculus, Strabo and Thucydides all record various eruptions, one so destructive as to cover the town of Lipari in ashes in the 4th century BC. Monte Vulcanello, on the extreme north of the island, rose out of the sea only in 183 BC. Not surprisingly, Vulcano was the only Aeolian uninhabited in antiquity. The main crater, the Fossa (1,125ft), has been popping off for centuries, last erupting in 1890 when it obliterated the alum-extracting industry of a Scotsman named Stevens, who once owned the island.

Composed of five different volcanic structures, Vulcano is a bizarre island of strange colours and bitter odours. The ancients believed that Hephaestos, god of fire and blacksmiths, had his headquarters on the island; in the Middle Ages Vulcano was thought to be the entrance to Hell. San Bartolomeo, it was said, separated Lipari from Vulcano to protect his island from its eruptions. Hell's gateway or not, Vulcano is one of the most visited of the Aeolians, especially by Italians who come to bathe in the mud in a setting worthy of the late, lamented Fellini.

Hold Your Nose

The emergence of Vulcanello off the north coast, connected by a narrow isthmus, conveniently formed the island's two harbours: **Porto Ponente** (for pleasure boats), lined with warm black sand, and **Porto di Levante**, where hydrofoils and ferries dock (only the vehicles of islanders are permitted, so don't try to bring your car). Your sensibilities are immediately insulted by smelly sulphurous fumes from the steaming fumaroles on the isthmus.

Immediately north of the Porto di Levante is the great rock known as the **Faraglione della Fabbrica** where alum was once extracted (alum, a whitish astringent mineral, is mainly used in fixing dyes). The colours here – ochres, yellows, reds and oranges – look as if they themselves came out of the dyeworks of some other-worldly Fauvist painter, who painted the earth around the two portside hot springs of **Acqua del Bagno** and **Acqua Bollente**. In these shallow pools of stinking mud the pale rubber-capped heads of bathers bob up and down surreally as they wallow in its amazing restorative virtues. If you join them, follow your soak with a wash in the sea (in this case, whoever jumps in, first or last, is a rotten egg). But even on the beach you can't escape the murmurs of the volcano: underwater fumaroles cause the sea to bubble, creating Mother Nature's own Jacuzzi, although sulphur deposits on the seabed give the coast a scabrous appearance and you have to take care not to scald yourself. In another part of the port, miniature but disconcerting geysers sometimes shoot warm mud into the air.

There are hotels and restaurants at each of the ports, and most of the island's 400 people live nearby, in a disarming Legoland of little rustic houses and pretty flower gardens that defy the busy mud-pies by the sea.

Where to Stay

Vulcano ✉ 98050

Most of Vulcano's hotels close between October and April; as in Lipari, it is especially important to book ahead from July to mid-September. The highest price refers to August, when half-board is often mandatory; the lowest price refers to springtime and/or June. Expect to pay something in the middle in the other months. Because of the volcanic activity, camping is forbidden.

Sea House Residence, Via Porto Ponente, t 090 985 22 19. If you feel like passing a few days undisturbed, you can get a reasonably price apartment (up to four people), and try preparing your own Aeolian cuisine.

★★★★**Les Sables Noirs**, Porto di Ponente, t 090 985 24 54, *www.framon-hotels.com* (*luxury*). Named after its beach of volcanic black sand, this is the island's oldest and best hotel. The rooms are bright and pure Mediterranean, and it has an oasis-like garden of palms and a pool. Quite lovely. *Closed Nov–March.*

★★★**Arcipelago**, Vulcanello, t 09 09 85 20 02 (*expensive*). For somewhere totally up to date, come to this lonely place, by the sea 2km from the village. *Closed Nov–Feb.*

★★★★**Eolian**, Porto Ponente, t 090 985 21 51, *www.eolianhotel.com* (*expensive*). Offers 80 Aeolian-style rooms on the sea, and plenty of water sports for its guests. *Closed Nov–Feb.*

★★★**Mari del Sud**, Porto Ponente, t 090 985 3250 (*moderate–expensive*). Perfectly comfortable, and with a restaurant. *Closed Nov–March.*

★★★**Conti**, Porto Ponente, t/f 090 985 20 12, *www.netnet.it/conti* (*moderate, half-board*

only in Aug). One of a few less expensive choices, overlooking the black sands, and worth staying at if you wash up on Vulcano out of season.

★★**Faraglione**, t 090 985 20 54, *www.linea futura.it/hotelfaraglione* (*inexpensive–moderate, half-board only year round*). Built right into the rock opposite the hydrofoil dock in Porto di Levante; ask for one of the three rooms with a balcony overlooking the large garden.

★**Hotel Torre**, Via Favaloro 1, Porto di Levante, t 090 985 23 42 (*inexpensive*). Cheapest of all, this is the island's basic option.

Eating Out

Beware: prices erupt on Vulcano in summer.

Da Vicenzino, Porto di Levante, t 090 985 20 16 (*moderate*). A friendly place with more variety than most, good fish, and hefty portions. *Closed winter.*

Il Diavolo dei Poli, Porto di Levante, t 090 985 30 34 (*moderate*). Reliable, near the port, with good pasta dishes.

Da Maurizio, Porto di Levante, t 090 985 2426 (*moderate*). A charming place with a pleasant garden and perhaps the best food of all, a bit pricey but worth it for an unforgettable cuttlefish pasta. *Closed Nov–Easter.*

Maria Tindara, Via Provinciale 38, t 090 985 30 04 (*moderate*). A green oasis up in Pianoconte, offering local cuisine as well as a few rooms with bathrooms.

Maniaci, Gelso, t 090 985 22 42 (*moderate*). Members of the Maniaci clan, Pina and Toni, run two places in out-of-the-way Gelso. The menus are mainly fish, and it's up to you to decide if they're all really maniacs. *Closed Nov–Easter.*

Around Vulcano by Land

The only bus on Vulcano takes the only road up to **Vulcano Piano**, a scenic drive across the island past the ruins of the church of **Sant'Angelo**, shattered by an earthquake in the 1950s. Most of the houses at Vulcano Piano are used as summer residences. There are a few bars and small restaurants, and many opportunities for quiet walks in the woods or among the sheep grazing on the hillsides.

From Porto di Levante it is an hour's walk (in sturdy shoes!) up to the summit of the **Gran Cratere di Vulcano** (or Vulcano della Fossa). The barrier that blocks the path halfway up marks the line beyond which the comune of Vulcano takes no responsibility for whatever befalls you. When you reach a fork in the path, take the more leisurely right-hand one, unless you're prepared to scramble.

On the way up you'll pass the obsidian vein at **Pietre Cotte** ('cooked rocks') and clouds of smoke rising from the side of the mountain, near the red rocks. Farther up, a large number of 'bread crust' volcanic bombs lie scattered about from the 1890 eruption. Above them at 1,500ft is the eerie hollow of the great crater, more than 1,520ft in diameter. The acrid carbonic gases from its fumaroles are stifling. The floor is solid (there's a platform part-way down) but the magma is not far under the surface, measured by the instruments round the rim that send data back to the geophysical observatory in Lipari. Bereft of any vegetation, the whole area of the crater would look at home on the moon; from the highest point of the mountain you certainly get a moon's-eye view of the entire Aeolian archipelago.

Across the isthmus from Porto di Levante you can climb the much cuter crater of **Vulcanello**, of toy-like volcanic spouts and stinking fumaroles. Passing the villas clinging to its slopes, the path ascends to the top of the calico baby volcano. Inside the crater you can step into an equally colourful cave, where alum was once extracted. The 'bread crust' bombs it last emitted in 1888 created a '**valley of monsters**' of lava formations, reached by way of Vulcanello's pine forest path.

Around Vulcano by Sea

Unless you are something of an alpinist, the only way to see the rest of the island is by boat. Ask a local fisherman to take you around the island or contact Vulcanomare on Via Reale 39, who cruise around the island for around €15. (*t 090 985 3064*). Made up of both ancient and more recent lava, the coasts of the island are rough, rugged and almost unfailingly spectacular. Sailing between Lipari and Vulcano in the narrow **Bocche di Vulcano** – 1km wide and adorned with sea monoliths – is a quite stupendous experience.

On the south side of the island, beneath the tallest mountain, Monte Aria (1,500ft), are two lighthouses, **Faro Vecchio** and **Faro Nuovo**, and the tiny, somewhat forgotten village of **Gelso** (*served in the summer by bus*). Although there are no hotels or rooms here, you can stop off for lunch. On the west side of Vulcano there is a fine beach at **Spiaggia Lunga**, near the pretty **Punta di Capo Secco**, and the mother of all boulders called **Pietro Quaglietto**.

Salina

The twin volcanoes that gave Salina its ancient name, Didyme, are long extinct –
Monte Fossa delle Felci (3,155ft), the tallest peak in the Aeolian archipelago, and
Monte dei Porri (2,821ft). From a distance the island looks like a child's drawing –
simple, painted green (unlike the other Aeolian Islands, Salina is endowed with
natural springs), with two rounded mountains and a smooth coastline. Tourism has
made few inroads here, and most of the 2,290 inhabitants earn their living from the
land, producing tons of capers for export and most of the Aeolians' sweet tawny DOC
Malvasia di Lipari. Despite its name, Salina no longer has any salt pans, although
these used to be an important industry at Lingua.

Santa Marina Salina

Santa Marina Salina, the main port, is a straggling little village at the foot of the
Fossa. Like every other town on Salina, it has little to 'see' or 'do', but offers much in the
way of peace, quiet and friendliness (indeed many of the inhabitants are returned
Australian immigrants). By the lighthouse to the north a **Bronze Age settlement** once
flourished, and among the finds here was a necklace of Egyptian beads, a popular
style in Mycenaean days. Similar necklaces have also been discovered in England.

South of Santa Marina, the road leads some 3km to **Lingua**. Its small lake, once used
as a salt pan, is separated from the sea by a pebble beach, where the water is
renowned for its clearness. In the 18th century the ruins of an Imperial Roman villa
were noted here, but they have since sunk into the ground. On the slopes behind
Lingua and Santa Marina, several **Roman tombs** have been excavated.

Thanks to the efforts of environmental groups, Salina is kept as pristine as possible,
a fact appreciated increasingly by migratory birds. Well-maintained forest paths from
Santa Marina lead up to the summit of **Fossa delle Felci** (about two hours' climbing –
no cars allowed), from where on a clear day you can see not only all of the Aeolian
Islands, but also Reggio di Calabria and Mount Etna. The upper part of the mountain
is a wildlife preserve.

Around Salina

The coastal road north of Santa Marina passes many curious **offshore formations** of
lava and basalt, and lonely beaches of pebbles and rock. Much of the land is neatly
cultivated, although for lack of labour large tracts have become overgrown. The first
village on the route is **Malfa** in the north, located on a wide plain overlooking the sea.
West of here lies **Pollara** near the natural arch of **Punta di Perciato**, the only place on
Salina where you can see the white pumice proving the island's volcanic origins; the
last eruption took place here in 10,000 BC. This is also where *Il Postino* was filmed
(that poignant tale of the postman and the poet) which does nothing to detract from
its stunning beauty; the sea stretches away like a mirror.

Between Malfa and Leni, in the saddle between the twin volcanoes known as
Valdichiesa, is the **Santuario della Madonna del Terzito**, built in 1630 and the religious

Getting Around

Ships and hydrofoils to Salina call at Santa Marina Salina and Rinella. All villages are connected by good roads, and Salina's **bus** schedules coincide with the arrival of the hydrofoils. If you're only on the island for a day, consider Nicola De Pasquale's **mini-bus tours**; you'll usually find him waiting at the port.

Where to Stay

Malfa ✉ 98050

★★★Signum, Via Scalo 15, t 090 984 42 22, *www.hotelsignum.it* (*expensive*). Intimate and friendly, built in the Aeolian style and furnished with antiques. Owner Clara has paid magnificent attention to detail and created a magical hotel– an oasis of calm with a garden full of tumbling jasmine and fluttering butterflies. The pool seems to flow into the horizon and into the sea. The restaurant is one of the best on the island.

★★★Hotel Santa Isabel, Via Scario 12, t 090 984 4018, *www.santaisabel.it* (*moderate–expensive*). If you can't get into the Signum go round the corner (on the way to the beach) to the more modest Isabel which also has stunning views and has been recently completely refurbished. It now has rather hip and comfortable accommodation. *Closed Nov–Mar.*

★★Punta Scario, Via Scario 8, t 090 984 41 39 (*moderate, half-board only in July–Aug*). Another modest option near the Signum. *Closed Nov–mid-Mar.*

Santa Marina Salina ✉ 98050

★★★Mamma Santina, Via Sanità 40, t 090 984 30 54, *www.mammasantino.it* (*expensive, half-board only in summer*). *Closed Nov–mid-Mar.* Clean and friendly, with great views from the top floors and some fabulous furniture, good food and a. swimming pool.

★Punta Barone, Lungomare Giuffrè 8, t 090 984 31 72 (*inexpensive–moderate, half/full board only*). Aeolian-style, family run hotel featuring comfortable rooms, some with sea views.

Il Defino, Località Lingua, t 090 984 30 24, *www.ildelfinosalina.com* (*inexpensive*). Apartments to rent.

★La Marinara, Lingua, t 090 984 30 22 (*inexpensive*). *Closed Oct–May.* Another perfectly serviceable small hotel with a friendly feel, clean and comfortable.

centre of the island. Pilgrims flock here on the main feast days of Mary, especially the Assumption (15 August).

Leni, another small community, overlooks the tiny fishing port of **Rinella** at the end of a steep winding road. The small beach down below has a series of grottoes behind it. Fishermen will often take you on brief excursions along the coast – westwards to the **Grotta di Racina** or eastwards to the **Grotta di Basalto** at Punta Grottazza, which easily wins the prize as the loveliest cave on the island (it can also be reached from Lingua).

Filicudi

Twenty kilometres west of Salina, little Filicudi is not to everyone's taste, but most who come are willing to sacrifice modernity for the rarefied pleasure of a tranquil, crystal sea. Yet despite the difficulties it presents, Filicudi has been inhabited off and on since the 18th century BC. The Greeks called it Phoinikodes, referring either to its abundant ferns or (according to Strabo) to its palms. They left behind an inscription near Pecorini, and later peoples left the numerous terraces cut like grand stairways in the mountains; although many of these have since been abandoned, from a distance

Rinella ✉ 98050

**L'Ariana, Via Rotabile 11, t 090 980 90 75, www.hotelariana.it (*inexpensive–moderate*). Near the beach and with a decent restaurant.

Tre Pini, t 090 980 91 55. Rinella's campsite. *Closed Oct–April.*

Eating Out

The restaurants are unpretentious on Salina. In particular look for dishes with capers and fish, topped off with a glass of malvasia.

Malfa

Hotel Signum, Via Scalo 15, **t** 090 984 42 22, (*moderate*). Book ahead as there is no menu and you have to make your choices in advance. The freshest ingredients go into Aeolian dishes that are excellently cooked and served with utter charm. The terrace is beautiful too. Dinner only.

Santa Marina Salina

Nni Lausta, Via Risorgimento 188 **t** 090 984 3486, www.isolasalina.com (*moderate*). Chef/owner Fabio Giuffre is not just one of the most entertaining characters you can

hope to meet, he is also a true original in the kitchen. Using fresh local ingredients, Fabio invents dishes drawing on global influences to turn traditional Aeolian cuisine into something approaching genius. Go before Fabio becomes the star he seems destined to be. World class food without a doubt, and at a bargain price. *Closed Oct–Easter.*

Portobello, t 090 984 31 25 (*moderate*). Traditional restaurant offering good seafood and pasta. *Closed Wed and Dec–Easter.*

Rinella

Da Peppino, t 090 980 91 06 (*moderate*). The best choice in Rinella, serving the normal range of Aeolian dishes based on the capers-olives-aubergine theme, fish and straightforward grilled meats. *Closed outside high season.*

Lingua

A Cannata, t 090 984 31 61 (*inexpensive*). Another trattoria strong on local dishes. *Closed Fri.*

Il Delfino, t 090 984 30 24 (*inexpensive*). A good trattoria serving Aeolian specialities.

Bar Alfredo, like the others also on the seafront. The best *granitas* on the Aeolians.

they give the island a distinctly striped-look. Much of these empty spaces is now owned by the film-directing Taviani brothers. The 450 inhabitants of Filicudi mostly live from the sea. Although the coral they once gathered is virtually gone, men still harvest sponges as well as fish. The crystal sea around Filicudi draws scores of divers in the summer. To organize a dive, contact the Lipari tourist office.

Capo Graziano

Filicudi Porto, where the ships and hydrofoils call, is one of the three communities on the island. A long stony beach curves towards the promontory of Capo Graziano, where in the 18th century BC a settlement was founded on the natural rock terrace some 270ft above sea level, the successor to an even earlier, but completely indefensible village on Filicudi's plains. Capo Graziano itself was abandoned and extensively resettled all the way up to the slopes of Montagnola, its prosperity based on Aegean trade – potsherds from Mycenae and the Cyclades from 1500 BC were discovered here. In 800 BC Capo Graziano was destroyed.

The foundations (*not visitable*) of 20 oval-shaped huts have been uncovered, and the ceramics found here, with undulating scratched designs, gave their name to the Capo Graziano culture (1800–1400 BC). All South Tyrrhenian ceramics are now in the

Museo Archeológico in Lipari, but one of the huts contains the smooth rocks of what appears to be a prehistoric altar. The necropolis of Capo Graziano extended up the steep flanks of Montagnola, where people were buried in communal graves in the rock, much like those found in Sicily.

Around Filicudi by Land and Sea

From Filicudi Porto you can climb the tallest of Filicudi's three peaks, **Fossa Felci** (2,319ft), passing through Rocche di Ciauli and Val di Chiesa, the main village of Filicudi, where the large church of **Santo Stefano** (1650; *rarely open*) perches on the rim of an ancient crater. From here the path winds through the palms, broom and ferns that dominate the island's flora, up to the summit and its charming views. The only proper road on the island, built in the mid-1970s so that cars could replace mules, connects Porto with the other seaside village of **Pecorini**, where the aforementioned ancient Greek inscription may be seen on the rocks.

From here, or Porto, you can **hire a boat** to circle round the island, the highlight of a stay on peaceful Filicudi. The west coast is particularly lovely, with a 300ft volcanic obelisk called **La Canna** towering out of the sea, covered with seagull nests. Next to it is another rock, the black **Scoglio di Montenassari**. A pointed natural arch forms the entrance to the marvellous **Grotta del Bue Marino** ('of the sea bull', after the hooded Mediterranean monk seals that once lived there). Enter this large cavern in a small boat, or swim around its ample perimeter; the intense silence and ever-changing light patterns are pure magic. Other **grottoes** include the deep Maccatore and Perciato. The steep precipice **Rupi della Sciara** and the **Fortuna** coast offer further insights into the aesthetics of volcanic landscaping.

Alicudi

Westernmost of the Aeolians, and one of the most remote islands in the entire Mediterranean, Alicudi is the round green bump of a volcanic cone floating on the

Where to Stay and Eat

Alicudi ✉ 98050
★Ericusa, Via Regina Elena, **t** 09 09 88 99 02
(*inexpensive, half-board only in July–Aug*).
Apart from a handful of private homes that
open their doors to visitors, this is the only
place to stay. It's a few metres from the

beach, and the trattoria at the hotel (*inexpensive*) has tasty food, although no one
knows from one day to the next what's
going to be on the menu (ferries bring provisions only twice a week in the summer, and
sometimes just once a month in the winter,
when the population plunges to 15 souls).
Closed Oct–May.

sea, a miniature version of Filicudi, although in comparison Filicudi seems like a
metropolis. Its ancient name, Ericusa, was derived from the heather that still covers
its 1.9sq miles. In 1904, 9th-century BC tombs were discovered at Fucile, but it is not
known if Alicudi was ever permanently settled in ancient times; lacking any natural
defences, it may have been used only as a burial ground.

The gently sloping eastern part of the island is corrugated with green terraces and
has the only village on Alicudi, **Alicudi Porto**. Among the humble pink-and-white
houses scattering the terraces there is only one prominent building, the church,
prettily sited at the top of a small stairway.

High above Porto is the steep Serra della Farcona where women used to hide
from the pirates in a spot called the **Timpone delle Femmine**. Higher still is the
depression of the very old crater, the 'harp string' **Filo dell' Arpa** (2,025ft). Be careful,
however: the heights of Alicudi have recently been colonized by Germans, who are
said to have their own resident witch. Western Alicudi is too steep for houses or
farming, but there are small scattered beaches and natural grottoes made by the
wind, such as the **Grottazzo**. The few outsiders who visit Alicudi come mainly for the
perfectly limpid water and the excellent fishing, especially for the Mediterranean
lobster, the *aragosta*. Note that the only means of transportation on the rocky slopes
of the island are the local donkeys, invariably miserably overloaded.

Panarea

Panarea, smallest (1.3sq miles) but one of the prettiest Aeolian Islands, was 'discovered' in the 1960s by a handful of Milanese industrialists who beautifully restored
the island's old houses as hideaways in the olive groves. Film buffs know it from
Antonioni's *L'Avventura*. Today it's still the most fashionable Aeolian, but low-key and
relaxed, where the rich and famous come for a dose of *dolce far niente*.

Panarea originally was much larger, but the volcano that created the island sank,
leaving a little archipelago, of which Panarea is queen. Known in ancient times as
Euonymos ('of good omen'), it was the site of an early settlement at Piano Quartara
(contemporaneous with Capo Graziano on Filicudi), as well as a later settlement at
Punta Milazzese (1400–1250 BC), a culture that produced the zigzag ceramic designs
more often associated with Minoan civilization on Crete.

There's only one paved road on Panarea, where the houses are spread across
three hamlets – Ditella, San Pietro and Drauto. Electricity was installed only in 1988.

Getting Around

Boats can be rented in San Pietro for visiting Basiluzzo. Other than that, the only transport available on Panarea is your feet.

Where to Stay

Panarea ✉ 98050

There are no bargains on this miniature St-Tropez, and only a couple of places that remain open between October and April. A number of people have rooms to let: ask around or pick up the list at the Lipari tourist office.

**Raya, Costa Galletta, near San Pietro, t 090 983 013, www.hotelraya.it (luxury, half-board only in Aug). The most exclusive and elegant hotel, assuring absolute peace and privacy. Built in the form of a little hamlet on several levels, each room has a private bath, and terrace overlooking the sea. There's a garden, restaurant and a small port with boats to hire for island excursions. Closed Nov–Mar.

***Albergo La Piazza, San Pietro, t 090 983 154 (expensive–luxury). It has a garden, a lovely terrace and a pool. Closed Nov–Easter.

***Hotel Cincotta, San Pietro, t 090 983 014 (expensive–luxury). Provides similar facilities to La Piazza, with an even larger terrace. Closed Nov–Mar.

***Lisca Bianca, San Pietro, t 09 09 83 004 (expensive–luxury). Has a pleasant garden but no restaurant. Closed Nov–Mar.

**Hotel Tesoriero, San Pietro, t 090 983 098 (moderate–expensive). A cheaper alternative to the Lisca Bianca, run by the same family. Closed Nov–Mar.

*Rodà, Via San Pietro, t 090 983 006 (inexpensive–moderate, half-board only in July–Aug). A bit lower on the chic thermometer. Closed Nov–Mar.

Eating Out

As on the other islands, the catch of the day features prominently on all the restaurant menus, but prices tend to be a little higher – especially on items such as wine, which has to be 'imported' from Sicily. Because it's a stopping-off point for daytrippers, Via San Pietro has a number of places on the small harbour, all offering pasta and seafood.

Cincotta, Via San Pietro, t 090 983 014 (expensive). This hotel-restaurant is also worth trying out, even if you're not staying over. Closed Oct–Mar.

Da Pina, Via San Pietro, t 090 983 032 (expensive). Has a good, generous menu showcasing fish. Closed Oct–Mar.

Da Paolino, Via Ditella, t 090 983 008 (moderate). Owned by a fisherman, the fish served on the terrace of this restaurant comes guaranteed as fresh as you can get. Closed Oct–Mar.

La Sirena, Via Drautti 4, t 090 983 012 (moderate). Among the better establishments in Panarea to fill up for the day. Closed Oct–Easter.

By the little quay at San Pietro there is a locally used hot spring. Another lingering reminder of Panarea's volcanic past is the off-shore rock of Bottaro, where underwater fumaroles make the sea seem to boil.

Punta Milazzese

From San Pietro it's an hour's walk south, or a leisurely sail, to the landing at **Cala Junco**, a lovely natural rock pool hemmed in by dark cliffs of outlandish volcanic prisms. Beyond Cala Junco crooks the thin knobby finger of Punta Milazzese, a basalt-walled promontory where, in 1948, 23 stone oval huts were excavated (you can visit, but there are only a few old stones to see). Between 100 and 200 people lived here and maintained religious cults at Calcara and Punta Cardosi. Some of the pottery found at Milazzese bears an evocative script similar to Minoan Linear A. In approximately 1250 BC, however, this Neolithic settlement was gutted by fire and ruined by

Bronze Age tough-guys, who used their new metal-working technology mainly to destroy. *Plus ça change...*

North of the village of Ditella, **Calcara Beach** is reached by following a hairpin path down the rocky cliffs that comprise much of Panarea's coast. At Calcara fumaroles have left the stone a variety of colours. In places steam still rises from the ground, and patches of sea and land are quite hot. In Neolithic times the fumaroles were apparently worshipped or feared as infernal gods, and deep pits were dug on the beach to receive their offerings.

From Drauto another path leads towards the Contrada Castello; from here you must make your own way up the terraces to the highest point of Panarea, the **Timpone del Corvo** (1,254ft), with splendid vistas of Strómboli and its active volcano. Just below Punta del Corvo, archaeologists have found traces of a Neolithic cult at Punta Cardosi.

Basiluzzo

No one coming to Panarea will want to miss a tour of its unique cluster of weird rocks and islets. One islet, the **Dattilo** (Greek for finger yet pyramidal in shape), was until recently used by the islanders as a pasture for their sheep, which they would ferry back and forth in boats. Now it's home to seagulls. The mountainous east coast of the island has a cluster of strange formations of hardened lava, like **Pizzo Falcone** above San Pietro. An unusual submerged shelf created by an ancient seismic disturbance extends from here, and on it, poking over the sea, are shoals and peculiar natural knick-knacks, the largest of which is the fascinating islet with the Byzantine name, **Basiluzzo**.

Made of stratified lava in delicate shades, Basiluzzo is formed into giant columns and pipes. By the landing point the ancient Roman dock wavers under the water and, if it's very clear (often you can see 60ft down), you can make out traces of a hamlet dating from 2600 BC – built before Panarea's volcano sank into the sea. Traces of Roman habitation dot the entire islet. It's uncertain whether the Romans were attracted by the uncanny beauty of the place, or merely used the islet as a cruel prison for political deportees; traces of mosaics found on Basiluzzo suggest the former. The rosemary and capers growing on the little plain of the islet are harvested by the people of Panarea. The other rocks and islets in the area are also remarkable, in particular the multi-coloured **Lisca Bianca** and **Lisca Nera**.

Strómboli

In the 1950s Strómboli became a household name with Rossellini's really awful *cinéma vérité* film of the same name starring Ingrid Bergman, and it is still the best known of the Aeolians for its active volcano. As islands go, Strómboli is a newborn, only 40,000 years old, and has yet to settle down. Its belching cone is the first thing you see if you begin your island odyssey from Naples, 211km away. Jules Verne fans will remember it as the exit of the heroes in *Voyage to the Centre of the Earth*.

Getting There and Around

Boats and hydrofoils arrive daily in Scari from Milazzo, Naples (in summer) and the neighbouring islands (*see* p.243). At least once a week one of the Milazzo steamers calls at the island's second port, tiny Ginostra. Otherwise, the island's regular transport is shoe leather.

Where to Stay

Greater Strómboli metropolitan area, sometimes called Strómboli town, is where you'll find most of the hotels. Unless you've booked, don't expect to find anything resembling a room between mid-July and mid-September. Half-board is mandatory as noted. A list of private rooms for rent is available from the tourist office on Lipari.

Strómboli Town ✉ 98050

****La Sirenetta Park Hotel, Via Marina 33, Ficogrande, t 090 986 025 (*expensive–luxury, half-board only two weeks in Aug*). The loveliest hotel of all in Strómboli, with a huge pool on a terrace overlooking the sea and gorgeous rooms. *Closed Nov–Mar.*

***La Sciara Residence, Via Soldato Barneao 5, t 090 986 121 (*expensive, half-board only in Aug*). A 62-room hotel with resort facilities and a pool. *Closed mid-Oct–April.*

***Villaggio Strómboli, Via Regina Elena, Piscita, t 090 986 018 (*moderate–expensive*). The hotel has sporting facilities and organizes boat excursions. Every room has its own mini-bar. *Closed Nov–Mar*

*Villa Petrusa, Via Soldato Panettieri 4, Piscita, t 090 986 045 (*moderate*). A reasonable option from among the cheaper hotels on Strómboli. *Closed Nov–Feb.*

*Stella, Via F. Filzi 14, San Vincenzo, t/f 090 986 722 (*inexpensive–moderate; cheaper rooms are without private bathrooms*). This rather funky but quiet place is basic, and (for the island) dirt-cheap.

*Miramare, Via Nunziante 3, t 090 986 047 (*inexpensive–moderate*). Small and smart place with good views from its terrace restaurant. *Closed Nov–Mar.*

Ginostra ✉ 98050

*Locanda Petrusa, Via Soldato Panettieri, t/f 090 981 23 05 (*inexpensive–moderate, without private bathrooms*). If all the other listed hotels are too near civilization for your liking, this is a quiet and simple place to stay; its 12 double rooms all have a view. *Closed Nov–Feb.*

Eating Out

Strómboli Town

Ai Geki, Vico Salina 12, Scari, t 090 986 213 (*expensive*). Another good choice.

Barbablu, Via V. Emanuele 17, t 090 986 118 (*expensive*). Good reliable food.

Da Zurro, Via Picone 18, Scari, t 090 986 283 (*expensive*). Strómboli doesn't have much of a reputation in the kitchen; however, this place is known for its fish. *Closed mid-Nov–Easter.*

Miramare, Ficogrande, t 090 986 047 (*moderate*). A reliable choice. *Closed Oct–Easter.*

Ginostra

Puntazza (*inexpensive*). Of the three basic *trattorie* at Ginostra that ensure summer daytrippers don't leave hungry, this has the best food, local wine and great pizzas.

Little has changed since the 2nd century AD, when Pausanias succinctly observed: 'On Strongyle, "the round island", you may see fire coming up from the earth.' This may sound dangerous for the 400 inhabitants of Strómboli, but it's not – all volcanic activity takes place on the Sciara del Fuoco, confined by the nature of the mountain itself. From the two parishes on the northern part of the island, all you can see are puffs of smoke, and at night only the apogees of the fireworks.

The Greater Strómboli Metropolitan Area

Visitors disembarking at **Scari**, the main port, are met by three-wheeled vehicles offering to ferry your luggage up the hill to your hotel, for only they can manoeuvre in the narrow village streets. **San Vincenz**o, the 'centre', is named after its large parish church of San Vincenzo Ferreri, which overlooks the village and the bizarre islet of Strombolicchio. Here, and at San Bartolo, the other parish, the **whitewashed houses** swagged with bougainvillea are among the best examples of the Aeolian style. Most of the tourist amenities on the island are to be found here or below on the beautiful black sand beach of **Ficogrande** ('big fig').

Yet these settlements have a half-abandoned, melancholy air. The light, perhaps because it is filtered through gaseous volcanic burps and steam, is strange and uncanny. Although tourists come by the thousand in the summer, and there are some posey bars and discos to keep them off the streets, no one seems to want to live permanently on this rarest of islands, and the delicious white wine and malvasia of Strómboli, subtly flavoured by the volcanic soil – said to be the finest in the Aeolian Islands – is now scarce for lack of labour.

On Top of the Volcano

Malcolm Lowry's unhappy characters sloshed their way to trouble *Under the Volcano*, but Strómboli offers you the chance to get on top of the situation. A recent law requires you to make the ascent with a guide (not a bad thing – it's tricky and potentially dangerous), and the **A.G.A.I. office**, at Via Pola 1 (*down the steps from Piazzale San Vincenzo*; **t** *09 09 86 263*, **t** *09 09 86 211*; *open April–Oct daily*), has been set up to make this easy. You can find a guide from the Associazione Guide Alpine Italiane (AGAI) below Piazza San Vincenzo (**t** *090 986 211*), and arrange to spend a night on the rim; additionally guides touting for business hang out in the piazza in the morning; or ask at the shop Totem Trekking, opposite the church. It may be best value to reserve a couple of days in advance, and form a group of 20 to 30.

Although the ascent doesn't require any special skills, it's not advisable for young children or anyone with trouble walking. Bring a sturdy pair of trainers, a windcheater and warm pullover (the summit of Strómboli is the very citadel of the wind god, and he's lusty enough to blow cinders into every orifice in your body), perhaps two litres of water, snacks, a powerful electric torch (available for rent from the A.G.A.I. office) and a sleeping-bag in which to wake up to the spectacular view of the day dawning over the archipelago. The best time to make the climb is at a full moon, beginning around 5pm, allowing time to see the sun set.

The ascent takes three or four hours and the descent perhaps another two. There's a more vertical ascent for climbers, but take care: two or three people are killed every year taking stupid risks.

If you're not up to making the complete ascent, from the west end of San Bartolo it is about half an hour's walk to the **Osservatorio di Punta Labronzo** (follow the signs painted on the lanes). The Osservatorio, at the northernmost point of the island, offers a fine view of the volcano; come at night with binoculars to see the volcanic sparks. The ascent to the summit continues from here along paths cut through the cinders wandering every which way over the rocks.

The peak, or the **Serra Vancura** observation point, at 2,781ft, is covered with sand which has a nasty tendency to blow into your eyes. However, from here you have an excellent view of the crater 639ft below; the amount of volcanic activity, the wind and your own stamina will determine how much closer you get. It is an extraordinary sight.

Strómboli has given its name to the constant, explosive nature of a certain type of volcano: every 10 minutes red sparks flare up in an enormous fountain of fire, accompanied by appropriate deep rumblings inside the volcano. On busy nights the volcano spews chunks of molten volcanic debris and smouldering magma down the infernal Sciara del Fuoco; and when the fog gathers around the crater, the effect is even more eerie. On good nights (little wind and no bitter volcanic gases), it is easy to stay up until dawn, always a magnificent sight from a mountain-top, and particularly breathtaking on top of the world's most active volcano.

A more leisurely way to watch Strómboli blow its top is to take one of the **evening boat excursions** in the summer to the base of the startling Sciara del Fuoco. The contrast between the verdant hills of the rest of the island and the hellish black slag of the Sciara couldn't be greater, and, while the volcano isn't as immediate or awe-inspiring as when you make the big climb, the red sparks spraying over the side of the Sciara provide a memorable sight.

Ginostra and Strombolicchio

Other possible boat excursions are to **Ginostra** and Strombolicchio. Ginostra (which has a population of just 22) lies at the edge of the Sciara del Fuoco, on the far western side of Strómboli. This remote hamlet – much diminished through widespread emigration to Australia and America – has literally the smallest port in the world: no more than two tiny fishing boats can fit in at a time. Lava rocks in the sea form a natural protective wall against the frequent violent storms. The fishermen and their families who have remained in Ginostra are amongst the hardiest of all Italians, their parish served by an Australian priest, a real character, who performs mass in the tiny church amongst the sugar-cube houses, many built on ledges of black lava. The only contact that Ginostra has with the outside world is by sea, either from other parishes on the island, or the steamers from Milazzo. A path leads up in two hours from Ginostra to the crater, but it's steeper and rather harder to follow.

One last excursion by sea is to **Strombolicchio**, a couple of kilometres off the north coast of Strómboli. From the distance this sheer mass of volcanic rock looks like a Gothic cathedral; it is surrounded by strange currents, and its spires turn out to be petrified monsters. Between 1920 and 1927, some 200 concrete steps were hewn in Strombolicchio's side, leading up to the lighthouse, a vital installation in these frequently violent seas. Until around fifty years ago, at *festa* time, the people from Strómboli would hop over in their boats to dance on the high terrace of the lighthouse – and magical it must have been beneath a full moon.

Ionian Coast

13

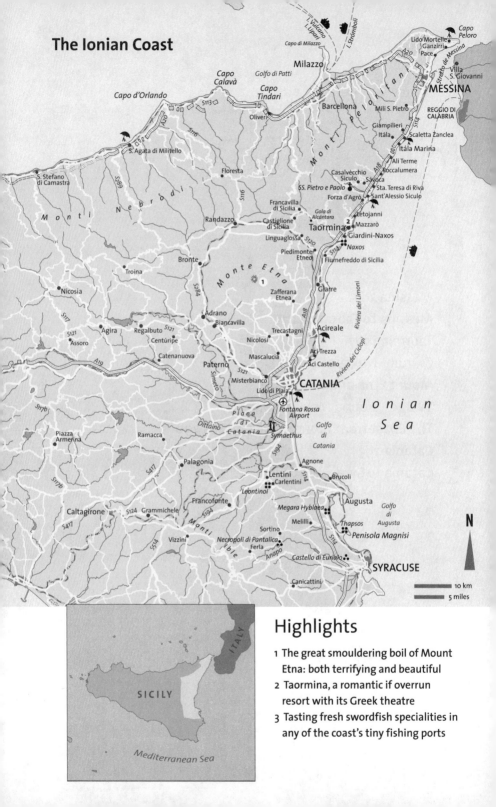

The Ionian Coast

T. Vulcano
I. Lípari
I. Strómboli
Capo di Milazzo
Capo Peloro
Lido Mortelle
Ganzirri
Pace
Milazzo
Golfo di Patti
Capo Calavà
Capo Tindari
MESSINA
Villa S. Giovanni
REGGIO DI CALABRIA
Capo d'Orlando
Oliveri
Barcellona
Mili S. Pietro
S. Agata di Militello
Giampilieri
Itála
Scaletta Zanclea
Itála Marina
S. Stefano di Camastra
Floresta
Casalvécchio Sículo
Ali Terme
Roccalumera
Sávoca
SS. Pietro e Paolo
Sta. Teresa di Riva
Sant'Alessio Sículo
Monti Nébrodi
Francavilla di Sicília
Gola di Alcántara
Letojanni
Randazzo
Castiglione di Sicília
Forza d'Agro
Mazzarò
Taormina
Giardini-Naxos
Monti
Linguaglossa
Naxos
Nicosia
Bronte
Piedimonte Etneo
Fiumefreddo di Sicilia
Troina
Monte Etna
Zafferana Etnea
Giarre
Adrano
Biancavilla
Riviera dei Limoni
Agira
Regalbuto
Centúripe
Trecastagni
Nicolosi
Acireale
Assoro
Catenanuova
Mascalucía
Aci Trezza
Paternò
Misterbianco
Aci Castello
Riviera dei Ciclopi
Piazza Armerina
Ramacca
Lido di Plaia
CATANIA
Fontana Rossa Airport
Ionian Sea
Dittáino
Piana di Catania
Golfo di Catania
Symaethus
Palagonia
Agnone
Brucoli
Lentini
Carlentini
Francofonte
Leontínoi
Augusta
Caltagirone
Grammichele
Megara Hyblaea
Golfo di Augusta
Melilli
Thapsos
Penisola Magnisi
Vizzini
Sortino
Necropoli di Pantalica
Ferla
Anapo
Castello di Euríalo
SYRACUSE
Canicattini

N

10 km
5 miles

SICILY
ITALY
Mediterranean Sea

Highlights

1 The great smouldering boil of Mount Etna: both terrifying and beautiful

2 Taormina, a romantic if overrun resort with its Greek theatre

3 Tasting fresh swordfish specialities in any of the coast's tiny fishing ports

The approach to Messina, 'The Gateway of Sicily', is striking however you go about it, and awe-inspiring if you have the good fortune of sailing in from the north past the surging cliffs of Calabria and into the magnificent Strait, braving Odysseus' old nemesis, the six-headed monster Scylla and whirlpool Charybdis.

But this is only the introduction to Sicily's most stunning coast. After Messina itself, the shore to the south is framed by smoking, snow-capped Mount Etna, the deep-blue sea and a luxuriant growth of palms and citrus trees, most famously at the celebrated resort of Taormina, where newlyweds come to swoon and spoon in one of the most enchanting settings in Italy. Here too is a dense array of hill towns, and the metropolis of eastern Sicily, strange, decaying, Baroque Catania.

Messina

Two giants, Mata and Grifone, founded Messina in a magnificent setting at the foot of the Monti Peloritani, overlooking the Strait, but on property that has periodically been swept clean by earthquakes. Hence Sicily's third city (pop. 273,810) is also the island's most modern one, but not oppressively so in spite of its tragic history; its postwar charms (and there are a few, if discreet) are all the more delightful for being unexpected.

History

Strategic Messina has been important since ancient times. It was initially colonized in the 8th century BC by Cumaeans and Chalcidians who called it Zancle (sickle) after the shape of its harbour. In 493 BC, Zancle was captured by Anaxilas, tyrant of Rhegium across the Strait, who renamed it Messana after his native Messenia in Greece. When the Carthaginian general Himilco destroyed the town in 397 BC, Syracuse rebuilt it; after the death of Syracuse's tyrant Agathocles, the city thought it a wise move to welcome in his renegade mercenaries, the Mamertines (sons of Mars). But rather than protect Messina, the Mamertines massacred the entire population and took over large areas of Sicily and Calabria as well. When Hieron II of Syracuse gave them a dose of their own medicine, the Mamertines went whining off to Rome for assistance, giving the Republic its first excuse to intervene in Sicily. Once the Roman fox was in the hen-house, Cicero graciously honoured Messina as a 'great and wealthy' ally of Rome.

Later, Byzantine to the core, Messina fell to the Arabs in 843, but, as elsewhere, its Saracen rulers were content to collect taxes and let the Greeks pretty much get on with their lives. A Byzantine army, aided by Norman allies, briefly reconquered Messina in 1038. In 1061, 500 Normans under Roger de Hauteville secretly sailed at night over the Strait, taking a long, unexpected route to the south, while the beefed-up Saracen defences had all been concentrated to await them north of Messina. The Normans captured the city, their first victory in Sicily and the bridgehead for their conquest of the island, almost without a fight.

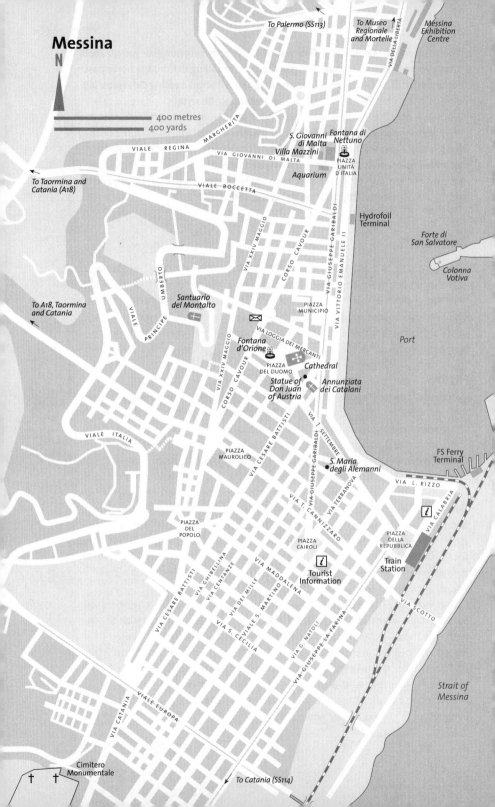

Messina

N

400 metres
400 yards

To Palermo (SS113)

To Museo
Regionale
and Mortelle

Messina
Exhibition
Centre

VIA DELLA LIBERTA

VIALE REGINA MARGHERITA

VIA GIOVANNI DI MALTA

S. Giovanni
di Malta
Villa Mazzini

Fontana di
Nettuno

PIAZZA
UNITÀ
D'ITALIA

Aquarium

VIALE BOCCETTA

To Taormina and
Catania (A18)

VIA XXIV MAGGIO

CORSO CAVOUR

VIA GIUSEPPE GARIBALDI

VIA VITTORIO EMANUELE II

Hydrofoil
Terminal

Forte di
San Salvatore

Colonna
Votiva

VIALE PRINCIPE UMBERTO

Santuario
del Montalto

PIAZZA
MUNICIPIO

Port

To A18, Taormina
and Catania

VIA XXIV MAGGIO

VIA LOGGIA DEI MERCANTI

Fontana
d'Orione

PIAZZA
DEL DUOMO

Cathedral

CORSO CAVOUR

Statue of
Don Juan
of Austria

Annunziata
dei Catalani

VIALE ITALIA

VIA I SETTEMBRE

VIA CESARE BATTISTI

PIAZZA
MAUROLICO

S. Maria
degli Alemanni

FS Ferry
Terminal

VIA GIUSEPPE GARIBALDI

VIA T. CANNIZZARO

VIA TERRANOVA

VIA L. RIZZO

VIA CALABRIA

PIAZZA
DEL
POPOLO

PIAZZA
CAIROLI

PIAZZA
DELLA
REPUBBLICA

i

VIA CESARE BATTISTI

VIA GHIBELLINA

VIA CENTANZE

VIA MADDALENA

VIA DEI MILLE

VIALE S. MARTINO

Tourist
Information

i

Train
Station

VIA S. CECILIA

VIA G. NATOLI

VIA GIUSEPPE LA FARINA

VIA SCOTTO

VIA CATANIA

VIALE EUROPA

Strait of
Messina

Cimitero
Monumentale

To Catania (SS114)

Richard the Lionheart and Other Disasters

Under the Normans, the Strait was safe for Christian shipping for the first time ever, and Messina boomed, especially when the Crusaders sailed through. One, however, named Richard the Lionheart, behaved very badly when he wintered here with King Philip Augustus. He arrived in September 1190 in a foul mood because his sister Joanna, widow of William II, wasn't being paid her just revenues by Tancred. Tancred quickly paid Joanna off, but the King of England wanted more and went off in a huff; he tossed the monks out of Messina's Monastery of the Saviour, the most important Greek monastery in Sicily, and installed his own troops.

It was the last straw for the citizens of Messina, who rioted and locked the English out of the city gates. Richard was furious, but discussions to bring about a peace seemed to calm him down until crowds of citizens were heard shouting insults at the English. Richard, never one to control his temper, immediately called his troops and set them on the city, leaving it a smouldering ruin – with the banners of England flying triumphantly from the walls. To add insult to injury, Richard took a number of citizens as hostages and built a large wooden castle called Mategriffon, 'Greek-curber', just outside the city's walls.

Tancred dipped deep into his pockets to buy peace with Richard, whom he needed as an ally against Hohenstaufen claims to Sicily. Richard was appeased and even gave Tancred a rare gift – the sword Excalibur, recently discovered in Arthur's tomb at Glastonbury. In April, Richard's extraordinary globe-trotting mother, Eleanor of Aquitaine, arrived in Messina with his fiancée Berengaria of Navarre in tow; as it was Lent, the wedding had to be postponed, and Berengaria and Joanna sailed with Richard to the Holy Land. Without Richard's help, Tancred and Norman Sicily fell to Henry Hohenstaufen a few weeks later.

Messina resisted the grasping Charles of Anjou in 1282, but in the 1530s received another Charles, the Fifth, who lavished monuments on the city. In 1571, Messina saw off the fleet that defeated the Turks at Lepanto, making Messina a household name – Shakespeare set *Much Ado About Nothing* here. In 1674–8 Messina rebelled against the Spanish, with the aid of Louis XIV; when the French pulled out, the Spanish punished the city, most of all by revoking its privileges as a free port.

This initiated a streak of bad luck that few cities can match. In 1743, the plague killed 40,000 in Messina; in 1783 an earthquake demolished the city; in 1848 the Bourbon Re Bomba, Ferdinand II, bombarded the city fiercely from the sea to quell Sicilian cries for independence. There was a cholera epidemic in 1854, another earthquake in 1894, and then, on 28 December 1908, the most devastating tremor of all, killing 84,000 inhabitants in their beds in the small hours of the morning. The coast sank 19 inches into the sea, altering the dreaded currents of the whirlpool Charybdis so that it no longer posed a threat to sailors. The rebuilding of Messina had scarcely finished in 1943 when Allied bombs flattened it again.

The Big Sickle

Messina's striking sickle shape is immediately apparent as you sail into port or stroll along portside Via Vittorio Emanuele II. The very tip of the sickle is marked by a

Getting There and Around

Magazzini Piccolo in Viale S. Martino; tickets sold on board.

By Air

The nearest airport is at Reggio di Calabria. Cavalieri buses leave for the airport from Autosilos Cavalotti, **t** 090 771 938.

By Train

All trains from the Italian mainland stop at Messina via FS Ferries; call **t** 090 675 234 for information. Trains run regularly to Milazzo, Cefalù and Palermo, and south through Taormina, Catania and Syracuse.

By Ferry and Hydrofoil

There are frequent ferry crossings to Villa San Giovanni on Caronte-Tourist Ferry Boats, **t** 090 41415 (every 10–15mins) or the FS line, call **t** 848 888 088; less often there are FS ferries to Reggio di Calabria.

There are hydrofoil departures from Reggio di Calabria (15min trip; every half hour). In the summer (June–Sept) hydrofoils leave Messina for the Aeolian Islands on the SNAV line (**t** 090 364 044 or 090 662 506) several times a day; in winter, once a day. Hydrofoil tickets and information are available from Cortina del Porto, **t** 090 364 044; departures are opposite the Jolly Hotel.

By Bus

The popular Taormina–Giardini-Naxos–Catania–Randazzo and Bronte route leaves from Piazza della Repubblica (station); the company is Interbus, **t** 090 661 754. The SAIS office, **t** 090 771 914, has information about services to Catania and its airport, Palermo and Enna. For Milazzo (for the Aeolian Islands), Giuntabuses, **t** 090 673 782, leave Via Terranova 8, near the station, every 40mins or so. Capo d'Orlando, Brolo, Patti and Tindari are served by TAI, **t** 090 675 184, from opposite the

Tourist Information

APT, Via Calabria 301 bis, **t** 090 640 221/674 236, *www.messinaonline.too.it* (*open Mon–Sat 8.30–6.30*); AAST, Piazza Cairoli 45, **t** 090 293 5292/293 6294 (*open Mon and Sat 8.30–2, Wed 8.30–2 and 3–6.30*). Good city information: *www.messinacitymap.com*.

Where to Stay

Messina expects more business travellers than tourists and comes up short in reasonably priced accommodation.

******Grand Hotel Liberty**, Via 1 Settembre 15, ✉ 98123, **t** 090 640 9436, *www.framon-hotels.com* (*expensive*). Art nouveau style predominates in this luxury option opposite the train station.

******Jolly Hotel Dello Stretto**, Via G. Garibaldi 126, ✉ 98100, **t** 090 363 860, *www.jollyhotels.it* (*expensive*). Modern, centrally located and with air-conditioning, this is similar in atmosphere to the Royal Palace hotel.

******Royal Palace**, Via T. Cannizzaro 224, ✉ 98123, **t** 090 6503, *www.framon-hotels.com* (*expensive*). This is an expense-account favourite fitted out with air-conditioning and every other comfort.

*****Paradis**, Via C. Pompea 441, Contemplazione, ✉ 98168, **t** 09 03 10 682 (*moderate*). An option if you have a car. If not heavenly or meditative, it is certainly more than adequate.

*****Excelsior**, Via Maddalena 32, ✉ 98123, **t** 090 293 14 31 (*inexpensive*). An attractive and well-kept older hotel, also central.

marble **Madonna** high on a column, its base inscribed *Vos et ipsam civitatem benedicimus*, a passage taken from the letter written by the Virgin to Messina (*see below*). Directly behind it stands the Spanish **Forte di San Salvatore**, built in 1546 by Viceroy Ferrante Gonzaga on the site of the Greek monastery hijacked by Richard the Lionheart. The Spaniards also built the even larger Cittadella in the middle of the sickle in 1682–8 to keep a foot on the neck of the rebellious Messinese; its ruined

**Panoramic, SS113, Colle S. Rizzo, ✉ 98124, t 090 340 228 (*inexpensive*). A little hotel with a garden and grand views.

*Touring, Via N. Scotto 17, t 090 293 88 51 (*inexpensive*). An unremarkable cheaper option near the station. Best to avoid the noisy ground floor.

*Locanda Donato, Via Caratozzolo 8, t 090 393 150 (*budget*). Out on Capo Peloro, by the lake, this is a tranquil alternative.

*Mirage, Via N. Scotto 1, t 090 293 88 44 (*budget*). Another basic budget choice near the railway station.

Eating Out

Messina does itself proud in the kitchen, with specialities naturally based on swordfish (*pesce spada*). Also look for *'ncasciata* (short pasta dressed with a meat sauce, meat patties, hard-boiled eggs, peas, fried aubergine, sausage and cheese, all baked together in a pie dish).

Another local speciality is *pesce stocco a ghiotta*: the reason why Italian ports like Venice, Ancona and Messina are so fond of stockfish – dried cod – when there's so much fresh fish about dates back to tastes acquired from the Crusaders. In Messina it is prepared *a ghiotta* (fried and then stewed in a rich sauce of tomatoes, onion, olives, pinenuts, sultanas and garlic).

At Easter, look for *sciuscieddu*, made of chicken stock, curd and meatballs.

The province of Messina produces the least wine of any in Sicily. However, the best wines to try are Capo Bianco, Cariddi, Mamertino and red DOC Faro.

The classic Messinese pastry is black or white *pignolata* (crispy doughnut sticks covered with dark or white chocolate).

Alberto, Via Ghibellina 95, t 090 710 711 (*expensive*). An *elegantissimo* establishment out towards Mortelle, offering a wide assortment of *antipasti* and everything you can possibly make with swordfish. Put on your gladrags and be sure to book ahead. *Closed Mon and Sun eve.*

Da Piero, Via Ghibellina 121, t 090 718 365 (*expensive*). Come here for a first-rate introduction to the island's cuisine, and especially its swordfish, but expect to pay at least €50 for a full meal. *Closed lunch and Sun.*

Osteria del Campanile, Via Loggia dei Mercanti 7, t 090 711 418 (*moderate*). This bargain near the Piazza del Duomo has outdoor tables where you can dine on delicious *involtini di pesce spada* (stuffed swordfish fillets grilled on a skewer), *papardelle monte e mare* (pasta with mushrooms) or pizzas. *Open late, but closed Sun except in July and August.*

Taverna del Polipo Guercio, Via Centonze 32, t 090 719 542 (*moderate*). Come to this bustling place and you're likely to be eating alone with the locals. *Closed Sun and Aug.*

Capitano's, Via Dei Mille 88–90. A lively place serving some of the best pizzas in the province (*inexpensive*). *Closed Mon.*

Opera Prima, Via Laudamo 28, t 090 345 111. Sit in the pleasant summer garden to enjoy a variety of wines and snacks.

Del Pópolo, Piazza del Pópolo. Another inexpensive place with tables in or out and a delicious *pasta alla Norma* (*inexpensive*). *Closed Sun and mid-Aug.*

Billé, Piazza Cairoli 7, t 090 718 311. A *pasticcerie* famous throughout Messina for its *pignolata*. *Closed Tues.*

Pisani, Via Tommaso Cannizzaro 45, t 090 293 81 58. Another well-known *pasticcerie*. Here they stuff their *pignolata* in a *cannolo* of chocolate. *Closed Thurs.*

walls now contain the **FS Ferry Terminal**. Messina in the 1700s was famous for its 'curtain' of noble, four-storey buildings with wrought-iron balconies that overlooked the port like one great terrace, nicknamed the Palazzata. Earthquakes and bombs have destroyed even the restoration of the palaces, but their postwar replacements, if hardly as elegant, still make a handsome impression.

Just inland, Via Garibaldi has two churches that have survived all the upheavals, the first, **Santa Maria degli Alemanni**, just barely. Built in the early 1200s by the crusading Teutonic Knights, this was one of Sicily's few Gothic churches. The Messinese apparently disliked the style as much as the rest of the Italians, and deserted it in the 1400s; rather heavy restoration work is under way.

North on Via Garibaldi, the 12th-century Norman **Annunziata dei Catalani** has survived in better nick, covered with patterned brick- and marble-work and crowned with a little dome to create a charming Arab-Byzantine hotchpotch. It appears to be half sunk below the streets; the modern ground level shows the amount of earthquake rubble Messina is built on. Behind the church is a 16th-century **statue of Don Juan of Austria**, 24-year-old natural son of Charles V and hero of the Battle of Lepanto (1571), shown with his foot on the head of the Turkish commander Ali Bassa. Bronze plates on the base depict scenes from the battle, which effectively put an end to Ottoman threats to Western Europe. Sicily, on the front lines – Malta had just withstood a terrible siege – was especially grateful.

The Cathedral and its Busy Campanile

Just in from the Annunziata is the heart of medieval Messina, the Piazza del Duomo and Messina's **cathedral** (*open daily 7.30–12 and 4–6.30*). Built by Roger II in 1160, and last restored after bombs in the Second World War caused it to burn for three days, this incorporates fragments that have miraculously survived – charming 15th-century reliefs of country life and a portal pieced together from bits, including two lions from the 1300s. It was here that the angelically handsome William II married the 15-year-old Joanna Plantaganet in 1177.

Inside the cathedral are restored treasures: Antonello Gagini's *John the Baptist*, and part of the tomb of the English Archbishop of Messina, Richard Palmer, who died in 1195. On the high altar, note the bronze group of the *Madonna della Lettera*, the Virgin handing a letter to an embassy from Messina. The story goes that Messina was converted by St Paul in AD 42, but the result was a terrible famine. In pity, the Virgin sent a ship full of food to Messina without any crew, and wrote a letter blessing the city. Although the original letter was lost in one of Messina's disasters, the cathedral preserves a copy. This wasn't the only holy letter floating around the Mediterranean: Constantinople had one written by Jesus Christ himself until it was destroyed in a 12th-century revolt. Agrigento preserves one from His unholy adversary (*see* p.174).

As it is, the cathedral is upstaged by its huge **campanile** with an astronomical clock built in Strasbourg in 1933 and reputedly the largest in the world, telling the year, the date, the phase of the moon and the location of the planets. But even that is upstaged by the pageant of its clockwork bronze automata: the lion waves his banner and roars three times, the cock flaps his wings and crows, and Dina and Clarenza, Messina's heroines in the Sicilian Vespers, take turns ringing the bell. Jesus pops out of the tomb, the dove circles a model of the Santuario del Montalto as it rises from the ground (the real one can be seen on the hill to the left), and the Virgin gives her letter to the dignitaries of Messina, all to a scratchy recording of Schubert's 'Ave

The Elusive Antonello

Antonello was born in Messina some time before 1430. Like many a painter, his first biography appears in Vasari, who wrote that Jan van Eyck taught him the secrets of oil painting in the Low Countries. Antonello in turn introduced it to Domenico Veneziano in Venice. Domenico brought the new technique to Florence and was murdered by the jealous Andrea del Castagno.

What Vasari wrote is logical (except for the fact that Domenico continued to paint after Andrea del Castagno died) and there are so many years unaccounted for in Antonello's life that it will never be disproved. A century of detective work by art historians, however, has produced an alternative biography for Sicily's greatest contribution to the Renaissance.

Growing up in a city ruled by Aragon, they say, Antonello was surrounded by Catalan art, at the time deeply influenced by the new naturalism in Italian and Flemish art. At the age of 25 he went to Naples and entered the workshop of the painter Colantonio, who was celebrated for his ability to imitate van Eyck and his oil techniques. In 1457 Antonello was in Messina, where he painted in a strongly Flemish style, with great attention to detail; the next record has him returning home again three years later. From where? Rome, probably, where he may have met Piero della Francesca and Frenchman Jean Fouquet; at least, after 1460 his compositions show a new serenity, clarity and architectural modelling. Then there's a lacuna, from 1465 to 1471, after which his paintings show an even greater sensitivity and power, a synthesis of the best in Flemish and Italian art. At any rate, by 1475 Antonello was in Venice, where he painted the *Pala di San Cassiano* (now in fragments, in Vienna), a work that had a powerful influence on Venetian painters, who copied his modelling and form. The Venetians also loved his portraits – always done in the three-quarter view, in the Flemish style (there's one in Cefalù), and remarkable for their pioneering light, shadow and texture, and intense psychological depth. In autumn 1476 Antonello was back in Messina, where he remained until his death in 1478.

Maria'. It's best to be here at midday when you get the full symphony of sounds which can be rather alarming if it takes you by surprise.

In front of the cathedral is the beautifully restored **Fontana d'Orione** (1547) by Florentine Angelo Montorsoli, a pupil of Michelangelo. Along with Mata and Grifone, the hunter Orion is one of Messina's legendary founders; the crocodile-wrestling putti below him represent the Rivers Tiber, Ebro, Nile and Camaro. The latter is little more than a torrent, but it was the construction of an aqueduct bringing its waters to Messina that occasioned the fountain.

North along Via Garibaldi

Via Garibaldi continues north from Piazza del Duomo past the massive **Municipio** (1934) and the 19th-century **Teatro V. Emanuele** to the public gardens of **Villa Mazzini** (*open until sunset*) and its **Aquarium** (*open Tues–Thurs 10–12, Fri 10–12 and 4.30–6.30*), filled with Mediterranean sea creatures.

Across the street, engulfed by the Prefecture, is **San Giovanni di Malta** (*under restoration, to visit call t 090 661 747*), an elegant Mannerist church from the 1500s that has managed to hold itself together. On the seafront here, in Piazza Unità d'Italia, splashes another work by Montorsoli, the **Fontana di Nettuno** (a copy; the original was moved to the museum after its castration by some delinquents from Palermo).

Museo Regionale

Open April–Sept Mon, Wed, Fri and Sun 9–1.30; Tues, Thurs, Sat 9–2 and 4–7; Oct–March Mon, Wed and Fri 9–2, Tues, Thurs and Sat 9–2 and 4–7, Sun 9–1. last entry 30 mins before closing; adm.

From Piazza Unità d'Italia, Via della Libertà continues past the vast Messina exhibition centre to the **Museo Regionale**, a noisy and polluted 2km walk of no charm whatsover or a simple hop on bus 8 from the station. A much bigger museum building is under construction next door.

The museum houses works salvaged from Messina's catastrophes – a 13th-century Catalan *Crucifixion* and a *Virgin and Child*, perhaps by Laurana and said to represent the features of Eleanor of Aquitaine, all overshadowed by two major paintings by **Caravaggio**, both commissioned by Messina and finished in 1609, the year before his wretched death on a Roman beach: the *Adoration of the Shepherds*, a deceptively simple triangular composition, and the powerful *Raising of Lazarus*, one of his most disturbing works, in which Lazarus's hand rises stiffly in the unrelieved dark void that occupies the entire upper half of the large canvas.

The other star of the collection is the five panels of the earthquake-damaged but lovely polyptych, *Madonna Enthroned between SS. Gregorio and Benedict* (1473), by **Antonello da Messina**. Museum keepers are plentiful and vigilant: they follow you step by step through the rooms.

Other Sights in Messina

If you have a car, you could try a **scenic drive** along the avenues in the hills over Messina, the *circonvallazione a monte*, offering panoramic views over to the Calabrian coast. At the southern end of the city, above Piazza Dante, the **Cimitero Monumentale** (*open daily until sunset, with a lunch break*) is a popular attraction, not only for its views but for its amazing 19th-century and Liberty-style statuary. Messina also has several bookshops devoted to Sicilian authors and subjects: try the **Libreria Pizzullo**, Via dei Mille 60.

Inland from Messina head uphill, northwest on SS113 towards the Tyrrhenian coast, to **Gesso**, a village believed to be of Saracen origin. The ethno-anthropological museum here displays instruments from the local Peloritani musical culture, such as bagpipes, simple and double clarinets and oboes for use during ceremonial processions. The Kyklos Association which is connected with this museum has released CDs of traditional songs from this area.

Messina to Taormina

The Strait of Messina

The Fretum Siculum has been on the map since the dawn of Western civilization, when Odysseus's ships were almost wrecked by Scylla, apparently not a monster but a rock that made eerie noises in the wind, now gone but remembered in the name of Scilla in Calabria; the Sicilian shore hosted Charybdis, who may not have been a whirlpool as much as violent currents. Hot summer days sometimes produce a mirage that dramatically distorts the coast of Calabria, called *fata Morgana* after the enchantress Morgan la Faye. And what is she doing in this sunny clime? When the Normans brought the tales of Roland with them to Sicily, they also brought the legends of King Arthur and transplanted them deep in the fertile Sicilian imagination. Mount Etna became the fairy kingdom of Mongibel, where Morgan lived and where her sprites entrapped Arthur.

Crossing the Strait has posed a challenge since the Second Punic War, when the Romans, having captured Hannibal's war elephants in Palermo, lacked the ships to send the heavy pachyderms across, and ended up floating them on rafts strapped to large, empty jars. Some historians believe that, when the Normans transported their horses over the Strait to capture Messina in 1061, it was with recently gained know-how from Byzantium; Sicilian knights with William the Conqueror applied the lesson five years later when they crossed over to England from Normandy. Lately there has been talk about building the world's longest suspension bridge over the Strait, or a tunnel, or a suspended underwater tunnel called the Archimedes Bridge, proposed by British engineer Alan Grant, that would be anchored to the sea-bed with adjustable steel cables. A major hurdle to building any link is the fact that it has to be able to withstand a major earthquake; at present those interested in the venture are holding back, pondering the financial mess of the Channel Tunnel.

Swordfish and Capo Peloro

The Strait swarms with swordfish, the quarry of fishermen from the small villages of charming names (Paradiso, Contemplazione, Pace) that dot the headland towards Capo Peloro. If you are lucky you'll see their fishing boats, as curiously shaped as their prey, topped with a thin ladder-like mast, from which one man spots the swordfish and, as the boat sails off in hot pursuit, instructs the harpoonist perched precariously on the end of the extremely long, thin prow.

Further north along the cape lies **Lago Ganzirri**, a popular weekend destination and particularly lively in the summer months when there are nightly pop concerts. Mussel is farmed on Ganzirri's lake so this is a great place for seafood. Most restaurants are concentrated on the small strip between the lake and the sea and the accommodation here is much cheaper than in Messina. Capo Peloro is the easternmost corner of Sicily. From here a huge power cable stretches over the Strait, supported by two monster pylons to permit ships to pass beneath. Just beyond it, facing the Tyrrhenian Sea, is the favourite beach of the Messinese, **Lido Mortelle** (*frequent bus from*

Messina), which gets crowded in the summer. Mortelle has open-air film shows throughout July and August, twice a night.

South to Taormina

The Ionian Coast south of Messina is fringed with small towns and beaches wedged between the Monti Peloritani, the handmaidens of Dame Etna. The closer you get to Taormina, the more spectacular the scenery, whether you go by car or train. If you're driving and in a hurry, take the A18 autostrada; it's a toll road whenever the attendants aren't on strike. The other main road, the parallel SS114, is the solidly packed main street of what seems a single town, with lots of delays as far south as Santa Teresa di Riva. If there's no hurry, there are lots of beaches along the way – you'll find one under any of the little bridges that carry the train tracks that follow the SS114. **Acqualadrone** is perhaps the nicest of the beach towns along this coast.

Norman Churches, Mummies and Mud

Above Mili Marina, in the hills near Mili San Pietro, directly across the Strait from Reggio di Calabria, there is a lovely old Basilian monastery church, **Santa Maria**, founded in 1082 by Count Roger, whose son Jordan was buried there 10 years later. Pick up the key from the Mili San Pietro priest, who will direct you down to the church – now set in the middle of a pig farm. **Giampilieri Marina** is an old resort nearby, and further south is another, **Scaletta Zanclea**, its beach set below the mountains where the melancholy ruins of a **13th-century castle** moulder quietly away. From here, you can take a 3km detour up to the hill village of **Itála** to see a Norman church in much better nick: **San Pietro**. Built in 1093 on a site where the Normans had defeated a Muslim army, the restored church retains its dome and graceful brick arcading of interlaced arches along the sides.

The coastal road continues to the spa of **Ali Terme**, with its mineral springs and two **mud baths** (*one is open June–Oct, t 0942 701063; the other is open May–Dec, t 0942 715029*), located on a wide stretch of beach. Above Santa Teresa di Riva, the next town on the coast, **Sávoca** was once the haunt of cut-throat *banditi* who lived in the ruined castle; today it's a picture-perfect Sicilian hill village – good enough for Hollywood to shoot part of *The Godfather* here, safely distant from the real Mafiosi out west, who probably would have doubled their usual protection rates. Sávoca's church of **San Michele** has a good Gothic porch, but the real attraction here are the small **catacombs** (*open Tues–Sun April–Sept 9–1 and 4–7, Oct–March 9–12 and 3–5*), with mummified bodies, a tidier miniature of the macabre galleries in Palermo. Only people of a certain social status enjoyed this treatment after death. To have your mortal remains preserved, dressed up in Sunday best and exposed to public admiration was a matter of the highest prestige.

The best of this area's Norman churches lies 3km above Sávoca, in citrus groves near the village of Casalvécchio Siculo. **SS. Pietro e Paolo** was built by a certain Master Gerard the Frank in 1172 for Basilian (Orthodox) monks. Situated on the banks of the Fiumara di Agro, the building reflects the lavish Norman-Byzantine decorative ideal, with local lava added for a multicoloured effect. All the Greek monasteries along the coast here were founded by monks fleeing the Iconoclastic persecutions in the 8th century. They survived Arab rule, and prospered greatly under the Normans, who found their cooperation extremely useful in maintaining control over the Greeks living in their new domains. (If it's locked, seek out the man with the key, and tip him.)

Forza d'Agrò

South of Santa Teresa, watching the traffic on the *autostrada* go by from its tremendous 1,410ft balcony, Forza d'Agrò is a pretty medieval village, dominated by a **16th-century castle**, now defending the local cemetery. Forza's main church, 16th-century **Sant'Agostino**, contains a beautiful painting by Antonio Giuffré of *Three Angels Visiting Abraham*, and a medieval gonfalon. Just before Taormina, **Capo Sant' Alessio**, with its castle perched on the 397ft cliffs, offers a striking view from the window of your train or car. Below it lie the growing resorts of **Letojanni** and **Sant'Alessio Siculo**, both with wide beaches.

Taormina

Taormina is Sicily's resort *extraordinaire*. Europe's leisured classes began to winter here at the start of the 20th century; among these were D. H. Lawrence, who had a villa from 1920 to 1923 in Via Fontana Vecchia. Filled with fine medieval buildings, bougainvillea-scented squares, bustling cafés and boutiques, and shady groves of lemons and oranges, Taormina enjoys a year-round season, and its spectacular situation is enhanced by the looming eminence of blue, snow-capped Mount Etna. The view from the Greek theatre is one of the most impressive in all of Sicily.

Sadly. like many famous resorts, Taormina has become a victim of its own fame and its picturesque perfection is sometimes barely visible under the constant tide of tourist bodies and prices are higher than elsewhere in Sicily. If you can manage not to be swept away by this tide, the little hill village that Taormina once was can still be found and enjoyed, mostly between October and April, when you will also have a better chance of spotting elusive Etna as the days are at their clearest then.

History

Taormina was founded in 358 BC, after Dionysius of Syracuse destroyed the ancient colony of Naxos below. Andromachus, father of Timaeus the historian, took the refugees of Naxos to Tauromenium, as it was then known; later, Andromachus was the only tyrant to join Timoleon, the new ruler of Syracuse, in his efforts to restore democracy in Sicily. During this time the town prospered (the Romans made it a privileged *civitas fœdecata*) but later it erred in supporting Pompey against Octavian, who as Augustus turned it into a strategic military colony. The Saracens destroyed Taormina in 902, but then rebuilt it. In 1410 the Sicilian parliament deliberated here in electing a new king for the island when the Aragonese line died out with Martin II. In the Second World War, Marshal Kesselring made Taormina his headquarters, and the town consequently suffered bomb damage.

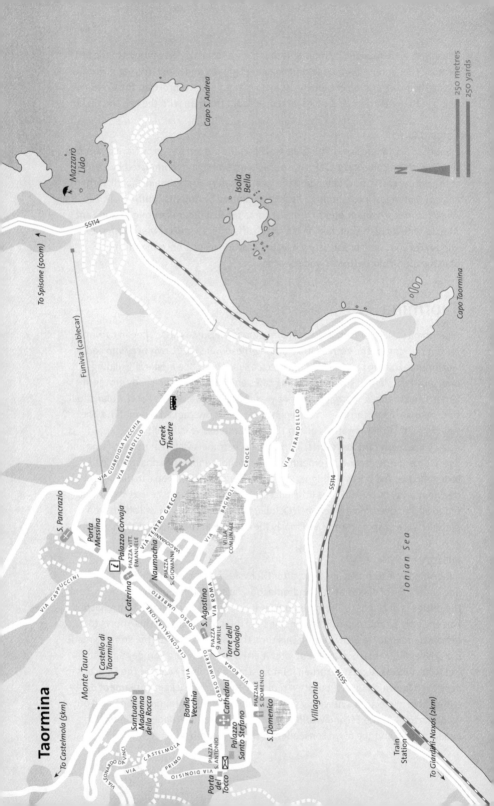

Taormina

To Castelmola (5km) →

← To Spisone (500m)

Funivia (cablecar)

SS114

Mazzarò Lido

Capo S. Andrea

Isola Bella

Capo Taormina

Ionian Sea

Monte Tauro

S. Pancrazio

Porta Messina

Palazzo Corvaja

VIA CAPPUCCINI

VIA GUARDIOLA VECCHIA

VIA PIRANDELLO

Greek Theatre

VIA TEATRO GRECO

VIA GIOVANNI DI GIOVANNI

Naumachia

PIAZZA VITT. EMANUELE

S. Caterina

PIAZZA S. GIOVANNI

CORSO UMBERTO

CIRCONVALLAZIONE

VILLA COMUNALE

VIA BAGNOLI CROCE

VIA PIRANDELLO

SS114

S. Agostino

PIAZZA 9 APRILE

VIA ROMA

Torre dell' Orologio

Castello di Taormina

Santuario Madonna della Rocca

VIA LEONARDO DA VINCI

Badia Vecchia

CORSO UMBERTO PRIMO

VIA CASTELMOLA

Cathedral

PIAZZA S. ANTONIO

Palazzo Santo Stefano

S. Domenico

PIAZZALE S. DOMENICO

Porta del Tocco

VIA DIONISIO

VIA ROMA

Villagonia

SS114

Train Station

To Giardini-Naxos (2km) →

N

250 metres
250 yards

Getting There and Around

From the Taormina Nord exit off the *autostrada*, take picturesque Via Luigi Pirandello, also the route of the buses from the railway station Taormina-Giardini; get off the bus at the Porta Messina, or look for a parking space (rare) – if you don't stop here you'll be up on top of the mountain before you know what hit you. Buses from Catania or Messina stop at the terminal on Via Pirandello, about 0.5km below the town.

Taormina is connected with its main beach, Mazzarò, by the *funivia* (cable-car), which runs every 15mins from 8am to 8pm (until 1am in summer). There are also **buses** down to Capo Taormina, Letojanni, and up to Castelmola. Other destinations include Giardini-Naxos, Catania and the Gola di Alcàntara. For the daily **coach excursions** to Mount Etna, Agrigento and Piazza Armerina, see the travel agents along Corso Umberto. Taormina is connected by **train** with, among other places, Messina, Catania, and Syracuse; the rail station is a period gem.

Tourist Information

Palazzo Corvaja, Piazza Santa Caterina, t 0942 23 243, *www.gate2taormina.com* (*open Mon–Fri 8–2 and 4–7, Sat 9–1 and 4–7, in summer also Sun 9–1*).

Sports and Activities

Taormina's main beach, **Mazzarò**, has every facility, including restaurants – as have other beaches in the area, such as **Lido Spisone** and **Lido Mazzeo** and the coves around pretty **Isola Bella** and **Capo Taormina**. Most visitors like to spend a day on a hike through the **Gola di Alcàntara** (*see* below), easily reachable by car or by bus from Taormina. There are municipal

tennis courts next to the Villa Comunale, and a number of places to rent a **bike or scooter** – for the Alcàntara gorge, or the wild and empty hills to the west of Taormina; for the really ambitious, the Rifugio Citelli near Etna's craters is only 50km away. For **diving** visit the Nike Diving Centre onthe road of Isola Bella (t 0942 47534, *www.divenike.com*). Now that the Isola Bella is a nature reserve there is much more to see underwater. For **helicopter tours** of Etna, Taormina and the area, call t 800 188488, *www.thesauron.com*.

Where to Stay

Taormina is packed with luxurious accommodation, both in the town and on the panoramic drives around it. Note that, where two prices are listed, the higher refers to high-season rates.

Taormina ✉ 98039

Luxury–Expensive

★★★★★Grand Hotel Timeo, Via Teatro Greco 59, t 0942 23801, *www.framon-hotels.it* (*luxury*). The first hotel in Taormina, the setting right below the Greek theatre is unbeatable and the views are panoramic. Furnished with real style and elegance, the service is smooth and the pool and terrace glamorous. Everything a luxury hotel should be.

★★★★Excelsior Palace, Via Toselli 8, t 0942 23 975, *excelsior@tao.it* (*luxury*). One of many hotels here with a spectacular location, and a pool set on a prom overlooking the Bay of Naxos.

★★★★★San Domenico Palace, Piazzale San Domenico 5, t 0942 23 701, *www.thi.it* (*luxury*). Top of the hotel list in Taormina and occupying a 15th-century monastery; its pool has a reputation as the loveliest in town but in reality feels rather narrow and cramped. Service can be patchy but there is nothing to

To Piazza Vittorio Emanuele

From sea level, Via Pirandello winds up past villas, hotels, the Anglican church of St George and the *funivia* station before finally flowing into **Porta Messina**, Taormina's front door. To the right is the church of **San Pancrazio**, built on the site of a temple to Serapean Zeus; the cella foundations are still visible. To the left, under the gate, fault the luxurious rooms, fabulous garden and great views. Its rates by far the steepest in Taormina.

★★★★**Hotel Villa Ducale**, Via Leonardo da Vinci 60, t 0942 28 153, *www.hotelvilladucale.it* (*expensive*). Converted from an old family villa, the rooms are individually furnished in the old Sicilian style, with all mod cons and private terraces. There is also a superb patio overlooking the view, for enjoying the delicious buffet breakfast or drinks in the evening; plus a free taxi service to the beach and charming service.

★★★**Villa Belvedere**, Via Bagnoli Croce 79, t 0942 23 791, *www.villabelvedere.it* (*expensive*). Another well-positioned villa-hotel with a garden terrace and pool, built in 1902 as a grand hotel. *Closed Nov–Mar.*

★★★★**Villa Fabbiano**, Via Pirandello 81, t 0942 626058 (*expensive*). This castle-like hotel is situated just below the town.

★★★★**Villa Paradiso**, Via Roma 2, t 09 42 23 922 (*expensive*). Few visitors notice this lovely hotel right on the edge of the old quarter. It has balconies and views of Etna from many rooms, and a good restaurant.

Moderate

★★★**Bel Soggiorno**, Via Pirandello 60, t 0942 23 342 (*moderate*). Great views can also be had from here, in smaller and quieter surroundings. *Closed Nov–Dec.*

★★★**Isabella**, Corso Umberto 58, t 0942 23 153, *www.gaishotels.com* (*moderate*). This is a good bet right in the centre of town.

Inexpensive–Budget

Taormina may be a posh resort, but it is by no means out of most people's reach – on the contrary, there is a wide range of accommodation for under €80.

★**Pensione Svizzera**, Via Pirandello 26, t 0942 23 790 (*inexpensive–moderate*). This place also has fine views. *Closed Dec–Feb.*

★★**Hotel Victoria**, Corso Umberto 81, t 0942 23372 (*inexpensive–moderate*). If you want to be in the heart of things, this is a comfortable place to stay, with a terrace that overlooks the Corso, so you can people-watch as you eat your breakfast.

★★**Villa Greta**, Via Leonardo da Vinci 44, t 0942 28 286 (*inexpensive*). A welcoming and well-kept, family-run place, though it's a bit of a climb up from the centre.

★★**Villa Chiara**, Via Don Bosco 10, t 0942 62 54 21 (*inexpensive*). Just north of the Corso, right in the centre, this place has air-conditioning and television in some rooms. *Closed Oct–March.*

Locanda Diana, Via Giovanni 6, t 0942 23 898 (*budget*). Come here for rock-bottom prices; it's in the centre near Porta Messina.

Locanda Moderno, on the SS114, t 0942 51 017 (*budget; slightly more expensive rooms with bathroom*). Another bottom-rung bargain, near the station and well below the town.

Near Mazzarò and Spisone Lidos
✉ 98030

★★★★**Villa Sant'Andrea**, Mazzarò, Via Nazionale 137, t 09 42 23 125, *www.framon-hotels.com* (*luxury*). The best choice in Mazzarò, this restored 19th-century villa has lovely rooms and an even lovelier subtropical garden – and even its own beach.

★★★★**Lido Méditerranée**, Spisone, t 0942 24 422 (*moderate*). This is an elegant old establishment, one of a fair share of hotels along the beaches under Taormina. The only trouble with Spisone is the noise from the railway line. *Closed Nov–Feb.*

★**Pensione Villa Caterina**, Mazzarò, Via Nazionale 155, t/f 09 42 24 709 (*moderate*). A good bet if you want to be right on the beach without paying the price. *Closed Nov–Feb.*

★**Villino Gallodoro**, Mazzarò, Via Nazionale 147, t 0942 23 860 (*inexpensive*). Cosy, bright,

lies the old town, along the pedestrian main street, **Corso Umberto I**, well-scrubbed, shoulder-to-shoulder with tourists and lined with smart cafés, ice cream parlours, designer boutiques and shops selling ceramics and tacky lava art. The Corso leads to Piazza Vittorio Emanuele, site of the magnificent **Palazzo Corvaja**, built in the 14th century and decorated in the local fashion with black lava and pink and only metres from the sea. *Closed Oct–Easter.*

Campeggio San Leo, Capo Taormina (off the SS114 south of Mazzarò), **t** 0942 24 658. The only campsite in the area.

Eating Out

If a few of Taormina's restaurants have been spoilt by having to cater for too many tourists, competition is fierce, and most do their best.

Angelo alla Terrazza, Corso Umberto 38, **t** 0942 24 411 (*expensive*). Also has a strong following. *Closed Thurs between Nov–Feb.*

Casa Grugno, Via Santa Maria de Greci, **t** 0942 21208 (*expensive*). Catalan-style 16th century farmhouse where Austrian chef Andreas Zangerl is ambitious with his menus, so don't expect traditional fare.

Granduca, Corso Umberto 172, **t** 0942 24 983 (*expensive*). A fashionable eaterie inside an old *palazzo*, considered to be one of the best restaurants in Taormina. Sicilian specialities are served, with a view over the Greek theatre; they also do excellent pizzas for around €10. *Closed Wed.*

Vicolo Stretto, Corso Umberto I 6, **t** 0942 24995 (*expensive*). Off the Corso on what must be Sicily's narrowest streets, this specializes in Sicilian dishes perfectly prepared. The terrace is lovely but service can be patchy. The *caponata* is heavenly. *Closed Mon in winter.*

A Zammàra, Via Fratelli 15, **t** 0942 24 408(*expensive*). Just off Corso Umberto, you'll be seated in an orange garden and served old Sicilian dishes with style. *Closed Wed except in Aug.*

La Botte, Piazza Santa Domenica, **t** 0942 24 198 (*moderate*). Can be great or awful, depending on your luck; there's a traditional Sicilian menu or inexpensive pizzas,

accompanied by a great wine list. The place has won prizes, and the locals seem to love it.

A Casitta, the village of Graniti. **t** 0942 47047 (*moderate*). It's worth making the journey a few kilometres up the Alcántara valley to be plies by endless antipasti by owner Pippo Lembo. Authentic Sicilian fare at very reasonable prices.

La Bouganville, Via Bagnoli Croci 88, **t** 0942 625218 (*inexpensive*). Opposite the Vila Comunale this is a perfect lunch stop with a sunny terrace and equally sunny service. There is a good set menu at €11 and the food is very fresh and tasty.

Bar Vitelli, Sàvoca. At the very entrance of town, this is a good spot for a coffee, or something stronger. Sit beneath the vine-laced pergola and watch the world pass by at medieval pace. You may recognise the bar from the wedding scene in *The Godfather.*

Pasticceria Etna, Corso Umberto I 112. The place to stock up on almond sweets in all shapes and forms.

Entertainment

From July to September, the city runs an arts festival called **Taormina Arte** (*www.taormina-arte.com*), with a full schedule of concerts, films and plays – many held in the transcendent setting of the Greek theatre.

One of the most important displays of Sicilian folklore takes place (funding allowing; not every year) at the end of May/beginning of June – **Il Raduno del Costume e del Carretto Siciliano**. Traditional puppet shows are performed, as well as folksongs and dances, and painted carts trundle around.

On most Fridays there's a **puppet show** at 5.30 in the Teatro San Nicola by the cathedral or in the Giardino Púbblico.

white pumice stone. Once the seat of the Sicilian parliament, the palace now houses the tourist office and **Museo d'Arte e Tradizioni Popolari** (*open Tues–Sun 9–1 and 4–8*), displaying nativity scenes, ex-votos, furniture and captivatingly quaint 19th and early 20th-century tableaux of saints whose miraculous interventions appear as comic-book thought bubbles depicting peasants suffering such mishaps as losing an eye playing tennis and falling off a merry-go-round. **Santa Caterina d'Alessandria** (*open daily 8am–one hour before sunset*), also in Piazza Vittorio Emanuele, was built in the 1600s over the **Roman Odeon**; next to the church are some of the seats, brick steps and part of the stage. Some **Imperial Roman baths** have been excavated towards the beginning of Via Teatro Greco, located behind the police station.

The Greek Theatre

Open daily 9am until one hour before sunset.

Via Teatro Greco, naturally enough, leads to Taormina's Greek theatre (the stage for arts events during summer). The ancient Greeks, some doltish scholars argue, had little thought for views, but dug their theatres out of the hills wherever it was most convenient. Yet here in Taormina it's hard to imagine that they didn't give the backdrop at least a thought – indeed, you have to wonder how drama could ever compete against such a spectacular panorama of sea, jutting coastline, rolling hills and a smouldering volcano. The theatre itself was originally constructed in the 3rd century BC and rebuilt in their characteristic brick by the Romans in the 2nd century AD; then it was given a stage building to shut off the view and, used exclusively for gladiatorial bouts. Some 333ft in diameter, it is the second largest in Sicily, after the theatre in Syracuse, and, although the cavea has fallen somewhat into disrepair, the scena is very well preserved. The columns above the theatre belonged to a portico which once encircled the cavea.

Down Corso Umberto I

Back to the Corso, in the main shopping area of town, steps descend to the so-called **Naumachia**, a Roman cistern that is now a small public garden, flanked by 18 Roman arches supporting houses along the Corso. In lively Piazza Nove Aprile, the **Belvedere** offers fabulous views down to the sea, and there are two churches, **Sant'Agostino**, built in 1488, and, at the top of the steps, the 17th-century church of **San Giuseppe**, converted into a library and art gallery. Passing beneath the **Torre dell'Orologio** (12th century, restored in the 17th) you enter the Borgo Medievale, the oldest and most charming quarter of Taormina, still retaining an Arabic touch or two, especially in its street plan.

The **cathedral**, in Piazza del Duomo, is a simple structure from the 13th century, with a later rose window and some fine paintings inside, including a polyptych of 1504 by Antonello de Saliba. Piazza del Duomo has a small **fountain** (1635) by the Montorsoli schoo. Below, the 16th-century **San Domenico** convent, used as German headquarters during the war, is now a luxury hotel. The end of the Corso is closed by the **Porta del Tocco** (1440). In **Piazza S. Antonio**, the town's western limit, a tiny church has been totally given over to housing a huge, ostentatious crib scene. Down the steps, off Piazza Sant'Antonio, the **Palazzo del Duca di Santo Stefano** (*open daily 9–12.30 and 3–6*), one of the last palaces built by the Normans in Sicily, is one of the town's best-looking buildings, now a sculpture museum displaying statues by Giuseppe Marzullo, a contemporary Sicilian sculptor. Above the Corso, on Via Dionisio Primo, stands the battlemented tower of the 15th-century **Badia Vecchia** (the old convent), with its wide, pointed windows.

Below the town, on Via Bagnoli Croce, is one of Taormina's greatest delights – one few tourists ever see, though it is a popular venue for post-wedding photographs. The **Villa Comunale** – or **Jardino Pubblico** – (*open daily 9–10, summer 8.30–12midnight; free*), a century ago the private garden of a Scots woman who had to leave Britain in a hurry after an affair with the future Edward VII, is now one of the most beautiful public parks anywhere, an exotic garden with fanciful brick pavilions (one a five-storey Italianate pagoda with rickety wooden balconies like a tree house), a 'stone circle' (complete with sacrificial picnic tables), a torpedo memorial to Italian sailors and a terrace with tremendous views. Those ubiquitous Taormina feral cats are particularly profuse in this garden, thanks to hand-outs.

Taormina has its own **cable car**, which takes you down to a **beach** – not one of Sicily's best, with shingle and some obtrusive hotels too close for comfort. The free public areas are very limited.

Castelmola

For another superb view of the surrounding region, you can go on foot (Via Circonvallazione to the Mulattiera Castel Taormina) or by car (Via Castelmola) to the **Santuario Madonna della Rocca** and the **Castello di Taormina** – of little interest in themselves, but commanding unforgettable panoramas.

For an even better view, ascend to **Castelmola**, 5km up the mountain from Taormina, and a pleasant enough walk in itself (or take the bus). There is another medieval castle, but the village is most famous for its almond wine, which you can readily try in the local bars, and it's on sale in several shops. If it's not heady enough, continue towards Castelmola's cemetery, where a road heads up steeply to **Monte Venere** and its col, a 90min walk rewarded with a sublime vision of Etna, the coast, and the mountains retreating into the hinterland. There are some magnificently scenic, empty roads to nowhere reaching out from here.

Giardini-Naxos

Just down the hill from Taormina, Giardini-Naxos is Sicily's fastest-growing resort, with its long beach of golden sand, modern hotels, swimming pools, garden district of Contrada Recanati and convention centre.

Yet while the Giardini half is as new as anything in Sicily, Naxos (signposted from Giardini, on Capo Schisò) was nothing less than the first Greek colony on the island. These first pioneers found Giardini's sands as attractive as do modern sun-worshippers – the ancient Greeks beached their ships rather than anchoring them in deep harbours.

Getting There

Giardini-Naxos is linked by bus with Taormina, Messina and Catania. The Gola di Alcántara can be reached by bus from Taormina.

Tourist Information

Giardini-Naxos: Via Tysandros 76/E, facing the beach. **t** 0942 51 010 (*open Mon–Sat 8.30–2 and 4–7*).

Where to Stay and Eat

Giardini-Naxos ⊠ 98035

This stretch of the coast is a popular riviera for many Italian families.

****Naxos Beach Hotel**, Via Recanati 26, **t** 0942 51 551 (*expensive*). Huge, and situated on the shore with a pool and tennis court.

***Arathena Rocks**, Via Calcide Eubea 55, **t** 0942 51 349 (*moderate*). Smaller and more personal, with a good restaurant.

Villa Mora Via Naxos 47, **t** 0942 51 839 (*inexpensive*). Central, clean, friendly and very efficiently run.

*La Sirena**, Via Schisò 36, **t** 0942 51 853 (*budget, half-board only in August*). One of several *pensioni*, this pleasant place has a restaurant (*inexpensive*) that serves the old favourite, pasta with aubergine, and a small selection of fish and meat dishes.

La Cambusa, Via Schisò (*moderate*). A good option if you want to eat by the sea (at the end of the road by the pier, with a sign for 'Terrazza sul Mare').

Noemi, up in the hills at Gallodoro, **t** 0942 37 162 (*moderate*). Don't eat a thing until you arrive: for €25 a head you can fill up on a wonderful set menu that includes everything from *antipasta* to the excellent house wine, *grappa* and coffee.

Ancient Naxos

Founded *c.* 750 BC, the name of this first Greek colony derives from the Cycladian island of Naxos, but most of the original colonists are thought to have come from Euboea and Ionia. They found the native Sikels easy to encroach on, and before long the Naxians were founding their own colonies.

Troubles, however, were never far away, in the form of the newer but more powerful Dorian Greek settlements. With few defences, Naxos was attacked in turn by Hippocrates of Gela (495 BC) and Hieron of Syracuse (476 BC), and survived, only to choose the wrong side in the battle between Athens and Syracuse. In retaliation, the Syracusan tyrant Dionysius the Elder razed Naxos in 403 BC, selling its citizens into slavery. He gave the territory back to the Sikels, though they preferred the heights of Taormina, and eventually the Naxians who escaped bondage settled there as well. The city by the sea was heard from no more.

The Excavations

Open daily 9am until one hour before sunset.

The well-ordered site of ancient Naxos is built on the ancient, level stream of lava that forms Capo Schisò; it enjoys a beautiful setting, with both the sea and Mount Etna for a backdrop. The remains are scant, but so are the visitors.

Archaeologists so far have uncovered the polygonal city walls, the remains of two temples believed to have been part of a celebrated sanctuary of Aphrodite, and two kilns; the street plan (a new layout superimposed on the more ancient one), along with some Hellenistic tombs, suggests that at one time settlers returned to Naxos. An old Bourbon fort on the cape has been converted into a **Museo Archeológico**, chronicling the history of the site into the Byzantine era; among the exhibits are terracotta ex-votos from the temple of Aphrodite, coins from the 5th century BC, and antefixes, or architectural roof ornaments, with female figurines and the head of fertility-wine god Silenus, who was especially associated with the colony for the heady wines it produced.

The Gola di Alcántara (Alcántara Gorge)

Open daily 9am until one hour before sunset; adm, €7 including boots.

From Giardini you can take a walk on the wild side: through the dramatic, volcanic wonderland of the Gola di Alcántara, or Alcántara Gorge, carved by the river of the same name through the hardened basalt of one of Etna's ancient eruptions, 64ft deep and a mere 9ft wide in some places. Like a multi-layered Russian torte, the basalt of the steep walls has revealed a variety of colours when sliced; along the way is a host of unusual stone formations sculpted by the elements. To enter the gorge, head up 17km on SS185 to the parking area, where a lift awaits to lower you into the scenic abyss. It is very commercial here, with a restaurant and bar and shop, but do get the boots or salopettes that they offer here as the water is freezing and you definitely need rubber boots to get a grip on the bottom. It isn't a country stroll: take your bathing suit and don the rubber boots. If you can, try to avoid the picnic scrum on Sundays. Plenty of tour buses depart from Taormina.

At the western end of the gorge, a couple of kilometres beyond the parking area, lies **Francavilla di Sicilia**, with a medieval castle and bridge spanning the Alcántara; the ruins near the bridge belong to a domed Byzantine church.

Mount Etna and Around

I do not think I shall ever forget the sight of Etna at sunset; the mountain almost invisible in a blur of pastel grey, glowing on the top and then repeating its shape, as though reflected, in a wisp of grey smoke, with the whole horizon behind radiant with pink light, fading gently into a grey pastel sky. Nothing I have ever seen in Art or Nature was quite so revolting.
Evelyn Waugh

If you happen to make the crossing of the Strait on the clearest of days, Etna will be part of your welcome to Sicily, perhaps with a plume of smoke above its crater. Usually you won't see it at all, due to the entourage of clouds its heat tends to create. In fact, you may spend a week around the volcano, even circumnavigating it, and never catch a glimpse of the terrible cone at its summit. Which is all just as well – when you do see it, it is perhaps the most disturbing sight nature can offer on this planet. Doubtless Etna takes some joy in reminding us how small we are. This great smouldering boil that pushed itself nearly 11,000ft up from the sea covers a larger

Getting Around

For many, the ascent up the mountain is the highlight of a visit to Sicily, though disappointingly the summit is often swathed in cloud. The main route up is from the south, the **Strada dell'Etna**, beginning in Catania. If you do not have a car, there is a daily bus (AST) at 8am from Catania's Stazione Centrale to Rifugio Sapienza that returns at 4pm, plus plenty of tour excursions, which can easily be arranged by travel agents in Catania and Taormina; these supply the necessary outer wear for the top of the volcano (it's freezing and gusty up there, even in August). The trip takes an entire day.

You can drive or take the bus to Refugio Sapienza and from there cobble together a visit to the crater. But bear in mind that the Refugio is teeming with souvenir shops and lost-looking tourists mulling over how they will get to the crater.

It's better to organise a visit with a specialist operator with expert vulcanologists. the Gruppo Guide Alpine Etna Sud (**t** 095 791 4755) take a group of ten every morning at 9 along iwth their vulcanologist.

Another possibility is the **jeeps** which leave every half hour from the disused cable car stop or SITAS mini-bus from Nicolosi (buses from Catania) to the Torre del Filosofo.

You can pick up the secondary approach, **Etna Nord**, by following the signs south of Taormina; watch carefully for the signs, otherwise you may end up on an unplanned safari of the lower slopes.

The very beautiful small towns and villages at the foot of Etna can easily be visited on the **Circumetnea Railway**, from Corso delle Provincie 13 in Catania (**t** 095 541 111, **t** 095 541 250, *www.circumetnea.it*); to see everything take the 8.45am train or earlier. *See* also pp. 289–293.

Specialist tours of the area are offered by **GeoEtna Explorer** who organise nature excursions in the area led by expert geologists, *www.geoetnaexplorer.com*. **Parco dell'Etna** also offer different itineraries to the crater, call **t** 095 82 1111, *www.parcoetna.it*.

Better still, cross Etna on **horseback** with Centro Ippico Amico del Cavallo, **t** 095 461 882, *www.amicodelcavallo.it*.

Tourist Information

Linguaglossa: Piazza Annunziata, **t** 095 643 094 (*open Mon–Sat 9–12 and 3–6.30, Sun 9–12.30*).

Nicolosi: Via Garibaldi 63, **t** 095 911 505/090 911 784 (*open Mon–Sat 8.45–1 and 4–9*).

Where to Stay and Eat

Nicolosi ✉ 95030

There aren't many places to sleep under the volcano, so it is strongly advised to ahead to avoid getting stuck.

★★★Biancaneve, Via Etnea 163, **t** 095 911 176, (*inexpensive*). Fifteen kilometres from both Etna and the sea; pool, tennis, and access for the disabled are added pluses.

Rifugio Sapienza, **t** 095 911 062 (*budget*). Again, do ring ahead to book at this mountain refuge.

Camping Etna, Via Goethe, **t** 095 914 309. A pleasant campsite in the pinewoods. *Closed Nov–April.*

Grotta del Gallo, Via Madonna delle Grazie 40, **t** 095 911 301 (*inexpensive*). This restaurant serves delicious Sicilian dishes. *Closed Mon and Nov–Dec.*

Zafferana Etnea ✉ 95019

★★★Airone, Via Cassone 67, **t** 095 708 18 19, *www.hotel-airone.it* (*moderate*). In a lovely location, with a garden; good if somewhat pricey meals; have breakfast in the bar.

★★★Primavera dell'Etna, Via Cassone 86, **t** 095 708 23 48, *www.hotel-primavera.it* (*budget*). Not everyone's taste, but well provided with facilities: tennis, games for the kids, disco, restaurant and pizzeria.

Bronte

Conti Gallenti, Corso Umberto I. This *pasticceria* puts Bronte's pistacchios scrumptious cakes and ice creams. *Closed Tues.*

Randazzo

Veneziano, Via dei Romano 8, **t** 095 799 13 53 (*inexpensive*). A good place to come for reasonably priced home-cooked lunch. *Closed Mon, and Sun eve.*

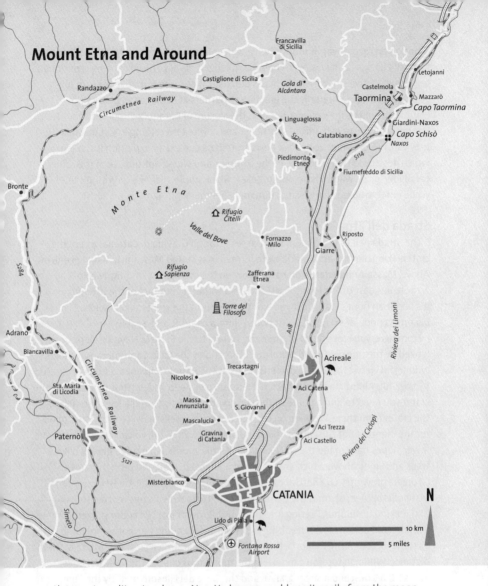

Mount Etna and Around

Francavilla di Sicilia

Castiglione di Sicilia

Gola di Alcántara

Castelmola

Letojanni

Randazzo

Taormina

Mazzarò

Capo Taormina

Circumetnea Railway

Linguaglossa

Giardini-Naxos

Calatabiano

Capo Schisò

Naxos

Piedimonte Etneo

Fiumefreddo di Sicilia

Bronte

Monte Etna

Rifugio Citelli

Fornazzo -Milo

Riposto

Valle del Bove

Giarre

Rifugio Sapienza

Zafferana Etnea

S284

Adrano

Torre del Filosofo

Riviera dei Limoni

A18

Biancavilla

Acireale

Circumetnea Railway

Trecastagni

Sta. Maria di Licodia

Nicolosi

Aci Catena

Massa Annunziata

S. Giovanni

Mascalucia

Aci Trezza

Paternò

Gravina di Catania

Aci Castello

Riviera dei Ciclopi

S121

Misterbianco

CATANIA

Simeto

Lido di Plaia

N

10 km

5 miles

Fontana Rossa Airport

area than metropolitan London or New York – you could see it easily from the moon. As unpredictable as any volcano, it has the power to bring death and destruction to tens of thousands in a day's work, whenever it has a mind to.

At 10,902ft, Mount Etna (in Arabic 'Gibel Utlamat' – hence the Sicilian name Mongibello) has little to do with the rest of Sicily's geology. Vulcanologists say its career began under the sea, gradually rising to become part of the island. More than 135 eruptions have been recorded, beginning in 475 BC, when both Pindar and Aeschylus described the awesome volcanic explosion. Several eruptions in the Middle Ages reached the sea; from that time come the Norman legends of King Arthur and his knights – according to the Sicilians, they sleep beneath Etna to this day. The worst eruption on record was in 1669, when a wide gap opened up from the summit to the town of Nicolosi, and lava overwhelmed much of Catania. The volcano has continued to be quite active since then, if not as ruinously.. It erupted from five vents in July 2001, necessitating not only the erection of barriers at Sapienza to protect the complex from the flow of lava, but also the closure of Catania's airport as the towering plume of ash drifted southeast and covered everything in Catania in a fine grey ash. In December 2002, lava flows from Etna caused an explosion in Sapienza which destroyed two buildings in the complex and wiped out the use of the cable cars. Now locals watch its smoke intensely. Black smoke means everything's fine, while white smoke means watch out, frail ephemeral humans.

Strada dell'Etna

The Strada dell'Etna from Catania passes through **Gravina di Catania**, where the craters Pomiciari di Santa Maria were formed in 1381, and **Mascalucia**, a wine centre. Above, **Massa Annunziata**'s orchards grow on the cooled lava of 1669. **Nicolosi**, at 2,290ft, lies east of the Monti Rossi craters, another by-product of the 1669 fireworks; it's about an hour's walk up if you want to peer into the smoking pits. Nicolosi has become a popular ski resort, with two ski lifts, a chairlift and a cable-car.

From here, you cross fields of more recent lava to the **Serra la Nave** ski slopes, over-looked by the fine old Grand Hotel dell'Etna, and to the **Casa Cantoniera**, which has wonderful views. The Strada dell'Etna ends at the **Rifugio Sapienza**, a hostel operated by the Club Alpino Italiano at 5,822ft. Here you can sleep and eat, but to ascend to the crater you need to find a guide to the **Observatory** (9,650ft), and a jeep or coach to the crater from there. Working on the veteran party-goer's premise that ash is good for the plants, if not the carpet, the same applies to Etna: the volcanic deposits on the lower slopes have made the soil extremely fertile, producing orange groves, olive trees and vines, above which are scattered orchards of fruit and pistachio trees.

Forests grow up to 6,888ft; above that height the only plant is the *spino santo* (*Astigalus aetnensis*) amid the barren lunar landscape of volcanic matter, smoking and reeking of sulphur. Peering into the multiple depths of the crater is a remarkable, sublime and perhaps even revolting experience, depending on your temperament – as is the view of Sicily, Calabria, the Aeolian Islands and, on a clear day, Malta far in the distance. While on top you can take in the monstrous chasm, the **Valle del Bove**, whose sides descend a sheer 2,742ft, and the **Torre del Filosofo** built by the Romans to celebrate Hadrian's ascent of the volcano, and named after history's first known vulcanologist, the philosopher Empedocles from Agrigento, who mysteriously disap-peared from the crater in 433 BC leaving, according to legend, only his slippers at the edge of the rim.

The **Ascent of Etna Nord**, commencing off the SS114 at Mangano, climbs up to **Zafferana Etnea**, a charming summer resort with many hotels, which escaped the flow in 1992 by the skin of its teeth thanks to several well-aimed lumps of concrete dropped from helicopters. It has long been famous for its honey (especially orange blossom) and claims to produce 40 per cent of the national output. Catch the market on Friday or visit Fresta on Via Garibaldi 237, **t** 095 708 1979 for the perhaps most delicious and subtly-flavoured honey you will taste.

Beyond is **Fornazzo-Milo** with views of the Valle del Bove. Here a road branches off to the alpine refuges Citelli (5,710ft) and Sucai (5,210ft), while the main road goes to **Linguaglossa**, a newer ski resort amid tall trees, with a national ski school and the four ski lifts on the Piano Provenzana. In Linguaglossa you can pop into the **tourist office**, which has a showcase room of Etna's minerals, flora and fauna; the **Chiesa Madre** has some exquisitely carved 18th-century wood panels and stalls. There is also a good market for souvenirs in the Piano Provenzana.

Villages around Mount Etna: on the Circumetnea Railway

One of the great train rides of Italy, or possibly anywhere, the Circumetnea trundles its way at no great speed around the base of Etna through an exhilarating blend of scenery. If you are starting from Taormina, you need a reasonably early start. To do it anti-clockwise, you could start from Riposto or Giarre (mainline trains); otherwise begin from Catania, where a metro connects the rail station with the Circumetnea rail station (some way off). Direct trains take 3hrs 30mins, but you'll probably have to change at Randazzo, itself worth a stop anyway.

Paternò is the first important stop along the tracks, 20km west of Catania, with a nearly cubic Norman **castle** at the top of the town, built in 1073 by Count Roger. The views from the top are so good that the Germans used it as an observation post during the Second World War. Here Frederick II of Aragon died on his way to Enna. There are some good frescoes in the chapel of **Santa Barbara**, and the convent of **San Francesco** is a French Gothic affair from the 15th century. **Biancavilla**, 15km from Paternò, glistens with its orange groves; **Adrano**, the next station a few kilometres further on, was founded in 400 BC by Dionysius I of Syracuse as Adranon, named after the Sikel god whose temple was near the site. The **castle**, another founded by Count Roger in the 11th century, has been turned into a prehistory museum and art gallery (*open Mon–Fri 9–1 and 4–7*). Near here are a few vestiges of the **Greek wall**, and the **Chiesa Madre**, also Norman, incorporating columns from an ancient Greek temple. The harsh cold stone of the 18th-century church of **Santa Lucia** (*open daily 7–10am*) is softened by the elegant palms of the **Vittoria Gardens** below; you could be in Spain. At Easter, Adrano presents a passion play, one of the most famous in Sicily. Near Adrano is the recently excavated Sikel town of **Mendolito** (8th–6th centuries BC), where a long, as yet untranslatable, inscription in Sikel was discovered, along with a treasure-trove of bronze artefacts.

Bronte and Randazzo

The Circumetnea continues round to **Bronte**, a town founded by Emperor Charles V in 1535. In 1799, Ferdinand III of Naples elevated Bronte to a dukedom when he bestowed it on Nelson for services rendered: the admiral had whisked the king away to Palermo just as the French were entering Naples (*see* 'Parco della Favorita', p.95). The ducal seat in Bronte, **Castello di Maniace** (*open 8am–one hour before sunset*) was founded by Margaret of Navarre in 1173 as a convent, marking the site where the Byzantine general George Maniakes defeated the Saracens in 1040. Although Nelson died before ever setting eyes on it, his heirs, the Bridports, held on to Castello di Maniace until 1978; now the town has taken over and is slowly restoring the interior. In his day, Nelson received a cool £3,000 annually from his dukedom, much of it derived from the pistachio orchards that envelop the town; Bronte, after all, is the Pistachio Capital of Italy, producing a small but rarefied crop harvested in September and October, but only in odd-numbered years.

Bronte has two curious **literary associations**. In 1905, the Scottish poet Fiona Macleod (William Sharp) died here, and he lies buried under an Ionic cross. The second is a result of the obsession a certain Rev. Patrick Prunty had for Nelson, so strong that he changed his name to Brontë (adding an umlaut to the 'e' for effect). He then had three daughters, Emily, Charlotte and Anne, who made the name famous in places where no one has ever heard of Bronte, Sicily.

Five kilometres out of Bronte, an agrotourist reconstruction of a typical rural settlement of bygone days, the **Museo dell'Antica Civiltà Locale** (*open daily 7–1 and 2–5*), is centred on an Arab-Norman building dating from around AD 1000, which was for centuries inhabited by monks skilled in making paper and curing animal skins. On display are the tools of their craft, together with others used over the centuries by local artisans, a mini zoo where Tibetan goats are crossbred, and, of all things, a chastity belt.

Randazzo, under the north slopes of the volcano, is the largest and perhaps the most interesting village of Mount Etna, and site of a popular Sunday-morning wood, textile and metal-work market. Although built out of lava, it has never succumbed to an eruption, and has preserved its medieval atmosphere, although it suffered Allied bombardments when the Nazis made it one of their last strongholds in Sicily. The private **Museo Vagliasindi**, on the Corso, No.265 (*open Mon–Sat 9–6; to see it, ask the owner*), houses a good collection of finds from a nearby Greek necropolis.

The town's **Cathedral of Santa Maria** dates from the 13th century. **San Niccolò** is a hundred years younger, with later additions and a few Gagini works. **San Martino** has a lovely campanile, although the church itself was damaged in the war. Next to the church the restored 13th-century **castle-prison** bears bullet holes which commemorate the final German defeat in August 1943. From here the Circumetnea continues to the winter resort of Linguaglossa (*see* 'Strada dell'Etna', above).

The Coast from Taormina to Catania

The crowded and often messy coast here is loaded with campsites, castles and beaches. Starting from the north, **Calatabiano** has a lofty medieval castle, north of which are steps descending into the Gola di Alcántara (*see* 'Giardini-Naxos', above). **Giarre**, farther south, is a wine-producing centre and the first coastal stop on the

Circumetnea Railway; Via L. Sturzo is lined with handicraft shops and manufacturers; Giuseppe Cicala, at No.59, is one of the last to make authentic Sicilian puppets.

Acireale

A mere infant among the cities of Sicily, Acireale (pop. 46,000) is no older than AD 1326, founded after the big eruption of 1169 had turned most of this coast into a bed of lava. This Aci is 'royal' as a special privilege granted by the Spanish kings, who took it under their personal rule. Acireale is built on streams of lava, and has become an attractive tourist centre for its sandy beach, the **sulphur baths at Santa Venera** (*open Mon–Sat 7–12*, **t** *095 601 508, www.terme.acireale.gte.it*), the 'most beautiful Carnival in Sicily', and its venerable ice-cream-making tradition, dating back to the days when it made use of Etna's snow. Sited on cliffs 500ft above the sea, Acireale was rebuilt after the 1693 earthquake, giving it a pleasant Baroque core around

Land of the Cyclopes

Beyond Giarre begins the kingdom of the Acis – at least nine towns and villages share this prefix. From the ancient Greeks there is record of a village called Akis, probably somewhere near Aci Trezza. This gave its name to the River Aci, which vanished in the Middle Ages when a lava flow from Etna made the waters change their course.

In Greek mythology, the river sprang out of the earth where the shepherd Acis died, murdered by Polyphemus, the Cyclops, for jealousy of the maiden sea nymph Galatea. Polyphemus had done the deed in approved Cyclopean fashion, flattening the poor shepherd with a great boulder. He later tried to serve Odysseus and his men in the same fashion. The mighty one-eyed Cyclopes, once a race of smiths who had crafted the thunderbolt for Zeus, had decayed to a race of herdsmen without gods or laws; cannibalism was only one of their more unpleasant habits. Polyphemus had captured the Greeks and already dined on a few of them, when Odysseus got him drunk and put out his eye. The next morning, when the Cyclops rolled back the big stone that covered the mouth of his cave, the Greeks made their escape by hiding under the bellies of Polyphemus's sheep, which shared the cave with him. Once safely (so he thought) on his ship, Odysseus couldn't resist a mocking goodbye to the blind Cyclops, who responded by tossing after him the great boulders that can be seen today off the coast near Aci Trezza, called by the Sicilians I Ciclopi.

The fiery cauldron of Etna, of course, was the Forge of Hephestos (Vulcan), god of all smiths. Who knows but that behind the vast complex of religions, fairy tales and garbled travellers' accounts that underlies the *Odyssey* and the rest of Greek mythology, there may be a real memory of ancient craftsmen – the same fellows who get credit for building the 'Cyclopean' walls of the oldest cities of Italy and Greece. Perhaps the figure of the Cyclops represents the Greek opinion of the native inhabitants of Sicily, who had culturally known better days when the Greeks found them, in the 8th century BC. As a final note, the town of Bronte (*see above*), on the other side of Etna, recalls Brontes, son of Mother Earth and father of all the Cyclopes.

Getting Around

Acireale is on the train line between Catania and Taormina. There are also frequent buses stopping at most towns along this stretch of coast.

Tourist Information

Acireale: Corso Umberto 179, **t** 095 89199 (*open June–Sept Mon–Sat 8–2 and 4.30–7.30; Oct–May Mon–Fri 8–2 and 4–7, Sat 8–2*).

Where to Stay and Eat

Acireale ✉ 95024

****Aloha d'Oro, Via A. de Gasperi 10, **t** 095 768 7001, *www.hotel-aloha.com* (*moderate–expensive, half-board only in Aug*). The best bet in Acireale, with a pool, proximity to the sea, and the best restaurant in the area (*expensive*), featuring superb fish soup, meat grilled over an open fire and irresistible ice cream. Apart from the fine Sicilian specialities there are very satisfying pizzas for around €7.

****Park Hotel Capomulini, at Capo Mulini, **t** 095 877 511, *www.parkhotelcapomulini.it* (*moderate–expensive, half-board only in Aug*). A great favourite, mainly because of its pleasant setting and seawater pool and other fitness centre facilities that are the result of recent refurbishment.

La Timpa, Via Santa Maria La Stella 25, **t** 095 764 81 55. Acireale's campsite.

Bettola, **t** 095 876 352 (*inexpensive*). One of a number of restaurants in Santa Maria La Scala, a little fishing village at the port just below the town. They'll serve you up the day's catch along with some fine Sicilian white wines.

Panoramico, on the Acireale–Santa Maria Ammalati road, **t** 095 885 291 (*inexpensive*). Delicious specialities from sea and land, and homemade ice cream, are served here. *Closed Mon.*

Aci Castello ✉ 95020

Aci Castello is really within in the suburbs of Catania.

****Grand Hotel Baia Verde, Via Angelo Musco 8, Cannizzaro, **t** 095 491 522, *www.baiaverde.it* (*luxury*). Overlooking the sea, each room has a living area and terrace all arranged round a pool area strung with palms. Inviting in the extreme.

****Catania Sheraton, Via A. da Messina 45, Cannizzaro, **t** 095 271 557 (*expensive*). This sumptuous hotel has luxury rooms and some delectable things on offer in its restaurant (*expensive*) and a beach across the road.

***Excelsior Palace Terme, Via delle Terme 103, Acireale, **t** 095 768 8111, *www.shr.it/ excelsiorpalace.html* (*expensive*). A 19th-century grain mill that has been converted into this big modern hotel with a pleasant pool and arrangements with the thermal baths for treatment programmes.

Villa delle Rose, Via Nazionale 15 (*moderate*). Throughout the summer and at weekends this trattoria is packed with Catanese, who come to enjoy the view from the saloon and the seafood from the Gulf of Catania. Very good *pasta alla Norma. Closed Mon and Nov.*

Pizzeria (*inexpensive*). Look out for the pizzeria that sits at the foot of the Norman castle and has a view of the bay, and is ideal place for watching the evening *passeggiata*. On the menu is a wide selection of *antipasti* and pizza, with mussels as a regular feature.

central Piazza del Duomo and Piazza Vigo. Here, the monuments include the **cathedral**, with a 19th-century neo-Gothic façade by G. B. Basile and a lavish interior, and the adjacent **SS. Apostoli**. The **Palazzo Comunale** (1659) is an example of bizarre Spanish-Sicilian Baroque.

The **Biblioteca Zelantea**, in Via Marchese Siciliano (*open Mon–Fri 10–7*), is a library, museum and art gallery, which has some beautiful drawings and a painting attributed to Rubens. The **Teatro dei Pupi**, on Via Alessi (*under restoration, ask tourist office* *for information*), gives performances in the summer; there are lovely views of Etna from the **Villa Belvedere** park on the northern edge of town.

Just inland from Acireale is **Trecastagni** ('the three chestnut trees'), with one of the most beautiful Renaissance churches in Sicily, the **Chiesa Madre**, built by the sculptor Antonello Gagini. Here, on the night of 9 May, thousands pay tribute to the Three Saintly Brothers (Cirino, Alfio and Filadelfo) with fireworks; the next day, barefoot pilgrims dressed all in red run up from Santuario dei Santi Martiri to the Chiesa Madre, where they light candles to the three saints, then run back. Traditional carts pulled by bedecked horses and mules, and Catanians on bicycles, accompany the valiant runners.

Aci Castello

Aci Castello, facing the islets of the Cyclopes, derives its name both from Aci and from the **castle** built in 1297 by Roger di Lauria, who rebelled against Frederick II of Aragon. So impregnable was this fortress that only by building wooden siege towers the same height (an old Greek and Roman trick) could Frederick reduce it. The castle, a splendid gaunt structure resembling the prow of a beached ship, contains a new **Museo Archeológico e Geologico** (*open June–Sept, Tues–Sun 9–8; Oct–May, Tues–Sun 9–1 and 3–5*); the whole overlooks the sea, the strange rocks of the Cyclops, and the throng of holidaymakers from Catania who have made the 'Riviera dei Ciclopi' the most popular stretch of coast in the province. Nearby is **Aci Trezza**, a lively offshoot of Aci Castello, with streets jammed with cars, bars and people in summer.

Catania

By any measure, this is western Europe's most degraded city, and the Catanese have no one but themselves to blame. Unlike Palermo or Naples, this city does not have the Mafia or the Camorra to suck its blood (though there is evidence the Mafia has made great inroads here in the last decade). Neither can it claim poverty as an excuse: Sicily's second city and main business centre (pop. 338,000) makes quite a good living from trade and industry. In fact there are two Catanias: the modern, up-to-date suburbs on the north and west, where almost all the Catanese have fled, and the once-beautiful Baroque centre, now surrounded by a blackening lava-paved inferno of trash, crime and despair. Perhaps things are changing: a few brightly restored old buildings do stand out among the general ruin, and a group of centre-left politicians have recently taken control of the city's notoriously crooked government. But, for now, you can cruise the streets of this perfect dystopia and enjoy the aroma of an urban carcass that is rotting away.

A few years back, when the mayor of Catania proposed making a bid for the Mediterranean Games, people turned out in big demonstrations against it – the anti-games leaders weren't shy about saying that the embarrassment of showing their city off to the world would be a little too much to take. The rest of Sicily doesn't much

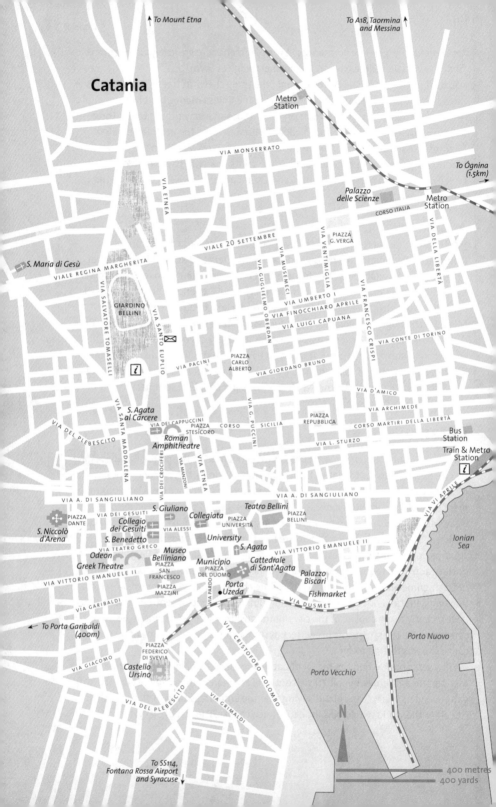

Catania

To Mount Etna

To A18, Taormina and Messina

Metro Station

VIA MONSERRATO

To Ógnina (1.5km)

Palazzo delle Scienze

CORSO ITALIA

Metro Station

VIA DELLA LIBERTÀ

VIA ETNEA

VIALE 20 SETTEMBRE

PIAZZA G. VERGA

S. Maria di Gesù

VIALE REGINA MARGHERITA

VIA SALVATORE TOMASELLI

GIARDINO BELLINI

VIA SANTO EUPLIO

VIA CUGLIELMO OBERDAN

VIA MUSEMECI

VIA UMBERTO I

VIA FINOCCHIARO APRILE

VIA LUIGI CAPUANA

VIA VENTIMIGLIA

VIA FRANCESCO CRISPI

VIA CONTE DI TORINO

VIA PACINI

PIAZZA CARLO ALBERTO

VIA GIORDANO BRUNO

VIA D'AMICO

VIA ARCHIMEDE

VIA SANTA MADDALENA

S. Agata al Carcere

VIA DEL CAPPUCCINI

PIAZZA STESICORO

Roman Amphitheatre

VIA DEI CROCIFERI

VIA MANZONI

VIA ETNEA

CORSO

VIA G. PUCCINI

SICILIA

VIA PUCCINI

PIAZZA REPUBBLICA

VIA L. STURZO

CORSO MARTIRI DELLA LIBERTÀ

Bus Station

Train & Metro Station

VIA DEL PLEBESCITO

VIA A. DI SANGIULIANO

VIA A. DI SANGIULIANO

VIA VI APRILE

Ionian Sea

S. Niccolò d'Arena

PIAZZA DANTE

VIA DEI GESUITI

Collegio dei Gesuiti

S. Benedetto

VIA ALESSI

VIA TEATRO GRECO

S. Giuliano

Collegiata

PIAZZA UNIVERSITÀ

University

S. Agata

Teatro Bellini

PIAZZA BELLINI

VIA VITTORIO EMANUELE II

Odeon Greek Theatre

Museo Belliniano

PIAZZA SAN FRANCESCO

Municipio

PIAZZA DEL DUOMO

Cattedrale di Sant'Agata

Palazzo Biscari

VIA VITTORIO EMANUELE II

PIAZZA MAZZINI

VIA PARDO

Porta Uzeda

Fishmarket

VIA DUSMET

VIA GARIBALDI

To Porta Garibaldi (400m)

PIAZZA FEDERICO DI SVEVIA

VIA CRISTOFORO COLOMBO

Porto Nuovo

VIA GIACOMO

Castello Ursino

VIA GRIMALDI

Porto Vecchio

VIA DEL PLEBESCITO

To SS114, Fontana Rossa Airport and Syracuse

N

400 metres
400 yards

care for Catania; in fact, far surpassing any political issue, the city has become the favourite subject for Sicilian graffiti.

History

Chalcidians from Naxos founded Catania in 729 BC, on the fertile plain known as the Laestrygonian Fields, named after the cannibalistic Laestrygones in Book 10 of the *Odyssey*; in spite of such unpromising neighbours, it prospered from the first. Catania's tyrant Carondas drew up a code of laws in the 7th century BC which were adopted by all the Ionian colonies of Magna Graecia. The Syracusans under Hieron I took the city in 476 BC and exiled its inhabitants, but in 461 the Catanians triumphantly returned and sent Hieron's Doric colonists packing.

An ally of Athens, Catania was the Athenians' base in the ill-starred Great Expédition, and suffered the consequences when Dionysius of Syracuse sold the inhabitants into slavery in 403 BC. Himilco the Carthaginian, Timoleon and Pyrrhus, followed by the inevitable Romans, trace the domination of the city up until Christian times. Augustus rewarded Catania for having supported him in the civil war against Pompey. In AD 253 Catania's patron, Sant'Agata, patroness of wet-nurses, bell-founders and jewellers, suffered martyrdom by having her breasts lopped off; she has been carrying them around on a plate, like Santa Lucia's eyes, in the city's churches to this day.

In the early Middle Ages, Catania suffered a series of terrible disasters. A major Etna eruption and earthquake devastated the city in 1169, and it was sacked twice, first by Henry IV, then by Frederick II. In 1669, the worst eruption in Etna's history buried much of the city in lava and, before it could recover, the 1693 earthquake destroyed almost everything else. However, with their usual resilience the Catanians rebuilt the city better than ever under the direction of the great Palermitan architect Vaccarini, who made Catania into the showcase of Sicilian Baroque. They built well. Northern Europeans in the 18th and 19th centuries made Catania a popular stop on the 'Grand Tour'; many wrote in amazement that a city they had never heard of should present so majestic and noble an aspect.

The coming of the railway and industry in the 19th century brought a great increase in population and wealth, and the city spread out in all directions. Catania suffered as much as any place in Sicily from bombardments in 1943, when scores of its monuments suffered damage. More trouble came a year later, when demonstrations against the right-wing government installed by the Allied occupation turned into a full-scale revolt and the burning of the town hall.

Catania's decomposition since the war has been profound and continuous. Ironically, while the city's economy has become the most developed and forward-looking in southern Italy, earning Catania the title 'Milan of the South', the corruption and incompetence of its successive city governments have become responsible for an urban crisis as severe as that of Naples.

But Catania is a tough town, one that nature has wiped off the map no fewer than seven times, and one that has immediately rebuilt itself on each occasion. The city's

Getting There and Around

By Air

Flights arrive from Palermo, Venice, Bologna, Rome, Milan and Naples. The airport is at Fontana Rossa, 6km from town. The terminal is at Corso Sicilia 105; buses leave from here, Piazza del Duomo and Piazza Stesícoro for the airport. A Giunta bus links the airport to Milazzo (for the Aeolian Islands), and other buses for Enna/Palermo and for Agrigento also make stops here.

By Bus and Train

Catania is on the Messina–Syracuse train line. There are also trains direct from Enna, Caltanissetta and Palermo, and the rest of Sicily with a change or two. Ditto for buses. Catania is the hub of all transport in eastern Sicily and you may have to back-track to Catania (from Syracuse, for example) to reach more distant cities. Buses for most points within Catania province (Etna villages and Acireale) and for the rest of Sicily leave from the Stazione Centrale, on Piazza Papa Giovanni XXIII; many stop at Piazza Bellini in the centre. The main hubs for city buses are the Stazione Centrale and Piazza Stesícoro, on Via Etnea.

The narrow-gauge Circumetnea (see pp.289–93), which calls at the major villages around Mount Etna, leaves from its station, reached by metro from the main train station.

Tourist Information

Via Cimarosa 10, off Via Etnea just south of the Giardino Bellini, t 095 730 6211, www.apt.catania.it (open daily 9–8); Fontana Rossa Airport, t 095 730 62 66 (open daily 7am–10pm). For information on Mount Etna call in at the Club Alpino Italiano, Via Vecchia Ognina 169 (guides available for climbers) or ask at the tourist office. Many Etna tours set off from Catania (the jumping-off point for activities in the area.

Where to Stay

Catania gets plenty of businessmen but few tourists, and the available accommodation reflects this.

Luxury–Expensive

****Katane Palace Hotel, Via Finocchiaro Aprile 110, ✉ 95129, t 095 747 0702, www.katanepalace.it (expensive–luxury). Opened in 2002 in yet another restored palazzo. Sound-proofed rooms with fax and internet point are elegantly furnished and there is an excellent restaurant Il Cuciniere (see below).

*****Grand Hotel Excelsior, Piazza G. Verga 39, ✉ 95129, t 095 747 6111, www.thi.it (expensive). Extremely comfortable.

****Villa del Bosco, Via del Bosco 62, ✉ 95131, t 095 733 5100, www.hotelvilladel bosco.it (expensive). South of Via Grimaldi (near the port), this elegant converted palazzo features all mod cons as well as a frescoed room by artist Jean Zuber.

Moderate–Budget

***Hotel del Duomo, Via Etnea 28, ✉ 95124, t 095 250 3177, www.hoteldelduomo.it (moderate). Small classic hotel right in the heart of historical Catania, in a building that dates back to 19th century.

***Novecento, Via Ventimiglia 35, ✉ 95124, t 095 310 488, www.hotelnovecento catania.it (inexpensive). Good value with an art nouveau-style interior and well-picked period furniture.

***Savona, Via Vittorio Emanuele II 210, ✉ 95124, t 095 326 982 (inexpensive). Decent clean rooms in the centre of town.

perfect mascot, the grinning, endearingly ugly elephant made of hard Etna lava that stands in front of the cathedral, shows nothing of grace but plenty of energy, strength and determination; maybe some day Catania will use these qualities to raise itself up again.

*Moderno, Via Alessi 9, t 095 326 250, www.albergomoderno.it (budget). Spartan but acceptable, again in the centre.

*Pensione Bellini, Via Landolina 41, t 095 715 0969 (budget). Basic but very friendly in the centre (south of Piazza Bellini); garage.

There are several campsites on the southern edge of town, along Viale Kennedy and by the beach at Ógnina.

Eating Out

Catania can cook, no doubt about that. Arab and Spanish influences have had a marked effect on the cuisine, making it distinct from that of the rest of Italy; specialities include *scacciata*, at Christmas, with anchovies, fresh cheese, pepper and sauces, stuffed in a pastry envelope; *cannelloni alla Catanese*; and the ever-popular *pasta alla Norma*, with basil, aubergine and tomato sauce. Favourite wines are Trecastagni and Lo Sparviero dell'Etna (reds), Castelriccio (rosé) and Ciclope-Mazzullo (white).

Costa Azzurra, Via de Cristoforo 4, at Ógnina beach, t 095 494 920 (expensive). This place has achieved a wide reputation for its adventurous cooking, using truffles, clams and the freshest of vegetables, especially aubergine, in a number of original and delicious ways. To complete the meal they always have a good choice of cheeses and ice cream. Closed Mon.

Il Cuciniere, Katane Palace Hotel, t 095 747 0702 (expensive). Eastern Sicilian cuisine is a speciality of chef Carmelo Chiaramonte who uses the highest quality local produce. Numerous wines from the Etna region.

Osteria i 3 Bicchieri, Via S. G. al Duomo 31, t 095 715 3540 (expensive). Owned by one of the premier wine producers in the area. there are over 1,000 different wines in the restaurant (just north of Piazza Duomo), as

well as a cigar room and wine bar featuring live jazz. Closed Sun and Mon lunch.

La Siciliana, Viale Marco Polo 52, t 095 376 400 (expensive). One of Sicily's finest restaurants. Apart from the wonderful array of seafood, the roast lamb and breaded cutlets deserve mention, as do the vegetables and salads. Some very decent white wines are available, as well as the special red, Cerasuolo di Vittoria. You'll need to take a taxi to get there. Closed Sun eve and Mon.

Pagano, Via De Roberto 37, t 095 537 045 (moderate). They take great pains to produce authentic Catanese food here – of particular note are their pastas, stews and rice dishes, helped down with a bottle of Torrepalino dell'Etna. Closed Sat lunch.

Sicilia in Bocca, Via Dusmet 31–35, t 095 250 0208 (moderate). Original feted Catanese seafood restaurant (a new branch has opened in Piazza Lupo, t 095 746 1361) beloved of Catanese glitterati and some of the freshest seafood in town.

Marrakesh, Via Landolina 52 (inexpensive). South of Piazza Bellini: the best couscous in town. In the summer they set up their tables in the midst of live music, mostly jazz. Closed lunchtimes and Tues.

Nievsky, Scalinata Alessi 15–17, t 095 313 792 (inexpensive). Organic and fair-trade produce goes into Sicilian, Greek and Cuban dishes. There is Internet access here, Nievsky is the centre of Catania's alternative scene and at night, a lively crowd hangs out on the steps here. Closed Sun lunch and Mon.

Stella Antica Friggitoria Catanese, Via Ventimiglia 66, t 095 325 429 (inexpensive). An institution since 1830, serving quite wondrous concoctions from the frying pan. Closed Mon.

Tripoli, Via Pardo (inexpensive). One of a few good, cheap and popular trattorie around the fishmarket.

Piazza del Duomo

In the centre of the Piazza del Duomo, the Baroque showcase at the heart of the city, stands a fountain, with the elephant made of lava supporting an obelisk on its back – **Catania's symbol**. The obelisk was brought from Egypt, originally having served as a turning-post in the Roman circus. It must have been a prominent monument ever since; the Arabs called Catania the 'city of the elephant'. Vaccarini turned the statue into a fountain, perhaps inspired by the famous one built by Bernini in Rome's Piazza Minerva; Napoleon was so struck with the symbol (wherever he saw it) that he incorporated the elephant-obelisk emblem into several buildings in Paris, and planned to build a colossal one in the Place de la Bastille.

The elephant smiles benignly towards the **Cattedrale di Sant'Agata**. A Count Rosa founded the church in 1094, but following the eruption and the earthquake it had to be rebuilt, only the three apses of lava having survived from the original Norman structure. The façade was designed by Vaccarini; the columns on its lower half came from the Roman amphitheatre. Inside are the tombs of Bellini and the Aragonese Viceroy Fernandez d'Acuna (1494, in the chapel of Sant'Agata). The saint's relics are only displayed on high feast days – Agata's veil, said to have descended from an ancient icon of Isis, is credited with halting the lava flow in 1669, and the Catanese have been using it for the same purpose ever since. A fresco (1675) in the sacristy, portrays Etna's attack on Catania. In Roman times the whole cathedral square was the site of a huge **baths complex** (*sometimes open, ask at the tourist office*), whose entrance is to the right of the cathedral façade.

Also in the Piazza del Duomo are the **Municipio** (1741), with ornately decorated windows, another work of Vaccarini; and **Porta Uzeda**, an 18th-century archway through which you will find a small park where old men sun themselves and suspiciously eye all foreigners. In a corner of the *piazza*, the **Fontana dell'Amenano** holds the waters of a mysterious underground river that flows through the city.

On any morning except Sunday, have a look in the streets behind the cathedral, around the Baroque Palazzo Biscari; Italy's most chaotic and colourful **fishmarket** takes place here, with sights and colours you won't soon forget. **Palazzo Biscari** (1737; *visits by appointment, t 095 715 2508*), partially built on Catania's old city wall, is one of the grandest in town, with its wealth of putti and caryatids. It was the home of the important noble family who assembled the great archaeological collection now locked up in the Castello Ursino; Goethe visited it, and wrote about it in his *Italian Journey*.

Just to the north of the cathedral, across Via Vittorio Emanuele II, **Sant'Agata** with its huge dome is one of Vaccarini's most impressive churches – one of seven city churches dedicated to Catania's patroness, not counting the cathedral. In the desperate quarter east of Piazza del Duomo, in Piazza Bellini, is the **Teatro Bellini** (1890; *visits Mon 9.30–10.30am*), one of the largest and richest theatres in Europe, where operas are performed in winter and spring; it's worth attending whatever is on if you can, if only to see the incredible interior, surrounded by five levels of gilt boxes, and crowned with a ceiling fresco called *The Apotheosis of Bellini*.

Piazza Mazzini and the Castello Ursino

Two main streets, Via Garibaldi and Via Vittorio Emanuele II, run west from the Piazza del Duomo. Via Garibaldi leads to the elegant **Piazza Mazzini**, with its arcades of Roman columns from a basilica that once stood here. The effect of this little *piazza*, as with all of old Catania's numerous squares, is somewhat tarnished by its use as a car park. Just beyond, to the left, Via Castello Ursino leads directly up to the **Castello Ursino** in the Piazza Federico di Svevia. Built by Emperor Frederick II to intimidate local hotheads after he sacked the city, the castle was restored in the 19th century after being damaged by the 1669 eruption. Only the huge, ponderous keep remains – most of the rest is under lava – but it is still properly grim and impressive. For an example of how nature likes to reshape this city every few centuries, consider that when Frederick built the castle it stood on the shore, which thanks to Etna's bounteous flows is now over 600 yards to the east.

The castle contains the **Museo Civico** (*open Tues–Sat 9–1 and 3–6, Sun 9–12.30*), with the Biscaris's archaeological collection, objects from the Convento di San Niccolò, and an example of the Sicilian carved and painted carts. You may never get to see them: it's been closed for well over a decade under the pretence of 'restoration'. There may still be a few items of interest inside that haven't yet been stolen. There is the usual talk of it reopening soon.

Bellini's House and Via dei Crociferi

On the other side of Piazza Mazzini, at the intersection of Via Vittorio Emanuele, is Piazza San Francesco, where you'll find the **Museo Belliniano**, at No.3 (*open Mon–Sat 9–1.30; Sun 9–12.30*), with mementoes of composer Vincenzo Bellini, born here in 1801, the son and grandson of organists. His career was short but sweet. His first opera, written in 1825 while studying at the conservatory in Naples, attracted attention in the right quarters. The next year he was commissioned to write *Il Cirata* for La Scala; it caused a sensation.

Like Rossini, Bellini wrote expressly for the singers of the day, but with a lyricism and melodic beauty that made him the uncontested maestro of *bel canto*: success followed success with *I Capuletti ed i Montecchi* (1830), *La Sonnambula* and *Norma* (both 1831; the latter remains one of the most challenging roles in opera for sopranos). He had just finished his last work, *Puritani* (1835), when he suddenly fell ill and died, aged 33, and was buried in Paris's Père Lachaise cemetery. The museum contains some original scores, and stage models of some of the scenes of his works.

Next to it, you may pass beneath an archway called the **Arco di San Benedetto**, built, according to local legend, in a single night in 1704. This is the entrance to the famous **Via dei Crociferi** (*closed to traffic*), one of the prettiest streets in Sicily. Catania's wealthy Benedictine monks, the story goes, had been refused permission to erect their arch, which did not fit in with the rebuilding plans after the 1693 earthquake – so they presented the authorities with a *fait accompli*. Via dei Crociferi was the centre of the action in those times, with noblemen and religious orders queueing up to build churches and palaces on the most prestigious street of the new Catania. Many of the palaces are now used by the university, including the **Collegio dei Gesuiti**, with a cloister by Vaccarini; the architect also contributed **San Giuliano** (1739), with its curving façade. The Benedictines, however, built the most imposing church on the street, the 1713 **San Benedetto**.

The Greek Theatre and San Niccolò d'Arena

Round the corner on Via Teatro Greco, the **Greek Theatre** (*entrance at No.47; presently closed but may reopen in 2004*) can be seen on the left. The present structure actually belongs to the Roman era, built in the 2nd century AD, on the site of the Greek theatre where Alcibiades spoke to gain support for the Athenian cause. Next to it are the ruins of the **Odeon**, used mostly for concerts. Both are made of lava, which was originally covered with a refined layer of marble stucco.

Near the northern end of Via dei Crociferi, take the steep, tree-lined Via dei Gesuiti or Via Sangiuliano up to **Piazza Dante**, a beautiful Baroque semicircle much deteriorated through lack of care. This height was the acropolis of Greek Catana. Facing Piazza Dante is the gigantic church and monastery of **San Niccolò d'Arena** – surely one of the oddest, spookiest monuments in Sicily. The Catanese call it 'mastodonic', from the unfinished columns of its façade, sticking up like tusks. The largest church on the island, with the second largest convent in Europe (after the Mafra in Portugal), it was begun in the 16th century but never finished, then restored in 1735 after an earthquake destroyed it. It isn't finished now, and it never will be. The vast interior is fitfully undergoing badly needed renovation to stave off what seems an inevitable collapse, but if the door is open you can peep in and see the huge organ, of 2,916 pipes – its builder, Donato del Piano, was buried underneath it. Another feature is the meridian line on the transept floor, decorated with signs of the zodiac. If you want to risk a visit up to the fragile 205ft dome for its view, apply to the sacristan, if you can find him. The equally huge **Convento di San Niccolò** now houses a library and astrophysical observatory, but they too suffer from the Catanese indifference.

If you're tempted to explore the hallucinatory neighbourhoods to the south of San Nicolò, head west along Via Garibaldi, then cross Via Plebiscito, a winding boulevard that follows the course of Catania's medieval walls. Beyond this, the **Porta Garibaldi** is as spectacular and strange a decoration as any city could ask for, a great Baroque monumental arch from Bourbon times, built in parfait stripes of green and white stone.

Via Etnea

Back at Piazza del Duomo, Via Etnea (*closed to traffic until 10pm*), the gloomy main street of Catania, cuts straight across the city, with a view of Mount Etna at its very end. Every evening the most enthusiastic *passeggiata* in Sicily takes place here, the pavements crammed with ice-cream-eating Catanese peering in the windows of the many shoe, silver, jewellery and baby-clothes shops. At the end of the street, near Piazza del Duomo, is the **university** with the pretty **Collegiata** church, a royal chapel built by the Bourbons in 1768. The university itself, Sicily's first, was founded by Alfonso V of Aragon in 1434.

Further up, Via Etnea gives on to the **Piazza Stesícoro**, site of a major urban bus stop, a Bellini monument, and the remains of the 2nd-century **Roman amphitheatre** (*closed*). This was one of the largest amphitheatres in the Roman world, capable of seating some 16,000. A painting on the site shows the amphitheatre in its glory,

before the Ostrogoths started using it as a quarry (those barbarians at it again – in
fact the honest Goths had outlawed the vicious Roman games, and were using the
amphitheatre's stone to rebuild public monuments and churches). All the marble
facing has worn away to expose the lava foundation. Here, according to tradition,
Sant'Agata suffered martyrdom. Only a fraction of the work is exposed; the rest sleeps
in peace under the surrounding buildings.

From here, Via dei Cappuccini leads past the church of **Sant'Agata al Carcere**, built
on the supposed site of Agata's prison. It has a beautiful 13th-century door from the
old church of Sant'Agata la Vetere, the ancient cathedral. Beneath the ruined church
of San Euplio, in Piazza Stesícoro, is a Roman **hypogeum** (*closed*).

Via Etnea continues north to the grandiose main post office and the **Giardino
Bellini** (*open daily 8am–sunset*), one of the prettiest public gardens in Sicily, meticulously maintained – unlike the rest of Catania's public places. The exotic plants in the
park range from Brazilian araucavias to what the Catanese believe is the world's
largest fig tree. The floral clock and calendar on the hillside are unique in Sicily.

Along the northern end of the park runs the main street of many names – Viale
Regina Margherita here, Viale Venti Settembre and Corso Italia farther east. **Santa
Maria di Gesù** stands to the northwest of the park; Antonello Gagini designed the
chapel doorway and sculpted the *Madonna with the Angels* inside.

East Catania and the Beaches

There's little reason ever to cross Via Etnea: the areas between it and the sea are the
foulest Catania has to offer, disfigured even more by a witless urban renewal
programme of the 1950s that never got more than half finished. At Corso Italia 21 is
the **Palazzo delle Scienze**, near the modern Piazza Giovanni Verga. (The Geology,
Mineralogy and Vulcanology Museums near by are all currently closed to the public.)
Not surprisingly, Catania has one of the best schools of vulcanology anywhere. The
train station stands amidst the worst of the slums by the sea, near a **fountain** of the
'Rape of Persephone', floodlit at night.

The nearest beaches to the city are **Ógnina**, a pretty place with lava cliffs, to the
north, and **Lido di Plaia** to the south (bus D in the summer from Piazza Giovanni
Verga and Via Etnea). Near Lido di Plaia there's the airport at Fontana Rossa and, at
the mouth of the River Simeto, the **Riserva Naturale Orientata**, a wildlife reserve (*an
information office, on the SS114 across from the Cavallino Bianco restaurant, has information about guided tours*).

Catania to Syracuse

Augusta

The Plain of Catania, south of the city, is drained by the Rivers Simeto and Dittáino,
but there's little to tempt the traveller to stop – for at least 13km south of Catania it's
nothing but airport and squalid industrial wastelands. In between Catania and
Syracuse, below the honey-producing Monti Iblei that inspired Theocritus' bucolic

Getting Around

Lentini and Augusta are on the train line between Syracuse and Catania. Frequent buses from Catania and Syracuse serve most towns in the area, particularly Augusta, Lentini and Carlentini. Megara Hyblaea can be reached only by car. Pántalica is best visited as a day trip from Syracuse, organized by various travel agencies.

poetry, lies Augusta, Italy's main oil port, a naval base, chemical works, and in general a thoroughly awful place, metamorphosed irreparably by a big industrial plan of the 1950s financed by the government. The road from Augusta to Syracuse is almost surreal with its mesh of coloured pipes and tubes and industrial gewgaws.

Like Syracuse, Augusta is built on an islet connected by a bridge to the mainland. Frederick II founded the city on the site of the ancient Xiphonia in 1232 for refugees from Centuripe and Montalbano. Most of the original buildings were destroyed in the 1693 earthquake and again in the 1943 air raids, although the 17th-century **cathedral** and two **16th-century towers** along the Porto Megarese survive. The **Municipio** still sports Stupor Mundi's imperial eagle over the door. Augusta's main interest for the tourist, however, is its proximity to the excavations of Megara Hyblaea (*see* below) and the beach resorts at **Brucoli** and **Agnone**.

Lentini and Carlentini

Inland from Augusta is **Carlentini**, founded in 1551 as a fortress town for the inhabitants of Lentini. From here one can visit **Lentini** itself, the second oldest Greek colony in Sicily, after Naxos. Founded by the Chalcidians on the site of an early Sikel town, Leontinoi soon became important as an agricultural centre. Syracuse ruled over the city for most of its existence, though in the mid-5th century BC, in a brief interlude of independence, it became allied with Athens and sent the renowned orator Gorgias to the Athenian assembly to plead for protection from its old master. When Syracuse attacked Leontinoi in 427 BC, the Athenians jumped at the chance to send aid. Although the Syracusans eventually made a treaty with them, the Athenians used the Leontinoi conflict as one of their major justifications for the Great Expedition a few years later. Leontinoi, like Syracuse, sided with Carthage in the Second Punic War, and was also attacked by the vengeance-seeking Romans; however, unlike Syracuse, Leontinoi was granted no mercy, and the Romans beheaded 2,000 citizens for desertion, in accordance with their law.

The medieval town of Lentini fell flat in the 1693 earthquake, although you can still see the ruins of Frederick II's **castle**. Lentini was the birthplace of Frederick's court poet and falconer Iacopo Mostacci, or Iacopo da Lentini, whom Dante credited with inventing the sonnet and being the first to write in vulgar Italian:

Canzonetta novella
va canta nova cosa;
levati da mattino
davanti a la più bella
fiore d'ogni amorosa,
bionda più ch'auro fino:

Lo vostro amor, ch'è caro,
donatelo al Notaro
ch'è nato da Lentino.

('Delicate song of mine/Go sing thou a new strain/Seek, with the first sunshine/Our lady, mine and thine – /The rose of Love's domain,/Than red gold comelier./Lady, in Love's name hark/To Jacopo the Clerk/Born in Lentino here' – translation by Dante Gabriel Rossetti.)

In Lentini, the **Chiesa Madre**'s right-hand nave was a built-over 3rd-century Christian hypogeum; also note the beloved 9th-century Byzantine icon of the *Madonna Odigistria*. At the **Museo Archeológico**, in Via Piave (*open Tues–Sat 9–2*), are items from various stages of the town's history. The remains of ancient **Leontinoi** lie between Lentini and Carlentini, spread over two hills, Metapiccola and San Mauro. Traces of the early Sikel town may be seen on Metapiccola, while around San Mauro are remains of Leontinoi's defences, a Hellenistic necropolis and part of the south gate to the city.

A Plunge Inland: Francofonte and Vizzini

From Lentini, SS194 leads up 13km to **Francofonte**, which disputes with Vizzini the claim to be the setting for Verga's story and Mascagni's opera, *Cavalleria Rusticana*, as well as Verga's *Mastro Don Gesualdo*. In the church **Santa Maria di Gesù** the altarpiece of the *Madonna and Child* (1527) is by Antonello Gagini. **Vizzini**, just off SS194, 1854ft up in the Monti Iblei, stands on the site of ancient Bidis, mentioned by Cicero.

Along the Coast: Megara Hyblaea

Across the bay from Augusta (signposted on the SS114) is **Megara Hyblaea** (*open daily 9am–one hour before sunset*), founded in 729 BC by the Greeks of Megara. This site, at the mouth of the River Cántera, was originally inhabited in the Neolithic period. Pantalica, the Sikel king of Hybla, offered it to the Greek colonists, whose manufacture of ceramics brought considerable prosperity. Gelon of Syracuse destroyed the city in 483 BC; he settled the rich in Syracuse, and sold everyone else into slavery. Timoleon had the site resettled, but the Consul Marcellus delivered its *coup de grâce* in 214 when the new town defied the Romans. Important excavations were begun here by the French in 1948.

A part of the ruins has been covered by the sea; those visible on land are always open and include parts of two walls: the older, larger one, now outside the railway tracks, and the much smaller circuit from Timoleon's day near the shore. There remains a Doric temple, possibly dedicated to Aphrodite, an irregularly shaped agora with two long stoas, archaic tombs, and some Hellenistic houses built around peristyle courtyards. Megara Hyblaea's Antiquarium is closed, but it's no great loss: the most interesting finds are in the museum in Syracuse.

Melilli, Thapsos and Pántalica

Melilli, 5km inland from Megara Hyblaea, is famous for the festival of San Sebastiano which takes place every 4 May. Here, in return for a favour from the saint, parents promise that their children will take part in the procession of San Sebastiano – as stark naked as the saint himself, when Roman archers made him a vertical pincushion. The discarded clothing is later given to the poor children of the town. At **Cava Secchiera**, near Melilli, are some prehistoric rock-cut tombs.

East of Melilli, out on the Magnisi peninsula, are the ruins of **Thapsos**, the largest Bronze Age town in Sicily (the nearest town is Priolo Gargallo, and the excavations are 2.5km away, near the lighthouse). Dating from the 14th century BC, the settlement consists of circular, multi-roomed huts, only recently discovered, as well as an area of neat rectangular blocks and streets – a proper little city. Most interesting are the tombs carved out of the rock with cupolas, where vases imported from Mycenae and Malta have been found. Thapsos gave its name to the Bronze Age culture on Sicily, and is known for the bizarre vases on pedestals you can see in the Syracuse museum. Around the beginning of the first millennium BC the inhabitants of Thapsos were forced inland, perhaps to Pántalica.

West of Melilli the road leads through the Anapo Valley to **Sortino**, which has an impressive church. Roads from either Sortino or the village of Ferla (the view from Ferla is much better), farther west, can take you to the vast Bronze Age necropolis of **Pántalica** (*open 9am–one hour before sunset*), spread along the cliffs in the deep valleys of the Anapo and Calcinara Rivers. The settlement of Pántalica, dating from 1200 BC, when invaders forced the coastal residents to move inland, is now believed to be the legendary Sikel town of Hybla. Few traces remain of this: one building, perhaps the anactoron or palace, along with signs of a wall. In the surrounding cliffs, however, are some 5,000 family tombs carved in the rock like a honeycomb, attesting to the large size of ancient Hybla. In the 8th century BC, Pántalica was abandoned for reasons unknown. Later, threatened like the Sikels by invaders on the coast, the Byzantines sought shelter at Pántalica and expanded the tombs for dwellings. Two small chapels remain from this period. In the spring, look out for the wild Sicilian orchid which punctuates the landscape.

Syracuse
and the Southeast

14

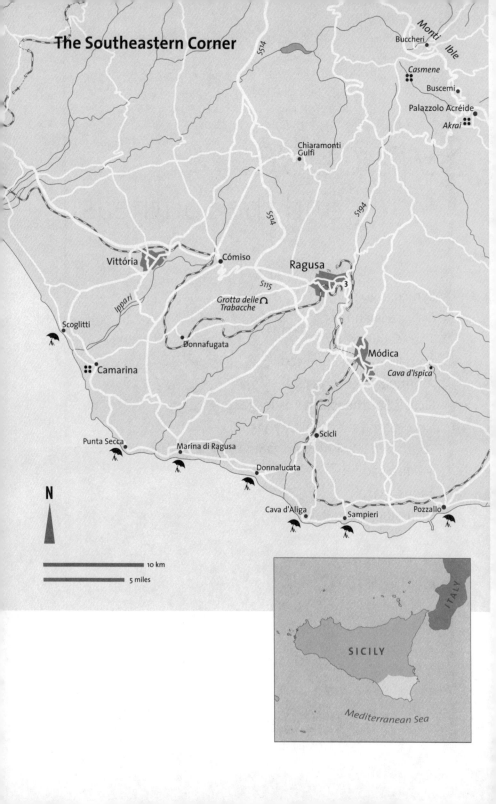

The Southeastern Corner

Monti Ible

Buccheri

Casmene

Buscemi

Palazzolo Acréide

Akrai

Chiaramonti
Gulfi

SS14

SS14

SS194

Vittória

Cómiso

Ragusa

3

SS115

Grotta delle
Trabacche

Ippari

Scoglitti

Dónnafugata

Móldica

Camarina

Cava d'Ispica

Punta Secca

Marina di Ragusa

Scicli

Donnalucata

N

Cava d'Aliga

Sampieri

Pozzallo

10 km

5 miles

ITALY

SICILY

Mediterranean Sea

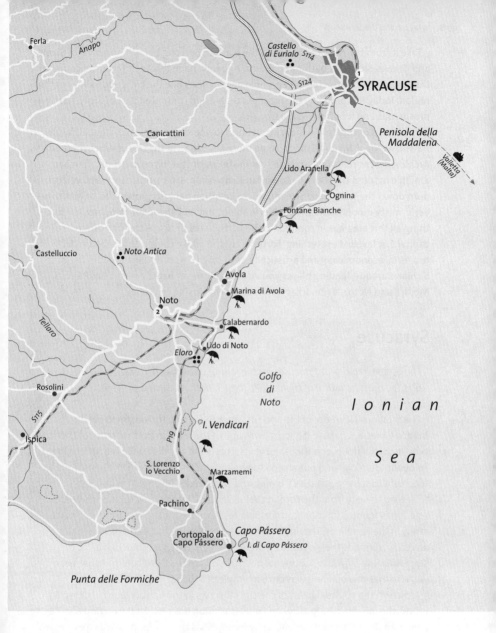

Highlights

1 Wandering the streets and ruins of Syracuse, the New York of the ancient world
2 The icing-sugar façades of the churches and palaces of Noto, a masterpiece of Sicilian Baroque
3 Ragusa, a subtle and gently decaying hill town, set in a rugged landscape of dry stone walls and olive trees

Take it from the Neolithics – this is the place to be. Long before the arrival of Sikels and Greeks, Sicily's Neolithic and Bronze Age folk made this their favourite corner of the island; their distinctive pigeon-hole necropolises line the cliffs and valleys of the region. Today it is probably the most peaceable and contented part of Sicily, relatively prosperous and free from Mafia troubles.

Syracuse is of course the main attraction. Nowhere else does the splendid, fatally flawed world of Magna Graecia come more alive than in the city of Aeschylus and Archimedes; as ruins go, Syracuse's seem still warm, set in the midst of a fine and amiable modern city. Outside town, landscapes come in surprising variety: you can punt down the lush Cyane stream, where Egyptian papyrus grows wild, or hike over eerie, misty moors in the Monti Iblei with nothing but sheep for company. The one thing all this area has in common is the Earthquake of 1693 – this one deserves a capital E: it levelled everything. Fortunately, the quake caught southeastern Sicily in top form, economically and artistically. Each town was carefully rebuilt in the best Sicilian Baroque, lending places you've probably never heard of – such as Ragusa, Módica and Noto – a remarkably refined air that lasts even today.

Syracuse

*I had often heard that Syracuse was the largest of the Greek cities,
and the most beautiful of them all. Its fame is not undeserved.*

Cicero

The fabulous New York of the ancient Greek world, the thriving metropolis of Magna Graecia, Syracuse (Siracusa) was one of the most important cities of the Western world for over a thousand years. This is the city that whipped Athens in the Peloponnesian War and put an end to her imperial dream. Later, Plato came here to teach philosophy to Syracuse's tyrant, and Archimedes invented his brilliant machines to defend the city from the Romans. Yet if Syracuse retains only ruins of its Golden Age, it has found a far more comfortable, less troublesome role as a civilized place rarely in the headlines. The light is sharp and brilliant – that, perhaps more than anything, reminds the visitor of its Greek founders. Other reminders wait at every step: walk into Syracuse's cathedral and you will see the Doric columns that bear witness that this building was once a temple of Athena.

Although the spiritual heart of the city still rests in the narrow lanes of Ortygia Island, the inexorable urge towards modernization has pushed the commercial centre deep into the adjacent mainland. Only recently has the city (pop. 120,000) expanded out to approximate the physical area of ancient Syracuse.

History

According to Thucydides, ancient Syracuse (from Suraka, the Phoenician name of a nearby marsh) was founded in 733 BC by colonists from Corinth, who usurped the native Sikels. The location was ideal: the offshore islet of Ortygia could easily be defended, the plains facing it were fertile, and the natural harbour offered immense

Syracuse

To Castello Eurialo

To Catania (SS114)

EPIPOLAE

VIA NECROPOLI GROTTICELLI

VIALE TERACATI

VIALE TICA

Necropoli dei Grotticelli

Via dei Sepolcri

Grotta dei Cordari

Latomia di S. Venera

RIZZO

VIA LATOMIA DEL CASALE

LUOGO NEDO NADI

VIA BASSA AGRADINA

Latomia dei Cappuccini

Greek Theatre

VIALE G.E.

Orecchio di Dionisio

Latomia Intagliatella

S. Giovanni

VIA A. VON PLATEN

VIA SEBASTIANO

S. SEBASTIANO

Villa Landolina

VIA POLITI LAUDIEN

VIALE

Latomia del Paradiso

NEAPOLIS

Museo Archeológico

Catacombs of Vigna Cassia

VIA PORDENONE

GIULIO EMANUELE RIZZO

VIALE PARADISO

VIA AUGUSTO

VIALE

TEOCRITO

Ara di Ierone II

Roman Amphitheatre

Sant. della Madonnina delle Lácrime

VIA TORINO

VIA CAVALIERI

Santuario di Demeter e Core

To A18, SS114 and Catania

VIALE PAOLO ORSI

ACHRADINA

VIA TESTAFERRATA

VIA GORIZIA

S. Lucia

VIA ENNA

TYCHE

PIAZZA DELLA VITTORIA

VIA RAGUSA

PIAZZA S. LUCIA

VIA TEVERE

CORSO GELONE

MONS. CARABELLI

CADORNA

VIA AGRIGENTO

RIVIERA DIONISIO IL GRANDE

VIALE ERMOCRATE

Train Station

PIAZZA D. REPUBBLICA

VIA TRAPANI

MONTEGRAPPA

VIA STATELLO

Arsenal Byzantine Baths

PIAZZA EURIPIDE

Porto Piccolo

Ionian Sea

Ginnasio Romano

VIA F. CRISPI

LUOGO GILIPPO

VIA DELL'ARSENALE

VIA ELORINA

VIA A. DIAZ

VIA REGINA MARGHERITA

Pantheon of the Fallen

To Ragusa and Noto (SS115)

PIAZZA MARCONI

FORO SIRACUSANO

CORSO UMBERTO

VIA TRIPOLI

VIA MALTA

VIA BENGASI

PIAZZA DELLA POSTA

LUNGOMARE DI LEVANTE

Ponte Nuovo

VIA C. BATTISTI

Porto Grande

PIAZZA PANCALI

Tempio di Apollo

VIA TRENTO

VITTORIO

S. Pietro

VIA RESALIBERA

CORSO MATTEOTTI

VIA MIRABELLA

CORSO CAVOUR

Palazzo Montalto

VENETO

Porta Marina

FORO ITALICO

VIA SAVOIA

VIA MAZZINI

PIAZZA ARCHIMEDE

S. Filippo

VIA DELLA MAESTRANZA

Palazzo Lanza

S. Lucia alla Badia

VIA GEMELLARO

V. E. SETTIMO

VIA RODA

Cathedral

ORTYGIA

VIA NIZZA

Capitaneria di Porto

PIAZZA DEL DUOMO

Palazzo Arcivescovile

Tropical Aquarium

Palazzo Bellomo

Fonte Aretusa

VIA CAPODIECI

V. CASTELLO MANIACE

S. Martino

N

Castello Maniace

400 metres

400 yards

Getting There

By Train

There are frequent services to and from Messina (3hrs), Catania (1.5hrs) and all stations in between, plus less frequent trains to Noto (40mins), Módica (2hrs), Ragusa (2.5hrs), Gela (4hrs) and Licata (4hrs). For information t 848 888 088. For shorter trips such as Noto, buy your ticket from the newsagent's stall on the station platform.

By Bus

There are twelve to fourteen buses a day Mon–Sat, plus four on Sundays to and from Catania; about twelve daily to Noto; ten daily Módica–Ragusa; eleven a day Mon–Sat to Lentini; eleven daily to Palazzolo Acréide; twelve daily to Avola; one daily Mon–Sat to Piazza Armerina (but at useless times, making a day trip unfeasible), five express daily Mon–Sat, three on Sun to Palermo, and buses to many other towns in the province. AST buses (t 0931 462 711) depart from the bus station in Piazza della Posta over the Ponte Nuovo in Ortygia, the Interbus (t 0931 66710) bus station is in Via Trieste, round the corner.

Getting Around

For the Greek theatre and the other archaeological sites in Neapolis, there are about a dozen different **bus** lines – all begin at the post office on Ortygia. No.11 goes closest to Castello Eurialo. There are also buses that run regularly to the nearby beaches.

There's no regular schedule, but a **boat** called the *Selene* makes cruises around the city's two harbours April–Oct, starting from the mainland Porta Marina (t 368 317 0711, *wwwortygiatour.cjb.net*).

Tourist Information

Via San Sebastiano 43–5, near the Museo Archeológico, t 0931 67 710, t 0931 481 232, t 0931 481 200, *www.apt-siracusa.it* (open daily 8.30–2 and 3.30–6.30); Via della Maestranza 33, Ortygia, t 0931 464 255,

t 0931 65 201 (*open Mon–Sat 8–2 and 4.30–7.30*). Kiosk at the train station.

Where to Stay

Syracuse ✉ 96100

Avoid any place around Corso Umberto: it's a noisy, charmless street, and you'll wish you were on Ortygia instead, where most of the streets are surprisingly quiet. There are one or two agencies that offer apartments for rent (ask the tourist office for details).

Luxury–Expensive

★★★★**Hotel Roma**, Via Roma 66, Ortygia, t 0931 46 56 26, *www.hotelroma.sr.it* (*expensive–luxury*). Built in 1880, this delightful hotel has recently been reopened after being restored to elegance with all mod cons in all 36 rooms, some with disabled access and private garage in the heart of Ortygia.

★★★★**Grand Hotel Villa Politi**, Via Politi Laudien 2, t 0931 41 21 21, *www.villapoliti.com* (*expensive*). Near the Latomia dei Cappuccini, in a quiet garden setting with a pool and tennis courts.

★★★★**Grand Hotel**, Viale Mazzini 12, Ortygia, t 0931 46 46 00, *www.grandhotelsr.it* (*moderate–expensive*). An old palace first opened as a hotel in 1905. Extensive restoration has taken in the city's medieval walls and throughout kept the art deco character. The rooms are spacious and the restaurant has panoramic views over the port. A bus shuttles guests to a private beach

Villa dei Papiri, Cozzo Paantano, Fonte Ciane, t 0931 721 321, *www.villadeipapiri.it* (*moderate–expensive*). Enticing *agriturismo* in a 19th-century farmhouse set in 32 acres of fertile land in the Ciane Saline nature reserve (a 10min drive from Syracuse) with its abundance of Egyptian papyrus growing wild. Rooms are splendid and come with their own kitchen.

Moderate–Budget

L'Acanto, Via Roma 15, t 0931 212 70, *www.pc-serv.net/l'acanto* (*moderate*). This wonderful B&B on Ortygia offers rooms or, better still, self-contained, centrally located flats at extremely reasonable prices.

★★★Gran Bretagna, Via Savoia 21, Ortygia, **t** 0931 68 765, *www.hotelgrandbretagna.it* (*moderate*). This welcoming and well-kept *pensione* is the best, though not the cheapest, of the less expensive places that can be found around the rail station or on Ortygia.

★★★Relax Hotel, Viale Epipoli 159, **t** 0931 74 01 22, *www.hotelrelax.it* (*moderate*). Farther out in a quiet suburban environment close to Castello Eurialo. The rooms are average, but if it's hot the fantastic swimming pool will more than compensate.

Il Casale, Via delle Fornaci 103, Contrada Isola, **t** 0931 721 107, *www.ilcasalebb.com* (*inexpensive–moderate*). Blissful family-run B&B 700 yards from the beaches of Capo Murro di Porco, close to Syracuse and with a lovely garden. The rooms have been restored with traditional Sicilian materials and the friendly owner is a mine of local information (ask her for details of deserted little coves). *Closed Jan and Feb.*

★Aretusa, Via F. Crispi 75, **t** 0931 24 211, *www.hotelaretusa.it* (*budget*). A very plain collection of rooms near the railway station.

★Pantheon, Via Foro Siracusano 22, ✉ 96011, **t** 0931 21 010 (*budget*). A nice, old-fashioned *pensione* of the sort that is gradually becoming extinct in Italy.

Fontane Bianche, Loc. Fontane Bianche, **t** 0931 79 03 33. A campsite near the beach. *Closed mid-Oct–mid-May.*

Eating Out

Syracuse chefs boast of their *pasta fritta* (sweet balls of pasta covered with honey), *tonno alla marinara* (tuna fish with onions and spices) and stuffed artichokes.

Agricola Limoneto, outside Syracuse on the SS124, **t** 0931 71 73 52, *www.emmeti.it/ limoneto* (*expensive*). If you have a car, book for one of the superb five-course lunches served out of town amid lemon groves. There's no menu, but all the ingredients are grown on the estate and couldn't be fresher. The farm also has some charming bed-and-breakfast rooms.

Jonico-a Rutta 'e Ciauli, Riviera Dionisio il Grande 194, **t** 0931 65 540 (*expensive*). Come here for a taste of real Syracuse and Sicilian cooking. Apart from traditional pasta dishes and seafood, the menu promises exotic things such as smoked pork belly and a choice of cheeses from Ragusa. This, with a fine view from the terrace, and a mini ethnographic museum. Reservation recommended. *Closed Tues.*

Pescomare, Via Landolina 6, Ortygia (*expensive*). This restaurant is a favourite among locals and expatriates. Sit under a leafy canopy and enjoy Sicilian specialties.

Archimede, Via Gemmellaro 8, Ortygia, **t** 0931 69 701 (*moderate*). Perhaps the classic Syracusan restaurant, with waiters who remember the town as it looked in the photos on the walls. The seafood *antipasti* buffet is a good place to start. *Closed Sun eve.*

La Foglia, Via Capodieci 31, Ortygia, **t** 0931 66 233, *www.lafoglia.it* (*moderate*). A couple of doors away from the museum at Palazzo Bellomo, the artistically ambitious restaurateurs here serve inventive food with a leaning towards the organic and vegetarian.

Il Porticciolo da Piero, Via Trento 24, Ortygia, **t** 0931 61 914 (*moderate*). Just steps from the daily fishmarket, and you are sure to find the day's catch cooked up simply and without fuss. *Closed Mon.*

Nonna Margherita, Via Cavour 12, Ortygia (*inexpensive*). There's very good pizza to be had at this popular place.

La Siciliana, Via Savoia 17, Ortygia, **t** 0931 68 944 (*inexpensive*). Another neighbourhood favourite for that evening pizza. *Closed Mon.*

L'Incontro, Via Landolina 21, Ortygia, **t** 0931 23 32 448. This café-bar is a very agreeable place to find yourself if you want a few gifts to take home. You can taste Sicilian specialities such as Marsala wine, orange-blossom honey, anchovies and capers, and they can post it home for you if you're overloaded. Free coffee while you browse.

Vino Enoteca Salaria, Via Roma 86, Ortygia, **t** 0931 46 30 04. A basic but colourful wine shop where the food is served to accompany the wines you are tasting. This is a good place to try a selection of Marsalas and other wines.

The Athenian Expedition

Shortly after Hieron's death, in 466 BC, Syracuse turned democratic, while its power and influence across the Mediterranean was growing with each passing year. Athens grew jealous of this new rival, and feared for its own allies and interests in western Greece, especially considering that Syracuse was allied with Sparta, Athens' arch-enemy, in the Peloponnesian War. After the great victory over the Spartans at Pylos in 424 BC, where Spartan soldiers surrendered for the first time ever, the Athenians became even cockier than usual. In the citizens' assembly of 415 BC, demagogues, including the brilliant pervert Alcibiades, convinced them that first Syracuse and then the rest of Sicily was ripe for plucking. The largest force any Greek power had ever collected, including 134 triremes, the greater part of the Athenian navy, set forth in the summer of 415 BC. Alcibiades and Nicias, the experienced general who had opposed the expedition, were co-commanders.

At first, the Syracusans refused to believe the news and, even when they learned the Athenians had been well received at Catania, they did not seem too perturbed; they sent an army to Catania – but the clever Athenians took the chance and sailed to Syracuse, setting up a camp. The Athenians defeated the returning Syracusans, and went back to spend the winter in Catania. Alcibiades, called back to Athens to stand trial by his political enemies, defected to the Spartans.

The following year, the siege began in earnest – according to the peculiar fashions of the 5th century BC. The Athenians built a fort called the 'circle' outside the city walls, and from it tried to extend a wall of their own round the city. The Syracusans, under an able new Spartan commander named Gylippos, started a counter-wall of their own to cut the Athenians off. Indecisive skirmishes and naval battles continued through 414 BC, until Gylippos managed to capture the Athenian forts on Plemmyrion Point across from Syracuse's Porto Grande, cutting off the Athenian supply route. After a pair of naval defeats, in which the Athenians were unable to use their superiority in the enclosed space of the harbour, the Syracusans strung a chain of ships across the harbour's entrance. The dazed, exhausted Athenians, whose retreat had already been postponed too long by the erratic command of Nicias, now made a last desperate attempt to break out by sea. It failed. The former masters of the seas, having lost all their ships, now made a pathetic retreat south, by land, where they were surrounded and destroyed.

'This was the greatest Hellenic achievement of any war, at once most glorious to the victors and most calamitous to the conquered; they were utterly defeated at all points, and their sufferings were terrible in every way. Fleet and army perished from the face of the earth...' Such was the judgement of Thucydides. Indeed, this surprise victory over the most powerful city of its day could only give a mighty boost to Syracuse's prestige. On the other side of the coin, the miserable Athenians captured at Syracuse were kept in the quarries (*latomiae*) under inhuman conditions. Few ever returned to Athens; the story goes that only those who were able to recite passages of Aeschylus or Euripides, the two favourite poets of the Syracusans, were ever let out again.

possibilities for maritime activities. It wasn't long before the oligarchs of Syracuse were founding colonies of their own on Sicily, at Akrae and Camarina, increasing the city's sphere of influence to the borders of Gela and Megara Hyblaea.

In 485 BC political turmoil within Syracuse caused the oligarchs to invite Gelon, the tyrant of Gela, to take control of the city. Gelon realized the potential of the Porto Grande and made Syracuse a sea power; on land he annexed Megara Hyblaea and moved much of the population of his native Gela, and that of Camarina, to Syracuse. It was Gelon, in alliance with Theron of Akragas, who defeated the massive Carthaginian attack on Himera in 480 BC.

Two years later, Gelon was succeeded by his brother Hieron, a precursor of the archetypal Renaissance tyrant: cruel yet cultured, a passionate lover of poetry, patronizing and surrounding himself with the greatest talents of his time – Simonides, Pindar and Aeschylus. Pindar praised Hieron's victories in the chariot race, and Aeschylus is thought to have written *Prometheus Bound* and *Prometheus Unbound* in Syracuse, where they had their debut. Militarily, Hieron led the Greeks in defeating the Etruscans at Cumae, near Naples (474 BC), expanding the Syracusan sphere of influence halfway up the Italian peninsula.

Syracuse's Golden Age

Hermocrates, democratic leader of Syracuse during the siege (*see* 'The Athenian Exhibition', below), was murdered soon after in a political plot; one of his supporters, the ambitious Dionysius, took power as tyrant in 407 BC. Dionysius was also a poet, and wrote numerous tragedies which he entered year after year in the festivals of his near-namesake, only to be begrudged a prize by the Athenians. However, in 368 BC, when Athens sought an alliance with Syracuse, the festival judges suddenly found Dionysius' entry a work of genius, whereupon Dionysius celebrated his long-sought victory so lavishly that it killed him.

Unfortunately – or perhaps fortunately – none of Dionysius' poetry has come down to us, and history remembers him instead for his military genius. He constructed the fortress and walls on the strategic Epipolae ridge, where the Athenians had mounted their siege, which proved to be the linchpin of the city's defence during his campaign to rid Sicily of the Carthaginians. In this, however, Dionysius never quite succeeded, despite his efforts to gather engineers from all over Greece and Italy to design new weapons. Most spectacular of these was the catapult, which was instrumental in the Greeks' victory over the Carthaginians at Motya in Western Sicily (*see* p.145).

Under Dionysius, Syracuse became a powerful empire, with bases as far afield as the Adriatic Coast, but his son Dionysius II was rather ineffectual, despite Plato's efforts to make him a philosopher king according to the ideals of the Republic. When Dion, uncle of Dionysius II and friend of Plato, at last grew tired of his nephew's tyranny, he rose to overthrow him, and was in turn assassinated for acting the tyrant.

The year 343 BC found Syracuse in a bad way. Fearing a new Carthaginian offensive, the citizens appealed to mother Corinth for aid and were sent Timoleon, a man of justice and peace who, after overthrowing all the petty tyrants of Sicily, established democracy and made a peace treaty with Carthage.

Timoleon's good works lasted through his lifetime, but when he died in 336 BC the internecine bickering among the Greeks began again, eventually bringing the bellicose adventurer Agathocles to power in 317 BC. Throughout his rule, Syracuse was at war, conquering most of Greek Sicily except for Akragas. When Agathocles died in 289 BC, without an heir, his fragile empire crumbled.

In the confusion that followed, the Carthaginians saw their chance and sailed into the Porto Grande – this time deterred by Pyrrhus of Epirus, who came to the rescue at the request of Syracuse and Akragas (this is the fellow who would later be famous for his meaningless 'Pyrrhic victories' against the Romans). Once again, the barbarian threat temporarily served to unite the Greek factions.

The Roman Conquest to the Present

The Syracusans elected Hieron II, one of Pyrrhus' officers, as their new ruler (275–216 BC). As wise as he was long-lived, Hieron II proved a blessing to the city. Besides making a treaty with the Romans, and supporting them in the First Punic War, he improved the laws and life of the Syracusans, redesigning the Neapolis quarter of the city and building the mammoth altar to Zeus the Giver of Freedom (or 'Zeus Eleftherios'). Theocritus, the first writer of idyllic poetry, frequented the court of Hieron II, who also patronized his talented and scientific cousin, Archimedes.

Hieron II was succeeded by his grandson, Hieronymus, who made the mistake of pledging allegiance to Hannibal, in 215 BC, when the Carthaginian was at the height of his power. This brought down the wrath of Rome in the form of the Consul Marcellus, who laid siege to Syracuse. Here the Romans faced not so much the defending army of a city as the genius of one man – Archimedes. Despite all his technological tricks, the Romans prevailed when the city's gates were opened by traitors. Archimedes was slain, despite express orders to capture him (as the story goes, the genius was so wrapped up in his reading that he refused to notice the officer sent to capture him, finally making him so angry that he ran Archimedes through). From then on Syracuse dwindled in importance, although it became capital of the Romans' new province of Sicily.

The Romans, still half-barbarous, with no art of their own, always admired Syracuse for its beauty; Verres, the notorious governor prosecuted by Cicero, admired it so much that he tried to take it all home with him before he was caught. Syracuse suffered more in rebel attacks during the Slave Wars. Reconstruction did not occur until the time of Augustus, when the amphitheatre and other works in Neapolis were built. Christianity found Syracuse a fertile field in its early days, especially after St Paul stopped for three days en route from Malta to Rome.

In the 5th century AD, the Vandals put an end to Roman rule. In 535, Belisarius captured Syracuse from the Ostrogoths in the name of Byzantium. One of the Eastern emperors, Constans, moved his capital from Constantinople to Syracuse in 663, but he died five years later when a homesick servant clipped him over the head with a soap dish. The court lost no time in returning to Constantinople. A key Byzantine port, Syracuse was besieged and destroyed by the Arabs in 878. Recaptured temporarily by the Byzantines under George Maniakes in 1038, the city was reclaimed once and for all by Count Roger in 1105. Under the Normans, Syracuse regained some of its former prosperity. From 1361 to 1536 the Camera Regionale sat at Syracuse, although many of the fine palaces of that period were felled in the 1693 earthquake. The city also suffered from both Allied and Luftwaffe bombings 250 years later.

Ortygia Island

Ortygia (Greek for 'quail'), a name associated with the goddess Artemis, originally referred to the whole of Syracuse, but later became sole property of the island. Much of the island fell into decay a century ago, when the mainland extensions became populated, but lately the Syracusans have begun a game attempt at restoring the old houses of the quarter, especially around the Fonte Arethusa.

Two bridges connect the island to the mainland: the main one, **Ponte Nuovo**, leads to the large Piazza della Posta and the adjacent Piazza Pancali, which boasts the ruins of the Doric **Tempio di Apollo**, excavated in 1943. Dating back to the mid-6th century, this was the first large temple built by the Greeks in Sicily. Two of its columns and part of the cella walls have been reconstructed, though it is still hard to imagine what the temple originally looked like; it seems to have performed service as both a church and a mosque before it disappeared. Painted terracotta fragments from the cornice are in the Museo Archeológico, offering a chance to see how colourful and exotic a Greek temple looked before the classical age. From here, Corso Giacomo Matteotti leads up to **Piazza Archimede**, the old heart of Ortygia. Its 19th-century **fountain** has been confusingly dubbed 'the Fonte Arethusa', but this isn't the real one. Note the **Palazzo Lanza** (15th century), and the Banco d'Italia, housed in a medieval Catalan building. Just off the *piazza*, on Via Montalto, the **Palazzo Montalto** (1397) offers an inspired example of the Chiaramonte style, with its delicately mullioned triple windows.

Piazza del Duomo

Just to the south, this is one of Sicily's most elegant squares. It fills up with coachloads of daytrippers by 10am, but if you can get here before them, you can drink your coffee in atmospheric peace. At night, with the buildings lit up, it is one of the most magical places in Sicily to have a nightcap. The site was sacred even in Sikel times. Here the 5th-century BC Greeks dedicated a temple to Athena in thanksgiving for their victory at Himera. This temple was adapted by the Christians, and became the **cathedral** (*open 8–12 and 4–7*) in 640 under Bishop Zosimus. Further remodelling took place under the Normans, and, when the front toppled in the 1693 earthquake, Andrea Palma designed the sumptuous Baroque façade (finished 1754), a complex composition that teases the eye with tricks of light and depth. It is one of the last Baroque works in Italy, and one of the best. You can spot the original Greek Doric columns outside, semi-immersed into the more recent outer wall; within the columns columns are even more apparent as they trace the skeleton of Athena's temple. The first chapel on the right is the baptistry, containing an ancient Greek marble font resting on Norman bronze lions; the panels of intricate Cosmatesque decoration on the walls give an idea of how the church looked in medieval times. This is followed by the Cappella di Santa Lucia, patroness of Syracuse. At the far end of the same aisle is the Cappella del Crocifisso, with a painting of St Zosimus by Antonello da Messina, and one of St Marcian attributed to the school of Antonello, which also painted the 13 panels in the sacristy (door in the chapel).

Other buildings in Piazza del Duomo include the **Palazzo Arcivescovile**, housing the Biblioteca Alagoniana with its 13th-century manuscripts; the church of **Santa Lucia alla Badia**, with another delightful façade, begun in 1695 after the earthquake; and the **Municipio**, a palace built in 1633 by Giovanni Vermexio, with a lovely Baroque courtyard, built over ruins which house the small Ionic **temple antiquarium** (*usually open in office hours*). The tall, graceful Ionic temple, perhaps dedicated to Artemis, was begun next to the temple of Athena *c.* 525 BC. Models of both can be seen in the Museo Archeológico.

Fonte Arethusa and Around

From Piazza del Duomo, take Via Picherali west to the seafront and the **Fonte Arethusa**. Now populated by ducks and planted with papyrus, this beautiful freshwater spring, so close to the sea, fascinated the ancient Greeks. According to them, the nymph Arethusa was being pursued by the river god Alpheus through Arcadia in Greece, when she begged Artemis, the goddess of virginity, to save her from the god's embrace. Artemis obliged by turning her into a fountain, in which form she fled under the sea to Sicily, with Alpheus in hot pursuit, both rising up in Ortygia, where their waters were mixed. Strabo claimed that a cup thrown in the River Alpheus, in Arcadia, would turn up in Arethusa's fountain in Syracuse. The potent symbolism of an underground river was highly significant in the esoteric circles of the Renaissance. Learned academies were known as 'Arcadian'. In England, Sir Philip Sidney wrote his masterpiece, *Arcadia*, long before Coleridge's opium dream that produced *Kubla Khan* ('where Alph the sacred river ran...').

On a more mundane level, Nelson replenished his fleet from the fountain before the Battle of the Nile; perhaps the luxuriant papyrus along its edges brought him luck. Recently the fountain has been lovingly restored, and a small **tropical aquarium** (*open 10–8.30*) installed nearby. The papyrus also grows at the Cyane spring west of the city (*see p.323*), and other places, and local artisans put it to use. Signs near Arethusa point you to a **Papyrus Museum** (*open Tues–Sun 9–1.30*) and other shops. North of the fountain extends the promenade called the Foro Vittorio Emanuele II, or **Foro Italico**; at the far end stands the 15th-century **Porta Marina**, with Gothic inscriptions.

A few steps further south is a tiny but very tempting bathing **beach**, with a postage-stamp area of sand and a small terrace, and a very small admission charge.

On the southernmost tip of Ortygia rises the **Castello Maniace**, named after George Maniakes, the Byzantine who, with Norman help, recaptured the city from the Muslims. Rebuilt by Frederick II in 1239, the keep is 165ft square but only two-thirds of its original height. Now a barracks, it can be visited only with permission from the superintendent of archaeology (**t** 09 31 48 11 11). Beneath the castle you can also visit the imaginatively named **Bagno della Regina** (Queen's Bath), actually an ancient underground reservoir.

Museo Regionale d'Arte Medioevale e Moderna

The only other building from Frederick's time on Ortygia is the **Palazzo Bellomo** (Via Capodieci), although later additions almost overwhelm the original building. The *palazzo* now contains the **Museo Regionale d'Arte Medioevale e Moderna** (*open Mon–Fri 9–1.30, Sun and hols 9–12.30; adm*). The collection includes architectural fragments from ancient to medieval times, which share the ground floor with a number of sculptural works by the Gaginis, notably Antonello's elegant Renaissance tomb of Giovanni Cardinas, an important nobleman of the late 15th century who is also remembered by an Antonello da Messina portrait upstairs. The paintings, on the first floor, include altarpieces moved here from local churches, showing the Sicilians' artistic conservatism and their love of colour and rich gold backgrounds. Many of the works are by foreigners, especially Venetians; others show a Catalan influence, like the naive, brilliant 15th-century *Altarpiece of San Lorenzo*. The stars of the collection, though, are the damaged *Annunciation* by Antonello da Messina, and one of Caravaggio's masterpieces, the *Burial of St Lucy* (1608), in which the artist greatly distorted the size of the gravediggers to create a memorable vision of mindless brutality. Besides paintings, there are painted ceramics from the Muslim era, drawings, furniture, reliquaries and crafts.

Opposite, **San Martino** (*open for services*) is a 6th-century basilica, although most of what stands now is from the 14th century. It houses a fine 15th-century triptych of the *Madonna and Child*. The Opera dei Pupi performs traditional marionette shows in summer; the city is currently restoring a theatre for it, and in the meantime you can visit their **workshop** (*ask at the tourist office for details*). Two other churches of interest lie at the opposite end of Ortygia: Baroque **San Filippo** in Via Vittorio Veneto, a fine street of 17th-century Spanish mansions, and **San Pietro** round the corner, in Via San Pietro, founded in the 4th century by St Germanus. You can still make out its original form as a Roman basilica despite later alterations.

The Mainland

In the Middle Ages, stricken Syracuse shrank into the easily defensible island. In the 19th century, it began to expand outwards once again. The ancient quarter of Achradina, across the bridge from Ortygia, was laid out in a new grid of streets, and the site of the Greek agora was made into the large square called Foro Siracusano, now dominated by the Fascist-built war memorial, the **Pantheon of the Fallen**. Between the railway station and the **fishmarket**, on Via Elorina (*open mornings Mon–Sat*), are the ruins known as the **Ginnasio Romano** (*open daily 9–1*), although they actually encompass a small 1st-century theatre, its cavea picturesquely flooded.

Archaeologists believe it was constructed for the minority who still appreciated drama after gladiatorial contests became the fare at the far larger Greek theatre.

Borgo Santa Lucia

The quarter Borgo Santa Lucia, to the east, is named after Syracuse's patroness, who, after various torments, was stabbed in the neck in 304 on the site of the church of **Santa Lucia** (*open daily 9–12 and 4–6*). Rebuilt in 1629, a few elements remain of an original Norman church, including the doorway, rose window and two ancient cruci-fixes in the apse. St Lucy was kept here until 1030, when George Maniakes sent her body off to Constantinople; the Venetians, incurable relic-pirates, stole her from there in 1204. In expectation of her imminent return in 1630, an octagonal sepulchral chapel was built by Giovanni Vermexio. The chapel is still empty, although not for lack of trying: a few years back, some Sicilians nabbed her relics from Venice's Santa Geremia, meaning to bring her home, but they reconsidered and gave her back (on her name day), and there she remains. Then there is the confusion over her form of martyrdom. Lucy is usually portrayed carrying her eyes on a platter, like a waitress with an order of eggs sunnyside-up; she is invoked by sufferers of eye diseases. The association with eyes is derived from her name, which means light; her festival on 13 December is most enthusiastically celebrated in Sweden, where she brings the hope of light to the land of the midday moon. Beneath the church is a vast series of cata-combs (*closed*), the oldest in Sicily – used by the Christians since the 2nd century – and the second largest in Italy, after those in Rome. A small underground chapel has traces of Byzantine paintings.

Also in Borgo Santa Lucia, on Via dell'Arsenale, are the rather scanty remains of the ancient **arsenal**, and, next to it, the Byzantine **bath-house**, where Emperor Constans was so piquantly murdered. Imagine for a moment that there had been no soap dish, and the Byzantine capital had remained in Syracuse; history would have been completely different, maybe even nicer.

The *Latomie* and the Catacombs

If you were to sweep all of old Syracuse into one big pile, its volume would appar-ently be about five billion cubic metres – that is the amount of stone taken since Greek times from the string of *latomie*, or quarries, that bound the northern edge of town. A landmark since Thucydides' day, they often helped in defence, and have been used since for everything from prisons to gardens (Dionysius, the poetical tyrant, filled them with people who didn't appreciate his verse, most famously the lyric poet Philoxenes, who couldn't stop laughing at one of his recitals).

The first *latomia* is in the ancient quarter of Tyche, the working-man's neighbour-hood of Greek Syracuse, to the north of Borgo Santa Lucia. Where the Riviera Dionisio il Grande and the Via Politi Laudien meet is the entrance to the **Latomia dei Cappuccini**, quarries begun in the 6th century BC. Once the horrible dungeon of the captured Athenian soldiers, these are now the peaceful **gardens of the Capuchin friars** (*closed*). To the west, on Via August von Platen, are the **Catacombs of Vigna**

Cassia (*currently closed*), from the 3rd century BC, with a few traces of paintings, and the **Protestant Cemetery of Villa Landolina** (*open daily 8–5*), located in a small *latomia*, where the refined and soulful German Romantic poet August von Platen is buried. Von Platen would have got on fine with Shelley and his other English contemporaries: his most famous lyric begins, 'He who has once looked on Beauty with his eyes, Is already given over to Death'. He spent some time mooning around the ruins here, and then died.

In the vicinity (Via San Giovanni) is the ruined church of **San Giovanni**, built on the site of the first cathedral of Syracuse, rebuilt by the Normans, then destroyed by the 1693 earthquake – although the fine rose window somehow managed to escape intact. There is much more to see there than first meets the eye; beneath the church is the only part of the city's labyrintine catacombs (second only in scale to Rome's) that are accessible to visitors (*open Wed–Mon 9–1 and 2.30–5*). The tour begins in the crypt, where the first Bishop of Syracuse, St Marcian, was martyred in the 3rd century. The symbols of the four Evangelists are carved on the columns of the chapel, which also contains an altar on the site where St Paul is said to have preached to the Syracusans, the pillar where St Marcian was martyred, and what is believed to be the first painting of Santa Lucia, a fine work dating back to the 4th century. The guided tour takes you further underground through the astonishing catacombs, used from Roman times until well into the 6th century (the bodies have since been reburied elsewhere). In places you can still spot traces of early Christian paintings, and incised decoration with Christian symbols. For the most part, however, there are honeycombs of empty niches within an eerie, labyrinthine underworld. The city's catacombs owe their origins to the Greeks, who created an underground system for supplying water to the city: reservoirs were linked by tunnels (which became the catacomb tunnels) and fed by shafts still visible today.

Back outside, you will already have noticed the **Santuario della Madonnina delle Lácrime** (*open daily 7–12.30 and 4–7*), across Viale Teocrito, built to house a small, factory-made statue of the Madonna which wept for five days in 1953. This 251ft concrete shuttlecock, eerily dominating the city, has certainly divided the true believers from the rest of the Syracusans. The sanctuary was completed a few years ago, and a colossal statue of the Madonnina was bolted on top.

Museo Archeológico Paolo Orsi

Open daily 9–1 and 3.30–6.30; closed Mon morning and Sun evening.

Across Viale Teocrito from the sanctuary and a step away from the **San Giovannicatacombs** is the Museo Archeológico, which houses perhaps the greatest hoard of Greek art between Athens and London. Set in a palm-shaded park, the museum is a modern building that is spacious but clearly not in a brilliant state of repair. Its namesake Paolo Orsi was Sicily's greatest archaeologist, of whom the Syracusans are very proud.

More than enough is on display to fill an entertaining half-day, starting with a very thorough grounding in the talented cultures that occupied Sicily before the Greeks.

This is a seriously didactic museum, and, besides an overwhelming amount of art and artefacts, there are photographs and plans of their major sites, and lots of historical information (in Italian). The parade of pottery starts off with the intricate incised and painted designs of the **Neolithic peoples**. The cultural unity Sicily enjoyed in Neolithic times was shattered by invasions from the mainland *c.* 3000 BC, when the story begins to get complicated. Among the contributions of the **Thapsos and Castelluccio folk** and the rest, you can trace the beginnings of figurative art from the first shy snakes, fish and birds. The next important invaders, the **Sikels**, were much better at jewellery – something warrior societies (like the Celts, and the barbarians that overran Rome) often have in common, whatever the age.

The Greek section begins with a large exhibit on the excavations at **Megara Hyblaea** (*see* p.303); though small, this is the Greek town that has been most thoroughly excavated, and has provided a good deal of our knowledge about Greek life in Sicily. Archaic Greek art is well represented in the rooms that follow, including some hints of tendencies that were uniquely Sicilian, like the 5th-century **metopes** with floral designs, unlike anything ever seen in Greece. The collection's star exhibit is the notoriously voluptuous ***Landolina Venus*** (a Roman copy of a Hellenistic work), excavated in the grounds of the museum itself; just as remarkable are the more maternal statue of an unknown goddess suckling twins, and the sarcophagus of Valerius and Adelphia, with its biblical scenes.

From Syracuse itself, there are reconstructions of the **temple of Athena** (now the cathedral) and the slim, graceful **Ionic temple** that stood next door – marking an architectural revolution of Hellenistic times. In ancient times, just next to the site of the Madonnina delle Lácrime, there stood a sanctuary of Demeter and Core; the best from among the thousands of terracotta **ex-votos** are on display here. Terracotta was also used for most of the architectural decoration; note the striking **Gorgon**, with its winged horse Pegasus who, according to a version of the legend, was born from her blood.

The chronology currently ends there, though plans for a much-needed Roman section are in the pipeline.

Archaeological Zone

Open daily 9am until two hours before sunset; adm.

The Archaeological Zone is in Neapolis (a rather grindingly dull walk from Ortygia, worth avoiding if possible), the 'new city' quarter of Syracuse built by Hieron II. Largely abandoned in the Dark Ages, Neapolis suffered even more at the hands of that most destructive of emperors, Charles V, who in 1526 ordered Neapolis to be demolished to use the stone for fortifications, at the same time as he was trashing the Alhambra in Spain, and a year before his army would sack Rome. The ruins are still very impressive, even the much pilfered **Ara di Ierone II** (Altar of Hieron II; 241–215 BC), over 540ft long, dedicated to Zeus Eleftherios. Hieron II built this altar in honour of Timoleon's expulsion of the tyrants, which the ancient Syracusans commemorated annually with a

The Wizard of Syracuse

Give me motion and extension, and I can move the Earth.

attributed to Archimedes

Looking back at Greek Sicily, it's hard not to be depressed: so much talent gone to waste, so much brilliance, and little but ruins to show for it. Like Leonardo da Vinci, the great genius Archimedes (*c.* 287–212 BC) was forced by circumstances to spend much of his brain's precious time on military matters – finding ways to keep the barbaric Romans out. As General of Ordnance, Archimedes was busy designing ingenious war machinery to defend the city. His contraptions dropped 600lb lead weights on to the Roman scaling engines, and his grapnels were lowered to snatch the Roman ships in the harbour, lift them up by their hulls, and spill their crews into the sea. According to Diodorus Siculus, a historian whose strangest stories have a way of turning out to be true, Archimedes even reflected the sun's rays with mirrors to ignite the more distant Roman ships. That would be difficult: it would have required a very large set of mirrors, a precise mechanism for focusing them, and a non-moving target. You can bet he probably tried.

Archimedes' real love, however, was mathematics. He discovered the ratio of the surface of a right circular cylinder to that of a sphere inscribed within it (if you think that's simple, try it yourself). It was a spectacular trick for his time, leading to many mathematical discoveries; it explains the strange figures on his tomb. Among many other useful things, Archimedes found a reasonably accurate value for pi, and made the first orrery, a working model of the heavenly bodies (the Romans stole it, although a mosaic picture of it survives at Soluntum). He worked a lot with levers and the theory of mechanical advantage; beyond doubt his greatest invention was the block and tackle, or compound pulley – none of the works of the Romans, nor of the medieval cathedral builders, could have been raised without it.

Everyone knows the story of Archimedes racing out of his bathtub and down the street shouting 'Eureka!' Hieron II had commissioned a golden crown to present to the gods at Delphi. When the work was finished he began wondering how he could know for sure that the work was really all gold, and he set his cousin Archimedes the task of finding out. Sitting in the tub, and watching the water level rise, Archimedes suddenly considered how objects displace water – and so discovered the principle of specific gravity. He had a lump of gold made, the same mass as Hieron's crown; dipping them both in a vase, he noted that the crown displaced more water – hence another, lighter metal was concealed within it, increasing the bulk of the crown. Thus Archimedes proved conclusively that the goldsmith, like everyone else in the Hellenistic Greek world, was a crook.

great sacrifice. Such altars, the most famous of which was the Altar of Zeus at Pergamon, were much in vogue in Hellenistic times. Although only the base of this one remains, it does give an idea of the size of the public monuments built by the western Greeks.

The Greek Theatre

This grandeur is also evident in the Greek theatre carved out of the living rock. One of the largest in the world, it measures 455ft in diameter and seats 15,000. The original theatre was probably of wood, and probably from the 6th century BC. In later incarnations, this was one of the top venues of the Greek world. Aeschylus' *The Persians*, and his Prometheus plays, saw their debuts here, among many other works, and native Syracusan Charmides produced the first classical comedies. Sicilian Greeks always enjoyed the lighter side: later Syracusan stars included Sophron and Rinthon, the inventors of classical mime. We usually think of Greek theatres as semicircular, but there is architectural evidence that the stage where these works were performed was actually trapezoidal in shape.

Rebuilt in its present form by Hieron II, it was later partially reconstructed by the Romans, in that decadent time when few people cared for real theatre any more. Their major contribution was a stage building, shutting off the panoramic view that the Greeks loved as backdrop for their theatre; only the substructures of this remain. The Romans staged gladiatorial matches here, and flooded the orchestra for mock naval engagements (*naumachiae*). Along the top of the seats are inscriptions dedicating various parts of the theatre to gods and to the family of Hieron II. As in ancient times, Greek dramas are still performed here, though only in summer (*ask the tourist office for details*). Above the theatre runs a long terrace called the **Via dei Sepolcri** (Street of Tombs), with mostly Byzantine graves. The largest niche is a nymphaeum built by Hieron II, where the waters of an ancient aqueduct still cascade. West of the theatre, the very ancient **Santuario di Apollo**, sacred since the 7th century BC, may be visited, along with the equally primitive **Teatro Lineare**, where the seats consist of 17 steps carved into the hillside; this may have been used for political assemblies.

Orecchio di Dionisio and the Roman Amphitheatre

East of the Greek theatre is the **Latomia del Paradiso**, whose main attraction is the odd **Orecchio di Dionisio** (Ear of Dionysius), an artificial cavern 211ft long and 69ft high, of uncertain purpose, known for its excellent acoustics (as demonstrated in song by the tour guides as they take parties in – or try for yourself). Caravaggio christened it after its ear-shaped entrance, although some have speculated that the tyrant Dionysius incarcerated political prisoners here so that he could listen to their conversations. Next to the cavern is the man-made **Grotta dei Cordari** (Ropemakers' Cave), used for centuries – the cool, humid air inside made naval ropes hold their shape better. In the same area are the **Latomia di Santa Venera** and **Latomia Intagliatella**, leading to the major burial ground of Greek times, the **Necropoli dei Grotticelli**. An adjoining Roman-era cemetery includes a **tomb**, sculpted with a pediment, that has long been called (falsely) the tomb of Archimedes.

One enters a separate section of the Archaeological Zone through another gate (but with the same ticket), to the **Roman amphitheatre** built in the 3rd century AD. Like the Greek theatre, it is one of the largest of its kind, measuring 462ft across, though not quite as jaw-dropping (for that reason it might be worth visiting first). From the corridor below the front seats, the wild beasts and gladiators would enter the arena, in the centre of which is a mysterious pit. The names of wealthy patrons can be seen inscribed on some of the seats. In summer the theatre is sometimes used to stage concerts – details from the tourist office.

Around Syracuse

Castello Eurialo

Open daily 9am until one hour before sunset.

One interesting excursion from Syracuse (city bus 11) is to Castello Eurialo. After the defeat of the Athenian expedition, the relieved Syracusans sat back and took stock. They realized how close they had come to defeat themselves, and that the Achilles' heel of their defences had proved to be the long Epipolae ridge that sloped down to the city from the northwest, where the Athenians had built their fort and tried to wall off the city. The only way to prevent this from happening again would be to fortify the entire ridge, creating an enclosed area far larger than Syracuse itself. New walls were started, and Eurialo, at the top of the ridge, was begun by Dionysius the Elder in the early 4th century BC, and later modified by Archimedes.

Euryalos means 'broad nail' in Greek, and the castle defended the crucial inland supply route to Syracuse in times of siege. Three great trenches, connected by under-ground passages, were constructed to repulse the rapidly evolving machines of war. The castle, with its five huge towers, was only part of the vast 27km system of defence designed by Dionysius, the longest of any Greek city. Unfortunately, the defenders surrendered without a fight to the Roman Marcellus in 212 BC; the Romans had attacked during a festival of Aphrodite, goddess of love, and most of the defending soldiers were away from their posts. The castle, though in ruins, is the best-preserved example of Greek defensive works in the world; it also affords an excellent view of the Syracusan plain below.

Sights West and South of Syracuse

The **Olympieion**, the scant but picturesque ruins of a Doric temple of Olympian Zeus, 1.5km west of the city, can be reached by buses 21, 22, 23 and 24. Still standing on the right bank of the River Cyane are two columns and part of the stylobate. This suburban temple, fortified during the war with Athens, played a key role in the fighting as the base of the Syracusan cavalry. The Athenians had neglected to bring enough horses, and the riders who holed up here, able to raid at will from behind enemy lines, drove the Athenians crazy and contributed as much as anyone to the final victory.

From here you can walk to the **source of the Cyane** ('blue' in Greek), the river where Hades opened up the earth and took Persephone down below, after abducting her at Lago Pergusa. It is named after Persephone's nymph, who wept so much at the goddess's disappearance that she turned into a spring. Along the banks of the Cyane grows the exotic papyrus, reputedly a gift to Syracuse from the Hellenistic ruler Ptolemy Philadelphus of Egypt. It grows wild nowhere else outside North Africa. A leisurely way to visit the Olympieion and the Cyane is a one-hour trip by small motor-boat (*departures between 10–5, April–Oct*, **t** *0931 69076*).

When you've had your fill of ruins, consider a dip at one of the chain of beaches to the south. **Pantanelli** is the closest, with the more organized **Lido Arenella**, **Fontane Bianche**, **Lido Sayonara**, etc. farther on. The deep blue of the sea is matched in intensity by the glistening green of the citrus groves, but be warned – you will not be 'getting away from it all'. Fontane Bianche has superb beaches but in season is a huge, noisy, over-organized resort such as only the Italian seaside can produce: self-service cafés, lines of umbrellas, and, above all, a constant and deafening racket of pop music and people. You'll pay to park, swim, shower, use the loo, and so on. There is only one free public beach. In the summer there are concerts at the southern end of the beach.

Sicily's Southeastern Corner

At the three points of mystic Trinacria (*see* map, p.199) we find Tràpani, Messina – and, at the third, nothing at all. Nevertheless, this corner, dominated by the rugged Monti Iblei and the river valleys that run down from them, has plenty worth seeing. In ancient times, especially before the arrival of the Greeks, it was often the most important and heavily populated part of the island, and so there is no shortage of ruins to inspect. Almost every village and town here suffered greatly from the earthquake of 1693; it was a relatively prosperous time for the area, and all were ambitiously rebuilt with a frosting of glorious Baroque.

Inland from Syracuse: Palazzolo Acréide

The scenic SS124, west from Syracuse, takes you up into the mountains, and to Palazzolo Acréide, successor of ancient Akrai, the first Syracusan colony, founded in 664 BC on a high hill. Its ruins are the most extensive in the province after Syracuse itself: a 15min walk from the modern centre takes you there. The **Archaeology Zone** (*open daily 9–12.30 and 3–one hour before sunset*) includes a small (600-seat) but well-preserved Hellenistic theatre, Roman silos and mills, the *bouleuterion* (council chamber), and the foundation of the agora. Behind the theatre are two quarries, the **Intagliata** and the **Intagliatella**, one containing Byzantine tombs, the other niches of a hero cult, with a carved relief. Another *latomia*, more mysterious and one mile from the Archaeology Zone (follow the signposts), contains the **Templi Ferali**, two great chambers with niches and inscriptions in honour of the deceased. Below, in an enclosure, are the '**Santoni**' – 12 eroded reliefs representing various aspects of the goddess Cybele, the orgiastic Phrygian version of the Great Goddess, whose worship was widespread in Greek Sicily, and later in Rome; she appears here – the archaeologists say – with Hermes, corybantes (her priests), lions and other divinities.

Palazzolo itself is a Baroque charmer with a complete lack of tourist facilities; it was relocated back near ancient Akrai after the medieval town, a few miles away, was ruined in the 1693 earthquake. There is a museum, the **Casa Museo**, in Via Machiavelli (*open daily 9–1 and 3.30–7*), with a fine ethnographic collection in an early 20th-century peasant home. Among the churches, note the asymmetrical **Chiesa dell'Annunziata** – Antonello da Messina's famous *Annunciation* in the Syracuse museum was painted for this church; also the *Madonna with Child* by Laurana, in the church of the **Convento dei Minori Osservanti**; and the exuberant Baroque interior of **San Paolo**, in Piazza Umberto.

Just to the north of Palazzolo, people in the village of **Buscemi** are developing an interesting folk 'museum', spread around several sites: a weaver's workshop, a *frantoio* (oil presser), etc. Contact Mr Rosario Aquaviva (**t** 09 31 87 82 73) to set up a tour. Another colony of Syracuse, **Casmene** (founded 644 BC), is located on top of Monte Casale, northwest of Palazzolo. The scenic river valleys around Casmene offer more than the excavations themselves, and the difficult access to the site makes it a destination for the adventuresome. **Buccheri**, the closest village to Monte Casale, is a modest summer resort, surrounded by forests and pretty views. Between Palazzolo and Syracuse lies another hill town, **Canicattini**, from where speleologists can visit the **Grotta del Monello** (Little Rascal's Cave), with stalactites. The **cemetery** of Canicattini is a true Baroque city of the dead.

As a prelude to Baroque Noto, there is **Avola**, south of Syracuse, another town destroyed in 1693 and rebuilt on a new site. Like Grammichele (*see* p.208), Avola has a hexagonal plan, centered on Piazza Umberto I. The plan, and many of the major buildings, such as the Chiesa Madre, was the work of royal architect Angelo Italia.

Noto: Baroque's Ideal City

Noto stands out as sharply as one of the magical towns described in Italo Calvino's *Invisible Cities*: a new city, designed and built of golden, sun-drenched sandstone in the finest Sicilian Baroque, it is unabashedly theatrical, tacitly admitting, in its set *piazze*, broad sweeping stairs, and the confectioner's façades of its churches and palaces, that all the world is indeed a stage. Sicilians call it a 'garden of stone'. Then, out of the blue, it was discovered that even a fantasy city could be in grave danger of total collapse.

Noto was born of destruction, when its parent, now called Noto Antico, fell prostrate in the great 1693 earthquake. Despite the damage and loss of life, the townspeople began rebuilding on the old site. The government had other plans, however, and they were forced to up-sticks to a new town, located several miles away. The great priest-architect Rosario Gagliardi, Paolo Labisi and Vincenzo Sinatra, laid out a new street plan in accordance with the ideals of the early 18th century to set off their architecture: rational and symmetrical, with straight streets, stairs and sloping *piazze*, to play perspective games with the eye. And when this Baroque paragon was finished, there was nothing more for it to do but sink discreetly into the national daydream and collect dust.

The rude awakening occurred in September 1986, when a long-overdue structural survey discovered that Noto was so fragile that the slightest tremor of the earth would make it go down like a house of cards. Nuns were evacuated from convents, the *corso* was closed to traffic, the museum locked up. A conference was quickly called and, when the powers-that-be voted yes to Noto, the work of propping up the foundations of the city's monuments began.

All the effort notwithstanding, the cathedral's cupola collapsed in 1996 after a particularly bad storm, and this building, as awell as many others, are bound to be crisscrossed with scaffolding for decades to come. The renovation work is extensive but Noto is still well worth a visit.

Walking in Noto

For the full effect, enter Noto through its monumental gate, the **Porta Reale** (1838), siphoning traffic into Noto's majestic main street, **Corso Vittorio Emanuele**, which the planners placed along the flank of a hill, the better to build the wide ballroom stairs beloved of Sicilian Baroque. The *corso* pierces three grandiose set-piece *piazze*. The first is adorned with the elliptical convent of **Santa Chiara** (*open daily 9–12.30 and 4–7*), attributed to Gagliardi, which contains a *Madonna* by Antonello Gagini saved from old Noto, **San Francesco** (1745, *open daily 9–12.30 and 4–7*), at the top of the cascading steps, with the horizontal contrast of the monastery of **San Salvatore** (1703; *closed*), running parallel to the stairway. The monastery houses the **Museo Archeológico**, an interesting collection of finds from Eloro and Noto Antica, recently opened after a lengthy restoration.

The next square along the *corso*, **Piazza Municipio**, is Noto's most important. Three flights of steps ascend to the monumental cathedral of **San Nicolò** (or Corrado Gonfaloniere, as it is also known), named after the town's patron saint, which has twin bell towers. One of the last structures to be completed (1770), its cupola collapsed in a storm and is still being rebuilt. Next to it stands the **Palazzo Vescovile** and, opposite, the beautiful, arcaded **Palazzo Ducezio** (town hall, *open daily 9–12.30 and 4–7*), built in 1746 by Vincenzo Sinatra, the Neoclassicist among Noto's architects. The effect is completed by another church, **San Salvatore**, and the **Palazzo Landolina di Sant'Alfano**.

The *corso* then enters a third square, **Piazza Sedici Maggio**, where a pretty little garden contains a fountain with a statue of Hercules, salvaged from Noto Antica. Noto's food market gathers here every Monday morning and on the first and third Tuesday of every month. Facing this is the **Teatro Vittorio Emanuele** (*for programme t 0931 896 655 or ask at the tourist office; open daily 8.30–12.30 and 4–8*), finished in 1842 and recently restored, and the beautiful convex façade of **San Domenico** (1727; *under restoration*), by Gagliardi; adjacent is a former **convent**, now containing a library and municipal museum. Off the *corso*, up and down bumpy cobbled streets made for mountain goats, you can seek out more works by Gagliardi: the concave church and *collegio* of the **Gesuiti** (1730s) and the **Carmine** (1743), a journey into the Rococo.

Getting There and Around

Noto can be reached by **train** from Syracuse. There are **buses** from Syracuse to Noto, Palazzalo Acréide, Avola and numerous other towns in the region. There are also numerous buses and trains between Ragusa, Módica, Ispica and Noto. The Cava d'Ispica is accessible only by **car**.

Tourist Information

Noto: Piazza XVI Maggio, **t** 0931 573 779, *noto.apt@tin.it (open Mon–Sat 8–2 and 3.30– 6.30, Sun 8.30–1.30).*

Where to Stay and Eat

There are plenty of places to stay in Noto as long as you don't mind *pensione* and rented rooms (which often come with a private bath and cooking facilities) The tourist office has information on them all.

Noto ✉ 96017

★★★Hotel della Ferla, Via A. Gramsci, **t** 0931 576 007, *www.hotelferla.it (moderate)*. Modern, comfortable 15-room hotel on the edge of the historic centre, and with a garage. Set in a garden filled with olive and orange trees.

★Stella, Via F. Maiore 44, **t** 0931 835 695 *(inexpensive, less without bath)*. A good choice *pensione.*

Il Giglio, Piazza Municipio, near the cathedral, **t** 0931 838 640 *(moderate)*. You can expect some typical Sicilian dishes at this trattoria, or good homemade ravioli with ricotta, as well as culinary surprises like paella – the owner's wife is Spanish.

Neas, Via Rocco Pirri 3, **t** 0931 573 538 *(moderate)*. Sicilian fare and seafood serves in interior honeycombed with stone arches. The terrace is nice too.

Carmine, Via Ducezio 1, **t** 0931 83 87 05 *(inexpensive)*. Very much a family concern, with wholesome fare – try the *coniglio alla stimpirata* (rabbit with olives and mint). *Closed Mon.*

Bar-Gelateria Constanza, Via Silvio Spaventa. A good place to try the local sweets and pastries.

Noto Marina ✉ 96017

★★★Eloro, Contrada Pizzuta, **t** 0931 81 22 44, *www.teorematour.it (expensive, full board only in Aug)*. The facilities here include a swimming pool, a tennis court, a beautiful private beach, a playground for the tots and 230 rooms.

★★Jonio, Viale Lido 1, **t** 0931 81 20 40, *hoteljonio@hotmail.com (inexpensive)*. A very servicable place to stay, though not exactly elegant.

★Korsal, Loc. Marina, **t** 0931 81 21 19 *(budget)*. This is the basic option in town.

Avola ✉ 96017

★Ancora, Via Lungomare, **t** 0931 82 28 75 *(budget, half-board only in summer)*. A range of no-frills rooms are offered at this *pensione*. The adjoining restaurant-pizzeria *(inexpensive)* is a useful bonus, and serves up a nice *pizza alla marinara*, and a range of fresh seafood.

★Mignon, Via Maugeri 37, **t** 09 31 82 17 88 *(budget)*. A bargain-price *pensione* handily located near the beach.

Portopalo di Capo Pássero ✉ 96017

★★Jonic, Viale V. Emanuele 19, **t** 0931 84 26 15, *www.jonichotel.com (budget–inexpensive, half board only in Aug)*. Of the few hotels here, this one has rooms with their own bathrooms.

Vendicari ✉ 96017

Il Roveto, C. da Roveto, on the Noto–Pachino road, **t** 0931 66024, *www.roveto.it (inexpensive)*. This *agriturismo* is the only place to stay near the wonderful beach of the Vendicari nature reserve. Has self-contained apartments in a restored old farmhouse, which get booked quickly in the summer (when the minimum stay is three nights). There is also a good restaurant *(moderate)* which uses produce from the farm.

Rosolini ✉ 96017

Locanda del Borgo, Via Controscieri 11, **t** 0931 850514 *(expensive)*. Head to this renovated castle to eat innovative dishes that make the best of traditional regional techniques.

Among the palaces, the **Palazzo Villadorata**, on Via Corrado Nicolaci (1737–60; *open daily 9–1 and 3–6, admission*), stands out. No other building in Noto, or anywhere else outside Bagheria, exposes so well the fantastical tastes of Sicily's 18th-century nobility. Only the Salone delle Feste hints at its former splendour inside while it is adorned with lovely wrought-iron balconies and battalions of Baroque grotesques: nymphs, lions, horses and putti in squads of five under each window.

San Carlo at the bottom of Via Nicolaci (*open daily 9–12.30 and 4–7, adm*) has the best views of Noto's rooftops sweeping all the way down to the sea from its bell-tower. Up on the hill of Noto Alto, where the streets become increasingly austere, the principal monument is **SS. Crocifisso** (early 1700s; *under restoration*), a large basilica; inside is a statue of the *Madonna della Neve* (1471) by Francesco Laurana.

South and West of Noto

Around Noto

The meagre remains of **Noto Antica**, ancient Netum, lie some 20km from Noto on Monte Alviano, off the road to Palazzolo Acréide. Founded according to tradition by the Sikel king Ducetius, in the 5th century BC, Netum came under the rule of Syracuse. It was the only town to resist the despoliations of the praetor Verres with any success, and was also the last bastion of the Saracens, before their surrender to the Normans in 1091. Never rebuilt after the earthquake, Noto Antica remains a wild, total ruin, which includes parts of a Norman castle, the gateway, churches and tombs (earliest of which are two Sikel necropolises excavated in the vicinity). It's a poignant place to explore on foot: from the town gateway a track leads into the ruins of the city, past the still imposing Torre Reale, and on towards shattered remains of houses and palaces.

West of Noto Antica, **Castelluccio** (*open daily 9–1*) was a prehistoric settlement, inhabited between the 18th and 14th centuries BC. The great archaeologist Paolo Orsi excavated the site, and gave its name to the early Bronze Age culture of eastern and central Sicily. You can see the remains of the village and necropolis, though all portable finds are now in the Museo Archeológico in Syracuse.

South Along the Coast to Capo Pássero

Besides archaeological sites, there are also a number of beaches which can easily be reached by bus from Noto: from north to south, **Lido di Avola**, **Marina di Avola**, **Calabernardo** and **Noto Marina**. Just south of the last is **Eloro**, or ancient Helorus (*open daily 8–2*), founded by the Syracusans in the 7th century BC, at the mouth of the River Tellaro. It has recently been excavated: at the entrance to the site stand the Pizzota Column (a Hellenistic funeral monument), and the Santuario di Demeter e Core, both outside the well-preserved city walls. Within, a small theatre and the grandiose stoa of the 2nd century BC have been uncovered.

The coastal road continues down to the isolated beaches at **Vendicari**, at the foot of an old coastal watchtower. The surrounding lagoons have been designated a wildlife sanctuary and are home to egrets, herons and flamingoes while the nature reserve designation keeps developers at bay from one of Sicily's finest beaches. Trees are few here, in this flat land of cane and rocks. It is slowly being developed: near Pachino, at the southernmost tip of Sicily, come fine beaches at **Marzamemi** and **Portopalo di Capo Pássero**, both heading for resort status after starting life as simple fishing villages based around the old *tonnaras*.

You can **hire a boat** to explore Isola di Capo Pássero, and even tinier islets in the area, or the truly isolated parts of the coast around Punta delle Formiche to the west. Just north of Pachino, at the farm **San Lorenzo lo Vecchio**, the skeleton of a Hellenistic temple, transformed into a Byzantine church, may be seen incorporated into the farm buildings.

Ispica and the Cava d'Ispica

On the road from Noto to Ragusa, the first town you meet will be **Rosolini**. This has to be one of the dustiest little nowheres in Italy, but even it has an interesting site and a wonderful restaurant in a castle (see p.327). Beneath the **Castello del Principe** (1668) are catacombs and an early Christian **crypt** (*open daily 9–7; winter 9–1.30*), with three irregular naves carved out of the rock.

Five kilometres from Rosolini is **Ispica**, known as 'Spacca' in the Middle Ages. Like many of the surrounding towns, Ispica was destroyed in the earthquake of 1693, but re-emerged to become a busy agricultural centre. The **town hall** is a 1906 Liberty-style work of Ernesto Basile, and the church **Santa Maria Maggiore** is decorated with Baroque frescoes. What's left of pre-earthquake Ispica can be visited outside the modern town at the **Parco della Forza** (*open daily 9–7.30, until 5 in winter*): ruins of a castle, palaces, churches, walls, and a long underground staircase that led to an emergency water supply dating from prehistoric times to the Renaissance. As most of the stone was used for new buildings, there isn't that much to see.

Between Ispica and Módica is the **Cava d'Ispica** (*open daily 9–7.30, until 5 in winter*), a gentle 14km-long gorge in rugged country, fascinating for its signs of continuous habitation from the Bronze Age to the early 20th century: catacombs and cave dwellings carved in the rock face, silent testimonies of hardship and courage, mostly from the 5th–13th centuries. Many of the caves were inhabited by Byzantine monks, as in Apulia and in Cappadocia; some were expanded into chapels, and bits of fresco painting survive.

Pozzallo, south of Ispica, was once the port for Ragusa, and has a 14th-century tower and a fine wide sandy beach which is often empty, even in summer. British troops led by Montgomery landed here in 1943, joining with US troops to capture Gela, the first European ground to be recaptured by the Allies in the Second World War. Outside town a number of salt water ponds have been reclaimed and are now protected as they are the final stops for birds migrating to Africa.

The catamaran goes to Malta twice a day in August and less frequently the rest of the year (*www.virtueferries.com*, **t** 0932 954062).

Módica

Módica, the ancient Motyka, is one of the oldest towns of Sicily, the medieval fief of the Chiaramontes, and another Baroque showcase rebuilt after 1693. From Arab times through the reign of the Aragonese, it was capital of the county of Módica (roughly the modern province of Ragusa). At the beginning of the 18th century it was the fourth largest city in Sicily, though since then it has gradually lost its position as top town in the area to Ragusa.

Rather than standing high on a mountain-top, like most other ancient Sicilian towns, Módica is oddly hidden in a deep valley among the lonely limestone hills of the region: you won't see it until you're practically in it. The torrents that pass through Módica, and helped make it a defensible site, flooded the town in 1902; now dammed, and covered over, they are the main thoroughfares, Corso Umberto and Via Giarratana. Módica may no longer be 'the Venice of Sicily', but it is still a lovely town, where the houses on the hills peer discreetly over the shoulders of their neighbours, and many of the streets are stairways. It gave the world the now practically forgotten 1959 Nobel prizewinner for literature, Salvatore Quasimodo.

Getting There

Módica is on the train line between Syracuse and Ragusa. The journey to Syracuse takes about 40mins, and to Ragusa about 25mins.

Tourist Information

Corso Umberto 251, **t** 0932 753 324 (*open Mon–Sat 8.30–1.30 and 3–8, Sun 8.30–1.30*).

Where to Stay and Eat

***Hotel Relais**, Via Tommaso Campanella 99, **t** 0932 754 451 (*inexpensive–moderate*). Recently-opened *palazzo* sensitively renovated and offering good views of the town. Rooms are individual in style and comfortable.

Bristol, Via Risorgimento 8B, **t 0932 76 28 90 (*inexpensive*). This appealing little place is located a couple of kilometres out from Módica's centre.

***Motel di Módica**, Corso Umberto I, **t** 0932 94 10 22 (*inexpensive*). A modern hotel outside the centre, with its own parking.

Il Tetti di Siciliano, Via Cannata 24, **t** 0932 942 843, *siciliando@tin.it* (*budget*). A stone's throw away from the cathedral, this charming little hotel has a particularly inviting terrace, frescoed ceilings in the dining room and balconies in all the rooms that provide great views. It also holds art and crafts courses.

Fattoria delle Torri, Vico Napolitano 17, **t** 0932 75 12 86 (*expensive*). One of the best restaurants in the region, this serves a selection of memorable Sicilian dishes – and makes a worthwhile place to seek out for pork dishes that this corner of the island is renowned. Reservation recommended. *Closed Mon and Sun eve.*

Gargantua, Corso Umberto 261, **t** 0932 752 927 (*expensive*). Ring ahead to book on of the five tables in this barrel-vaulted resturant serving fresh seasonal food. *Closed Mon and Sun eve.*

L'Arco, Piazza Corrado Rizzone (*inexpensive*). You'll find excellent food, *vino locale* and friendly service, at this trattoria located in the central square by the bus station. *Closed Mon.*

Antica Dolceria Bonaiuto, Corso Umberto I. Stop here for something really different – *i'mpanatigghi*, a sweet made of meat and chocolate.

Módica Bassa

Módica consists of two towns, the upper and the lower. In Módica Bassa are the main shopping streets, the bus and train stations, etc. Most of Módica's monuments are strung along the main axis, Corso Umberto I. Starting from the southern end, Baroque **Santa Maria delle Grazie** was built in 1624 to house a miraculous icon, and its adjacent convent, now used as a town library and the **Museo Cívico** (*open Mon–Sat 9–1*), has a small collection on Sicilian traditions and folk arts. Past Piazza Buozzi, the *corso* skirts more Baroque churches: the **Carmine** and **San Francesco**, next to the town hall (the area between these churches was the centre of Módica's ancient Jewish community). Then comes **San Pietro**, an ambitious work atop a stairway, similar to San Giorgio (*see* below). Farther up are some fancifully decorated post-earthquake noble palaces, notably the **Palazzo Tedeschi**, next to San Pietro, and the **Palazzo Marmenti**.

In Via Marchese Tedeschi, in the other river valley, is the 18th-century church of **Santa Maria di Betlemme**, where the highest point of the great flood is marked by a plaque. Inside are two interesting chapels, the Gothic Cappella del Sacramento, and another with a colourful presepio of a century ago, with dozens of figures in traditional costume, made by ceramic artists from Caltagirone.

San Giorgio

From almost anywhere in town, you can see Módica's pride and symbol, the 18th-century church of San Giorgio, in Módica Alta, a building reminiscent of San Giorgio in Ragusa, and perhaps designed by its architect, Gagliardi. Dominated by its huge central spire, the church has a beautiful ornate façade beckoning at the summit of a monstrous Baroque stair of 250 steps. San Giorgio is purely decoration – there's not much inside worth climbing the steps for. But if you do make it up to the quiet streets of Módica Alta, there are more **Baroque palaces** in and around the main street, Corso Regina Margherita; take Via Pizzo to the **Belvedere Pizzo** for the best view over the city. The old conventual church on top of Módica Alta, **Santa Maria di Gesù**, now . houses a prison.

Ragusa

In these parts, the contrast between town and countryside is extreme, even for Sicily – two busy, large towns, and between them scarcely a house or flock of sheep on the sparse limestone hills. The 18km between Módica and Ragusa, however, will be memorable either way you take it: along the old road, in the picturesque valley of the Irminio, or on the faster, modern SS115, a carnival ride on endless, soaring viaducts, created by Italy's masterful highway engineers.

Ragusa is Módica writ large, one of the most picturesque hill towns in Sicily, and not nearly as visited as it deserves to be, with its decaying, flamboyant Baroque buildings hugging the sides, its slow pace of life – why the tourists don't troop in here is some-

Getting There and Around

By Train

Ragusa is well served by trains to and from Syracuse (via Scicli, Módica and Noto) and Licata (via Donnafugata, Cómiso and Vittória) many times daily; the station is at Piazza del Popolo. The 20min journey between Ragusa and Módica is quite spectacular, alternately looping through tunnels and revealing huge breathtaking vistas.

By Bus

From Piazza del Popolo on the AST line: about seven a day to Noto and Syracuse, three for Palermo and Agrigento, two for Gela and Camarina, plus frequent services to all the towns of Ragusa province, including eight a day in season for Marina di Ragusa. City buses 1 and 3 link Ragusa Superiore's Piazza del Popolo with Ragusa Ibla.

Tourist Information

In Ragusa Ibla, Via Capitano Bocchieri 33, t 0932 62 14 21, www.ragusaturismo.it (open Tues–Sun 9–2 and 3–7).

Where to Stay

Ragusa ⊠ 97100

For those on a tighter budget there are three campsites around Camarina.

***Hotel Il Barocco**, Via Santa Maria La Nuova 1, t 0932 652 397, www.ilbarocco.it (moderate). Opened in 2003, this small hotel has pleasant rooms in a converted carpenter's workshop (it's bigger than it sounds). There is a restaurant and ice cream parlour round the corner.

****Mediterraneo Palace**, Via Roma 189, t 0932 621944, www.mediterraneopalace.it (moderate). Just over the Ponte Nuovo this posh hotel is aimed at the business market, but has great views.

***Montreal**, Via S. Giuseppe 10, t/f 0932 62 11 33, hotelmontreal@sprintnet.it (inexpensive–moderate). One of the most comfortable place to stay in Ragusa; rooms have air-conditioning.

***Kroma**, Via G. D'Annunzio 60, t/f 0932 62 28 00 (inexpensive). Another good bet.

***San Giovanni**, Via Transportino, t/f 0932 62 10 13 (budget). Offers good-value rooms, some with en suite facilities.

Marina di Ragusa ⊠ 97100

Eremo della Giubliana, Contrada Giubliana, t 0932 669 119, www.eremodellagiubliana.it (luxury). A gem of a hotel offering just 11 rooms in 15th century fortified monastery where the Knights of St John took refuge on their way to Malta. Attentive service and fabulously elegant throughout with a garden, pool and an accomplished restaurant serving Ragusan recipes made with produce from their own land, at a very reasonable price. A real find.

***Hotel Terraqua**, Via delle Sirene 35, t 0932

thing of a mystery. Set in a rugged, dry landscape of maze-like stone walls, carobs and olives, scented with the wild mint, rosemary and lemon balm that lend a delicate taste to the local honey (praised by Pliny), Ragusa's colours, grey and austere, become subtle and quietly beautiful as the eye adjusts; 'it needs patience and love to be understood and accepted', as the poet Quasimodo wrote.

The most exciting thing to do in Ragusa is to take the hair-raising bus from the new part of town, Ragusa Superiore, to the ancient hilltop island of Ragusa Ibla, plunging down narrow winding streets. Yet, just past Santa Maria delle Scale, the marvellous panorama of old Ibla opens up, crowned by the dome of San Giorgio. For more thrills, come back on the last Sunday of April, when there is a pageant presenting scenes from St George's life: his fight with the dragon, Emperor Diocletian and the sorcerer Atanasio, accompanied by allegorical figures of Hunger, War and Faith.

615600, *www.framon-hotels.com* (*expensive*). Private beach, two swimming pools, a restaurant overlooking the lush garden, marble in the lobby.

Eating Out

Ragusa tends to fare much better with its restaurants than its hotels.

Antica Macina, Via Giusti 129, Ibla, **t** 0932 24 80 96 (*expensive*). This restaurant runs a close second to U'Saracinu. *Closed Mon.*

Da Carmelo, Lungomare Andrea Doria (*expensive*). Head for this no-nonsense eatery where the road brings you out to Marina di Ragusa. It's in a lovely position right on the beach. *Closed Mon.*

Duomo, Via Capitano Bocchieri 31, **t** 0932 651 265 (*expensive*). Stunning food served in surroundings to match – it's located in front of the cathedral. The only potential problem in the summer is the cacophonous sound of the live band.

Majore, Via Martiri Ungheresi 12, **t** 0932 92 80 19 (*moderate*). Chiaramonte Gulfi boasts this, one of Sicily's best-known restaurants, run by the same family for over a century and famous for its range of dishes based on pork – try for example the sausage or *costata ripiena* (stuffed pork chop). *Closed Mon.*

Le Mole, Contrada di Chiara, **t** 0932 92 60 66 (*moderate*). Another excellent restaurant in the same price range, set in a farmhouse with mini-apartments. *Closed Mon.*

U' Saracinu, Piazza del Duomo, Ibla, **t** 0932 24 69 76 (*moderate*). This is the place to eat in town, specializing in the best of local cooking. *Closed Sun.*

Vecchio Fienile, Strada Provinciale 18, km4, **t** 0932 93 03 77 (*moderate*). This restaurant built into a converted barn is also worth a stop. *Closed Wed.*

Villa Fortugno, **t** 0932 66 71 34 (*moderate*). Located 5km along the road to Marina di Ragusa, this large restaurant serves delicious *ravioli di ricotta*, pork dishes (*cavatelli al sugo di maiale*), and great traditional desserts also based on ricotta.

Del Castello, **t** 0932 61 92 60 (*inexpensive*). This trattoria set in the stalls of the castle at Donnafugata serves some of the better food in the area.

Orfeo, Via S. Anna 117, **t** 09 32 62 10 35, Ragusa Superiore (*inexpensive*). A popular spot for having a spot of lunch, with free TV entertainment thrown in. On Friday nights you indulge in eight courses of pasta for an absurdly modest price. *Closed Sun.*

Osteria del Braciere (*inexpensive*). If you have a car, try this local favourite in the village of San Giacomo, northeast of Ragusa, where the good food is plentiful and inexpensive.

Casa del Formaggio, Corso Italia 330, Ragusa Superiore. Come to this place to try out Ragusa's specialities – *caciocavallo* and *pecorino* cheeses made from sheep's milk. Local wines including Ambrato and Cervasuolo can also be tried here.

History

The town of Ragusa, perched atop a hilly ridge, is divided into two parts, the lower of which – Ragusa Ibla – was the site of the original Sikel town of Hybla Heraea, one of their major settlements. Conquered by the Greeks and Romans in 258 BC, Hybla Heraea declined, only regaining some of its former importance when Count Roger created the county of Ragusa for his son in 1091, although in 1296 Manfred Chiaramonte incorporated it into the powerful county of Módica. This became the most powerful fiefdom in Sicily. Later kings rued its semi-independence under the counts of Chiaramonte, Cabrera and Henriquez-Cabrera, who only begrudgingly tipped their hats to Palermo, and paid their tribute only when the king's army came to collect it. This state of affairs lasted into the 18th century, and it was rather more benevolent to the local population than might at first be thought, with its unique set of laws uniting townsmen and farmers in a common cause, such as the reconstruction of towns after earthquakes. After the 1693 earthquake, work was begun on Ragusa Superiore, which remained a separate town from Ibla – and its main rival – until they were united in 1926, when the new Ragusa became the provincial capital. A little oil strike, early in the 20th century, turned Ragusa into a minor industrial centre, bestowing such blessings as big smelly asphalt plants, now largely shut down. The new town boomed, but Ragusa remains a city of great charm.

Ragusa Superiore

Ragusa Superiore is the address of most of the city's businesses, as well as the **Museo Archeológico** (*open daily 9–2 and 3–6.30*), located on Via Natelelli, off Via Roma. The museum contains a chronologically arranged collection of artefacts from the province, especially from the important Syracusan colony of Camarina: well-preserved painted vases of the 6th century BC, imported from Attica, terracotta figurines of the goddess Demeter, in her flowerpot hat, and the mosaic pavement of an early Christian church, decorated with animals.

Across the bridge (Ponte Nuovo) from the museum, **Piazza della Libertà** is a civic centre from the 1930s, a showcase for the Mussolini regime in Sicily, and one of the most ambitious examples of Fascist town design outside Rome; it was called 'Square of the Empire' back then. Traces of the old Fascist symbols and slogans, though effaced, can still be made out, and one sign still proclaims the 'Chamber of the Corporations', the regional economic organ of Mussolini's Corporate State.

In the other direction, from the museum, Via Roma leads to Piazza San Giovanni, site of the large Baroque cathedral of **San Giovanni Battista** (*open for mass*), with its imposing façade and campanile; inside, note the richly ornate stucco decorations in the interior of the cupola, and another 18th-century terracotta presepio.

High on the isthmus dividing Ragusa Superiore from Ragusa Ibla stands the 15th-century **Santa Maria delle Scale**, 'of the stairs' (*open daily 9–12*), one of the few buildings to survive the earthquake, though reworked in the 1600s. Of the original, the portal and pulpit beneath the campanile remain; a 16th-century bas relief inside is a work of the prolific Gagini. There are fine views from the terrace, and a choice of routes to Ibla: the 242 steps below the church, or the winding Corso Mazzini.

Ragusa Ibla

Before the earthquake of 1693, this may have been one of the most impressive cities in Sicily. Destruction was quite complete, sweeping away the Arab-Norman castle and scores of churches and palaces. Rather than abandon the site, however, the Iblaeans decided to rebuild it exactly as it was, retaining the labyrinth of alleys that goes back to the time of the Arabs, or the Sikels, or God only knows when.

In Ibla's narrow lanes and midget squares, the genteelly dilapidated palaces more often than not serve as planters for weeds and wild flowers; little Baroque monsters lurk just under the balconies and roofs. It all looks particularly good lit up on a balmy summer's night with the festival atmosphere of the *passagiata* and live music. Crowning all is the high-domed, high-fronted masterpiece of Rosario Gagliardi of

Noto, the **Basilica di San Giorgio** (1738). One of the finest examples of Sicilian Baroque, its elegantly vertical convex façade is perfectly sited on a curving stair above the palm-lined Piazza del Duomo. The interior is quite plain, save for the great dome over the crossing, more glass than stone. Outside Sicily, by Gagliardi's time, Baroque was on its last legs. But this dome, entirely in the spirit of the Age of Enlightenment, and much more graceful than anything the northern Europeans were doing, stands as evidence that the Sicilian architects were not as behind the times as one might think. The cathedral treasure, which includes Byzantine religious items dating back to the 7th century, may be seen on request.

Corso XXV Aprile leads from San Giorgio to the heart of Ibla: **Piazza Pola**, the Piazza Maggiore of medieval times, where Ibla's old **Municipio** still stands, next to another fine church attributed to Gagliardi (or an imitator), **San Giuseppe**, its convex façade making it a little brother to San Giorgio. At the end of the *corso*, the park called the **Giardino Ibleo** (*open daily 8–8*) has views towards the sea, as well as a number of churches in and around it: the 15th-century portal of the original Gothic-Catalan **San Giorgio Vecchio**, which collapsed in the earthquake, is near the park's entrance; in the lunette there's a weathered relief of St George and the dragon. Inside the park is **San Giacomo** (*open Fri and for Sun mass*), rebuilt from a 14th-century original.

Excursions from Ragusa

From the city, roads fan out towards various points along the coast. On the way to the beaches around Camarina, **Punta Secca** or **Marina di Ragusa**, you could detour to the **Grotta delle Trabacche** (11km from Ragusa), with its large 4th-century catacombs, or farther south to the **Castello di Donnafugata** (*open daily 9–1; with restaurant, see above*). Giuseppe di Lampedusa borrowed the name Donnafugata for the country house of his Salina family in *The Leopard*, though the village he had in mind was the one where he spent his own childhood summers, Santa Margherita di Bélice. This place is a bit fictional too, a medieval palace rebuilt in the late 19th century by Baron Corrado Arezzo, senator and mayor of Ragusa, and decked out in Venetian Gothic trim. There are over a hundred rooms with early 20th-century furnishings, an art collection that includes a work by Filippino Lippi, even a garden maze, all evoking the twilight world of the Sicilian aristocrats as well as di Lampedusa's novel.

If you haven't had enough stately Baroque ensembles, there's still **Scicli**. Directly south of Ragusa and Módica, Scicli is a pleasant and sleepy town with more than its share of 18th-century churches and palaces, but happily so far off the tourist track that you are bound to have it almost to yourself (save the elderly inhabitants). From here the road forks for the beaches at **Donnalucata**, **Cava d'Aliga** and **Sampieri**.

Camarina

On the coast west of Marina di Ragusa, Camarina was a Syracusan colony founded in 598 BC. One of the Greeks' most important commercial towns, it always found itself in just the wrong place, geographically and politically. Syracuse, its mother city, showed its maternal affection by razing Camarina on three separate occasions. The Carthaginians got in a good sack, and the Romans finally put the town out of its misery in 258 BC. Little remains of Camarina, set on a low hill overlooking the sea, though the foundations of a 5th-century **temple of Athena**, the grid-pattern street plan and part of the wall, can all be made out. The 6th-century BC necropolis yielded many interesting objects, some of which are in Ragusa, and others in the small **museum on the acropolis** (*open daily 9–1 and 3–8; adm*).

Cómiso and Vittória

West of Ragusa, after a stunning descent from the Monti Iblei, the road leads into the more fertile lands around the River Ippari. Attractive, unheralded **Cómiso**, another town that was rebuilt after 1693, was ruled by the Naselli d'Aragona family from the 15th to 18th century; their 14th-century **castle** has recently been restored. Near the town centre, in the Piazza delle Erbe, **San Francesco** (finished 1478), contains the Cappella Naselli and the sepulchre of Count Gaspare Naselli by Antonello Gagini, one of his finest tombs. Just off the *piazza* is an interesting **19th-century building** (*open Mon–Sat 9–1 and 3–7*), which once held the town's market – Cómiso is an agricultural centre. But Baroque is the dominant note in the town's *palazzi* and churches, especially the 17th-century **Santa Maria delle Stelle**, with its tall narrow dome, similar to the dome crowning the vast **Basilica dell'Annunziata**. The **Fonte Diana** once supplied water for the Roman baths, now under the Municipio; the **library** displays a surviving mosaic. Cómiso's high vines produce excellent table grapes and Ambrato wine.

Neighbouring **Vittória**, city of peaches, spring produce and Cerasuolo wine, was named after its 1607 foundress, Vittoria della Colonna, the daughter of a viceroy. Although the rest of the town isn't much to write home about, Vittória has two elegant *piazze*, surrounded by Baroque and Neoclassical buildings, especially the one containing the handsome church of **Madonna delle Grazie**, and the adjacent Neoclassical **Teatro Comunale** (*visits by request at the town hall*), which Berenson, in his *Trip to Sicily*, described as 'one of the best European theatres in this style'. **Scoglitti**, some 16km away on the coast, with a pleasant wide beach, a few restaurants and one hotel, is the beginning of the 'Gela Riviera'.

Despite its name, **Chiaramonte Gulfi** is an inland village north of Ragusa, famous in Sicily for its food. Few towns in Sicily have such a jolly and contented air about them – maybe there is a connection. The town sits on a hill, bordered on the south by lush pine forests that provide a striking contrast with the landscapes around Ragusa and Módica. From the public gardens you can see Cómiso, Vittória, Caltagirone, the beach at Gela, and (on a clear day) Etna in the distance.

Language

Just as vernacular poetry first appeared in Europe during the late 11th century in the south of France, when the first troubadours came in contact with the love poetry of Muslim Spain, so the first poetry in vernacular Italian came out of 13th-century Sicily, when Emperor Frederick II presided over the last chapter of the island's multiracial golden age. In Sicily's subsequent insularity, this pre-Dante Italian developed into a unique dialect, characterized like other southern Italian dialects by the predominance of the letter U (as in the popular saying *Quannu 'u' to' diàvulu ieve a scola, 'u miu era già prufissuri* – 'When your devil went to school, mine was the teacher'). Sicilian has a huge vocabulary of its own; the better bookshops sell fat Sicilian–Italian dictionaries. There is a sense of medieval chivalry in the use of some Sicilian words: one common adjective for describing something nice or pleasant in Sicilian is *grazioso* (graceful), as opposed to the plain Italian *bello*, while the favourite offensive word is *cornùto*, which means horned and implies you have an unfaithful spouse. Linguistically, Sicilian is a rich feast, full of often surprising contributions from early Latin, Greek, Arabic, French and Spanish.

Sicilian has gone the full circle of other minority languages in Europe. Unification in the 19th century meant the teaching of Italian in schools, and nothing but Italian in the media, until many young people looked at the language that their grandparents and parents spoke at home as something backward. Now intellectuals are making an effort to keep it alive both as a spoken language and as a literary one, publishing more books in Sicilian every year and promoting classes in schools. This attempt to preserve the language ties in with a fearsome sense of identity: scorned by mainland Italians – especially those from the north – as '*Terroni*' (people of the earth), Sicilians retaliate by calling northern Italians '*Polentoni*', after polenta, a common cornmeal dish which on its own is mushy and flavourless.

Although you will hear Sicilian spoken, especially by old people in villages (it outfoxes even the Italians, so don't expect to understand a word), not to worry: you can get by very well in Sicily with a little Italian. If you stick to big cities and resorts such as Taormina, Cefalù and Lipari, you can probably even get by with English.

The fathers of modern Italian were Dante, Manzoni and television. Each did their part in creating a national language from an infinity of regional and local dialects. The Florentine Dante, the first 'immortal' to write in the vernacular, did much to put the Tuscan dialect in the foreground of Italian literature. Manzoni's revolutionary novel *I Promessi Sposi* (*The Betrothed*) heightened national consciousness by using an everyday language all could understand in the 19th century. Television in the last few decades has been performing an even more spectacular linguistic unification: although the majority of Italians still speak a dialect at home, school and at work, their TV idols still insist on proper Italian.

Perhaps because they are so busy learning their own beautiful but grammatically complex language, Italians are not especially apt at learning others. English lessons, however, have been the rage for years, and at most hotels and restaurants there will be someone who speaks some English. In small towns and out of the way places, finding an Anglophone may prove more difficult. The words and phrases below should help you out in most situations, but the ideal way to come to Italy is with some Italian under your belt: your visit will be richer, and you're much more likely to make some Italian friends.

For wining and dining vocabulary, *see* the **Food and Drink** chapter.

Pronunciation

Italian words are pronounced phonetically. Every vowel and consonant (except 'h') is sounded. Consonants are the same as in English, except the 'c', which, when followed by an 'e' or 'i', is pronounced like the English 'ch' (*cinque* thus becomes 'cheenquay'). Italian 'g' is also soft before 'i' or 'e', as in *gira*, pronounced 'jee-ra'. 'Z' is pronounced like 'ts'.

The consonants 'sc' before the vowels 'i' or 'e' become like the English 'sh', as in '*sci*', pronounced 'shee'; 'ch' is pronouced like a 'k', as in Chianti, kee-an-tee; 'gn' as 'ny' in English (*bagno*, pronounced 'ban-yo'); while 'gli' is pronounced like the middle of the word 'million' (Castiglione, for example, is pronounced 'Ca-steely-oh-nay').

Vowel pronunciation is: 'a' as in English father; 'e' when unstressed is pronounced like 'a' in 'fate', as in *mele*, but when stressed can be the same or like the 'e' in 'pet' (*bello*); 'i' is like the 'i' in 'machine'; 'o', like 'e', has two sounds, 'o' as in 'hope' when unstressed (*tacchino*), and usually 'o' as in 'rock' when stressed (*morte*); 'u' is pronounced like the 'u' in 'June'.

The accent usually (but not always!) falls on the penultimate syllable. Also note that, in the big northern cities, the informal way of addressing someone as you, *tu*, is widely used; the more formal *lei* or *voi* is commonly used in provincial districts.

Useful Words and Phrases

yes/no/maybe *si/no/forse*
I don't know *Non lo so*
I don't understand (Italian) *Non capisco (italiano)*
Does someone here speak English? *C'è qualcuno qui che parla inglese?*
Speak slowly *Parla lentamente*
Could you assist me? *Potrebbe aiutarmi?*
Help! *Aiuto!*
Please/Thank you (very much) *Per favore/(Molte) grazie*
You're welcome *Prego*
It doesn't matter *Non importa*
All right *Va bene*
Excuse me *Mi scusi*
Be careful! *Attenzione!*

Nothing *Niente*
It is urgent! *È urgente!*
How are you? *Come sta?*
Well, and you? *Bene, e Lei?*
What is your name? *Come si chiama?*
Hello *Salve/ciao (both informal)*
Good morning *Buongiorno (formal hello)*
Good afternoon, evening *Buonasera (also formal hello)*
Good night *Buonanotte*
Goodbye *Arrivederla (formal), arrivederci, ciao (informal)*
What do you call this in Italian? *Come si chiama questo in italiano?*
What?/Who?/Where? *Che?/Chi?/Dove?*
When?/Why? *Quando?/Perché?*
How? *Come?*
How much? *Quanto?*
I am lost *Mi sono smarrito*
I am hungry/thirsty/sleepy *Ho fame/sete/sonno*
I am sorry *Mi dispiace*
I am tired *Sono stanco*
I am ill *Mi sento male*
Leave me alone *Lasciami in pace*
good/bad *buono; bravo/male; cattivo*
hot/cold *caldo/freddo*
slow/fast *lento/rapido*
up/down *su/giù*
big/small *grande/piccolo*
here/there *qui/lì*

Days

Monday *lunedì*
Tuesday *martedì*
Wednesday *mercoledì*
Thursday *giovedì*
Friday *venerdì*
Saturday *sabato*
Sunday *domenica*

Numbers

one *uno/una*
two/three/four *due/tre/quattro*
five/six/seven *cinque/sei/sette*
eight/nine/ten *otto/nove/dieci*
eleven/twelve *undici/dodici*
thirteen/fourteen *tredici/quattordici*
fifteen/sixteen *quindici/sedici*

seventeen/eighteen *diciassette/diciotto*
nineteen *diciannove*
twenty *venti*
twenty-one *ventuno*
thirty *trenta*
forty *quaranta*
fifty *cinquanta*
sixty *sessanta*
seventy *settanta*
eighty *ottanta*
ninety *novanta*
hundred *cento*
one hundred and one *centouno*
two hundred *duecento*
one thousand *mille*
two thousand *duemila*
million *milione*

one way *semplice/andata*
return *andata e ritorno*
first/second class *prima/seconda classe*
I want to go to... *Desidero andare a...*
How can I get to...? *Come posso andare a...?*
Do you stop at...? *Ferma a...?*
Where is...? *Dov'è...?*
How far is it to...? *Quanto siamo lontani da...?*
What is the name of this station? *Come si chiama questa stazione?*
When does the next ... leave? *Quando parte il prossimo...?*
From where does it leave? *Da dove parte?*
How long does the trip take...? *Quanto tempo dura il viaggio?*
How much is the fare? *Quant'è il biglietto?*
Have a good trip *Buon viaggio!*

Time

What time is it? *Che ore sono?*
day/week *giorno/settimana*
month *mese*
morning/afternoon *mattina/pomeriggio*
evening *sera*
yesterday *ieri*
today *oggi*
tomorrow *domani*
soon *fra poco*
later *dopo/più tardi*
It is too early *È troppo presto*
It is too late *È troppo tardi*

Transport

airport *aeroporto*
bus stop *fermata*
bus/coach *autobus/pullman*
railway station *stazione ferroviaria*
train *treno*
platform *binario*
taxi *tassì*
ticket *biglietto*
customs *dogana*
seat (reserved) *posto (prenotato)*

Buying Tickets

One (two) ticket(s) to Naples, please *Un biglietto (due biglietti) per Napoli, per favore*

Driving

near/far *vicino/lontano*
left/right *sinistra/destra*
straight ahead *sempre diritto*
forward/backwards *avanti/indietro*
north/south *nord/sud*
east *est/oriente*
west *ovest/occidente*
round the corner *dietro l'angolo*
crossroads *bivio*
street/road *strada/via*
square *piazza*
car hire *noleggio macchina*
motorbike/scooter *motocicletta/Vespa*
bicycle *bicicletta*
petrol/diesel *benzina/gasolio*
garage *garage*
This doesn't work *Questo non funziona*
mechanic *meccanico*
map/town plan *carta/pianta*
Where is the road to...? *Dov'è la strada per...?*
breakdown *guasto/panne*
driving licence *patente di guida*
driver *guidatore*
speed *velocità*
danger *pericolo*
parking *parcheggio*
no parking *sosta vietata*
narrow *stretto*
bridge *ponte*
toll *pedaggio*
slow down *rallentare*

Useful Hotel Vocabulary

I'd like a double room please *Vorrei una camera doppia, per favore*

I'd like a single room please *Vorrei una camera singola, per favore*

with bath, without bath *con bagno, senza bagno*

for two nights *per due notti*

We are leaving tomorrow morning *Partiamo domani mattina*

May I see the room, please? *Posso vedere la camera?*

Is there a room with a balcony? *C'è una camera con balcone?*

There isn't (aren't) any hot water, soap, *Manca/Mancano acqua calda, sapone,*
 light, toilet paper, towels
  luce, carta igienica, asciugamani

May I pay by credit card? *Posso pagare con carta di credito?*

May I see another room please? *Per favore potrei vedere un'altra camera?*

Fine, I'll take it *Bene, la prendo*

Is breakfast included? *E' compresa la prima colazione?*

What time do you serve breakfast? *A che ora è la colazione?*

How do I get to the town centre? *Come posso raggiungere il centro città?*

Shopping, Services, Sightseeing

I would like... *Vorrei...*

Where is/are... *Dov'è/Dove sono...*

How much is it? *Quanto costa questo?*

open/closed *aperto/chiuso*

cheap/expensive *a buon prezzo/caro*

bank *banca*

beach *spiaggia*

bed *letto*

church *chiesa*

entrance/exit *entrata/uscita*

hospital *ospedale*

money *soldi*

newspaper (foreign) *giornale (straniero)*

pharmacy *farmacia*

police station *commissariato*

policeman *poliziotto*

post office *ufficio postale*

sea *mare*

shop *negozio*

room *camera*

tobacco shop *tabaccaio*

WC *toilette/bagno*

men *Signori/Uomini*

women *Signore/Donne*

Further Reading

Azis, Ahmed, *A History of Islamic Sicily* (Edinburgh University Press, 1953). The best account of the period in English.
Blok, Anton, *The Mafia of a Sicilian Village 1860–1960* (Polity Press, 1979). Micro-historical.
Blunt, Anthony, *Sicilian Baroque* (Weidenfeld & Nicolson, 1968). A classic, and a good read.
Brea, Luigi Bernabo, *Sicily Before the Greeks* (Thames & Hudson, 1957). A definitive account.
Brydone, Patrick, *A Tour through Sicily and Malta* (London, 1790). The most entertaining of travellers' accounts.
Bufalino, Gesualdo, *The Plague Sower*, *Night's Lies* (Collins Harvill/Macmillan, 1990). Essential novels by Sicily's most important living writer and island psychoanalyst.
Calvino, Italo, *Italian Folktales* (Harcourt Brace Jovanovich, 1980). A delight.
Campbell, Rodney, *The Luciano Project: The Secret Wartime Collaboration of the Mafia and the US Navy* (McGraw Hill, 1977). An exposé of Lucky Luciano's role in the Allied liberation.
Cronin, Vincent, *The Golden Honeycomb* (Hart Davis/Dutton, 1954). Entertaining, informed traveller's account (the golden honeycomb was Daedalus' gift to Aphrodite at Erice).
Demus, Otto, *The Mosaics of Norman Sicily* (London, 1950). The authority on the subject.
Dolci, Danilo, *Report from Palermo* (in the UK, *To Feed the Hungry*), *Outlaws and Sicilian Lives* (Orion Press/Pantheon). Accounts of events and people, in devasting prose.
Durrell, Lawrence, *Sicilian Carousel* (Viking, 1977). About himself and his friends.
Finley, Moses, *A History of Sicily: Ancient Sicily to the Arab Conquest*, published in a 3-volume set with Dennis Mack Smith's *Medieval Sicily 800–1713* and *Modern Sicily After 1713* (Chatto & Windus/Viking, 1984). The best all-round history of Sicily in English.
Goethe, J. W., *Italian Journey* (trans. W. H. Auden and Elizabeth Mayer, Penguin, 1982).

Not only a fascinating period piece, but plenty of speculation on the Ur-plant thrown in for free.
Lampedusa, Giuseppe Tomasi di, *The Leopard* (Collins Harvill/Fontana, 1972). The Sicilian novel.
Lewis, Norman, *The Honoured Society* (Eland/Hippocrene, 1984). The classic, highly readable account of the Mafia. Also *The March of the Long Shadow* (Secker & Warburg) about postwar Sicily.
Maxwell, Gavin, *The Ten Pains of Death* (Dutton, 1959). Interviews and life in Scopello.
Norwich, John Julius, *The Normans in Sicily* (Penguin, 1992). Fat, compelling, delightfully written volume.
Pirandello, Luigi, *Henry IV*, *Six Characters in Search of an Author*, *Short Stories* (Methuen). The provocative classics from the 1920s by Sicily's Nobel Prize-winning playwright.
Randall MacIver, David, *Greek Cities in Italy and Sicily* (Clarendon Press, 1931).
Runciman, Steven, *The Sicilian Vespers* (CUP, 1988). Blow-by-blow account of the uprising.
Sciascia, Leonardo, *Candido* (a satire), *The Day of the Owl* and *Equal Danger* (thrillers), *The Wine Dark Sea* (short stories) (Carcanet/Paladin, all 1980s). Sicily's great 20th-century writer.
Shawcross, Tim and Martin Young, *Mafia Wars* (Fontana, 1988).
Simeti, Mary Taylor, *On Persephone's Island* (Knopf, 1986), *Sicilian Food* (or *Pomp and Sustenance*) (Random Century, 1989). An American view on Sicilians and their customs. Also *Bitter Almonds* (William Morrow, 1994), recollections of life in the convent, with recipes.
Trevelyan, Raleigh, *Princes Under the Volcano* (Macmillan, 1972). The English connection.
Verga, Giovanni, *Mastro Don Gesualdo* (trans. D. H. Lawrence), *The House by the Medlar Tree*, *Cavalleria Rusticana* (Daedalus, 1980s). Short stories, 19th-century Greek tragedies.

Glossary

Agora: ancient Greek marketplace.
Ambones: twin pulpits in early churches.
Antefix: decorative protrusion on the corner of the roof of a Greek or Roman temple.
Architrave: lower part of a temple's entablature.
Badia or **abbazia**: an abbey or abbey church.
Baglio: originally a *massaria* (*see* below) in western Sicily, later used as a warehouse.
Basilian: Orthodox monks, after St Basil, the 4th-century founder of Orthodox monasticism.
Basilica: a rectangular building divided into three aisles by rows of columns.
Camposanto: a country graveyard.
Cardo: the traverse street of a Roman castrum-shaped city.
Capital: the decorative piece placed at the top of a column to support an architrave or arch.
Caryatid: supporting pillar or column carved into a standing female form.
Castrum: a Roman military camp, always rectangular, with straight streets and gates.
Cavea: the semicircle of seats in a classic theatre.
Cella: the enclosed sanctuary of a temple.
Chthonic: of gods, fertility and death.
Comune: commune, referring to the governments of free cities in the Middle Ages. Today it denotes any local government.
Confraternity: a religious lay brotherhood.
Corinthian Order: characterized by fluted columns and acanthus-leaf capitals.
Cyclopean walls: ancient fortifications built of enormous, irregularly polygonal blocks.
Dammuso: typical domed house of Pantelleria.
Decumanus: street of a Roman castrum-shaped city parallel to the longer axis.
Doric Order: characterized by unfluted columns and fairly simple round capitals.
Entablature: the architrave, frieze and cornice of a classical building.
Exedra: semicircular recess.
Ex-voto: figurine, painting or silver pendant given in gratitude to a god or saint.
Faraglione: a large rock or boulder in the sea.
Forum: central square of a Roman town.

Fossa: volcanic crater.
Fresco: wall painting in which pigment is applied to wet plaster.
Fumarola: spurting outlet of volcanic steam.
Ghibellines: one of the two medieval parties, supporters of the Holy Roman Emperor.
Guelphs: the opposition party to the Ghibellines, supporters of the Pope.
Hypogeum: underground burial chamber, usually of pre-Christian religions.
Intarsia: work in inlaid wood or marble.
Ionic Order: known for its elegant fluted columns and the distinctive curl of its capitals.
Kore or core: a young girl; also Persephone.
Kouros: a boy, or Archaic Greek male figure.
Latomia: a tufa quarry, especially in Syracuse.
Macchia: *maquis*, Mediterranean scrubland.
Massaria: large farm, a descendant of the Roman country estate or *mansio*.
Metope: panel on the frieze of a Doric temple.
Misteri: tableaux in Holy Week processions.
Naumachia: a mock sea battle performed in a flooded amphitheatre.
Nymphaeum: nymphs' temple near a spring; later a kind of summer gazebo.
Pantocrator: Christ 'ruler of all'.
Pediment: gable on façade of ancient building.
Peribolos: a temple precinct and its area.
Peristyle: a colonnaded garden court.
Piscina: a Roman tank or pool.
Putti: flocks of Italian Baroque cherubs.
Quattrocento: the 1400s.
Sesi: early, *nuraghe*-type structures.
Stentinello: early Neolithic culture making pottery with geometrical or seashell imprints.
Stylobate: base of columned temple or building.
Telamon: male caryatid (*see* above).
Termae: baths.
Tholos: a circular building, a form often used for Greek tombs.
Tophet: shrine for human sacrifice.
Transenna: marble screen separating the altar area from the rest of an early church.
Triclinium: the main hall of a Roman house.

Index

Main page references are in **bold**. Page references to maps are in *italics*.

Sicily touring atlas

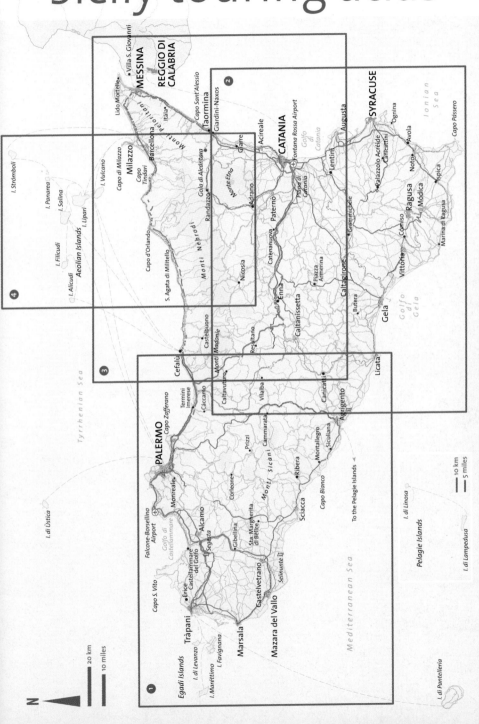

Capo S. Vito

S. Vito lo Capo

▲ Monte Mónaco

Golfo
di
Castellammare

Mácari

Monte Cófano ▲

Riserva Naturale
dello Zingaro

Castelluzzo

Custonaci

Scopello

Lido di S. Giuliano

Erice

S187

Alcamo
Marina

Tràpani

Valderice

Baglio
Messina

Castellammare
del Golfo

I. di Levanzo

Grotta del Genovese ◠

Alcamo

Castello di Punta Troia

Levanzo

Salt Pans

Monte
Bonifato

Maréttimo

Egadi Islands

Nubia

Paceco

S113

Segesta

I. Maréttimo

Favignana

Birgi Airport

S115

Calatafimi

I. Favignana

Salt Pans

Pianta de
Romano

I. Grande

Motya

I. S. Pantaleo

Salemi

Stagnone Islands

S188

Gibellina

Gibellina
Vecchia

Capo Lilibeo o Boeo

Sta. Ninta

Marsala

Calamita
Vecchia

S113

Partanna

Lido Mediterraneo

S115

Petrosino

Lago di Trinità

Castelvetrano

SS. Trinità di Délia

Belice

A29

S115

Mazara del Vallo

Campobello
di Mazara

S115

Cave di Cusa

Selinunte

Marinella

Porto Palo

Punta Granitola

I. di Pantelleria

N

Mediterranean Sea

10 km

5 miles

1

Tyrrhenian Sea

Aeolian Islands

Naples/Livorno
Genoa/Cagliari

I. di Ustica

Falcone-Borsellino
Airport

Sferracavallo

Mondello Lido

Monte Pellegrino

Golfo di
Palermo

Capo Zafferano
Soluntо
Porticello

Terrasini

Carini

Boccadifalco

PALERMO

Bagheria

Sta. Flavia

S. Martino
delle Scale

Castellaccio

Golfo di
Termini Imer

Trappeto

Montelepre

Monreale

Villabate

Altavilla
Milicia

S. Nicola l'Arena

S285

Partinico

S624

Misilmeri

Trabia

Termini Imerese

Himera
Buonfornella

Piana degli
Albanesi

S113

S. Giuseppe
Jato

Portella
della
Ginestra

Lago di Piana
degli Albanesi

Cáccamo

S285

Caltavuturo

S. Cipirello

S118

Cefalà Diana

S520

Camporeale

Ficuzza

Bosco della Ficuzza

S121

Vicari

S285

Rocca
Busambre

Mezzojuso

S624

S528

Corleone

S189

Lercara
Fridi

Poggioreale

Salaparuta

Sta. Maria
del Bosco

Prizzi

S188

Vilalba

Sta. Margherita
di Belice

Bisacquino

Monte
Adranone
Excavations

Monti

Sambuca
di Sicilia

Sicani

Cammarata

S180

Castello
Manfredonico

Mussomeli

Bivona

Caltabellotta

Casteltermini

Campofranco

Monte
S. Calogero

Ribera

S115

Platani

S. Angelo
Muxaro

S640

Capo S.
Marco

Sciacca

Aragona

Racalmuto

Eraclea Minoa

Montallegro

Raffadali

Canicatti

Capo Bianco

Siciliana

Siciliana Marina

Agrigento

Porto
Empedocle

Valley
of the
Temples

Favara

Naro

S323

Lido Rossello

S. Leone

I. di Linosa

Palma di
Montechiaro

Marina di Palma

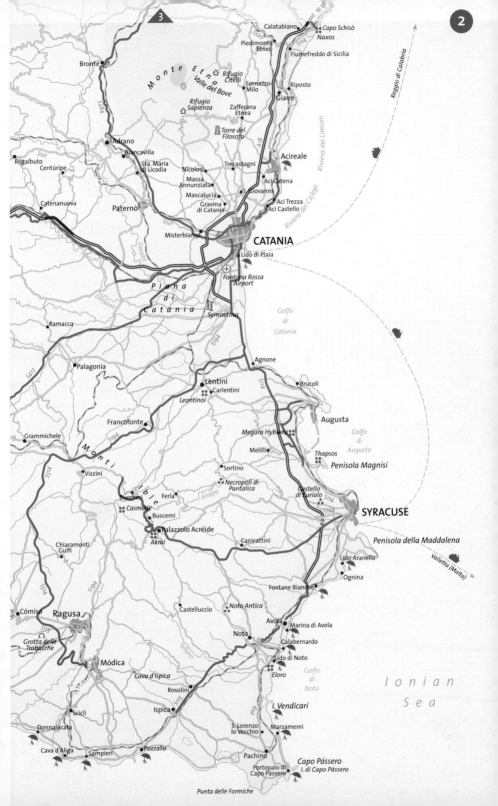

2

Palermo
Palermo

T y r r h e n i a n   S e a

I. Alicudi
I. Salina
I. Lipari

Capo d'Orlando
Brolo
Naso
Capri Leone
S. Agata di Militello
S. Marco d'Alunzio
Frazzanò
Marina di Caronia
Acquedolci
Longi
Cefalù
Castel di Tusa
S. Stefano di Camastra
S. Fratello
Alcara li Fusi
Santuario di Gibilmanna
Halaesa
Tusa
Lago Biviere di Cesarò
Isnello
Mistretta
Monte Soro
Collesano
Castelbuono
M o n t i   N e b r o d i
Portella Femmina Morta
Castel di Lucio
M o n t i   M a d o n i e
Geraci Siculo
Portella del Contrasto
Caltavuturo
Polizzi Generosa
Troina
Petralia Sottana
Gangi
Petralia Soprana
Castellane Sicula
Sperlinga
Bosco di Sperlinga
Nicosia
Lago Pozzillo
Resultano
Leonforte
Agira
Regalbuto
Centúripe
Assoro
Villarosa
Calascibetta
Catenanuova
Sta. Caterina Villarrosa
Enna
Monte Sabucina
Pergusa
Lago di Pergusa
S. Cataldo
Vassallaggi
Caltanissetta
Pietraperzia
Aidone
Morgantina
Ramacca
Delia
Piazza Armerina
Villa del Casale
Palagonia
Mazzarino

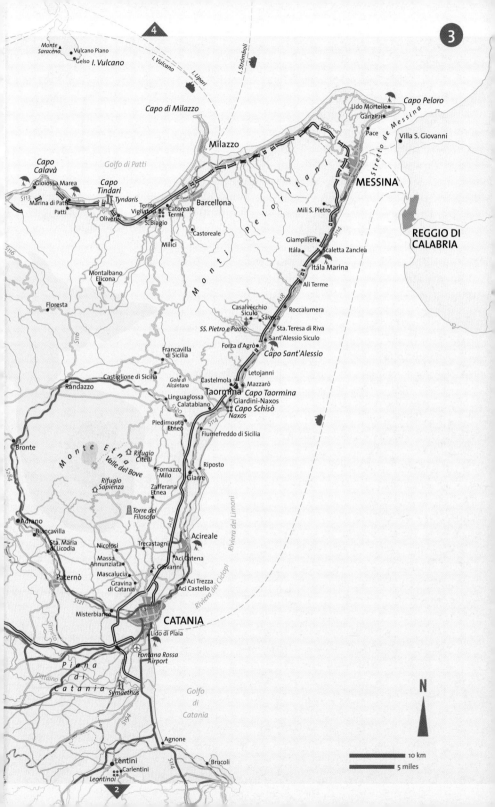

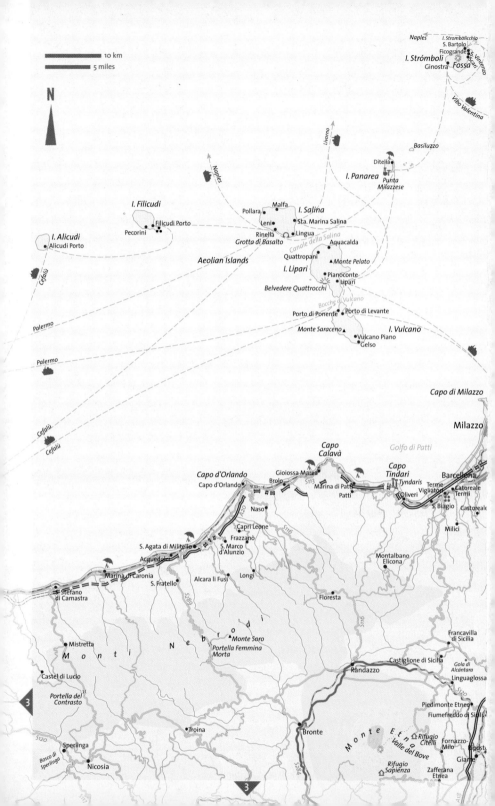